NATURAL
RESOURCE
ECONOMICS–

AN INTRODUCTION

NATURAL RESOURCE ECONOMICS—

AN INTRODUCTION

Barry C. Field

Department of Resource Economics
University of Massachusetts—Amherst

Boston   Burr Ridge, IL   Dubuque, IA   Madison, WI
New York   San Francisco   St. Louis
Bangkok   Bogotá   Caracas   Lisbon   London   Madrid   Mexico City
Milan   New Delhi   Seoul   Singapore   Sydney   Taipei   Toronto

McGraw-Hill Higher Education

A Division of The **McGraw-Hill** Companies

NATURAL RESOURCE ECONOMICS

Published by Irwin/McGraw-Hill, an imprint of The McGraw-Hill Companies, Inc., 1221 Avenue of the Americas, New York, NY 10020. Copyright © 2001, by The McGraw-Hill Companies, Inc. All rights reserved. No part of this publication may be reproduced or distributed in any form or by any means, or stored in a database or retrieval system, without the prior written consent of The McGraw-Hill Companies, Inc., including, but not limited to, in any network or other electronic storage or transmission, or broadcast for distance learning.

This book is printed on acid-free paper.

1 2 3 4 5 6 7 8 9 0 FGR/FGR 0 9 8 7 6 5 4 3 2 1 0

ISBN 0–07–231677–2

Editor-in-chief: *Gary Burke*
Senior sponsoring editor: *Lucille Sutton*
Editorial assistant: *Joanna Honikman*
Marketing manager: *Nelson Black*
Project manager: *David Sutton*
Production supervisor: *Pam Augspurger*
Supplement coordinator: *Louis Swaim*
Cover design: *Susan Newman Design, Inc.*
Compositor: *Shepherd, Inc.*
Typeface: *10/12 Palatino*
Printer: *Fairfield Graphics, Inc.*

Library of Congress Cataloging-in-Publication Data

Field, Barry C.
  Natural resource economics : an introduction / Barry C. Field
     p. cm.
  Includes index.
  ISBN 0-07-231677-2 (alk. paper)
  1. Natural resources. 2. Environmental policy. 3. Sustainable development. I. Title.

HC85 .F54 2000
333.7—dc21   00-036976

http://www.mhhe.com

ABOUT THE AUTHOR

Barry C. Field is Professor of Resource Economics at the University of Massachusetts in Amherst. Previously he taught at the University of Miami and The George Washington University. He received his B.S. and M.S. degrees from Cornell University, and his Ph.D. from the University of California at Berkeley.

At the University of Massachusetts he has devoted many years to teaching natural resource economics to students at all levels, and has worked to develop an undergraduate major in environmental and resource economics.

Professor Field is the author of numerous articles on resource and environmental economics.

To Martha

CONTENTS

PREFACE

One of the major themes of human concern as we launch into the next millennium is how we should shape and manage our relationship to the natural world. On one side of the issue are those who believe that we are exhausting and degrading natural resource endowments to such an extent that the future welfare of the human community itself is threatened. On the other are those who believe that the technological and institutional challenges of natural resource scarcity can be overcome given sufficient amounts of human effort and ingenuity. Most people are probably somewhere in the middle: concerned but hopeful.

Wherever one stands on the ecological spectrum, it is clear that future outcomes depend to a great extent on the human decisions that are made about resource use. Natural resource economics represents one way of framing and analyzing these decisions. By "analyze" we mean developing an understanding of why resource decisions are made the way they are and how they might be improved upon. Natural resource economics focuses on resource valuation, economic incentives, and the institutional arrangements that will give us the utilization and conservation decisions we want.

The basic structure of the book is to start out with a few preliminaries, then cover some fundamental principles of economics, discuss how these principles apply to the general question of natural resource use, and then move to a series of topical chapters—each of which treats a particular natural resource. Finally, the last two chapters look at natural resource issues as they are encountered in developing countries. There may be too many chapters to cover in a single semester course. In this case it should be easy to cover the basics, and then select the applications chapters that instructors and students find most interesting and relevant.

Each chapter ends with a summary, list of key words, some questions for further discussion, a brief reference to some sites on the worldwide web that might be useful, and a short list of selected readings. Neither the selected readings nor the web site lists are comprehensive in any way. Given the massive proliferation of sites on the web and the large scientific literature on natural resource issues, the lists at the end of each chapter can cite only a tiny fraction of the material that students might find interesting and informative. They are meant simply as a way to help students get their feet in the door, should they want to push further with any of the ideas of the chapter.

In this sense the book is a companion to my earlier work, *Environmental Economics: An Introduction* (McGraw-Hill, 2nd edition, 1997). The latter treats issues of environmental pollution and the management of environmental quality in the same fashion, and has found a wide audience. It is used primarily for introductory courses, but on occasion also for more advanced courses. My hope is that the present work will find the same niche.

ACKNOWLEDGMENTS

Like most textbooks, this book is the result of many years' teaching in the classroom. So my deepest debt is to the thousands of students who have sat in my classes over the years. Without their faces, reactions, and feedback, the book could not have been written, and if I have been able to present the material in a way future students find comprehensible and meaningful, it is all these earlier students who can take most of the credit.

Many thanks to the economists who have read all or part of the manuscript and offered their comments: Anne E. Bresnock, California State Polytechnic University; Richard Bryant, University of Missouri; Nick Gomersall, Luther College; Douglas Parker, University of Maryland; and Keith Willet, Oklahoma State University. Their insights and reactions have made the book much better than it would have been without them.

Very special thanks to the people who helped me produce the book: to Darleen Slysz, for her incredible work with the word processor and keeping the project organized, and to Eileen Keegan for her fine work with the graphics. Thanks also to Lucille Sutton, Joanna Honikman, and David Sutton at McGraw-Hill, who saw the book through to completion.

Finally, deep thanks and love to Martha, who read every word more than once, who encouraged me onward, and who kept trying to explain to the kids why daddy had to write all those words.

INTRODUCTION

This first section contains two introductory chapters. Chapter 1 offers a brief tour through some of the major natural resource issues facing us today. The objective is to become acquainted with them in commonsense terms before we launch into an analysis of these problems in later chapters. The second chapter covers some of the essential terminology that will be used throughout the book.

IMPORTANT ISSUES IN NATURAL RESOURCE ECONOMICS

In this book we apply some relatively simple, but powerful, economic princi- ples to the study of natural resource conservation and use. The emphasis will be on **analysis:** why resources are used as they are, and what specific steps can be undertaken to use them at a rate that is socially beneficial for all. It may sometimes seem that the emphasis is more on refining the analytical principles than on applying them in useful ways. To underline the fact that the analytical models are not of interest per se but merely allow us better to come to grips with real-world problems, we start by taking a brief, descriptive excursion through a number of important contemporary natural resource issues. The aim, in other words, is to get an overview of the kinds of problems that are dealt with in **natural resource economics,** before launching into the study of the analytical tools that are brought to bear on them.

NATURAL RESOURCE ADEQUACY

The longest-running issue in natural resource economics is undoubtedly the **resource adequacy** issue. Given that contemporary economies use relatively large amounts of many types of natural resources as "inputs" to production and consumption, we must ask ourselves a few serious questions: Will future supplies of these resources be sufficient to support the economic needs of our children, grandchildren, and succeeding generations indefinitely? Or will natural resource shortages ultimately become so severe as to threaten, and perhaps lead to a collapse of, future standards of living?

This is not a new concern. Before the industrial revolution, when economies were tied more closely to local resource endowments, fears of local shortages of items such as wood and water were very common. When the industrial revolution did arrive, with its heavy reliance on coal, concern shifted to the possibility that that resource, since it was nonrenewable, would grow scarce and cause collapse.

In more recent years, the **energy crisis** of the 1970s provoked a great deal of soul searching and dire commentary about resource scarcities and economic collapse. It is true that modern economics uses prodigious amounts of energy per unit of output; that is, they are very energy-intensive. But the runup of energy prices of the early 1970s was in fact a political phenomenon, not connected at all with real scarcity factors. Furthermore, the price increases led to very important amounts of energy conservation, as users sought ways to reduce their energy consumption. By 1990, unfortunately, few people still gave much thought to energy conservation, since the real prices of such important items as gasoline had declined to pre-1970s levels.

But the dilemma still remains. The largest part of the energy system of the western world is based on nonrenewable resources: petroleum, coal, and natural gas. Has the inevitable crisis in energy supplies, and by extension other critical natural resources, simply been pushed off into the future? There is probably no way of answering this definitively to everybody's satisfaction. People who think about the likelihood of a natural resource scarcity–induced economic collapse tend to distribute themselves along a spectrum running from extreme **pessimism** to extreme **optimism.**

The pessimist side goes back at least to Thomas Malthus, whose famous treatise on population was based on the notion that human population growth would inevitably outstrip the ability of nature to provide sustenance in ever-increasing amounts.[1] In the early 1970s an influential work on the pessimist's side was published titled *The Limits to Growth*.[2] This study used large-scale computer simulation models with complicated feedback mechanisms to arrive at the conclusion that natural resource scarcities, along with several other factors such as increased pollution, would lead to precipitous declines in the output of modern economies, beginning early in the twenty-first century. And pessimist studies continue to appear.[3]

---

[1] T. R. Malthus, *An Essay on Population,* London, 1798.

[2] Donella H. Meadows et al., *The Limits to Growth: A Report for the Club of Rome's Project on the Predicament of Mankind,* New York, Universe Books, 1972.

[3] A recent one is Mark Hertsgaard, *Earth Odyssey, Around the World in Search of Our Environmental Future,* Broadway, BDD, 1999.

The pessimists can point to history to support their view. George Perkins Marsh, in his influential historical study[4] of the relationships of humans to their natural environments, begins with an allusion to the Roman Empire:

> The Roman Empire, at the period of its greatest expansion, comprised the regions of the earth most distinguished by a happy combination of physical advantages. . . . The abundance of land and water adequately supplied every material want, ministered liberally to every sensuous enjoyment. . . . If we compare the present physical conditions, . . . we shall find that more than half of their whole extent . . . is either deserted by civilized man and surrendered to hopeless desolation, or at least greatly reduced in both productiveness and population.

At the other end of the spectrum are the extreme optimists. Natural resource scarcities will surely occur in the future, they admit. But human beings have the capacity to overcome this challenge, largely by finding **substitutes** for resources that get scarce and by eventually bringing population growth under control.[5]

The optimists can also call upon history to support their position. When England began to experience severe wood shortages, along came coal technology upon which to build the **industrial revolution.** When coal started becoming scarce, petroleum technology was developed. When serious food scarcities threatened the burgeoning populations of Asia, the **green revolution** was initiated to increase food production potential. When domestic energy prices increased rapidly in the 1970s, American producers and consumers demonstrated a surprising ability to adjust technologies and behaviors so as to conserve energy. In other words, history provides many examples of technology shifts and resource conservation in the face of increasing natural resource shortages. This has led many people to be optimistic about our abilities to respond, without catastrophic results, to natural resource scarcities of the future. Of course this does not rule out the need for many local adjustments that will be burdensome in the short run, especially to people whose livelihoods are tied directly to supplies of the scarcer resources.

Perhaps it is fair to say that most of us lie somewhere between the extremes on this issue: We are concerned, certainly, but there is a sense that this is not a situation that we are incapable of ameliorating to a large extent if the right steps are undertaken. This brings up a further question: How are we to know when real natural resource scarcity is about to put a serious crimp in economic welfare? To be able accurately to forecast when some essential natural resource will become seriously restricted in supply, we would need complicated

---

[4] George Perkins Marsh, *Man and Nature, 1864,* Belknap Press of Harvard University Press, Cambridge, MA, 1965, pp. 7–9.

[5] A good early example of the optimist school is the report put out by the Hudson Institute, a think tank specializing in trying to discern future trends; see Herman Kahn, William Brown, and Leon Martel, *The Next 200 Years,* New York, William Morrow and Company, 1976. A more recent optimist work is Julian Simon, *The Ultimate Resource 2,* Princeton University Press, Princeton, NJ, 1996.

models incorporating predictions about population growth, the rate of techno-logical change, the rate of new discoveries, and so on. It is very difficult to build economic models that explicitly account for all these factors.

Long-Run Price Changes

But there is another way. Many natural resources are traded on organized markets; most of these are international in scope with hundreds of partici-pants on the demand and supply sides of the markets. All the different views held by these participants regarding the present and future demands and sup-plies of the resources in question get registered on one element of the market, namely, the **price** of the resource. Resource prices, in other words, tend to dis-till out the preponderant views about present and future resource scarcities.[6] Thus the main focus of resource economists in the study of natural resource scarcities has been to examine the historical paths of the prices of these re-sources. Rising prices would signal increasing scarcity, whereas steady or de-clining prices would signal the absence of scarcity.

Actually, there does not seem to be any long-run tendency for natural re-source prices—at least prices of the traditional resource-type commodities—to increase. It is more generally true that prices have historically decreased, de-spite the huge demographic growth that has taken place over the last few cen-turies. Some prices have shown temporary rises, but the long-run trend has been downward. The primary reason for this has been massive technological change in extraction, transportation, and refining. Whether we can expect the indefinite continuation of technological transformations to the degree we have enjoyed in the recent past is a much debated issue.

Natural Resource Substitution

A key relationship within the long-run scarcity phenomenon goes under the prosaic name of **natural resource substitution.** It is perhaps a human trait for living generations to project thoughts of permanence onto situations that are, especially in the long run, quite changeable. Familiarity with contemporary technologies leads us to discount the idea that the situation could be very dif-ferent. But over the long sweep of history, patterns of natural resource use have changed dramatically, at least in the developed world. What history shows is a series of large and small natural resource substitutions in response to changing conditions of scarcity and price. There is every reason to believe that substitutions in the future will work toward relieving future resource shortages. One possible example is discussed in Exhibit 1-1. This is the substi-tution of salt water for freshwater sources to provide for the needs of humans.

---

[6] Of course other factors also affect prices, so we must be careful in trying to identify a scarcity signal in all the real-world noise. We must also remember that resource prices will normally not reflect any environmental costs of their extraction—a factor that will become increasingly impor-tant in the years to come.

EXHIBIT 1-1

DESALINATION: AN INCREASINGLY POPULAR OPTION

Areas with water shortages, especially in high-income countries, are turning increasingly to desalination plants to supplement water resources. In the 1980s, the number of plants producing more than 100 cubic meters per day increased dramatically, from 3,527 plants in December 1986 to 7,536 plants operating in 120 countries in December 1989. At that time, global capacity (either installed or contracted) was estimated at nearly 13.3 million cubic meters per day, roughly a 13-fold increase since 1970.

Desalination plants are now common in areas that can afford the relatively high cost such as Saudi Arabia, Kuwait, and south Florida. Measured by percentage of total global capacity, Saudi Arabia is the world leader with 27 percent; followed by the United States, 12 percent; Kuwait, 11 percent; and the United Arab Emirates, 10 percent.

Large plants, such as the 1 million cubic meter per day Jubail plant in Saudi Arabia, usually use the distillation process, in which salt water is heated and the resulting steam condenses into fresh water. The main distillation process—the multistage flash process—has declined from 67 percent of total capacity in 1984 to about 56 percent in 1989, but it still plays a significant role in very large plants and in dual-purpose plants coupled with power generation. Smaller plants typically use reverse osmosis, which uses high pressure to force salt water through a screen that filters out both suspended and dissolved solids. Reverse osmosis climbed to about 31 percent of total global capacity by 1989, up from 20 percent in 1984.

Desalination is still three to four times more expensive than conventional sources of fresh water, costing 40–60 cents per 1,000 liters of brackish water and $1.05 to $1.60 per 1,000 liters of sea water. As the technology improves, however, and the cost of conventional fresh water increases, desalination plants are likely to become more popular and the costs are likely to continue to decline slightly. There is greatly increased interest, for example, in building distillation plants alongside electric utilities and using the waste heat from power generation to drive the desalination process.

About 65 percent of all plants are treating sea water and 27 percent are treating brackish water. Desalination plants are increasingly being used for applications other than removing salt, such as the treatment of effluent waters, of river water to obtain water for boilers, of groundwater that has been polluted by nitrates and pesticides, and of municipal water to make ultrapure water for the electronics industry.

Source: From *World Resources 1992–93: A Guide to the Global Environment* by World Resources Institute. Copyright © 1992 by World Resources Institute. Used by permission of Oxford University Press, Inc.

The future will probably see a further drop in the costs of desalination, and as this happens the shift to the oceans for our water supplies will have vast impacts, economically and politically, on current water supply systems.

Substitution occurs not only among resources, but also between natural resources and other types of inputs. In fact **resource conservation** can be thought of as a particular type of substitution. During the 1970s, high energy prices encouraged a great deal of substitution, in this case of capital-type inputs (e.g., new energy-saving machines) for energy inputs, which produced a substantial amount of **energy conservation.** A major role for natural resource economics is to study the future potential for scarcity-mitigating resource substitutions.

SOCIALLY OPTIMAL RATES OF RESOURCE USE

As a way of coming to grips with the issue of whether society is using its natural resource assets wisely, looking at long-run trends in resource prices may seem rather indirect. A more satisfying approach might be to focus on the **rates** at which particular resources are used and to try to answer the question of whether these rates are the best ones from the standpoint of society. The study of **socially optimal natural resource utilization rates** is a major part of natural resource economics. "Optimal" means "best" according to some specified criteria. Optimal use rates depend on many factors, such as the value of the resource in alternative uses, rates of natural replenishment, environmental factors, expected demographic and technological trends, and so on. The challenge to those who would study these matters is to use theories and models that will capture the important complexities of the real world, but give results that are comprehensible to the average person.[7]

Exhibit 1-2 illustrates some of the difficulties of trying to determine optimal utilization rates. The problem here is setting **annual catch rates** for particular fisheries. One concept that fisheries biologists and administrators have used is **maximum sustained yield,** the maximum allowable catch that can be sustained over many years. But fish stocks may fluctuate from year to year for a variety of reasons. So an allowable catch that is reasonable in a year of relative abundance may not be in years of scarcity. From an administrative/political standpoint it may not be possible to vary allowable catch rates annually: The pressure will be to set the rates at the same level for a period of years. For a fisheries administrator the problem is how to set long-term catch rates in a fluctuating ecosystem.

Again, the relevant criterion for evaluating natural resource use rates is **social optimality.** But society is composed of many people and groups, and what is optimal for one may not be so for another. If a decision or course of action is socially optimal, it presumably means that it is the best, taking into account all the expected consequences and implications flowing from the decision or action. In later chapters we will try to give substance to this somewhat abstract notion.

IDENTIFYING THE SOURCES OF NATURAL RESOURCE MISMANAGEMENT

A natural extension of identifying optimal natural resource use rates is the issue of diagnosing the reasons why actual rates of use are often not optimal. The job here is one of studying the **causes of resource mismanagement.** To diagnose instances of mismanagement calls first for a specific criterion that can be used to recognize cases of mismanagement. In economics the primary criterion is **efficiency;** a second one of great importance is **equity.** A natural

---

[7] In economics a "model" is a simplified way of depicting how important factors (e.g., resource use rates, technical change, population growth) are interrelated and how changes in one factor can affect changes in others.

EXHIBIT 1-2

UNCERTAINTY, RESOURCE EXPLOITATION, AND CONSERVATION:
LESSONS FROM HISTORY

Donald Ludwig, Ray Hilborn, Carl Walters

For some years the concept of maximum sustained yield (MSY) guided efforts at fisheries management. There is now widespread agreement that this concept was unfortunate. Larkin concluded that fisheries scientists have been unable to control the technique, distribution, and amount of fishing effort. The consequence has been the elimination of some substocks, such as herring, cod, ocean perch, salmon, and lake trout. He concluded that an MSY based upon the analysis of the historic statistics of a fishery is not attainable on a sustained basis. Support for Larkin's view is provided by a number of reviews of the history of fisheries. Few fisheries exhibit steady abundance.

Harvesting of irregular or fluctuating resources is subject to a ratchet effect: during relatively stable periods, harvesting rates tend to stabilize at positions predicted by steady-state bioeconomic theory. Such levels are often excessive. Then a sequence of good years encourages additional investment in vessels or processing capacity. When conditions return to normal or below normal, the industry appeals to the government for help; often substantial investments and many jobs are at stake. The governmental response typically is direct or indirect subsidies. These may be thought of initially as temporary, but their effect is to encourage overharvesting. The ratchet effect is caused by the lack of inhibition on investments during good periods, but strong pressure not to disinvest during poor periods. The long-term outcome is a heavily subsidized industry that overharvests the resource.

Scientific certainty and consensus in itself would not prevent overexploitation and destruction of resources. Many practices continue even in cases where there is abundant scientific evidence that they are ultimately destructive. An outstanding example is the use of irrigation in arid lands. Approximately 3000 years ago in Sumer, the once highly productive wheat crop had to be replaced by barley because barley was more salt-resistant. The salty soil was the result of irrigation. E. W. Hilgard pointed out in 1899 that the consequences of planned irrigation in California would be similar. His warnings were not heeded. Thus 3000 years of experience and a good scientific understanding of the phenomena, their causes, and the appropriate prophylactic measures are not sufficient to prevent the misuse and consequent destruction of resources.

Political leaders at levels ranging from world summits to local communities base their policies upon a misguided view of the dynamics of resource exploitation. Scientists have been active in pointing out environmental degradation and consequent hazards to human life, and possibly to life as we know it on Earth. But by and large the scientific community has helped to perpetuate the illusion of sustainable development through scientific and technological progress. Resource problems are not really environmental problems: They are human problems that we have created at many times and in many places, under a variety of political, social, and economic systems.

Source: Reprinted with permission from *Science,* Vol. 260, April 2, 1993, pp. 17, 36. Copyright 1993 American Association for the Advancement of Science.

resource is being managed efficiently if it is producing the maximum net value to society. "Producing" in this case means more than conventional extractive activities; it also includes values that resources produce when they are not used in traditional ways, but rather are conserved for ecological purposes or other nonextractive roles. A natural resource is being used equitably if the distribution of the net benefits flowing from its use is regarded as fair. Economic analysis can identify situations that are efficient; judgments about what is fair must come from the political system.

In a market economy, natural resource mismanagement can arise from two major sources: (1) the difficulties private markets encounter, in some circumstances, of functioning efficiently, and (2) misguided public policy and public regulation.

Exhibit 1-3 discusses three cases of misguided policies in the United States. They deal essentially with the way laws have been used to subsidize users of natural resources on the public domain. In many cases this happens because laws that were originally enacted for one purpose stay on the books even though conditions change. So a mining law, for example, that may have been reasonable when it was enacted in 1872, has become a means of subsidizing mining operators because conditions in the industry are vastly different now, while the law remains unchanged. And because the subsidies create powerful political constituencies, present-day legislatures are unable to change the laws.

Throughout the book we will encounter many cases like this, where public resources policy enacted at one point in time, or in the pursuit of certain objectives, has had effects that are inefficient and/or inequitable. Likewise, we will encounter situations where private markets, left to themselves, will lead to natural resources mismanagement. This obviously creates a dilemma. If private natural resource markets are functioning inefficiently, but effective public policy is too hard to get, what do we fall back on? We obviously have to fall back on making choices between imperfect alternatives—an idea we will deal with throughout the book.

PRESERVATION VS. EXTRACTION: VALUATION OF THE ALTERNATIVES

In their ancient, historical role, natural resources were thought to be merely raw materials to be extracted or otherwise physically converted or used to support economic growth and the advancement of material welfare. They were regarded as **inputs** to fuel the economy and the production of the full range of goods and services desired by consumers. They still play this role. But in recent decades another role has become widely recognized and appreciated: the value of natural resources in terms of the **nonextractive** services they provide—scenic values, support for outdoor recreation, biodiversity preservation, and simply the preservation of a meaningful natural heritage.

The opposition between the motives of extraction and preservation has produced some monumental conflicts in this century. One of the first and best known was the fight in the early years of the century over converting the Hetch-Hetchy Valley within Yosemite National Park from a scenic natural wonder to a massive dam and reservoir to supply water to San Francisco. A similar fierce debate occurred in the 1960s and 1970s over the construction of a dam in Glen Canyon, Utah, that changed a place of great natural beauty to a

EXHIBIT 1-3

PUBLIC SUBSIDIES AND NATURAL RESOURCE UTILIZATION

One important factor leading to excessive natural resource use can be public subsidies that go to natural resource users as a result of past resource policies. The following is from the Economic Report of the President, 1997.

Current policies toward natural resource use are mainly rooted in past legislation intended to stimulate the economies of the West and encourage settlement of the region. These policies facilitate the development and exploitation of natural resources.

Subsidized Use of Federal Public Lands. Most uses of Federal public land are currently subsidized in one of at least three possible ways. First, a subsidy can exist when the price to the user is less than the government's cost of overseeing the activity. Second, a subsidy may exist when users of Federal lands pay the government a price below that paid for the similar use of comparable privately owned lands. Finally, resource users may receive a subsidy if they pay the government less than the opportunity cost of the land's use, which is defined as the value of the highest alternative use of the resource. The type and amount of subsidy offered on Federal lands vary with the nature of the activity and with the location of the land.

Public grazing fees are almost always below private fees and may not even cover the government's cost of administering the grazing program.

The subsidy offered to ranchers is small, however, compared with that given to miners taking hardrock minerals such as gold, copper, silver, and uranium: miners do not pay the government any significant revenue or fee for hardrock minerals extracted from Federal public lands. This policy, established in the 1872 General Mining Law, bestows a large subsidy on private mining companies.

Timber extraction from Federal public lands is also subsidized, although the subsidy is more subtle than those for mining and grazing. Generally, the USFS subsidizes timber extraction from public lands by collecting less in timber sale revenues than it spends on timber program costs.

Federal water projects constructed and managed by the Bureau of Reclamation, the Army Corps of Engineers, and the Natural Resource Conservation Service of the U.S. Department of Agriculture are all highly subsidized. For example, projects constructed by the Bureau of Reclamation embody a number of different subsidies. These include interest-free repayment for capital invested in irrigation facilities, limitation on repayment association with "ability to pay" guidelines that do not necessarily reflect changing economic or market conditions or individuals' income, and the repayment of costs above an irrigator's estimated ability to pay by using hydropower revenues far in the future.

Recreational use of Federal public lands is also heavily subsidized: in many areas fees paid by recreational users do not cover the costs of maintaining the resource for recreation. The Park Service spends around $250 million annually to provide visitor services at its 374 parks, monuments, and historic sites. Entrance fees raise only $80 million annually.

Source: Economic Report of the President, Government Printing Office, Washington, D.C., 1997, pp. 216–218.

large flat-water recreation area. Conflicts continue today: the cutting of old-growth forests vs. preserving endangered species; the drilling for oil in designated wilderness areas; the expansion of ski resorts vs. the preservation of forest habitat; the growth of off-road motor vehicles vs. the preservation of natural peace and quiet, and so on.

In the extraction/preservation debate there are a number of important tasks for resource economists. One is to try to look deeply into the **basic nature of the choice** that confronts society in these cases. Preserved resources are usually unique; extracted resources usually are not. Extraction often results in irreversible changes of natural resource assets; preservation normally does not. In light of these factors, normal principles of rational choice may suggest that we adopt conservative decision strategies that will prolong our natural resource options. We will discuss this topic at greater length later in the book.

Another important role for economics in these cases is in **valuing the consequences of the preservation** option. Extracted resources are normally (not always) sold in markets; think of petroleum, timber, agricultural land, and commercial fish. The values that society places on these resources are registered in **market prices** for such products as oil, wood, and land. These are often well-organized, competitive markets where prices reflect the give-and-take between consumer desires and natural scarcities. The preservation option, on the other hand, usually does not involve the market. In many cases this is a problem to be rectified, and one of our tasks will be to explore new possibilities for market-based resource policies. But another critical task is to develop and apply analytical tools to measure the value of nonmarket resources, for example, resources such as **ecosystem services,** which do not move through markets. Resource economics has developed some special techniques for doing this, as we shall see.

A third important contribution that economics can make to this debate is in assessing the economic consequences of shifting resources from extractive to preservation uses, especially the consequences in terms of the **distribution of costs.** Programs to reduce or change the extraction rates of particular resources will usually have important impacts on the extractive industries formed for this purpose. Proposals to reduce timber harvesting in a certain region, for example, will impact people in transport and mill operations in that region. Plans to reduce fishery catch rates will require cutbacks in employment in the fishing fleet. Very often the costs of preservation programs are disproportionately borne by relatively small groups of people. It is important for economic analysts to identify this situation when it exists and to help provide the data and analysis on which compensation might be devised.[8]

PROPERTY RIGHTS AND NATURAL RESOURCES

How people use, and abuse, natural resources is not simply a technological matter, but more importantly a result of the economic institutions[9] that guide

---

[8] This does not preclude that economists are advocates for one position or another, but that it is essentially a political role, not an analytical one.

[9] "Economic institutions" refers broadly to the rules and organizations that govern economic activity in any particular society. Such things as laws governing property rights and commercial transactions, court systems, patent and copyright laws, and policy organizations like legislatures and regulatory agencies are all examples of institutions.

our decisions and behavior. Especially important in this respect are **property rights institutions:** the laws, customs, and regulations governing the rights of people to have access to, and utilize, natural resources of different types. All human societies have property rights institutions, though not necessarily the same ones. How different property rights systems affect human uses of natural resources is a major issue in natural resource economics.

One important topic is how different types of property rights—public or private, individual or collective—affect the types of uses to which natural resources are put and the resulting rates of utilization. Another important problem is how the physical features of different natural resources (e.g., the fugitive nature of wild fish or the regional variations in water abundance) affect the property rights that are most appropriate to the resources. A third is how new types of property rights might evolve to help resolve certain difficult natural resource problems.

Exhibit 1-4 discusses an example of the latter. It deals with the shift from an **open-access system** of fisheries management to one based on **private property**

EXHIBIT 1-4

RIGHTS-BASED FISHING: TRANSITION TO A NEW INDUSTRY

North Atlantic fisheries off New England and maritime Canada have collapsed, and throughout the world yields from many ocean fishing grounds are declining precipitously. Reversing the process may require abandoning the tradition of free and open access to the ocean's resources in exchange for a "closed-access" system based on property rights.

The story is certainly not news: many of the world's ocean fisheries are being pushed toward possibly ruinous declines. True, we have yet to see skyrocketing prices or long lines at the seafood counter. Long-established fishing communities, however, are threatened, as are some traditional, often centuries-old ways of life. Sporadic armed conflict has even broken out in some territorial waters. And the equilibrium of coastal marine ecosystems, already taxed by pollution and other development pressures, is further threatened by progressive decimations of many marine species and populations.

Many Americans may be aware of the collapsed North Atlantic fisheries off New England and maritime Canada. The problem, though, is global and growing, and we know why: overfishing. The practice results from the tradition of free and open access to fishery resources that itself stems from the traditional principle of freedom of the

seas. As a result of overfishing, too many fishermen and manufacturers now pursue and process fewer and fewer—and generally smaller—specimens.

Broad command-and-control regulatory approaches, typically based on some version of open access, clearly are not working. Management areas, for instance, seem to be too large to reflect accurately the local conditions and interests of the fishermen themselves. Even when control has been regionalized, as in the United States with its nine regional fisheries management councils, the decisionmaking powers tend to reside in those with vested interests in short-term gains rather than the long-term health of the fisheries. Ocean fisheries management needs the cooperation of those who work the seas, much of the preservation of terrestrial biodiversity and ecosystem management require the willing assistance of private landowners.

EXHIBIT 1-4—*Continued*

RIGHTS-BASED FISHING: TRANSITION TO A NEW INDUSTRY

Would creating and using property rights among fishermen work to control both open access and overcapacity—and, thereby, overfishing? Systems could be designed to set quotas on catches permitted or limit the number of licenses issued. Such systems have in fact been used around the globe with increasing frequency since the 1970s, but mostly at local and regional levels. Such *rights-based fishing* assumes that fishermen, if allowed exclusive use rights and thus included more directly in fisheries management decisions, will clearly see the benefits of managing for the long-term health and productivity of their fisheries.

Exclusive user rights have long been used by small-scale local fishermen with fishery resources adjacent to their own community, especially for relatively sedentary animals like shellfish. Expanding this to larger fisheries and more mobile sealife remains a challenge (although tuna companies in the Philippines have successfully controlled local access by limiting the type of fishing gear used). The goal in all cases, though, is to convey more authority for the use of a fishery, including monitoring and surveillance, to its primary users.

New Zealand has become the leader in ITQs (individual transferrable quotas), with thirty-two species-specific agreements. Australia is a close second: its division with Japan of much of the southern bluefin tuna fishery is illustrative. Using relatively low quota allocations, many in the Australian part of the fishery had to decide whether to buy more quota or sell out. In the two years following the start of the ITQ system for that fishery, the number of boats in use dropped by 50 percent. Researchers estimated that the capital so employed in the boats was $10 to $12 million less than under other management schemes. The system also focused catches on larger, more valuable specimens, with the value of the catches increased three- to fourfold.

Some Problems

Unfortunately, bycatch—the inadvertent capture of unsought species —is not necessarily reduced substantially though quotas could be set for bycatch to encourage fishermen to work other areas of the fishery with less bycatch potential or (in some fisheries) to invest in equipment that would minimize bycatch. Also, the introduction of a property-rights regime does not immediately, or even necessarily, result in a leveling out of the rate of fishery stock depletion. And those fish that move between the biologically arbitrary 200-mile-wide territorial waters and the high seas present another challenge to property-rights regimes, much as they do to the present system.

Enforcement also remains a problem, with the intrusions of foreign boats and fleets especially vexing. Poaching may always be with us, and assigning surveillance and monitoring to property owners seems unlikely to change that. Even more damaging and difficult to resolve can be legal fishing at the very edges of the 200-mile limit. Small-scale fishermen looking ever-farther afield can so intrude, as can "pirate" trawlers using illegal equipment such as fine-meshed nets. Usually, however, the legal industrial fleets of huge trawlers present the greatest challenge. Designed to catch and process a ton or more per hour, these giants can effectively clean out much of any fishery. Negotiating and enforcing international agreements may prolong the full transition to a rights-based industry.

Source: Adapted from Resources for the Future, *Resources,* Issue 124, Summer 1996. Reprinted by permission.

rights. Ocean fisheries have historically been treated as an open-access resource: The fish are converted to the ownership of whoever gets there first and puts the most effort into catching them. This has led repeatedly to overfishing and reduced fish stocks. The system of **individual transferable quotas** (ITQs) is an attempt essentially to create marketable property rights in fish. If it works, it could lead to reduced pressure on marine resources by taking advantage of the normal incentives that owners have to preserve the values of their assets. We will discuss this in detail in Chapter 19.

THE USE OF BENEFIT-COST ANALYSIS IN NATURAL RESOURCE DECISIONS

In 1966 the U.S. Congress enacted a law aimed at preserving endangered species.[10] It authorized the federal government to purchase land for the conservation of threatened species and the protection of their required habitats "insofar as possible." The language in which these statutes were written in effect allowed the relevant public agencies to make what they regarded as "balanced" decisions on species protection, weighing the apparent benefits of certain preservation decisions with the costs of these decisions.

Then in 1973 Congress passed the Endangered Species Act (ESA). This was a time of great activity in federal environmental and resource policy. Advocates of new laws and more encompassing public initiatives put great stress on the benefits to be produced by these efforts, and paid relatively little attention to their costs. Thus, the language of the ESA was very different from the earlier laws; it essentially directed the agencies to protect endangered species no matter what the cost. Certain amendments of 1978 provided some flexibility by creating a mechanism whereby exemptions could be granted to the strict requirements of the law. The terms of the original act still hold, however, in that they do not permit the Secretary of Interior to take costs into account in making decisions about endangered species. Once a species is listed as endangered or threatened, it is supposed to be protected at all costs.

But although the political language appears to be unambiguous and uncompromising, real life is more complicated. With goals in conflict, restrictions on budget resources, and imperfect knowledge, decisions simply cannot be made without compromises and trade-offs. These can be made out of sight, as it were, in the recesses of the bureaucratic process. Or they could be done more overtly, by bringing **benefit-cost analysis** explicitly to bear. Benefit-cost analysis is simply an attempt to account for and compare, within the same analysis, all the benefits and costs of particular courses of action. It was developed many years ago to evaluate federal water projects like dams. In recent years many people have taken the view that it ought to be applied more broadly to all the natural resource and environmental decisions made in the public sector. Needless to say, this is a controversial issue.

---

[10] Public Law 89-669, signed on October 15, 1966.

Regarding the endangered species act, benefit-cost analysis would require that economists estimate both the costs of taking action to preserve particular species and the benefits of so doing. The costs are the values forgone if resources are preserved for the support of an endangered species. The benefits are the values that citizens place on having the species preserved, adjusted for the probability that the species would survive anyway in the absence of the specific preservation action under consideration. Exhibit 1-5 discusses some of the benefit-cost analyses that resource economists have done on plans to protect the spotted owl.

In Chapter 8 we will examine the principles of benefit-cost analysis and some of the techniques that economists have developed for applications in cases of natural resource problems. Although the political controversy will no

---

EXHIBIT 1-5

THE ECONOMICS OF SPOTTED OWL PRESERVATION

The spotted owl is an endangered species that lives in the forests of northern California and Oregon. Logging of a forest makes it useless as spotted owl habitat, so ensuring the survival of the animal implies restricting the harvest of forests where they are located. This has implications for those whose livelihood depends on logging. Trying to reach a compromise between preservationists and loggers has been difficult and conflict-ridden.

Resource economists have sought to illuminate the conflict by applying benefit-cost analysis to the plans for spotted owl preservation.

In a benefit-cost framework there are two relationships to consider: the costs of achieving higher probabilities of spotted owl survival; and the benefits in terms of the social value of the preserved spotted owls.

Claire Montgomery and Gardner Brown looked closely at the cost side.[1] They worked closely with wildlife biologists to determine how the spotted owl's survival probabilities (the probability—50 percent, 90 percent, etc., that the spotted owl would not become extinct sometime in the next 150 years) were related to the amount of their forest habitat; some of which, but not all, is located in old-growth forests of Oregon.

They then estimated the amount of owl habitat that consisted of harvestable forest, and therefore the amount of such forest land that would have to be withdrawn from potential harvest to achieve particular survival probabilities. They then estimated the lost value of timber production from these withdrawn acres.

On the benefit side, Daniel Hagen, James Vincent, and Patrick Welle[2] estimated the social value of preserved spotted owl population. They did this through what is called a "contingent valuation" survey, essentially a technique of polling a large number of people about how much they would be willing to pay in terms of increased taxes, or the increased costs of building materials, in order to prevent the extinction of the spotted owl. Their results are that the value of benefits per year, to the average household, of preserving the spotted owl, was between about $50 and $150.

[1]Claire Montgomery and Gardner M. Brown, Jr., "Economics of Species Preservation: The Spotted Owl Case," *Contemporary Policy Issues,* X (2), April 1992, pp. 1–12.

[2]Daniel A. Hagen, James W. Vincent, and Patrick G. Welle, "Benefits of Preserving Old-Growth Forests and the Spotted Owl," *Contemporary Policy Issues,* X, (2), April 1992, pp. 13–26.

doubt continue on the appropriate role of benefit-cost analysis in public programs, the important approach from an analytical point is to keep working on making it better in terms of its applicability and the accuracy of the results it produces.

LAND-USE ISSUES

In the ebb and flow of public concern about high-profile natural resource issues—like endangered species, mining in national parks, and grazing fees on the public range—it is sometimes easy to overlook one resource problem that is faced virtually every day by communities everywhere: **the use of the land.** Land is a resource in the sense that it is capable of producing distinctive goods and services; it is also a resource because it is the spatial plane on which most human activity takes place. Humans use portions of the earth's surface for a myriad of different uses: housing, work locations, roads and other transportation corridors, farms, parks, and wilderness areas. Land is also the critical supporting medium for other biological resources of all types.

In most countries of the developed world, decisions on how particular pieces of land will be devoted to particular uses are made through a complex mixture of private land markets and public oversight. Land markets in the United States are extremely well developed, with sophisticated surveying, deed registration, title transfer practices, and courts to adjudicate disputes. But there is a long history of public intervention in land issues, both to provide essential public services like roads, to regulate the economic and technical impacts that adjoining or propinquitous parcels of land have on one another, and to manage human impacts on portions of the natural environment. In doing this, communities have developed a large arsenal of regulatory tools, such as zoning, conservation restrictions, subdivision regulations, and outright land purchase.

The story in Exhibit 1-6 discusses a technique used by many states to try to preserve agricultural land uses. In certain places, agricultural preservation is important for cultural, scenic, and/or food supply reasons, and so efforts have been made to look for ways of slowing the rate at which agricultural land is converted to other uses, such as home lots. The approach is **development rights purchase,** whereby public authorities purchase only the right to develop from farmers, leaving them with the remaining rights on their land and the freedom to farm the land as they wish. This allows some farmers to continue farming but also to realize a large share of the development value of their lands. This clearly improves their financial positions, and the hope is that it will enable them to continue operating the farms. This may be easier because of the tax advantages stemming from sale of the development rights.

It is not hard to see how economic analysis has an important role to play in cases like this. Local land markets are usually very finely tuned institutions; they normally react quickly to new stimuli (e.g., rumors of a new office building going up in town), and they can be very hard to guide in particular directions because of the substantial incentives they give to participants. The effects

EXHIBIT 1-6

PRESERVING FARMLAND. COWS IN TRUST

PAWLET, VT.—In the south-western corner of the state of Vermont, where mountains rise above farmland and the Mettowee River is full of trout, Tim and Dot Leach, the owners of Woodlawn Farm, have decided to sell the development rights of their 350-acre dairy farm to the Vermont Land Trust. It was not an easy decision. In giving up their right to sell the land at its market value, the Leaches have placed a conservation easement on it, a legal agreement between landowner and land trust that restricts development of the property. They still own the land and their children will inherit it, but it must be kept open and available to farming.

To compensate them, the Vermont Housing and Conservation Board puts a lump sum in the Leaches' bank account, with cash from the state matched by local charities. It may be less than half what the property is worth on the open market.

The Leaches are part of a conservation movement which started in Vermont in 1977 and has grown, over 20 years, into 1,100 non-profit regional and local land trusts dotted through the 50 states. As a result, over 4m American acres have already been preserved from encroaching subdivisions, shopping malls and other commercial developments. Vermont alone has saved 110,553 acres. The six New England states have most land trusts, more than a third of the total: Massachusetts has 121, more than vast California's 116. According to the Land Trust Alliance, the umbrella organization for these groups, new trusts are appearing at a rate of one a week.

It was uncertainty about the future that made the Leaches decide to put Woodlawn Farm in trust. The four Leach children are the seventh generation to live on the farm since the early 1800s. For the past 90 years Woodlawn has been a dairy farm, an endangered species in America's north-east. Mr. Leach has built up the herd and added an automated milking parlour; he now runs one of the highest-yielding milk operations in the state. Yet the volatility of milk prices has been a constant worry. "You can go from doing well to doing poorly," says Mr. Leach. "You don't know what will happen next."

Mr. Leach was suspicious when the Mettowee Valley Conservation Project, an arm of the Vermont Land Trust, moved to the valley ten years ago. "The idea of a land trust is not traditional. My stubborn Yankee conservative nature rejected the idea for years," he says. From the project's point of view, Woodlawn Farm was exactly what it was looking for: a solid, well-managed working farm with a history. As a bonus, the Leaches also allowed access to hunters, fishermen and snowmobilers. Public access is not a requirement for Vermont land-trust farm, but it helps.

Joan Allen, the project director of the Mettowee Valley land trust, says that competition to take part in the land trust programme is fierce. It takes a while to apply and even longer to be appraised by the local agency and state offices. In the final stage, farm-owners have to appear before the Vermont Housing and Conservation Board in Montpelier, the state capital, to answer questions. More than 100 farms, most of them dairy ones, apply in Vermont each year. This year, 37 farms reached the final stage; there was money for only 11.

Not everyone agrees that selling development rights to a land trust is the wisest choice for the landowner. The conservation easement, the legal tool that makes the deal work, is meant to be permanent. Although the children can inherit, they lose their rights to develop the land, even down to such details as adding a septic tank. This means that the value of the property is diminished. Yet the alternative, in most cases, is stark: they would be able to stay in farming.

Critics also say the land trust movement is elitist. It benefits the upper and upper-middle classes, the argument goes, by the

(continued)

EXHIBIT 1-6—*Continued*

PRESERVING FARMLAND. COWS IN TRUST

strict standards it imposes to protect the land: growth control, open space, maintained eco-systems and the preservation of town or village character. With land-trust-monitored farms in the neighbourhood, houses and land prices may go up, taking them out of the middle-class market.

Robert Rakoff, a professor at Hampshire College in Amherst, Massachusetts, has studied land-trust conservation in the northeast. In a letter to the *New York Times* on

March 23rd, he concluded that in many cases farming disappears anyway and what is protected is scenic open space. He calls it a "cultural shift toward the passive consumption of nature." The Leaches, and many like them, will hope it is not as passive as all that.

Source: The Economist, May 17, 1997. © 1997 The Economist Newspaper Group, Inc. Reprinted with permission. Further reproduction prohibited.

---

of development right purchases may be to protect land from development, but not necessarily to ensure that farming continues actively to be preserved. We will look at some of the major dimensions of land economics in Chapter 14.

NATURAL RESOURCE ACCOUNTING

In 1997 the **gross domestic product** (GDP) of the United States was $8,111 billion. This figure is an estimate of the total value of "final" goods and services produced in the economy, that is, goods and services supplied to households and other consumers. Among the countries of the world, increases in GDP are normally associated with growth and progress. They support growing populations and make it possible to enjoy increases in per capita wealth and human welfare.

But conventional GDP measures are deficient in a number of respects. One important problem is that they measure only the value of goods and services that move through markets. So, for example, the value of volunteer work done in the country is not included, nor is the value of work done in the household by members of those households. Another problem is that they do not allow for **natural resource depletion.** Adjustments are normally made for the depreciation of human-produced capital goods—buildings, equipment, and the like—which, in the normal functioning of an economy, will be used up to some extent. Deducting capital from gross economic output leads to a measure of net output.

But depreciation may also occur in a society's **natural resource capital.** The production of conventional goods and services requires inputs from the natural environment, both in traditional forms, such as minerals, timber, water, and agricultural land, and also in the less widely recognized nontraditional services such as biological diversity, carbon fixation, and nutrient recycling. Natural resources supply important scenic resources basic to the large outdoor recreation industry. The resource base from which these goods and services are supplied can clearly be depreciated as a result of their use. Quantitatively, resources such as minerals used today reduce the stock available for future generations. Qualitatively, ecosystems may be impacted so much that they lose productivity, as in the case, for example, of soil erosion.

This has led some people to think about what is called **natural resource accounting.** This focus involves two types of work: The first is to estimate the value of ecosystem services provided by a country's natural resource endowment, so that they could be included along with standard output measures in the national economic accounts. An example of this is the measurement of flood control values produced by many forested areas or the wildlife preservation values produced by public parks or other wildlife refuge areas. As mentioned above, resource economists have worked to develop ways of accounting for these nonmarket service flows. The other part of the natural resource accounting effort is to assess the total value of the natural capital stock, so that we can determine the extent to which that stock is being depleted. Estimating natural resource accounts is an important task of **ecological economics,** a new specialty within economics, in which researchers try to combine the principles of economics and ecology to produce a more powerful way of looking at the role of natural resources and the impacts of economic activity on natural resource systems.

INTERNATIONAL NATURAL RESOURCE CONFLICTS

Natural resources historically have been the source of much conflict among countries of the world. As nations pursue their economic growth and development goals, these conflicts are likely to become more frequent and severe. Water resources have been a major issue, as Exhibit 1-7 discusses. Fights over surface water have led countries to the brink of war. Conflicts over access to productive fisheries have continued to flare up, though some of the basis for these has been removed with the 200-mile exclusionary zones now claimed by most countries. Differences over rights to mine deep sea minerals may become more common as undersea mining technology continues to improve. Conflicts over access to undersea petroleum deposits continue in some parts of the world. Understanding the genesis of, and possible solutions to, international conflicts clearly calls for an understanding of how international law and international political institutions function, or often don't function. Bilateral treaties are often the result when a resource is shared between just two countries (e.g., the Pacific Salmon dispute between Canada and the United States). Multilateral agreements are required when multiple countries are involved (e.g., the regional seas treaties sponsored by the United Nations).

Economics comes into the question when we want to understand the magnitude of natural resource values that are affected, in total and for the individual countries involved in disputes, and how these relative values might shift according to different patterns of agreement. Economic efficiency is involved, because it is important to be able to establish how a resource might be used so as to maximize its net social value. How the total gets divided is also extremely important, because fairness becomes an even more critical factor when it is the representatives of sovereign states who are doing the negotiating.

EXHIBIT 1-7

WATER AS A SOURCE OF INTERNATIONAL CONFLICT

Kenneth D. Frederick

From Canada to Mexico, from Africa to the Middle East, from Asia to Europe, conflicts and the potential for conflicts are growing over the availability of water. While sharing water resources has long been divisive, today's rising environmental, social, and financial costs of managing Earth's most abundant and renewable natural resource exacerbate these perennial tensions. Easing such tensions becomes imperative at a time when demands for water are rising. The greater efficiencies achievable by integrated resource management, developing water markets, and price incentives may prove the best ways to achieve this end. . . .

Several factors underlie virtually all international conflicts over water and pose problems for managing and allocating it efficiently and equitably. These include the variability and uncertainty of supplies, the interdependencies among users, and the increasing scarcity and rising costs of freshwater. Because water is a "fugitive" resource—naturally flowing from one location and one state (liquid, gas, or solid) to another—individuals and countries have incentives to capture and use the resource before it moves beyond their control but little, if any, incentive to conserve and protect supplies for downstream users.

Rivers and lakes that border multiple countries, rivers that flow from one country to another, and aquifers that underlie more than one country are international resources: the use of the resource by one country affects the quantity or quality of the resource available to another country. Such situations are numerous: about 200 river basins are shared by two or more countries. Thirteen are shared by five or more countries, and four basins—the Congo, Danube, Nile, and Niger—are shared by nine or more countries. Shared watersheds comprise about 47 percent of the global land area and more than 60 percent of the area on the continents of Africa, Asia, and South America. . . .

The competition for water in the Middle East is so intense that lasting peace in the region is unlikely in the absence of an agreement over shared water use. . . . Outstanding issues and potential sources of conflict include the allocation and control of the Jordan River, the use of the aquifers underlying the West Bank, and Jordanian objections to the construction and operation of Syrian dams on the Yarmuk, the major tributary of the Jordan River. Water has already been the source of armed conflict in the region between Syria and Israel, once in the 1950s and again in the 1960s. . . .

When the Indian subcontinent was partitioned between India and Pakistan in 1947, longstanding conflicts over the Indus River became overnight an international issue between two hostile countries. The partitioning divided the basin physically and split an established irrigation system between the two countries without specifying how the waters were to be divided. . . .

The breakup of the Soviet Union has also converted some formerly domestic water issues into potential international conflicts. Water scarcity and conflicts are particularly acute in the five former central Asian republics of the Soviet Union that share the flows of the Amu Dar'ya and Syr Dar'ya rivers. . . .

The lack of clear property rights to international water resources is an obstacle to more efficient resource management and to the resolution of water conflicts. Two extreme and opposing doctrines have been proposed for establishing property rights over international waters. The doctrine of unlimited territorial sovereignty states that a country has exclusive rights to the use of waters within its territory. . . .

The contrasting doctrine of *unlimited territorial integrity* states that one country cannot alter the quantity and quality of water available to another. . . .

EXHIBIT 1-7—*Continued*

WATER AS A SOURCE OF INTERNATIONAL CONFLICT

In the absence of bargaining, both of these doctrines are likely to lead to inefficient outcomes. . . .

In practice, international water disputes generally have moved away from the extreme positions implied by these two doctrines and toward a doctrine of *equitable and reasonable use.* . . .

Equity considerations and historical use have been more important than efficiency in the management of both domestic and internationally shared water resources. Relatively few precedents demonstrate the potential advantages of efficient integrated management of an entire hydrologic unit.

Yet, as water becomes increasingly scarce, the potential benefits of integrated management—and of institutions that enable scarce resources to be transferred among competing uses in response to changing conditions—will grow. Institutions that perpetuate inefficient water use will become increasingly costly and unstable. Inflexible and inefficient international agreements, which must be self-enforcing, may not be sustainable.

Source: Resources for the Future, *Resources,* Spring 1996, Issue 123, Washington, DC. Reprinted by permission.

NATURAL RESOURCES AND ECONOMIC DEVELOPMENT

Throughout the world, countries with delayed economies are struggling to push forward the material standards of living of their citizens and the added security and human welfare this implies. In this process there are important questions about the role of natural resources. Natural resources are **necessary** for economic growth. But "necessary" in this case does not mean that they be located within the same political unit, since there are many cases where countries without large endowments of natural resources have had strong growth. But they are not **sufficient** for economic development, as is proved by examples of resource-rich countries where growth has not been strong. In addition, questions of **sustainable natural resource use** abound: To what extent should nonrenewable resources be used to spur development? To what extent should the productivity of renewable resources be tapped to support short-run development initiatives? Will current resource use patterns seriously undermine other important aspects of the development process?

Important questions like these have to be faced by all developing countries, especially those that are relying on natural resource capital to provide a major impetus to development. The oil deposits of the Middle East, and now of the Caspian Sea Basin, the timber resources of many South American and Asian countries, the minerals of some African countries, the massive coal deposits of China—these are all cases of natural resource capital that is expected to fuel economic growth and development. Major questions exist, both as to the extent of the resources and the ways they should be utilized to achieve efficiency and sustainability. Exhibit 1-8 has a story about some of the repercussions flowing from attempts to develop a massive timber harvesting industry in a vast area of western China. Some of the negative ecological implications of the

---

EXHIBIT 1-8

CHINA TO REPLANT OVER-HARVESTED FORESTS

Joe McDonald

Kong Yifu felt lucky to get a job in a county lumber yard last year. Wrestling pine logs onto trucks was hard work, but it paid better than farming in mountainous western China.

Soon, Kong will lose that job, joining thousands of unintended economic casualties of an attempt to restore the dwindling forests of Sichuan province.

Logging was banned Sept. 1 in much of western Sichuan as part of stepped-up conversation efforts across China spurred by breakneck development's damage to the environment. After a summer of devastating floods made worse by logging that left bare hillsides unable to catch rain, Chinese leaders could no longer ignore the environmental costs.

The logging ban will wipe out more than 45,000 timber jobs, according to the Sichuan government. It is keeping those workers employed for now by paying them to replant forests they once cut.

Timber companies in Sichuan have been required since 1981 to plant one sapling for each tree cut. But few did. And forests receded as demand grew for paper, disposable chopsticks, furniture, building materials and other wood products.

Land covered by forest in Sichuan has shrunk from more than 40 percent in the 1940s to 20 percent today, forestry officials say. Land affected by erosion has nearly doubled, and the province loses 600 million tons of soil a year.

Plans call for replanting 350,000 acres, and logging is banned on 11 million acres. Violators can be sentenced to up to five years in a labor camp.

Similar tree-planting projects are under way or planned in provinces scattered throughout China. In Ningxia in the northwest, a grant from Germany is paying to plant 21,500 acres of trees.

In Sichuan, officials acknowledge that towns dependent on logging will suffer traumatic changes. But they talk optimistically about developing orchards, tourism, manufacturing and cement production.

An end to logging makes financial sense to the Sichuan government. Its timber industry has lost money for years, surviving on treasury-draining subsidies.

The Western Sichuan Logging Co. in Lixian lost $1.3 million last year, said its president, Qian Lishun. The company was renamed the Western Sichuan Forestry Bureau this year and put in charge of conservation.

The winding road to Bipeng Gorge offers a sobering glimpse of the economic future envisioned for the area by the government. Smoke pours from cement factories. Hills along the Min River have been dynamited into rubble for raw materials.

The government plans to build more cement plants, but at the same time wants to promote the area's natural beauty for tourism.

Tourism companies have visited to plan nature outings, said Peng Huangshi, chief engineer for the provincial Department of Forest Industries. But there are no investment commitments yet.

"If anyone wants to invest, we warmly welcome them," he said.

Source: Associated Press, October 11, 1998. Reprinted by permission.

---

project, especially impacts on the hydrological regime of the Yangtze River, have led to a major cutback in the extent of the timber sector and a substantial change in the way the remainder is being managed.

The final two chapters of the book are devoted to problems of some important economic aspects of natural resources and economic development.

SUMMARY

Long-run natural resource adequacy has been a traditional issue in natural resource use. Many people have predicted resource scarcities that will undermine economic growth, but these have not occurred yet. Opinion about when it might happen in the future is divided among optimists, pessimists, and those in the middle. A major challenge to adequacy in natural resource economics is whether long-run price increases in natural resources are imminent. Other resource issues are the shift from extractive to nonextractive forms of natural resource use, the determination of optimal rates of use, the study of policies to bring about these optimal rates, the role of natural resources in developing countries, how basic economic institutions such as property rights regimes affect resource use rates, and international natural resource conflicts.

USEFUL WEB SITES

For general reviews of current natural resource issues, log on to

- Resources for the Future (http://www.rff.org), a resource and environmental think tank in Washington, DC, that pioneered the application of economic analysis to these problems.
- Environmental Defense Fund (http://www.edf.org), a public interest group that emphasizes economic analysis.
- World Resources Institute (http://www.wri.org), for an international perspective.
- National Institute for the Environment (http://www.cnie.org).

Public agencies are good sources of overview material, such as

- United States Department of the Interior (http://www.doi.gov).
- Natural Resources Canada (http://www.nrcan.qc.ca).
- United Kingdom Department of Environment, Transport, and the Regions (http://www.detr.gov.uk).

SELECTED READINGS

Knight, Richard L., and Sarah F. Bates (eds.): *A New Century for Natural Resources Management*, Island Press, Washington, DC, 1994.

Krutilla, John V.: "Conservation Reconsidered," *American Economic Review*, 57 (4), 1967, pp. 777–786.

Macdonnell, Lawrence J., and Sarah F. Bates (eds.): *Natural Resource Policy and Law, Trends and Directions*, Island Press, Covelo, CA, 1993.

Miller, Alan S.: *Gaia Connections: An Introduction to Ecology, Ecoethics, and Economics*, Rowman and Allenheld, Lanham, MD, 1991.

Portney, Paul R., and Ruth B. Haas (eds.): *Current Issues in Natural Resource Policy*, Resources for the Future, Washington, DC, 1982.

Prescott-Allen, Christine, and Robert Prescott-Allen: *The First Resource*, Yale University Press, New Haven, CT, 1986.

Repetto, Robert C.: *World Enough and Time: Successful Strategies for Resource Management*, Yale University Press, New Haven, CT, 1986.

CHAPTER 2

NATURAL RESOURCES AND THE ECONOMY

An **economy** is a means by which a group of people provide themselves with adequate, and perhaps improving, levels of material and social welfare. In general, we associate economies with societies defined by national boundaries: the U.S. economy, the Japanese economy, the South African economy, and so on. Sometimes, however, we speak of the **global economy,** or of subnational economies such as one for a particular region or community.

All individuals play two roles in an economy, as producers and as consumers. In managing their economy, a society makes critical decisions about goods and services, including how much, when, and where to provide these services and the means through which this will be accomplished. They also make fundamental decisions about how these goods and services will be distributed, about who among them will have access to them and on what terms. In a market-type economy, these decisions result from the voluntary interactions of producers and consumers through **market institutions.** Such decisions are normally accompanied by varying degrees of public oversight and regulation through **governmental institutions** of different types.

Society is surrounded by, or encompassed within, a natural world. There are many ways of describing that natural system in physical terms. **Population ecology** leads us to account for it as a collection of interacting populations of organisms, subject to growth and change according to evolutionary principles and the impacts of a host of external events. A natural extension of this to the nonbiological part of nature is to think in terms of stocks of minerals and fossil fuels, subject to chemical and physical laws. **Ecosystem ecology** puts the focus on the processes of ecosystem functioning, such as how energy flows among different trophic levels, how biophysical elements move along certain pathways, and how gases and particulates move through the atmosphere. The aim here is to clarify how various biotic and abiotic processes contribute to these ecosystem functions. Of course these two perspectives are closely related; functions are impossible without populations and vice versa.

At any point in time nature can be described by a series of variables specifying the **quantitative** and **qualitative** status of the system. The quantitative variables consist of stock variables (e.g., acres of forest, tons of marine biomass) and flow variables (e.g., energy striking the surface of the earth, wind speed), while the qualitative variables describe important features of the resources (e.g., parts per million of air pollution, salinity and temperature of water) at particular points of time. Biological and physical laws describe how these variables are transformed from one time to another.

A fruitful way of thinking about the natural resource system and its relationship to human welfare is to think of it as a **stock of natural capital** which, in conjunction with other types of inputs, yields useful **goods and services.** The word "**capital**" has been used historically in economics to refer to a stock of human-produced artifacts, such as tools, machines, and buildings.[1] The concept of "**natural capital**" is useful because it combines the notion of nature-provided inputs with the idea that their quantity and quality can be affected by human actions.

Natural capital, in conjunction with other inputs, produces a wide variety of goods and services. We can discuss these under two rubrics, as depicted in Figure 2-1: The arrow labeled (*a*) depicts the flow of **natural resource products and services** into an economy. **Natural resource economics** is the study of this flow using the analytical tools of economics. We must think of this broadly, as encompassing both traditional extractive uses and the services provided by natural resource preservation. The arrow labeled (*b*) represents the flow of

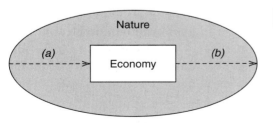

FIGURE 2-1
Nature and Economy

---

[1] There are other recognized types of capital: **working capital,** the financial assets that permit the continuity of production and consumption, and **human capital,** the capacities and capabilities of human beings.

materials and energy **residuals** back into the natural world. This flow is the main subject of **environmental economics.**

Which particular parts of the natural world have value depends on the characteristics of the society/economy in question. At any point in time an economic system will contain a variety of **technological capabilities** (e.g., different modes of production, distribution, and communication), **economic, legal, and regulatory institutions** (e.g., private business firms, a court system, commercial law, public agencies), and an important array of **demographic factors** (e.g., tastes and preferences, population sizes, skill levels, educational institutions). It is these technological, institutional, and demographic facts that make natural resources out of arbitrary elements of nature. One-hundred years ago petroleum was not a natural resource, nor was bauxite or uranium. Sixty years ago, water resources as the provider of recreational services were almost unknown. In recent years **biological diversity** has become an important natural resource. One hundred years from now some feature of the natural world that is currently unknown may have great social value—and may be, in other words, a valuable natural resource.

So the notion of natural resources as portions of the natural world that have value must be understood in the broadest sense. We must recognize that there are dimensions of nature that may become directly utilized only at some distant time when human institutions are very different from those of today. Some of these factors are totally unknown at the present time. Thus social value also incorporates what we would regard as the future potentials of the natural world, in addition simply to those being used today.

The return flow labeled (b) in the diagram highlights services being provided by nature in the form of a "sink" for the reception of wastes. Some of these wastes may be rendered more benign through changes that are produced by the **assimilative capacity** of the environment. Some may accumulate and produce various types of negative impacts on human welfare and the health of the ecosystems comprising the natural world.

There is clearly a close relationship between natural resource economics and environmental economics. The laws of physics assure us that what is taken in by the economy, in terms of material and energy, must eventually come out. So the decisions undertaken in the context of flow (a) will have a lot to do with the problems that have to be addressed under flow (b). But convention, and the advantages of dividing the whole subject into several manageable portions, leads us to a focus in this book on the resource side of the system.[2]

Some might argue that this way of framing things tends to imply that the worth of the natural world is exclusively, or primarily, in terms of its significance for human beings:[3] Nature, it is sometimes said, has value in and of it-

---

[2] Those who would like a similar treatment of environmental economics may want to look at *Environmental Economics: An Introduction,* by Barry C. Field, 2nd ed., McGraw-Hill, New York, 1997.

[3] This is termed the "anthropocentric" point of view.

self, independent of the wishes of people. We leave it to philosophers to argue about whether nonhuman organisms or entities of the natural world express values for different states of that world. This book is about how human values lead people to make decisions about natural resources. Some of these decisions may involve our preserving elements of the natural world in their undisturbed state, insofar as this can be done. We may be led to this out of a motive simply to be good **stewards** of nature, or because we are fearful of our ignorance about how nature affects human welfare. But these are as clearly the expression of human values as is the cutting down of a tree to make 2 × 4's.

SOME TERMINOLOGY

Natural resources have been critical for human welfare since people first started to walk the earth several million years ago. And conflicts over resource use have no doubt been a permanent part of this long history. In this book we take an analytical perspective on problems of natural resource use, applying somewhat formal methods and principles of social rationality to issues that engender great contention and conflict in the real world. We should be familiar with some of the main terminology that this history has produced.

Of course the primary concept is natural resource **conservation.** Battles have been fought over the meaning and application of this word.[4] It clearly has something to do with saving—or reducing—waste, but historically it has been used to cover everything from dam building, so as to reduce the "waste" implied by water runoff, to a state of moral commitment from which to launch political attacks on all the supposed villains of economic excess. Today we may say that conservation is the idea of using natural resources at a rate that is, in some sense, **socially** optimal. Of course, what is optimal for one person or group is not the same as what is correct for another, but the term does seemingly connote a course of action that finds an appropriate balance among diverse motives and avoids action that leads to waste and excessive damage.

One fault line that continues to run through public discussion is that between resource **development** and resource **preservation.** Development refers to actions that transform natural resources to a greater or lesser extent, presumably with the intent of increasing their contribution to the welfare of human beings. Preservation, on the other hand, connotes putting resources aside in a state of nonuse or in a state such that whatever use is allowed basically maintains the original status of the resource. An important modern version of this term is **scientific preservation,** in which the conflicts over development and preservation are analyzed and illuminated with sound scientific tools, especially the tools of natural science, rather than consigned solely to the emotionally charged conflicts of the political struggle. The most recent incarnation of

---

[4] See the well-known monograph of Samuel P. Hays, *Conservation and the Gospel of Efficiency. The Progressive Conservation Movement, 1890–1920,* Harvard University Press, Cambridge, MA, 1959.

this concept is **ecosystem management,** the idea of resource management decisions based on sound principles of ecological science.

THE RANGE OF NATURAL RESOURCE SERVICES

A minimal classification of natural resources would perhaps be: land resources, water resources, and air resources. But we need to move well beyond this delineation if we are to get a more complete understanding of the number and variety of goods and services that nature provides. As a first step in this direction we distinguish between **use values** and **nonuse values.** Use value implies that attributes of nature are being utilized in some sense. This sense may be the classic one, such as when water is used to irrigate crops, which are then harvested and consumed. The sense of use may not involve traditional consumption. White-water rafting and bird watching are activities that use resources in a different sense. Scenic values involve use only in the sense that natural resources are simply present to the senses.

Nonuse values, on the other hand, are values expressed by human beings simply for the **existence** of natural resources. Existence may be related to prospects for future use, called **option value,** or the desire to leave a healthy ecosystem to future generations, called **bequest value.** People may not be using a resource at present, but may prefer actions that will ensure that the resource is available in the future, should they or future generations wish to utilize it later; in other words, it is worth something to preserve the option. But true existence values, not linked to present or possible future use, also exist. They may of course be harder to assess and measure in particular cases, but they are nonetheless real and relevant to the full set of incentives that motivate human decisions.

Table 2-1 contains a catalog of use values. These are broken down into **extractive** and **nonextractive** resources. Extractive resources are those subject to some process of physical removal from their natural surrounding and perhaps physical transformation during their use. Classic cases include the mining of ores of various types, and the harvesting of timber and its conversion to building materials. Commercial fishing, and much recreational fishing and hunting, are also extractive. It is common to use the term **natural resource products (or commodities)** to refer to quantities of physical resources that have been removed from nature and made available for use.

Nonextractive resources are those that yield valuable services without being removed from their natural setting. The classic case of a nonextractive resource is resource-based recreation, such as backpacking and river rafting. Many resources produce both extractive products and nonextractive services. Forests may produce both timber and backpacking. Water can be used for municipal and industrial water supplies and for boating.

Another important nonextractive resource service is **ecosystem protection.** One part of a resource system provides support and protection for other parts. Wetlands, for example, are usually integral parts of wider hydraulic systems,

TABLE 2-1
CLASSIFICATION OF NATURAL RESOURCES

	Natural resource products and services	
Natural resource	Extractive	Nonextractive
Minerals	Nonfuel (bauxite) Fuel (coal)	Geological services (weathering)
Forests	Forest products (timber)	Recreation (backpacking) Ecosystem protection (flood control, CO_2 sequestration)
Land	Fertility	Space, scenic values
Plants	Food and fiber (agricultural crops, wild food crops) Biodiversity products (medicinal plants)	
Terrestrial animals	Food and fiber (farm animals, wild game) Biodiversity products (genetic variability)	Recreational services (bird watching, ecotourism)
Fisheries	Food (saltwater and freshwater fish)	Recreational services (recreational fishing, whale watching)
Water	Municipal and industrial supplies, irrigation	Recreation (boating)
Meteorological services	Energy sources (geothermal)	Energy sources (solar) Global radiation balances Radio spectrum Natural disasters

so their protection is important in providing protection for water resources that are subject to direct extraction, such as groundwater aquifers. Forests often provide important services in flood control and the regulation of water quality. Land and water resources in coastal areas provide important services in terms of mitigating storm damage.

The newest resource, **biological diversity,** is perhaps a special type of extractive resource. Diversity is not a feature of one ecosystem or species or gene, but of a collection of them. But the justification for preservation of diversity is often expressed in extractive terms, as a source of diversity-type products like medicines and plant characteristics. Diversity may also be important in general ecosystem maintenance. Preservation of diversity normally implies a shift away from traditional types of extractive activities.

We normally think of nature as the repository of useful goods and services, but it also supplies negative services, that is, services that may have negative value, at least to human beings. In an average year natural disasters—

earthquakes, floods, volcano eruptions—cause enormous damage around the world. Some of these are exacerbated by human impacts on natural resources, e.g., deforestation. In all cases the need is for intelligent adjustments to manage these impacts at acceptable levels.

The dividing line between extractive and nonextractive is sometimes ambiguous. Some extractive resources are not necessarily transformed during use or are entirely lost to nature. Water that is extracted from an aquifer or river and used for irrigation may flow back into the hydraulic system at a different location, although possibly in diminished quantity and perhaps also degraded in terms of quality. The flow of zoo animals is extractive in the sense that they are removed from their natural habitats, but no physical conversion is involved. Soil fertility may be thought of as extractive in one sense, in that agricultural practices may lead to its temporary or permanent diminution. In another sense it is nonextractive, since appropriate steps can be taken for its maintenance.

MODELING RESOURCE SERVICES

There are several other ways of distinguishing among types of natural resource goods and services. In order to discuss them, however, we will adopt a slightly more formal approach. In later chapters we will be using simple analytical models to examine various natural resource problems. The material that follows in this section will give us a chance to start thinking in ways that are somewhat more formal and abstract, but that preserve the essence of the resource situations we will want to study.

Natural resource management decisions are complex because they involve connections and trade-offs between the present and the future. The connections stem from the characteristics of the resource itself, such as its biology or chemistry, and the way they are impacted by human use. Consider a situation in which there are just two time periods, period 0 and period 1. In effect period 0 could stand for today and period 1 for some time in the future, but to keep it simple think of period 0 as this year and period 1 as next year.[5]

The basic structure of a general resource use and charge problem can now be set up in the following way. Suppose that there is a certain quantity of a resource available at the beginning of period 0. During that period the resource is "used" in some amount. It is easiest to think of "use" in this case as extraction in the traditional sense. But we also interpret it in other ways. The other thing that may happen during the first period is some amount of replenishment or growth of the resource, the amount of which depends on the type of resource involved. All these factors contribute to the quantity of the resource available in period 1.

---

[5] Natural resource economics is about time, so we need a way of indexing events in different time periods. The convention that we follow throughout the book is to index today, or the present period, with a zero (e.g., q_0). Subsequent periods follow along; next year is indexed with a one (e.g., q_1), the next with a two, and so on.

We can express the basic relationship as follows:

Amount of resource available in period 1 (S_1)	$=$	Amount of resource available in period 0 (S_0)	$-$	Amount of the resource used in period 0 (Q_0)	$+$	Increment to the resource in period 0 (ΔS)

It is easier to write this expression in terms of the symbols shown in parentheses under each one; thus

$$S_1 = S_0 - Q_0 + \Delta S$$

The critical term is ΔS, representing the added increment of the resource that becomes available during period 0.[6] By interpreting ΔS in different ways, we can use the basic expression to describe many different types of resources.

Nonrenewable Resources

The most straightforward application of the general expression would appear to be a **nonrenewable resource.** For a **known deposit** of such a resource, we have $\Delta S = 0$; that is, there is no replenishment or increment of the resource. This being the case, the basic accounting expression becomes $S_1 = S_0 - Q_0$; the quantity available in the next period is the quantity that was available at the beginning of the present period minus the quantity used in this period. The classic example is a mineral deposit containing a given quantity of material. It is true that very long-run geological processes may be creating new deposits, but in terms of the time spans that are relevant to generations of human beings, total quantities are effectively fixed in amount.

A resource in one circumstance may be renewable; in another circumstance it may not be. Groundwater is held in underground geological formations, or aquifers. In this case, ΔS is the **recharge quantity,** the quantity that flows into the formation during a year. In some cases ΔS is essentially zero, making that aquifer a nonrenewable resource. In other cases $\Delta S > 0$, making it a renewable resource.

The basic character of nonrenewable resource changes if we move from considering a single deposit to considering **all known deposits.** Over a period of time, **exploration and development** can add to the quantity of the known stock. In this case ΔS is the quantity added to existing stocks through discovery and development. In fact this makes the situation quite complex because "new" deposits come in a variety of forms. For example, a deposit can be new in the sense of recent geological discovery, or it may be "new" in the sense that we have a new technology capable of making use of it, as compared to last year when it was geologically known but essentially beyond our reach.

---

[6] The symbol Δ is often used to denote the change in a variable of interest.

What this tells us is that the distinction between renewable and nonrenewable resources is only partly a physical one. It is also partly an economic one. The decision to put more effort into resource exploration is an economic one; it uses resources and has certain potentials in terms of benefits. Resource development, based on human actions, can convert cases that seemingly involve nonrenewable resources into cases of renewable resources.

Recyclable Resources

Certain nonrenewable resources may be **recyclable.** A portion of the resource used in period 0 can be recycled back to add to the available supply in period 1. Here the basic expression may be rewritten as:

$$S_1 = S_0 - Q_0 + \alpha Q_0$$

where α is a percentage indicating the proportion of the first year's use that is returned via recycling. Here two basic decisions are to be made, the utilization rate Q_0 and the recycling ratio α.

Renewable Resources

A **renewable resource** is one that replenishes itself in some fashion. In this case $\Delta S > 0$, so the quantities available in period 1 are affected by the replenishment process. This may be a biological process, as for example in the case of fisheries or timber. For a forest, the amount of wood (in, e.g., cubic feet) in year 1 is what existed at the beginning, minus that which was harvested during period 0, plus the biological growth increment of the timber that was not harvested. The size of the growth increment will be related to the size of the population and also other features of the ecosystem, such as climate.

Most biological growth processes involve **accumulation** to some degree; the resource growth adds to the resource stock. Certain types of renewable resources are nonaccumulating. Consider a free-flowing river, for example. Each year a certain (no doubt fluctuating) amount of water comes down the river; this is a meteorological and geographical fact of life. But it flows by a given point and then is gone. Thus the annual replenishment does not add to any preexisting quantity. In this case our basic relationship changes to the following:

$$S_1 = \Delta S$$

The amount of the resource available in period 1 now does not depend on the rate of use during period 0.

Of course if somebody were to build a reservoir on the river, the situation would change. Now the incoming flow would augment whatever was left in the reservoir from the previous year, changing a nonaccumulating resource into an accumulating one, at least to some degree. Another example of a nonaccumulating renewable resource is the incoming stream of solar energy that strikes the earth each year. The stream itself is nonaccumulating, though of course all the biological processes it makes possible on earth represent accumulating phenomena.

This accounting expression can be applied to land resources, but it will look different according to the exact way we define the resource. If we write the formula for the total land area in a given geographical region, such as a town, the expression is simply $S_1 = S_0$. In other words, the total area is fixed and unchanging (barring political changes in town boundaries). But if we define our resource of interest as, for example, land devoted to a particular use, such as housing developments, wetlands, or land in agriculture, it would look like

$$S_1 = S_0 - Q_0 + \Delta S$$

where Q_0 is the amount of acreage taken out of that use during the year (e.g., number of acres devoted to new housing development) and ΔS is the amount of land put back into that use (e.g., wetlands restored, if our S variable of interest is acreage of wetlands).

An important feature of some natural resources is **reversibility,** expressed in terms of either quantity or quality. Usage of a natural resource is reversible if it is possible that $S_1 > S_0$. By definition, utilization of a nonrenewable resource is irreversible, at least as long as we are talking about a particular deposit. Most renewable resources are reversible; if extraction is lowered sufficiently, the natural replenishment will cause the stock to increase, at least up to some biological maximum. But many renewable resources, especially biological resources, may have **thresholds** that, once past, render the resource irreversibly changed. The classic case is a population of wildlife in which the number of adults falls below a level sufficient to support reproduction greater than mortality, and hence evolves irreversibly toward extinction. More complex cases occur, for example, where characteristics of species diversity change in an ecosystem sufficiently to set in motion forces that bring about permanent changes in many structural and functional features of that ecosystem.

SOME WORDS ABOUT ECONOMICS

This is a book about **economic analysis.** To analyze something means to examine its basic structure and the cause-and-effect relationships that govern the way it works. So to analyze the problems of saltwater fisheries, for example, we will try to understand the basic **bioeconomic** operation of the interconnected system that includes the growth and decline of fish stocks together with the human fishing effort expended on them. When we look at the role of natural resources in economic development and growth, we must try to understand the main linkages between natural resource stocks and such things as imports, exports, and rates of growth in **gross domestic product (GDP).**

To pursue these analyses we need (1) to look at the data that tell us what has happened historically and what the current situation is with respect to particular natural resources, and (2) to develop simple analytical models with which to explore the interconnections among the important elements of each situation. A "model" in economics is an explanatory construct built up from some underlying principles and concepts, and used to examine the behavior of the economy, or some part of it. For example, the market model is built up from underlying principles of supply and of demand. The model we will use to look at issues of wildlife management contains both economic and biological concepts. A prime feature of economic models is that they are abstract. You got a little taste of that in the preceding section where we explored the differences among different types of resources. A model is abstract when it focuses on underlying relationships and leaves out the many factors that are not relevant to understanding those basic relationships. It is not to say that the factors left out are unimportant, only that they are not considered important in the present context. Often factors are omitted to make a model simple and easy to understand.

Natural resource problems vary over a continuum from relatively small, local issues (which are nevertheless of great importance to local communities), to larger regional problems, to all-encompassing national and global issues. The models that economics uses to study these problems must range commensurately in terms of scope and applicability. It is standard to divide economics into microeconomics and macroeconomics. Microeconomics (or just "micro" as it is often called) proceeds on the basis of detailed models of individual behavior—of consumers, producers, policy makers, and so on. These models are normally "aggregated" up so that we can derive conclusions about the performance of groups of people. Studying how individual households make choices about their use of water in and around the home—so that we might predict the affects, for example, of a tax on water use—is a problem in microeconomics. So is a study of how the logging industry in, say, Oregon, might respond to a new set of regulations on habitat preservation.

Macroeconomics, on the other hand, takes economies as a whole as the basic unit of analysis. A study on how the U.S. economy might respond to higher energy prices would probably be conducted with a macroeconomic model, one which deals directly with relationships among macro variables, such as the overall rate of unemployment, rates of economic growth, and changes in the growth patterns of major industry groupings. Another type of macroeconomic study would be one that looked at how important a role natural resource endowments have played in a country's historical pattern of economic growth. Still another would be a study to adjust commonly published measures of macroeconomic performance, gross domestic product (GDP), for example, to take into account natural resource depletion.

Many resource problems fall between these two types, and make use of both. One natural resource issue that is very common around the world is the performance of a local or regional economy that is based to some degree on the exploitation of a natural resource (e.g., logging or mining), a resource that other groups are trying to have preserved in a natural state. A major factor in trying to determine the best course of action in such a case is knowing how the regional economy is in fact affected by changes in the availability of the resources. To get to the bottom of this we may call on both microeconomics (e.g., how will firms, workers, and consumers behave if the rates change) and macroeconomics (e.g., how will developments in the national economy affect demands for the resource). The conclusion to be drawn from this is that many resource issues call for several different types of analyses, so we need to be ready with a full array of tools to carry them out.

Another important distinction that needs to be made is that between **factual statements** and **value judgments.** In economics this is usually referred to as **positive economics** (factual) and **normative economics** (values). If somebody does an analysis of the rates at which mineral mining has grown over the last century or of the way timber prices have trended over the last few decades, they are engaged in positive economics, that is, what has actually happened in the use of these resources in these time periods. Similarly, if somebody studies how log prices and interest rates affect the rate of deforestation in some region or how fishers will respond to certain restrictions on their harvesting practices, they are also engaged in positive economics: How the world actually works, in terms of the interconnections of economic variables and the resulting rates of output, prices, and so on.

Statements as to what people **ought to do,** on the other hand, come under the heading of normative economics. If an economist recommends limiting the catch season for a certain species of fish or initiating certain policy changes to reduce the rate of soil erosion, he or she is engaging in normative economics, because the recommendations require placing value judgments on different outcomes that could result from different types of behavior.

For us to make headway in better managing the globe's natural resources, both types of economics are necessary. Policies need to be enacted and pursued, with the explicit or implicit value judgments they contain. But these policies should be based on our best understanding of how the economies and natural systems work. Activists, who are anxious to get on with doing something, are often impatient with analysts who are engaged in strictly positive analysis. The prime motivation of the latter is that better knowledge about how things actually work will allow better policies to be pursued.

THE POLITICAL UNIT PROBLEM

In the chapters that follow we will use several criteria to evaluate the performance of natural resource–using individuals and firms, and of public agencies pursuing natural resource management policies of different types. Issues of **economic efficiency** and **equity** will be encountered, as will the idea of **sustainability** in resource use. When we use such concepts, we must do it from the perspective of some specific political unit. Not political in the sense of bringing particular value judgments to the analyses, but in the sense of looking at things from the perspective of a given group of people. If we talk about some course of action that is economically efficient, or equitable, or sustainable, from the **social** standpoint, we have to be clear about which particular society we have in mind.

Often, economic policy and performance are evaluated from a nationalistic perspective. We will examine, for example, the policies pursued by U.S. officials to manage the stocks of fish in the coastal waters around the country. The United States has the responsibility of establishing and enforcing fisheries regulations in its own coastal waters, as other countries do in theirs. Should these policies be evaluated in terms of how well they represent the interests of the U.S. citizenry, or all of North America, or some other unit? The answers one gets may differ, depending on which perspective one takes. Exhibit 2-1 discusses a particularly interesting example of this problem in central Asia.

The problem exists also at the local and regional levels. Suppose we wish to evaluate the economic efficiency aspects of a local wetlands protection regulation. Should we evaluate this strictly from the standpoint of the one community where the wetlands is located, the region, the state, or the country? In fact

---

EXHIBIT 2-1

THE CASPIAN SEA

The Caspian Sea is a California-size body of brackish water in southeast Asia. The northern half is quite shallow, and is the main home of the Caspian sturgeon fishery, the primary world source of caviar. At various points around its borders, and within the sea itself, petroleum deposits have been exploited in the past. In recent years the pace of petroleum-related activity has heated up in the region, and many people feel that there could be a boom in oil exploration and development in the next few decades, depending on developments in the middle eastern oil fields and the building of pipelines to get the oil to export markets.

Large increases in onshore and offshore oil development and production will have huge implications for environmental quality of the region, especially through their impacts on the aquatic environment of the Caspian Sea. The people of the region will be faced with important and difficult issues about the appropriate balance between economic growth and environmental protec-

tion. Identifying and achieving this balance will be hard in light of the environmental uncertainties, political realities, and the economic aspirations of people in the region. But the Caspian Sea is bordered by five different countries (Azerbaijan, Iran, Kazakhstan, Russia, and Turkmenistan). Suppose we are trying to evaluate the performance of one of them, say Kazakhstan, regarding the use of Caspian resources and, especially, the development of petroleum resources in the Caspian basin. Suppose further that we are evaluating the cost effectiveness of Kazakhstan's planned program for protecting the water quality of the Caspian during its petroleum exploration activities. If we were to do this solely from the perspective of this one country, we might get a different answer than if we approached it from the standpoint of all the Caspian countries together. But if we do it from the standpoint of Caspian society in general, what particular group of people should we include?

there is a bumper sticker that reads "Act Locally, Think Globally," which would seem to imply that we ought to evaluate all local programs like this in global terms. The upshot of this discussion is simply to make it clear that when we use criteria like efficiency, or equity, **from the social standpoint,** we need to be clear about which particular society we are talking about.

SUMMARY

Natural resource economics is the study of how the flow of goods and services derived from natural resources is, and ought to be, managed in today's world. Resource management problems derive from the underlying technological, institutional, and cultural factors that characterize an economy. **Natural resource economics** focuses on resource flows into an economy, whereas flow out of that economy back into nature is studied under **environmental economics.** There is a great variety of types of natural resource goods and services. One way of thinking about the differences among them is to take a basic accounting identity of resource use, $S_1 = S_0 - Q_0 + \Delta S$, and then alter its several terms to describe natural resources with specific characteristics. The most basic distinction between natural resources is that between **renewable** and **nonrenewable** resources. Characteristics such as **recyclability** and **reversibility** are very important. When we consider natural resource management issues, we must be very explicit about the **political unit** to which the analysis is applicable.

KEY TERMS

Natural resource
Economic, legal, and regulatory
  institutions
Natural resource services
Extractive vs. nonextractive resources
Use values vs. nonuse values
Natural resource products
  (commodities)
Ecosystem protection

Nonrenewable resources
Recyclable resources
Renewable resources
Positive and normative economic
  statements
Microeconomics and macroeconomics
Economic models
Political unit problem

QUESTIONS FOR FURTHER DISCUSSION

1 Identify several cases where certain features of the natural environment, which were not regarded as natural resources in the past, are now thought of in those terms.
2 How might the **basic resource formula** be cast so as to represent the occurrence of natural disasters (i.e., characteristics of nature that have negative values rather than positive values)? How about a natural attribute such as soil fertility?
3 Distinguish between use values and nonuse values in natural resource economics.
4 Consider a particular natural resource issue, for example the allocation of scarce water supplies among competing uses in the western United States. Give an example of a positive statement and a normative statement in the context of this problem.

5 Suppose we are studying the extraction rates of copper ore in the United States over the last decade. There are both macro and micro factors that affect these rates. Give several possible examples of each type.

USEFUL WEB SITES

For a broad perspective on the goods and services produced by natural resources:

- International Society for Ecological Economics (http://www.isee.org).
- Sustainable Earth Exchange for Educators (links to a wide variety of web sites for resources and the environment) (http://www.class.csupomona.edu/earth.html).

For help in interpreting graphs:

- The web page for the book has a section on using and interpreting graphs. See www.mhhe.com/economics/field. Also, the main site (http://www.mhhe.com/economics) has an interactive section (called the Leading Indicator) with a graphing routine.

SELECTED READINGS

Adams, David A.: *Renewable Resource Policy,* Island Press, Washington, DC, 1993.

Hays, Samuel P.: *Conservation and the Gospel of Efficiency,* Harvard University Press, Cambridge, MA, 1959.

Herfindahl, Orris C.: "What Is Conservation?" in *Three Studies in Mineral Economics,* Resources for the Future, Washington, DC, 1961.

Howe, Charles: *Natural Resource Economics,* John Wiley, New York, 1979, Chapter 1.

Poljman, Louis P. (ed.): *Environmental Ethics, Readings in Theory and Application,* Wadsworth, Belmont, CA, 1998.

Randall, Alan: *Resource Economics,* John Wiley, New York, 1987, Chapters 1 and 2.

BUILDING BLOCKS

To understand how natural resources are used and to formulate policies that might influence these rates of use in desirable directions, two strands of knowledge must be brought together: knowledge of how the natural ecosystem itself functions and knowledge about human behavior. The first comes from scientists such as biologists, ecologists, meteorologists, earth scientists, and the like. The second comes from social scientists such as economists, political scientists, and sociologists. In this book the emphasis is on economics, the science that deals with values, incentives, and institutions governing the allocation of productive resources[1] and the production of goods and services. This section is devoted, therefore, to the study of a number of primary concepts and relationships in economics. Economics is a very cumulative subject. The more complex theories and models used to study complicated real-world problems are always built up from the core concepts. Thus the ideas studied in this chapter, though very simple and rather abstract, are going to be vital to the various natural resource models we develop later to look at specific resource issues.

---

[1] "Resources" has two meanings in economics: On the one hand it is short for "natural resources," on the other it is often used to refer to all inputs, both natural and otherwise, that are used to produce goods and services. The context is usually sufficient to distinguish the one being used.

Virtually any human action affecting natural resources use rates has two consequences: on the one side it will normally create goods or services that have value; on the other side it will entail costs. This is true whether the action is of a private or public firm extracting or otherwise using a natural resource, or whether it is some organization, such as a government agency, that is pursuing an explicit conservation objective. The discussion will be organized around these two sides; first we discuss **willingness to pay** and **demand** on the output side, and then we get into **opportunity cost** and **supply** on the input side.

CHAPTER 3

WILLINGNESS TO PAY/DEMAND

The first requirement is to develop some notion of **value.** "Value" is a word with many interpretations, but in economics it means the worth that a person or group of persons places on something, such as a particular good or service or state of the world. The basic assumption is that individuals are possessed of a set of underlying **tastes and preferences** that determine these relative values.

WILLINGNESS TO PAY

To make visible this notion of value in a way that it can be observed and measured, we use the idea of **willingness to sacrifice.** The value that a person puts on something is the amount they are willing to sacrifice to obtain that something, which may be a good, or service, or state. Sacrifice what? It could be anything. For a hermit the best index might be the time needed to produce some item. In a monetized economy it makes most sense to measure it as willingness to sacrifice generalized purchasing power. Thus we use **willingness to pay** as our fundamental concept: The value a person places on a good or service is what they are willing to pay to get that good or service.

What determines how much a person is willing to pay to obtain something? Clearly individual tastes and preferences are paramount. Some people are willing to pay a lot to visit the Grand Canyon; others are not. Some people are willing to pay a lot for white-water recreation opportunities; others are not.

Some people place a high value on trying to preserve the habitat of unique animal and plant species; others do not. It is obvious also that a person's **wealth** affects the willingness to sacrifice; the greater their wealth, the better a person can afford to pay for various goods and services. Willingness to pay, in other words, also reflects **ability to pay.** Willingness to pay also depends upon the state of one's knowledge and experience. For a person who has never left the city, for example, a backpacking experience may open up new opportunities and essentially shift a person's preferences.

What a person is willing to pay, and what they end up actually having to pay in concrete situations, are two different things. Willingness to pay is a representation of underlying tasks and preferences. A person may be willing to pay a maximum of $6.50 to visit a particular beach for a day. What they actually have to pay will depend on circumstances. Maybe it is a town beach with no admission fee or perhaps a privately operated beach with a $5 entrance fee.

Willingness to Pay Illustrated

Consider an individual and some arbitrary good or service. We need a way of representing graphically that person's willingness to pay for the item in question. We will use simple numbers for illustrative purposes.

Assume that the person has none of the good to begin with. We ask her, or perhaps deduce from watching her spend her money, how much she would be willing to pay for a single unit of a good rather than go without. Suppose this is some number, such as $38 pictured in the top of Figure 3-1. We then ask, assuming she already has one unit of this good, how much she would be willing to pay for a second unit. According to Figure 3-1, her answer is $26. In similar fashion, her willingness to pay for each additional unit is depicted by the height of the rectangle above that unit: $17 for unit 3, $12 for unit 4, and so on. These numbers depict a fundamental relationship of economics: the notion of **diminishing willingness to pay.** As the number of units consumed increases, the willingness to pay for additional units of that good goes down.

Quantity data (e.g., consumption, production) often have a **time dimension** such as pounds consumed per month or year, or tons produced per year. To remind ourselves of this, we could index our variables with a time indication, such as Q/t. In the interests of notational simplicity we will sometimes leave out the explicit time designator, but you should remember that it is in the background.

It is not very convenient to work with diagrams that are step-shaped as in the top of Figure 3-1. Assume that people can consume fractions of items in addition to integer values (e.g., pounds of potatoes consumed per week). What this does is produce a smoothly shaped **willingness-to-pay curve,** such as the one pictured in the bottom of Figure 3-1. In effect the steps in the willingness-to-pay curve have become too small to see, yielding a smooth curve to work with. On this smooth function we have singled out one quantity for illustrative purposes. It shows that the willingness to pay for the third unit is $17.

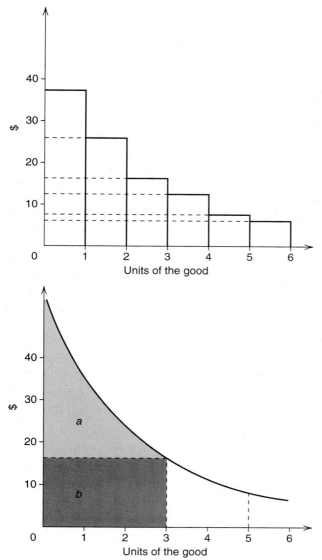

FIGURE 3-1
The Concept of Willingness to Pay

The concept in use here is more exactly called **marginal willingness to pay.** Suppose a person is already consuming two units of this good; according to Figure 3-1, that person would be willing to pay $17 for a third unit. This is the marginal willingness to pay—in this case, for the third unit. "**Marginal**" thus describes the additional willingness to pay for one more unit. So the height of the rectangles in the top of Figure 3-1 and the height of the curve in the bottom graph show the marginal willingness to pay for this good.

The **total willingness to pay** for a given consumption level refers to the total amount a person would be willing to pay to attain that consumption level rather than go without the good entirely. Suppose the person is consuming at a level of three units; her total willingness to pay for consuming this quantity is $81, which is in fact the sum of the heights of the demand rectangles between the origin and the consumption level in question ($38 for the first plus $26 for the second plus $17 for the third). This corresponds, in the smooth version of the willingness-to-pay function, to the whole area under the marginal willingness-to-pay curve from the origin up to the quantity in question. For three units of consumption, the total willingness to pay is equal to an amount represented by the combined areas *a* and *b*.

Marginal Willingness to Pay and Demand

There is another way of looking at these marginal willingness-to-pay relationships. They are more familiarly known as **demand curves.** An individual demand curve shows the quantity of a good or service that the individual in question would demand (i.e., purchase and consume) at any particular price. For example, suppose a person whose marginal willingness-to-pay/demand curve is shown in the bottom part of Figure 3-1 is able to purchase this item at a unit price of $17. The quantity he would demand at this price is three units. The reason is that his marginal willingness to pay for each of the first three units exceeds the purchase price. He would not push his consumption higher than this because his marginal willingness to pay for additional quantities would be lower than the purchase price.

An individual's demand/marginal willingness-to-pay curve for a good or service is a way of summarizing his personal consumption attitudes and capabilities for that good. Thus, we would normally expect these relationships to differ somewhat among individuals because individual tastes and preferences vary. Figure 3-2 displays several different demand curves. Panel (a) shows

FIGURE 3-2
Typical Demand/Marginal Willingness-to-Pay Curves

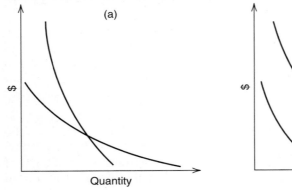
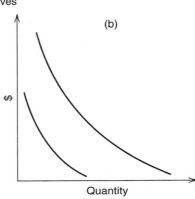

two demand curves, one steeper than the other. The steeper one shows a situation in which marginal willingness to pay drops off fairly rapidly as the quantity consumed increases; the other marginal willingness to pay, although lower to begin with, goes down less rapidly as quantity increases. These two demand curves could represent the case of one consumer and two different goods or services, or the case of two different consumers and the same good or service.

Panel (b) of Figure 3-2 also has two demand curves; they have the same general shape, but one is situated well to the right of the other. The demand curve lying above and to the right shows a good for which the marginal willingness to pay is substantially higher than it is for the same quantity of the other good. What could account for the difference? They might represent the demand curves of two different people for the same good. But there are other possibilities. How much a person is willing to pay for something obviously depends on how much money she has; more than likely the higher her income, the more she is willing to pay. So the two demand curves in panel (b) could apply to the same individual and the same good, but at two different points in time, the one to the right being her willingness to pay after she has had a substantial increase in income.

There is another way of looking at the two demand curves of panel (b), one that may be very important for the application of these ideas to natural resource assets. People's tastes depend on a variety of psychological and historical factors that are hard to pin down and describe but are nevertheless real. They depend in part on the experiences that people have and the information they gather over time about the qualities of different goods and how they feel about them. So, for example, the demand curve to the right could be the same consumer's demand curve for a good for which his appreciation has increased over time. Perhaps they are demand curves for outdoor wilderness experiences, the one to the left applying before much is known about this type of activity and the one to the right applying after the person has had wilderness experience and learned to enjoy the activity. Other factors are information and psychology; the demand curve on the right might be a person's demand for a good before an announcement of the presence of pesticide residues in it, with the curve on the left being the demand curve after the announcement.

Note that the demand curves are in fact nonlinear, rather than straight lines. A straight-line demand relationship would imply a uniform change in the quantity demanded as its price changes. For most goods, however, this is unlikely to be true. At low prices and high rates of consumption, studies have shown that relatively small increases in price will lead to substantial reductions in quantity demanded. At high prices and low quantity demanded, however, price increases have a much smaller effect: They produce much smaller reductions in quantity demanded. This gives us a demand relationship that is convex to the origin, that is, relatively flat at low prices and steep at higher prices. Exhibit 3-1 discusses this in terms of the demand for gasoline.

EXHIBIT 3-1

THE DEMAND FOR ENERGY FOR TRANSPORTATION

People sometimes think of their demands as somewhat fixed, according to their lifestyles. This is often the way people think of their demand for gasoline, for example. Actually, researchers have found these relationships to be somewhat more flexible. In general, as the price of gasoline rises, the total consumption of gasoline declines: Although individual responses will differ, depending upon peoples' circumstances and preferences, the total will decline.

At relatively low prices, gas consumption is high; because of the low cost of driving, people use their cars with little restraint. At somewhat higher prices, many (though not necessarily all) people begin to think about curtailing unessential driving, perhaps going to the supermarket only once per week rather than two or three times, and riding with somebody else to the movies on the weekend. At still higher prices more thought is given to reducing unessential driving, and at very high prices people have the incentive to car-pool, switch to public transit, buy more fuel-efficient vehicles, or, in the long run, move closer to their place of work.

This implies that the demand for gasoline might be shaped as in the diagram. At low and moderate prices, increased prices will lead to substantial drops in aggregate consumption because, paradoxically as it might seem, the higher the level of consumption, the easier it is to find ways of cutting back. So the demand curve is relatively flat in this range. But at higher prices where most of the driving is for essential purposes, further price increases lead to smaller drops in consumption, and hence a steeper demand curve.

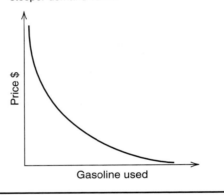

Economics is sometimes misunderstood as assuming that people are driven only by thoughts of their own welfare, that they are complete egoists. Because these are individual demand curves, they do indeed summarize the attitudes of single individuals, but this does not imply that individuals make decisions with only themselves in mind. Although some people focus only on themselves, most people are influenced by other powerful motives that affect their demands for different goods, including altruism toward friends and relatives, feelings of civic virtue toward their communities, and a sense of social responsibility toward fellow citizens. Individual tastes and preferences spring from these factors as well as from more narrow considerations of personal likes and dislikes.

Aggregate Willingness to Pay/Demand for Private Goods

In examining real-world natural resource issues, the focus of attention is usually on the behavior of groups of people, not single individuals. It could be all people in a single community or region, or all people in the country. It could

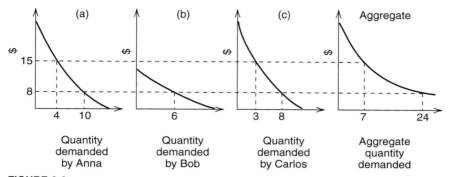

FIGURE 3-3
Aggregate Demand/Marginal Willingness-to-Pay Curve for a Private Good

even be all people in the world. The **aggregate marginal willingness-to-pay curve** is the summation of the marginal willingness-to-pay curves of all the individuals in the group of interest.[1] The aggregate marginal willingness to pay for water by people in California, for example, is the curve that one gets from adding together the individual marginal willingness-to-pay curves for water (in terms, say, of the number of gallons used per month) of all the residents of California.

Figure 3-3 depicts the derivation of a simple aggregate marginal willingness-to-pay curve, in this case by adding together (horizontally) the marginal willingness-to-pay curves of each of the three people in this group. A good like this, which can be consumed in separate and possibly different amounts by each of the individuals in a group, depending on their preferences and wealth positions, is called a **private good.** The total amount consumed in this case is simply a sum of the individual quantities consumed. Cantaloupes are a good example, as are cars, fishing trips, and 2 × 4's. At a marginal willingness to pay of $8, consumption is 10, 6, and 8 units for, respectively, Anna, Bob, and Carlos. Thus total consumption at $8 is 24. At a marginal willingness to pay of $15, aggregate consumption is 7 units (4 for Anna, none for Bob, and 3 for Carlos).

Aggregate Willingness to Pay/Demand for Public Goods

Many of the goods and services produced by natural resources are not private goods, for which we add together the consumption levels of different people to get total consumption. Rather, they are called **public goods.** A public good is one that when it is made available to one person, automatically becomes available to others as well. A good example is a signal broadcast by a radio station. When the signal is sent out, it is available to anybody within range

---

[1] Remember that total willingness to pay is the area under the MWTP curve of each individual consumer, whereas aggregate willingness to pay is a summation over a number of individuals.

TABLE 3-1
AGGREGATE MARGINAL WILLINGNESS TO PAY FOR RESTORING BALD EAGLES

Extent of restoration	Marginal willingness to pay (MWTP)			
	Anna	Bob	Carlos	Aggregate
Low	50	10	25	85
Moderate	30	5	10	45
Extensive	10	0	5	15

who has a receiver. Furthermore, this type of public good is available to every individual in essentially the same quantity; in other words, the amount that one person listens does not diminish the amount available to other potential listeners.

Goods and services are defined as public or private in microeconomics because of their **technical characteristics,** not because of whether they are produced by public agencies or private firms. If a radio station "scrambled" its signal, and then rented unscramblers to subscribers, the signal would then be a private good. Public agencies may provide private goods (publicly provided flood insurance, for example); private firms may provide public goods (the radio station example). And the difference between public and private goods is not that the former is in some sense of greater social importance than the latter. It is strictly a distinction based on the technical characteristics of the good in question.

To find the aggregate marginal willingness to pay for a public good, we must proceed somewhat differently from the case of a private good. Consider a program designed to reestablish a certain species of wildlife in a region, for example the restoration of the bald eagle in New England. Let the group of people involved consist of three individuals, the same three we mentioned above. Their individual marginal willingnesses to pay are listed numerically in Table 3-1. Three alternative discrete levels of restoration are identified: "low," "moderate," and "extensive," corresponding, for example, to the number of adult animals that would be expected to survive under each scenario.

The marginal willingness to pay (MWTP) for Anna, Bob, and Carlos are as shown. For example, Anna would be willing to pay $50 for a light restoration program, and $30 more if it were increased to a moderate level, and so on. Bob has a lower marginal willingness to pay than Anna, and Carlos lies between the other two in terms of MWTP. The restoration of the bald eagle is a public good, in the sense just described. If it were carried out for one person it would be available to others as well. To find the aggregate marginal willingness to pay in this case, we add together the individual MWTPs corresponding to given "output" levels (in this case different levels of restoration). This is done in the last column of Table 3-1.

Figure 3-4 shows the derivation of the aggregate marginal willingness to pay in graphical terms. In contradistinction to the private good, where the ag-

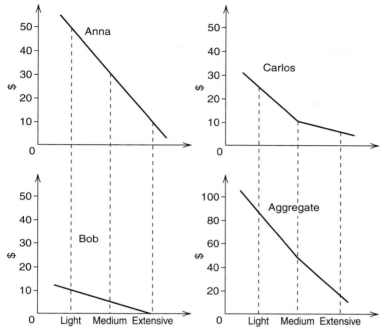

FIGURE 3-4
Aggregate Marginal Willingness to Pay/Demand for a Public Good

gregate MWTP is found by adding individual curves horizontally (i.e., adding quantities of the three individuals corresponding to the same MWTP), we instead add the individual curves together vertically (i.e., the marginal willingness to pay of the three individuals corresponding to the same quantities on the horizontal axes).

Willingness to Pay and Benefits

We now come to the idea of **benefits.** Benefits is one of those ordinary words to which economists have given a technical meaning. The word "benefits" clearly implies being made better off. If someone is benefited by something, her position is improved—she is better off. Conversely, if benefits are taken from her, she is worse off. How do we confer benefits on somebody? We do this by giving her something she values. How do we know that she values something? We know by the fact that she is willing to sacrifice, or willing to pay, for it. Thus, the benefits that people get from something are equal to the amount they are willing to pay for it.

The logic behind this definition of "benefits" is quite strong. It means we can use ordinary demand curves to measure the benefits accruing to people from given quantities of a good or service. For example, Figure 3-5 shows two demand curves, and on the horizontal axis two quantity levels are indicated.

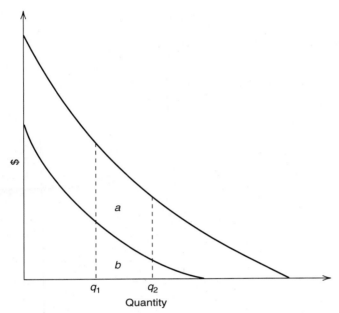

FIGURE 3-5
Willingness to Pay and Benefits

Suppose we wish to estimate the total benefits of increasing the availability of this item from quantity q_1 to quantity q_2. Benefits are measured by willingness to pay, and we know that total willingness to pay is measured by areas under the demand curve—in this case the area under the demand curves between quantity q_1 and quantity q_2. So for the lower demand curve the benefits of such an increase in availability are equal to an amount shown by area b, whereas benefits in the case of the higher demand curve are equal to the total area $a + b$.

The logic of this seems reasonable. The people with the higher demand curve must place a greater value on this item; whatever it is, they are willing to pay more for it than the people whose demand curve is the lower function. This is in agreement with common sense. The more people value something, the more they benefit by having more of that something made available, or, to say the same thing a different way, you can't damage people by taking away from them something that they don't value.

This is a fundamental notion underlying natural resource economics. It underlies, for example, questions such as the benefits conferred on people when natural resources are used in production, as compared to the benefits they would provide if preserved. It underlies the question of evaluating the impacts of environmental programs and policies undertaken by local, state, and federal governments. This is its strength—the fact that it is based on a clear notion of the value that people place on different things.

But the idea also has shortcomings. For one thing, demand and, therefore, benefits are often very hard to measure when natural resource questions are concerned, as we will see in later chapters. For another, we have to remember that demand curves are critically affected by the **ability to pay** for something as well as preferences. In Figure 3-5, for example, the lower demand curve could represent a group of people with lower incomes than those with the higher demand curve. The logic of the argument would lead to the conclusion that the increase in quantity of $q_2 - q_1$ would produce fewer benefits among lower-income people than among higher-income people. This may not be a very equitable conclusion, depending on the circumstances. Thus, although the logic of the concept is clear, we have to be careful in using it, especially when we are dealing with groups of people with diverse income levels. To do so, we must find out as clearly as possible how the various natural resource policies and programs, present or proposed, affect people at different income levels. We discuss this at greater length in later chapters.

One other possible problem exists in using conventional demand curves to measure benefits. An individual's demand for something is clearly affected by how much he knows about it; a person would not be willing to pay for a good if, for example, he were ignorant of its very existence. In Figure 3-5, the higher demand curve might be the demand for a biodiversity product after it is found to contain a promising pharmaceutical product, while the lower demand curve shows demand before this fact becomes known. This is not especially surprising; people do after all become more knowledgeable about things over time as a matter of education, experience, and the availability of information. But people's views about the importance of particular resources and the place of nature in their lives are often blown back and forth almost from day to day, by the media, by the scientific press, and so on. Care must be exercised in taking people's demand curves of the moment, influenced as they are by all kinds of real and imagined factors, as true expressions of the benefits of actions affecting natural resources. They are highly relevant, but they need to be taken with a certain amount of caution.

Willingness to Pay Over Time

Problems in natural resource economics are particularly complex because the **time factor** plays a major role in them. Decisions made today, or this year, will have consequences in future years. Trade-offs are necessary because present and future willingness to pay, and present and future costs, are involved. We talked above about willingness to pay as it applied to the consumption of a certain quantity of a good or service. The assumption was that we were working with events in the present. But consumers are usually involved with streams of consumption over a series of periods. If a person buys a car, for example, the services of the car will be realized both today and in the future over its service life. The consumption of necessities such as food, clothing, and shelter by definition occur over a series of years, not just a single one. Thus consumers can be thought of as having a willingness to pay not just for current consumption, but also for a stream of consumption quantities extending into the future, as pictured in Figure 3-6. This shows a sequence of willingnesses to

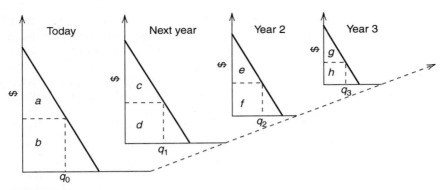

FIGURE 3-6
Willingness to Pay over Time

pay, for the current quality q_0, and for a sequence of future quantities, q_1, q_2, q_3, and so on.

The problem immediately presents itself of adding up willingness-to-pay amounts over a string of years to find the total willingness to pay for the over-all sequence. How can (or should) values of willingness to pay (or of cost, as we shall see in the next chapter) occurring in different time periods be added together. The standard answer to this is by discounting future values.

DISCOUNTING

Discounting involves applying a discount factor to future values in order to convert them into **present values.** Most people readily understand **compounding.** If a sum of money equal to $M is put in a savings account at an interest rate of r, the value after one period of compounding is given by the formula

$$\$FV = \$M(1 + r)$$

The formula compounds the present value ($M) into the future value (FV). If M is left in the bank account at r percent interest for t periods, then the future value is found by compounding the present value t times, thus,

$$FV_t = M(1 + r)^t$$

As an example, if M = $1,000, r = 0.04, and t = 6, the future value is

$$FV_6 = \$1,000(1 + 0.04)^6 = \$1,265$$

Discounting is the reverse of compounding. It is a procedure for finding the present value corresponding to some future value. Discounting answers the question: If I expect to receive something of value in the future, what is it worth today? Or, for example, if someone promised you a sum of money next year or a lesser sum of money this year, which is the better deal? Algebraically, the expressions for present values are simply the ones above but rearranged to get present value (which we will now call PV instead of M) on the left hand side. Thus, for example, the present value of a sum equal to $FV to be realized one period from now, at a discount rate of r, is

$$\$PV = \frac{\$FV}{(1 + r)}$$

Suppose somebody gave you an IOU stating that they will pay you $100 one year from now, and that the discount rate is 4 percent. The value of that IOU is the present value of that future $100, and is found with the expression:

$$\$PV = \frac{\$100}{(1 + 0.04)} = \$96.15$$

This means that $100 one year from now is the same as having $96.15 today, based upon a discount rate of 4 percent.

Suppose the IOU was for $100, but to be given to you 5 years from now rather than after just one period. Then the present value of the IOU would be:

$$\$PV = \frac{\$100}{(1 + 0.04)^5} = \$85.48$$

What discounting does is to translate future values into a single metric, that of present value. So, for example, if we had numerous different future values occurring in various future years, we can convert them all to present values and aggregate them in those terms. For example, suppose the IOU given to you specifies the following payment schedule:

	Year[2]					
	0	1	2	3	4	5
Payment	$100	$100	$150	$150	$50	$50

[2] We are assuming that the payments are made at the beginning of each year. Remember the convention that the present period is indexed 0 and is not discounted, next period is indexed 1 and is discounted one period, etc.

The present value of this stream of payments[3] is found as follows:

$$PV = \$100 + \frac{\$100}{(1+r)^1} + \frac{\$150}{(1+r)^2} + \frac{\$150}{(1+r)^3} + \frac{\$50}{(1+r)^4} + \frac{\$50}{(1+r)^5}$$

If the discount rate is 4 percent, this present value sum is equal to $545.18.

Now we are able to aggregate the willingness-to-pay amounts shown in Figure 3-6. The present value of the stream of total willingness to pay is equal to

$$PV_{(WTP)} = (a+b) + \frac{(c+d)}{1+r} + \frac{(e+f)}{(1+r)^2} + \frac{(g+h)}{(1+r)^3} + \cdots$$

The areas under the curves at each quantity for each year are the values of FV for that year. The same approach is used to find the present value sum of a sequence of costs. Note that the discount rate is set equal to zero, all the discount factors go to unity, and we are just adding up the annual values without alteration. For progressively higher discount rates the present value aggregate becomes smaller and smaller, because the denominators in the present value formula get progressively larger. At very high discount rates the discounted future values become very small compared to current values.

SUMMARY

The primary way of registering value in economics is through **willingness to pay.** This does not mean that "money is the only thing of value," but only that willingness to sacrifice is the underlying concept, and a monetary index is the most convenient index of making it visible. We introduced **marginal** and **total** willingness to pay, for individuals and for groups of individuals (called **aggregate** measures). Willingness-to-pay curves are more familiarly known as demand curves. We distinguished between two fundamental types of goods: **private goods** and **public goods.** The difference lies in the technical nature of the goods and not in the institutional means chosen to supply them. The step from individual to aggregate willingness-to-pay curves has to be carried out differently for the two types of goods. People's willingness to pay for something normally extends over **time,** and this presents the problem of adding up willingness-to-pay amounts that occur in different time periods. This is done through **discounting,** which is essentially the reverse of the compound interest process.

---

[3] A generalized way of writing this is $PV = \sum_{t=0}^{6} \frac{FV_t}{(1+r)^t}.$

KEY TERMS

Value

Marginal willingness to pay

Total willingness to pay

Aggregate willingness to pay

Demand

Private good

Public good

Benefits

Ability to pay

Discounting

QUESTIONS FOR FURTHER DISCUSSION

1 We talked about willingness to pay for a good or service. How does the concept apply to an act of strict preservation, in which the flow of goods and services from a natural resource is put at zero?

2 There are ways of expressing value alternative to using willingness to pay. Can you think of some?

3 Calculate the present value of the following sequence of willingnesses to pay: this year, $100; next year, $150; year 2, $150; year 3, $50. Use a 5 percent discount rate. Recalculate using a discount rate of 8 percent. What is the effect of using a higher discount rate?

4 Is a movie theater a public good? How about a "public" telephone? A lighthouse? A bus? The music you are playing on your stereo?

5 Suppose your house or apartment has become very cluttered and messy and needs to be cleaned. As you proceed through the tasks of cleaning, how does the marginal willingness to pay for more cleaning change? Which tasks generate the greatest impact or benefit, and which tasks the least?

USEFUL WEB SITES

Several web sites put together by economists feature introductory text material:

- *Essential Principles of Economics: A Hypermedia Approach,* by Roger A. McCain of Drexel University (http://william-king.www.edu/top/prin/txt/Eco Toc.html); Chapter 5 contains an introduction to demand theory
- *Cybereconomics: A Semi-Interactive, Almost-Multimedia Way to Learn Economics,* by Robert E. Schenk, of St. Joseph's College (http://ingrimayne. saintjoe.edu/econ/ TitlePage.html); See the chapter on "The Logic of Choice."
- *Essential Microeconomic Principles,* by John Bouman, of Howard Community College (http://www.howardcc.edu/social_science/microbk.htm), unit 2

Some of the most successful commercial web sites are based on letting people express their willingness to pay for various items:

- For airline tickets, http://www.priceline.com
- For almost anything else: http://www.ebay.com
- The Chicago Board of Trade (http://www.cbot.com) has an on-line auction featuring the demand and supply of recyclables (under programs and services of CBOT's EcoCenter)

SELECTED READINGS

The subjects covered in this and in the next several chapters are treated in all introductory microeconomics textbooks. The best way to proceed, in order to get a longer treatment and deeper understanding of the ideas, is to consult the appropriate chapters of one of these books. Some of the more popular ones are the following:

Baumol, William J., and Alan S. Blinder: *Microeconomics, Principles and Policy,* 8th ed., Harcourt Brace Jovanovich, Dallas, TX, 1999, Chapters 5, 7, 8.

Boyes, William, and Michael Melvin: *Economics,* 4th ed., Houghton Mifflin, Boston, MA, 1999, Chapter 3.

Heilbroner, Robert L., James K. Galbraith, and Thomas Beveridge: *The Economic Problem,* 9th ed., Prentice-Hall, Englewood Cliffs, NJ, 1990, Chapter 8.

Lipsey, Richard G., Peter O. Steiner, and Douglas D. Purvis: *Economics,* 11th ed., HarperCollins, New York, 1992, Chapter 4.

McConnell, Campbell R., and Stanley L. Brue: *Economics,* 14th ed., McGraw-Hill, New York, 1998, Chapters 23 and 24.

Parkin, Michael: *Economics,* 5th ed., Addison-Wesley, Reading, MA, 2000, Chapters 7, 10.

Samuelson, Paul A., and William D. Nordhaus, *Economics,* 16th ed., McGraw-Hill, New York, 1998, Chapters 6, 8.

Schiller, Bradley R.: *The Microeconomy Today,* 8th ed., McGraw-Hill, New York, 1999, Chapter 2.

Waud, Roger N.: *Microeconomics,* 5th ed., HarperCollins, New York, 1992, Chapters 4 and 5.

CHAPTER 4

COSTS/SUPPLY

It is now time to move to the other side of the picture and consider **production costs.** Even though some things in life may be free (though it is getting harder and harder to think of any), it is generally true that the production of anything will require the expenditure, or using up, of things that have economic value: To get **outputs** it is necessary to use **inputs.** This is clearly true in the case of the traditional extractive processes; inputs are required to harvest natural resource commodities. But it is just as true in the case of nonextractive resources. Natural resource preservation is not just "nonuse"; it is in general a more activist activity that requires the expenditure of productive resources to be effective.

This chapter covers the fundamentals of cost: important general cost concepts, the depiction of relationships between costs and output levels, and some very important notions of cost that are specifically useful in looking at natural resource issues. It is easy sometimes to concentrate on the role of the benefits that flow from natural resource utilization and preservation, while overlooking the cost side. But courses of action that are "best," or "optimal," for society clearly cannot be distinguished without taking both sides into account.

OPPORTUNITY COST

The most fundamental notion of costs in microeconomics is **opportunity cost.** Production processes, traditional or otherwise, require the expenditure of "inputs" to produce "outputs." The costs of inputs used to produce a particular output are the values those inputs would have produced had they been devoted instead to their next best production opportunity.

Suppose somebody is engaged in commercial fishing. The operation requires equipment, fuel, materials of various types, crew to operate the boat, and so on. All these inputs could have been devoted to something else: The crew could have worked elsewhere, the supplies could have been used by some other person, fuel could have been consumed in another operation, the inputs represented by the fishing boat itself could have been devoted to some other type of capital good, and so on.

The opportunity costs of these inputs are the values they would have produced in their next best alternative. Opportunity costs include "out of pocket" cash costs but are much wider than this. Suppose that the fisher has a spouse who keeps the books and does the accounting for the fishing operation and that this person receives no monetary compensation for doing the job. Although this input service has no cash cost, there is an opportunity cost, represented by what the spouse could have earned if he had worked in his next best alternative.

Another important kind of opportunity cost that usually does not show up as a monetary cost is the **environmental cost** of a production process. Suppose that one is producing writing paper using inputs of capital, labor, energy, and raw materials and that in producing the paper various pollutants are introduced into a nearby stream. These pollution costs are part of the true opportunity costs of manufacturing the paper, even though they do not show up as cost items in the firm's profit-and-loss statement.

The idea of opportunity cost is relevant to many types of situations. The examples above refer to production of some physical output. For a public agency the opportunity cost of spending resources on one program include the forgone benefits of using them on another program. For a student, the opportunity cost of studying more for one final exam is the lower grade on another exam for which study time is reduced.

Of course it is usually impossible to know exactly what the next best opportunity is for a given collection of inputs. The usual approach, therefore, is to use the **market prices** of inputs as a measure of their true opportunity cost. This requires that the markets exist and that they are subject to competition. For many inputs (like the water quality affects discussed above) markets may not exist, in which case other means have to be found for determining true opportunity costs.

COST CURVES

In the models of natural resource use of subsequent chapters we will make use of graphical representations of costs. The primary relationship is the one between the rate at which something is produced and the costs of that production. Just as in the previous chapter it is useful to distinguish between a marginal concept and a total concept. Here we distinguish between **marginal costs** and **total costs** of production.

Marginal cost is defined as the **change in total cost** resulting from a one-unit change in the quantity of output. Consider the top panel of Figure 4-1. It shows a step-shaped marginal cost function. The graph is laid out as before:

FIGURE 4-1
Marginal Cost

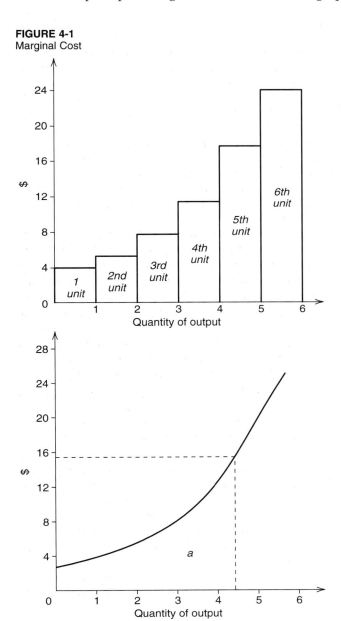

quantity on the horizontal axis and a monetary index on the vertical axis. Remember that this quantity variable has a **time dimension,** such as quantity of output per year. The graph shows that it costs $4 to produce the first unit; next it shows that if production were to be increased from 1 to 2 units, total costs would **increase** by $5. Producing one more unit—the third—would **add** $8 to total costs, and so on. The height of the rectangles depict, in other words, the **marginal cost** of producing additional units of output. Marginal cost works in both directions. It is the added costs, the amount by which total costs increase when output is increased by one unit, and it is also the cost savings if production were to decrease by one unit. Thus, the reduction in output from four to three units would reduce total costs by $12, the marginal cost of the fourth unit.

It is inconvenient to work with step-shaped curves, so we make the assumption that the firm can produce intermediate quantities as well as integer values. This gives a smooth marginal cost curve, as shown in the bottom panel of Figure 4-1. This curve now shows the marginal cost for any level of output. For example, at an output level of 4.5 units, marginal cost is slightly less than $16.

Marginal cost curves can be used to determine **total production costs.** On the stepped marginal cost curve of Figure 4-1, the total cost of producing five units is equal to the cost of the first unit ($4), plus that of the second ($5), plus that of the third ($8), the fourth ($11), and the fifth ($18). This total is $46; geometrically this is equal to the total area of the rectangles above the first five units of output. Analogously, in the smoothly shaped version of the marginal cost function, the total cost of producing a given quantity is the dollar amount equal to the area under the marginal cost curve between the origin and the quantity in question. So, for example, the total cost of producing 4.5 units of output is given by the area marked *a* in the figure.

THE SHAPES OF COST CURVES

Marginal cost curves summarize the important technical and economic characteristics of a production process. The height, shape, steepness, etc., show the quantities of inputs required to produce different levels of output. Figure 4-2 depicts several marginal cost curves. Panel (a) shows a very common situation: Initially marginal costs decline as output increases, but then increase at larger output levels. Suppose the production process involved is the generation of electricity. Here quantity refers to kilowatt-hours produced per year. At low levels of output the plant is not being fully utilized; thus, as output increases, marginal costs actually decline. But suppose we are dealing with the **short run,** a time short enough that the size of the plant cannot readily be expanded. At higher output rates, the capacity of the plant is approached. Machinery must be worked longer, additional people must be hired, and so on. Thus marginal cost begins to increase. As the capacity of the operation is neared, these problems become more acute. To continue to increase output, more extraordinary measures are required, which can only be done at a high cost; thus, marginal cost in-

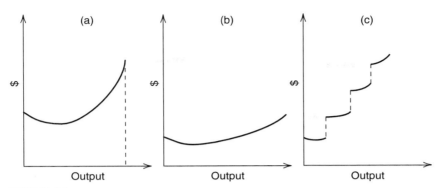

FIGURE 4-2
Marginal Cost Curves

creases even more. A point may come at which it becomes almost impossible to increase output further, which is the same as saying that the marginal costs of production at this point increase without limit. This limit is indicated by the vertical dashed line in panel (a) of Figure 4-2.

This marginal cost curve depicts an important generic characteristic of all marginal cost curves, namely, that of **increasing marginal costs.** Although marginal cost may initially decline, it will always increase, eventually, as output becomes large enough. These increases are related to certain underlying factors, such as increased plant utilization, the need to reach farther away for raw materials, and the inevitable higher management costs that accompany larger operations. Virtually all economic studies of particular operations and industries demonstrate increasing marginal production costs, and this fact will be an important shaping element in our later discussions specifically related to natural resource use.

Panel (b) of Figure 4-2 shows a marginal cost curve similar in general shape to the one in panel (a), but with less pronounced curvature. In particular, although this marginal cost curve eventually increases, it does so less steeply than the first one. This is more typical of a **long-run marginal cost curve;** that is, one where enough time is available for operators of the firm to adapt fully to an increase in the rate of output. In the short run, the power plant has a certain capacity that is basically fixed; but in the long run, there is time to expand the size of the plant by adding generating capacity. For larger outputs the marginal costs of this higher plant will be lower than those of the smaller plant. But even in these long-run situations marginal costs will eventually increase, as is depicted in panel (b). In later discussions we will assume long-run marginal cost curves, unless specified otherwise.

Panel (c) in Figure 4-2 shows a more complicated case. Here the marginal cost curve increases, but in a discontinuous, or jumpy, fashion. These jumps might, for example, be associated with the need to shift to newer and larger machines or to hire more individuals as the firm's output gets larger.

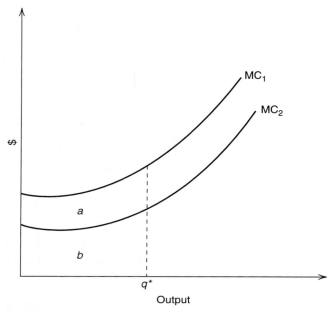

FIGURE 4-3
Technical Change

Technical Change

Marginal cost curves can be used to depict **technical change.** In effect, technical improvements—in, say, operating procedures or equipment—normally make production less costly. Graphically, this shifts the relevant marginal cost curve downward, as is depicted in Figure 4-3. Not only does marginal cost shift downward, but the total costs of producing any particular rate of output also go down. Suppose, for example, a technological improvement shifts production from MC_1 to MC_2 in Figure 4-3. The total cost of producing an output rate of q^* goes from $(a + b)$ to b.

Technological change is a driving force behind costs and prices in most industries, especially natural resource extractive industries. Exhibit 4-1 discusses the rapid changes that have been made over the last few years in petroleum discovery and extraction costs. Essentially this pushes the marginal cost function down and thus, as we discuss in the next section, the **supply curve** for the good or service in question.

MARGINAL COSTS AND SUPPLY

Supply is a word used to describe the quantities of a good or service an organization will produce and make available to consumers during some period of time, like one year. A critical factor in the operation of any economic system is what quantities of output firms and other entities will choose to produce—their

EXHIBIT 4-1

THE NEW ECONOMICS OF OIL

Crude-oil prices have been careening like steel balls in a pinball machine this autumn in response to news and rumors from the Middle East. In the first few days of October, the threat of armed conflict between Iran and Iraq sent crude prices soaring from $20 a barrel to almost $23, before sinking back down again.

Even as the world is reminded of the vulnerability of its oil supply, consumption is soaring. Americans have fallen in love with gas guzzlers such as the Ford Expedition. In newly prosperous developing countries, ordinary people can afford cars for the first time. A recent survey in the *China Youth Daily* found that 75% of Beijing families planned to buy a car within the next five years.

Are we in for another oil crisis? . . .

Perhaps. But there's another, quite different scenario—namely, that oil prices, adjusted for inflation, won't rise at all over the long term. They may even fall. Why? First, because producers in the Mideast and elsewhere need the cash from oil too much to let their supply be interrupted for long, despite political and military skirmishing. Second, and more important, because demand growth can't push prices upward as long as it is balanced by supply growth. And the supply curve for oil—the amount offered at any given price—is being pushed steadily outward, thanks to technology.

Technological advances are slashing the costs of finding, producing, and refining oil, creating a new economic calculus for the oil industry. The new alchemy runs from three-dimensional seismology to exotic wells that sit on the ocean floor, in some cases eliminating the need for billion-dollar offshore production platforms. Says Shell Oil Chief Executive Philip J. Carroll: "Technology always drives down cost. I don't think its effect in this industry will be any different. . . ."

The progress already achieved through technology is mind-boggling. The average cost per barrel of finding and producing oil has dropped about 60% in real terms over the past 10 years, while proven reserves are about 60% higher than in 1985. And these official figures far understate the amount of accessible oil in the ground. Smith Rea Energy Associates Ltd., a London-based researcher, figures that the world's oil producers could add 350 billion barrels to their proven reserves if they counted all the oil that has become affordable to recover because of the latest breakthroughs. That sum is equal to nearly 14 years' worth of worldwide consumption.

The new economics of oil are built on advances in every corner of the vast oil industry. In refining, for example, more gasoline and diesel are being squeezed out of every barrel of oil because of more efficient catalysts and the elimination of processing bottlenecks. In the U.S., the oil industry closed 29 refineries since 1990 and still increased output by 105,000 barrels a day.

Even bigger strides have come in finding and producing oil. For exploration, there are now "geosteering" drill bits that snake down, across, even up again to follow the trail of oil miles underground. Sensors that do magnetic resonance imaging—like the MRI machines in hospitals—peer ahead of a drill bit to find the least expensive route to black gold. Exxon Corp. says such technologies have helped it cut exploration costs by 85% in 10 years.

Deep waters that were once off limits to oil explorers are suddenly accessible, partly because of advances in floating rigs. Computer-controlled thrusters keep drilling ships and floating rigs in place even in stormy seas. The thrusters "know" which way to nudge the floating craft because of coordinate readings from global-positioning satellites. . . .

Just emerging from laboratories at Amoco, Exxon, Syntroleum, and South Africa's Sasol are ideas for producing synthetic oil from its underground partner—natural gas. The concept is to reassemble plentiful and cheap natural gas into petroleum liquids such as methanol or refined products such as diesel or gasoline. . . .

Source: Reprinted from November 3, 1997 issue of *Business Week* by special permission, copyright © 1997 by The McGraw-Hill Companies, Inc.

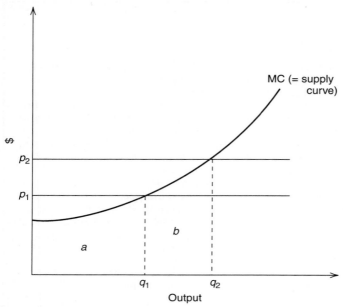

FIGURE 4-4
Individual Marginal Cost and Supply

supply decisions, in other words. The principle extends to the use of natural re-sources: A basic question is whether organizations involved in the manage-ment of natural resources will choose the "correct" output rates, from the standpoint of society.

Individual Supply Curves

An **individual supply function** depicts the quantities of a good or service that a firm will produce and make available. On the assumption that a firm has the goal of maximizing its net income, it turns out that its supply function is none other than its marginal cost curve. Consider Figure 4-4. It shows the rising marginal cost curve for a firm harvesting, say, timber. The quantity axis shows the annual quantity of timber delivered to saw mills, in cubic feet during a given time period. Suppose the delivered price of timber is p_1, on the vertical axis. Define **net income** as total revenue minus total costs. The firm would maximize its net income by harvesting q_1 cubic feet of timber. At any output level less than this, $MC < p_1$, so a firm could increase its net income by increas-ing output. At any output level above this, $p_1 < MC$, so a firm is actually pro-ducing items the marginal cost of which is higher than the price; in this case, the firm should reduce output if it wishes to maximize its net income. If the price of delivered timber rises to p_2, the firm, if it is a net-income maximizer,

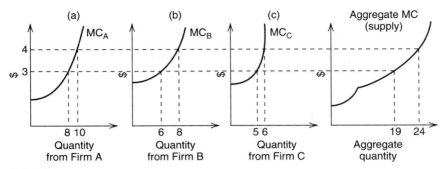

FIGURE 4-5
Derivation of Aggregate Supply from Individual Firm Supply Curves

would increase its quantity supplied to q_2. Thus the marginal cost curve essentially functions as a supply curve, showing the quantities that will be supplied at different prices.

Aggregate Supply

In most of the natural resource issues discussed in later chapters, attention focuses not on single firms but on resource-using industries, that is, groups of firms all producing the same, or similar, outputs. So the relevant concept in this case is the **aggregate supply curve,** which shows how much of a good or service an industry group would supply at various prices. The idea is analogous to the aggregate demand curve discussed in Chapter 3.

The aggregate supply curve for a group of firms is simply the aggregate marginal cost curve for that group of firms, which is derived by summing together all the marginal cost curves of the firms comprising the industry. This is depicted in Figure 4-5. The first three panels show the marginal cost curves of the three firms comprising this industry. The panel on the far right shows the aggregate marginal cost, or industry supply, curve. It is found by summing the individual marginal cost curves horizontally. For example, at a price of $3, firms A, B, and C would produce, respectively, 8, 6, and 5 units of output. So the aggregate supply at this price is 19 units. At a price of $4, the individual quantities supplied by firms A, B, and C would be 10, 8, and 6 units, respectively, so aggregate supply at this price would be 24 units of output.

PRESENT VALUE OF COST

In the last chapter we applied the procedures of present value analysis to time streams of benefits. It is also useful in evaluating future time streams of costs. Resource development or protection programs normally extend over long periods of time, with costs being incurred each year throughout their life. This is pictured in Figure 4-6.

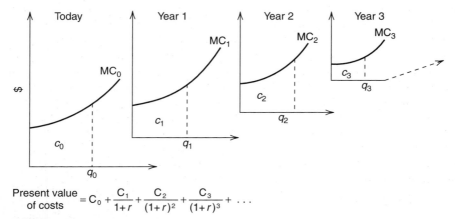

$$\frac{\text{Present value}}{\text{of costs}} = C_0 + \frac{C_1}{1+r} + \frac{C_2}{(1+r)^2} + \frac{C_3}{(1+r)^3} + \cdots$$

FIGURE 4-6
Present Value of a Stream of Costs

Costs in the current period (C_0) are equal to the area under today's marginal cost curve (MC_0) up to today's rate of output (q_0). Likewise, the expected marginal cost curves of future periods are shown, together with the expected rates of output and total costs that will be incurred in each period. The formula for determining the present value of this stream of costs is

$$\frac{\text{Present value}}{\text{of costs}} = C_0 + \frac{C_1}{1+r} + \frac{C_2}{(1+r)^2} + \frac{C_3}{(1+r)^3} + \cdots$$

where r is the rate of discount.

TAXES AS COSTS

A major part of the study of natural resource economics is the analysis of public policies for resource development and protection. A key part of this is looking at how private firms and individuals will react to various types of public policies and regulations. One type of regulation frequently used in natural resource industries is **taxes,** for example **severance taxes** (taxes on quantities of resource harvested), income taxes, and levies on the use of certain types of inputs.

A frequently asked question is whether a particular tax applied to a firm or group of firms would lead them to make changes in, say, the amount of a resource harvested. We can examine this question with the help of the ideas discussed above. Suppose there is a firm with the marginal cost curve as depicted by MC in Figure 4-7. If it sells its output at a price of p_1, it will produce a total output of q_1 units. Now we have the following principle: Any tax that has the effect of shifting the MC curve will lead the firm to change output; any tax that

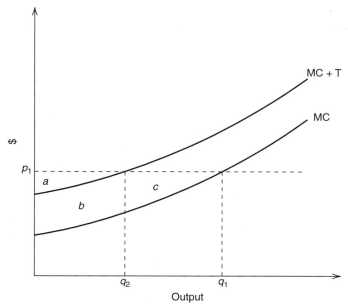

FIGURE 4-7
Taxes as Costs

does not shift the curve will leave output unchanged. Suppose, for example, that authorities levy a tax per unit of output; that is, for each unit of output produced, the firm must pay a certain unit tax to the public authority. This would have the effect of shifting the marginal cost curve upward, to the line labeled MC + T. And this would lead the firm to reduce its output[1] to q_2.

On the other hand, suppose a profits tax were applied, that is, a tax of some percentage of the total net income made by the firm. At an output level of q_1, the total net income of the firm would be an amount equal to the area $a + b + c$. Because of the proportionate nature of the tax, the rate of output that maximizes net income is unaffected. This tax affects neither the marginal costs of producing the output nor the output's price. So in this case the profits tax creates no incentives for the firm to shift its rate of output.

SUMMARY

The prime topic of this chapter was **economic cost.** The most important notion of cost is that of **opportunity cost.** The opportunity cost of producing something is the maximum value that could have been produced of something else

---

[1] In the diagram the assumption is made that the tax will not affect output price. This is unrealistic in practice, but is made here to keep things simple.

if the good or service in question had not been produced. We distinguished among **marginal costs, total costs,** and **aggregate costs,** and we discussed the importance of **technology** in determining costs in any concrete situation. We linked marginal costs with supply functions; the key factor in this case being the profit-maximizing incentives of market-oriented firms. We discussed also the issue of discounting future costs to find the **present value of costs,** and the question of how firms treat some taxes as costs.

KEY TERMS

Opportunity cost	Supply
Marginal cost	Present value of cost
Total cost	Technology and costs
Aggregate cost	Taxes as costs

QUESTIONS FOR FURTHER DISCUSSION

1 How does the concept of opportunity cost apply to the following situations:
   a A piece of land that is to be devoted to a public park
   b An abandoned railroad that is given to a community for constructing a bike path
   c The costs of diverting water from a river to irrigate nearby farmlands
   d The costs of clear-cutting timberland
2 Contrast private and social costs in the following situations:
   a Electric power production
   b Strip mining
   c Timber harvesting
   d Ecotourism
3 What are the major factors behind shifts in supply functions? Illustrate this with an example from a natural resource–based industry.
4 Determine the present value of costs for the following time profile of costs:
   $C_0 = 10$
   $C_1 = 8$
   $C_2 = 6$
   $C_3 = 5$
   Do this for discount rates of 4 percent and 6 percent.

USEFUL WEB SITES

The economics textbook sites listed at the end of the preceding chapter can be consulted for material on costs and supply functions:

- McCain (Drexel University) site: Chapters 7 and 8.
- Schenk (St. Joseph's College) site.
- Bouman (Howard Community College) site: unit 2.

SELECTED READINGS

A statement similar to the one at the end of the last chapter is appropriate here. Consult the appropriate chapters (those dealing with cost concepts) of one of the main microeconomics textbooks currently available:

Baumol, William J., and Alan S. Blinder: *Microeconomics, Principles and Policy,* 8th ed., Harcourt Brace Jovanovich, Dallas, TX, 1999, Chapters 5, 7, and 8.

Boyes, William, and Michael Melvin, *Economics,* 4th ed., Houghton Mifflin, Boston, 1999, Chapter 3.

Heilbroner, Robert L., James K. Galbraith, and Thomas Beveridge: *The Economic Problem,* 9th ed., Prentice-Hall, Englewood Cliffs, NJ, 1990, Chapter 8.

Lipsey, Richard G., Peter O. Steiner, and Douglas D. Purvis: *Economics,* 11th ed., HarperCollins, New York, 1992, Chapter 4.

McConnell, Campbell R., and Stanley L. Brue, *Economics,* 14th ed., McGraw-Hill, New York, 1998, Chapters 23 and 24.

Parkin, Michael: *Economics,* 5th ed., Addison Wesley Longman, New York, 2000, Chapters 7 and 10.

Samuelson, Paul A., and William D. Nordhaus: *Economics,* 16th ed., McGraw-Hill, New York, 1998, Chapters 6 and 8.

Schiller, Bradley R.: *The Microeconomy Today,* 8th ed., McGraw-Hill, New York, 1999, Chapter 2.

Waud, Roger N.: *Microeconomics,* 5th ed., HarperCollins, New York, 1992, Chapters 4 and 5.

CHAPTER 5

EFFICIENCY AND SUSTAINABILITY

In this chapter we bring together the two main concepts that were introduced earlier: **willingness to pay** and **marginal cost.** Combining these two ideas leads to a major concept used throughout economics, that of **economic efficiency.** The notion of efficiency is used in positive economics to help explain how people in fact behave in the real world. It is also a tool of normative economics, as a criterion for judging outcomes, such as for evaluating in specific instances whether the rate at which individuals are using a natural resource is the best one from the standpoint of society as a whole.

We look at economic efficiency from two angles: **state efficiency** and **dynamic,** or **intertemporal, efficiency.** A state of affairs that is efficient in the static sense is one that is efficient strictly from the perspective of a single time period, in particular the present one. In the spring a farmer plants a crop, later harvesting it and shipping it to market. A timber harvesting firm cuts down a number of trees this year and also ships them to market. A public agency allows a certain number of visitors into a park this year. These decisions will be efficient in the static sense if they are undertaken in light of the consequences flowing from them this year only.

Dynamic, or intertemporal, efficiency means a situation that is efficient when account is taken not only of the present year but all future years as well. A decision is intertemporally efficient if it takes into account all the consequences flowing from it, those occurring this year and those in the future. If there are no future consequences stemming from today's decision, a static perspective is sufficient also to achieve dynamic efficiency. Consider the farmer. There is essentially no connection between this year's decision as to how many acres to devote to cantaloupes and anything that will happen in future years. This decision can be made, and harvests produced, with essentially no future consequences.[1] In this example a decision made only on static grounds will capture all the consequences that are involved.

But this is not true for the company doing the logging. Cutting down and replanting trees this year means there will be no trees to cut on this parcel until such time as the new trees mature. There are clearly future consequences flowing from today's decisions. Pumping petroleum out of an underground deposit is also a decision of this type; pumping more today means having less to pump out in the future. In cases like this decisions made only on static grounds (considering only current consequences) will be very different from those made on dynamic grounds (considering both current and future consequences).

The next two sections deal, respectively, with static and dynamic economic efficiency. After that we turn to the idea of **sustainability,** an idea that has become widely popular in recent years as a possible alternative, or additional, criterion for evaluating the long-run consequences of natural resource decisions.

STATIC EFFICIENCY

To understand the notion of **static efficiency** we bring together the two major concepts of the last chapter, marginal willingness to pay and marginal cost. This is done in Figure 5-1. The horizontal axis depicts alternative quantities of the output of a good or service and the vertical axis has a value scale. The MSC curve represents **marginal social cost,** that is, the marginal costs to all of society of producing this good or service. The MSB curve represents **marginal social benefits,** which are measured by the marginal willingness to pay of all members of society for this good or service. Both MSB and MSC curves are aggregate relationships. They represent the summed marginal willingness to pay and summed marginal cost relationships of all the people and firms in our "society." Since nothing and nobody is left out, they are called "social." The rate of output that is socially efficient is the one that yields the maximum **net benefits to society.**[2] Net benefits refer to the total benefits of the thing that is produced minus the value of the resources used up to produce it. The total benefits of a quantity of output are given, as we saw earlier, by the area under

---

[1] This is not to suggest that all farming decisions are essentially static, of course. Things can be done today that clearly will have an impact on the future, say, through affecting future soil fertility.

[2] The difference between "efficiency" and "social efficiency" is the degree of inclusiveness. Efficiency is a condition of maximum net benefits, and could apply to a single firm, community, or country. Social efficiency is efficiency pertaining to the full, all inclusive, society.

the social marginal willingness-to-pay curve. At a quantity of q^* in Figure 5-1, the total social benefits of output are equal to the area labeled $a + b$.

Total costs are equal to the area under the social marginal cost curve. For the quantity q^* in Figure 5-1, this is shown as area b. Thus the **net social benefits** of the output level q^* is $(a + b) - b = a$. Net benefits are equal, in other words, to the difference between the area under the social marginal willingness-to-pay curve and social marginal cost curve.

It is straightforward to show that q^* is the rate of output that maximizes the net social benefits associated with the production of this good or service. To do this, take some other output level, such as q_1 in Figure 5-1. The net benefits of this output are derived as follows:

$$\text{Total benefits: } a + b + d$$
$$\text{Total costs: } b + c + d$$
$$\text{Benefits} - \text{costs: } a - c$$

In other words, net social benefits are equal to what they would have been had output been q^*, **minus** the quantity c. We can conclude that net social benefits are definitely lower at q_1 than at q^*. In fact this same conclusion can be drawn[3] about any output that is different from q^*.

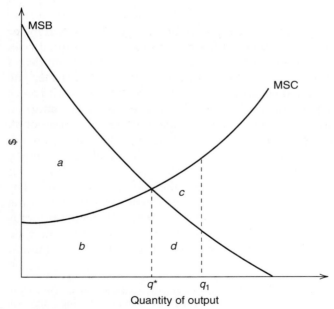

FIGURE 5-1
Static Social Efficiency

---

[3] To see this, pick some output level below q^* and label the resulting areas. Then follow through the arithmetic the same way.

Of course the condition that identifies output level q^* uniquely is that MSB = MSC at that output. The notion of efficiency involves a trade-off between willingness to pay and production costs. To the left of q^*, an additional unit of output would add more to social benefits than to production costs (i.e., marginal willingness to pay exceeds marginal cost) while to the right of q^* the opposite is true. At q^*, therefore, these two quantities are in balance, marking the socially efficient rate of output.

The reason this is called static efficiency is that it is based on a balance between two contemporaneous, or current period, quantities. Quantity of output, marginal benefits, and marginal cost are all values pertaining to the current year; there is nothing in this simple model that applies to some other time period, for example, future period marginal costs as they might be affected by this period's output rate.

DYNAMIC (INTERTEMPORAL) EFFICIENCY

By **dynamic** or **intertemporal efficiency,** we also refer to a state of affairs in which there is a maximum of net benefits; but now benefit and cost categories are extended to include not only those of the present period, but also the **future consequences** flowing from today's decision. Consider Figure 5-2: It shows a series of marginal benefit and marginal cost curves, one set for each year starting with the current year and stretching into the future. Dynamic, or intertemporal, efficiency now requires choosing a **time series of output quantities,** not just one. And since time is involved, our criterion for that decision now becomes to choose the one time series of quantities that gives the **maximum present value of net benefits.**

Which particular time series of outputs will maximize the present value of the net benefit stream depends on whether and how the different q's are linked together. Suppose they were not linked. Suppose, for example, that Figure 5-2 refers to the farm case mentioned above. In this case there is no connection

FIGURE 5-2
Time Profile of Net Benefits Associated with a Series of Outputs

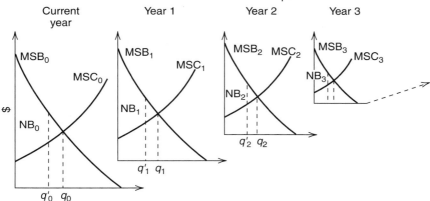

between the time periods. Intertemporal efficiency would be achieved by selecting the statically efficient output rate in each time period, shown in the figure as $q_0, q_1, q_2, \ldots$. But suppose there is a connection. Maybe there are extraction rates for a small mineral deposit, in which case we can't change output in one year without having to change it in some other year or years. Our intertemporally efficient time path of outputs might now be something like $q_0', q_1', q_2', \ldots$

Let us look explicitly at the criterion to be maximized in the search for intertemporal efficiency. It can be written as follows:

$$\begin{array}{r} \text{Present value of} \\ \text{net benefits} \end{array} = \begin{array}{c} \text{Net benefits} \\ \text{in year 0} \end{array} + \begin{array}{c} \text{Net benefits} \\ \text{in year 1} \end{array} \frac{1}{1+r}$$
$$+ \begin{array}{c} \text{Net benefits} \\ \text{in year 2} \end{array} \frac{1}{(1+r)^2} + \ldots$$

or

$$\begin{array}{r} \text{Present value of} \\ \text{net benefits} \end{array} = \begin{array}{c} \text{Net benefits} \\ \text{in year 0} \end{array} + \begin{array}{c} \text{Sum of all discounted} \\ \text{future net benefits} \end{array}$$

The present value of net benefits can be thought of as consisting of a sum; the first term in the sum is the net benefits in the current period, while the second term shows the net benefits of all future periods **discounted** by the appropriate factors. Dynamic efficiency requires that current and future rates of use be chosen that make this sum as large as possible. What makes things complicated is that there is normally a **trade-off;** decisions that increase the net benefits of using a natural resource in the present period often have the effect of decreasing net benefits from the resource in the future. It is this problem of finding the appropriate balance between present and future that characterizes the concept of dynamic efficiency.

Clearly, the discount rate plays a critical role in intertemporal efficiency. In Chapter 3 we covered the mechanics of discounting, and here we use it to convert future net benefits into their present values. Our idea of intertemporal efficiency depends, in other words, on the notion that future net benefits of natural resource use are to be discounted in order to determine their present values. Discounting future net benefits to help identify social efficiency is controversial. And controversies rage over what the discount rate actually should be. We take up these issues later in the chapter.

We can take the last expression and convert it into marginal terms. Remember that "marginal" refers to the extent to which something changes. Thus if there is a one-unit change in today's rate of resource use, we have

Change in the present value of = net benefits	Change in benefits of present period	–	Change in costs of present period	+	Change in discounted value of future net benefits
(MNB)	(MB)		(MCC)		(UC)

which can be rewritten, using the indicated designators:

$$MNB = MB - MCC + UC$$

The designator MCC can be thought of as "marginal current costs"; that is, marginal costs incurred in the current period. UC stands for **user costs.** User costs, in other words, is the name that will be given to the change in the discounted value of future net benefits. Anything that affects these future net benefits, in other words, is expressed through what we are calling user costs.

If the choices of today's output actually have no future consequences, then these user costs would be zero; in effect, we would be back to a static situation. The decision about how many acres of cantaloupes to grow this year on a 100-acre farm is strictly a static decision. There are no future consequences flowing from this decision, only contemporary ones; hence, user costs in this case are zero.[4] Or suppose the decision is how much water to take out of a passing river to irrigate some crops. Increasing or decreasing the amount withdrawn is not likely to have an impact on future water availabilities in the river, hence the user costs of the water are zero.

But in cases where user costs are not zero, intertemporal efficiency requires that today's rate of output be set so that today's marginal willingness to pay is equal to the sum of today's marginal costs and user costs. This is depicted in Figure 5-3. This shows the current year market for a natural resource good or service, for example, the number of units (tons, barrels) of a resource harvested or extracted, or the number of acres of land devoted to a park or wildlife refuge. MCB (for marginal current benefits) shows society's valuation of this resource-based good or service in the present period, while MCC shows the social costs of harvesting or extracting or otherwise making it available this year. To repeat, if this were a static problem, these would be the only relevant relationships and the efficient rate of output would be q_0^1. But assuming there is a user cost of some amount, this has to be added to today's harvest cost, giving the overall marginal cost function labeled MTC (= MCC + UC). The intersection of this curve with MCB gives q_0^* as the intertemporally efficient rate of output in the current period.

User cost is, in effect, the factor that accounts for the future resource-related consequences of today's decisions. Think of user cost as being a single term that is used to show the discounted present value of the sum of all future consequences stemming from today's decisions. Clearly, the higher the user cost, the more will the MTC curve diverge from the MCC curve, in other words, the bigger the difference between dynamic and static efficiency. The exact form that user cost will take depends on the problem at hand. If the problem is a simple one, say, with just two time periods and a strictly nonrenewable resource, user cost will be simple also; it will be equal to the discounted value of

---

[4] As mentioned, however, we could think of a scenario in which this would not be the case; for example, the cantaloupe production might have an impact on future land productivity.

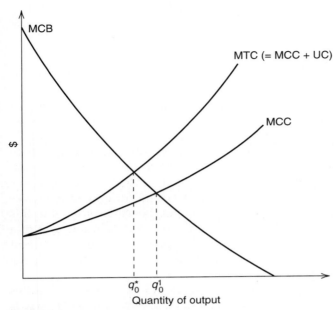

FIGURE 5-3
Intertemporally (Dynamically) Efficient Rates of Output of a Natural
Resource Good or Service

extracting one less unit next year. But if the situation is complex, user cost will
also be complicated. Suppose the issue is how current output decisions affect
future species diversity over the next century. This is a biologically complex,
difficult-to-measure, long-run problem. User cost in this case will be very hard
to estimate. Conceptually, however, it is clear. It is the present value of all the
future consequences arising from today's natural resource use decisions.

Natural Resource Rents

The **in situ price** of a natural resource is its price **as situated in the natural
world.** The stumpage price for wood, what it sells for on the stump, is an in
situ price, whereas the price of timber delivered to a mill is not, because that
price includes the stumpage value plus the cost of harvesting. The landed
price of fish is not an in situ price, because that price reflects both the in situ
value of the resource and the costs of catching it and getting it to market. The
in situ price of copper ore is the price of a ton of copper in the ground, before
it is extracted and delivered to a refinery. The price of land to be used for
farming, or to build houses on, is an in situ price.

In natural resource economics in situ price of a natural resource is commonly called its **resource rent.** In a sense it is the value of something that the

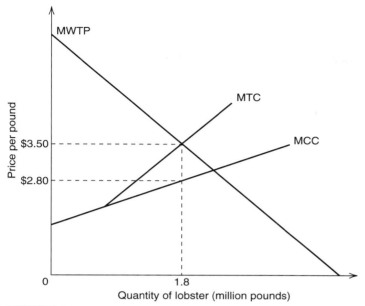

FIGURE 5-4
The Lobster Market

workings of nature itself has made available. Consider Figure 5-4, which shows the marginal willingness-to-pay curve for lobsters by people vacationing in New England in a recent year. The intertemporally efficient quantity of lobsters is 1.8 million pounds, and the efficient price is $3.50 per pound. The marginal harvesting cost at this level of catch is $2.80 per pound. At a catch of 1.8 million pounds, the marginal rent of lobsters is the market price minus marginal harvesting costs, or $3.50 – $2.80 = $0.70. Note that this is a **marginal value;** it applies to the marginal thousand pounds of lobsters when total output is at 1.8 million pounds. If we take the **marginal lobster rent** of $0.70 and multiply it by 1.8 million pounds, we get a **total lobster rent** of $1.26 million. In other words resource rent can be either the rent on the marginal unit of resource, in which case we can call it the **marginal rent;** or the rent on the total harvest, or in some cases the total stock, in which case we can call it the **total rent.** Marginal rent has different names in different situations: In timber economics it is usually called the **stumpage price;** in mineral economics it is often called the **royalty rate.**

Look again at Figure 5-4 and compare it to Figure 5-3. At 1.8 million pounds of lobster, MTC is equal to $3.50 while marginal harvesting cost (MCC) is $2.80, so $3.50 – $2.80 = $0.70 is the user cost. At the margin, in other words, resource rent and user cost are exactly the same, at least when we are dealing with a situation that is intertemporally efficient. This might make you ask, why use two terms to refer to the same thing? The answer is that the terms tend to emphasize two slightly different perspectives: User cost refers to the value of future consequences of today's decisions, whereas rent refers essentially to a price. But it is very informative to realize that these are two different perspectives on exactly the same thing.

We have to be careful in discussing the idea of resource rent. It refers to a price, not necessarily to a social value. A price is a market phenomenon. If there is no market, there can be no rent. If resources produce services that do not pass through markets, then the rent for these resources will not reflect these services. We will have many occasions in later chapters to consider this fact.

IS IT APPROPRIATE TO DISCOUNT?

Intertemporal efficiency, which maximizes the welfare of the present generation, involves discounting the future values of benefits and costs. This is a controversial issue. Discounting appears to put a lesser value on future net benefits than on net benefits occurring closer in time. Furthermore, discounting is done from the perspective of the current generation. Is this fair to future generations? By discounting are we not giving short shrift to the interests of future generations, who apparently are not around to represent themselves? There are many who feel that discounting is essentially anticonservationist; by putting a higher value on today's output relative to future output, we tilt the production profile toward the present. How valid is this objection? There are several different parts to this question, which we will take up in turn.

One question to ask is whether people actually discount in practice, in their everyday lives. And the answer here is yes. The fact that there are positive rates of interest in the world is partly a reflection of the fact that people place a higher value on something today than on that same something happening off sometime in the future. Direct research has also been done on the discount rates applied by people. In one recent study a large number of people were queried on the question of trade-offs between public programs that would save a certain number of lives today as compared to other programs that would save some larger number of lives at varying distances in the future. By asking enough people to choose among enough different combinations, it was possible to find out the relative values among which they were indifferent, and therefore their implied discount rate. For example, if a person responded that she was indifferent between a program that would save 10 lives today and one that would save 500 lives 50 years from now, the implied rate of discount that the person is applying to these payoffs is about 8 percent.[5]

---

[5] To find this we find the r that makes the following equation hold true: $10 = \dfrac{500}{(1+r)^{50}}$.

The results of this research are shown in the following tabulation[6]:

Length of time period (years)	Implied discount (%)
10	12.0
20	9.0
30	7.0
40	6.0
50	5.0
60	4.8
80	4.2
100	3.8

These results show that the farther in the future is the event being considered, the lower is the discount that people apply to it. For events that are only 10 years distant, the average rate of discount was about 12 percent; for events that will happen in 50 years, the discount was 5 percent; and for 100 years, the discount was 3.8 percent.

Since people (in both their consumer and producer roles) do discount, on average, in their everyday lives, may we not take this as implying that we ought to discount when assessing the social desirability of natural resource use rates? Some observers have taken the position that when individuals use some positive rate of discount to evaluate future benefits and costs, they are demonstrating a defective capacity for weighing the future consequences of their actions; they are being myopic. To believe this, one has to believe that people who discount are somehow less in touch with the benefits and costs that impinge upon them than are certain observers. This is not only condescending, it is also scientifically dubious—especially so when we are looking at the behavior of people at markedly different wealth levels. People with low wealth positions clearly have an incentive to put heavy weight on near-term payoffs over future ones. It is not easy to see how the lives of these people would be improved by asking them in effect to put more weight on distant (in time) values and less on the immediate requirements of making a living and supporting their families.

From the perspective of the **current generation,** therefore, the arguments for discounting future benefits and costs are reasonably compelling. The rub comes when we wish to factor in the welfare of **future generations.** Does discounting put future generations at a disadvantage relative to those people alive today? Or to put it the opposite way, does discounting tend to improve

---

[6] The study is reported in Maureen L. Cropper, Sema K. Aydede, and Paul R. Portney, "Rates of Time Preference for Saving Lives," *American Economic Review,* 87(2), May 1992, pp. 469–472.

the welfare of today's generation at the expense of future generations? Would we be better off today if our grandparents had used lower discount rates in their decisions? If future generations could somehow have a seat at today's table, would they agree with the discounting practices of today's decision makers? If we could show that future generations will be better off if people alive today discount the future, we could argue that discounting was both efficient and fair to the future. But can we show this?

The first point to be made is that higher discount rates are not invariably anticonservationist; in fact, plausible circumstances exist in which low discount rates work against conservation rather than the reverse. In the 1960s, natural resource policy makers in Washington were wracked by a dispute over the choice of discount rates to be used in water development projects like large-scale dams built for purposes of flood control and irrigation. The major dam-building public agencies, the Army Corps of Engineers (Defense Department), the Bureau of Land Reclamation (Interior), and the Soil Conservation Service (Agriculture) all evaluated their proposals with relatively low discount rates.[7] The effect of using those low rates was that it allowed them to justify many water development projects, which had high up-front construction costs and relatively low future annual benefits. The low discount rates led to relatively high aggregate benefits because future benefits were not heavily discounted. Low discount rates in this case led to greater dam building, thus working against the goal of preserving natural habitats, though of course it also worked toward the goal of providing larger amounts of water for traditional extractive uses (see Exhibit 5-1).

We must also be aware of the role of the discount rate at the **macroeconomic level.** In general, low discount rates are associated with higher rates of economic growth. This is because low discount rates spur investment, which enhances growth rates. But higher rates of economic growth, by leading to higher rates of economic activity (production and consumption) in the future, will thereby cause a greater demand for natural resource inputs than would otherwise have prevailed. The lower discount rate leads to greater future demand for natural resources.[8]

Can a present generation make itself better off by adopting a resource utilization rate that reduces the long-run productivity of the resource base? Think of a single farmer, age 52 years, who plans on retiring at 60 and doing some traveling to see the world.[9] Might this farmer be tempted to work the farm at

---

[7] The rates were tied to historical yields on government bonds, in such a way that made them much lower than current rates.

[8] For a technical discussion of this see: Bob Rothorn and Gardner Brown, "Biodiversity, Economic Growth and the Discount Rate," in Timothy M. Swanson (ed.), *The Economics and Ecology of Biodiversity Decline: The Forces Driving Global Change,* Cambridge University Press, Cambridge, England 1995, pp. 25–40.

[9] This example was inspired by Alan Randall, *Resource Economics,* 2nd ed., John Wiley, New York, 1987, pp. 128–129.

EXHIBIT 5-1

LOW DISCOUNT RATES AND DAM CONSTRUCTION

In the 1950s and 1960s, three large federal agencies had very active dam-building programs. The U.S. Army Corps of Engineers built large main-stem dams primarily for flood control and navigation purposes, the Bureau of Reclamation (in the Department of Interior) specialized in large western dams whose primary purpose was providing water for irrigation, and the Soil Conservation Service (in the Department of Agriculture) built smaller upstream flood control dams. Many of these dams were controversial because they massively changed the rivers' functions and substituted flat water resources for previously free-running water resources. The time profiles of costs and benefits for most of these dams were characterized by very high initial costs followed by many years of relatively low annual benefits. During the heyday of dam construction, the dam-building agencies strove to get congressional authorization for their projects. To do this they had to show essentially that the present value of their benefits exceeded the present value of their costs. But, although most costs were incurred immediately, most benefits accrued only in the future. How to ensure that the present value

of estimated future benefits would exceed costs? Use a low discount rate.

Suppose, for example, a planned dam has the following cost and benefit streams (in millions of dollars):

	Year					
	0	1	2	3	...	50
Costs	10					
Benefits	0.5	0.5	0.5	0.5	...	0.5

Using a 5 percent discount rate, we get a present value of costs of $10 million and a present value of benefits of $9.1 million; so the benefits are lower than the costs in present value terms. But using a discount rate of only 3 percent gives a present value of benefits of $12.9. So the project could be authorized at 3 percent but not at 5 percent, which illustrates why the agencies were interested in using relatively low discount rates to evaluate their proposed dams.

Low discount rates do not necessarily mean greater conservation.

too high a rate for the next 8 years, so as to gain somewhat higher incomes in these years that could then be added to the retirement fund? The critical question is, what will he do with the farm at the end of the 8 years? One obvious alternative, since there is a ready market for farmland, is to sell it and add those proceeds to the retirement fund. But running down the short-run productivity temporarily to lift earnings will reduce the sale price of the farm, because it means that he will be selling an asset of less long-run value. In other words, he faces a trade-off between temporarily increasing incomes but reducing the sale price at the end of the 8-year period. Note that this is essentially an intergenerational trade-off, because the sale of the farm basically hands it along to the next generation. The procedure that solves this little problem from the standpoint of the farmer is to calculate the present value of the sum of the incomes over the 8-year temporary period plus the sale price at the end of the period. It is important to see that discounting, at a positive rate of discount, in effect incorporates the regard for future generations, as long as the value of the asset (in this case the farm) can be transferred to future generations. This is, of course, what markets do.

But even granting this argument, might there not be cases where the negative consequences of today's natural resource use are so far in the future that people simply are unlikely to take them into account? Even with a very low discount rate, the present values of these very distant consequences may be so low that people of today may be led simply to disregard them.

EFFICIENCY AND INTERGENERATIONAL EQUITY: THE ISSUE OF SUSTAINABILITY

There is another way of thinking about this problem of balancing the interests of distant future generations with those of people today. In the last couple of decades the concept being used increasingly to deal with this is **sustainability.** The idea of sustainability was emphasized in a well-known 1987 report done by a United Nations–sponsored group set up to, among other things, "propose long-term environmental strategies for achieving sustainable development."[10] It is worth noting that "sustainable" here is used as an adjective for "development." The Commission recognized, in other words, the desirability of future economic development, especially for those parts of the world where per capita wealth levels are currently very low. The objective, however, is to do whatever is necessary to make this development "sustainable."

Sustainability has come to be a rallying cry and an organizing principle for much of the subsequent public discussion about natural resource and environmental policy. In that arena it has clearly served to encourage a longer-run perspective in policy discussions and decisions. But is it a useful criterion for evaluating resource use decisions? In order to answer this, it has to be defined more explicitly. According to the Commission report, sustainable development is "development that meets the needs of the present without compromising the ability of future generations to meet their own needs."[11] Without getting into arcane discussions of the meaning of words like "compromise" and "needs," one way of interpreting this operationally might be the following: Any actions on the part of people today that would make future generations worse off than we are today is to be called nonsustainable. Sustainability implies, therefore, that future generations are to be no worse off than today's generation.

But worse off in what respect? Suppose we insist that it be in the sense of the physical supplies and availabilities of natural resources. The condition for sustainability would be that future generations should have no smaller sup-

---

[10] The Report is titled *Our Common Future,* done by the **World Commission on Environment and Development** (Oxford University Press, 1987). (This Commission was often called the Brundtland Commission, after its chair, Gro Harlem Brundtland of Norway.)

[11] *Our Common Future,* p. 43.

plies than currently exist. There is no particular conflict between this and intertemporal efficiency when the subject is **renewable resources.** Intertemporal efficiency normally implies constancy of the resource stock through time, which would be in agreement with this particular notion of sustainability. For **nonrenewable resources,** however, there is obviously a problem if sustainability is to be defined in terms of physical availability. In this case any positive rate of extraction today obviously must lead to reduced availabilities at some time in the future.

Sustainability defined in terms of physical quantities might still be a viable idea if it were interpreted as nondiminution of the total of natural resources rather than any particular single resource. In this case the drawing down of a nonrenewable natural resource could perhaps be compensated for by augmenting supplies of a renewable resource. We might, for example, increase the acreage of preserved ecosystem in one region as quantities of coal or some other mineral are extracted elsewhere.

But the practical usefulness of a procedure like this is open to question. A basic problem is knowing the "exchange" ratios between resources, for example how many acres of preserved wetlands are worth 1 ton of extracted coal or other mineral. To make this approach feasible, we switch from a physical-units notion of sustainability to one that is based on value. This would make it possible to assess different resources in terms of a common metric that allows comparison and aggregation. If natural resources are converted to values, then an injunction to preserve them in terms of their aggregate value is at least operationally feasible, whether or not the rule makes sense in terms of preserving or enhancing human welfare.

A Political Unit Problem

It may seem odd to bring in at this time what appears to be a political problem, but doing so will help get to the bottom of the sustainability question. Suppose we wish to have a concept of sustainability that is applicable to any political jurisdiction: countries, states, regions, or communities. But some political areas are well endowed with a range of natural resources, whereas many are not. It may be reasonable to say that sustainability in the United States as a whole requires that the value of the national resource stock be nondiminishing; it is probably not reasonable to require the same of each and every country and community.

Suppose there were a community, or small country, only modestly endowed with some nonrenewable resource. Sustainability in the above sense would require that community to replace the nonrenewable resource with some other resource as the former is drawn down. But there may be no such resource with which to do this. If there is no such resource, this is not a very useful objective. Nor would it be for any community whose resource endowment consists of a preponderance of some nonrenewable resource.

Sustainability, Broadly Considered

The basic problem here is that sustainability is being defined too narrowly. A better approach is to recognize that human welfare is based on both natural resource capital and other forms of productive capital, in particular **human capital** and **produced capital.** Human capital refers to the human capacities and capabilities that usually result from experience, training, and education. Human capital should also be defined broadly to include **intellectual capital,** basically ideas and operating procedures, improvements which are important to advances in human welfare. Produced capital refers to such things as machinery and buildings, but also includes investments in physical infrastructure (such as roads and ports) that are so important for the productivity of any economic system.

Sustainability in a broader sense now becomes the following: Use of a nonrenewable natural resource is sustainable if the value of the resource used up is matched by capital investments of equal value in other natural resources or in productive nonresource capital. This concept of sustainability can be used to evaluate decisions in political units of any size, from small communities up to nation states and the global economy.

To be able to apply this definition of sustainability, we must have a measure of the extent to which the value of nonrenewable resource stocks are reduced as a result of current extraction. To think about this, we can go back to the concept of **user cost.** User cost is a measure of the present value of future net benefits sacrificed as a result of today's extraction. If compensating investments can be made sufficient to offset the user costs of a nonrenewable resource extraction, sustainability will be attained despite the gradual drawing down of the resource.

Remember that we are trying to adapt a notion of sustainability to the case of a nonrenewable resource. For renewable resources the problem is less acute; sustainability in this case implies the continued availability of the resource to future generations, and this is not likely to be in great conflict with standard economic efficiency criteria.

SUMMARY

In this chapter we dealt with two primary criteria for evaluating performance: **efficiency** and **sustainability.** Economic efficiency is a situation in which net benefits to society are at a maximum. We distinguished between **static** and **dynamic,** or intertemporal, efficiency. A rate of output that is efficient in the static sense is one that maximizes the **net benefits of the current period** only. Intertemporal efficiency requires the maximization of the **present value** of the stream of net benefits, starting today and extending into the future. We defined the concept of **user cost** as the present value of all future consequences stemming from a small change in today's rate of output. If there are no future consequences, user cost is zero, so static and dynamic efficiency amount to the same thing. We also introduced the concept of **natural resource rent,** which is basically the price of a natural resource **in situ.** Intertemporal efficiency implies **discounting** future benefits and costs, an idea around which there is controversy. To deal with very long run, intertemporal, issues, the concept of sustainability has become popular. We discussed several possible definitions of this term, and concluded that to be most useful it had to be understood as applying to general measures of welfare, not just to specific resources.

KEY TERMS

Static efficiency

Dynamic (intertemporal) efficiency

User cost

Natural resource rent (marginal and total)

Sustainability

QUESTIONS FOR FURTHER DISCUSSION

1 Prove that the rate of output that equates MSB with MSC is efficient in the static sense. Apply this idea to a problem involving the preservation of a natural resource.

2 What happens to the statically efficient rate of output when there is a technical change in the mode of production such as new satellite-based resource exploration techniques? When there is population growth?

3 How would the intertemporally efficient time path of output be affected by a zero discount rate?

4 What are the future costs associated with:

   a Extracting coal from an open-pit mine?

   b Harvesting timber in an ecologically sensitive area?

   c Taking steps to preserve a wetland?

5 A small community has discovered a mineral deposit within its borders. How can the community extract this deposit sustainably?

USEFUL WEB SITES

Refer to the web sites of the economics texts listed after Chapters 3 and 4:

- McCain (Drexel University) site: Chapter 3.
- Schenk (St. Joseph's College) site: Costs are treated in the section on "The Firm and Its Constraints."
- Bouman (Howard Community College) site: unit 2.

Sustainability is the new organizing concept, and there are many sites that feature it, at least in the title:

- Sustainable Earth Exchange (http://www.class.csupomona.edu/earth.html).
- International Institute for Sustainable Development (http://iisd.ca).

SELECTED READINGS

For reading about the general notion of efficiency look again at an introductory microeconomics textbook, such as one of those listed at the end of Chapters 3 and 4. For reading about the ideas of efficiency as it is applied to natural resource use and sustainability, the following references might be useful.

Hackett, Steven C.: *Environmental and Natural Resource Economics*, M. E. Sharpe, Armonk, NY, 1998.

Heal, Geoffrey: *Economic Theory and Sustainability*, Columbia University Press, New York, 1998.

Page, Talbot: *Conservation and Economic Efficiency*, Johns Hopkins Press for Resources for the Future, Baltimore, MD, 1977.

Prato, Tony: *Natural Resource and Environmental Economics*, Iowa State University Press, Ames, IA, 1998.

Tietenberg, Tom: *Environmental and Natural Resource Economics*, 5th ed., Addison Wesley Longman, New York, 2000.

THREE

GENERAL NATURAL RESOURCE ISSUES

The previous section dealt with some fundamental building blocks that are used in microeconomics. In the present section we take a step closer to dealing with important natural resource issues, though we continue to work at the conceptual level for the most part. We live in a market system, and it is important to know how normal markets function in the case of natural resources. This is addressed in Chapter 6. Having inquired into the positive question, we then deal (in Chapter 7) with the normative question of what steps should be taken to ensure that we move in the direction of managing resources in a socially optimal way.

MARKETS AND EFFICIENCY

The last chapter was devoted essentially to definitional matters: what it means for a natural resource use situation, or any economic situation for that matter, to be efficient and/or sustainable. In this chapter we take up the question: Do markets involving natural resources normally function so as to give efficient or sustainable outcomes regarding the rate of use of resources? There are good reasons for pursuing this question. Virtually all developed economies in the world are **market economies;** that is, the primary social institution relied upon to make decisions about resource use is the private market. And in recent years most of the economies that once operated on the basis of decisions and directives of central planning authorities have rejected that approach in favor of greater reliance on private markets. So it is vital to understand the basics of how markets operate: when they give efficient results and when not, when public intervention might be called for and when not. We are particularly interested, of course, in the operation of markets for natural resource goods and services.

MARKET DEMAND AND SUPPLY

A market is a process where buyers and sellers negotiate transactions among themselves to transfer the ownership or use of a good or service at agreed-upon prices. Markets vary from the most primitive, two people meeting face

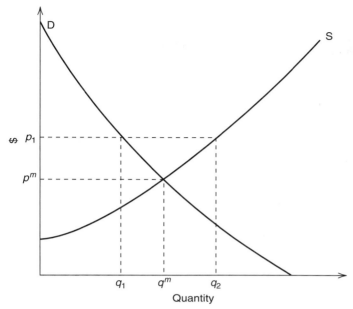

FIGURE 6-1
Basic Model of Demand and Supply

to face to trade a sack of potatoes in return for two hours' worth of labor; to the most sophisticated, a room full of people in electronic contact with their counterparts around the world buying and selling foreign exchange at prices that vary from minute to minute. But all markets essentially do the same job; they guide the flow of goods and services among buyers and sellers in terms of quantities and prices.

The basic market model, used to summarize these interactions, is shown in Figure 6-1. It shows two price-quantity relationships, one for demanders and one for suppliers. The **demand curve,** labeled D, shows the various quantities of the item that demanders will purchase at alternative prices. We met these types of functions in the previous chapter. They are based on the notion of willingness to pay, and their downward slope illustrates the principle of **diminishing willingness to pay,** as we discussed earlier.[1] It is important to see the demand curve as comprising a menu of possibilities. It tells not only what the quantity demanded will be at the present price, but also what it would be if the price were higher or lower.

The market demand curve summarizes the behavior of all the people who are in the particular market under consideration, those who have just bought something and those who might buy something if the price were lower. The

[1] See p. 42.

demand curve reflects their incomes, tastes and preferences, and other relevant economic factors of their circumstances. If any of these underlying factors change, the market demand curve will change.

The supply curve, labeled S, represents the behavior of sellers of this good or service. Its upward slope is a reflection of increasing marginal production costs, and its exact shape—how steep it is, how far to the right or left—is related to input prices used in production and the fundamental technologies employed in the production process. Like the market demand curve, a market supply curve basically consists of a large number of potential output levels, only one of which will be realized during any particular time period.

Market Quantities and Prices

Given the demand and supply curves as shown, there is only one price where the quantity demanded by consumers is the same as that supplied by producers: This is when the price is p^m, the quantity is q^m. At any other price, there is a discrepancy between quantity supplied and quantity demanded. At a price of p_1, for example, suppliers would attempt to supply q_2 units of this item, while demanders would desire only q_1 units. As long as the demand and supply curves remain the same, something has to give. Excess supply normally will lead to downward pressure on prices; as prices go down, the quantity demanded will increase. So market adjustments in this case will move prices and quantities toward the **equilibrium** pair, p^m, q^m.[2] Prices that are temporarily below p^m will lead to excess demand, that is, quantity demanded by consumers in excess of quantity supplied. This puts upward pressure on price and increases in quantity supplied toward the equilibrium levels.

In a dynamic economy we usually don't see prices and quantities that stay constant over a long period of time. That's because the underlying factors that affect the demand and supply functions are regularly changing. Demographic growth shifts demand curves, and technical change shifts supply curves, for example. Shifting expectations affect how demanders and suppliers will react on current markets. So over time we often see prices moving upward or downward and not necessarily coming to some resting place as in an equilibrium. But the model is still very useful, because it explains how the basic market process operates.

The essence of this process is that it is the interaction of buyers and sellers, actual and potential, that causes prices and quantities to adjust, normally toward some equilibrium level. For price-quantity combination p^*, q^* to materialize, it is not necessary for some economists first to figure out what they are,

---

[2] "Equilibrium" is a somewhat technical term in economics, referring to a situation in which all the various forces that would tend to cause a situation to adjust and change are in balance. An equilibrium is not defined as a state of affairs where everybody is happy in some sense. Consumers would like to see a lower price, suppliers would be happy to have a higher price. Equilibrium is simply a state of affairs where there is a balance between quality demanded and quantity supplied.

or for a politician or public administrator to intervene and enforce them by fiat. It happens as a result of the more or less unrestricted interactions and transactions among buyers and sellers.

MARKETS AND STATIC SOCIAL EFFICIENCY

Markets tend toward equilibrium values like p^m and q^m in Figure 6-1. But how do we know that these values represent those that are **socially efficient?** Refer back to Figure 5-1.[3] Social efficiency, identified as q^* in that model, is defined as the rate of output at which marginal social benefits (MSB) are equal to marginal social costs (MSC). Thus, at least two things have to be true for market outcomes to be socially efficient: The market demand curve and the MSB curve have to be the same, and the market supply curve and the MSC curve have to be the same. If these two conditions are met, markets will tend to generate socially efficient outcomes; if they are not met, markets will not be efficient.

Market demand curves register the willingness to pay of the participants in those markets. Thus, to say that the market demand curve must be the same as the MSB curve is to say simply that there are no sources of social value that are not registered by market participants themselves; in effect, nothing is left out. Similarly, market supply curves are based on the costs that impinge on the private parties who make up the supplying entities on the market—business firms, for example. Thus, to say that the supply function and the MSC function are the same is to say simply that there are no sources of cost to members of society that are not registered in those private cost/supply curves.

Our job, then, is to consider the conditions under which these relationships will be consistent, MSB and D, and MSC and S. But before this, one other condition has to be true for markets to be socially efficient: They must **be competitive.** Competition means that there are no possibilities for buyers and sellers to exert influence on the market; suppliers cannot band together and collude to produce a higher price; nor may buyers do anything on the other side of the market to force lower prices. Competition requires several things: a large number of buyers and sellers, so as to foreclose any one of them gaining a controlling position, and a set of rules defining the limits of acceptable behavior (you may outbid a rival, you may not physically trash their goods). Of course in real-world markets it hardly ever is a question of the simple presence or absence of competition, it is always a question of how much. "Acceptable" levels of competition are those which allow a market to achieve efficiency; competition that is either too weak or too strong will make it impossible for markets to do this.

Let us now return to the question of whether market demand curves and market supply curves are equal to, respectively, marginal social benefits and marginal social costs. We will first take up the cost question.

[3] See p. 72.

External Costs

To pursue this point we reiterate the distinction between social costs and private costs. Social efficiency is defined according to social costs, while supply curves are based on private costs. Under what circumstances might there be a discrepancy between the two? Consider the costs of harvesting the trees in a forest to get timber that will ultimately be turned into building supplies. Private costs in this case are the costs incurred by the logging companies to get the trees out of the forest: like labor, equipment, and fuel costs. These are the costs (which we have called marginal private costs, or MPC) that show up on the profit-and-loss statement of the logging companies at the end of the year. These private costs are legitimate social costs, because these inputs could have been used elsewhere in the economy to produce something else.

But in this case, the full social costs of logging may include other cost elements as well. The U.S. Forest Service may devote some resources to the operation, for example, in constructing logging roads into the forest. Social costs may also include ecological costs. Certain forests may have unique ecological values that are diminished as a result of the logging. These costs may be very difficult to measure in practice, but they are legitimate social costs nonetheless.

The difference between private costs and social costs is called **external costs.** External costs, in other words, are costs incurred by people who are not party to the decisions that give rise to them. In the forestry example the external costs result from the decisions of the logging companies, but they are incurred in part by others, in particular those people who place value on the ecological characteristics for the forest.[4]

As another example, consider a collection of paper mills located on a river. They produce paper and in the process emit residuals into the river. The water quality of the river is reduced, which leads to damages suffered downstream by recreators and communities using the river as a water supply source. This situation is illustrated in Figure 6-2. The market supply curve (labeled S) depicts the behavior of the supplying firms: the paper mills. The factors determining the shape and height of this supply curve are the costs that impinge directly on the profit-and-loss sheets of these mills—such items as labor costs, energy costs, raw materials, and buildings. These costs—and the technology of paper production—determine the quantity of inputs needed to produce various quantities of output, their marginal costs of paper production, and therefore the market supply curve of paper. But the downstream external costs are legitimate social costs that need to be included when determining the socially efficient rate of output of paper. The curve labeled MSC is the market supply curve plus the external costs (EC). MSC thus includes all the social costs of producing paper. Assume further that the demand curve D registers accurately the full social benefits of this product. Then the **socially efficient** quantity and price of paper are q^* and p^*, while the market will tend to settle at q^m

---

[4] It is of course true that many individuals running logging companies also place high values on the ecological services produced by forests.

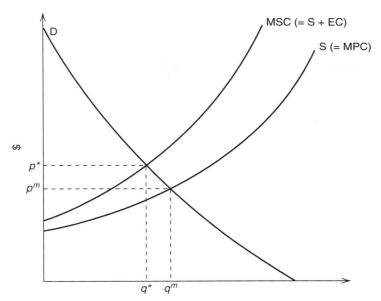

FIGURE 6-2
Market Performance in the Case of External Costs

and p^m. In other words, when environmental external costs are involved, normal market operations will tend to lead to **quantities that are too high and prices that are too low,** relative to socially efficient levels.[5] From a policy perspective the question is how to get these external costs **internalized,** so that the paper mills will choose output level q^* rather than q^m. We will focus on this in the next chapter.

External Benefits

On the other side of the market, to say that the demand curve must be the same as the social marginal willingness-to-pay curve is to say that the market demand curve must include all the social benefits arising from the consumption of the good or service in question. Nobody is left out; all benefits are included, no matter to whom they accrue. If, on the other hand, significant social benefits accrue to people who are not direct participants in the market in question, then the market results are unlikely to be efficient. They may also be regarded as inequitable.

External benefits can be present in the same direct way that external costs are present. Suppose I consider buying a new lawn mower. I evaluate the

---

[5] Note that even at q^* some external cost is present. Efficiency does not require, in other words, that all external costs totally disappear, only that they be properly included in the overall trade-off.

different models available and the important characteristics of each, especially their prices. Another important feature is their noise level; in general, I can get a quieter machine if I am willing to pay a somewhat higher price. In making my decision I try to balance these two factors (there are probably more factors involved than just these two, but we disregard them to keep the example simple) in terms of my own tastes and preferences and budget. But buying a quieter model would also confer benefits on my neighbors, in the form of a generally quieter neighborhood. For my purchase to be fully socially efficient, not just efficient from my own perspective, these other benefits need to be included. These are **external benefits;** they accrue to somebody other than the person making the decision that produces them.

Suppose I own a farm that contains, besides a certain area of cleared fields, an area of woods. I maintain the woods because I like to produce maple sugar from the maple trees that are on it. In making a decision about how much wooded acreage to maintain, I weigh the benefits in terms of revenues from maple sugar, with the costs in terms of not having the land available for pasture or cultivation. But suppose some interesting wild animals live in these woods. They are interesting perhaps because they are endangered or because people like to see them occasionally or simply know that they are there. The benefits produced by the wild animals are largely external benefits; they accrue to people who are not involved in the decision about how much of my land to keep in woods. When external benefits are involved, market outcomes will tend to be inefficient, the outputs responsible for the external benefits will be too small, and its price will be too low.

External benefits are present whenever **public goods** are involved. We introduced this concept in Chapter 3. A public good is a good that, once made available to one person, automatically becomes available to others. On Martha's Vineyard island off the southeast coast of Massachusetts, there are two medium-size lighthouses guarding the entrance to the main harbor. The one on the eastern headland was built privately, by Captain Daggett in 1878. The good captain, having built the lighthouse at his own expense, then approached the various companies and owners whose boats regularly came and went in the harbor, and asked them for contributions to help cover the costs of the lighthouse. At this point, Captain Daggett ran into the classic problem of private markets and public goods. The lighthouse was (and still is) a **public good:** Its services can be used by anybody using the harbor, whether or not they have contributed anything to its construction and operation.

When public goods are involved, private markets will find it difficult to supply socially efficient levels. Table 6-1 contains some numbers we saw earlier, in Chapter 3. They refer to the willingnesses to pay of three individuals for a program to restore bald eagles in a particular habitat. It also has a column showing the marginal cost of this program, which can be carried out at three different levels: light, moderate, or extensive. Comparing the aggregate marginal willingness to pay with the marginal cost shows that a moderate restoration program would be the one that maximizes net benefits to this society of just three people.

TABLE 6-1
BENEFITS AND COSTS OF RESTORING BALD EAGLES

	Marginal willingness to pay				Marginal cost
	A	B	C	Aggregate	
Light	50	10	25	85	40
Moderate	30	5	10	45	40
Extensive	10	0	5	15	40

Suppose, then, a private firm were to engage in this restoration program. It puts up the $80 required for a moderate-level program, and then asks the three beneficiaries for contributions, commensurate with their willingnesses to pay, to cover the costs. Because of the nature of the good involved, it now becomes possible for the individuals to **free-ride.** Free riding means holding back on one's contribution so as to get the benefits while bearing less of the cost. This is possible because it is a public good; once available, it produces benefits for everybody, regardless of how much or little they have contributed.

If everybody tries to free-ride,[6] then the firm doing the restoration is likely to experience a revenue shortfall relative to its costs. Knowing this was likely to be the case, they probably would not have undertaken the project in the first place. Thus private markets, in which transactions are concluded voluntarily and without coercion, will be hard put to supply the efficient levels of this type of good or service. Free riding will tend to reduce the revenues realized by sellers, thus weakening the incentive to produce and make them available in efficient amounts. This is why relatively few lighthouses are privately provided. In Captain Daggett's case, the free-rider problem led him, after just a few years, to sell his lighthouse to the state of Massachusetts, which could use tax revenues to maintain it.

Open-Access Resource

We come now to an important class of natural resources the utilization of which typically gives rise to external costs, and the effective management of which typically involves public goods and external benefits. For these reasons they are often overutilized and overdepleted. The resources in question are called **open-access resources.** An open-access resource is simply one that is open to unrestricted use by anyone who might wish to utilize it. The classic example has always been the ocean fishery. Until fairly recently most fisheries, for example the North Atlantic groundfish fishery, could be fished by anybody who had a boat and the appropriate gear. Another example is terrestrial

---

[6] Technically, a "free rider" is a person who pays nothing toward the public good, while a person who pays something but less than commensurate with their true willingness to pay is an "easy rider."

TABLE 6-2
AN OPEN-ACCESS RESOURCE: PUBLIC BEACH

Number of visitors	Individual marginal willingness to pay	Total willingness to pay (WTP)	Cost per visit	Total costs (TC)	Total WTP minus TC
1	$20	$20	$12	$ 12	$ 8
2	20	40	12	24	16
3	20	60	12	36	24
4	20	80	12	48	32
5	18	90	12	60	30
6	16	96	12	72	24
7	14	98	12	84	14
8	12	96	12	96	0
9	10	90	12	108	−18
10	8	80	12	120	−40

wildlife in North America; historically hunters have had unrestricted access to stocks of wild game, such as birds, deer, buffalo, or elk. Open-access resources need not be extractive resources. Public parks, where visitors may enter without restriction, are also open-access resources.

Open access typically leads to overuse. We can illustrate this with a very simple example, that of a small public beach. Being public, the beach is open to use by anybody who wishes to visit. This is somewhat artificial, of course, because today beach access is often restricted in some way, for example to citizens of a particular community. The use restrictions are usually a response to the problems stemming from open access. We can learn what these are by considering a simple numerical example of an open-access resource.

The essential data are shown in Table 6-2. This small beach lies a number of miles from a town center from which all the visitors originate. The first column shows the potential number of visitors that might make use of the beach on an average day; it runs from one to ten (it's a small beach). The next two columns show willingness to pay, first marginal and then total. Marginal willingness to pay is the MWTP, given that the number of visitors is currently at the level indicated. For example, if today there are two visitors, the marginal willingness to pay of the third is $20. Note—and this is critical—that MWTP stays constant at $20 until there are four visitors; after that it begins to fall off. The reason for this is congestion. At higher levels of visitation, the quality of the beach diminishes because of congestion, so the MWTP by additional visitors declines.

On the cost side, we assume that the cost of visiting the beach is the same for every visitor, $12. We are assuming that the travel costs for each of the visitors to get to the beach are basically the same. We assume that there are no entry fees charged at the beach. The fifth column shows total visitation costs.

The efficient level of beach visitation is evidently four people per day. This is the level that maximizes the net benefits of the beach. We will now see, however, that if beach access is uncontrolled, visitation will be higher than this efficient level. Suppose that there are currently four people using the beach and that a fifth is trying to decide whether to visit. The costs to the fifth visitor are $12, her willingness to pay is $18; her visit will apparently lead to net benefits of $6, so she visits. But a sixth person will also realize positive net benefits from a visit, as will a seventh. It is only when we get to the eighth potential visitor that net individual benefits fall to zero, and for the ninth and tenth visitors, they are negative. So we can reason that with open access, total visitation will go to 7 visitors and possibly to eight (if the MWTP for the eighth were just slightly higher). This is substantially higher than the socially efficient visitation level.

In this case open access leads to a substantial overshoot—excessive use rates relative to efficient levels. The main reason for this is what are called **open-access externalities.** These are externalities that the users of the resource inflict on one another in the form of diminished resource value.[7] In the beach case the diminished value stems from increased congestion. When the fifth prospective visitor is deciding whether to visit, she compares the gain she will have of $18 with the cost of $12 and acts accordingly. But in proceeding with her visit, she reduces the value of the beach to the four already there, from $20 to $18 for each one, a $2 loss times 4 visitors equals a total external cost of $8. This external cost is in fact equal to the individual gain of the fifth visitor and, for the sixth and seventh visitors, the individual gain would be less than the externality losses.[8]

The exact nature of the open-access externalities will differ from one type of resource to another. For the beach it was externalities in the form of beach congestion, which reduces the value of a beach visit. For hunters sharing a territory, including fishers working the same fishery, it is the added cost of harvesting, which stems from two sources: hunters more often intrude on one another, and higher catch rates mean lower stocks. We will run into this type of resource problem many times in the following chapters.[9]

---

[7] There was a famous paper written on open-access problems titled "The Tragedy of the Commons" (Garrett Hardin, *Science*, Vol. 162, 1968, pp. 1243–1248). Commons in this case refers to open-access resources, which are sometimes called commons, or common property. Hardin's example was an open-access pasture where individual farmers could graze as many animals as they wished. Here the open-access externality that leads to overuse of the resource is the diminution in the quality of the pasture as more and more animals are put on it.

[8] For the fifth, sixth, and seventh visitors, the situation is the following:

Visitor	Individual gain	External costs	Net gain
5	$18 - 12 = 6$	$2 \times 4 = 8$	−2
6	$16 - 12 = 4$	$2 \times 5 = 10$	−6
7	$14 - 12 = 2$	$2 \times 6 = 12$	−10

[9] It is not just natural resources that have the open-access problem. Roads that are open to anyone are also open-access assets; the external costs in the case of road congestion are the increased travel times that motorists inflict on one another.

Open Access and the Dissipation of Resource Rent

There is another important observation to be made with this simple example. At the efficient visitation level of 4 visitors, total willingness to pay is $80 and total costs are $48, for a net of $32. This $32 is actually a return attributable to the resource itself, in this case the beach. This is actually the **resource rent** being produced by the beach. A way of seeing this is to note that if the town authorities were to sell the beach to a private operator (and this is not a subtle hint for recommending this course of action; it's only to show the basis of the value of the beach), its price in a competitive market would be a reflection of this net valuation, because that would be the income earning potential of the beach to anyone who happened to own it.

Suppose the open-access visitation level of the beach had in fact gone to 8 people (the eighth is right on the margin, but let us assume they visit). At this level of use there is no rent; total willingness to pay is $96, as is total cost. Open access has led, in other words, to the **dissipation,** or disappearance, of all natural resource rent. The total value of the visitation is being absorbed by the visitation costs of the recreators; it is as if the natural resource responsible for the benefits, the beach, is essentially of zero value. Note also that at other visitation levels like 1, 2, 6, 7, and so on, the implied rent is positive but less than it is at 4 visitors. Another way of saying this is that the efficient use rate is the one that produces the **maximum natural resource rent.**

Overuse and rent dissipation are features of many natural resources: game resources harvested by recreational hunters, ocean fisheries harvested by commercial fishers, groundwater extracted by irrigators or municipalities, and so on. Clearly, the management issue in cases like this is how to reduce the rates of resource utilization to something approaching efficient levels. This is the subject of the next chapter.

MARKETS AND INTERTEMPORAL EFFICIENCY

Compare panels (a) and (b) in Figure 6-3. They represent two different versions of the output from, let us say, a group of timber companies. The output in this case is cubic feet of timber harvested during a particular year from a given geographical region. Panel (a) shows the classic market demand and supply curves. Panel (b) shows the socially efficient level of output, given by the balance of marginal social benefits and a function representing the total of marginal current costs and user costs. Will q_0^m and q_0^* be the same? Evidently they will be if all functions in the two panels are the same. Note that now the output has a time index; it is the output of the first period, recognizing that in the dynamic case this is just the first year of a multiple-period production program.

If there are no external benefits, then MSB = D. But on the cost side things are trickier. Panel (a) shows MCC (marginal current costs) and the supply function S. Here we have to recognize that there can be a difference in user costs seen from the private and social points of view. Private user costs incorporate

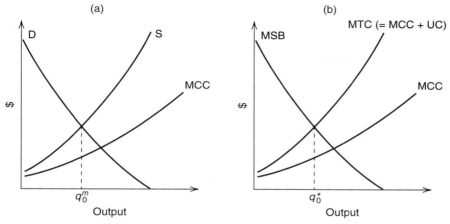

FIGURE 6-3
Markets and Intertemporal Efficiency

future revenue changes impinging on firms as a result of decisions made today. The market rate of output, labeled $q_0{}^m$, is based on private user costs. Will this output level be intertemporally efficient from the social viewpoint?

Panel (b) shows the MTC as the summing together of marginal current costs (MCC) and user costs (UC). In this case user costs are defined as future costs from the **social standpoint.** Evidently the market rate of output ($q_0{}^m$ in panel a) will be equal to the socially efficient rate of output ($q_0{}^*$ in panel b) if and only if the private user costs actually taken into account by suppliers are equal to the user costs considered from the standpoint of society as a whole.

Assume for the moment that there are no classic external costs of the type we discussed in the previous section (like emissions from pulp mills or ecological destruction by timber firms). Then the only way we can get a difference between S and MTC is for **private future costs** to be different from **social future costs.** For the most part, we are concerned with factors that may make private future costs lower than true social future costs, because when this is the case, the market rates of output will be too high relative to the output that is intertemporally efficient.

Markets and Discounting

There are several reasons why today's markets may function in ways that are not intertemporally efficient. Remember that the future costs of today's actions are in terms of **present value;** in other words, it is a future consequence **discounted** back to the present period. On the market this discounting will occur at discount rates that today's market participants apply, according to their own views about the affects of time and its impacts on relative values to themselves. But suppose, in some wider social sense, people typically apply discount rates that are too high. There have been many observers through the years who have thought that the average person is too short-sighted, that they do not put sufficient weight on the future effects of their actions. In other words, they use private discount rates that are too high.

If this is true, then future costs affecting decisions of market suppliers will be too low, relative to what might be called the socially efficient levels of future costs. And if this is indeed true, then contemporary natural resource markets will produce at levels that are too high and at prices that are too low, relative to the levels that are socially efficient. Of course, like a lot of other things, it is easy to say this on a conceptual level. It is harder to figure out if it actually happens in the real world.

Tenure Conditions

Private future costs reflect the present value of future net revenue consequences flowing from today's decisions. By tenure conditions we mean factors that determine whether people today are affected by all the future consequences flowing from their behavior. Consider a logging firm operating on a **timber concession** given it by the government of the region where the forest is located. Suppose the terms of the concession are only that it is nonrenewable and lasts for 5 years. The effect of this is to cut off the impact today of any consequences that are more than 5 years in the future. In this extreme case, for example, a logging firm would have no incentive to replant after harvesting the trees, because the benefits from doing this would occur well beyond the time limit of the concession. In fact, the terms of concession would sharply reduce private future costs and lead the timber companies to adopt something approaching a completely static viewpoint.

Another way in which private future costs can be attenuated (weakened, or reduced) is through a lack of future marketability. Suppose the timber concession mentioned in the previous paragraph is long-run (permanent, in fact), but that it cannot be sold. If and when the current logging company no longer wishes to harvest trees in this area, it must give the concession back to the regional government. This has the same type of impact as the time limit, though it would probably not be as extreme as that case in terms of its impact on private user costs. A market, in this case a market for standing timber and the land that it is on, is what allows the harvesting firm to profit from actions that maximize the value of that land. Without that possibility the firm would not have the incentive to avoid all actions that diminish the very long run productivity of the timber land. That is to say, the private future cost would be lower than social future costs of harvesting the timber.

Of course, relaxing the assumption made above on traditional externalities will also affect our conclusions. Suppose that one impact stemming from logging a particular piece of land this year is that higher rates of runoff and soil erosion will be experienced in the future. These are in effect future external costs, and would have the effect of making private future user costs lower than social user costs.

SUMMARY

The basic question undertaken in this chapter was: Under what conditions will private markets be **socially efficient**? Markets operate according to the conditions of **private demand and supply,** that is, according to the marginal willingness to pay and marginal production costs of the participants in the market. If these conditions include all social benefits and all social costs, then markets will be socially efficient. We looked at some cases where **external costs** and/or **external benefits** might be a problem. Environmental costs are important instances of external costs, and social efficiency in the case of these costs requires that they be **internalized** or that resort be had to direct public regulation. One important source of external costs is in the case of **open-access resources;** we examined the problem of **rent dissipation** in resources of this type. We also looked at what are called **public goods,** and saw that private markets in this case will lead normally to suboptimal output levels. Finally, we took up the question of markets and intertemporal efficiency, and focused on the question of the conditions under which the **future costs** facing resource users will be too low relative to socially efficient levels.

KEY TERMS

Market supply and demand	Open-access resources
Market prices and quantities	Public goods
External costs	Rent dissipation
External benefits	Markets and intertemporal efficiency

QUESTIONS FOR FURTHER DISCUSSION

1 Show that when external benefits are involved, market outputs and prices will tend to be too low relative to socially efficient levels.
2 What is the impact of a rise in market interest rates on the intertemporally efficient rate of today's output?
3 How does the free-rider problem apply to: (a) radio stations, (b) bus riders, (c) commercial fishers?
4 Refer to the open-access beach problem in the text of this chapter and Table 6-2. If the cost per day rose to $15, how many people would maximize the net benefits of the beach? And how many people would visit the beach under open access?
5 Roads (except for toll roads) are typically open-access. In what sense are the rents dissipated in this case?

USEFUL WEB SITES

The U.S. Environmental Protection Agency has a web page titled Economy and Environment that offers links on topics in environmental economics, which includes many of the concepts covered in this chapter.

• USEPA, Economy and Environment (http://www.epa.gov/economics).

For an on-line lecture on externalities, public goods, and market failure, see:

- (http://www.upei.ca/~rneill/canecpro/microprol.html).

SELECTED READINGS

Folmer, Henk, H., Landis Gabel, and Hans Opschoor: *Principles of Environmental and Resource Economics,* Edward Elgar, Aldershot, England, 1995, Chapter 2.

Hackett, Steven C.: *Environmental and Natural Resource Economics,* M. E. Sharpe, Armonk, NY, 1998, Chapters 3 and 4.

Kahn, James R.: *The Economic Approach to Environmental and Natural Resources,* 2nd ed., Dryden Press, Forth Worth, TX, 1998, Chapters 2 and 3.

Prato, Tony: *Natural Resource and Environmental Economics,* Iowa State University Press, Ames, IA, 1998, Chapter 5.

Tietenberg, Tom: *Environmental and Natural Resource Economics,* 5th ed., Addison Wesley Longman, New York, 2000, Chapter 4.

CHAPTER 7

PUBLIC POLICY FOR NATURAL RESOURCES

Public policy refers to the **collective actions** that people undertake through **governmental institutions.** These actions shape the terms under which natural resources are used. Collective action can be pursued at many levels, from the local neighborhood and community level to that of the country or even the world. The public institutions through which policy is pursued differ from level to level, region to region, country to country, and even from time to time.

In this chapter we review some of the major types of **policy alternatives** that are available in a market economy to manage natural resource conservation and utilization. Although the discussion is conceptual to a large extent, we use natural resource examples to illustrate general cases. We are moving closer to the later chapters, which will focus more deeply on issues involving specific natural resources. The objectives are, first, to understand that there are different types of natural resource policies and, second, to assess the applicability of these policies in different circumstances. Policy decisions are not simply technical exercises: They are full of conflict and political controversy. Benefits and costs are involved, but so are political ideologies and strategies. We are not going to deal here with the political dimensions of the public policy process. The goal is, rather, to clarify the economic/incentive aspects of different policy approaches so that we can identify which approaches represent the best course of action for particular circumstances.

THE OBJECTIVES OF PUBLIC POLICY

To say "best course of action" implies that we have a good idea what the **objectives** of public policy should be or, to say it another way, what **criteria** should be used to judge the effectiveness of different resource policies. Controversies over public policy occur for many reasons, one of which is disagreement and/or lack of clarity about policy goals. The most important of these goals are the following.

Economic Efficiency

The attraction of economic efficiency is that it takes into account both the benefits and the costs of taking an action. Efficiency in the use of natural resources implies that the natural assets of society are being utilized in a way that **maximizes their net benefits** to the members of that society. So efficiency would seem to be a reasonable goal for any policy that purports to be in the public interest. A policy that is efficient, or moves toward efficiency, is to be preferred over one that is not, other things equal.

It needs to be said loudly and clearly that efficiency does not presuppose that market values are to be preferred over nonmarket values. Efficiency does not require, in other words, that some strictly monetary aggregate, akin to current gross domestic product (GDP) or gross community product (GCP),[1] be maximized. Many benefits from natural resources, particularly when we are talking preservation rather than commercial harvest, are hard to measure. But the very essence of social efficiency is that all benefits, including nonmarket benefits, are to be counted.

Although efficiency as a goal may be fairly noncontroversial in the abstract, its actual realization in any particular resource-using circumstance is likely to be problematic and contentious for several reasons. One is that people differ in terms of the values they place on different outcomes. If what is involved is a private good, this is not a problem. Some people like cantaloupes and some don't, and it is perfectly plausible for some people to eat lots of cantaloupes and for others to eat few of them. But if what is involved is a public good, production can be only at one level, which by definition is the same for everybody. Thus, conflicts can easily occur as to what that one level should be.

But perhaps the major difficulty leading to conflicts over the achievement of efficiency is the **information problem.** Everyone may agree in the abstract that we want to maximize net social benefits, but how can we be sure that this is being achieved in any particular case? Policies differ in terms of the amount and kinds of information needed in order to achieve outcomes that are reasonably efficient.

---

[1] This is the total monetary output of people living within a given community.

Equity

To be **equitable** means to be **fair.** Just because a resource use plan is efficient doesn't mean it is fair. Fairness has to do with how the overall benefits and costs of natural resource use are **distributed** among subgroups of the overall population. Suppose a local community has an important deposit of a nonrenewable resource, such as petroleum. From an economywide perspective, efficiency might call for extraction of the deposit at a rapid rate; depletion of this one deposit may have relatively little national significance, because it is only one of many. From the standpoint of the community, however, it may have great significance. It may represent the primary source of nonhuman wealth in the community. What is an efficient extraction program at the national level may be regarded as unfair at the local level.

One of the major issues in contemporary natural resource economics is that of **preservation vs. extraction.** A local community may have an important resource, such as an expanse of standing timber or a large body of water. Overall national efficiency may call for preservation of these resources or for their utilization at relatively low rates. But this might be regarded as unfair to local communities that rely on these resources for an economic base. For example, a town may rely on fees from timber or mineral sales to finance its schools.

Public resource policies (indeed virtually any type of public policy) very often are characterized by a distributional disconnect regarding their benefits and their costs. It is often the case that either (1) benefits are widely spread among the population while costs are localized or (2) benefits are localized and the costs are widely dispersed. These spreads are illustrated numerically in Table 7-1. The numbers represent benefits and costs from three possible policies as they would accrue to five different individuals. Policy A has benefits and costs that are evenly distributed among the population of five individuals. Policy B has evenly distributed benefits but concentrated costs; costs are

TABLE 7-1
ALTERNATIVE DISTRIBUTION OF BENEFITS AND COSTS

		Individuals				
	Total	1	2	3	4	5
Policy A						
Benefits	100	20	20	20	20	20
Costs	80	16	16	16	16	16
Policy B						
Benefits	100	20	20	20	20	20
Costs	80	40	10	10	10	10
Policy C						
Benefits	100	80	5	5	5	5
Costs	80	16	16	16	16	16

proportionately much higher for Individual 1 than for the other individuals. Policy C has evenly distributed costs but concentrated benefits.

In the case of Policy B total net benefits are positive. However, there are four people for whom individual net benefits are positive, and one for whom they are very negative. An example might be the Endangered Species Act (ESA). Overall, the ESA may have positive net benefits. The benefits of this act are presumably widely diffused, in the sense that all citizens enjoy the benefits (especially the "nonuse" benefits). The costs, on the other hand, are very likely to be concentrated, especially on those individuals owning land where endangered species are found.

In the case of Policy C total net benefits are also positive, but there are four individuals for whom net benefits are negative and only one for whom they are strongly positive. The reason for this is that benefits are so highly concentrated. An example of this might be a beach restoration project, which has substantial benefits locally but few beyond the local area and for which the costs are spread in a very diffuse pattern among general taxpayers.[2]

Another important social dimension of the equity issue is how policies treat people who have different amounts of wealth. Markets are clear in at least one major respect, resources tend to flow toward people who have not only the willingness to pay but also the **ability to pay.** The tastes and preferences of people who lack adequate wealth are relatively unrepresented in normal markets. They may or may not be underrepresented in **political markets.** If they are underrepresented, then charitable or humanitarian causes must take over, and that support may or may not be very strong in particular circumstances.

A major equity issue in current resource controversies is the balance to be struck among the generations, the generation that is here now and the ones that will be around in the future, even the distant future. This is the major focus of the concept of **sustainability,** which refers essentially to the idea that current generations should not undertake actions today that will create conditions making it substantially more difficult for future generations to achieve today's living standards.

Flexibility

The primary national statute governing mineral exploration and extraction on public land in the United States was enacted in 1872. Although it has been significantly amended several times since then, many of the central provisions of that early mining law still apply. The price for purchasing, or "patenting," a mineral claim is still $5 an acre, for example, just as it was when the law was passed. This is an example of a seriously inflexible natural resource management policy. Conditions in mineral industries have obviously changed a lot since the nineteenth century, as have conditions elsewhere in the economy. As

---

[2] Note that if the three programs were voted on by the five individuals, Policies A and B would be approved by a majority, whereas C would not.

a matter of common sense, if the law was appropriate for the conditions of the nineteenth century, it is unlikely to be appropriate today. Largely for political reasons, however, the law does not change.

This suggests another important criterion for evaluating natural resource policies, namely, how well they adapt to changing circumstances. "Changing circumstances" in economics means essentially two general things: changes on the demand side in terms of social factors and values that affect the willingness to pay for different goods and services and changes on the supply side that affect the availability of resources. As an example on the demand side, major shifts have occurred in recent decades in the concerns that people have about preserving natural resources, as well as in the development of a very substantial natural resource–based outdoor recreation sector. Policies that were appropriate in an era when natural resource development and extraction was a prime objective are not likely to be prudent when values shift strongly toward preservation. As an example on the supply side, urban growth, in terms of number of people and their geographical spread, has led to great reductions in the availability of accessible open land in urban and suburban regions. Policies that guided urban growth in times when open space was ample may not be appropriate when it gets increasingly scarce.

Other things equal, policies that adjust and evolve more or less automatically to changing resource availabilities and human values are to be desired over policies that do not.

Enforceability

Public policies are the outcomes of a political process, in which groups and interests collide and compete, striving for support and influence. The maneuvering and coalition building that go on produce political theater as much as substantive actions. One result of this is that laws are frequently enacted without addressing the enforcement issue. Sometimes they are simply unenforceable at a reasonable cost. Often it is simply assumed that enforcement will be carried out with vigor and with ample resources, but this is never true in the real world. Enforcement resources are always scarce, which is why the **enforceability** of laws and regulations is an important criterion.

TYPES OF PUBLIC POLICIES

In a fundamental sense, the policy problem refers to the question of how to bring about a state of affairs in which people's private behavior is also socially appropriate. There are basically only two general ways of doing this. One is to structure the system so that the **incentives** people face will lead them to make decisions that are simultaneously both in their own best interests and in society's best interest. The other way is to institute **direct controls** that limit the actions of people through fiat, or involve direct public production and/or distribution. These options can be further broken down as follows:

I **Incentive-based policies**
  A **Market/property rights policies:** Many natural resource problems can be attributed to inadequate or inappropriate property rights governing access to the resources. The most effective way to solve the problem may be to institute a new system of property rights. Essentially this means establishing and enforcing a new set of rules governing **property rights** and **market transactions,** and then letting the rate of use of natural resources be established by voluntary interaction among suppliers and demanders.
  B **Government-sponsored incentive policies:** Public agencies employ such devices as taxes and subsidies to structure the incentives facing resource users.
II **Direct public action**
  A **Command and control policies:** Public authorities establish direct controls on individual actions, enforcing these controls with standard legal enforcement practices.
  B **Direct public production:** Public agencies themselves own natural resources and themselves pursue programs of production and distribution.

We can best distinguish among these options by considering a specific natural resource. Barnstable Bay on Cape Cod is a large, relatively shallow embayment that contains extensive areas of productive shellfish flats. For many years these resources were open to harvest by any person who was a bona fide resident of the community and had the minimal equipment necessary for the job. For a long time this sufficed, in the sense that the number of fishers and quantities harvested did not substantially reduce the productivity of the clam beds. Around the middle of the twentieth century, however, this began to change, as the number of summer recreators in town began to grow and the commercial shellfish market experienced rapid expansion. This brought added fishers, greater pressure on the fishery, and declining yields in terms of quantity and quality. The problem in this case was one of **open access,** a concept that was introduced in Chapter 6. What are the options for reducing the overfishing and moving toward the efficient utilization of this resource?

Property Rights Policies   In this case the town would divide the bay into a relatively large number of parcels (the water is shallow so markers can be used, or shore points can be used for reference). It would then lease or sell these parcels to individual fishers, who would be free to make their own harvest decisions on their parcels. The leases would be long-term, so leasees would have time to take advantage of long-run management plans, such as seeding the areas with young clam stock and systematically rotating harvest plots within their overall leaseholds. The leaseholds may be bought and sold among fishers. The job of the town shellfish officer now is to keep a record of who holds each parcel, and then make sure that trespassers do not encroach on anyone's holding.

Government-Sponsored Incentive Policy   The town could simply levy a tax per bushel of clams harvested on fishers in the bay. The tax could be different for commercial and recreational diggers, and for different sizes of clams. In effect the tax now becomes a new operating cost for clam diggers. By shifting their cost curves upward, the expectation is that the quantity of clams dug in the bay would decrease, simply as a result of fishers responding to the new financial conditions of harvesting and not because of any direct controls on their operations. The job of the shellfish officer is to get accurate data on the quantity of individual harvests, and then send out and collect the tax bills.

Direct Command and Control   The town of Barnstable would establish a set of rules governing the harvesting of shellfish in the bay. It already has a rule limiting access to town residents; different rules could be set for year-round residents and for summer residents. Rules could be established for the maximum allowable individual harvest per day or per year. Rules could be set for the type of fishing gear that would be allowed, for the minimum size of clam that could be kept, and so on. In this case the town shellfish officer would be instructed to take whatever steps were necessary to enforce the rules, such as surveillance, monitoring of landings, examination of financial records, and the like.

Direct Public Production   The town of Barnstable, or some other public agency, might go into direct production itself, asserting ownership of the resource, hiring people to do the fishing, selling or giving away the clams, and distributing revenues in whatever way it chooses. A town shellfish officer would patrol the clam beds to make sure there is no unauthorized clamming.

In the real world, of course, mixtures of policy measures are possible. For example, direct controls on harvest quantities can be combined with a tax; private property rights may be combined with rules on clamming operations; and so on. Mixtures are very common. Private ownership of land resources is a dominant system in most western countries. But these ownership institutions are also usually accompanied with rules that limit the uses to which land may be put, as well as taxes on land. Many public parks and forests in the United States (direct government production) make use of entrance fees (financial incentives) and harvest concessions (property rights) to control resource use. The reason for discussing them separately is to make clear the way each works and, especially, the conditions that have to be met for them to achieve efficient and equitable resource use rates.

In the rest of the chapter we consider each one of these alternatives in more detail. To do this, we work with a simple numerical example. Consider the data in Table 7-2, which show the costs and returns of a small clam fishery. The second column is catch per fisher. From 1 to 4 fishers, this is 20 pounds per day. From 5 fishers up, the catch per fisher goes down because of open-access externalities the fishers inflict on one another; more fishers create congestion and greater scarcity, so the catch rates go down. The larger the number

TABLE 7-2
DAILY COSTS AND RETURNS FROM CLAM FISHERY

Number of fishers	Catch per fisher (pounds per day)	Total catch (revenue)*	Cost per fisher	Total costs	Net returns per fisher	Aggregate net returns
1	20	20	$12	$ 12	8	$ 8
2	20	40	12	24	8	16
3	20	60	12	36	8	24
4	20	80	12	48	8	32
5	18	90	12	60	6	30
6	16	96	12	72	4	24
7	14	98	12	84	2	14
8	12	96	12	96	0	0
9	10	90	12	108	-2	-18
10	8	80	12	120	-4	-40

*On the assumption that each unit of shellfish has a market value of $1.

of fishers, the more the decline. The third column shows total catch, which, if we assume the clams sell for $1 per unit, is also equal to total revenue. The last three columns show, respectively, costs per fisher (assumed the same for all fishers), total costs, net returns per fisher, and aggregate net returns (total revenue minus total costs).

You will no doubt recognize these numbers. They are the ones we used to illustrate the concept of an open-access resource back in Chapter 6, except that there they were used to illustrate the problem of visitors to an open-access beach. The rent-maximizing number of fishers is 4, as we can tell by looking at the last column. But the open-access number of fishers will tend toward 8, because the returns per fisher are positive up to this point. The policy question is, how do we achieve a reduction in fishers to efficient levels?

PRIVATE PROPERTY RIGHTS

The overuse of many natural resources can be attributed to the fact that **property rights** to these resources are either ill-defined or not adequately exercised. By this diagnosis, for example, the rent on open-access resources is dissipated, in whole or in part, because the resource does not have an owner, or owners, who will limit its use in order to maximize its value. Consider the following scenario:

A large expanse of remote land contains areas of forests, natural meadows, sizeable streams and several rivers. Over the years substantial amounts of the forests have been logged and some of the meadows have been used for grazing cattle. Many people have also pushed into the area, on the logging roads and trails, to pursue a variety of outdoor recreation activities: hunting, backpacking, canoeing, and camping. In fact in recent years use of the region became so heavy that the natural resources started to be damaged, for example, by erosion from heavily used lands, water pollution, fires attributable to humans, littering, and a growing scarcity of certain game animals.

There are calls for intervention by the state department of natural resource management. But the land is currently owned by several dozen large private landowners. The landowners themselves are aware of the resource degradation and the public access that is causing it. They decide that they can act together to reduce this damage and, furthermore, provide themselves with a modest but significant flow of income. What they do is create a number of controlled access points into the area, and then begin charging entry fees to people who want to use the area. The landowners create a small firm whose job is to manage the resources of the region and the outdoor recreators who make use of them. One of the first things they do, for example, is to set some rules for the logging companies who are allowed access, so that logging practices will not substantially impact the outdoor recreation values of the region.

What we have here is an example of resource management pursued through the use of **private property institutions.**[3] The essence of social efficiency is that natural resources be used in ways that maximize their net value to society. The essence of the property rights approach is to define these rights clearly enough so that private owners, in pursuing their own personal interests in maximizing their own wealth, will simultaneously maximize the net benefits flowing from the resource.

The property rights approach to our clam-bed problem is, therefore, to convert the clam beds to private property. It will then be in the interests of the owners to adopt levels of use that maximize the value of the resource. In the numerical example the owner(s) would have the incentive to limit entry to 4 fishers and to defend the boundary of the resource so that the level of extraction does not exceed that level. In fact, however, incentives would go beyond this. In an open-access situation, nobody would invest in efforts to, for example, seed the clam bed or cultivate it so as to increase long-run yields. If somebody were to do this, others could move in to reap the benefits. But privatizing the resource would change this: By allowing owners to exclude others, there would be an incentive to invest in these long-run improvements.

Privatization could be accomplished in various ways. In many instances resources of this type have been privatized informally through self-organization and management by the users without the official sanction of public authorities. Exhibit 7-1 recounts a case of this type, dealing with the harbor gangs of Maine who have sought in effect to privatize portions of the lobster fishery of that state. In some cases, like the example of the forest owners discussed above, boundaries already exist and it is up to the existing owners to agree on joint action to maintain them and manage the resource. In others, new boundaries may be specified and the resource distributed in some way to new owners. In the case of the Barnstable Harbor clam fishery, long-term leaseholds

---

[3] The example is in fact taken from real life. The group of landowners is called North Maine Woods, Inc.

EXHIBIT 7-1

THE MAINE LOBSTER GANGS—INFORMAL PRIVATIZATION

The coast of Maine is heavily indented and studded with small islands. It is also the locale of a very rich lobster fishery. Lobsters are sea creatures, the legal status of which historically has been an open-access resource. But to avoid the excessive harvests and overfishing that open-access resources normally experience, the lobster fishers of Maine have resorted to informal privatization. They have done this through means of harbor gangs, which are informal groups of fishers in each harbor who establish and enforce boundaries around "their" particular harbors or islands. The boundaries do not have legal status but are enforced anyway, essentially through trashing (or threats thereof) the gear of interlopers, that is, people from outside the harbor. Of course, the ability of any harbor gang to do this effectively varies. Where it is small and close-knit (consisting, for example, of family relatives around a smallish island), exclusion can be quite effective. In bigger harbors with more diverse populations and greater demand for lobsters, exclusion is more difficult to pursue and so is less complete. There are other formal, legal constraints in effect also, for example, on minimum sizes for harvested lobsters.

History shows many cases like this, where an open-access resource is privatized to a greater or lesser extent by informal user groups. It demonstrates the potential gains that can be obtained by moving in the direction of private property. When there is open access, there will be rent dissipation. When access is limited, rents will become positive and will accrue to the people doing the excluding (unless they are partially taxed away).

Source: Information on the Maine harbor gangs can be found in James M. Acheson, *The Lobster Gangs of Maine,* University of New Hampshire Press, Hanover, NH, 1988.

---

were identified by boundary markers and these were distributed to some of the people who had been in the clam fishery for many years.

Irrespective of how they are initially distributed, property rights must have several important characteristics if they are to lead to socially efficient resource use. They must be:

1 Complete (or reasonably so)
2 Enforceable at reasonable cost
3 Transferable
4 Combined with a complete set of competitive markets

Complete   A fancy way of saying this is that the property rights must not be **attenuated** in any way relevant to the use to which they will be put. In other words, they must not be limited in any way that would reduce the incentives of the owners to search out the way(s) that maximize their value. Suppose the clam-bed leases in the Barnstable case were limited to 1 year, after which they could be rescinded and given to somebody else at the discretion of the local authorities. This would undermine the incentives of leaseholders to make long-run (anything over 1 year) investments to increase the productivity of the leasehold. Or suppose the authorities required that the clams be harvested using a certain type of harvesting technology. This would weaken the incentive for the owners to search out the least-cost method of harvesting clams within the circumstances of this leasehold.

In actual practice, all property rights are attenuated to some extent. For purposes of protecting the public health, owners do not have the right to use their property in a way that would injure others. But the extent of legitimate restrictions is a controversial issue. The people digging clams on private leaseholds in the bay presumably do not have the right to drive large pilings down and construct a hotel on stilts in the middle of the harbor. This would seem to be a restriction that is obviously conducive to the public welfare. But in some circumstances restrictions of this type might foreclose value-increasing courses of action on the part of the owners.

Enforceable, at Reasonable Cost   By enforceable we refer to two things: (1) that would-be trespassers can be excluded at reasonable cost and (2) that owners can be effectively enjoined from using their property in ways that are illegal. **Exclusion** has two dimensions, technical and legal. The **technical** side is the physical means available for stopping trespassers: the ability to mark boundaries, the use of fences in the case of some land boundaries, the costs of surveillance, and so on. The **legal** side relates to whether boundaries are recognized by legal authorities. Both factors are important. In many cases natural resources that are legally open-access resources have been essentially "privatized" by individuals or groups who take it upon themselves to exclude certain outsiders. The Maine lobster gangs are an instance of this. There have also been many cases where property, which legally is owned by defined individuals or groups, is still subject to open access because the costs of excluding encroachers is simply too high relative to the gains the owners would achieve by so doing.

The other part of enforceability is that it must be possible to stop the owners themselves from using their resources in ways that are illegal. We talked in the previous section about the need to have property rights relatively unconstrained. By the same token it is always true that some legal constraints will be found necessary, and constraints of this type have to be enforceable. In most countries there are legal requirements that forestry companies are supposed to follow in harvesting timber—for example, limits on clear cutting. If these limits are not enforceable because of, say, the costs of detection, then they obviously cannot be effective.

Transferable   Suppose I operate a farm on land leased from the community. It is a long-term lease, but it is not transferable. As long as I wish to farm, I can occupy the land. I may even be able to pass it on to my sons and daughters. But I cannot sell it to third parties. Suppose I am thinking of retiring and moving into town. Since I have no heirs, I must relinquish the land at that point in time. This situation effectively reduces to me the **user costs** of mining the fertility of the soil and the productivity of whatever other natural assets exist on the farm (a small groundwater aquifer, for example). It reduces the incentive to maintain the maximum market value of these natural assets, because in effect they are not marketable.

Restrictions on transfers of natural resource assets are a ubiquitous feature throughout history. This is particularly the case with agricultural land. Early farming communities in developed countries, and many existing communities in developing countries, have placed restrictions on selling land to nonresidents. The reasons for this are primarily social and political. If a community's land is the only productive asset it has, it will not wish to see, on either efficiency or equity grounds, that asset falling into the hands of people outside the community. It is only when people have other good alternatives that they will be comfortable with the idea of full and unfettered transferability.

The Presence of Markets   Suppose I own a piece of forest land that I currently use for light timbering and wood pasture for a small herd of cattle. Suppose also that in my region there is some pressure to convert forest land into house lots; some nearby land has already been converted, and the suburban area is expected to continue to spread. Markets for agricultural land and for suburban land are well developed, meaning that there are well-recognized prices for land devoted to these uses; these prices register the social value of these services producible by the land. Suppose my land is also well recognized by biologists as an area of rich biodiversity. In technical terms, the land apparently produces **biodiversity preservation services,** which would be reduced if the farm is either cultivated more intensively or converted to house lots.

If a market exists such that I could obtain a revenue flow equal to the value of these biodiversity services, this flow would be capitalized into the price of the land, which then would function as an opportunity cost of devoting the land to some other use.[4] But if no such market exists, land prices will not reflect these other ecological services that they produce. Market prices for land having unique biological attributes will be too low, relative to land that does not. For private property to lead to efficient resource use patterns, markets must exist so that owners can capture the full value of the services produced by the resource in question. Only then can we be sure that resources will be devoted to the uses that maximize their social value.

Property rights arrangements have efficiency implications; they also have important distributional, or equity, implications. If the clam beds in Barnstable Harbor are allotted to private owners, many people who used to dig clams there may not be able to do so anymore. If an open-access woodland is changed to restricted entry (in the sense of entrants having now to pay for use), local people who used to be able to enter the area may find themselves excluded, especially if their incomes are low. Suppose a resource that was once used widely in an open-access framework is now privatized in the hands of a relatively small number of owners who wish to keep it for their exclusive use. These examples point out that property rights solutions to resource issues will normally have important distributional consequences.

---

[4] For a discussion of land prices and the capitalization of service flows, see Chapter 14.

GOVERNMENT-SPONSORED INCENTIVE POLICIES

A **government-sponsored incentive policy** is one in which regulatory authorities try to shift the incentive aspects of a situation so that resource users will be motivated voluntarily to adjust their behavior in the direction of efficiency. Plans of the sort normally involve taxes or subsidies, or a combination of the two.

Taxes

Consider again the situation depicted in Table 7-2. Suppose authorities now institute a charge of $7 per day per fisher, which acts essentially as an entrance fee that all fishers must pay to gain access to the fishery. This does not change the fundamentals of the fishery, in terms of the harvest rates, harvest costs, and the efficient number of fishers. What it does change is the financial incentives facing each fisher. **From the standpoint of the fishers,** the Cost-per-Fisher column now consists of $19 throughout rather than $12. We know that in an open-access situation entry will increase up to the point where marginal cost (in this case $19) equals average harvest value. This now occurs at a rate of 4 fishers (actually it occurs between 4 and 5 fishers; we are assuming that fishers come only in integer values). The tax, in other words, has shifted the costs of the fishers so that now, even with no direct control over entry, the number of fishers will stop at 4, the socially efficient level. However, from a **distributional standpoint,** the tax approach is quite different from the property rights approach studied earlier. With the $7 tax, the Net Returns column can now be divided as follows:

Number of fishers	Net returns		
	Total	Accruing to fishers	Tax receipts
1	$ 8	$ 1	$ 7
2	16	2	14
3	24	3	21
4	32	4	28
5	30	−5	35
6	24	−18	42
7	14	−35	49
8	0	−56	56
9	−18	−81	63
10	−40	−110	70

Distributionally, then, the tax transfers most of the rent of the fishery from the pockets of the fishers to the coffers of the taxing authorities. In the property rights approach the total rent shared by the 4 fishers would be $32; in the tax approach it would be $4, and the authorities would get the other $28. Of course, such distributional consequences reduce the political attractiveness of using taxes to achieve efficient resource utilization rates.

In order for an efficient tax to be applied, authorities must have accurate knowledge of the cost and revenues of the typical fisher. This is a central weakness of this approach, because the only reasonable place for the authorities to get this knowledge is from the operators themselves. Note that a standard income tax will not have the desired efficiency effects. A normal income tax would take a certain percentage of a fisher's net income. Suppose a 50 percent income tax rate were applied to the fisher example in Table 7-2. The Returns-per-Fisher column would change as if those numbers were all multiplied by 0.5. But the open-access number of fishers would still be 8. To have the desired efficiency effect, in other words, the tax has to be levied per unit of effort (i.e., per fisher) or per unit of harvest. This puts more burden on the taxing authorities, in terms of getting accurate enough information to identify the efficient tax level.

Subsidies

It may not seem obvious, but a cleverly designed system of **subsidies** could have the same efficiency effects as a tax, with entirely different distributional consequences. Suppose the clam fishery is currently operating at open-access levels (i.e., there are 8 fishers on the fishery). The authorities now step in and offer a subsidy of $7 to each fisher **who will refrain from fishing.** Now consider the eighth fisher; this individual is essentially just breaking even: $12 of catch and $12 of cost. He clearly would be better off by taking the subsidy and ceasing operations that year. The same could be said for the seventh fisher (current net gain of $2, as compared to the $7 subsidy), the sixth, and the fifth. But at 4 fishers, no further reduction would occur because the marginal return ($8) is greater than the subsidy.

For this subsidy to have the appropriate efficiency effects, authorities would have to stop people entering the fishery solely for the purpose of obtaining the subsidy by quitting. This means the authorities must have a reasonably accurate knowledge of the open-access level of the fishery, together with the cost and revenue situation of the typical fisher, so that the subsidy could be set at the correct level. It needs to be stressed that this is a very particular type of subsidy. It is essentially a payment to individuals in return for their reduced use of the resource in question; the objective is to affect the rate at which the resource is used. Subsidies in the real world are seldom like this; they usually have a redistribution objective to transfer income, often from the general taxpayer to favored groups or sometimes to individuals. Natural resource industries have often been favored in this respect:

- Many governments around the world have offered financial aid to fishers; in the United States, for example, the federal government has at times taken steps to reduce the costs of purchasing fishing boats.

- Federally constructed irrigation dams have sold water to farmers and ranchers at below-cost prices.
- Publicly owned land has been leased to ranchers for grazing purposes at extremely low prices.
- Mineral operators have had access to federal land at very low prices.
- In many countries timber companies have won timber harvesting concessions at very low prices.

It is universally the case, of course, that recipients of subsidies never think of them as such, but instead as revenues justified by conditions that are special to their particular circumstances. For the most part, however, they are subsidies gained through the political process, which in most cases have the effect of increasing the rate of use of the affected resource over what it would be without the subsidies. We may regard these as **governmental failures,** where political initiative has been used, not to rectify cases of inefficient use of natural resources, but simply to shift income toward favored groups.

In such cases, a social gain is to be had at no cost, by simply lifting the subsidy. Figure 7-1 depicts the case of an item the production of which is subsidized (through, for example, a subsidy on some important input, such as energy). The real social marginal cost curve (i.e., not counting the subsidy) is MC, while the subsidized marginal cost curve, which determines the effective market supply curve, is MC minus the subsidy, that is, MC − S. The subsidy

FIGURE 7-1
Inefficiency Caused by Subsidized Production

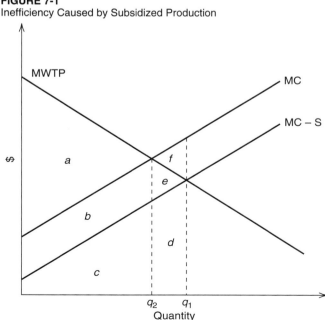

lowers the effective marginal cost curve. Thus, the market output will be q_1, which is somewhat larger than the socially efficient output q_2. At q_2 the net social benefits would be $(a + b + c) - (b + c) = a$; whereas at an output level of q_1, net social benefits are $(a + b + c + d + e) - (b + c + d + e + f) = a - f$. (Remember that although the market output is determined by the subsidized marginal cost curve, net social benefits are still determined by MC, the unsubsidized marginal cost curve.) Thus, a discontinuance of the subsidy would produce a social gain equal to the area f. In effect society would gain simply because it moves to a position that is socially efficient from one that is not.

So why then don't governments end subsidies of this sort? The answer is that although there will be a gain to society, there may not be a gain to each and every group or individual in society. Ending subsidies means ending the flow of redistributed income toward certain groups. Thus, it is in the interests of these groups to use the political process to preserve the subsidies. One should not necessarily conclude that it is individual firms and industries who are always the recipients of subsidies. In many countries consumers in general are the subsidized group. Many developing countries, for example, subsidize the prices of energy and food; in such cases, it is politically very difficult to get rid of the subsidies.

DIRECT CONTROLS

The direct approach to controlling natural resource use, often called the **command-and-control** approach, is simply to enact a regulation specifying, for example, maximum use rates, then using normal means (like monitors and police) to enforce the regulations. In the Barnstable Harbor case the town could establish a regulation saying that only the first 4 fishers to apply would be allowed and after that no further entry would be permitted. Anybody else caught harvesting clams would be arrested and fined. Many different types of controls have been used in different circumstances.

1 An upper limit on the total quantity of fish caught annually from a certain fishery; after the limit is reached the fishery is closed.
2 A limit on the specific uses to which a piece of land may be put, for example, zoning regulations.
3 A limit on the quantity of water that particular users may withdraw each year from a nearby river.
4 A limit on the number of people who are allowed access to a state or national park.
5 A limit on the quantity of timber that may be harvested from a given parcel of land.

The command-and-control approach to regulation appears to be simple and straightforward, deceptively so. Consider Figure 7-2. It shows the market demand (D) and supply (S) of a natural resource; left to itself the market quantity would settle down at q^m. But suppose there are additional costs not being

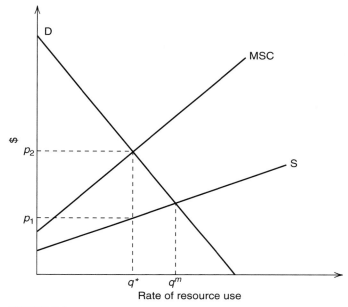

FIGURE 7-2
Direct Controls

taken into account by the market suppliers—ecological costs associated with producing timber, for example. After having studied the situation, the authorities decide that the true social cost function is MSC and that the socially efficient rate of output is q^*, not q^m. A regulation is therefore promulgated stating that the maximum allowable production is q^*.

Rather clearly, if a direct regulation like this is to achieve efficiency, the regulators must have good knowledge of the underlying costs and benefits. In order to identify a policy target level like q^* in the figure, they must know not only the nonmarket ecological costs that the market is currently leaving out, they also must have a good idea about private production costs, as well as the market demand curve. Regulation of this type, therefore, places a very substantial **information burden** on the public agencies responsible for regulations. This burden will be higher than is apparent in Figure 7-2. If q^* is an **aggregate output limit,** this may have to be broken down into individual output limits for the firms making up the aggregate. And to do so effectively requires information about the cost structure of each of these firms. Information on costs of this type usually must come from the regulated community itself, which puts a substantial burden on the agency to get data that is reasonably accurate.

A major issue of the command-and-control approach is the **enforcement** process. Suppose output has been reduced by regulation to q^* in Figure 7-2. At that point, the market price is going to be p_2, whereas the marginal costs of production are at p_1. Any producing enterprise that can find a way to produce one more unit of this item will profit by an amount equal to $p_2 - p_1$. We might call this the **incentive to be noncomplaint.** The more restrictive the regulation, the larger will be this incentive. This is not to say that regulations of this type are never justified. Historically, direct command-and-control regulations are the primary way that public policy has been pursued. In many cases, however, the enforcement part of the whole process has been overlooked.

DIRECT PUBLIC PRODUCTION

The last policy approach to be discussed in this chapter is **direct government production.** In the case of Barnstable Harbor, the town in this case would claim title to the clam flats. They would appoint a "clam production committee," which would hire clam diggers, police boundaries, sell the harvested clams on the open market, and deposit the proceeds (the rents) in their own bank account. These funds could then be used by the town for whatever purpose it chooses. In fact, this is analogous to privatization, but in this case the owning and acting organization is a public body rather than a private firm.

In fact, direct public production of this general type appears in many places. Public parks at community, state, and national levels operate in this general way, as do national forests, national monuments, and the like. Much of the original public domain in the United States is still in public ownership. In many other countries whole sectors (electricity production, banking) have been nationalized at various times, although at present the trend seems to be going the other way.

In principle there is nothing to stop a natural resource–owning public organization from using that resource in a socially efficient way. To do this, it would have to function much as a private firm would, with the added proviso that it include all external costs and benefits, as well as nonmarket costs and benefits, in its deliberations. In actuality, of course, it is difficult for political firms to function in this way. The incentive for private firms to move toward efficiency is that they are **residual claimants;** that is, they get to keep the net revenues or, in the case of natural resources, the resource rents. But public agencies are seldom in this situation. Revenues collected by public firms usually go into general revenues rather than into the specific bank account of the agency itself. Expenditures of the agencies are not constrained by collected revenues but by budgets that are enacted in the context of a political decision process in which outcomes are a result of the play of interests and influences by affected individuals and groups. The question is whether public agencies involved in direct production can assess and balance these various interests so as to get close to something that qualifies as a socially efficient outcome. In some cases they may, and in other cases they may not.

In the case of natural resources, public production often takes the form of allowing private firms to have access to public domain resources under controlled conditions. That is, the legal title to the in situ resources remains for the most part with the public, but the extraction is actually done by private firms who harvest and sell the resources. The contractual terms of these arrangements, and therefore the prices paid for the resources, varies from one resource to another, as Exhibit 7-2 summarizes.

Contracts of this type have been controversial in recent years and are destined to become more so. Critics often charge that the prices at which public domain resources are sold are often lower than their fair market values. Users of the resources normally argue the opposite. Managers of the public domain are under increasing pressure to shift resource use away from extractive and toward nonextractive uses. And the environmental impacts stemming from the extraction of public domain resources are becoming a growing concern. In subsequent chapters we will revisit this issue as we discuss particular natural resources.

MARKET FAILURE/GOVERNMENT FAILURE

In the previous pages we have focused on the many ways that a society has of managing its natural resource endowment. All approaches to resource management involve collective action of one sort or another. In some cases this consists of the collective establishment of a legal system of property rights and markets, after which natural resource use rates are determined through the decentralized interactions of buyers and sellers. At the other extreme is direct public production. And there are many types of policy intervention involving combinations of public and private actions. The usual justification for overt public action of one type or another is that strictly decentralized property rights and markets don't give results that are socially equitable and efficient. This is called **market failure,** and is linked usually to such problems as the presence of externalities, public goods, and myopia on the part of present generations. When these kinds of problems are present, private markets are incapable of operating efficiently and public policy is called for.

But there is a danger here of evaluating alternative public policy intervention only in terms of what might be called **ideal types,** that is, policy as it would work in theory if it were conducted by totally selfless public servants who always acted in the public interest using good information on possible outcomes. But this is never true. Public policies are normally pursued in a highly politicized environment by public servants who usually mean well but who have their own views of where the public interest lies and who work with information that is usually incomplete and often biased. So public policies in practice are never likely to give the results that they would appear to promise in theory. A way to describe this is **government failure.** Government failure can happen in many ways:

- Regulations are enacted but **inadequately enforced.**
- Regulations are enacted that create **perverse incentives,** making situations worse instead of better.

EXHIBIT 7-2

PROGRAMS THROUGH WHICH THE U.S. GOVERNMENT SELLS PUBLIC DOMAIN RESOURCES

Timber Sales

Responsible agencies: Forest Service (Department of Agriculture); Bureau of Land Management (Interior).

Method: Agencies prepare annual sale programs and individual timber sales; prior to sale the timber is appraised. Sale contracts are offered for sale through competitive bids at oral auctions, with the appraised values acting as minimum acceptable bids.

Grazing Permits

Responsible agencies: Bureau of Land Management (Interior) and Forest Service (Agriculture).

Method: Agencies identify grazing allotments and determine number and timing of grazing; allotments are associated with nearby ranches and usually remain with permitters permanently. Fees are set on a base value (set at $1.23 per animal unit month in 1966) and adjusted by indices of livestock prices and ranch operating costs.

Hard-Rock Minerals

Responsible agency: Bureau of Land Management (Interior).

Method: Claims to areas believed to contain minerals may be made for a fee of $10 and $100 per year thereafter for holding it open. When a valid claim is shown to have recoverable minerals, the minerals may be developed, with or without a patent. A patent application, if approved, gives claimant full title to the surface and mineral rights, at a cost of $2.50 per acre.

Onshore Oil and Gas

Responsible agency: Plans prepared by Bureau of Land Management (BLM); administered by Minerals Management Service (Interior).

Method: BLM determines leasable tracts; these are offered for sale in competitive oral auctions, with the highest bidder awarded the contracts. Leaseholders must pay an annual fee of $1.50 per acre, replaced by a royalty of 12.5 percent of the value of production once production begins.

Offshore Oil and Gas

Responsible agency: Minerals Management Service (Interior).

Method: Agency prepares 5-year leasing plans on leasable tracts, and periodically offers leases for competitive bidding. Sealed bids are normally used, and bidders may make bonus bids, but royalty rates must be at least 12.5 percent and profit shares at least 30 percent.

Mineral Materials

Responsible agency: Minerals Management Service (Interior)

Method: Includes common varieties of minerals such as sand, gravel, cinders, clay, etc. Sales are made at market value, as determined by appraisal, with newspaper advertising preceding sealed or oral bids. However, up to 100,000 cubic yards may be sold non-competitively.

Water

Responsible agency: Bureau of Reclamation (Interior).

Method: Once federal projects are completed, irrigation water is delivered at rates specified in long-term contracts. Factors affecting rates are the reimbursable costs of project, amount of irrigable land in a project area, annual operations and maintenance costs, land class and ownership, and irrigator's ability to pay. Normal rates vary from less than $1 to almost $20 per acre-foot of water.

Source: Compiled from Ross W. Gortz, "Federal Sales of Natural Resources: Allocation and Pricing Systems," Congressional Research Service, Report 97-15, *Engineering News Record,* January 3, 1997.

- Laws and regulations are enacted in the name of efficiency but in reality are **redistributive;** that is, they are attempts by one group to wrest resources away from another group.
- Laws are enacted in the name of correcting **market failures,** whereas the real objective is to protect the privileged position of an existing group with respect to the use of a natural resource.
- Laws and regulations are pursued that essentially require information that public agencies do not have and cannot get.

The implications of this are the following: When considering the possibility of public policy, it is not correct to compare the results we are getting from an imperfectly functioning market system with what we would get from a perfectly designed and implemented public policy. Instead we have to compare imperfect markets with perhaps equally imperfect public policies. In many cases it may be far more effective to determine why markets are not functioning efficiently and solve that problem, than to engage in overt activist public policy. In many cases the opposite will be true.

POLICY CENTRALIZATION/DECENTRALIZATION

The example used earlier in this chapter concerned the management of a local natural resource (a clam bed) by a single community (the town of Barnstable). The resource is local in the sense that it occupies a small part of the territory of the town and in the sense that the question of whether the clam stock is large or small is not a matter of great concern beyond the town's borders. The relevant government body was the town itself, acting through whatever agencies and units were established to deal with the issue. Suppose, however, that the particular species of clam found in the Barnstable clam beds is a unique species found nowhere else, as far as anyone knows at the present time. Now it is reasonable to ask the question: Is the local government still the appropriate place to solve this management question? Might it now be desirable to have this resource case addressed at a higher level of government, either the state or perhaps the federal level?

This is the **centralization/decentralization** problem in natural resource policy.[5] What is the appropriate governmental level at which particular natural resource issues should be addressed? In the United States we can distinguish four main levels: local (the single community), county, state, and federal. The importance of county government varies from region to region. We could perhaps also speak of a regional level, taking in several states. Historically, certain resource issues have been addressed at the federal level (fisheries regulation, managing national parks and forests), whereas others have typically been local (land-use issues).

---

[5] Of course it's a problem that exists in all types of policy areas, not just natural resource policy.

The general principle for assigning a particular natural resource issue to one or another level of government is fairly clear. It should be addressed at the lowest level of government whose geographic scope encompasses all the relevant benefits and costs of the problem.[6] The reason for this rule is that it will make it easier to compare the benefits and costs of the problem and achieve the balance between them that efficiency requires. Most of the benefits and costs of the original Barnstable case are local. Thus the community forum is the one where people can most directly comprehend them and confront the trade-offs that are involved. Political processes at the state and federal levels would not be able to do this as effectively.

Real difficulties come up, however, when the geographical spread of benefits and costs are quite different, as they often are in natural resource issues. Consider again the version of the clam bed case in which the clams are an endangered species. In this case the benefits of preserving them may accrue widely, to all citizens who place a high value on preserving species and encouraging diversity. But the costs of a regulation to limit harvesting below locally efficient levels are concentrated locally. This is a very common pattern in natural resource issues. Widely dispersed benefits argue for a state or federal role; localized costs argue for a local perspective.

The use of markets solves this problem to some extent. When clams are harvested and sold, they presumably go into at least a regional, or perhaps national, market. With established prices for clams, the local clam-managing individuals and groups have an easy way of assessing the benefits produced by digging the clams. But this only works if there are ready markets for the resource. No private market exists for species uniqueness. There is no way for people who value this characteristic of the clams to buy units of it. It might be possible for people to buy the clam bed and preserve the species, if public authorities allowed this sort of thing. The public good aspect of this would still have to be solved, of course.

So, how are the clam beds of Barnstable Harbor managed? The harbor is divided into two areas. In one area long-term leases are granted to commercial fishers who manage and harvest clams on their own leaseholds. The other area is fished as an open-access resource by town residents who must obtain clam digging permits from the town. The leasehold section of the harbor is overseen by the state of Massachusetts, while the permit section is managed by the town of Barnstable.

SUMMARY

Public policy involves collective action to influence the rate and manner in which natural resources are used. There are many types of policy approaches,

---

[6] Wallace E. Oates, "Thinking about Environmental Federalism," in Wallace E. Oates (ed.), *The RFF Reader in Environment and Resource Management,* Resources for the Future, Washington, DC, 1999, p. 119.

each with strengths and weaknesses. To choose among different policies for a particular situation, one must have in mind some criteria with which they will be evaluated. The criteria discussed were **efficiency, equity, enforceability, and flexibility.** The four types of policies evaluated for addressing resource issues were the creation of **property rights, government-sponsored incentive programs, command and control regulations,** and **direct governmental production.** No one policy approach is likely to be the best for all situations; which one is best will depend on the characteristics of the problem, the presence of appropriate social institutions and infrastructure, the capabilities and objectives of public officials, and other factors. The chapter also discusses the issues of **market failure** vs. **government failure** and the appropriate governmental level for addressing particular public policy problems.

KEY TERMS

Public policy

Policy criteria (efficiency, equity,
  enforceability, flexibility)

Incentive-based policies

Property rights

Command-and-control approach

Public production

Residual claimant

Conditions on property rights
  (complete, enforceable, transferable,
  presence of competitive markets)

Market failure

Government failure

Policy decentralization/centralization

QUESTIONS FOR FURTHER DISCUSSION

1 Give an example of a policy that is efficient but not equitable, and of one that is the opposite. Do you think that, in general, efficient policies are likely to be equitable, and vice versa?
2 Suppose, in the clam fishing example introduced in Table 7-2, a tax is applied per pound of clams harvested, rather than per fisher day. This tax, in other words, works to lower revenues rather than raise costs. At what level should the tax be set to bring about the socially efficient use level?
3 Besides income (rich vs. poor) and generations (today vs. future), what other demographic and social factors might be important in assessing the fairness of resource policies?
4 From a political perspective, why do subsidies and property rights policies often get more support than taxes and command-and-control policies?

USEFUL WEB SITES

For information about federal policy initiatives and developments:

- U.S. Department of the Interior (http://www.doi.gov)
- Natural Resources Defense Council (http://www.nrdc.org)
- League of Conservation Voters (http://www.lcv.org)

- Findlaw (http://www.findlaw.com/lawecon); search on environmental law
- Environmental Law Institute (http://www.eli.org)

For news and views of using property rights and free markets:

- Public Interest Research Center (http://www.perc.org)
- Center for Private Conservation (http://www.cei.org/cpc)

For information on environmental issues at the community level:

- Local Government Environmental Assistance Network (http://www.lgean.org)

A good source on state level issues is the environmental atlas feature of the:

- Resource Renewal Institute (http://www.rri.org)

SELECTED READINGS

Anderson, Terry L., and Donald R. Leal: *Free Market Environmentalism*, Westview Press, Boulder, CO, 1991.

Conrad, Jon M.: Resource Economics, Cambridge University Press, Cambridge, U.K., 1999.

Hackett, Steven C.: *Environmental and Natural Resource Economics*, M. E. Sharp, Armonk, NY, 1998.

Organization for Economic Cooperation and Development, *Renewable Natural Resources, Economic Incentives for Improved Management*, OECD, Paris, 1989.

Tietenberg, Tom: *Environmental and Natural Resource Economics*, 5th ed., Addison Wesley Longman, New York, 2000.

FOUR

NATURAL RESOURCE ANALYSIS

Many resource development and utilization programs and projects are undertaken by agencies in the public sector. Many are also undertaken by individuals and firms in the private sector. Whatever the case in a particular instance, it is important that society be able to assess in quantitative terms the net benefits flowing to its members. In the next two chapters we will look at techniques that economists have developed to do this. In Chapter 8 we will look at several different types of analysis that can be pursued, devoting most of our time to **benefit-cost analysis.** In Chapter 9 we will look at problems of **resource valuation,** especially problems of measuring resource flows in nonmarket situations.

CHAPTER **8**

PRINCIPLES OF ANALYSIS

Each year federal, state, and local governments pursue all sorts of policies and regulations designed to impact on the ways natural resources are used. Controversies swirl around these actions: whether they are effective, whether the trend should be toward more or toward less public regulation, whether we should have more or less reliance on private markets, and so on. Effective policy, even effective monitoring of markets, requires high-quality information and the presentation of that information in ways that facilitate action. Good analysis does not necessarily produce good decisions. But bad analysis will almost certainly contribute to bad ones.

In this chapter we examine some of the alternative **types of analysis** that are undertaken by policy analysts. Most of the chapter will be devoted to **benefit-cost** analysis, since this is the technique most frequently used. Before examining the basic principles of benefit-cost analysis, however, we look briefly at several other modes of analysis.

IMPACT ANALYSIS

"Impact" is a very general word, meaning the influence that one set of events has on another. In general, impact analysis seeks to measure the impact of a public action, such as a regulation, on a designated sector of the society/economy. Several different types of impact analysis are important in natural resource economics.

Environmental Impact Analysis

An **environmental impact analysis** is essentially an identification and elaboration of all repercussions of a designated activity on all or part of the **natural and environmental resource base.** Many countries have laws requiring that environmental impact analyses be carried out before a substantial public program or project is undertaken. Analyses are sometimes required also of private actions. In the United States, the relevant law is the **National Environmental Policy Act of 1970** (NEPA). This law requires that agencies of the federal government conduct environmental impact assessments of proposed laws and "of other major federal actions significantly affecting the quality of the human environment." Over the years this has been interpreted to include any actions funded in part or regulated by the federal government, even though the actions may be undertaken by private parties. Many states have analogous laws governing state-funded projects.

The end result of an environmental impact analysis is an **environmental impact assessment** (EIS), sometimes called an Environmental Impact Report (EIR). An EIR is supposed to contain the following information:

- a description of the environmental impact of the proposed action,
- any adverse environmental effects that cannot be avoided should the proposal be implemented,
- alternatives to the proposed action,
- the relationship between short-term uses of man's environment and the maintenance and enhancement of long-term productivity, and
- any irreversible and irretrievable commitments of resources that would be involved in the proposed action should it be implemented.[1]

For the most part EIR's are the work of natural scientists, such as biologists, hydrologists, and ecologists. The main job is to try to clarify the linkages that will spread the impact of a project through the ecosystem and to estimate the qualitative and quantitative repercussions it will have on the various characteristics of that system. These could be impacts on fish and wildlife, the functioning of the water system, or land and plant resources. The objective is to get a clear and comprehensive picture of how these resources are likely to be impacted. The emphasis is not, however, on placing **values** on these resources—on estimating the worth, for example, of losing 20 nesting pairs of spotted owls, or the value associated with moving certain plant species closer to extinction, or the social costs of losing 50 acres of wetlands.

It would appear that valuation could wait until physical impacts are identified, but this may not be possible. Suppose, for example, a certain forest area is

---

[1] Council of Environmental Quality, "Environmental Quality 1984," Washington, DC, 1985, p. 513.

to be preserved for wildlife protection, and also to be left open to hikers and backpackers. The extent of the human impact on the region will depend in part on the number of people who visit. This includes not only the direct impact of the recreationists on the site in question, but also related impacts such as those stemming from added automobile traffic in the region. To predict these behavioral factors with reasonable accuracy, it is necessary to have good analytical information on consumer (in this case recreationist) demand for this type of natural resource reservation. Economic analysis is the prime source of studies of this type.

Economic Impact Analysis

When interest centers on how particular public or private actions affect certain dimensions of an economic system, we speak of **economic impact analysis.** The perspective might be local, for example, how the opening of a community or regional park will affect local employment rates. It might be national, for example, how a new law on harvesting timber in national forests will affect the price of building materials. It could even be global, for example, how a treaty on protecting biodiversity will impact the economic growth rates of certain developing countries.

The range of economic impacts that may be of interest is very wide, for example,

- Employment numbers (or unemployment rates), total or in certain industries
- Household incomes
- Rates of technical change in certain resource extraction industries
- Rates of inflation
- Trade balances with other countries

Exhibit 8-1 discusses an economic impact analysis recently done by the U.S. Fish and Wildlife Service. The primary concern of the study was to estimate the impact of a wildlife refuge on employment levels and incomes of people living in the vicinity of the refuge. The refuge in this case is located in Wisconsin.

Any impact analysis is only going to be as good as the underlying economic data and model used to do the study. The more one knows about how the affected economies normally function, the better is one able to estimate the impacts that can be expected from whatever public or private program is being evaluated. Economic impact analysis may also be merged into environmental impact studies. It is also important when it comes to evaluating natural resource conservation and preservation initiatives. Many of the target resources have historically been harvested for consumptive uses; forests have been logged, fisheries have been harvested, farmland has been cleared. In most cases these activities have led to the growth of local extractive industries, firms engaged directly in harvesting, transportation, and sometimes a certain amount of processing. Secondary service industries have often appeared to

EXHIBIT 8-1

ECONOMIC IMPACTS OF HORICON NATIONAL WILDLIFE REFUGE

Description

Horicon NWR encompasses the northern two-thirds of Horicon Marsh, a 32,000-acre internationally recognized wetland in central Wisconsin. Sometimes called the "Everglades of the North," Horicon Marsh is the largest freshwater cattail marsh in the United States. The refuge includes 16,956 acres of wetlands and 4,309 acres of upland habitat. It is managed to provide habitat for nesting and migrating waterfowl.

The primary recreational activity on the refuge is wildlife watching. . . . Most visitors come in the fall to see the vast flocks of migrating waterfowl and the changing foliage. . . . Fishing, as well as deer and small-game hunting, are permitted in some areas. . . . Waterfowl hunting is not permitted on the refuge, but the southern third of the marsh, which is managed by the Wisconsin Department of Natural Resources, is a premier waterfowl hunting area. . . .

Area Economy

The population of Dodge and Fond du Lac counties has been stable over the last 30 years. The economy of the region is highly diversified. Much of the land is devoted to dairy farming for cheese production, but there is also a strong industrial and government services base. Mayville hosts several metal fabrication plants. Horicon is the home of John Deere's lawn tractor factory. . . . In addition, the area is an hour away from Milwaukee and Madison, so many people commute to work in these cities and their suburbs. . . .

Activity Levels

The Refuge Management Information System (RMIS) recorded 133,810 visitors during FY 1995. Of this number, 80,724 used the nature trails, 2,079 hunted, and 284 fished. . . .

Refuge staff estimate that 90 percent of non-consumptive use visitors live more than 30 miles from the refuge, many of them in the cities of Milwaukee and Madison, which are within a 1-hour drive. Little public hunting land is available in this area of Wisconsin, so hunters travel some distance to reach the refuge. The refuge staff estimate that 60 percent of hunters are local residents. . . .

Regional Economic Analysis

The fall influx of non-resident, non-consumptive visitors generates most of the spending from Horicon visitation. . . . Non-resident refuge visitors spent about $1.8 million in the region [in 1995]. When all of the spending had cycled through the economy, the refuge generated $1.4 million in final demand, $582,000 in employee compensation, and 41 jobs. . . .

In total, refuge visitors spent $1.9 million in the region. The total effect of this spending was $1.53 million in final demand, $616,000 in employee compensation, and 44 jobs, . . .

Fish and Wildlife Service spending for payrolls, operations, and maintenance of Horicon was $333,000 in FY 1995. This spending is an additional stimulus to the local economy that was not included in the impact calculations.

Source: Excerpted from: U.S. Fish and Wildlife Service, "Banking on Nature: The Economic Benefits to Local Communities of National Wildlife Refuge Visitation," Washington, DC, USFWS, July 1997, pp. 40–42.

serve the people involved with the direct extractive activities. It is only natural for politicians and policy makers to be concerned with the welfare and status of the people in these firms, and the impacts on them of alternative proposals for utilizing the resources in question.

COST-EFFECTIVENESS ANALYSIS

Suppose a community has decided that it needs to increase the capacity of its public water supply system. Assume that to accommodate future expected population growth, the community has decided it must find an additional 100,000 gallons of water per day. There are, we suppose, a number of ways it could do this: drill several new wells into an aquifer that is currently not being used, hook up to the system of a neighboring town that has (at least for now) some excess water, build a new reservoir, plug the leaks in the existing system, find a way of getting consumers to reduce their use, and perhaps some others. A **cost-effectiveness analysis** would estimate the costs of these different alternatives to compare them in terms of costs per thousand gallons of water available for use by town residents. A cost-effectiveness analysis, in other words, takes as given the objective of the project, in this case the 100,000 gallons of additional water, and then costs out the different ways of reaching this objective.

Cost effectiveness is particularly useful in cases where there is wide agreement on the objective but not on how to reach it. It does not attempt to measure the objective in the same value terms as costs, but expresses it in terms of some physical target that is to be obtained. Examples, besides the water supply increase mentioned above, include the preservation of an endangered species; the reduction of fish harvest by, say, 50 percent; the reduction of soil erosion by some percentage; and the reduction of aggregate electricity consumption by some amount. But cost-effectiveness analysis cannot tell us what goals are worth, nor compare the value of resources used up in a program with the value of the objective achieved. For this we must broaden the analysis.

BENEFIT-COST ANALYSIS

Suppose an energy company was contemplating the construction and operation of a group of electricity-generating windmills. Since the company is "bottom line"–oriented, it would want to study the **commercial feasibility** of the windmills before it made a commitment to the plan. It would estimate as clearly as possible its costs of production: construction costs, including connecting the windmills to the power grid, operating costs, periodic maintenance, and so on. It would also estimate its expected revenues, based on the electricity prices it expected, wind conditions, etc. It would then compare expected revenues with expected costs and come to a decision on the commercial feasibility of the venture.

Benefit-cost analysis is an analogous exercise for projects and programs undertaken in the public sector. What is being explored in the case of benefit-cost analysis is not commercial feasibility (though commercial aspects may enter in) but **social feasibility,** in the sense of whether the benefits to society exceed the costs to society of undertaking particular courses of action. One very important difference in practice is that, whereas commercial revenue/cost analysis deals only with inputs and outputs that move across markets, benefit-cost analysis typically involves estimating the value of both market and **nonmarket inputs and outputs.**

Benefit-cost analysis was originally developed in the United States in the 1930s as a tool for studying natural resource decisions in the public sector—specifically to study water resource decisions of federal agencies. The primary applications were the dam building programs of the U.S. Army Corps of Engineers (Department of the Army), the Bureau of Reclamation (Department of the Interior), and the Soil Conservation Service (Department of Agriculture). At the time, each agency operated under a somewhat different set of purposes and objectives. In the Flood Control Act of 1936 it was stated that federal dam projects would be justified if "the benefits to whomever they accrue are in excess of the estimated costs." The agencies were instructed to develop a common set of principles for studying the benefits and costs of these projects, which were eventually codified in the *Green Book* published in 1950.[2] In recent years benefit-cost analysis has been applied to a wide range of government programs, such as environmental protection measures, health care programs, and highway construction projects.

Benefit-cost analysis has led two intertwined lives in natural resource policy making. The first has been among its practitioners—economists inside and outside the public sector who have developed the techniques, searched for the needed data, and sought to improve the quality of the results in different types of applications. (The primary goal of the rest of this chapter, in fact, is to consider briefly some of these procedures.) The second has been its political life among the administrators and legislators who have major ideological and political interests in the public programs to which it has been, or might be, applied. In the abstract, few people can be against the idea of having better analysis and more rational decision making in the public sector. But in its concrete application, good analysis can be politically controversial, because it can give results that are contrary to the interests of politicians, agencies, and interest groups.

In 1980 President Reagan issued Executive Order 12291, which required all agencies to conduct benefit-cost analyses of all proposed new regulations issued by federal agencies. His motive was to place a new hurdle in the way of agencies issuing new regulations, since he was committed to a strong antiregulation political agenda. In the 1990s this effort has been revived by Republican Congresses, which have sought to require benefit-cost analyses of all new federal regulations and programs.[3] Proponents argue that this would ensure that no public programs would be approved unless the social costs are adequately considered along with the benefits. Opponents frequently argue that since it is usually harder to measure benefits than it is to measure costs, a requirement like this will make it more difficult to pursue socially beneficial public programs.

---

[2] U.S. Federal Interagency River Basin Committee, Subcommittee on Benefits and Costs, "Proposed Practices for Economic Analysis of River Basin Projects," Washington, DC, 1950.

[3] And the Reagan order was essentially reaffirmed, though in somewhat weaker form, by President Clinton, in his Executive Order 12866 of September 1993.

Natural resource and environmental groups have often been in this latter category, primarily on the grounds that the benefits of public programs to preserve natural resources are often difficult to estimate with accuracy. This may be changing, however, as new analytical techniques are developed. Exhibit 8-2 describes a case where environmental groups are attempting to use benefit-cost analysis as a weapon in their fight to have timber harvesting operations stopped within national forests. Others may be coming around to the view that it is quite possible to justify current environmental and resource regulations on benefit-cost grounds; in fact, even tighter regulations can be justified in many cases.

In the last chapter we discussed major policy approaches to managing natural resources. One of these was private property and the reliance on private markets to determine how resources will be used. In this case it has been argued that benefit-cost analysis is not needed. If market prices correctly represent all social costs and all social benefits of an activity, then standard commercial feasibility analysis, like the one done by the windmill company, is all that is needed to ensure that resource decisions are in the **public interest.** But this is a fairly extreme position. Although a move in the direction of private markets may be desirable, it can never be a universal policy, good for all circumstances. Such factors as public goods, distributional consequences, intergenerational issues, and externalities will always be with us. Thus, there is always going to be a need for evaluating public programs, as well as private decisions, to assess their social consequences. Benefit-cost analysis is going to be necessary in these cases.

The Basic Framework

As the name implies, benefit-cost analysis involves measuring, adding up, and comparing all the benefits and costs of the public project or program under study. There are essentially five steps in a benefit-cost analysis, each of which has a number of components:

1 Decide the overall perspective from which the analysis is going to be done; which "public" is the relevant one?
2 Specify clearly the project or program under study.
3 Describe quantitatively the inputs and outputs of the program, that is, all the physical consequences that will flow from it.
4 Estimate the social values of all these inputs and outputs; in effect, estimate the benefits and costs.
5 Compare these benefits and costs.

Decide on the Perspective   Benefit-cost analysis is a tool of public analysis, but there are actually many publics. A benefit-cost analysis of a new town park or a wetlands preservation regulation might be done strictly from the perspective of the local community; that is, the objective may be to estimate

EXHIBIT 8-2

CRITICS WHIPSAW THE FOREST SERVICE

Brad Knickerbocker

The United States Forest Service is a bit like comedian Rodney Dangerfield, whose main laugh line is "I don't get no respect."

Environmentalists think it does the bidding of the logging, mining, and ranching industries. Those who make their living from national forests say the agency too often capitulates to "preservationists" more interested in obscure plant and animal species than in hard-working rural folks. Budget hawks say it wastes hundreds of millions of dollars a year, and its policies are continually under pressure by lawmakers.

The latest round came last Thursday when a coalition of environmental groups and businesses filed suit in federal court in Vermont. They want to halt logging on all federal land until the Forest Service compares the economic benefits of a standing forest versus a pile of logs or wood chips.

Perhaps all this political tussle is not surprising, given that the Forest Service, a $3 billion, 30,000-employee organization, controls 192 million acres—with all the wealth and emotional ties to nature that represents. But these days, the agency is under unusual pressure.

Conservative members of Congress charge that the agency is conducting an illegal lobbying campaign to advance its policies, one some lawmakers think is too "green" in its approach to timber cutting and cattle grazing.

From the opposite quarter, meanwhile, conservation groups in Oregon and Washington State recently filed suit to stop the Forest Service from swapping land with corporate owners. Such deals are meant to consolidate "checkerboard" holdings that date back to 19th-century railroad land grants while making commercially valuable timberland available to loggers and mill owners.

The U.S. Department of Agriculture (the Forest Service's parent agency) is investigating the land-exchange program, which critics say does not include enough environmental protection.

Environmentalists and fiscal watchdog groups also criticize the Forest Service for, in effect, subsidizing the timber industry through the below-cost sale of rights to log billions of board-feet of timber. The GAO recently reported that from 1995 to 1997 the federal government lost just over $1 billion.

Industry defenders say managing national forests for timber production as well as wildlife and recreation supplies the nation with wood and paper products while providing thousands of jobs for rural communities. But that argument does not mollify critics, who point to environmental degradation.

"All too often, these logging-based revenues have come at the expense of damaging clearcuts, eroded soils, degraded water quality, and impaired fish and wildlife habitat," says Rep. George Miller of California, senior Democrat on the House Resources Committee.

Forest Service Chief Michael Dombeck concedes that the agency must adjust to an era in which public values demand a different approach—one that emphasizes "watershed health and integrity" over commodity production.

Even though the timber program has decreased by 70 percent in less than 10 years, timber production still drives the priorities and the reward system, and that needs to change, Dr. Dombeck told a meeting of foresters in September.

the benefits and costs impinging on town residents only. An analysis of a federal regulation would probably be done from the standpoint of all people living in the country, while a global treaty on natural resource use might be undertaken considering the entire population of the earth as the public.

Specify the Project   This involves a complete (as complete as possible) specification of the project or program, including its location, timing, groups involved, and connections with other programs. In any benefit-cost analysis some assumptions have to be made. Will the economy continue to grow? At what rate? Will population growth continue? Will another public agency continue with a related project? Assumptions such as these have to be made as transparently and as realistically as possible right at the beginning.

There are two basic types of public programs for which benefit-cost analysis may be done:

1 Physical projects that involve some type of direct public production such as irrigation water delivery canals, beach restoration, park trails and visitor centers, logging roads, and habitat improvement projects.
2 Regulatory programs aimed at enforcing laws or practices such as restrictions on certain types of activities in national parks or monuments, land-use regulations, regulations to control commercial or recreational fishing, and regulations covering imports of endangered species. This includes also many financial-type programs like fees charged for grazing cattle on public range, subsidies offered for switching to more energy-efficient equipment, and royalty payments made by miners on public lands.

Measure Inputs and Outputs   For some projects this will be relatively easy. The engineering staff will be able to provide a reasonably complete picture of a water supply system, in terms of what it will take to build and operate it over time. The inputs required to lay out a trial system or to carry out a wetland restoration may be fairly easy to estimate. But many types of data outputs will be more difficult to measure. How many visitors can be expected in this wilderness area or at this wildlife viewing area? How might fishers, who are subject to regulations of one type, adjust their operations in an attempt to continue harvesting fish? How fast can we expect industries to grow that would supply essential equipment to backpackers, white-water rafters, or snowmobilers?

A particularly challenging aspect of this analytical element is that virtually all projects and programs extend over time, usually over long periods of time. So the job of specifying inputs and outputs requires making **predictions** about the future, and these are always going to be subject to some uncertainty, perhaps a lot of uncertainty. How does one predict population growth or rates of technological change in the medium-term future? Long-term ecological relationships are also likely to be highly uncertain. What will wolf restoration do in the long run to elk populations? How much will the survival probabilities of the spotted owl increase if we restrict logging in a defined region?

To answer such questions puts a great premium on being able to draw on diverse sources of expertise and data—like engineers, soil scientists, wildlife biologists, hydrologists, economists, published data, new survey data, and private data collected for other reasons. Benefit-cost analyses are costly in terms of time and expense. To search for existing data or to conduct surveys to get new data takes money and effort. Furthermore, all benefit-cost analyses will be pursued with limited budgets. There is no hard-and-fast rule on how much it takes to do a benefit-cost analysis, other than the principle that the bigger the budget, the better chance one has of getting better information and more accurate results.

Value Inputs and Outputs   This step involves putting values on the items estimated in the last step, in essence to estimate the benefits and costs of the project or program. We could do this in any units we wish, but typically this implies measuring benefits and costs in monetary terms. This does not mean in market-value terms because in many cases we will be dealing with effects, especially on the benefit side, that are not directly registered on markets. Nor does it imply that only monetary values count in some fundamental manner. It means that we need a single metric into which to translate all the impacts of a project or program in order to make them comparable among themselves as well as with other types of public activities. Ultimately, certain impacts of a program may be irreducible to monetary terms because we cannot find a way of measuring how much people value these impacts. In this case we must supplement the monetary results of the benefit-cost analysis with estimates and discussions of these intangible impacts.

Compare Benefits and Costs   Once all benefits and costs have been estimated as well as possible, it's time to take the last step, which is to compare them. There are two ways of doing this:

1 **Net benefits:** Total benefits minus total costs gives net benefits.
2 **Benefit-cost ratio:** Total benefits divided by total costs gives the benefit-cost ratio, the value of benefits produced per dollar of cost.

To understand what is involved in very general terms, consider the numbers in Table 8-1. They are illustrative but realistic numbers for the construction and operation of a new wildlife refuge. The purpose of the refuge is to provide visitors with opportunities both for wildlife watching and, at certain times of the year, hunting and fishing. Another purpose is to provide continued habitat for several species of threatened wildlife.

The refuge involves three types of costs: the costs of acquiring the land, the costs of constructing the refuge, and the annual costs of operating it. The latter costs include the costs of handling the visitors to the refuge and the costs of maintaining both the constructed facilities and the habitat of the refuge. There are also three types of benefits. **Nonconsumptive benefits** include the benefits accruing to those visitors whose primary purpose is wildlife viewing. Benefits

TABLE 8-1
ILLUSTRATIVE RESULTS: BENEFIT-COST ANALYSIS
OF A NEW WILDLIFE REFUGE

	Estimated annual (dollars)
Costs	
Land purchase	153,000*
Construction	
Visitor center	142,000*
Trail system	64,000*
Operation and maintenance	
Personnel	187,000
Other	63,000
Total	609,000
Benefits	
Wildlife watchers	143,000
Hunters and fishers	627,000
Species preservation	A[†]
Total	770,000
Net benefits: $161,000 + A[†]	
Benefit-cost ratio: 1.26 + a[†]	

*These are the **annualized costs** of initial one-time outlays. Essentially they are the annual payments necessary to cumulate up, at a given interest rate, to the total initial outlay over the life of the project.

[†]A and a are used to account for the factors that are non-quantifiable in monetary terms.

to hunters and fishers are the **consumptive benefits** of the refuge. There are also **species preservation benefits** flowing from the refuge, but since we have not been able to develop a realistic measure of these, they are entered as an amount equal to A. Net benefits and the benefit-cost ratio are shown at the bottom, the first with the indeterminate amount "A" included, and the second with an adjustment factor designated "a."

Scope of the Project

Should we devote 1,500 acres to the proposed new public park, or should it be more or less? Should forest clear-cuts be limited to 100 acres, or would 150 acres be better? Should we manage the wolf population at 1,000 individuals, or at some higher or lower level? The example in Table 8-1 relates to a wildlife refuge of some given size, but how do we know that this is in some sense the optimum size? Although benefit-cost analyses are done for programs/projects of a given size, we must also keep in mind that these could be smaller or larger. Even in the case of a regulation, which would seem to be an either/or proposition, there is a question of how many resources to devote to its enforcement, which gets us right back to the problem of scope.

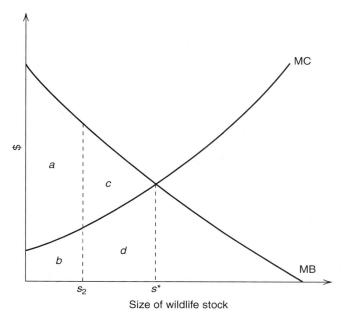

FIGURE 8-1
Scope of a Project

   To explore this issue conceptually, consider Figure 8-1. It shows several relationships pertaining to the size of a project, which in this case is assumed to be the maintenance of a wildlife stock. The horizontal axis indexes the stock size, measured in terms of the number of adult individuals in the stock. The curve labeled MB shows **marginal benefits,** that is, it shows how much total benefits will change when there is a small change in stock level. Note that it decreases to the right, which is a reflection of the fact that the total benefits go up less and less rapidly as the stock level increases. The MC curve shows **marginal cost,** which is the amount by which costs change as the stock level changes. This function increases to the right, a reflection of the fact that the total cost curve shown in panel (*a*) gets increasingly steep at higher stock levels.

   The optimal size of wildlife stock is shown as s^*; this is the stock size where marginal benefits and marginal costs are equal. The problem when we do a benefit-cost analysis of a specific project is that we cannot be sure whether we are dealing with a plan such as s^* in the figure or one at some other level, such as s_2? How can we be sure, for example, that the program analyzed in Table 8-1 is close to the **efficient size,** that is, the size that **maximizes net benefits**?

   Very often a benefit-cost analyst will be faced with studying a project of predetermined size. That is, the size of the project or program will have been established already, perhaps by engineers (in the case of a structure like a windmill farm), wildlife biologists (in the case of a wildlife refuge or wildlife restoration plan), or ecologists (in the case of a new national or state park). In these cases the size, or scope, of the programs has been established on physical grounds, and the benefit-cost analysts must confirm whether this is desirable from a benefit-cost perspective.

The procedure that can be pursued to shed light on this question is **sensitivity analysis.** This refers to the practice of recalculating benefits and costs for several alternative programs, some that are larger than the one shown in the table and some that are smaller. If the program shown in the table is indeed appropriately scaled, each of the alternatives will have lower net benefits. On the other hand, suppose the plan shown in Table 8-1 corresponds to the one shown as s_2 in Figure 8-1. In this case the net benefits shown in the table correspond to an amount equal to $(a + b) - b = a$ in terms of the areas shown in the figure. Sensitivity analysis in this case would allow the analyst to evaluate a larger effort, say, something that would maintain a wildlife stock in the vicinity of s^*. This analysis would show higher net benefits than s_2 (the net benefits would be $(a + c)$.

The With/Without Principle

In doing benefit-cost analyses, we must proceed according to the with/without principle: That is, we must compare the situation that would result if the program or project were pursued with what it **would have been** had the program been rejected. What is sometimes done instead is to compare results with the program with what the situation was **before** the program. But this can lead to false conclusions about the efficacy of the program.

Suppose, for example, we are trying to evaluate the benefits and costs of a wildlife restoration project. The population of the target animal is currently quite low, and the program involves, let us say, captive breeding and release. The benefits come from recreational viewing and are directly related to the size of the population. Estimated benefits are the following:

Before the program	$ 10,000
In the future without the program	$ 5,000
In the future with the program	$ 33,000

It would be a mistake to estimate program benefits at $23,000 ($33,000 − $10,000). This is a before/after comparison. But the base level, if the program is not pursued, is $5,000 rather than $10,000. This is because it has been predicted that there will be some attrition of the stock in the absence of the restoration program. Thus, the basis should be taken as $5,000, meaning that the benefits ascribable to the program are $28,000 ($33,000 − $5,000) rather than $23,000. This is not to imply that a with/without perspective will always give higher benefits than a before/after study. Often the opposite will be the case. If a certain population of wildlife is expected to increase moderately in the absence of a program, the with/without benefits would be larger than the before/after results.

Discounting

In Chapter 3 we discussed the mechanics of **discounting.** Discounting is a way of determining the value today (present value) of benefits and costs that will accrue at some future time. Since virtually any public program or project involving natural resources will extend beyond a single time period (e.g., year), a way has to be found to add benefits that occur in different time periods, and likewise with costs that occur in different time periods. Consider the following illustrative numbers, showing net benefits for two different projects, each of which extends over 4 years (in actuality, of course, most programs will extend much longer than this, but 4 years is enough to illustrate the general principle involved).

	Net benefits ($) in year[4]				Total (undiscounted) net benefits
	0	1	2	3	
Program A	20	20	20	20	80
Program B	50	10	10	10	80

If we simply sum the undiscounted net benefits across the 4 years, we get the same total for each, $80. But the **time profile** of benefits is quite different between the two plans: Program A has an equal distribution of net benefits across the 4 years, while Program B has most of its net benefits in the very first year, after which they are substantially lower for the last 3 years. From an intuitive standpoint we might regard Program B as somewhat more valuable because a much greater proportion of its net benefits are concentrated nearer in time. What we need is a way of **weighting** the net benefits accruing in different periods to reflect how near or distant in time they are. This is what discounting does. Thus, to compare the net-benefit streams in a way that allows for differences in their time profiles, we calculate the **present value** of total net benefits for each program. Using a discount rate of 6 percent, we get the following:

$$PV_A = \$20 + \frac{\$20}{1 + 0.06} + \frac{\$20}{(1 + 0.06)^2} + \frac{20}{(1 + 0.06)^3} = \$73.45$$

$$PV_B = \$50 + \frac{\$10}{1 + 0.06} + \frac{\$10}{(1 + 0.06)^2} + \frac{10}{(1 + 0.06)^3} = \$76.73$$

The Effects of Discounting

Note that in both programs the discounting has lowered total net benefits relative to the undiscounted totals. This is because discounting weights a dollar of

---

[4] Remember that we are following the convention that the current period is indexed with zero, and is not discounted.

net benefits accruing in the future at less than a dollar of net benefits accruing today. But the discounting affects Program A more than Program B, because a larger proportion of the net benefits of A occur in later periods, whereas the time profile of the net-benefit stream of B is concentrated more toward the present.

Discounting, then, allows us to compare projects or programs that have very **different time profiles of net benefits.** Consider the following net-benefit profiles for two alternative programs.

	Time period			
	0	1	2	3
Plan A				
Benefits	50	50	50	50
Costs	30	30	30	30
Net benefits	20	20	20	20
Plan B				
Benefits	100	50	25	25
Costs	50	40	15	15
Net benefits	50	10	10	10

The undiscounted sums of the net-benefit streams are the same; there are a total of $80 of net benefits in each of the plans. If we had to make a choice between the two plans, and we chose not to discount, we could essentially flip a coin between them. But suppose we discount net benefits, say, at 5 percent. Then the discounted stream of net benefits for the two projects would be

$$A = \$74.47$$
$$B = \$77.23$$

After the discounting, Program B has higher present value of net benefits than does Program A. The discounting has increased the relative value of the plan that produces its net benefits earlier in time. Or, to say the same thing, discounting penalizes projects in which the net benefits occur farther out into the future.

Discounting and Future Generations

The logic of a discount rate, even a very small one, is inexorable. A thousand dollars, discounted back over a century at 5 percent, has a present value of about $7.60. The logic is even more compelling if we consider a future cost. One of the reasons that environmentalists have looked askance at discounting is that it can have the effect of downgrading future damages that result from today's economic activity. Suppose today's generation is considering a course of action that has certain short-run benefits of $10,000 per year for 50 years, but that, starting 50 years from now, will cost $1 million a year **forever.** This may be somewhat similar to the choice faced by current generations regarding nuclear power or global warming. To people alive today, the present value of that perpetual stream of future cost discounted at 10 percent is only about $85,000. These costs may not weigh particularly heavily on decisions made by the current generation. The present value of the benefits ($10,000 a year for 50 years at 10 percent, or $99,148) exceeds the present value of the future costs. From the standpoint of today, therefore, this might look like a good choice, despite the perpetual cost burden placed on all future generations.

Choice of the Discount Rate

Because discounting is a way of aggregating a series of future net benefits into an estimate of present value, the outcome depends importantly on which particular discount rate is used. A low rate implies that a dollar in 1 year is very similar in value to a dollar in any other year. A high rate implies that a dollar in the near term is much more valuable than one later on. Thus, the higher the discount rate, the more we would be encouraged to put our resources into programs that have relatively high payoffs (i.e., high benefits and/or low costs) in the short run. The lower the discount rate, on the contrary, the more we would be led to select programs that have high net benefits in the more distant future.

The choice of a discount rate has been a controversial topic through the years, and we can only summarize some of the arguments here. First, it is important to keep in mind the difference between **real** and **nominal** interest rates. Nominal rates are those one actually sees on the market. If you take a nominal rate and adjust it for inflation, you get a real interest rate. Suppose you deposit $100 in a bank at an interest rate of 8 percent. In 10 years your deposit would have grown to $216, but this is in monetary terms. Suppose over that 10-year period prices increase 3 percent per year on average. Then the real value of your accumulated deposit would be less; in fact, the real interest rate at which your deposit would accumulate would be only 5 percent (8 percent – 3 percent), so in real terms your deposit would be worth only $161 after the 10 years.[5] If the cost estimates are expected real costs, that is, adjusted for expected inflation, a real interest rate is used for discounting purposes. If our cost estimates are nominal figures, a nominal interest rate is used in the discounting analysis.

The discount rate reflects the current generation's views about the relative weight to be given to benefits and costs occurring in different years. Even a

[5] These are slight approximations. The deposit would actually be worth $160.64, and the real rate of accumulation would be 4.89 percent.

brief look, though, will show that there are dozens of different interest rates in use at any one time—rates on normal savings accounts, certificates of deposit, bank loans, government bonds, and so forth. Which rate should be used? There are essentially two schools of thought on this question: the **time preference approach** and the **marginal productivity approach.**

According to the time preference approach, the discount rate should reflect the way people themselves think about time. Any person normally would prefer a dollar today to a dollar in 10 years; in the language of economics, they have a **positive time preference.** We see people making savings decisions by putting money in bank accounts that pay certain rates of interest. These savings account rates show what interest the banks have to offer in order to get people to forgo current consumption. We might, therefore, take the average bank savings account rate as reflecting the average person's rate of time preference.

The problem with this is that there are other ways of determining peoples' rates of time preference, and they don't necessarily give the same answer. Economists at Resources for the Future[6] completed a large survey in which they asked individuals to choose between receiving $10,000 today and larger amounts in 5 or 10 years. The responses yielded implied rates of discount of 20 percent for a 5-year time horizon and 10 percent for a 10-year horizon. These were substantially higher than bank savings rates at the time of the survey, which simply indicates that the actual discount rates people use may not be reflected well in standard market interest rates.

The second approach to determining the "correct" rate of discount is based on the notion of the **marginal productivity of investment.** When investments are made in productive enterprises, people anticipate that the value of future returns will offset today's investment costs; otherwise, these investments would not be made. The thinking here is that when resources are used in the public sector for natural resource and environmental programs, they ought to yield, on average, rates of return to society equivalent to what they could have earned in the private sector. Private sector productivity is reflected in the rates of interest banks charge their business borrowers. Thus, by this reasoning, we should use as our discount rate a rate reflecting the interest rates that private firms pay when they borrow money for investment purposes. These are typically higher than savings account interest rates.

Distributional Issues

From an efficiency standpoint the only thing that is relevant is total benefits and total costs; efficiency requires maximizing the difference between the two. But in many cases we will be interested also in how these benefits and costs are

[6] Resources for the Future (RFF) is a well-known Washington organization that specializes in natural resource and environmental economics research. It publishes a quarterly newsletter discussing its work. This information comes from RFF, *Resources,* No, 108, Summer 1992, p. 3.

distributed among the people and groups affected by the project or program. We talked about the importance of distributional issues earlier, particularly from a political economic perspective.[7] The political conflicts in which many natural resource issues get embroiled are often related to the fact that the groups who enjoy the benefits are not the same as those who bear the costs.

These are matters of equity, or fairness, which is why they can become so controversial. Another important aspect of distributional fairness in resource programs (or in any program, for that matter) is how they impact people with different income levels. This is a major issue in the **environmental justice** movement, and the same problems exist in natural resource projects. There are essentially two main dimensions of equity: horizontal and vertical. **Horizontal equity** means treating people in similar situations alike. From the standpoint of the income dimension, if all people in the same income class are treated alike, in the sense that they experience the same gain (or loss) in net benefits, then horizontal equity has been achieved. Suppose we have a wildlife restoration program that has the following benefit-and-cost profile for a typical urban resident and a typical rural resident:

	Urban resident	Rural resident
Benefits	80	120
Costs	40	80
Net benefits	40	40

Note that both benefits and costs of the rural resident are higher than for the urban citizen, but net benefits are the same for each. Thus, if these people have similar incomes, we would regard this situation as equitable in the horizontal sense.

On the other hand, suppose they do not have the same income. Suppose the rural dweller has an income half that of the urban person. Then there would be a question of equity in the vertical sense, because **vertical equity** refers to how programs impinge on people who are in different circumstances, in particular on people who are at different income levels. Consider the illustrative numbers of Table 8-2. They show monetary benefits and costs of three natural resource projects as they accrue to three different people with, respectively, a low (Person A), medium (Person B) and high (Person C) income. In the adjoining parentheses each number is shown as a percentage of the person's income. Take Project 1, for example. Although the net benefits accruing to each person are different, the percentage of income is the same for all three (1 percent). The project in this case has a **proportional impact;** it affects each consumer in the same proportion.

---

[7] See Chapter 7.

TABLE 8-2
VERTICAL EQUITY*

	Person A		Person B		Person C	
Income	$5,000		$20,000		$50,000	
Project 1						
Benefits	$150	(3.0)	$ 300	(1.5)	$ 600	(1.2)
Costs	100	(2.0)	100	(0.5)	100	(0.2)
Net benefits	$ 50	(1.0)	$ 200	(1.0)	$ 500	(1.0)
Project 2						
Benefits	$150	(3.0)	$1,400	(7.0)	$5,500	(11.0)
Costs	100	(2.0)	800	(4.0)	3,000	(6.0)
Net benefits	$ 50	(1.0)	$ 600	(3.0)	$2,500	(5.0)
Project 3						
Benefits	$700	(14.0)	$2,200	(11.0)	$3,000	(6.0)
Costs	200	(4.0)	1,000	(5.0)	1,500	(3.0)
Net benefits	$500	(10.0)	$1,200	(6.0)	$1,500	(3.0)

*Figures in the table show annual monetary values. Numbers in parentheses show the percentage of income these numbers represent.

Project 2, on the other hand, is **regressive;** it provides higher proportional net benefits to high-income people than to low-income people. Project 3 has a **progressive** impact because net benefits represent a higher proportion of the low-income person's income than they do of the rich person's income. Thus a natural resource project (or any project for that matter) is proportional, regressive, or progressive, according to whether the net effect of that project has proportionally the same, a lower, or a higher impact on low-income people as it does on high-income people.

Note that although the net effects of a project may be distributed in one way, the individual components need not be distributed in the same way. For example, although the overall effects of Project 2 are regressive, the costs of that program are in fact distributed progressively (i.e., the cost burden, measured as a percent of income, is greater for high-income people). In this case benefits are distributed so regressively that the overall project is regressive. This is the same in Project 3; although the overall program is progressive, costs are distributed regressively.

These definitions of distributional impacts can be misleading. A project that is technically regressive could actually distribute the bulk of its net benefits to poor people. Suppose a policy raised the net income of one rich person by 10 percent, but raised each of the net incomes of 1,000 poor people by 5 percent. This policy is technically regressive, although more than likely the majority of its aggregate net benefits go to poor people.

Although the terminology of horizontal and vertical equity are reasonably clear, it is usually very hard to figure out whether any specific real-world natural resource project or policy has a progressive or regressive impact. To know this, we must know both who the people are that are impacted and what their income levels are. This may be feasible if the analysis is dealing with a reasonably small group of people (e.g., water rights being transferred from a relatively small group of ranchers to a local community), but it is much less so if benefits and/or costs are widely dispersed (e.g., the benefits accruing to society at large from biodiversity preservation).

Dealing with Uncertainty

In each example used so far in this chapter we have assumed that benefits and costs are known **with certainty.** But reality is not like this, especially since the estimation of benefits and costs actually involves predicting the **future values** of variables going into the analysis, values that will often be quite distant in time. We have to recognize and deal with the fact that we can never know these future values with absolute certainty. How can we do this?

We need to recognize, first, that results like those shown earlier are in reality **point estimates** of uncertain situations. We may regard them as the **most likely outcome** to expect, even though we should not be surprised if actual events turn out otherwise. One possible way to acknowledge uncertainty is to estimate a **range** for net benefits (with sensitivity analysis). If one has only informal information about the likelihood of future events, it may be possible to make qualitative statements such as "we are highly confident that net benefits will fall somewhere within a range between $a and $b." If one can get better data on probabilities, it may be possible to derive statistical conclusions: "We are 90 percent confident that the net benefits will fall within a range between $c and $d."

Many natural resource issues involve **biological uncertainty.** In a study by Richard Bishop and his associates,[8] the objective was to measure the benefits and costs of a fish rehabilitation program in a part of the Great Lakes. The Wisconsin Department of Natural Resources was planning to put restrictions on current fishing activities so that the stock of fish (in this case yellow perch) would recover. But there was much uncertainty about biological relationships and how the stocks would respond to the lower levels of fishing activity. Bishop et al. analyzed the case by looking at six different **scenarios,** each one involving a different assumption about how fast and far the fish stock would recover. For each scenario they then estimated the potential benefits. The overall expected benefits were then found by averaging the benefits of the scenarios, with each scenario **weighted by its assumed probability of occurrence,** as in the following example:

[8] Richard C. Bishop, "Benefit-Cost Analysis of Fishery Rehabilitation Projects: A Great Lakes Case Study," *Ocean and Shoreline Management,* Vol. 13, 1990, pp. 253–274.

Scenario	Benefits ($ million)	Probability of occurrence	Benefits × probabilities ($ million)
I	40	.40	16.0
II	30	.20	6.0
III	20	.10	2.0
IV	10	.20	2.0
V	50	.05	2.5
VI	60	.05	3.0
Total		1.00	31.5

The summed benefits of $31.5 million in this case represent what are called **expected benefits.** Expected benefits (or expected costs, if the technique were used for estimating uncertain costs) may be thought of as **the most likely** outcome, given the uncertainty in the biological processes involved. The uncertainty is represented by the scenario probabilities, which in the case of the Bishop study were established by asking fishery biologists to evaluate the likelihood of each scenario. Note that the sum of the probabilities is unity: The six scenarios represent all possible outcomes.

Another source of uncertainty in benefit-cost analyses is **economic uncertainty.** Benefits and costs are based on assumed prices of inputs and outputs, and we know that relative prices can change through time. Very often the analysis will hinge on a strategic piece of economic information, the future course of which can only be assumed. For example, the benefits of wilderness areas are linked to the rapid rise in demand for outdoor recreation, such as backpacking, that has occurred in the United States over the last several decades. Will this activity continue to grow at the same rate in the future? Some assumption will have to be made about this growth rate if we wish to estimate the benefits of designating new wilderness areas.

Another source of uncertainty is the discount rate that should be used. Interest rates vary over time according to economic conditions, and there is no way of knowing with certainty what the rate will be 10 or 20 years from now. We may choose to overlook this and simply use today's rate, or perhaps calculate an average over the last, say, 10 years, to use in discounting future benefits and costs.

SUMMARY

In this chapter we looked at several ways through which economic analysts assess outcomes of natural resource decisions, especially those within the public sector. We looked at **cost-effectiveness analysis** and **economic impact analysis,** but reserved the bulk of our attention for **benefit-cost analysis.** Benefit-cost analysis is simply a technique of accounting for, and valuing, all outputs and inputs of public projects or programs. We considered the economic factors involved in finding the correct size or **scope** of the project: **discounting, distributional** issues, and the question of **uncertainty.**

KEY TERMS

Environmental impact analysis
Economic impact analysis
Cost-effectiveness analysis
Benefit-cost analysis
Net benefits
Benefit-cost ratio
With/without principle
Discounting

Political economy of benefit and cost
  distribution
Horizontal equity
Vertical equity
Uncertainty
Expected value
Biological uncertainty
Economic uncertainty

QUESTIONS FOR FURTHER DISCUSSION

1 Describe the difference between cost-effectiveness analysis and benefit-cost analysis as these would apply to the question of preserving biological diversity.

2 To restore a depleted fish population, it is often necessary to reduce or stop entirely the harvesting of the stock for a certain period of time. If we are evaluating the question of how long the period of reduced harvest should be, what impact would raising the discount rate have on our conclusion?

3 Suppose we are evaluating the benefits and costs of starting an ecotourism project where visitors will be given guided tours of a particularly rich habitat area. What are the main benefits and costs that should be enumerated?

4 Suppose we were doing an economic impact analysis of the project mentioned in question 3. How would this differ from the cost-benefit analysis?

5 Assume you have been asked to do a benefit-cost analysis of a habitat protection program to help preserve a certain endangered species of wildlife. What distributional issues might be important to examine in the course of your analysis?

6 In question 5, what are the sources of uncertainty that this analysis would have to deal with, and how might this be approached?

USEFUL WEB SITES

For material on resource valuation, discounting, and principles of benefit-cost analysis:

- Resources for the Future (http://www.rff.org).

For general information on benefit-cost analysis:

- United States Environmental Protection Agency (http://www.epa.gov) (search for benefit-cost analysis under projects and programs).

For information on project analysis and impact analysis:

- Bureau of Reclamation in the U.S. Department of Interior (http://www.usbr.gov) has an economics group handling project analysis and impact analysis.

SELECTED READINGS

Arnold, Frank S: *Economic Analysis of Environmental Policy and Regulation,* John Wiley, New York, 1995.

Dasgupta, Ajit K., and D. W. Pearce: *Cost-Benefit Analysis: Theory and Practice,* Barnes and Noble, New York, 1972.

Hanley, Nick, and Clive L. Spash: *Cost-Benefit Analysis and the Environment,* Edward Elgar, Aldershot, England, 1993.

Nas, Tevfik: *Cost-Benefit Analysis, Theory and Application,* Sage, Thousand Oaks, CA, 1996.

Sassone, Peter G., and William A. Schaffer: *Cost-Benefit Analysis, A Handbook,* Academic Press, New York, 1978.

Sugden, Robert, and Alan Williams: *The Principles of Practical Cost-Benefit Analysis,* Oxford University Press, Oxford, England, 1978.

CHAPTER 9

THE VALUATION OF
NATURAL RESOURCES

Having looked at the general framework of benefit-cost analysis, we now consider the question of how one measures the actual **values of input and output flows** in any given situation involving natural resource use. It is easy to say "put each resource to the use that maximizes net social value," but how do we measure what these values actually are in concrete situations? Consider the following scenarios:

- An oceanside community is contemplating the purchase of an expanse of shoreline to use as a town beach. It must buy the land from its current owners. What benefits will town residents receive from this public beach, and are the benefits substantial enough to warrant the purchase?
- The fish and wildlife agency of a midwestern state proposes to devote substantial resources to restoring bald eagles in portions of the state. What benefits and costs will accrue to residents of the state, and what benefits will accrue to nonresidents?
- Authorities managing a river in the West are under pressure to regulate its flow so as to provide better habitat for several species of fish downstream from a large impoundment. What social benefits will flow from such a policy?
- A private logging company is being asked to avoid large clear-cuts so that the effectiveness of a forest to control water runoff is not impaired. What are the net social benefits of this practice?

- A ranch owner in the West charges hunters a fee for hunting elk on his property. His annual revenues from this activity are about $200,000. Is this an accurate measure of the wildlife preservation benefits on this parcel of land?
- Congress is considering the establishment of a new national park in a western state. What benefits will accrue to people who visit the park, and what benefits will accrue to people who never visit the park?
- An area of wetlands is being altered to allow housing development to take place without any long-run decrease in the total amount of wetlands. But the change will result in the temporary loss of about 5,000 migratory waterfowl. It's expected that after 5 years the waterfowl stock will recover to its original level. What are the social costs of this temporary loss of waterfowl?
- An agency is considering the designation of a remote part of a forest as a wilderness area. It's expected that few people will actually visit the area because of its location. Are there significant social benefits from establishing this area despite the low visitation?

These diverse questions all call for valuation of resources or the service flows stemming from resource use. We do not have sufficient time and space to take up each one in detail. Thus in this chapter we try to deal with certain **principles of valuation** that can be adapted to specific circumstances.

MEASURING BENEFITS

Types of Benefits

We first make some distinctions among types of benefits. Perhaps the most important step is to distinguish between **active** and **passive** sources of value. **Active resource values,** sometimes called **use values,** are those stemming from situations where people come into direct contact with the resource in question. This can be divided into **consumptive** and **nonconsumptive** values. Consumptive values arise from what we have termed extractive resources: timber, minerals, recreational and commercial hunting and fishing,[1] and agriculture are examples. Nonconsumptive values (nonextractive resources) are resources that are utilized but not removed or diminished in quantity or quality, such as ecotourism, animal watching, boating, hiking, camping, and rock climbing.

    Passive natural resource values, sometimes called **nonuse values,** are involved when people place value on a resource independent of their actual use of the resource. Various motives have been suggested as the source of these values. Some of these are:

- **Option value:** People may be willing to pay to preserve a resource, or increase the likelihood of continued existence, because they may wish to utilize the resource at some undetermined future time. Example: Value

---

[1] But catch-and-release fishing may be regarded as a nonconsumptive activity.

expressed for maintaining or expanding national parks, with the possibility of later visits.

- **Existence value:** Willingness to pay to maintain the existence of resources even though no future utilization is likely. Example: Preservation of remote wilderness; steps taken to increase the survival probabilities of endangered species.
- **Bequest and gift value:** Willingness to pay to ensure that others, in both current and future generations, will enjoy a world in which the particular resources are present. Example: Willingness to protect open space so one's grandchildren will live in a world with ample amounts of this resource.

In the rest of this chapter we look at techniques that natural resource economists use to measure resource values of these different types.

ACTIVE (USE) BENEFITS

Benefits obtained when people actually use the resource in question, consumptively or nonconsumptively, are called active, or use, benefits. Use values can be further subdivided into those which are expressed through markets of one type or another, and nonmarket values. When markets are involved, interactions among buyers and sellers establish prices and quantities of transactions, which can often be analyzed to determine the willingness to pay of demanders and the marginal costs of suppliers. Market prices and quantities can be used to reveal these values in two ways. They can be used **directly** when the resource being evaluated is actually traded in its own right, and they may be used **indirectly** when what is being traded is not the resource itself but another good or service that is closely associated with it.

Direct Market Price Analysis

Suppose it is proposed that a dam constructed on a stream many years ago be removed. One impact of that removal is that it would restore a trout fishery on portions of the stream below the dam site. In making the decision, we would like to know, among other things, the net benefits this trout fishery would generate. It clearly has to be an estimate, because the trout fishery does not yet exist. But suppose there does currently exist elsewhere a private market in trout fishing. The suppliers in this case are certain people who control access to several trout streams, perhaps the riparian (or adjoining) property owners. "Production" in this case takes the form of maintaining good water quality and other conditions for a productive fish habitat, fishing access points, and the means of regulating entry. Demanders are the people who are willing to pay for access to this type of fishery. Suppose we look at existing operations and determine that the average price for a privately provided day of trout fishing is $25. May we use this value to estimate the benefits of our new trout fishery?

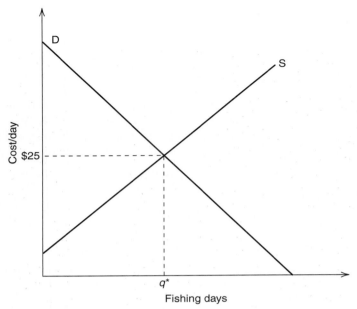

FIGURE 9-1
Market for Fishing Opportunities

Figure 9-1 shows the standard supply and demand functions of a market, which in the present case we suppose is the market for privately provided trout fishing. The price of $25 is the one that brings the quantity supplied into balance with the quantity demanded. On the assumption that there are no externalities on either side of the market and that the market is competitive, this price is an accurate indicator of both **marginal willingness to pay** and **marginal cost** at the number of fisher days represented by the quantity q^*. Therefore, if the new fishing area represents only a marginal addition to supply (i.e., if the market price of fishing days is not expected to change as a result of this new area coming on line) the $25 tells us what the marginal benefits are, and we can multiply this figure by the expected number of visits to get an estimate of total benefits. This must be done under the assumption that the new fishery will be reasonably similar to those now operating, in terms of the expected quality of the fishing.

When markets are present, they provide a good avenue for estimating resource values, because market participants are essentially revealing these values through their interactions. Thus, valuation of timber and minerals is often straightforward because they are traded on markets, both in situ (e.g., markets for trees on the stump) and as commodities after they have been harvested.

Market data may also exist to facilitate some nonextractive resource uses. Valuation of benefits from a public beach might be estimated from data on

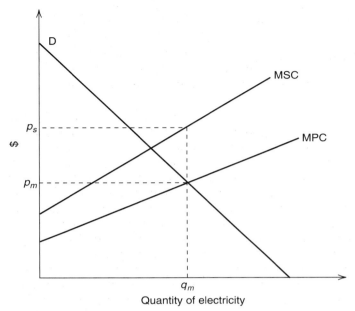

FIGURE 9-2
Market for Electricity with External Costs

visitations to private beaches, if enough of the latter exist in the study region. Or suppose there was a public policy conflict over taking steps to protect whales. The benefits produced by having abundant whales (at least some of the benefits) might be estimated by analyzing the whale watching market. The market suppliers in this case are the whales, together with the private boating firms that conduct whale watching excursions. The demanders are people who are willing to pay to be taken out to the parts of the ocean where they may eavesdrop on the whales. The prices, quantities, and costs in this market are the data we would analyze to get estimates of net benefits.

There may be many situations, however, where market prices do not give an accurate measure of social benefits. This would be true, for example, when environmental externalities are involved. Figure 9-2 presents the standard externality model introduced earlier,[2] in this case applied to the electricity market. D is the electricity demand curve, assumed to be an accurate representation of social marginal willingness to pay for electricity. MPC is the marginal private cost of producing electricity, and MSC is the marginal social cost of production. The difference is accounted for by the external costs of electricity generation, primarily air pollution. In the absence of anything (e.g., property rights changes or government policy) that causes these external effects to be

[2] See Chapter 6.

priced, the private market supply curve for electricity will be MPC, and the market price and quantity of electricity will be, respectively, p_m and q_m.

Suppose, now, that we are interested in building an array of windmills to generate power. It will be a relatively small addition to total electricity generation, but it will replace a part of the present polluting generating technology. Suppose the private cost of the windmill operation is the same as the conventional capacity. How do we value the power that the windmill project will provide? If we use simply the present market price for electricity p_m, we will be undervaluing the new power. This is because this new technology is valuable for two reasons: It produces power and it allows a reduction in the external costs coming from the electric power industry. The correct value to use in estimating the benefits of a small increase in windmill power is p_s, which is equal to the present price of power plus the current marginal value of external costs.

In many other cases market prices may not adequately represent the true social value of a natural resource–related good or service. This would be true, for example, where government subsidies or taxes lead to market prices that do not reflect true social opportunity costs. The search for correct prices to use in cases like this is a search for what economists call **accounting,** or **shadow** prices, which are simply prices that more correctly represent true economic scarcities than do the current or expected market prices. The use of shadow prices is especially important in cases where governmental policies of one type or another have produced these market distortions. We will see later that this is particularly important in developing countries.[3]

Indirect Market Price Analysis

Market prices, even when they have to be adjusted somewhat, are very useful for establishing the value of certain natural resources. But in many cases direct markets simply do not exist, or they exist in such rudimentary form that they do not provide good price data. In some cases the nature of the resource is such that direct markets are difficult to organize (e.g., air quality, which is a strong public good). In other cases government regulations have made it difficult or impossible for a market to form (e.g., wild game harvested within the country, which is illegal to sell on markets in the United States).

There are many such resources. An important natural resource in the United States is suburban wildlife, wildlife that exists in close proximity to areas of intensive human habitation. Issues related to the efficient management of these animals and plants will proliferate as urban sprawl continues at the same time that many people are changing their views about the value of wildlife. But there are no markets where people buy and sell the services of these wildlife. There may be some related markets, such as for hunting or bird watching, but these are likely to give only a very partial answer to the question of the true social value of these biological stocks. Or consider the

---

[3] See Chapter 20.

benefits associated with wilderness backpacking. Much of this activity takes place in remote publicly owned regions. Relatively little of the activity is arranged through private markets, though there may be related markets; for example, backpacking equipment is bought and sold in private markets, as are the services of wilderness guides.

In some cases activity in related markets can be studied to determine resource values. In such cases the value of the resource may be estimated **indirectly** by examining price, quantity, and quality data of the associated good or service in the related market.[4] As an example, consider the issue of open-space preservation in the suburbs. As suburban development in the United States has continued, more thought is being given to preserving some parcels in open space, like parks, visual buffers, and areas of ecological value. The costs of preservation are the value of development that they foreclose. These costs are fairly easily measured. But how can we assess benefits?

Although there is no market where people buy and sell units of open space directly, there is a closely related market in which open space can be expected to have an impact: the **suburban housing market.** The market for new and used houses is very active throughout the country. The price of a house is affected by many factors: the characteristics of the house itself and those of the neighborhood in which it is located. We assume that buyers purchase houses having the most desirable set of characteristics, given their incomes. One important neighborhood characteristic is the proximity of a house to open space or conservation land. These characteristics, if they indeed are valued (positively or negatively) by the average buyer, will be **capitalized** into the market prices of houses.

Since house prices in the suburbs are affected by many factors, what we need here is a large data set containing, for each house that was sold in a given time period, its transaction price and a description of all the characteristics that could be expected to have a noticeable impact on price. Among these would be, for example, the distance to the nearest significant parcel of open space. Statistical means can then be used to find out how this distance variable affects house prices and eventually to figure out the marginal willingness to pay that homeowners express for living close to preserved open space.

Another type of indirect market-price analysis is the **travel-cost approach.** This method takes advantage of the fact that people have to incur travel costs to visit the natural resource sites. Many resources, for example, are used by people for outdoor recreational purposes. Shoreline areas are used for picnicking, swimming, and fishing; coastal and interior wetlands are used for hunting and bird watching; forest and mountain areas are used for backpacking, camping, hunting; streams, rivers, and lakes are used for boating and fishing activities; and so on. The benefits people get from these experiences depend in large part on the qualitative characteristics of the resources: how broad the beach is, how good the fishing is, or how scenic the mountain trail is. However, most (though not all) of this activity takes place outside the market, in

---

[4] The name given to some of these studies is the **hedonic price approach.**

the sense that it does not involve direct transactions between recreators and private resource suppliers. So there are few direct market prices that could be used to estimate recreational demands for the resources.

Although recreators do not often pay direct admission charges to these resources, as they would going into a movie theater for example, they do normally have to spend money to make the visits. The costs of visiting a national forest, or a coastal wetland, or a distant lake, are the costs of traveling to these areas and engaging in the specific recreational activities chosen. Resource economists have developed techniques for deducing demand and benefit estimates by using these **travel costs as proxies** for the normal market prices that are used in market demand studies.

There are essentially two major components of travel costs: direct monetary costs such as fuel and en route lodging, and the value of the time that travelers require to get from home, or other point of origin, to the recreational site. Both types of cost would be expected to be higher for people living farther from the site in question. The procedure therefore is to survey visitors to recreation sites (and perhaps also nonvisitors in some cases), by asking questions in face-to-face interviews or via mail questionnaires. The surveys provide data on the number of visits (which could be zero), various components of travel costs, and relevant economic and demographic information (such as income levels, age, and educational attainment). These data can be analyzed to yield a demand curve for recreational visits.

Nonmarket Techniques

Resource economists have developed a special technique for estimating willingness to pay when direct or indirect market techniques are not available. It is called **contingent valuation,** and is a survey technique based on the straightforward idea that people's willingness to pay can be determined by asking them directly. The technique is called "contingent valuation" because it attempts to elicit peoples' valuations of contingent, or hypothetical, situations. In the absence of markets, people are essentially asked to choose as if there were a market for the resource in question.

Contingent valuation (CV) studies have been done for a long list of natural and environmental resources: endangered species, wilderness congestion, fishing experiences, clean air, view-related natural amenities, the recreational quality of beaches, and others. In fact, CV methods have spread into nonenvironmental areas, for example, the value of programs for reducing the risks of heart attacks, the value of supermarket price information, and the value of a seniors' companion program. Over time the method has been developed and refined to give what many regard as reasonably reliable measures of the benefits of a variety of public goods, especially environmental quality.

The steps in a CV analysis are the following:

1 Identification and description of the environmental quality characteristic to be evaluated
2 Identification of respondents to be approached, including sampling procedures used to select respondents
3 Design and application of a survey questionnaire through personal, phone, or mail interviews (in recent years, focus groups have sometimes been used)
4 Analysis of results and aggregation of individual responses to estimate values for the group affected by the environmental change

The central purpose of the questionnaire is to elicit from respondents their estimate of what the natural resource is worth to them. In economic terms this means getting them to reveal the maximum amount they would be willing to pay rather than go without the resource in question. A number of techniques have been used to get this response. The most obvious is to ask people outright to provide the amount with no prompting or probing on the part of the interviewer. Other approaches include using a bidding game, where the interviewer starts with a bid at a low level and progressively increases the value until the user indicates that their limit has been reached. Alternatively, the interviewer could start with a high figure and lower it to find where the respondent's threshold value is located. Another method is to give the respondents printed response cards with a range of values, and then ask the respondents to check off their maximum willingness to pay. Exhibit 9-1 shows some examples of questions used in several contingent valuation studies.

NONUSE (PASSIVE) BENEFITS

People may gain benefits from the preservation of the Grand Canyon, or a species of wildlife, or even a regionally significant wetland, even though they never expect to visit the Canyon or the wetland, or to directly observe the wildlife. These are called **nonuse benefits.** The evidence that benefits of this type exist is easy to see. A number of environmental organizations, the most widely known probably being the **Nature Conservancy,** raise money from donations to purchase and preserve important resource areas; it is highly unlikely that the average contributor expects to visit all the preserved sites. Thus a substantial proportion of the benefits obtained must be nonuse benefits.

We mentioned earlier some of the motives that could lie behind the existence of nonuse values and benefits.[5] Here we address the issue of how they might be measured. This is currently a topic of great controversy. There are those who feel that significant benefits will be missed if no attempt is made to measure nonuse values and include them in the overall evaluation of natural

[5] See p. 152.

EXHIBIT 9-1

EXAMPLES OF QUESTIONS IN CONTINGENT VALUATION STUDIES

Study to Estimate Certain Benefits of Better Water Quality in the Connecticut River

1 Have you heard about the Connecticut River salmon restoration program?
2 Did you make any donations for wildlife management or preservation last year?
3 Suppose that a private foundation is formed to take private donations and use them to support salmon restoration. What is the maximum donation you would make to this foundation?
4 What is your age?
5 How much money do you spend on entertainment each month?

Study to Estimate the Benefits of Outdoor Recreation in Northern New England

1 What is your favorite outdoor activity?
2 Please imagine that you have some time to enjoy the outdoor activity you gave in Question 1. Assume that the following options are the ONLY ones available. Please rate EACH option by using 5 for the option that you would DEFINITELY CHOOSE and a 1 for any option(s) that you would DEFINITELY NOT CHOOSE. If you are not sure, use 2, 3, or 4 to indicate the likelihood that you would choose each option.

OPTION 1:	OPTION 2:	OPTION 3:	OPTION 4:
Stay Home	Go to state park in Vermont	Go to Green Mt. National Forest	Go to White Mt. National Forest
	No garbage pickup Pit toilets 0 increase in wildlife population $1 access fee/visit	Full garbage pickup Pit toilets 25% increase in wildlife population $5 access fee/visit	Full garbage pickup Flush toilets 0 increase in wildlife population $2 access fee/visit
1 2 3 4 5 would would not do definitely do	1 2 3 4 5 would would not do definitely do	1 2 3 4 5 would would not do definitely do	1 2 3 4 5 would would not do definitely do

3 What is your age? _____ (number of years)

4 Are you: _____Female? or _____Male?

5 Excluding yourself, how many family members live with you? _____ (number of people)

resource benefits. There are others who think that nonuse values are largely insignificant compared to use values and that attempts to include them will normally lead to the inflation of total benefit estimates.

One possibility is to interpret the contributions that people make to groups such as the Nature Conservancy as estimates of the social benefits flowing from preservation of important natural resources. Nature Conservancy is a na-

---

EXHIBIT 9-2

THE OREGON WATER TRUST

In Oregon, as in most western states, water rights are something to fight over. One general source of conflict is between people who benefit from traditional water uses like irrigation and those who place greater value on instream uses. In 1987 Oregon passed a law that defined instream water rights. These are water rights that enhance fish, wildlife, habitat, recreation, water quality and navigation; the rights are defined for specific points or sections of streams, and are held in the same legal regard as other beneficial uses. What this does is create the incentives for people to acquire and hold these rights, thus assuring higher instream flows than would otherwise be the case.

In response to this new law the Oregon Water Trust (OWT) was formed in 1993, by a small group of individuals representing agricultural, environmental, legal and tribal interests. OWT's mission is to acquire water rights "through gift, lease, or purchase, and commit these water rights under the Oregon law to instream flows. . . ." Between 1994 and 1998 OWT spent $284,000 to purchase water rights and acquired an ad-

ditional $370,000 worth of water rights through donations. The OWT also leases water rights for shorter periods of time. They focus their efforts on small-scale transactions and negotiate primarily with individual farmers, ranchers, and landowners. At present they are also limiting their activity to a relatively small number of river basins in Oregon.

The OWT was helped in its original formation by a grant from the Northwest Area Foundation, a private group that helps nonprofit groups pursue innovative solutions to public problems. "Private foundations provide 90 percent of its operational budget, and corporations and individuals the remaining 10 percent. Roughly two-thirds of its acquisition budget comes from the private sector, and public funds provide the rest." These public funds come from agencies at the local, state, and federal levels.

Source: This information was taken from: Erin Schiller, "The Oregon Water Trust," Center for Private Conservation, Washington, DC, November 1998.

---

tional (in fact international) group; there are others of this scope, and there are many other regional and local groups that pursue essentially the same agenda and activities. Exhibit 9-2 discusses one such group, the Oregon Water Trust (OWT), whose basic purpose is the acquisition of water rights. OWT obtains funds from a variety of sources: individuals, private firms, private foundations, and public agencies. Clearly, these funds are an indication of the existence of social benefits coming from instream water flows relative to traditional water uses. And the fact that this is a somewhat local group helps pinpoint these benefits to a particular set of rivers and streams in Oregon. On the other hand, a large portion of the benefits from preserving instream flows may be direct use values accruing primarily to recreators; it is unclear how much of the total contributions made to OWT can be attributable to nonuse benefits produced by these particular streams and rivers.

Another potential problem with using contributions as a measure of willingness to pay for nonuse benefits is that the preserved resources that generate them are essentially public goods. There is no feasible means of excluding would-be beneficiaries when what is at issue is nonuse benefits, based on the simple knowledge that a resource has been preserved. When public goods are involved, private, market-related economic exchanges will undersupply the goods in question. Thus, there are conceptual reasons for thinking that private contributions to conservancy-type organizations will understate the nonuse values flowing from the resources they seek to preserve.

Since nonuse benefits are, almost by definition, independent of such factors as location or the consumption of other specific goods or services, hedonic and travel cost techniques are of no use in trying to measure them. This means that the only practicable means of assessing their magnitude is with **contingent valuation.** Contingent valuation studies have been controversial when measuring use values; they have been even more controversial when applied to nonuse values. This is because some of the problems inherent in the CV method become more acute in the case of nonuse benefits. Some of these are the following:

1 In the case of use values, beneficiaries may be presumed to be familiar with the resource whose valuation is being sought, through present or past contact with that resource. In the case of nonuse benefits, direct contact is not necessary, though it may have occurred in the past. Thus, there may be more ambiguity about the natural resource being evaluated, and the CV may be obtaining evidence of a general attitude rather than the valuation of a specific resource.

2 In many cases a person may experience both use and nonuse benefits from a natural resource. The difficulty then becomes how to distinguish between the two sources of value. A person living in proximity to a national park, for example, may get nonuse benefits from the knowledge that the park area is preserved and may also get direct use benefits from hiking or hunting in the area.

3 Where use values are concerned, it may be relatively easy to find out who the prime beneficiaries are. For visitors to a national park, for example, a survey will reveal the demographic characteristic of users. But this is not possible when nonuse benefits are involved. Thus, there is a real question about how wide the survey net should be cast to identify nonuse beneficiaries. If we are dealing with a certain species of wildlife in the Rocky Mountains, for example, should we survey people in the local community, the state, the region, or the country?

These, and other problems, make CV studies of nonuse values difficult, but not impossible. Researchers have investigated the magnitude of many nonuse values, such as the preservation of individual species of wildlife; the preservation of sites that have ecological or historical importance; and the characteristics of specific sites, such as water quality in a particular river or lake. Table 9-1 lists some of these studies.

TABLE 9-1
SEVERAL STUDY RESULTS DEALING WITH WILLINGNESS
TO PAY BY NONUSERS OF RESOURCES

Resource:	Protection of land through wilderness designation
Authors:	Walsh, Loomis, and Gillman
Results:	Respondents (expected nonusers) were willing to pay between $14 and $19 just to preserve areas in wilderness states.
Resource:	Humpback whales
Authors:	Samples, Dixon, and Gowen
Results:	Respondents' (nonusers') mean willingness to pay to preserve whales was between $35 and $60.
Resource:	Bald eagles and stripped shiners
Authors:	Boyle and Bishop
Results:	Respondents (expected nonusers) were willing to pay between $4 and $6 for shiner preservation and between $10 and $75 for eagle preservation programs.
Resource:	Whooping cranes
Authors:	Bowker and Stoll
Results:	Nonusers expressed willingness to pay between $21 and $70 for preservation programs.
Resource:	Salmon fishery in Fraser River Basin of British Columbia and fishing resources in southeastern United States.
Authors:	Described by Fisher and Raucher
Results:	Nonuse values approximately half of user values.
Resource:	Bald eagles, wild turkeys, Atlantic salmon, coyote
Authors:	Stevens et al.
Results:	Ninety-three percent of total willingness to pay was identified as nonuse value, only seven percent was use value.

Sources: Bowker, J. M., and John R. Stoll, "Use of Dichotomous Choice, Non-Market Methods to Value the Whooping Crane Resource," *American Journal of Agricultural Economics,* 70(2), 1988, pp. 372–381; Boyle, Kevin J., and Richard C. Bishop, "Valuing Wildlife in Benefit-Cost Analyses: A Case Study Involving Endangered Species," *Water Resources Research,* 23(5), 1987, pp. 943–950; Fisher, Ann, and Robert Raucher, "Intrinsic Benefits of Improved Water Quality: Conceptual and Empirical Perspectives," in *Advances in Applied Microeconomics,* V. Kerry Smith and Ann Dryden Witte (eds.), Greenwich, CT, JAI Press, 1984; Samples, Karl C., John A. Dixon, and Marsha M. Gowen, "Information Disclosure, and Endangered Species Valuation," *Land Economics,* 62(3), 1986, pp. 306–312; Stevens, Thomas H., Jaime Echeverria, Ronald J. Glass, Tim Hager, and Thomas A. More, "Measuring the Existence Value of Wildlife: What Do CVM Estimates Really Show?" *Land Economics,* 67(4), November 1991, pp. 390–400; Walsh, Richard G., John B. Loomis, and Richard A. Gillman, "Valuing Option, Existence, and Bequest Demands for Wilderness," *Land Economics,* 60(1), 1984, pp. 14–29.

MEASURING COSTS

We switch now to the cost side of benefit-cost analysis. All actions have cost consequences, whether this be costs of the obvious sort in classical natural resource extraction or costs of a more subtle kind when we consider resource preservation alternatives. It is easy to overlook the cost side, sometimes under the mistaken belief that "costs don't matter," or under the equally mistaken belief that they are easy to estimate. But costs often are difficult to determine accurately, and they do matter. The results of a benefit-cost analysis can be affected equally by over- or underestimating costs, as by over- or underestimating benefits. Furthermore, in the political realm it is almost axiomatic that options will be selected in the heat of political controversy and enthusiasm, without sufficient regard to the true social costs (or benefits) of the alternatives. All the more reason why the cost side of the analysis should be treated with as much importance as the benefit side.

General Issues

Cost analysis can be done on many levels. At its simplest it focuses on the cost to a single community or firm of a natural resource project or regulation, such as a new state park or a new community wetlands preservation plan. Although these cost estimates may still be hard to produce, the task is made relatively easy by the fact that the geographical extent or the physical nature of the programs is limited and well defined. At a higher level there are regulations or programs that affect relatively large groups: all timbering companies in the Northwest, all farmers in California, all consumers in the Northeast, for example. Here the job of collecting cost data is multiplied: Some sampling is usually necessary, and this will be complicated by a substantial amount of heterogeneity among the groups that must be studied. At the highest level are national cost estimates, for example, of the effects on the American economy of an international oil embargo.

There are two avenues through which social costs are incurred: the **opportunity costs** of using resources[6] in certain ways, and the **costs of price changes.** As discussed earlier,[7] the opportunity cost of using resources in a particular way is the highest-valued alternative use to which they might otherwise have been put. This alternative value is what society forgoes in using the resources in the specified fashion. Note the word "society." Costs are incurred by all sorts of individuals, firms, agencies, industries, and groups. Each will have its own perspective, and each will focus on those costs that directly impinge upon them. As we stressed earlier, social costs include **private costs** plus all other costs that are incurred as a result of resource use, that is, all **external** costs. Most people have an instinctive feel for the concept of opportunity cost;[8] the problem arises when we try to determine what that cost is in concrete circumstances. When an input has a market price, and the market is reasonably competitive, this price will normally be a good measure of its opportunity cost.

Price changes can create costs to producers and consumers that are somewhat different in concept than costs in the form of real resource expenditures.

---

[6] Remember that "resources" is a word that can have two meanings; it can be a short way of saying "natural resources," or it can be used as a general reference analogous to the word "inputs." Here it is being used in the second sense.

[7] See Chapter 4.

[8] For example, the opportunity cost of time is the relevant concept when allocating a fixed amount of time among several tasks.

In order to measure these costs, we need good data on the supply and demand functions for the markets on which prices change. Regulations on clear-cutting, for example, will change the costs of timbering and perhaps the price of lumber. Knowledge of the supply and demand factors on the timber market is necessary to predict these effects. It is conceivable that the appropriate statistical studies have been done to analyze these factors. If this is not the case, another approach is to carry out an engineering study to predict the effects of the regulation. We deal with these issues at greater length below.

Costs of Physical Facilities

Perhaps the easiest case to deal with is estimating the costs of a project that involves constructing and operating some type of physical facility like dams (and, in recent years, dam removal), irrigation works, parks with trail systems and visitor centers, animal refuges and restoration activities, or beach restoration activities. Most of the relevant costs here relate to the opportunity costs of the inputs used in the project, the **capital costs** of initial construction, and the annual **operating and maintenance** costs that will extend over the life of the project. The source of data on costs of this type is normally **engineering** or **scientific** authorities who can specify in detail the inputs needed for various phases of the projects.

Costs of Public Regulation

A great deal of public activity on natural resource issues is not related to physical projects, but to **public regulation** of private actions. Cost estimation in this case is usually more difficult because it requires knowing something about the costs of the private operations that will be affected by the regulations. As examples, consider the various regulations that public agencies pursue with private timber companies including specifications for clear-cutting, the use of chemicals in forest cultivation, and leaving intact certain wildlife habitat areas. The impacts of these regulations will work through shifting the costs of these private companies. This adds a major complication, however, since the cost shifts, by changing supply functions, may lead to output changes. This complicates the task of determining the costs of the regulation.

As an example, consider Figure 9-3. This diagram might depict the situation, for example, of a small regional forestry operation where local timbering companies are faced with a new regulation designed to protect the habitat of an endangered animal. Since this is a local impact only, it is not expected to have any influence on the national price of wood. In other words, the demand curve for timber harvested by the collection of local companies is flat, as depicted by the line marked D. Before the regulation their marginal cost curve, equal to their supply curve, was $MC_1 = S_1$. Thus, total output was q_1, total costs were $c + f$.

FIGURE 9-3
Costs of a Regulation on Timber Harvesters

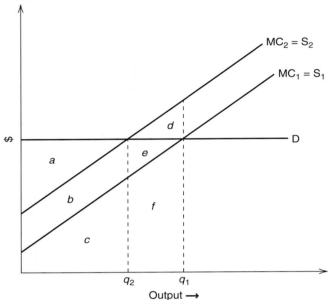

Output ⟶

The effect of the regulation is to increase the costs of harvesting timber, de-picted by an upward shift in the marginal cost curve to $MC_2 = S_2$. If output were unchanged, the total increase in costs would be measured by the area $b + e + d$. But the added costs, in the face of a constant price, will normally lead to output adjustments. In the depicted case, output would fall to q_2. One way of getting at the significance of the change is to look at net benefits before and after the change. Before the regulation they were $a + b + e$, whereas afterward, they are a; thus, there was a reduction in net benefits of $b + e$. Note that this is a number smaller than the cost increase for a constant output $b + e + d$. By the lowering of output, a part of the cost increase that would have been incurred in the absence of output change is avoided.

The information needed to measure the cost implications of the regulation includes (1) the extent to which the marginal cost/supply function will be shifted up by the regulation and (2) the extent of any output adjustments that firms will make as a result of the cost changes. Where does one get the cost data necessary to analyze the cost structure of an industry? Normally from the industry itself. Much of the data can be generated by **cost surveys,** in which questionnaires are sent to all, or a sample of, the firms in the industry in ques-tion. In effect, questionnaires are sent out to these firms asking them to supply information on the number of employees, processes used, costs of energy and materials, and so on. With a sufficiently detailed questionnaire and a reason-ably high response rate by firms, researchers hope to get a good idea of basic

FIGURE 9-4
Effects of a Regulation on Consumers

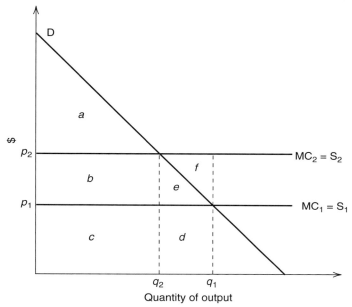

cost conditions in the industry and how they might be affected by regulations on natural resource use. Because the regulated firms themselves are the source of much of the cost data used to develop the regulations, there is clearly a question whether these firms will supply accurate data. By overstating the potential costs of adjusting to regulations, firms may hope to convince agencies to promulgate weaker regulations than they would if the agencies had an accurate idea of costs.

Another problem with cost surveys is that they are usually better at getting information on past data than on future costs under new regulations. Firms can probably report past cost data with more reliability than they can estimate future costs. But historical data may not be a good guide to the future, especially because environmental regulations, almost by definition, confront firms with novel situations and because future technological change can impact costs in major ways. In these cases it is common to supplement survey data with technical engineering data that can be better adapted to costing out the new techniques and procedures that firms may adopt.

Note that in Figure 9-4 the regulation led to an output reduction from q_1 to q_2. What this shows is the extent to which resources currently used in this industry will no longer be needed there. Certain inputs, for example energy and various types of material inputs, will be easily reduced. But inputs like labor are much more complicated. In a reasonably full employment economy, one could expect labor that is withdrawn from one industry to switch to another industry; the bigger the economy we are dealing with, the easier this will be. But adjustment problems, some temporary and others longer-run, can be quite challenging in cases like this. Not only is direct income from the affected industries reduced, but the secondary effects on support and service industries can be impacted. It is adjustment costs of this type that have made natural resource management politically sensitive in many cases, such as the reduction of parts of the timbering industry in response to forest regulation and the reduction in a fishing fleet in response to attempts to reduce overfishing.

Regulatory programs often produce other types of costs in the form of **increased prices** paid by consumers. The model of Figure 9-3 did not have this, because it was assumed that only a segment of a much larger industry was involved, and so the regulation would not be expected to affect output price. But with regulations affecting all, or a substantial portion, of an industry, consumers may experience **price effects.** These are costs in a sense different from the notion of opportunity costs. When prices paid by consumers change, there is a gain or loss in welfare: a gain to consumers if prices drop and a loss to consumers if they go up. Figure 9-4 gives the relevant analysis. Here there is a downward-sloping demand function and horizontal marginal cost/supply relationship. The initial price-quantity situation is p_1, q_1. A regulation is now enacted that has the effect of lifting the marginal cost curve to $MC_2 = S_2$. Price now rises to p_2, which makes consumers worse off. By how much? If we took the original quantity q_1 and multiplied it by the price increase, we would get an amount equal to $b + e + f$. But here again, we would expect consumers to respond to the price increase. In the figure, quantity drops to q_2. Looking at the change in net benefits brought on by the cost increase, we see that this comes out to be $b + e$.[9] The adjustment in quantity reduces the cost to consumers relative to what would have been the case with no quantity change.

To estimate this cost, especially to predict it ex ante, we must know not only what the change in cost will be, but also the **conditions of demand** in the industry. This is an important lesson. To measure the costs of the regulation, we must know both costs and the demand function facing the industry that we are studying.

SUMMARY

This chapter is devoted to a discussion of how analysts actually measure the benefits and costs flowing from specific natural resource utilization situations. Benefits can be classified as **consumptive** vs. **nonconsumptive** and as **use** vs. **nonuse.** Nonuse benefits of natural resources consist of **option, existence,** and **bequest** values. In many cases, **direct market prices** can be used to measure benefits of different types of natural resource use; sometimes these prices must

---

[9] Net benefits before the change are $(a + b + c + d + e) - (c + d) = a + b + e$. After the change they are $(a + b + c) - (b + c) = a$. Thus, the change is $b + e$.

be adjusted to take into account external costs and benefits. Market prices may also be used **indirectly,** in cases where natural resource use is closely connected to the consumption of a marketed commodity (e.g., the value of open space in the vicinity of houses). Travel cost analysis has frequently been used to estimate the benefits of outdoor recreation. For nonmarket benefits the most commonly used method is **contingent valuation,** which is essentially a survey technique in which respondents are asked directly about their willingness to pay for using natural resources in certain ways.

Cost measurement often seems easier than benefit measurement, but accurate cost estimates can often be difficult to estimate. In cases where physical-type projects are involved (e.g., dams, wildlife refuges, irrigation works) the relevant concept is **opportunity costs,** being the value the inputs could have produced in their next best alternative use. For regulatory-type programs (e.g., regulations on clear-cutting, regulations on access to fisheries), there may be both opportunity cost changes, as firms respond to the regulations, and costs to consumers stemming from **price changes** in markets for goods and services.

KEY TERMS

Active (use) values	Market prices as measure of value
Passive (nonuse) values	Shadow (accounting) prices
Consumptive values	Hedonic analysis
Nonconsumptive values	Travel cost analysis
Option values	Contingent valuation
Existence values	Opportunity costs
Bequest values	Costs of price changes

QUESTIONS FOR FURTHER DISCUSSION

1 Distinguish between use values and nonuse values in the specific case of preserving the quality of water in an underground aquifer. How might you measure the different types of benefits in this case?

2 A proposal is being made to ban the use of a particular type of gear used by vessels engaged in a certain saltwater fishery. Indicate conceptually how costs would be measured in this case. How might the necessary data be obtained?

3 What is the conceptual relationship between use values, consumptive values, and market values?

4 A proposal has been put forward to remove a dam on a river, which currently produces hydroelectric power. You have been hired to estimate the costs (not the benefits) of this action. What are the main types of costs in this case, and how might you go about measuring each type?

5 What types of questions might you put in a contingent valuation study being done to estimate the benefits of limiting timber harvesting in certain areas so as to preserve habitat for the spotted owl?

6 Select one of the scenarios given at the beginning of the chapter. Propose a way of answering the question posed in the scenario using one (or more) of the techniques discussed in the chapter.

USEFUL WEB SITES

See the material under nonmarket valuation at

- Resources for the Future (http://www.rff.org)

The USEPA's program in economy and environment has many links to work on benefits measurement:

- (http://www.epa.gov/docs/oppe/eaed/eedhmpg.htm)

Many countries have developed programs in benefits measurement, for example,

- Australian Bureau of Agricultural and Resource Economics (http://www.abare.gov.au).

For a private firm in the valuation business, see

- Damage Valuation Associates, Environmental Damage Valuation and Cost Benefit Web Site (http://www.damagevaluation.com)

SELECTED READINGS

Bateman, Ian, and Ken Willis (eds.): *Valuing Environmental Preferences: Theory and Practice of the Contingent Valuation Method in the U.S., EC, and Developing Countries,* Oxford University Press, Oxford, England.

Batie, Sandra, and Leonard Shabman, "Estimating the Economic Value of Wetlands," *Coastal Zone Management Journal,* Vol. 10, 1982, pp. 255–278.

Brookshire, David S., et al., "Valuing Public Goods: A Comparison of Survey and Hedonic Approaches," *American Economic Review,* 72 (1), March 1982, pp. 165–177.

Constanza, Robert, et al., "The Value of the World's Ecosystem Services and Natural Capital," *Nature,* Vol. 387, May 15, 1997, pp. 253–260.

Cummings, R. G., D. S. Brookshire, and W. D. Schulze, *Valuing Environmental Goods: An Assessment of the Contingent Valuation Method,* Rowman and Littlefield Publishers, Savage, MD, 1986.

Diamond, P., and J. Hansman: "Contingent Valuation: Is Some Number Better than No Number?" *Journal of Economic Perspectives,* Vol. 8, 1994, pp. 45–64.

Freeman, A. Myrick, III: "Nonuse Values in Natural Resource Damage Assessment," in Raymond J. Kopp and V. Kerry Smith (eds.), *Valuing Natural Resource Assets: The Economics of Natural Resource Damage Assessment,* Resources for the Future, Washington, DC, 1993, pp. 264–303.

Freeman, A. Myrick, III: *The Measurement of Environmental and Resource Values, Theory and Methods,* Resources for the Future, Washington, DC, 1993.

Hannemann, W. Michael: "Valuing the Environment through Contingent Valuation," *Journal of Economic Perspectives,* 8 (4), Fall 1994, pp. 19–44.

Hannemann, W. Michael, "Preface: Notes on the History of Environmental Valuation in the U.S.," in Stale Narud (ed.), *Pricing the Environment, The European Experience,* Oxford University Press, London, 1992, pp. 9–35.

Mitchell, R. C., and R. T. Carson: *Using Surveys to Value Public Goods: The Contingent Valuation Method,* Resources for the Future, Washington, DC, 1989.

Portney, Paul: "The Contingent Valuation Debate: Why Economists Should Care," *Journal of Economic Perspectives,* 8 (4), Fall 1994, pp. 3–18.

Smith, V. Kerry: "Lightning Rods, Dart Boards and Contingent Valuation," *Natural Resources Journal,* 1994.

Smith, V. Kerry: *Estimating Economic Values for Nature: Methods for Non-Market Valuation,* Edward Elgar, Cheltenham, England, 1996.

APPLIED NATURAL
RESOURCE PROBLEMS

The remainder of the book is devoted to the analysis of specific resource problems. Volumes could be written about each of these resources simply to describe all the challenging issues that currently exist. The physical, demographic, and economic diversity of the world, and of the United States itself, is so immense that it creates a corresponding diversity in natural resource issues. Major differences exist between eastern and western America in terms of the types of natural resource problems that are most important. This is also true of the north-south dimension. We cannot cover each resource comprehensively in the individual chapters. Rather, we shall survey some of the most important of these problems, and employ simple tools of economic analysis to clarify them and point toward their possible solution.

CHAPTER 10

MINERAL ECONOMICS

"**Mineral**" refers to the wide range of inorganic solid substances, which are normally found in or on the ground and which are used by humans for a great variety of purposes. We can distinguish between **fuel** and **nonfuel minerals;** the former will be covered in the chapter on energy. Nonfuel minerals can be further subdivided into **metals** and **industrial minerals.** The major classes of metals are the **ores,** such as iron, nickel, and bauxite, and the **precious metals.** Important classes of industrial minerals are the **natural aggregates** (crushed rock, sand, gravel), **cement, fertilizer minerals** (phosphate rock, potash), **abrasives,** and **gem stones.** Table 10-1 presents a list of the quantities and values of selected minerals produced in the United States in 1996. Of the metals, copper and gold together accounted for two-thirds of the total value of production. In industrial metals, cement, sand and gravel, and crushed stone represented about 70 percent of the total.

A mineral appears to fit the classic definition of the **nonrenewable resource,** one for which $\Delta S = 0$ in the terminology of Chapter 2. For a given deposit, the quantity of material would appear to be strictly nonreplenishable, hence one that can only be drawn down over time. In the next section we see that this state of affairs is somewhat ambiguous, because minerals normally exist in different **grades.** The notion of nonrenewability is sufficiently compelling in the case of minerals, however, that our first analytical job will be to explore conceptually the simple but classic question: Given that there is a

TABLE 10-1
U.S. PRODUCTION OF SELECTED MINERALS, 1996

	Quantity*	Value†	U.S. production as percent of world production
Metals			
Copper	1,920	4,610,000	12
Gold	321,000	4,030,000	14
Iron ore	62,200	1,770,000	6
Lead	426,000	459,000	15
Magnesium	133,000	455,000	—
Molybdenum	57,900	456,000	43
Silver	1,570	263,000	10
Other	—	957,000	—
Total	—	13,000,000	—
Industrial Minerals			
Boron	1,150,000	519,000	39
Bromine	227,000	150,000	50
Cement	78,270	5,631,000	5
Clays	43,138	1,709,800	—
Lime	19,100	1,140,000	16
Phosphate	45,400	1,060,000	32
Salt	42,900	1,060,000	22
Sand and gravel	941,800	4,497,000	24
Crushed stone	1,330,000	7,180,000	—
Other	—	2,853,200	—
Total	—	25,800,000	—

*Thousand metric tons, except gold, expressed in kilograms.
†Thousands of dollars.
Source: U.S. Geological Survey, Minerals Information, 1996, Statistical Summary, Washington, DC, USGS, 1998, Tables 1 and 9.

certain quantity of a nonrenewable resource available in a deposit, how fast should it be extracted and used? We then take up the broader question of **exploration, discovery, and development** of mineral deposits, where the question is no longer only how fast to run down known stocks but also how much to spend on finding new stocks. Finally, since minerals are the major component of materials, we focus on the economics of recycling.

GEOLOGICAL FACTORS AND COSTS OF EXTRACTION

Copper is widely distributed throughout the world. In fact the copper content of a randomly chosen bucket of the earth's crust contains 63 parts per million (ppm) of copper. But copper is actually mined in a selected number of spots, where the concentration of copper in the ore is substantially higher than this. It is high enough, in other words, that it can be extracted and refined at reasonable cost, with current extraction technologies. Thus, although copper (and

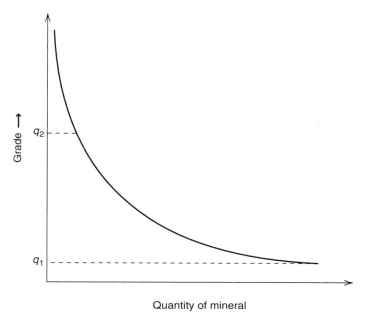

FIGURE 10-1
Relationship between Grade (Mineral Content per Quantity of Material)
and Total Quantity

most other minerals) is a nonrenewable resource in some ultimate physical sense, there is actually a long grade-quantity continuum like that pictured in Figure 10-1. Relatively few very high-grade deposits exist, but at progressively lower grades, the potential supply increases. Some very low-grade deposits, indicated by g_1 in the figure, correspond to average crustal abundance of the mineral, at which the potential supply is extremely large. The profile appears to be very definite, but it is actually quite speculative. Under technology available at present, there is some **cutoff grade,** such as the one indicated by g_2 in Figure 10-1, representing the minimum grade that can be economically extracted and refined. Geological exploration and conjecture may give us a reasonably good idea about how much is currently available at or above this cutoff grade, but how the relationship looks between g_1 and g_2 is much more uncertain. It may rise smoothly and steeply, or it may have bumps at various points. The actual relationship will be revealed only in the fullness of time, as geological theory and exploration progress.

Thus, as the mineral grade decreases, known and expected quantities increase. Also, as grade decreases, the costs of extraction and refining increase. So when it comes to the economics of extraction and supply for "nonrenewables" like minerals, there are essentially two questions to address: (1) Given a deposit of known quantity and grade, what is the socially efficient rate at which that deposit should be used up? (2) What is the economically efficient rate at which geological exploration should be pursued in order to expand our knowledge of known deposits? How much should be devoted, in other words, to geological exploration and discovery? We focus on these two questions in turn.

EXTRACTION ECONOMICS FOR A KNOWN STOCK

In this section we look at the simple economics of a nonrenewable resource in which the basic question is: Given that there is a known quantity of a nonrenewable resource, how fast should it be extracted and used? To address this in a simple but revealing way, we limit the analysis to just two time periods, this year and next year. A two-period analysis is clearly unrealistic, but the essence of efficiency in this case is the balance that is achieved between "today" and the "future," and the logic of this trade-off can be explored quite well with this simple model.

Suppose there exists demand or marginal willingness-to-pay curves for this resource in each of the two years, as shown by the MWTP curves of Figure 10-2 (a) and (b). They are the same. Today, the MWTP curve is known because it is happening now, and the assumption is that the MWTP curve of the next period is going to be like that of today's.[1] The marginal extraction cost curves, labeled MC_0 and MC_1, are also expected to be the same; they are, in fact, linear and sloped upward to the right, as depicted in the figure. These are assumed to be the aggregate marginal cost curves for a competitive extraction industry, that is, one composed of a substantial number of individual firms.

According to the situation depicted in Figure 10-2 (a) and (b), statically efficient extraction levels of this resource (identified by the condition MWTP = MC) are the same in each period: 200 units.[2] If the total quantity of resource available were greater than 400 units, there would essentially be no problem; the resource could be extracted at its static efficiency level in each period. The efficient multiple-period production plan in this simple case would be to produce the same output each year. But suppose the total amount of this resource were less than 400 units, for example 300 units. An extraction rate of 200 units each year for 2 years now would exceed the total availability of the resources; thus **extracting more today means having to extract less next year, and vice versa.** In order to determine our efficient intertemporal production plan, this overall limit on the amount of the natural resource must be taken into account.

It is easiest to work this problem out with a little algebra. Static efficiency required the choice of a single output rate, but it is now necessary to identify, simultaneously, two rates of output, one for the first year and one for the second. As mentioned above, the maximand in the multiple-year case is the

---

[1] Of course if the next period's MWTP curve is highly uncertain, this may add some complexity to the problem that we might want to explore, but for now we overlook this issue.

[2] Remember again the convention we are using. The present period is indexed with 0, and the next period with 1. Thus, q_0 and q_1 refer, respectively, to current (this year's) output and next year's output.

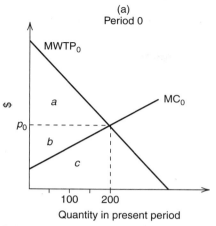
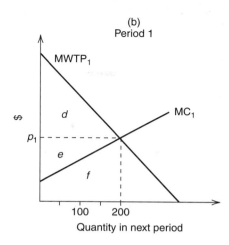

FIGURE 10-2
Extraction of a Nonrenewable Resource

present value of net benefits, which in the case of the two-period model is given as

$$\text{Present value of net} \atop \text{benefits (PVNB)} = \left(\begin{array}{c}\text{Net benefits}\\\text{in year 0}\end{array}\right) + \frac{1}{1+r}\left(\begin{array}{c}\text{Net benefits}\\\text{in year 1}\end{array}\right)$$

Remember that r is the discount rate.

The **trade-off** inherent in the intertemporal problem is depicted in the two terms to the right of the equals sign. Starting from some initial output levels q_0 and q_1, if q_0 is changed, it will change the first of the right-side terms in one direction, but also, through its impacts on q_1, will change the second of the terms in the **opposite direction.** If output increases in period 1, it must decrease in period 2. The two output rates that give a maximum of PVNB are the rates where the change in this year's net benefits and the change in next year's net benefits (discounted) are exactly offsetting. This condition can be written as

$$\text{Change in net} \atop \text{benefits in year 0} = \frac{1}{1+r}\left(\begin{array}{c}\text{Change in net}\\\text{benefits in year 1}\end{array}\right)$$

If the output in either of the years is changed a small amount, the change in net benefits is equal to MWTP − MC for that year. Thus, the last expression can be rewritten as

$$\text{MWTP}_0 - \text{MC}_0 = \frac{1}{1+r}(\text{MWTP}_1 - \text{MC}_1)$$

The intertemporally efficient time profile of extraction is the two extraction rates q_0 and q_1 that satisfy this equality.

Let us now shift from MWTP to price. Any quantity corresponds to a distinct level of MWTP. Any quantity also is associated with a distinct **market clearing price,** that price for which the quantity demanded exactly equals the quantity in question. In competitive situations, prices will adjust to their market clearing levels. In fact, the market clearing price for any quantity is the MWTP for that quantity, and so we can replace the last expression with

$$p_0 - MC_0 = \frac{1}{1+r}(p_1 - MC_1)$$

To draw out the implications of this last expression, consider an initial production profile in which $q_0 = q_1$, as depicted in panel (a) of Figure 10-3. Since

FIGURE 10-3
Panel (a): A Flat Productive Profile. Panel (b): An Intertemporally Efficient Production Profile

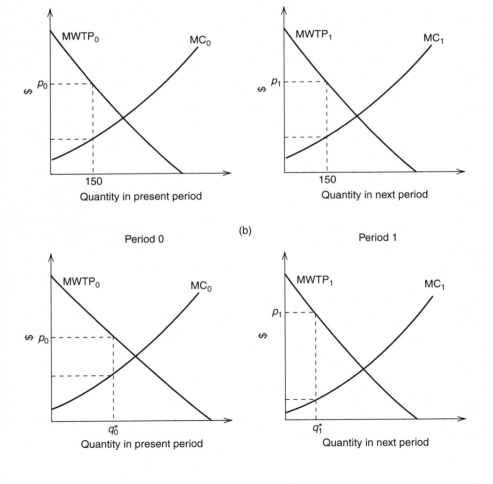

both marginal willingness-to-pay curves and marginal cost curves are the same in the two periods, this production profile would imply that $p_0 - MC_0 = p_1 - MC_1$. But if this were true, it would also be true that

$$p_0 - MC_0 \neq \frac{1}{1+r}(p_1 - MC_1)$$

as long as $r > 0$. This means that the equal production profile ($q_0 = q_1$) does not satisfy the condition for intertemporal efficiency. To satisfy that condition, the term on the left of the last expression must be reduced and that on the right must be increased.

The way to accomplish this is to increase q_0 and decrease q_1, because increasing q_0 will decrease $p_0 - MC_0$ as we move down the $MWTP_1$ curve, whereas decreasing q_1 will move us up the MWTP curve and therefore increase $p_1 - MC_1$. So this leads to the following conclusion: The dynamically efficient production profile involves a "tilt" toward the present, in the sense that extraction in the first year q_0 exceeds that of the second year q_1. This situation is depicted in panel (b) of Figure 10-3, with the efficient values of q_0 and q_1 labeled q_0^* and q_1^*.

Having found that intertemporal efficiency implies $q_0 > q_1$, we now see (on the assumption that the demand and supply curves are the same in each period) that it also implies $p_0 < p_1$. In other words, the efficient production profile also implies a rising price profile. In an intertemporally efficient situation, the **extraction profile is tilted toward the present** and the **price profile is tilted toward the future.**

Capital Values

The reason that extraction profiles are tilted toward the present is the presence of the discount rate. If the rate were zero, the efficient extraction profile would be flat. What is the economic logic behind this situation? To see this more clearly, remember the term that we introduced earlier: **resource rent.** Resource rent is the value of a marginal unit of the resource **in situ**—in other words, what it would be worth if somehow an extra unit of the resource could be added to the size of the deposit. The value of the rent in the first period is $p_0 - MC_0$, whereas the rental value in the second period is $p_1 - MC_1$. But efficiency requires that

$$p_0 - MC_0 = \frac{1}{1+r}(p_1 - MC_1)$$

which can be expressed as

$$Rent_1 = (1 + r)\, Rent_0$$

The optimal extraction profile is the one that yields a rent that rises at the rate of discount r.

In this perspective the mineral deposit is looked at as a form of capital asset. An efficient production profile is one that causes the value of this asset to appreciate at the same rate as other forms of capital that owners might hold. Finding the efficient extraction rate, in other words, is tantamount to maximizing the value of a portfolio of capital assets.

User Costs

Another informative way of analyzing the situation is with **user cost.** In this two-period example, an increase of one unit of extraction today means a decrease of one unit in period 1; the value of the latter would be a sum equal to the future marginal willingness to pay p_1 minus future extraction cost MC_1. The **user cost,** in other words, is $p_1 - MC_1$, and its present value is

$$\frac{1}{1 + r}(p_1 - MC_1)$$

Figure 10-4 shows a new version of the efficiency aspects of choosing a present period extraction rate, one that incorporates the user costs of first-period extraction decisions. The marginal willingness-to-pay curve is the same as before, as is the MC_0 curve, showing marginal costs of first-period extraction. The dotted curve that starts at $q_0 = q_0^0$ and goes up to the right is the user cost. At rates below q_0^0, user cost is zero, because at this rate or anything below, this first-period use is so low that it would not detract from availabilities in the next period.[3] The solid line labeled $MC_0 + UC$ shows the sum of marginal extraction cost and user cost. This curve intersects the $MWTP_0$ curve at an output level of q_0^*, which is the efficient rate of output in the first period. Compare this to the static efficiency level q_0^1.

As we discussed earlier, the concept of user cost provides a useful way of thinking about how efficient current and future extraction rates would be affected by changes in some of the factors in the model. Suppose, for example, that we expect the marginal extraction costs in period 1 to be higher than those of period 0, because smaller resource stocks make extraction more costly.[4] There is now another consequence of increasing first-period extraction rates, and this will have the effect of increasing the user cost. Current extraction, in other words, not only reduces future availabilities but also makes future extraction more costly. The increased user cost in period 0 implies that the first-period efficient extraction rate is decreased. So the expectation of future ex-

---

[3] For example, suppose the total availability is 300 units. We know that extraction in the next period would never exceed 200 units (refers back to Figure 10-1) because $MC > p$ beyond 200 units. Thus, if the use rate in year 0 is less than 100 units, there will be no economically relevant restriction on availability in year 1; that is, user cost below 100 units will be zero. Above 100 units, of course, user costs are positive and increasing, as pictured in Figure 10-4.

[4] In fact, for many resources, extraction costs have been decreasing for a long time Technological change has been the dominant factor in this long-run trend.

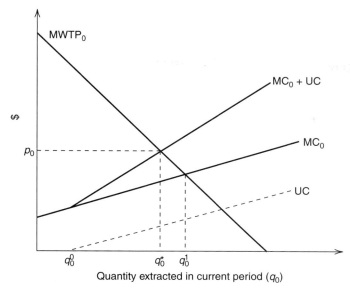

FIGURE 10-4
Efficient Extraction Rate in Current Period

traction cost increases results in a smaller degree of tilt in the time profile of extraction rates, as compared to the case of no increase in extraction costs.

Another future change that might be expected is population growth. This would have the effect, in our simple model, of pushing out the MWTP curve for the second period. And this would have the effect of increasing the user cost of extraction today. The implication is that the intertemporally efficient rate of extraction in period 0 would decrease. This is true of other factors, such as income growth, that have the effect of shifting out the future demand curve.

This abstract modeling exercise tells us something about a time profile of resource extraction that would be intertemporally efficient. We know that competitive markets with profit maximizing firms having good foresight will produce efficient use rates; this is true in both static and dynamic situations. So if we have a nonrenewable resource with a reasonably competitive extraction sector, we might expect to see the results we got above: diminishing extraction rates and increasing market prices over time.

In fact, for very few, if any, nonrenewable resources do we see this pattern in the historical record. Instead, we see, almost everywhere, **increasing extraction rates** and **declining prices.** How do we explain this? One immediately obvious factor could be increases in populations and in real incomes. By shifting out future demand functions relative to today's, this would lower current user costs and shift extraction profiles more toward the future. We might still expect prices to go up, however, as resource scarcities become more pronounced. Yet we do not observe them going up. Why?

RESOURCE EXPLORATION AND DEVELOPMENT

A major factor that we have to bring in at this point is the cost of natural resource **exploration, discovery, and development,** that is, the costs of adding to reserves. Individual deposits usually contain fixed quantities of a resource, but it is unlikely to be true that all deposits are currently known. In most cases, exploration and development can increase the inventory of known deposits. With continuous exploration effort, the stock of new deposits, or new reserves, may be pushed out more or less continuously. Of course the effectiveness of exploration and development will vary from mineral to mineral. We will see, for example, that some capable people are predicting a substantial falloff in the rate of discovery of new petroleum deposits in the world.[5] But for many minerals we may expect new deposits to be found and developed with some regularity.

Another important phenomenon is developments in extraction technology. Better extraction methods can make it possible to extract resources of lower grades. These new methods will expand the available inventory of extractable deposits, similar to the exploration process discussed above. Let us suppose that we can summarize these factors with what we will call a **resource discovery function.** As pictured in panel (a) of Figure 10-5, this shows the **marginal cost of expanding reserves.** It is drawn with a positive and increasing slope. At a reserve level of r_1 the marginal cost of an additional unit of reserves is c_1. Expanding reserves from r_1 to r_2 units would take a total of b dollars, and at r_2, marginal discovery costs would be c_2. Remember that we are talking here about the quantity of reserves, not the quantity of material extracted.

Panel (b) of Figure 10-5 depicts the supply and demand circumstances for reserves. The supply function is simply the marginal cost function depicted in the top panel. The demand function represents the willingness to pay by a firm or firms for additional quantities of reserve. The intersection of these curves shows the market price that will tend to be established for quantities of materials held in reserve. Furthermore, this price is sensitive to technological changes that take place in the reserve discovery function. These technological changes are represented by a downward shift in the resource discovery function. In the figure the marginal costs of discovery function shifts from MC_1 to MC_2. As it shifts downward because of these technical improvements, the price of reserve quantities goes down, and the quantity of reserves increases.

Consider now a firm that engages in resource extraction and exploration. It has essentially two big decisions to make: (1) how much to extract this year and (2) how much effort to devote to expanding reserves. These two decisions are closely related. A way of understanding this is to see that a firm (or group of firms) in this position has essentially two ways of adding to future stocks: (1) by reducing today's extraction rate and (2) by finding new stocks. If the

---

[5] See Chapter 11.

(a)

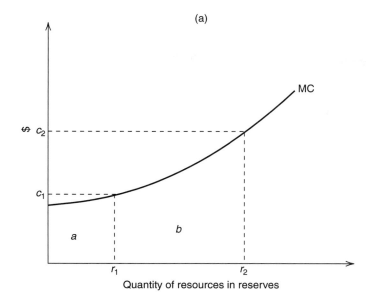

Quantity of resources in reserves

(b)

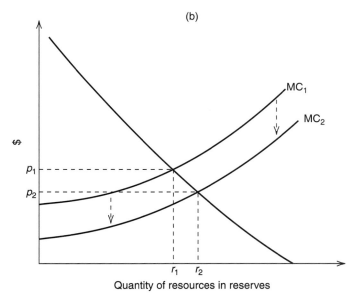

Quantity of resources in reserves

FIGURE 10-5
Resource Discovery Function

firm is making efficient decisions, it will adjust so that the marginal costs of these two activities are the same. But the cost of adding to reserves by cutting back today's extraction is simply the rental rate, or in situ price of the resource, while the cost of adding to resource stocks is the marginal cost of discovery. What this chain of reasoning allows us to conclude is that there is another important factor behind the perceived historical drops in mineral prices: the historical reductions in exploration and development costs.

NONRENEWABLE RESOURCES AND SUSTAINABILITY

With renewable resources it is not too hard to envisage long-run, or sustainable, rates of production. But with minerals this is not possible. Minerals, once used, are gone forever. How, then, can a nonrenewable resource be used in a sustainable fashion? There are two ways of doing this:

1 Consider mineral use, or the use of any particular mineral, as a transition process in which we will eventually shift to a substitute resource of greater abundance.
2 Invest the rents earned from current mineral extraction into other types of assets so as to maintain the overall productivity of the economy even though the supply of minerals diminishes.

Let us consider each of these ideas.

Switch to a Substitute

Recall that in our simple two-period model, the condition for an efficient time profile of production was

$$p_0 - MC_0 = (p_1 - MC_1)\frac{1}{1 + r}$$

which can be rewritten as

$$p_1 = \underset{\underset{\text{in second year}}{\text{Production costs}}}{MC_1} + \underset{\underset{\text{first year}}{\text{Rent in}}}{(p_0 - MC_0)} \quad \underset{\underset{\text{interest formula}}{\text{Compound}}}{(1 + r)}$$

This leads to the following conclusion: If extraction costs are constant, we should see the prices of nonrenewable resources increase through time. But how long will this go on? Eventually, if there were no substitutes, the price would get high enough to choke off economic growth, a nonsustainable result. But suppose there are high-priced but superabundant substitutes. For petroleum, a nonrenewable resource, there is solar energy, a substitute that is both renewable and in very large supply (except perhaps in polar regions of the

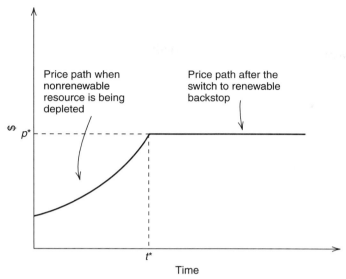

FIGURE 10-6
Long-Run Price Path with a Backstop Resource

world). At some relatively high price it will presumably be efficient to shift to this new resource, which is sometimes called a **backstop resource** or **backstop technology.** So in the very long run, the path of price might be expected to look like that depicted in Figure 10-6.

Up until year t^*, which of course may be a very long time in the future, the price rises in accordance with the expression above for the period during which the resource is being depleted. But when the price reaches p^* (at time t^*), the renewable backstop resource kicks in, and the path of price now becomes level, essentially forever. In other words, the nonrenewable resource has been extracted during a transition period; it has been a bridge resource allowing us to get eventually to the renewable one. Of course, several stages of nonrenewables could be depleted before reaching the final backstop (wood to coal to petroleum to solar). In the diagram this would give several more upward-trending price path segments before reaching the horizontal path.

How possible is this type of scenario? Perhaps much more plausible than we might be able to appreciate. We are talking of the extremely long run here, not the next few decades, or even the next half century. The average person finds it quite hard to extrapolate a long way into the future. But the average person is also a little nervous in assuming that a backstop resource will be available whenever an important nonrenewable gets very scarce, and also about the ability of ordinary humans to adjust to continually elevated rates of technical change. In some cases (solar energy, desalination, industrial diamonds) backstop technologies are sufficiently predictable now that we can believe in their future practicability. In many cases (production of food and clothing), however, future technical backstops are harder to visualize.

Invest Rents

Consider again the efficient extraction path studied above. One of its implications is that $q_1 < q_0$, that is, the amount extracted in the second period will be less than that of the first. Extractive resources of this type are usually not consumed directly by consumers, but are used to produce consumer goods. Suppose that to produce $10 of national income, you need exactly 1 ton of the nonrenewable resource, no more and no less.[6] This declining resource extraction path would also imply a diminishing consumption path (with no imports). This is not a sustainable profile, because sustainability means, at the very least, nondiminution. How can we convert this to a sustainable outcome? Suppose it is possible to produce the same output with fewer resources, provided that we substitute other forms of capital (say, tractors, fertilizers, better seeds, or better management) for the diminished natural capital. We can do this by investing in these other types of productive capital; in other words, the effects of the reduced resource use can be offset. Where does the money come from for investing in the other capital? From the **resource rents** earned from the extraction of the nonrenewable resources.

The conditions that need to be satisfied in order to have a sustainable (i.e., nondiminishing) consumption path have been worked out. It is essentially that the total stock of productive capital of the economy be nondiminishing. The total capital stock is equal to the stock of natural resource capital plus the stock of human-made capital. The latter can include both **machine-type capital** and, most importantly, **human capital.** To maintain this total capital stock, the rents achieved from extracting the nonrenewable resource must be invested in these alternative forms of capital.[7] This, then, is the rule for extracting a nonrenewable resource in a sustainable way.

MINERALS PRICES IN FACT

In theory, if nonrenewable resources are becoming more scarce, we should observe their prices rising. What has actually happened to these prices over the last few decades? Figure 10-7 shows the real prices of nine important minerals from the late 1960s to the early 1990s. In very general terms, there has been quite a lot of up-and-down movement in many of them, but certainly no

---

[6] In fact, over time this ratio has increased, that is, changes in the economy have reduced the resource intensity of production. But making this assumption here allows us to make a particular point more clearly.

[7] This is an application of the old idea of a **sinking fund.** When using a productive asset like a machine, one sets aside each year an amount equal to the **depreciation** of the machine, so that by the time the machine wears out, there will be just enough in the sinking fund to buy a new machine.

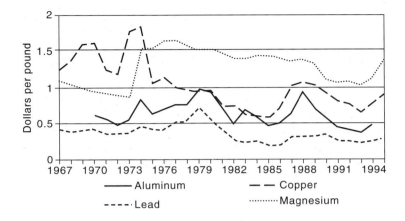

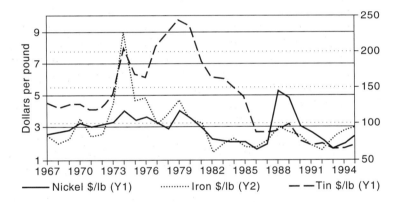

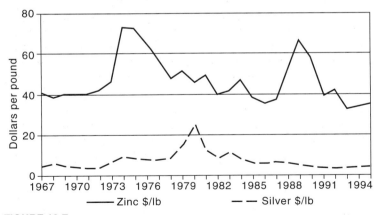

FIGURE 10-7
Real Prices of Selected Minerals, 1967–1995 (*Source:* Jeffrey A. Krautkraemer, "Nonrenewable Resource Scarcity," *Journal of Economic Literature,* 46(4), December 1998, pp. 2065–2107.)

discernible trend upward for any of them. There was a brief period in the early 1970s when the prices of many minerals shot upward. That was a time when many observers began talking ominously about how natural resource scarcities were about to threaten the world and bring the developed economies to a grinding halt. It did not happen.[8] In a few years most prices came right back down. Several prices spiked again in the late 1980s, but this was again followed by a marked drop. In real terms (i.e., after adjusting for the effects of general inflation), minerals prices were lower at the end of the period than they were in the 1960s.

There are two major factors behind this drop in prices. First, the market simply does not see a quantitative restriction in these resources, despite the fact that we are calling them nonrenewable resources. Certain deposits may be limited in quantity, and in some purely physical sense there must be some upper limit to their quantity, but this is simply not a relevant limitational factor from the standpoint of today's markets. When comparing present and projected human use with what we know about expected future availabilities, market participants simply see no particular reason why prices should go up in any relevant human-scale time frame.

The second factor causing prices to drop is technical change along the whole continuum of natural resource exploration, discovery, development, extraction, transportation, and processing. This is happening much faster than increases in demand, with the result that prices are being driven down over time. In the context of our simple model presented earlier in this chapter, it means simply that the costs in the second period are substantially lower than those of the first. In that case there is no reason for the price of the extracted mineral to increase; it will go down if the drop in costs is large enough.

Thus the big question is, can we expect technical change to continue into the indefinite future sufficient to forestall significant increases in mineral prices? Some people feel that technological change can be maintained indefinitely, but others believe that in the very long run it will be impossible to sustain for all time a phenomenon that is, after all, relatively recent in the history of the human race.

U.S. MINERAL IMPORT DEPENDENCE

A recurrent problem in U.S. minerals use is the heavy dependence on imports to supply domestic demands. Figure 10-8 depicts data on U.S. import

---

[8] This was the time of a famous wager between two public personalities on the future of resource prices. Paul Erhlich, an ecologist and strong pessimist about resource scarcity, made a widely publicized bet with Julian Simon, an equally strong optimist. Erhlich was to select five commodities (he chose nickel, tin, copper, chrome, and tungsten). He would hypothetically invest $200 in each commodity as of 1980. In 10 years he would calculate the real prices of the five items. If they had gone up in price from 1980, Simon would pay Erhlich the amount of the aggregate increase; if they went down Erhlich would pay Simon the amount of the aggregate decrease. In 1990 Erhlich sent Simon a check for $576.07.

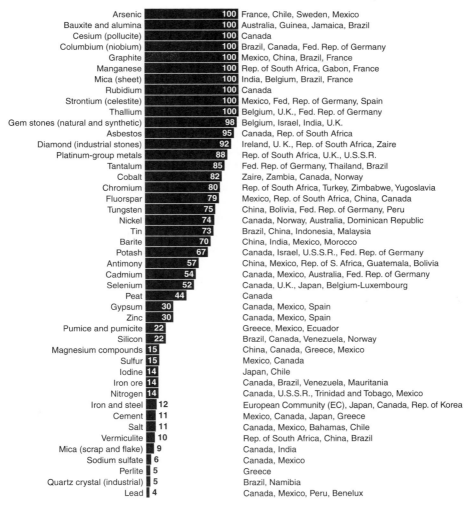

Arsenic	100	France, Chile, Sweden, Mexico
Bauxite and alumina	100	Australia, Guinea, Jamaica, Brazil
Cesium (pollucite)	100	Canada
Columbium (niobium)	100	Brazil, Canada, Fed. Rep. of Germany
Graphite	100	Mexico, China, Brazil, France
Manganese	100	Rep. of South Africa, Gabon, France
Mica (sheet)	100	India, Belgium, Brazil, France
Rubidium	100	Canada
Strontium (celestite)	100	Mexico, Fed, Rep. of Germany, Spain
Thallium	100	Belgium, U.K., Fed. Rep. of Germany
Gem stones (natural and synthetic)	98	Belgium, Israel, India, U.K.
Asbestos	95	Canada, Rep. of South Africa
Diamond (industrial stones)	92	Ireland, U. K., Rep. of South Africa, Zaire
Platinum-group metals	88	Rep. of South Africa, U.K., U.S.S.R.
Tantalum	85	Fed. Rep. of Germany, Thailand, Brazil
Cobalt	82	Zaire, Zambia, Canada, Norway
Chromium	80	Rep. of South Africa, Turkey, Zimbabwe, Yugoslavia
Fluorspar	79	Mexico, Rep. of South Africa, China, Canada
Tungsten	75	China, Bolivia, Fed. Rep. of Germany, Peru
Nickel	74	Canada, Norway, Australia, Dominican Republic
Tin	73	Brazil, China, Indonesia, Malaysia
Barite	70	China, India, Mexico, Morocco
Potash	67	Canada, Israel, U.S.S.R., Fed. Rep. of Germany
Antimony	57	China, Mexico, Rep. of S. Africa, Guatemala, Bolivia
Cadmium	54	Canada, Mexico, Australia, Fed. Rep. of Germany
Selenium	52	Canada, U.K., Japan, Belgium-Luxembourg
Peat	44	Canada
Gypsum	30	Canada, Mexico, Spain
Zinc	30	Canada, Mexico, Spain
Pumice and pumicite	22	Greece, Mexico, Ecuador
Silicon	22	Brazil, Canada, Venezuela, Norway
Magnesium compounds	15	China, Canada, Greece, Mexico
Sulfur	15	Mexico, Canada
Iodine	14	Japan, Chile
Iron ore	14	Canada, Brazil, Venezuela, Mauritania
Nitrogen	14	Canada, U.S.S.R., Trinidad and Tobago, Mexico
Iron and steel	12	European Community (EC), Japan, Canada, Rep. of Korea
Cement	11	Mexico, Canada, Japan, Greece
Salt	11	Canada, Mexico, Bahamas, Chile
Vermiculite	10	Rep. of South Africa, China, Brazil
Mica (scrap and flake)	9	Canada, India
Sodium sulfate	6	Canada, Mexico
Perlite	5	Greece
Quartz crystal (industrial)	5	Brazil, Namibia
Lead	4	Canada, Mexico, Peru, Benelux

FIGURE 10-8
Import Dependence for Selected Minerals (1992) (shaded area shows imports as a percentage of consumption) (*Source:* Oliver S. Owen and Daniel D. Chiras, *Natural Resource Conservation, Management for a Sustainable Future,* Prentice-Hall, Englewood Cliffs, NJ, 1995, p. 496.)

reliance for a number of the important industrial minerals. From time to time data like these are pointed to with alarm, as they seem to show how vulnerable the country would be to any actions that interrupt the flow of imports. The same issue exists in energy, especially petroleum, although the values involved in energy imports dwarf those of minerals. The **energy embargos** of the 1970s, engineered by the Organization of Petroleum Exporting Countries (OPEC), heightened fears that similar cartels of mineral suppliers could form and substantially raise the price of U.S. imports by restricting supplies.[9] How likely is this?

In the 1970s some bauxite producing countries sought to imitate the actions of OPEC and raise the export prices of their commodity. Similar actions were undertaken by some copper exporting countries. Neither effort was particularly successful. There is a wider appreciation now of the specific factors that apparently must be present if mineral producer **cartels** are going to be successful. A cartel is a group of producing countries (or a group of individual firms in the case of a private cartel) that act in concert to restrict supplies and raise prices. To be successful there are essentially two general requirements, one that is strictly economic and another that is more **political-economic.**

1 The demand for the commodity in question must be relatively price-inelastic; buyers will tend to purchase only slightly less even though the price increases.[10] In Figure 10-9 there are two demand curves, one steep (D_1) and one much less so (D_2). If quantity is currently at q_1 and the cartel is successful in restricting it to q_2, the price will increase much higher in the case of D_1 (to p_3) than in the case of D_2 (to p_2).
2 Enough countries to account for a substantial proportion of total production must be able to agree on, and enforce, joint action to limit supplies. They have to be collectively strong enough to be able to overcome the temptation each country will have to cheat on the agreement.

Condition 1 is satisfied quite well in practice. Minerals are **intermediate** goods; that is, they are used in the production of other goods rather than consumed directly. Their cost is usually a small fraction of the total cost of producing these goods. In the production of these goods it would normally take some time to develop substitutes for the metals in use. For both reasons, their consumption is unlikely to be particularly responsive to price. But one factor works in the opposite direction: the availability of supplies from countries that stay outside the cartel. Although the overall demand elasticity for a commodity may be low, for the output of countries in the cartel it could be relatively high if noncartel members are ready to make up cartel-sponsored supply reductions.

Condition 2 has several ramifications. Joint action is much more feasible if relatively few countries are involved. This is indeed the case with many minerals: World production is concentrated among a small number of countries. The

---

[9] High import dependence can lead to paranoid reactions. During the cold war there were those who were convinced that the Soviet Union was waging a "minerals war" against the United States.

[10] The **price elasticity of demand** measures the responsiveness of quantity changes to price changes along a demand function. It is defined as

$$\frac{\text{(percentage change in quantity)}}{\text{(percentage change in price)}}$$

Price-inelastic means that price changes do not produce large quantity changes. We will deal with this concept in greater detail in Chapter 17.

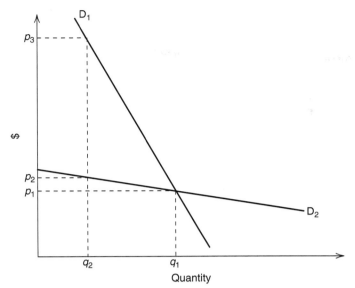

FIGURE 10-9
Quantity Restrictions and Price Increases

other major part of this, however, is that the countries must be able to make and to police agreements among themselves. In the past this has been the major weak point of attempts to form minerals cartels. Initial agreement is followed not long afterward by a breakdown in discipline and cohesion among the would-be participants. Even OPEC eventually succumbed to this problem, as well as to the problem of increased production by non-OPEC nations.

This phenomenon also needs to be looked at from the standpoint of the supplying countries. Many of these are developing countries, and many rely on exports of natural resource commodities, including nonfuel minerals, as important sources of income. In a later chapter on natural resources and economic development, we will revisit this issue from the perspective of the supplying countries.

OTHER POLICY ISSUES

Interest in minerals policy at the federal level in the United States waxes and wanes, generally in response to rapid price movements, either up or down. The Mining and Minerals Policy Act[11] of 1970 had the objective of making the federal government more active in encouraging the private mining sector in

(1) the development of economically sound and stable domestic mining, minerals, metals and minerals reclamation industries, (2) the orderly and economic development of domestic mineral resources, reserves and reclamation of metals and minerals

[11] Mining and Mineral Policy Act of 1970, PL 91-631, December 31, 1970, Vol. 84, *U.S. Statutes at Large,* p. 1876.

to help assure satisfaction of industrial, security and environmental needs, (3) mining, mineral and metallurgical research . . . and (4) the study and development of methods for disposal, control and reclamation of mineral waste products.

It did not outline specific steps to be undertaken to obtain these general objectives, however. Subsequently, the National Materials and Minerals Policy, Research and Development Act of 1980 was enacted. This law[12] directs the President to coordinate the relevant federal agency and private firm in programs of research and policy development to ensure adequate supplies of materials in the future. Note that the earlier law was in terms of "minerals" while the later law was written in terms of "materials," a more general term.

A problem that continues to gain some public attention is the possible revision of the **1872 Mining Law,** which regulates the prospecting and production of private minerals on public lands and which is still in effect. The law set up the **claim and patent system.** It allowed free access by prospectors onto public land and a system for filing claims on land found to contain economically significant minerals deposits. If the claim is developed, the prospector can have it patented, that is, converted to private ownership, at quite low prices. Critics over the years have sought to get the law changed, especially to raise significantly the prices that companies would have to pay to patent their claims and extract minerals from the public domain. One popular suggestion is to levy a federal royalty on produced minerals. In the present context a royalty is a tax based on the value of a commodity, such as a tax of "x" percent of the net value (price minus extraction costs) of a mineral delivered to the processing plant.

THE ECONOMICS OF RECYCLING

Recycling of nonrenewable resources serves both to reduce the draft on virgin supplies and to reduce the discharge of associated residuals back into the natural environment. Many resources change their chemical and physical nature so much during utilization that they cannot be recovered in useful form. This includes, for example, fossil energy resources, fertilizer minerals, and food resources such as fish and game. Other resources, however, finish their useful lives in forms that can be recycled as raw materials back into the production process. This includes many metals, wood and paper, and chemicals derived from petroleum.

The sequence of steps linking the initial removal of the material from the waste stream and its final reincorporation back into a final product can be complex both physically and economically.[13] It starts with the end users of the

---

[12] National Materials and Minerals Policy, Research and Development Act of 1980, PL 96-499, October 21, 1980, Vol. 94, *U.S. Statutes at Large*, p. 2306.

[13] It can also be very simple. Tag sales or garage sales link old users and new users together directly, so the entire recycling process is just a single transaction.

material in question; either they or some other entity must extract from the waste stream those materials destined for recycling. These materials then will often move through a sequence consisting of various combinations of steps: transporting, sorting, reconcentrating, reprocessing, and finally reuse. Sometimes these functions are accomplished by a single firm, but in most cases the activities of many different firms are coordinated by markets and by the forces of supply and demand that affect them.

There are several important questions when it comes to recycling. Suppose we target a particular material, say, aluminum cans. These can be manufactured from virgin raw material, the cost of which covers mining the bauxite, refining this into alumina and then aluminum, and finally manufacturing the cans. The cans can also be produced, in whole or in part, from used cans. The cost of the recycling covers retrieving them from the waste stream, reprocessing the aluminum, and then manufacturing the cans. There are several questions to ask here. First: What is the economically efficient level of recycling in this case? Next: Will current markets tend to produce this level of recycling, or is there a role for public oversight and perhaps intervention? If the answer to the latter is yes, what kind of policy is appropriate?

Figure 10-10 shows a very simple analysis of the recycling question; we can use it to look at how markets normally will function and the conditions under which they will be efficient. The demand curve, labeled D, shows the market

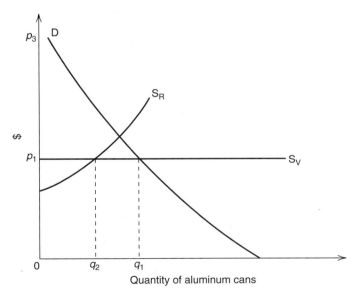

FIGURE 10-10
The Efficient Amount of Recycling

demand for aluminum cans. It's drawn with the standard downward-sloping shape; the higher the price, the fewer the cans demanded, and vice versa. S_V is the supply curve of aluminum cans using virgin raw materials. It's drawn quite flat, based on the assumption that additional quantities of cans can be produced from this source at roughly constant marginal cost. S_R is the supply curve of cans made from recycled aluminum cans; it is sloped upward rather steeply, based on the assumption that recycling is subject to increasing marginal costs.

This is an extremely simple model, but it can be used to reveal some interesting conclusions. According to this analysis, the total quantity of cans sold will tend toward q_1, given by the intersection of S_V and D. The price of cans will be p_1, which is the price established by the level of virgin production costs. This bears repeating: The factor governing the market price of cans is the **cost of production from virgin sources.** The quantity of recycled cans will be q_2; if recycled output were pushed beyond this, costs would rise above p_1, which would not be feasible in a competitive world. The quantity of cans produced from virgin material is $q_1 - q_2$, and the **recycling ratio,** the proportion of total cans that stem from recycled sources, is q_2/q_1.

Figure 10-11 looks at the different ways that are possible to get an increase in recycling. Panel (a) shows the result of a reduction in total demand for aluminum cans. This could come about through, for example, a shift to another type of container (glass, paper) or an overall reduction in consumption of whatever the cans contain. The demand curve is pictured as moving back from D_1 to D_2. This reduces total can production from q_1 to q_3, while leaving unchanged the production of recycled cans at q_2, thus increasing the recycling ratio. This is a revealing result. The recycling ratio was increased simply by decreasing total can output, without any direct intervention in the recycling process. This is because of the way the two supply sources (virgin and recycled) relate to one another. When overall production shifts, the adjustment is done entirely on the virgin supply side.

Panel (b) shows the effect of investing in the recycling industry. This lowers the cost of one or more of the recycling functions (collecting, transporting, reprocessing, remanufacturing), and is pictured by a rightward shift in S_R from S_R^0 S_R^1. This lowers the cost of producing any given amount of recycled cans, although the curve still slopes upward. Total can output at q_1 is unaffected, but recycled output increases from q_2 to q_3, and so the recycling ratio increases.

Panel (c) shows the effect of lifting the cost of virgin materials. The primary motivation for increasing recycling is to reduce the use of virgin materials, because of the environmental benefits this produces directly and because a smaller number of cans will be disposed of in the future. Suppose a tax were put on virgin materials, making them more expensive to the producers of cans. In effect this lifts the S_V line upward by the amount of the tax. This attacks the problem from both sides: Total can production drops from q_1 to q_3, and the output of recycled cans increases from q_2 to q_4.

(a)

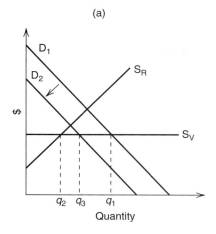

(b)

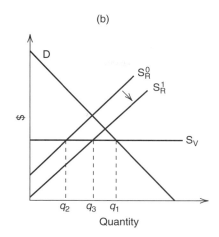

(c)

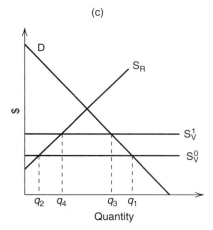

FIGURE 10-11
Ways of Increasing the Recycling Ratio

Which of these approaches is likely to be the most effective? Two factors are involved here: the shape of the functions themselves, and the ease with which they can be shifted. Consider the S_R function. Other things equal, the flatter this function, the greater impact will there be from a change like a tax on virgin materials; see panel (c). If the capacity of the present recycling sector tends to be fixed and inflexible, the function will be steep. If it is easy for the existing aluminum can recycling sector to expand or contract its output, given its present condition in terms of factors like the number of plants or the technology in use, the S_R function will be relatively flat. A rightward shift of S_R in panel

(b) can occur because of investment in additional recycling plants or adoption of better recycling technology, or a combination of both. The development of better recycling technology is, of course, a major pursuit in most modern economies. For aluminum cans and plastic soda bottles, new machines have mechanized the deposit return function.

Although this simple model shows some basic relationships, it cannot show how rapidly situations can change in the real world. Demand can shift because of demographic and economic changes; cost curves can change because technological factors underlying production, especially from recycled sources, will evolve, sometimes rapidly. In addition, macroeconomic factors and international trade developments can have substantial effects on resource prices and therefore on markets like the one analyzed in the model.

In the future we can expect to see modest increases in recycling in many sectors of the economy. One factor pushing this, which we have not highlighted above but is important nevertheless, is the increasing environmental costs of materials disposal. Working against this is the continued decline in the prices of virgin materials. The key to lifting recycling ratios in particular sectors will be in pushing out the S_R function in Figure 10-11. This means developing efficient recycling technologies and organizing effective recycling industries to close the loop between suppliers and demanders of recycled materials.

SUMMARY

This chapter reviewed some of the economic issues involved in extracting nonfuel minerals. These appear to be classic examples of **nonrenewable resources.** This is true in some ultimate physical sense, but the processes of **exploration and discovery** and the technological ability over time to utilize increasingly lower grades of ore give them the characteristics of a renewable resource for the foreseeable future. The first major topic of the chapter was a simple two-period model to explore economic issues involved in extracting a nonrenewable resource from a **known deposit. Time profiles of production and prices** were featured problems, and the role of **user cost** was explored. The processes of resource exploration and discovery were examined briefly. Technical change in resource discovery and extraction are the major factors behind the long-run drops in minerals prices. The question of the **sustainable extraction of nonrenewable** resources was explored, emphasizing the ideas of the **backstop resource** and the conditions for **investing of resource rents** to achieve sustainable incomes. After focusing briefly on the recent history of **minerals prices,** we looked at economic issues of import dependence and producer cartels. We considered some of the factors, such as the price elasticity of demand, that determine the probability that a cartel will be able effectively to raise prices and increase their incomes. Finally, we looked at a simple model of **recycling,** with special emphasis on the factors that produce changes in the **recycling ratio.**

KEY TERMS

Nonfuel minerals
Metals
Industrial minerals
Quantity-grade relationships
Time profiles of extraction and price
Capital values
User cost

Exploration and development
Nonrenewables and sustainability
Backstop technology
Import dependence
Producer cartels
Economics of recycling
Recycling ratio

QUESTIONS FOR FURTHER DISCUSSION

1 How is it possible to reconcile the theoretical results we got concerning increases in the prices of nonrenewable resources with the declines in actual prices that have occurred in the past and that are still going on?

2 How is user cost affected by the expectation that future demand for a resource will shift outward? What will be the impact of this on today's efficient rate of extraction?

3 What are some of the factors that could make social user costs different from private user costs in the case of mineral resource extraction?

4 Consider a three-period model of nonrenewable resource extraction. Lay out the maximization problem in a way analogous to the two-period model of the chapter, and determine the explicit expression for user cost.

5 Suppose you represented a country that was a heavy producer of cobalt. Several other major cobalt producing countries have suggested that you form an organization, restrict your exports, and drive the international price of cobalt higher. In considering the desirability of doing this, what are the major economic factors you should take into account?

6 Explain how changes could occur that produce increases in the quantity of materials recycled and, simultaneously, decreases in the recycling ratio.

USEFUL WEB SITES

The main U.S. government web site is the

- U.S. Geological Survey in the Department of the Interior, particularly the material dealing with minerals (http://www.usgs.gov/themes/minerals.html).

In Canada it is

Natural Resources Canada, Minerals and Metals Sector (http://www.nrcan.gc.ca/ms/efab/mmsdl).

Other public agencies in the United States and abroad that provide information and occasionally some analysis include

- Congressional Research Service. The CRS has done numerous reports on mining that are available through the National Institute for the Environment (http://www.cnie.org).
- Chamber of Mines of South Africa (http://www.bullion.org.za).

Some universities have units devoted to minerals studies, for example,

- Bureau of Economic Geology at the University of Texas (http:// www.utexas.edu/research/beg).
- Colorado School of Mines (http://gn.mines.colorado.edu:80/1/).
- Penn State Department of Energy, Environmental and Mineral Economics (http://www.ems.psu.edu/MnEc/).

Many minerals companies and associations have web sites with useful information, for example,

- LaFarge, a global construction materials company (http://www. lafarge.com).
- World Mine Cost Data Exchange (http://www.minecost.com/).

SELECTED READINGS

Barnett, Harold J., and Chandler Morse: *Scarcity and Growth: The Economics of Natural Resource Availability*, Johns Hopkins University Press for Resources for the Future, Baltimore, MD, 1963.

Gaffney, Mason: *Extractive Resources and Taxation*, University of Wisconsin Press, Madison, WI, 1967.

Humphries, Marc: *Mining Law Reform: The Impact of a Royalty*, U.S. Congressional Research Service, Washington, DC, No. 94–438, May 12, 1994.

Humphries, Marc: *The 1872 Mining Law: Time for Reform?* U.S. Congressional Research Service, Washington, DC, No. 89130, March 4, 1998.

Krautkraemer, Jeffrey A., "Nonrenewable Resource Scarcity," *Journal of Economic Literature*, 36(4), December 1998, pp. 2065–2107.

Landsberg, Hans H., and John E. Tilton, with Ruth B. Haas: "Nonfuel Minerals," in Paul R. Portney (ed.) (with the assistance of Ruth B. Haas), *Current Issues in Natural Resource Policy*, Resources for the Future, Washington, DC, 1982, Chapter 3, pp. 74–116.

Page, Talbot: *Conservation and Economic Efficiency, An Approach to Materials Policy*, Johns Hopkins Press for Resources for the Future, Baltimore, MD, 1977.

Slade, Margaret E: "Cycles in Natural Resource Commodity Prices: An Analysis of the Frequency Domain," *Journal of Environmental Economics and Management*, 9(2), 1982, pp. 138–148.

Slade, Margaret E: "Trends in Natural Resource Commodity Prices: An Analysis of the Time Domain," *Journal of Environmental Economics and Management*, 9(2), 1982, pp. 122–137.

Smith, V. Kerry, (ed.): *Scarcity and Growth Reconsidered*, Johns Hopkins University Press for Resources for the Future, Baltimore, MD, 1979.

Tilton, John: "The New View of Minerals and Economic Growth," *Economic Record*, 65(190), 1989, pp. 265–278.

CHAPTER 11

ENERGY

In the contemporary world, energy has two important dimensions. It is a critical input as a **power source.** This is especially true of modern, industrialized economies whose service and manufacturing sectors are based on huge systems of nonhuman power supply. It is also true, though perhaps in a different way, of developing countries that are tied more closely to basic sectors such as agriculture. And all people are dependent on incoming solar energy that supports photosynthesis and the production of plant and animal foods.

The other important dimension of energy use is as a source of **pollution.** Energy conversion—for example, the burning of fossil fuels—creates residuals that normally find their way into the environment. Carbon dioxide emissions from fossil fuel burning are implicated in global meteorological changes and the increase in surface temperatures that may result. Energy emissions from the conversion of nuclear fuels have been shown to have negative impacts on the health of humans and ecosystems. Heated water from the cooling systems of power plants has changed local ecosystems, and so on.

These two sides of the energy resource are closely connected, of course. If the amount of energy taken into a system for power purposes declines, then the energy-related emissions coming out the end of the system will decline, other things being equal. Underneath the simple aggregate of energy used, however, is the fact that many different forms of the input are in use, each with different environmental implications. So a shift from one type of energy source to another (coal to natural gas, or nuclear to solar, for example) will also change the environmental impacts of energy.

In this chapter we are going to focus on the power supply aspects of energy resources. This is by no means meant to imply that the emissions end of the process is unimportant, only that it accords with the idea that the book is meant to concentrate on issues of natural resource supplies.

ENERGY USE IN THE UNITED STATES: CONSUMPTION AND PRICES

The total consumption of energy of all forms in the United States was almost three times greater in 1996 than it was in 1950. Table 11-1 shows the consumption figures, in quadrillion Btus, for selected years during this period. Energy consumption increased very rapidly in the 1950s and 1960s, and much more slowly in the 1970s and 1980s. The rate of increase in the 1990s looks as though it will be higher than in the two preceding decades, but not as high as the earlier decades.

Behind aggregate figures like this, of course, a system of enormous complexity exists in terms of the diverse energy forms that constitute the supply, the various consuming sectors that generate the demand, and the avenues and pathways that link them together. Figure 11-1 provides some visual help for getting a perspective on this system. The data apply to 1996. Incoming flows on the left show amounts of energy supplied in terms of different energy types, and also according to whether it was produced domestically or imported. It shows, for example, that 72.61 quadrillion Btus (quads) of the total supply of 98.50 quads were supplied from domestic sources.[1] It also shows

TABLE 11-1
TOTAL ENERGY CONSMPTION IN THE
UNITED STATES, SELECTED YEARS,
1950–1996

Year	Consumption*	Percent change
1950	33.08	—
1960	43.80	32
1970	66.43	52
1980	75.96	14
1990	84.09	11
1997	94.20	12

*Expressed in quadrillion Btus.
 Source: U.S. Department of Energy, *Annual Energy Review,* Washington, DC, 1998.

[1] A Btu is a measure of energy. One Btu is the amount of heat required to raise the temperature of a pound of water by one degree Fahrenheit.

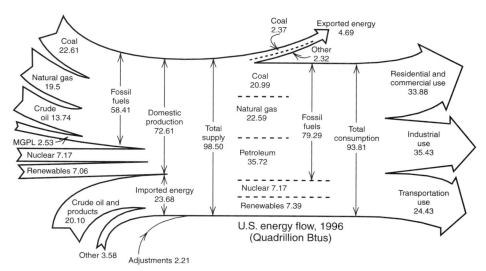

FIGURE 11-1
U.S. Energy Supply and Consumption, 1996 (*Source:* U.S Department of Energy, *Annual Energy Review,* Washington, DC, 1996.)

that imported oil amounted to 20.10 quads of the 33.84 total quads of oil supplied to the system, that is, about 60 percent of the total petroleum used by the U.S. economy in 1996. On the consumption side, fossil fuels accounted for 79.29 quads of the total of 93.81 quads consumed. As for the major use sectors, residential and commercial consumption and industrial consumption were very close in terms of total quantity (33.88 quads and 35.43 quads, respectively), while transportation consumed 24.43 quads of energy.

In the fall of 1973 members of the Organization of Petroleum Exporting Countries (OPEC) engaged in a coordinated effort to reduce exports of petroleum to the United States. The reasons for this action were strictly political, connected to events that were unfolding in the Middle East. In 1979 another, more severe supply restriction was arranged by OPEC. These years were described, by those living through them, as the years of the energy crisis. Vivid stories were passed around about long lines at gas stations, price gouging, and customers fighting one another. Many people were actually brought to believe that the price increases were more than just a political phenomenon caused by the OPEC cartel and that they actually had something to do with long-run energy scarcities. Many people who should have known better predicted permanent long-run increases in energy prices.

It has not turned out that way. Figure 11-2 shows the real prices[2] of four different sources of energy over the last four decades. For most people the most

[2] Real price are prices adjusted for inflation.

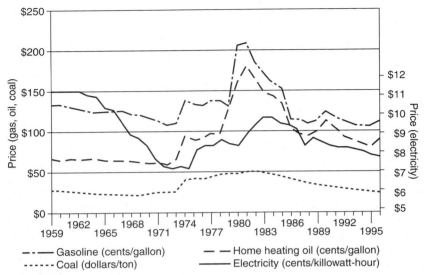

FIGURE 11-2
Real Energy Prices, 1959–1996 (*Source:* U.S. Department of Energy, *Annual Energy Review*, Washington, DC, 1996.)

direct indicator of energy costs is gas prices. In the gas price series, one clearly sees the price spikes during 1973 and during the year 1979–1980, but as of the mid-1990s the price of gas was lower or about at the same level it was immediately before the energy crisis. For several years it was actually lower than this, and most recently has started to increase. The story is roughly the same for the other energy forms; the 1970s were not the beginning of long-run price increases, but a temporary reversal of the real long-run trend, which is downward. Of course, past trends, even trends that have lasted for several centuries, are not a conclusive predictor of future trends. Despite the downward trends in energy prices, many people feel that real energy scarcities are possible in the not-too-distant future. We return to this below.

THE POLITICAL ECONOMY OF ENERGY MARKETS[3]

Material in the preceding section showed the relative size of the various energy flows in the system and aggregate prices as they have behaved over the last few decades. When we start to look in more detail at the entire energy setup, its full complexity begins to reveal itself. Obviously, a huge physical system—wells and mines, pipelines, tankers, trains, refineries, transmission lines—is required to move energy resources and products from start to finish.

[3] In writing this section I was greatly aided by Duane Chapman's book *Energy Resources and Energy Corporations*, Cornell University Press, Ithaca, NY, 1983.

There is also a large and complex institutional system—small and large private firms, markets, governmental bodies of all types, domestic and foreign entities, and consumers—that essentially manages the system. It is the people spread through these organizations whose decisions determine the size and character of the physical system and the quantity and timing of the energy flow within it. And it is they who determine how well the system works according to the various criteria with which it can be evaluated.

About 85 percent of the energy resources consumed in the United States are fossil fuels: coal, oil, and natural gas. If we were to characterize these industries briefly, we would say that they consist of small numbers of relatively large firms that are highly integrated. Take the petroleum industry, for example. The three primary phases of this industry are crude oil production and transportation, including importing; refining; and distribution and marketing. In the crude oil stage, roughly 20 firms control 80 to 90 percent of the activity in the United States, including ownership of petroleum reserves, extraction, and pipeline transportation. The largest companies involved here are household words: like Exxon, Mobil, Texaco, and Standard Oil of Ohio. These companies not only dominate domestic crude oil activity, they are active on a worldwide scale. In fact, for many of these companies their global activity, excluding that in the United States, is larger than that within the United States. It's also true that some U.S. subsidiaries of foreign companies are major players in the U.S. petroleum market; this includes such companies as British Petroleum, Royal Dutch Shell, and Phillips.

Petroleum refining and distribution are similarly dominated by a relatively small number of very large firms. What is more, these are essentially the same large companies that dominate the production side; these companies, in other words, are **vertically integrated** within the petroleum industry. Many of these companies are also **horizontally integrated;** they operate, often through subsidiaries or companies they have purchased, in other industries. Other energy companies are in, for example, the solar or coal industries. In some cases petroleum companies have acquired nonenergy companies or have been acquired themselves by firms in other industries. Change continues to characterize the petroleum industry. Prices in the latter 1990s hit very low levels, and this tended to encourage further concentration of the industry. Mobil and Exxon have recently merged, and other mergers are being explored.

The U.S. **coal industry** is somewhat less **concentrated;** that is, it contains a larger number of smaller firms than the petroleum industry. But most coal companies are actually owned by other firms, either other energy firms or firms in other basic industries such as power generation, steel production, and railroads. **Natural gas** is somewhat different. Gas production is to a large extent carried out by the large petroleum companies, since the technology is similar and much of the gas is located in or near petroleum deposits. Domestic transportation of gas, however, is almost entirely by pipeline, and the interstate gas pipeline network is owned and operated by pipeline companies. Although these companies are highly concentrated, they are to a large extent independent of the major gas and petroleum companies. On the consumption end, most natural gas distribution to industrial, commercial, and residential consumers is handled by gas utilities, which typically are companies that do not have major outside interests.

Given the competitive structure of the fossil fuel industries, the strategic aspects that result from the linkages to global energy markets, and the important role that energy plays in the domestic economy, it is easy to see why political and public authorities historically have focused so much attention on energy markets. This has tended to politicize energy markets in a major way over the last five decades, with numerous policy enactments, thousands of regulations, and the creation of a cabinet level Department of Energy in Washington around which pivots the political economy of U.S. energy markets. The concentrated structure of the industry has encouraged many to think of it as possessing excess monopoly power (or, in street parlance, as being a vast ongoing conspiracy against the public). The problem with this diagnosis is that, in theory, monopolies are supposed to be able to charge high prices and transfer wealth from consumers to the owners of the firms possessing the power. But it is obvious that the entire economy of the United States has been shaped historically by cheap energy, not expensive energy. So if monopoly power has been exercised by the energy companies, they must have done so with great subtlety. One can argue that energy prices have historically been too low, not too high. One extreme form of this argument is that energy companies have purposely kept the price of energy low so that consumers would become addicted to heavy energy use. The more reasonable version of this argument is that energy prices have not been high enough to cover the **external costs,** in terms of environmental damage, energy production, transportation, and use. This includes in particular the costs of air pollution stemming from energy conversion, of electricity and heat in power plants and industrial firms, and of mechanical energy in the nation's fleet of motor vehicles. Revisions in pollution control laws are called for in this case.

THE QUESTION OF ENERGY ADEQUACY

The actions by OPEC in the 1970s were political. The price increases of the time were not related to any fundamental changes in world petroleum supplies. Nevertheless, they served to focus people's attention on the basic **adequacy question:** When are the world's petroleum supplies going to be exhausted, and is this close enough in time that we need to start worrying about it now? For countries such as the United States (and other major energy importing countries such as Japan), energy adequacy has several important dimensions. On the one hand global energy supplies are clearly of major concern. Beyond this, however, is the issue that the bulk of these supplies, at least as far as petroleum is concerned, are elsewhere in the world, and so using them means relying on foreign suppliers, with all the political ramifications that may come from this situation.

Energy adequacy questions can be usefully broken down into three categories, based on the length of time that is considered:

1 In the short run (10 to 20 years?) how much should we try to switch to fuels other than petroleum? Nonpolluting fuels are of interest. The potential for wind power appears quite modest; solar power is cheaper but still expensive relative to fossil fuels and will require considerably more research and development before it becomes a viable alternative for the huge amounts of base load power that the system consumes. Natural gas appears to be a very viable substitute at the present time; a substantial switch in this direction is occurring and will help in terms of reducing carbon dioxide emissions.

2 In the intermediate run (20 to 50 years?) how long will the era of ample global petroleum supplies persist? Over the last several decades new discoveries have added to these supplies (North Sea, Alaska) and others are currently being touted (Caspian Sea), but these may have led us into a false sense of optimism about our ability to continue to make new discoveries in the future. Exhibit 11-1 contains an excerpt from a recent article written by several highly respected geologists, whose conclusion is that we will see a growing scarcity in world petroleum supplies in the near future. This concern is not universally shared, however.

3 Thus, in the long run (50 to 100 years?) the question is how we make a transition to a non-petroleum-based energy system. The answer to this is by no means obvious from our present vantage point. At one time nuclear power was thought to be the ultimate technology for the future (and some countries have indeed invested heavily in nuclear systems), but in the United States, at least, evolution in this direction has been almost totally derailed. Vast supplies of coal still exist, but a return to coal would have serious environmental costs. At the present time the important question is not which particular energy form should be adopted for the very long run—it is too soon for this decision—but how the search should be organized. Can the petroleum industry be relied upon to make the correct decision about very long run energy issues; is there a role for public research and development?

THE ECONOMICS OF ENERGY SELF-SUFFICIENCY

In the previous chapter we discussed the issue of the U.S. dependence on mineral imports. The same issue is extremely important in the case of energy. For better or for worse, the United States, and most other developed countries of the world, have energy systems that utilize large quantities of petroleum. As can be seen from the numbers of Figure 11-1, most of the petroleum used in the United States is imported. It was not always this way. In the early days of petroleum use, domestic sources were sufficient to meet demand. But in the latter half of the twentieth century with the boom in automobile transportation, foreign sources have become much more important. The OPEC[4] import

[4] Members of OPEC are Alegria, Indonesia, Iran, Iraq, Kuwait, Libya, Nigeria, Qatar, Saudi Arabia, the United Arab Emirates, and Venezuela.

EXHIBIT 11-1

THE END OF CHEAP OIL

"Global production of conventional oil will begin to decline sooner than most people think, probably within 10 years."

by Colin J. Campbell and Jean H. Laherrère

In 1973 and 1979 a pair of sudden price increases rudely awakened the industrial world to its dependence on cheap crude oil. Prices first tripled in response to an Arab embargo and then nearly doubled again when Iran dethroned its Shah, sending the major economies sputtering into recession. Many analysts warned these crises proved that the world would soon run out of oil. Yet they were wrong.

Their dire predictions were emotional and political reactions; even at the time, oil experts knew that they had no scientific basis. Just a few years earlier oil explorers had discovered enormous new oil provinces on the north slope of Alaska and below the North Sea off the coast of Europe. By 1973 the world had consumed, according to many experts' best estimates, only about one eighth of its endowment of readily accessible crude oil (so-called conventional oil). The five Middle Eastern members of the Organization of Petroleum Exporting Countries (OPEC) were able to hike prices not because oil was growing scarce but because they had managed to corner 36 percent of the market. Later, when demand sagged, and the flow of fresh Alaskan and North Sea oil weakened OPEC's economic stranglehold, prices collapsed.

The next oil crunch will not be so temporary. Our analysis of the discovery and production of oil fields around the world suggests that within the next decade, the supply of conventional oil will be unable to keep up with demand. This conclusion contradicts the picture one gets from oil industry reports, which boasted of 1,020 billion barrels of oil (Gbo) in "proved" reserves at the start of 1998. Dividing that figure by the current production rate of about 23.6 Gbo a year might suggest that crude oil could remain plentiful and cheap for 43 more years—probably longer, because official charts show reserves growing. . . .

According to most accounts, world oil reserves have marched steadily upward over the past 20 years. Extending that apparent trend into the future, one could easily conclude, as the U.S. Energy Information Administration has, that oil production will continue to rise unhindered for decades to come, increasing almost two thirds by 2020.

Such growth is an illusion. About 80 percent of the oil produced today flows from fields that were found before 1973, and the great majority of them are declining. In the 1990s oil companies have discovered an average of seven Gbo a year; last year they drained more than three times as much. Yet official figures indicated that proved reserves did not fall by 16 Gbo, as one would expect—rather they expanded by 11 Gbo. One reason is that several dozen governments opted not to report declines in their reserves, perhaps to enhance their political cachet and their ability to obtain loans. A more important cause of the expansion lies in revisions: oil companies replaced earlier estimates of the reserves left in many fields with higher numbers. For most purposes, such amendments are harmless, but they seriously distort forecasts extrapolated from published reports. . . .

Our analysis reveals that a number of the largest producers, including Norway and the U.K., will reach their peaks around the turn of the millennium unless they sharply curtail production. By 2002 or so the world will rely on Middle East nations, particularly five near the Persian Gulf (Iran, Iraq, Kuwait, Saudi Arabia and the United Arab Emirates), to fill in the gap between dwindling supply and growing demand. But once approximately 900 Gbo have been consumed, production must soon begin to

---

EXHIBIT 11-1—*Continued*

THE END OF CHEAP OIL

fall. Barring a global recession, it seems most likely that world production of conventional oil will peak during the first decade of the 21st century. . . .

Factors other than major economic changes could speed or delay the point at which oil production begins to decline. Three in particular have often led economists and academic geologists to dismiss concerns about future oil production with naive optimism.

First, some argue, huge deposits of oil may lie undetected in far-off corners of the globe. In fact, that is very unlikely. Exploration has pushed the frontiers back so far that only extremely deep water and polar regions remain to be fully tested, and even their prospects are now reasonably well understood. Theoretical advances in geochemistry and geophysics have made it possible to map productive and prospective fields with impressive accuracy. As a result, large tracts can be condemned as barren. Much of the deepwater realm, for example, has been shown to be absolutely nonprospective for geologic reasons.

What about the much touted Caspian Sea deposits? Our models project that oil production from that region will grow until around 2010. We agree with analysts at the USGS World Oil Assessment program and elsewhere who rank the total resources there as roughly equivalent to those of the North Sea—that is, perhaps 50 Gbo but certainly not several hundreds of billions as sometimes reported in the media. . . .

Last, economists like to point out that the world contains enormous caches of unconventional oil that can substitute for crude oil as soon as the price rises high enough to make them profitable. There is no question that the resources are ample; the Orinoco oil belt in Venezuela has been assessed to contain a staggering 1.2 trillion barrels of the sludge known as heavy oil. Tar sands and shale deposits in Canada and the former Soviet Union may contain the equivalent of more than 300 billion barrels of oil. Theoretically, these unconventional oil reserves could quench the world's thirst for liquid fuels as conventional oil passes its prime. But the industry will be hard-pressed for the time and money needed to ramp up production of unconventional oil quickly enough.

Such substitutes for crude oil might also exact a high environmental price. Tar sands typically emerge from strip mines. Extracting oil from these sands and shales creates air pollution. The Orinoco sludge contains heavy metals and sulfur that must be removed. So governments may restrict these industries from growing as fast as they could. In view of these potential obstacles, our skeptical estimate is that only 700 Gbo will be produced from unconventional reserves over the next 60 years.

Source: From *The End of Cheap Oil*, by Colin J. Campbell and Jean H. Laherrère. Copyright © 1998 by Scientific American, Inc. All rights reserved.

---

embargo of the 1970s seemed to demonstrate the vulnerability of the U.S. economy to the disruption of oil imports. For a time these imports declined, both absolutely and relative to total oil consumption. But in recent years imports have again started to increase, so that today (1999) they amount to about two-thirds of total U.S. petroleum consumption.

We can analyze this situation with the same type of model as was used in the previous chapter to analyze recycling.[5] There the two sources for materials

[5] See p. 192.

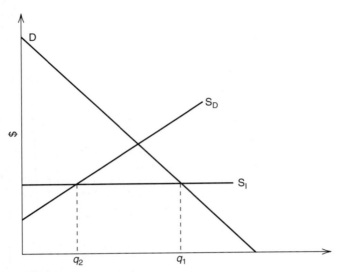

FIGURE 11-3
Input Dependence in Petroleum Markets

supply were virgin and recycled; here the two sources of petroleum production are domestic and foreign. Consider Figure 11-3; the overall aggregate demand for petroleum is labeled D, domestic supply is labeled S_D, and import supply is labeled S_I. Note that domestic supply is upward-sloping, while import supply is flat. Domestically, most petroleum deposits have been developed, and additional national production can be produced only at higher prices. On the import side, the assumption is that there is a going world price and that additional supplies could in fact be obtained at this price. This assumption may not be strictly accurate, but making it here allows us to set up and explore a reasonably uncomplicated model and derive clear conclusions. Total quantity consumed is q_1, while q_2 is the quantity produced from domestic sources. Thus imports are equal to $q_1 - q_2$, and the **import dependency ratio** (the proportion of total consumption imported) is $(q_1 - q_2)/q_1$. Note that the world price establishes the domestic price. If demand were to shift right or left, the changes in quantity would occur in imports, not in domestic production.

There are in this simple model only three ways of decreasing the import dependency ratio.

1 Increase the world price. Since this is a world price and not one set domestically, it can only be changed by other means such as an import duty that effectively increases the price to importers. Diagrammatically this would shift S_I upward, which would attack the import dependency ratio from two directions, lowering total consumption q_1 and increasing domestic output q_2.

2 Increase domestic supply, in effect shifting the S_D curve to the right. This leaves total consumption unchanged but would increase domestic production, thus cutting the import ratio.

3 Shift demand backward, for example, by pursuing a strategy of energy conservation. This would reduce total consumption but not domestic production, thus lowering the import ratio.[6]

Although we do not pursue this analysis in great depth, one can easily see that the relative effectiveness of these different approaches depends on a small number of **parameters.**[7] One of these is the price elasticity of demand for petroleum. If demand is relatively price-inelastic, then import tariffs will have little impact on overall consumption, so all of the adjustment will have to come via changes in domestic supply.[8] If S_D is relatively inelastic also, the import dependency ratio will be little affected by tariffs on imports.[9] Another important parameter is the extent to which energy conservation efforts can effectively shift back the demand function. We take up this question below.

The importance of these parameters was made manifest in the 1970s. The initial popular reaction to the OPEC price increase was that it would precipitate massive economic dislocation and transfer large amounts of wealth to the producing nations. According to this view, the U.S. economy was so energy-intensive that any reduction in energy supplies would be highly disruptive. This position was accurate in a limited way for the short run, but not at all for the long run. The runup in petroleum prices provided the incentive to explore new ways of energy conservation and new forms and sources of energy supply. In effect, the long-run demand curve for energy turned out to be much less inelastic than OPEC had originally thought. The eventual realization that this is indeed the case has very substantially tempered OPEC pricing policies in subsequent years.

One way that countries have sometimes sought to insulate themselves from unstable world markets, or future short-run price increases, is through **advance purchase and storage** (sometimes called **buffer stocks**). Materials put into storage can be taken out and added to market supplies in times of high prices, thereby putting downward pressure on these prices. In 1975 the U.S.

---

[6] There is another way of limiting imports, which is to do it quantitatively by establishing a quota on imports. This is a somewhat more complicated case to analyze, and we do not undertake it here.

[7] A parameter is a key variable which may take on different values that will affect critically the conclusions of the model.

[8] The price elasticity of demand for a good is equal to the percentage change in quantity demanded divided by the percentage change in its price. It is a way of describing the responsiveness of quantity changes to changes in price. Inelastic demand means that price changes do not lead to substantial changes in quantity supplied. The **price elasticity of supply** is equal to the percentage change in quantity supplied divided by the percentage change in price.

[9] Inelastic supply means that price increases do not call forth large increases in quantity; an elastic supply curve, on the other hand, is one in which relatively small price increases produce large increases in the quantity supplied.

Congress enacted a law providing for the creation of the **Strategic Petroleum Reserve** (SPR). Physically, it consists of huge underground caverns that can securely hold large quantities of petroleum for a reasonable length of time. Acquisition of oil for the SPR began in the late 1970s and continued until 1994, at which time the reserve contained about 600 million barrels of crude oil.

The economics of buffer stocks is reasonably straightforward, but of course there are many uncertainties. A major factor is how large the stocks should be. The higher the stocks, the greater the ability to protect the domestic market from international price stocks. But also the larger the stocks, the greater the cost. So one is essentially buying insurance, and the question is, how much insurance is enough? The U.S. SPR currently contains an amount of petroleum equal to about 2½ months of net petroleum imports. Is this sufficient to cushion substantially a supply disruption? The answer depends on many things: how thorough the supply reduction is, how much the price of energy is allowed to rise before the SPR is tapped, how much energy conservation is triggered by this price increase, and so on.

One problematic feature of a publicly sponsored storage effort like the SPR is that it continues to exist in the political domain, and therefore is subject to political manipulation. The SPR is supposed to be for emergency purposes. Several years ago, however, there was a temporary upward spike in gas prices because of a short-run glitch in the supply system. In order to be seen as doing something to protect consumers from this, Congress at that time put pressure on the Department of Energy to sell supplies from the SPR. More recently, Congress has mandated that oil be sold from the reserve to earn funds for covering its operating costs. Over the long run, of course, political actions like this will seriously reduce the economic potential of the SPR.

ENERGY CONSERVATION

Economic growth in the developed world has been accompanied in general by the copious consumption of energy. Events of the 1970s showed that in this type of world, **energy conservation** is a very viable alternative given the right incentives. Since prices have decreased, however, one hears less of this concept. For an energy importing country like the United States, energy conservation has important implications for national security. Energy conservation is important also in the battle against global warming.

What is energy conservation? It obviously has something to do with reducing energy consumption. But it turns out that this can be assessed in several different ways. Consider the following expression:

$$\text{Total energy consumed} = \text{Total number of people} \times \underbrace{\frac{\text{Income}}{\text{per person}} \times \frac{\text{Energy consumption}}{\text{per dollar of income}}}_{\text{Energy use per person}}$$

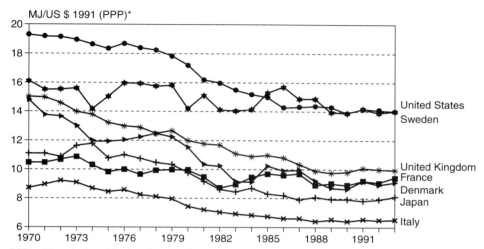

* MJ = Megajoules; 1 joule = 1 watt × 1 second; 1 megajoule = 948 Btu; PPP = purchasing power parity, a way of determining exchange rates between national currencies.

FIGURE 11-4
Primary Energy Consumption per Dollar of GDP, Selected Countries, 1970–1993 (*Source:* International Energy Agency, *Indicators of Energy Use and Efficiency,* Organization for Economic Development and Cooperative IFA, Paris, 1997, p. 48.)

Total energy use is clearly tied to total population. But for a given population, energy use is also related to income. Wealthier societies consume more energy; not only do consumers use larger amounts of energy as their incomes rise, but greater industrial and commercial energy consumption is what produces the higher incomes in the first place. What this alerts us to is the notion that not all reductions in energy consumption would qualify as energy conservation. The reduction in energy demand that results from an economic recession and falling incomes, although it reduces energy consumption, is not energy conservation, because consumption will increase again as soon as economic growth is reestablished.

Perhaps the best way of defining energy conservation is that it is a reduction in **energy use per dollar of income** (i.e., per dollar of economic activity). Figure 11-4 shows some recent history of this measure for the United States and for a number of other developed economies. For the most part these show declines during the period 1970–1993, although there was, and still is, a substantial spread among them. In the case of the United States the decline was most marked in the decade 1975–1985. Since that time, the index has diminished very little.

How to explain this development? There are essentially two ways of achieving energy conservation, which are depicted in Figure 11-5. The demand curves in the two panels show expected aggregate demand functions for energy in some future year, say 5 years from today. Panel (a) shows the

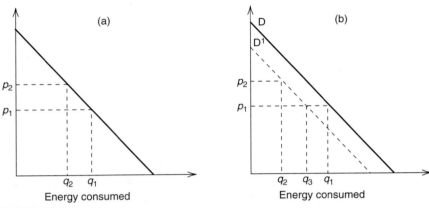

FIGURE 11-5
Two Types of Energy Conservation

impact of an increase in the price of energy. Suppose the current energy price is equal to p_1. If this price persists, then the quantity demanded of energy in our target year will be q_1. But if we have an increase in price for some reason, the quantity demanded of energy in that period will be only q_2 units. In this case, energy conservation consists of a price-induced movement up along a given energy demand function.

To some extent this is what happened in the 1970s in response to increases in the price of petroleum. In the very early days of the oil embargo in the fall of 1973, many observers took the position that this type of energy conservation was essentially impossible, that the economy used and required large amounts of energy, without which it could come to a grinding halt. Events proved otherwise. Paradoxically, it might seem, conservation may be easier the higher is the initial level of consumption. When energy use is very high, it is fairly easy to find ways to cut back consumption. Thus, consumers in 1973 found numerous ways to conserve energy in response to the price increases of the time (like turning off lights, running air conditioners a little lower, and going to the grocery store fewer times per week; these changes did not occur without a lot of grumbling, of course).

How much consumption will decrease in response to price increases depends in large part on the slope of the demand curve. For a given p and q, the steeper the slope, the less responsive quantity is to price; the less steep the slope, the more responsive. We can think of the aggregate demand curve for energy as being built up from all the individual demand curves in the economy of households, businesses, public agencies, and so on. Possibilities for price-driven reductions in energy consumption will, of course, vary widely among consumers, depending on their circumstances. The reduction in aggregate consumption is a result of all the individual adjustments made throughout the economy.

But this is not the whole story. It can't be, because energy prices are actually lower at the present time than they were in the 1960s, while consumption (per dollar of output) is today lower than it was then. Panel (b) of Figure 11-5 shows another way of achieving energy conservation. In this case the price increase to p_2 provides an incentive for technological developments that change energy consumption patterns: a shift to more energy-efficient equipment, machinery, appliances, and building methods. What these changes do is actually shift the expected demand function back. Instead of the demand curve at D 5 years hence, it actually occurs at the level indicated by the dashed demand curve labeled D^1. At the higher price p_2, consumption is now only q_2 and, should price drop back to the previous level, consumption would increase again but not back to the previous level. With D^1 and p_1, consumption would be at q_3, which is still less than the original level of q_1.

It is something like this that happened in the domestic energy market as a result of the 1970s price increases. The energy conservation depicted in panel (b) is more deeply rooted and **structural** than that of panel (a). It is conservation that may persist in the long run, even if energy prices were to return to previous levels. But in order to achieve this type of conservation, two things must occur: (1) **R&D (research and development)** has to be pursued to develop the more energy-efficient technologies and practices, and (2) the new techniques have to be **widely adopted** throughout the economy. The importance of energy prices here is that they are the primary **incentive** for the R&D and the widespread adoption rates. What we have seen in the 1980s and 1990s is the long-run impacts of the structural changes induced by the higher energy prices of the 1970s. What we will likely start to see in the twenty-first century are the longer-run impacts of the low energy prices of recent years.

ECONOMICS OF CAFE STANDARDS

The move away from petroleum that was spurred by the events of the 1970s is discernible in the residential and commercial sectors, and in the industrial sector (see Figure 11-6). But in transportation, petroleum consumption continues to advance in a major way. Serious amounts of petroleum conservation, therefore, hinge on doing something to reduce the demand for motor fuels. It was this thought that led the U.S. Congress to institute the CAFE program in the 1970s. CAFE stands for **corporate average fuel economy;** it is a program that requires the manufacturers of cars and light trucks to produce and sell vehicles that achieve, on average, a minimum mileage (miles per gallon) target. The mandated CAFE standards are the following:

Model year	Cars	Light trucks[10]
1978	18.0	—
1983	26.0	19.0
1988	26.0	20.5
1993	27.5	20.5
1998	27.5	20.5

[10] This category also includes sport-utility vehicles (SUVS).

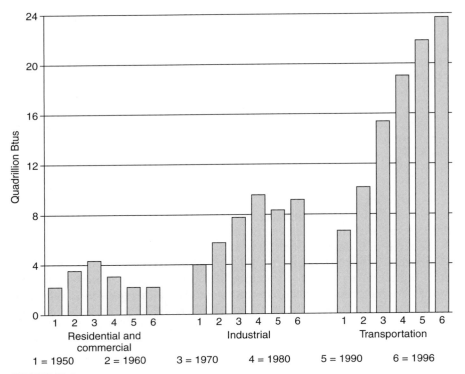

FIGURE 11-6
Consumption of Petroleum by Sector, Selected Years, 1950–1996, in Quadrillion Btus (*Source:* U.S. Department of Energy, *Annual Energy Review*, Washington, DC, 1996.)

The production of automobiles and trucks that get higher mileage is clearly an important part of overall energy conservation. But it makes a difference how this happens. The CAFE program is based on the notion that this has to be done by mandate. But in so doing, **perverse incentives** operate so as to undermine the effect of the program. Mandated increases in mileage lead, on the assumption that fuel prices are not affected, to the production of vehicles that are cheaper to drive, that is, those that have lower per-mile operating costs. But when the price of something goes down, consumers will buy more of it. So a reduction in driving costs will lead people to drive their vehicles more miles per year. This will lead to more fuel consumed, and the effect can offset to a great extent the impact of the fact that vehicles get better mileage. Thus total fuel consumption may decrease very little.

The critical parameter is the **elasticity of miles driven with respect to the cost of driving.** An elasticity is the ratio of two percentage changes, in this case miles driven in the numerator and cost of driving in the denominator. If this elasticity is –1, for example, a 10 percent reduction in the cost of driving will lead to a 10 percent increase in the number of miles driven. If people react more or less in this fashion, then the CAFE approach will produce very little in the way of reductions in total fuel consumption.

The conclusion is different if the increased mileage of the automobile and truck fleet were to increase because people had bought better mileage vehicles in response to increases in the price of fuel. In this case we would not expect to get a reduction in driving cost (cost per mile), and therefore no increase in miles driven. We would expect a substantial drop in total fuel consumption. This is another good example of how good intentions, if translated directly into public policy, can have unforeseen impacts. Although a vehicle fleet with higher average mileage is a good thing in terms of energy conservation, attempts to mandate it directly will not produce the intended effects. These can be obtained only by changing the incentives facing vehicle buyers and drivers themselves.

ECONOMIC ISSUES IN ELECTRICITY DEREGULATION

The energy sector is so important that it has always attracted public attention and political oversight. Major parts of the sector have at times been subject to public regulation, but just as in many other important sectors (airlines, trucking), the contemporary move is toward **deregulation.** Many years ago the **natural gas** sector was tightly regulated, especially through controls on prices. This has since been abandoned. The **electric power** industry has also been closely regulated historically, but here too contemporary events are pushing toward deregulation and vast structural change. In this section we take a very brief look at this phenomenon, especially at some of the changes that may occur in the industry.

The electric power system is extremely complicated, both technically and organizationally. Electricity is **generated** in a wide variety of **power plants;** large base load plants fired by nuclear, coal, or petroleum; middle-sized fossil-fueled plants; hydrofacilities; thousands of small plants using diesel engines, gas turbines, or other technologies; and new sources based on wind or solar power, geothermal resources, and so on. Electricity is transported long distances over a network of high-voltage **transmission lines.** The current system is highly integrated among states and internationally into Canada and Mexico. **Local distribution** networks, covering communities or relatively small regions, take the power from the transmission grid and transport it in usable form to the millions of retail customers in the urban and rural areas of the country.

Organizationally, the system is highly integrated vertically. We can depict the dominant business form, the one that deregulation is designed to change, as in Figure 11-7. The functions of electricity generation, transmission, and distribution are combined in a single, **integrated company,** which is granted monopoly rights to supply power to all consumers within a given region. Historically, a large, integrated form of business was considered necessary in the electricity sector to take advantage of the large **economies of scale** in the

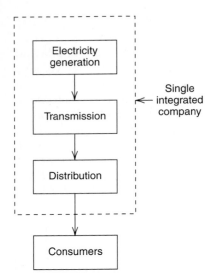

FIGURE 11-7
Electricity Generation: Structure of
the Large, Integrated, Public Utility

industry.[11] To get low generating costs, power plants had to be large. But it was not feasible to crisscross the land with competing sets of transmission and distribution lines. Hence an integrated system, in the hands of a single large company, was thought to be the best business form. And since this did not involve competition in any significant way, **public utility commissions** (PUCs) would provide public oversight and attempt basically to mandate the results that would have occurred in a competitive system if that had been possible.

The system as it exists incorporates many exceptions to this single integrated form of power company. Some communities own their own distribution systems and contract with outside power companies to provide them with power. Some communities may even have their own generating facilities, as may some large industrial operations. And the overall systems owned by a single power company are highly coordinated with those of other companies. Company A may use the transmission lines of Company B to reach some of its customers. One company may augment its own generation capacity by purchasing power temporarily from another company, and so on. Nevertheless the dominant single form is the integrated company as depicted.

Several things have happened in the last few decades to upset this pattern. In the 1970s the **Public Utilities Regulatory Policies Act of 1978 (PURPA)** created a new type of power source, called **qualifying facilities,** consisting largely of cogenerators[12] and small power producers that used renewable en-

---

[11] Economies of scale mean essentially that the long-run marginal production cost continues to decline with increasing output, until plant size becomes very large.

[12] Cogeneration means plants that produce both useful heat and electricity from the same fuel source (also called "combined cycle" generation).

ergy sources. PURPA required the large electric utilities to connect these qualifying facilities to the grid and purchase their power. Then in 1992 Congress
enacted the Energy Policy Act, which required that utilities open up the grid
to a large number of alternative energy sources, not just the ones covered by
the earlier law. Technological developments in electric generation have helped
push the system toward more competition. New combined-cycle gas turbine
plants, based on jet engine technology, have permitted the construction of
small power plants that have very low costs. Taken together, these changes
have moved substantially in the direction of opening up the system to the
forces of competition.

Competition is not an objective desired for its own sake, but for the positive
economic effects it is expected to have:

1 Competing firms will be motivated to produce at the lowest-possible cost
  and sell their electricity at the lowest-possible price; if they do not do so,
  other competitors may take their markets.
2 Competing firms will have the incentive to search for new, cost-reducing
  technological improvements in electricity generation and transportation.
3 Consumers will have wider choices which they may pursue to satisfy their
  own preferences. If a consumer wishes to buy "green power" (power from
  companies that use windmills, solar, or other renewables), for example,
  they can do this by searching for the appropriate supplier.

Alternative Structures in the Electricity Market

Figure 11-8 shows several possible deregulated structures for the electricity
market. Panel (a) shows a structure in which there is competition at the wholesale level but not at the retail level. The solid lines depict the contractual delivery route of electricity, and the dashed lines show the routes over which financial contracts are concluded. With wholesale competition only, consumers at
the retail level are still supplied by monopoly local distribution companies.
But the latter are free to contract with alternative power generators according
to price and whatever other factors are deemed important. In the pictured
case, the local company contracts with generator C for power. It must also pay
a grid company for transmission services. Since the aim of this is to foster
competition among generators, the presumption is that the grid company will
be independent of any of the generating firms.

ISO stands for **independent system operator.** With a multiplicity of generators all supplying the grid, and a multiplicity of local distribution companies
taking power from the grid, there are clearly serious problems in achieving
physical balance in the entire system. These are further complicated by the
day-to-day exigencies like power plants breaking down or storm-related damage to the system. Thus there is a role for a company whose primary job is operating the system. This might be the grid company itself, or perhaps a separate entity.

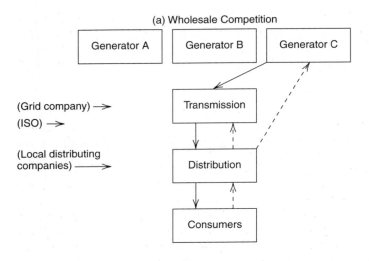

(a) Wholesale Competition

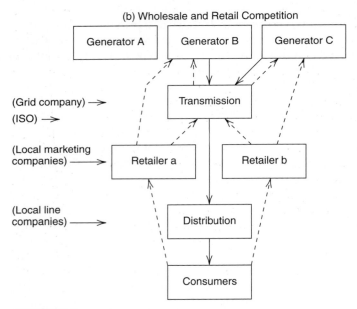

(b) Wholesale and Retail Competition

FIGURE 11-8
Alternative Structures for the Electricity Market

Panel (b) of Figure 11-8 shows a system that incorporates both wholesale and retail competition. In addition to alternative power generating sources, there are now alternative **local marketing companies** from among which consumers may choose. The local distribution lines are owned by a **line company,** whose job it is simply to maintain the physical system and distribute whatever power is contracted for among consumers and local marketing companies. Local marketing companies could take a wide variety of forms: private firms that sign up individual consumers in a community; all consumers in a particular part of town who decide to buy power together; a group of commercial users acting together; communities as a whole working through a cooperative, or perhaps through the normal town government; and so on. The local marketing companies, having brought together a number of local consumers, would contract for power with one or more of the generating sources. It might be a source actually owned by the local companies or by any other source with which appropriate contractual terms can be concluded.

Economic Issues

A huge number of problems must be worked out in making a reasonably smooth transition from the current system to a deregulated one. A considerable amount of public regulation will still be necessary, because there will still be only one set of transmission and distribution lines. These will continue to be monopoly operations, and so public oversight will be required to make sure these positions are not abused. One issue that has been very sensitive is that of cost recovery by the large utilities who have to pay for the systems built up under the previous regulated system. This is the problem of **stranded costs.** Public utility commissions historically had allowed the large utilities to set electricity prices high enough to cover the costs of the large generating plants they constructed. If electricity prices fall because of competition, how do these utility companies continue to get sufficient revenues to pay off the costs of these facilities?

Electricity deregulation also has implications for environmental matters. The overall impact of deregulation is supposed to be a substantial reduction in energy prices to consumers. This will lead to increases in the quantity of electricity consumed, other things being equal. This implies either developing new generating capacity or using the existing system at a higher rate. If the latter, we will have larger emissions from existing power plants, such as large coal-fired power plants in the Midwest that currently have excess capacity. If the former, emissions may not increase as much, for example, if the system shifts markedly toward natural gas as a generating fuel. On the other hand, electricity consumption in the eastern United States may use more hydropower imported from Canada, and there is controversy over the environmental and resource impacts of this power.

SUMMARY

Energy is a major resource underlying economic growth in the developed world. Energy prices were declining until the decade of the 1970s, at which time they rose dramatically for political reasons. Since then, prices have gone back down, in some cases reaching levels today that are below those of the

1960s. Questions of future energy adequacy are difficult to answer; on the one hand, people have been predicting energy shortages almost continuously over the last century. On the other hand, discovery, development, and technical change have continued so dramatically that shortages have not occurred. Some predictions today are that petroleum supplies will begin to tighten substantially over the next two decades.

The events of the 1970s produced considerable amounts of energy conservation, but the benefits of the conservation have gradually diminished, and energy use per dollar of economic activity is no longer decreasing in the United States. We looked at the attempt to mandate energy conservation through the CAFE program enacted by the U.S. Congress, and the perverse incentives this kind of approach produces. Finally, we looked at some of the great structural changes that electricity deregulation might entail and some of the economic and environmental consequences of this.

KEY TERMS

Horizontal and vertical industry
  integration
Industry concentration
Energy adequacy
Energy conservation
Price elasticity of demand for energy
Energy R&D
Energy independence
Import dependency ratio
CAFE standards

Perverse incentives
Elasticity of miles driven with respect
  to driving cost
Electricity deregulation
Wholesale electricity competition
Retail electricity competition
Independent system operator (ISO)
Public Utilities Regulatory Policies
  Act of 1978
Energy Policy Act of 1992

QUESTIONS FOR FURTHER DISCUSSION

1 Suppose gas costs $1 a gallon and the average car gets 20 miles per gallon. If Congress mandates that cars have to get 24 miles per gallon, by what percentage will this lower the costs of driving? If the elasticity of total miles driven (per year) with respect to the cost of driving is –1, by how much will total miles driven per year increase, assuming it is 10,000 miles at the beginning? How much will total annual gas consumption of the average car change as a result of the mandated program?

2 What has been the history of energy consumption in the United States over the last four decades, in terms of energy consumption per dollar of GDP (gross domestic product)? What political or economic factors account for this history?

3 Petroleum prices in the late 1990s have dropped to relatively low levels, and many producing countries have seen their export earnings shrink drastically. Why is OPEC apparently so weak these days that it cannot keep prices high? Is this situation likely to continue?

4 If electric power companies make their profits by selling electricity, why do these companies actively promote electricity conservation by consumers, which would tend to reduce the amount of electricity they sell?

USEFUL WEB SITES

For information on renewable energy in the United States:

- National Renewable Energy Laboratory (http://www.nrel.gov).

Information about the international energy market:

- World Coal Institute (http://www.wci-coal.com).
- Organization of Petroleum Exporting Countries (http://www.opec.org).

Information and analyses of the U.S. domestic energy markets:

- American Petroleum Institute (http://www.api.org).
- Energy Information Administration of the Department of Energy (http://www.eia.doe.gov).

Studies on energy use, particularly the economic implications of deregulation:

- Resources for the Future (http://www.rff.org).
- The Tellus Institute (http://www.tellus.org).

Information on the Energy Policy Act of 1992:

- (http://www.nfesc.navy.mil/energy/law_us/92epact).

Energy Issues in the Developed Economies:

- Organization for Economic Cooperation and Development (http://www.oecd.org).

SELECTED READINGS

Banks, Ferdinand F.: *Energy Economics: A Modern Introduction*, Kluwer Academic, Boston, 1999.

Bohi, Douglas R., and Michael A. Toman: *The Economics of Energy Security*, Kluwer Academic, Boston, 1996.

Brennan, Timothy J., et al.: *A Shock to the System, Restructuring America's Electricity Industry*, Resources for the Future, Washington, DC, 1996.

Chapman, Duane: *Energy Resources and Energy Corporations*, Cornell University Press, Ithaca, NY, 1983.

Congressional Research Service: *Electric Utility Restructuring Briefing Book*, Washington, DC (undated).

Federal Energy Regulatory Commission: "Promoting Wholesale Competition through Open-Access Non-Discriminatory Transmission Service by Public Utilities," RM95-8-000, Washington, DC, 1996.

Griffin, James M., and Henry B. Steele: *Energy Economics and Policy*, 2nd ed., Academic Press, New York, 1986.

Monroney, John R. (ed.): "Advances in the Economics of Energy and Resources," *Energy Supply and Demand*, Vol. 10, JAE Press, Greenwich, CT, 1997.

Peirce, William Spangar: *Economics of the Energy Industries*, 2nd ed., Praeger, Westport, CT, 1996.

CHAPTER 12

FOREST ECONOMICS

Forests cover about 30 percent of the land surface of the earth.[1] These forest resources are a heterogeneous collection, ecologically, socially, institutionally, and economically. Ecologically it's customary to distinguish between tropical forests (up to about 35° north and south latitude), temperate forests (35° to between 50° and 55° north and south latitude), and boreal forests (the high-latitude forests). Within the tropic band there are rain forests, moist deciduous forests, and dry-land forests. There are hardwood and softwood forests. There are expanses of natural forests (sometimes called "old growth" forests), forests modified by humans through use of various types, and human-made forests (sometimes called forest "plantations"). There are public forests and private forests, open-access forests and controlled-access forests. More than 60 percent of the world's forests are in seven countries (Brazil, Canada, China, Indonesia, Russia, United States, and Zaire); twenty-nine countries have more than half their land area in forests; forty-nine countries have less than 10 percent of their land area in forests.

Listed below are some of the major types of problems encountered in managing the world's forest resources:

1 The challenge of maintaining production of traditional forest outputs in keeping with expanding populations and economies. Recent trends in forest products consumption are discussed in Exhibit 12-1. They include wood for

---

[1] Eight thousand years ago this percentage was about 50.

EXHIBIT 12-1

TRENDS IN CONSUMPTION OF FOREST PRODUCTS

Global consumption of wood has expanded by some 36 percent (around 900 million m^3) over the past two and a half decades, reaching almost 3,400 million m^3 in 1994. Broad estimates suggest the value of this consumption in 1994 to be in excess of US$ 400,000 million, with industrial usage accounting for 75 percent of this. Slightly more than half of the wood volume was used as fuelwood, and the rest was used for a variety of industrial purposes. Fuelwood consumption expanded more rapidly than industrial roundwood consumption, growing by 60 percent to 1,890 million m^3 in 1994, while industrial roundwood consumption grew by 15 percent to almost 1,500 million m^3, although actually declining from a high of 1,720 million m^3 in 1990.

The decline in consumption from the 1990 level reflects both supply and demand conditions. A major factor was the continued dislocation of output in the Russian Federation where reported industrial roundwood removals were down substantially (around 50 percent from the 1990 level). The decline also reflected weak demand in the industrialized countries. Further, the supply of logs continued to be affected by restrictions on harvesting in North America and the main tropical Asian countries, increasingly due to environmental concerns. Some African countries also increased their restrictions on logging and export, both for forest management reasons and to encourage greater domestic processing.

World production of most individual forest products rose substantially in volume terms over the period 1970–94. Only sawnwood had a lower production in 1994 than in 1970. Output ranged from a minor fall in the production of sawnwood, to a 113 percent increase in paper and paperboard products. The slow growth for industrial roundwood masked the fact that coniferous roundwood production only increased by 1 percent, while that of non-coniferous roundwood grew by 48 percent. The main impact was post-1990, as production of both coniferous and non-coniferous roundwood had increased up to that point. Industrial roundwood and sawnwood both reached a peak in 1990 and then declined, mostly due to dislocation of output in the former USSR; recent levels have approached the 1990 high.

Growth rates for consumption of many commodities during 1980–94 have been slower than for the 1970–80 period in many regions.

The developing countries' share of total roundwood production has increased steadily from 49 percent in 1970 to 61 percent by 1994. They have increased their share of industrial roundwood from 17 percent to 33 percent.

For industrial roundwood, the most impressive changes have occurred, not for the leading consuming regions, but for the others: Africa's consumption nearly doubled to about 60 million m^3 between 1970 and 1994 with its share rising from less than 3 percent to 4 percent. South American consumption also rose from 3 percent to more than 7 percent. However, it was the growth of consumption in Asia that transformed the global balance: from consuming 15 percent of world industrial roundwood in 1970, Asia came to account for 21 percent (compared to about 20 percent for Europe) in 1994. Similar shifts have occurred for other commodities. For paper and paperboard the main developments have been the sharp declines in share of consumption by North/Central America and by Europe, mostly in favour of Asia which raised its share from 15 to 30 percent.

Source: U.N. Food and Agriculture Organization, *State of the World's Forests,* Rome, Italy, 1997, p. 50.

fuel, for manufactured products, and for the production of paper. Forests also produce many nontimber products, such as honey, nuts, oils, spices, pharmaceutical products, and cork products.

2 The shift in many developed countries from traditional types of forest uses to new forms of use, such as outdoor recreation.

3 The continued pressure, particularly in developing countries, to convert forest land to other types of land use, particularly subsistence and commercial agriculture.

4 The identification, valuation, and preservation of new types of forest services, such as biodiversity production, carbon sequestration, and ecosystem protection.

All these problems have technical aspects connected to the biological and technological factors affecting the growth of forests and their utilization. They also have important institutional and economic dimensions connected to the valuation and use of forest resources and the incentives facing those whose decisions impact the quantity and quality of forest resources. We clearly cannot deal, in a single chapter, with all the global issues in forest economics in all their specificity. But what we can do is try to lay out an analytical model with which the basic nature of these issues can be framed and analyzed.

FOREST HARVEST DECISIONS

We begin with what sounds like a very innocuous problem, but one that actually contains a perspective that can be used to analyze many of the issues involved in decisions about using forest resources. It's the problem of deciding **when to cut a tree.** Suppose there is a community that contains 1,000 acres of forest land. The objective of the community is to manage its forest land so as to maximize the sustainable value of the timber harvest. We suppose, for the moment, that there are no nontimber values involved. Whenever the community harvests a portion of its territory, it immediately replants that acreage. Assume also that the timber output of this community is small relative to the total market, so its harvest decisions do not affect the selling price of timber. How much of its acreage should it harvest each year?

A way of working into this is to focus on one representative acre of forest, which we assume to be covered with trees of roughly the same age. When should this acre be harvested? The answer lies in the combined effects of the biology and the economics of the situation. First, the biology, which in this case is wrapped up in the growth pattern of the trees. Many things affect how fast trees grow, but we will consider a generalized relationship like that shown in the numbers of Table 12-1, which are pictured in Figure 12-1. Growth rate is here related to the age of the tree. The total quantity of wood on the acre of trees grows modestly for the first several decades. In the third through fifth decades the growth rate is relatively rapid. In the sixth and later decades the rate slows down and eventually, at an age of about 100 years, be-

TABLE 12-1

TOTAL VOLUME, AVERAGE VOLUME, AND ANNUAL INCREASE IN VOLUME OF WOOD, BY
DECADES, OF ONE ACRE OF FOREST

Age of trees (years)	Total volume of wood (cu ft)	Average volume (cu ft/age)	Annual increase in volume (cu ft/yr)
0	0	0.0	0.0
10	80	8.0	8.0
20	200	10.0	12.0
30	400	13.3	20.0
40	720	18.0	32.0
50	1,360	27.2	44.0
60	1,660	27.7	30.0
70	1,840	26.3	18.0
80	1,960	24.5	12.0
90	2,040	22.7	8.0
100	2,090	20.9	5.0
110	2,090	19.0	0.0
120	2,090	17.4	0.0
140	2,090	14.9	0.0

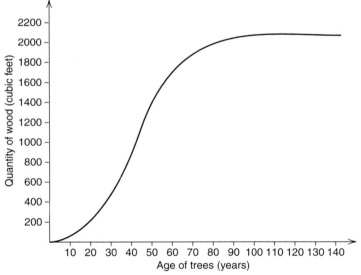

FIGURE 12-1
Total Volume of Wood by Age of Forest

comes zero. The columns of Table 12-1 show total and average volume of
wood, and the yearly growth rate, in successive decades of the forest's life.[2]
The average volume is simply the total volume in the forest divided by its age.

[2] Clearly the growth rates and volumes vary each year, but a table showing annual data would
be too big, and we can get what we need with a table based on decades.

It is possible to undertake various **silvicultural** steps to shift this growth function. For example, periodic thinning, or fertilizing, can increase the production of wood from a given acre of forest. It's also true that plant breeding can produce trees that grow faster. There has been enormous change through the years in the yield of timber that can be obtained from an acre of forest, in effect an increase in the volume figures shown in Table 12-1.

It is possible to make harvest decisions by reference only to the biological growth function. We might plan simply to maximize the amount of wood obtained at the time of harvest. This would imply delaying harvest until the forest achieved its maximum volume, around year 100. The problem with this is that we have to wait quite a long time to realize this harvest. Might it not be better to have a somewhat smaller harvest, in return for having it earlier in time?

One might think that it would make sense to cut at perhaps 60 years—when the average yield is the highest. Over, say, 1,000 years, this would yield about 27,666 cubic feet, as against a 100-year cycle, which would yield only 20,900 cubic feet in 1,000 years. In fact the 60-year cycle would yield the largest volume of any cycle, so it could perhaps be thought of as the **maximum sustained yield** for this forest. The question remains, however: Is this the harvest age that maximizes the net benefits of the forest to society?[3] Cutting at 50 years would produce less wood, but it would be available sooner. Thus there is a trade-off, and the solution depends as much on the values that society places on time as it does on the value of wood.

But the decision is somewhat more complicated. After the trees are cut, an acre of cleared ground will result. The optimal harvest time depends in part on what that land will be devoted to. We will assume, in keeping with the logic of the overall situation, that the land will be replanted with trees as soon as it is harvested and that this will be done each time the trees are cut, into the indefinite future. So what we are actually asking is: What is the optimal length of **timber harvest rotation** for our community? A "rotation" is a recurrent length of time, in years, between successive harvests of the same piece of land. A 40-year rotation, in other words, means that the typical acre of timber is harvested every 40 years. If we were to find, for example, that 40 years was the optimal rotation period, we would conclude that we should harvest one-fortieth of the thousand acres, or 25 acres, each year. A rotation pattern is pictured in Figure 12-2. The first harvest is made at t years from the beginning. Harvests are subsequently done at $2t$, $3t$, $4t$, and so on. Each harvest yields q cubic feet of timber. The question is: What is the socially efficient value of t?

A way of visualizing this problem is the following: Imagine that we are at the present time at the beginning of some year in the life of the trees on our acre. It doesn't matter which particular year it is. We ask the question: Should we cut the trees and send them to market this year, or should we wait and do it next

---

[3] Remember that for now we are assuming that the only thing of value is the trees for wood; we will relax this assumption later.

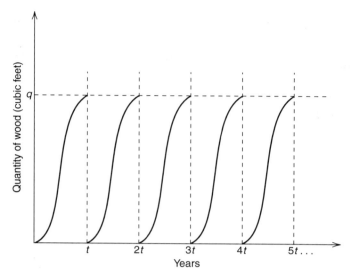

FIGURE 12-2
Typical Forest Rotation Pattern

year? This is really just a simple two-period problem, but it allows us to identify the efficient rotation period. If the decision is not to harvest this year, then next year the community will be faced with the same two-part comparison. So the community is essentially faced with a sequence of benefit-cost decisions. It compares the benefits of cutting this year with the costs, which are the returns they forgo because they won't have the trees to cut next year. In the early years of the trees' lives, the benefits of cutting are presumably less than those of waiting, because in these years the trees are growing rapidly. On the other hand, in later years when the growth rate is very low, the benefits of waiting would be very small compared to those of cutting today. At some point there will occur a tipping point, at which time the benefits of cutting are equal to, or slightly in excess of, those of waiting. This is the time to harvest the forest.

It's easier to look at this question with a little algebra. Define the following symbols.

V_0: The monetary value of the wood that would result if the forest were harvested this year

V_1: The monetary value of the wood that would be produced if harvest is delayed 1 year

$\Delta V = V_1 - V_0$: The value of the 1-year growth increment

C: Harvest costs, the monetary costs of felling the trees and getting them to market

r: Discount rate

S: The present value of all future net benefits when the forest is harvested with the optimal rotation period

The last term needs some explaining. We are actually trying to find out what the optimal rotation period is. To see the significance of S, pretend that after harvesting, the cleared land is going to be sold to somebody who is going to replant and then harvest forever at the optimal rotation period. The price the land would sell for is equal to the present value of the future stream of net benefits from following this course of action.

If the forest is harvested this year, the proceeds will be $(V_0 - C) + S$. This is the sum of $(V_0 - C)$, the net benefits of harvesting the timber, and S, the selling price of the land. If the harvest is delayed until next year, the present value of the proceeds will reflect the added growth, ΔV, and the revenue from selling the land next year. These must be discounted, giving

$$\frac{V_0 + \Delta V - C + S}{1 + r}$$

In this case both the realized yield next year and the selling price S must be discounted back one period. When the forest is young and ΔV is relatively large, the following inequality will hold:

$$\frac{(V_0 + \Delta V) - C + S}{1 + r} > (V_0 - C) + S$$

In other words, the net proceeds of waiting to harvest until next year will be greater than those of harvesting this year. But as the forest gets older, ΔV will eventually decline, and the net proceeds of harvesting this year will eventually become equal to those of waiting until next year. Thus the condition

$$\frac{(V_0 + \Delta V) - C + S}{1 + r} = (V_0 - C) + S$$

is the condition that tells when to harvest the forest.

The last expression can be reduced to the following[4]

$$\Delta V = (V_0 - C)r + Sr$$

What this amounts to is a benefit-cost type of expression. ΔV is the benefit received by waiting one more year for harvest, and $(V_0 - C)r + Sr$ is the cost of waiting. As long as the benefits of waiting exceed the costs, we put off harvest; when the benefits fall to the level of costs, it is time to harvest the trees.

---

[4] Multiplying both sides of the first expression by $1 + r$ gives: $(V_0 - C + S)(1 + r) = V_0 + \Delta V - C + S$. Isolating ΔV on the right gives $(V_0 - C + S)(1 + r) - (V_0 - C + S) = \Delta V$. Factoring gives $(V_0 - C + S)(1 + r - 1) = \Delta V$, which gives the result above.

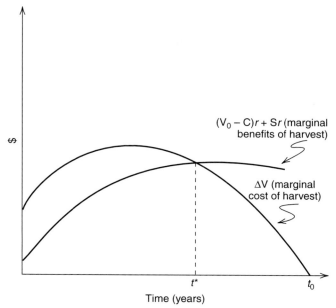

$(V_0 - C)r + Sr$ (marginal benefits of harvest)

ΔV (marginal cost of harvest)

t^*

t_0

Time (years)

FIGURE 12-3
Depiction of the Optimal Rotation

This solution is shown in Figure 12-3. The curve labeled ΔV shows annual growth increments at varying ages. Growth is low at the beginning, increases to a maximum (which corresponds to the point on the graph of Figure 12-1 where it reaches its steepest slope), then declines to zero again when the forest reaches its maximum biomass. The other curve in Figure 12-3 shows the right side of the last equation. As the volume of wood in the forest (V_0) increases, this function also increases, up to some maximum. The optimal rotation is identified by the intersection of these two functions; it is labeled as t^* on the horizontal axis. This can be interpreted in benefit-cost terms. $(V_0 - C)r + Sr$ is benefits of harvesting this year, while ΔV is growth forgone, or the costs, if harvesting is done this year.

Portfolio Choice

We can also interpret this as a portfolio choice, that is, as a choice about the form in which the community should hold its assets. Solving the last expression for r gives

$$r = \frac{\Delta V}{S + (V_0 - C)}$$

which we can interpret as an **asset portfolio** statement. The left side is r, which can be interpreted as the rate of return obtainable on general productive assets in the community. The right side is the rate of return we could expect if we let the trees stand for another year. What the solution for the optimal rotation gives us is a rule that says: Maintain the trees as long as the rate of return from so doing exceeds the rate of return on alternative assets. When the rate of return on the growing trees falls to that of alternative assets, harvest the trees and replant.

Factors Affecting the Efficient Rotation

We can further our understanding of this by looking at some of the factors facing the forest manager that, if they change, will change the efficient length of rotation. For example, suppose that **harvesting costs** increased substantially when a nearby logging mill closed and made it necessary to ship the logs a further distance. Note that harvest costs appear in one of the functions shown in Figure 12-3 with a minus sign. The impact of the increase in C is to shift the $(V_0 - C)r + rS$ function downward, thereby lengthening the optimal rotation period. In fact if harvesting costs become expensive enough, it may be efficient to refrain from harvest altogether, that is, the efficient rotation period might get pushed right out to t_0 in Figure 12-3. One way in which the social costs of harvest could increase is through **externalities** associated with timber cutting. If flooding or soil erosion are increased as a result of harvesting the timber, as they have in many of the world's watersheds, this essentially increases the social costs of harvesting. The effect, as we have seen, is to lengthen the optimal rotation.

Consider what happens to the length of the efficient rotation when the **interest rate** changes. For example, if the interest rate were to fall in the long run, this would tend to shift the marginal cost function down, that is, $(V_0 - C)r + rS$. The intersection of marginal benefit and cost curves would shift to the right, indicating that the efficient rotation would get longer. Note that if the interest rate were actually zero, the marginal cost curve would essentially disappear, moving t^* all the way to the right where $\Delta V = 0$. A zero interest rate implies that the return on alternative assets is zero, and so it is efficient to let the forest continue to grow until the natural growth rate falls to zero.

Suppose that timber became relatively more scarce, leading to an increase in the harvested **price of timber.** In this case the outcome on the efficient rotation period is ambiguous, because higher timber prices would increase ΔV, V_0, and S, though not necessarily all in the same proportion. So the interaction of the marginal benefit and marginal cost curves could shift either to the right or to the left.

Impacts of Nontimber Forest Values

It is now time to expand the analysis to recognize that forests typically produce other social benefits beyond the commercial values of the timber they supply, such as habitat for valuable animal species, watershed protection, outdoor recreation, preservation of biodiversity, and carbon sequestration. Conceptually, it may be easy to understand how one of these benefit categories would affect the socially efficient rotation length. In practice it may be very complex, because different factors are likely to impact the rotation in different amounts and in different directions, so if a number of them are involved in the case of a particular forest, the overall impact may be hard to sort out.

One major service produced by forests is **animal habitat.** Obviously, there are many different animal species that rely on forest resources, from tiny insects to large carnivores, and animals that are ground-dwelling, tree-dwelling, flying, and so on. Consider a situation involving only a single species. This is approximately true in the famous case of the northern spotted owl, which lives in old-growth forests of the northwestern United States. Its required habitat, in other words, is forest that consists of relatively old trees. Suppose we had a way of valuing our acre of forest in terms of contribution to spotted owl habitat, and expressing this in monetary terms. The function relating this value to forest age might look like that in Figure 12-4. The value is essentially zero until the forest is at least 60 years old; it then increases rapidly and reaches a maximum at around 100 years, and is constant thereafter. Let us assume also that the price of timber, and of forest land, is unaffected by its owl habitat value.

It is fairly easy to see how adding this value to the forest management decision would affect the choice of efficient rotation. The habitat value function, if added to the overall timber value function shown in Figure 12-1, would give a

FIGURE 12-4
Value of Forest as Spotted Owl Habitat, Related to Forest Age

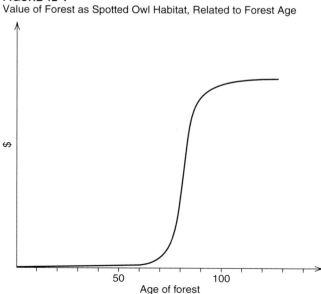

Age of forest

total value function like the earlier one but now with value for the older years increased somewhat. This would have the effect of pushing out the ΔV function in Figure 12-3. Since the owls do not have a commercial value (this would change if, for example, there were ecotourist industries that sold people owl-spotting tours in the forest), and the market value of the land is unaffected by the owls, the marginal cost function, expressed as $(V_0 - C)r + Sr$, of Figure 12-3 would be unchanged. This would give a new model as in Figure 12-5. The new marginal benefit function is shown as $\Delta V + H$. The ΔV term is the same as before; it is the increment in value of timber from another year's growth. The term H is annual value of the forest as owl habitat. The effect of adding H to the model is that it increases the optimal rotation. Several new marginal benefit functions are shown (the dotted lines), corresponding to higher values of H. The higher is the value, the more is the optimal rotation lengthened. The first dotted curve has an optimal rotation of t_2 years; if H is somewhat higher the rotation increases to t_3, and so on. In fact, if H becomes large enough, there will be no intersection with the marginal cost curve, indicating that the optimal rotation is essentially infinite, that is, social efficiency implies that the trees are never to be harvested.

While it may seem easy, at least conceptually, to factor a single species like the spotted owl into the situation, it is likely to be much more difficult to do this when a number of animal species are involved, and where the ecological factors affecting them differ. Deer, for example, may be advantaged in rela-

FIGURE 12-5
Optimal Rotation When Habitat for Spotted Owl Is Included

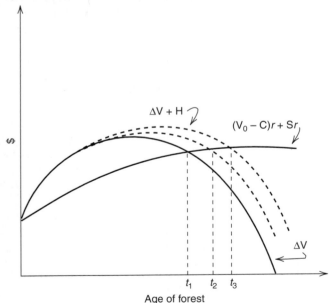

tively young forests, where the amount of available browse is relatively high. Certain insects may be advantaged in fully mature forests where there is an abundance of decaying wood. If the full habitat value of a forest is to be added to the timber value, some way would have to be found to develop some aggregate measure of habitat value from these conflicting elements.

Another nontimber value provided by forests is **carbon sequestration.** Global emissions of carbon dioxide from the burning of fossil fuels have produced elevated levels of carbon dioxide (CO_2) in the atmosphere. The consensus among atmospheric scientists is that this will lead to a significant long-run increase in global mean surface temperatures, which in turn will have major impacts on elements of the global ecosystem and the humans who depend on it. One obvious way of trying to ameliorate this process is to reduce CO_2 emissions. Another is to manage global forest resources so as to increase their capacity to absorb atmospheric CO_2.

Trees carry out photosynthesis to produce the glucose necessary for tissue growth and maintenance. The inputs into photosynthesis are atmospheric CO_2 and water. Thus growing trees absorb CO_2 from the air and in this way help ameliorate the buildup of CO_2 in the atmosphere. To sequester more carbon, there are two courses of action: (1) convert land currently in other uses (e.g., agriculture) into forest land and (2) manage existing forest land so as to increase the amount of carbon sequestered. If a forest is left standing, it will eventually reach and maintain a maximum biomass. At that point the carbon contained in the forest will be at a maximum, and this amount of carbon can be sequestered permanently by leaving the trees standing.[5] Can this performance be improved upon? If trees are immediately burned or destroyed after harvesting (as in land clearing for agriculture, for example), the carbon is immediately released back into the atmosphere. But if the timber is harvested and converted into building materials, the carbon stays sequestered until the materials decay. Suppose these building materials did not decay at all. Then by cutting trees and converting them to building materials, we are permanently sequestering the carbon. If there were a market for carbon sequestration services, the market values of timber would reflect both its value as building material and its value for carbon storage. In effect, the addition of the carbon sequestration function simply adds to the value of the timber in proportion to the amount of wood it contains, which is essentially the same as if there were an increase in the price of building materials. In this situation we would arrive at the same conclusion we had earlier in thinking about the impact of the price of timber on the length of the efficient rotation: It could push the efficient rotation in either direction.

But building materials do not exist forever; rather they decay at fairly rapid rates, depending on their form and use. A large proportion of the lumber market is used in the construction of buildings, particularly houses. The rate at which the housing stock decays would determine the rate at which the carbon

---

[5] Of course natural events like fires and hurricanes can affect this conclusion.

in the building materials is released into the environment. The critical factor is whether this rate is faster or slower than the growth rate of trees. If it is slower, then harvesting trees for building materials will increase the amount of carbon sequestered, relative to the quantity sequestered by leaving forests unharvested. If the decay rate is higher than the tree growth rate, the opposite conclusion holds.

One could envisage, at least theoretically, how a **carbon market** might work to motivate changes in silviculture practices and forest establishment practices that would lead to increased carbon sequestration. The market would allow forest owners to capture the value of stored carbon, thereby providing incentives for the appropriate decisions and trade-offs that would lead to efficiency in carbon sequestration. It would have to be a sophisticated market, for example, adjusting for the particular forest products into which trees are transformed if harvested. A problem with this is that the benefits of carbon storage are a massive public good, so private demanders are unlikely to materialize— which implies a program of public subsidies. Given the political context of most public subsidy programs, together with the uncertainties of the whole carbon sequestration process (see Exhibit 12-2), the likelihood that an efficient, or cost-effective, carbon sequestration subsidy program could be carried out is very small.

Optimal Clear-Cutting

Clear-cutting is the practice of harvesting all the trees in a particular area, as opposed to **selective cutting,** which means harvesting only those trees meeting certain criteria, such as species, size, or age. Clear-cutting is widely practiced in commercial forestry, and is controversial. Proponents point to harvesting cost savings and the advantages of promoting commercial forests that have trees of uniform characteristics. Opponents cite damages in terms of aesthetics, ecological integrity, watershed destruction, and reduced values for outdoor recreation.

It is relatively easy to frame the problem in conceptual terms. Suppose a company has a large forest from which it harvests timber on a 60-year rotation. On the assumption that it wishes to have a constant annual yield, in order to plan its workforce, and so on, it plans to harvest one-sixtieth of the forest each year. If the total forest contained 6,000 acres, this would mean they would harvest 100 acres each year. The harvesting pattern to be followed, in terms of clear-cutting, can vary over a wide continuum. On the one hand, it could be harvested as one large 100-acre clear-cut. At the other extreme, it could be harvested in 100 scattered 1-acre clear-cuts.[6] Or it could be harvested in any pattern between these two extremes: two 50-acre cuts, ten 10-acre cuts, and so on. Define n as the number of separate areas harvested in a year; thus $1 \leq n \leq 100$. The question is: What is the socially efficient value of n?

---

[6] We are assuming that one acre is the smallest possible harvest area.

EXHIBIT 12-2

FORESTS AND THE SEQUESTRATION OF CARBON

One important role that forests worldwide play is in the sequestration, or locking-up, of atmospheric carbon.

Forest management practices that can restrain the rate of increase in atmospheric CO_2 can be grouped into three categories: (i) management for carbon conservation; (ii) management for carbon sequestration and storage; and (iii) management for carbon substitution. *Conservation* practices include options such as controlling deforestation, protecting forests in reserves, changing harvesting regimes, and controlling other anthropogenic disturbances, such as fire and pest outbreaks. *Sequestration and storage* practices include expanding forest ecosystems by increasing the area and/or biomass and soil carbon density of natural and plantation forests, and increasing storage in durable wood products. *Substitution* practices aim at increasing the transfer of forest biomass carbon into products rather than using fossil fuel-based energy and products, cement-based products and other non-wood building materials.

The potential land area available for the implementation of forest management options for carbon conservation and sequestration is a function of the technical suitability of the land to grow trees and the actual availability as constrained by socioeconomic circumstances. The literature suggests that globally 700 Mha of land might be available for carbon conservation and sequestration (345 Mha for plantations and forestry, 138 Mha for slowed tropical deforestation, and 217 Mha for natural and assisted regeneration). The tropics have the potential to conserve and sequester the largest quantity of carbon (80% of the total potential), followed by the temperate (17%) and the boreal zones (3%). Natural and assisted regeneration and slowing deforestation account for more than half of the amount in the tropics. Forestation and agroforestry contribute the remaining tropical sink, and without these efforts regeneration and slowing deforestation would be highly unlikely.

Scenarios show that annual rates of carbon conservation and sequestration from all of the practices mentioned increase over time. Carbon savings from slowed deforestation and regeneration initially are the highest, but from 2020 onwards plantations sequester practically identical amounts as they reach maximum carbon accretion. On a global scale, forests turn from a global source to a sink by about 2010, as tropical deforestation is offset by carbon conserved and sequestered in all zones.

Using the mean cost of establishment or first costs for individual options by latitudinal region, the cumulative cost (undiscounted) for conserving and sequestering carbon ranges from about $250–300 billion at an average unit cost ranging from $3.7–4.6/t C. Average unit cost decreases with more carbon conserved by slowing deforestation and assisting regeneration, as these are the lowest cost options. Assuming an annual discount rate of 3%, these costs fall to $77–99 billion and the average unit cost falls to $1.2–1.4/t C. Land costs and the costs of establishing infrastructure, protective fencing, education and training are not included in these cost estimates.

While the uncertainty in the above estimates is likely to be high, the trends across options and latitudes appear to be sound. The factors causing uncertainty are the estimated land availability for forestation projects and regeneration programs, the rate at which tropical deforestation can actually be reduced, and the amount of carbon that can be conserved and sequestered in tropical forests. In summary, policies aimed at promoting mitigation efforts in the tropical zone are likely to have the largest payoff, given the significant potential for carbon conservation and sequestration in tropical forests. Those aimed at forestation in the temperate zone also will be important.

Source: Intergovernmental Panel on Climate Change, "Technologies, Policies, and Measures for Mitigating Climate Change," IPCC Technical Paper I, November 1996.

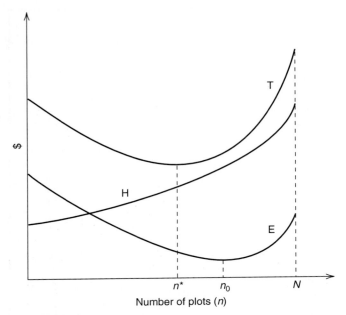

FIGURE 12-6
Efficient Clear-Cutting

In general we can identify two types of cost factors that vary with n. Harvest costs are one. As n increases, presumably the costs of harvesting timber would increase, owing to the need for the logging operation to visit an ever increasing number of scattered sites.[7] All the other costs we may lump under one category, called ecological costs. We would expect these costs to decrease as n increases, although once n gets relatively large, the costs may increase owing to the forest disruption on nonharvested acres when harvesters must visit many widely scattered cutting areas.

These relationships are pictured in Figure 12-6. Along the horizontal axis is the number of harvested plots (designated as n) varying from 1 up to some large number, say N.[8] The curve labeled H represents timber harvest costs, whereas the one labeled E shows ecological costs. The curve marked T shows total costs, and is the vertical summation of H and E. If harvesting were done simply to minimize harvesting costs, one large clear-cut would be called for, whereas if were done in such a way as to minimize ecological costs, clear-cuts of n_0 acres would be called for. The socially efficient number of acres lies between these two, at a value of n^*, where total costs are minimized.

Although it is relatively easy to discuss this on a conceptual basis, it would obviously be much harder to determine the actual number n for a specific situation. To do this, we would have to know the two cost functions H and E. It

---

[7] The spirit of this analysis is, of course, that the n areas are noncontiguous.
[8] N is the number of one-acre plots required to make up the total desired annual harvest area.

may not be too difficult to get the former—timber harvest companies presumably have good knowledge of their cost factors—but it is clearly a hard problem to measure ecological costs with a high degree of accuracy. Even without detailed knowledge of E, however, we can say that, as long as ecological costs are positive, the optimal clear-cut will be greater than one, the number that maximizes private profits.

INSTITUTIONAL ARRANGEMENTS FOR FORESTRY

Let us go back to the community with 1,000 acres of forest land, whose situation motivated the discussion about harvest decisions and the optimal rotation. We considered the logic of the optimal rotation when the commercial values of the timber are the only ones involved, and how the rotation decision might be affected by other factors. The next question is: How are efficiency and equity to be achieved under **alternative institutional arrangements**?

In the United States most commercial forest production is from private lands. A large part of this is from **industrial forest land,** consisting of relatively large parcels of timber land used primarily for harvesting timber. On these lands decisions are generally made with the objective of maximizing long-run net revenues. The extent to which these decisions also maximize social efficiency depends on whether unpriced outputs, on- or off-site, are taken into account by the decision makers. Some of these clearly are, because we know that private timber lands are often made available to hunters and hikers. Systematic data on these matters are not readily available, however.

Timbering is also carried out on nonindustrial timber lands. This is land held by owners who may produce some forest products, but for which timber output is not necessarily the primary goal. We can expect decisions in this case to be partially motivated by revenue considerations, but also to a large extent by the personal objectives of the landowners. Finally, some timbering is done on public lands, so that decisions on harvesting are made by public agencies. This is particularly the case in the developing world.

When an agency such as the U.S. Forest Service makes decisions about harvesting timber from national forests, its objectives and procedures are presumably dictated by its political mandate and the extent of the political/administrative conflicts in which it finds itself embroiled. We will address this issue in the next session. In the publicly owned forests of the developing world there are several major problems: (1) the shaping of the **commercial agreements** (called "concessions") entered into with private companies to extract timber from the public forests, (2) the continued use of forest resources by local groups who rely on the resource even though they do not technically own it, and (3) the terms under which the forest land may be converted to private ownership, which determines the incentives that prospective owners have to use the land in various ways.[9]

---

[9] For a discussion of some of these issues see Chapter 21.

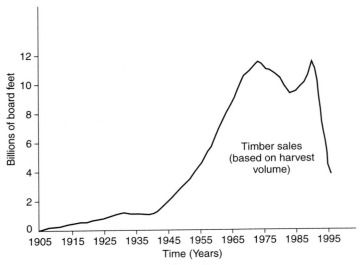

Timber sale levels are based on rolling average
harvest volume from 1905–1996.

Conversions from cubic foot to board foot
measures are approximate.

FIGURE 12-7
Historic National Forest Timber Sale Levels (*Data Source:* USDA Forest
Service, National Forest Timber Harvest, Washington, DC, undated.

TIMBER HARVESTING FROM NATIONAL FORESTS

The national forest system of the United States was begun in the late nineteenth century and now consists of 191 million acres of land in many different
sites around the country. During the first half of the twentieth century relatively little wood was harvested from national forests, but this changed after
World War II. Timber sales from national forests rose steeply to a peak of
about 11.5 billion board feet in the early 1970s. Since around 1990 timber sales
from the national forests have dropped by about 75 percent (see Figure 12-7).

The reason for the dramatic drop in these timber sales is the perceived shift
in relative valuations of the goods and services produced by national forests,
in particular an increase in the demand for services such as outdoor recreation
and ecosystem protection relative to the demand for harvested timber of the
traditional sort. The situation is depicted in Figure 12-8. The horizontal axis indexes the annual quantity of timber produced from national forests; the demand curve labeled D represents the marginal willingness to pay for that timber, and MPC represents the costs of harvesting it. If these were the only two
values involved, the efficient harvest level would be q_1. However, there are
other services produced by national forests, which for the most part are competitive with timber production. These are such services as opportunities for
various types of outdoor recreation, protection of biodiversity resources, sce-

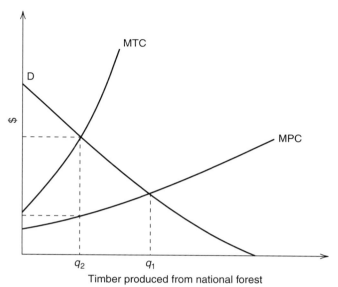

FIGURE 12-8
Efficiency with Nontimber Values

nic values, and such ecosystem protection services as flood control and soil erosion control. To a large extent these are use values, but nonuse values (e.g., existence value) are also important. On the assumption that the nontimber services diminish as the harvested timber quantity increases, they can be treated as an additional cost of timber harvesting. The curve labeled MTC in Figure 12-8 represents the total of marginal timber harvesting costs and marginal costs in the form of lost nontimber services. The difference between MTC and MPC, in other words, represents the marginal value of nontimber services being lost. According to this, full social efficiency requires that the timber harvest be reduced to q_2.

SUMMARY

This chapter first focused on the classic problem of when to harvest a tree. The decision involves a trade-off between the benefits one would receive immediately if it were harvested today, and the benefits of waiting, which are related to the rate at which the tree will grow in the next year. This basic model can also be used to look at cases where trees have value other than for timber, for example, for the provision of animal and plant habitat, a locale for outdoor recreation (e.g., hiking and hunting), and carbon sequestration. In all these cases, the optimal rotation is affected by benefit and cost values and the discount rate. We looked at a simple model that captured the major dimensions of the clear-cutting decision, and the reasons for the recent precipitous drop in sales of timber from national forests in the United States.

KEY TERMS

Optimal rotation
Biological growth function
Portfolio choice
Habitat values
Carbon sequestration

Carbon market
Optimal clear-cutting
Timber concessions
National forests

QUESTIONS FOR FURTHER DISCUSSION

1 Derive the condition for the optimal rotation when a forest also provides species habitat services.
2 How would the optimal rotation be affected when a forest is an important supplier of outdoor recreation services, such as backpacking and hunting? How would these factors affect the size of the optimal clear-cut?
3 How would decisions about managing forests for carbon sequestration be affected by the speed at which wood building materials decay?
4 Are privately owned or publicly owned forests likely to give the best results as far as achieving efficient management of forest resources?
5 Describe what is meant by the "portfolio choice" approach to managing renewable resource stocks like forests.
6 What are the types of benefits and costs that are involved when forests that were previously open to commercial forestry are now placed in preservation status?

USEFUL WEB SITES

The primary federal forest agency in the United States is the

- U.S. Forest Service (http://www.fs.fed.us)

Forestry programs are pursued by a number of public and private agencies:

- World Resources Institute, program on forests (http://www.wri.org/biodiv/foresthm.html)
- Food and Agriculture Organization of the United Nations (http://www.fao.org)
- United Nations Intergovernmental Program on Forests (http://www.un.org/esa/ sustdev/iff.htm)
- American Forests (http://www.amfor.org)
- European Forest Institute (http://www.efi.fi)

Most other countries have public forest agencies, such as the

- Canadian Forest Service (http://www.nrcan.gc.ca/cfs)
- Japan Ministry of Agriculture, Forestry and Fisheries (http://www.maff.go.jp/eindex. htm)

Many universities have schools of forestry, such as the

- University of Florida, School of Forest Resources and Conservation (http://www. sfrc.ufl.edu)
- Yale University, School of Forestry and Environmental Studies (http://www.yale.edu/forest/index.html)
- University of California at Berkeley (http://www.cnr.berkeley.edu/departments/espm/forestry.htm)

SELECTED READINGS

Adamowicz, W. L., et al. (eds.): *Forestry, Economics and the Environment,* CAB International, Wallingford, England, 1996.

Cubbage, Frederick W., Jay O'Laughlin, and Charles S. Bullock III: *Forest Resource Policy,* John Wiley, New York, 1993.

Ellefson, Paul V. (ed.): *Forest Resource Economics and Policy Research,* Westview Press, Boulder, CO, 1989.

Gorte, Ross W.: "Forest Service Timber Sale Practices and Procedures: Analysis of Alternative Systems," U.S. Congressional Research Service Report No. 95-1077-ENR, Washington, DC, October 30, 1995.

Hartman, Richard: "The Harvesting Decision When a Standing Forest Has Value," *Economic Inquiry,* Vol. 14, March 1976, pp. 52–58.

Newman, David H., and David N. Wear: "Production Economics of Private Forestry: A Comparison of Industrial and Nonindustrial Forest Owners," *American Journal of Agricultural Economics,* 75 (3), 1993, pp. 674–684.

Repetto, Robert, and Malcolm Gillis: *Public Policies and the Misuse of Forest Resources,* Cambridge University Press, Cambridge, England, 1988.

Sedjo, Robert A., Alberto Goetzl, and Stevenson O. Moffat: *Sustainability in Temperate Forests,* Resources for the Future, Washington, DC, 1998.

Sedjo, Roger A., R. Neil Sampson, and Joe Wisniewski (eds.): *Economics of Carbon Sequestration in Forestry,* Lewis Publishers, Boca Raton, FL, 1997.

CHAPTER 13

MARINE RESOURCES

Oceans and inland waters cover more than two-thirds of the surface of planet Earth. This aquatic ecosystem is the source of numerous products and services of value to humans and to the ecological health of the globe. The major ones include

Commercial fishing
Recreational fishing (including aquarium fish)
Transportation services
Shore-based and offshore recreation activities
Atmospheric and climate control
Mineral supplies

In this chapter we focus on the first of these: the exploitation of fish resources by commercially oriented harvesters. On a global basis, about two-thirds of this activity is to provide food for humans. The rest is fish for industrial purposes, such as producing fish meal to use as an animal feed. Figure 13-1 shows the trend over the last few decades of the total commercial fish harvest in the world and in the United States. In both cases the overall trend has clearly been up. The fish resource looms larger in some parts of the world than in others. In North America only about 7 percent of animal protein intake comes from fish, but in Africa this proportion is 21 percent and in southeast

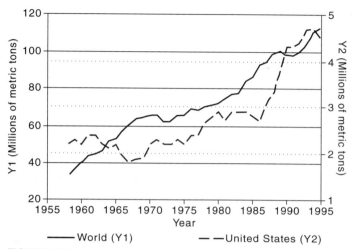

FIGURE 13-1
U.S. and World Commercial Fish Catches, 1958–1995

Asia it is 28 percent.[1] Of the total global catch, about 78 percent is saltwater-based (coastal and high seas), 7 percent is from inland fresh waters, and 15 percent is produced by aquaculture. The latter is a fast-growing segment of the total world harvest. World totals mask many changes that have taken place regionally and among different species of fish. Much of the growth in total harvest of recent years has been accounted for by lesser-valued species (sardines, pilchard) to which fishers have shifted their attention as some of the higher-valued species (cod, halibut) have become more scarce.

Within the United States, total commercial landings in 1995 were 4.5 million metric tons. This is about twice what it was 40 years ago. The total harvest has been fairly flat for the last 6 years. In 1996 the total value of commercial landings was about $3.5 billion. Just 15 years ago the Gulf of Mexico was the largest U.S. fishing region in terms of quantity of fish landed, but the largest today is the Pacific Coast/Alaska region. Table 13-1 shows the ten largest fisheries of the United States, by value.

CURRENT PROBLEMS IN MARINE FISHERIES

Major contemporary marine fisheries problems include

1 Overfishing, resulting in substantially diminished stocks of some species

---

[1] The data in this section come largely from the World Resources Institute, *World Resources, A Guide to the Global Environment, 1996–97,* Oxford University Press, New York, 1996; and U.S. National Marine Fisheries Service, *Fisheries of the United States, 1996,* Washington, DC, NMFS, 1997.

TABLE 13-1
TOP TEN U.S. FISHERIES, 1996

Fishery	1996 Landings ($ million)
Gulf shrimp	401.4
Pacific salmon	368.7
American lobster	241.8
Alaska pollack	238.1
Blue crab	147.1
Pacific cod	112.0
Sea scallop	101.8
Halibut	83.5
Pacific flounder	82.0
Pacific herring	69.7

Source: National Marine Fisheries Ser-vice, *Fisheries of the United States, 1996,* NMFS, Washington, DC, 1997.

2 Overcapitalization, that is, excessive investments in national fishing fleets
3 Water pollution that threatens spawning areas vital to the health of many marine species
4 Conflicts over fishing rights; intercountry (e.g., United States and Canada), and intracountry (Native American fishing rights within the United States or Canada).

In this chapter we deal primarily with the first two of these. They are, of course, closely related; too many fishers catching too many fish relative to what is known about the current size of the various fisheries. This situation is largely the result of the **open-access** nature of marine fisheries. Until recently, anyone who wanted to buy a boat and commence fishing could do so. The re-sult has been too many boats and a commensurate driving down of fish stocks. Historically, the opening up of new fisheries leads to a rapid influx of boats, overfishing, and, ultimately, depletion of the stocks. Figure 13-2 shows the landings profile of five historical fisheries of the United States, from 1837 to 1993. The profiles are remarkably similar and are probably representative of many other fisheries around the world.

Many countries have sought to regulate fishing to protect fish stocks, with mixed success. A major part of the problem is that public agencies have typi-cally relied on command-and-control measures that have not adequately ac-counted for the incentives facing fishers. It is also true that governments have usually been very much conflicted between the desire to avoid overfishing and the even stronger desire to protect the economic livelihoods of fishing communities.

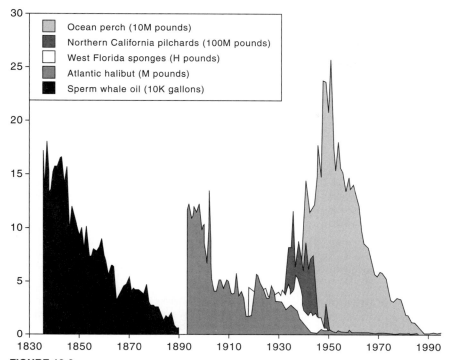

FIGURE 13-2
Profile of Landings for Five Historic Fisheries of the United States, 1837–1993 (*Source:* NMFS, *Our Living Oceans: The Economic Status of U.S. Fisheries, 1996*, U.S. Dept. of Commerce, NOAA Technical Memo NMFS F/SPO-22. Courtesy of Amy Gautam and Steve Edwards.)

U.S. FISHERIES MANAGEMENT INSTITUTIONS

The primary authority for fishery management in the United States is the **Magnuson Fishery Conservation and Management Act (MFCMA) of 1976.** Under this law, eight **Regional Fishery Management Councils** were established to pursue fishery management goals in their particular regions. The councils prepare **Fishery Management Plans** (FMPs) for the fisheries in their region that are in need of regulation. The councils, the states and other territories they include, and important species in each region, are shown in Table 13-2.

The councils are composed of public officials from the states and territories in the region, and from Washington, as well as "interested and knowledgeable members of the public," who have been, for the most part, representatives of the fish harvesting, processing, and distributing sectors. The FMPs prepared by the councils attempt to establish limits on total catches and regulations on such items as fishing gear, harvesting practices, and closure times as necessary for managing the fisheries.

TABLE 13-2
REGIONAL FISHERIES COUNCILS

Council	States and other territories	Species
New England	Maine New Hampshire Massachusetts Rhode Island Connecticut	Atlantic groundfish, Atlantic herring, sharks, sea scallops, swordfish, redfish, billfish, hake, pollack, red crabs, and American lobster
Mid-Atlantic	New York New Jersey Pennsylvania Delaware Maryland Virginia	Surf clam and ocean quahog, Atlantic mackerel, butterfish, squid, sharks, bluefish, swordfish, scup, dogfish, billfish, other flounder, sea bass, tile fish, and sea scallops
South Atlantic	North Carolina South Carolina Georgia Florida	Billfish, coastal migratory pelagics, sharks, swordfish, corals, spiny lobster, tropical reef fish, calico scallops, sea scallops, shrimp, and coastal herring
Caribbean	Virgin Islands Puerto Rico	Spiny lobster, shallow water reef fish, swordfish, migratory pelagics, mollusks, billfish, corals, deep water reef fish, bait fishes, sharks, and rays
Gulf	Texas Louisiana Mississippi Alabama Florida	Groundfish, calico scallops, shrimp, coastal migratory pelagics, reef fish, corals, squids, spiny lobster, sharks, stone crab, sponges, billfish, coastal herring, swordfish, and tropical reef fish
Pacific	California Oregon Washington Idaho	Salmon, anchovy, groundfish, pink shrimp, billfish, and herring
North Pacific	Alaska Washington Oregon	Tanner crab, Gulf of Alaska groundfish, king crab, high sea salmon, scallops, Bering Sea groundfish, Bering Sea clam, Bering Sea herring, Bering Sea shrimp, corals, dungeness crab, shrimp, and snails
Western Pacific	Hawaii American Samoa Guam	Billfish, bottomfish, precious corals, seamount resources, and spiny lobster

Source: Lee G. Anderson, "Marine Fisheries," in Paul R. Portney (ed.), *Current Issues in Natural Resource Policy,* Johns Hopkins Press for Resources for the Future, Baltimore, 1982, p. 167.

The widely held judgment on the performance of fisheries management councils has been recently stated by the National Marine Fisheries Service.

In terms of fisheries management objectives since implementation of the MFCMA, achievement of maximum sustainable yield has been the principal goal. A patchwork of legislation and subsequent regulations, centered on complicated and sometimes conflicting gear restrictions, quotas, trip limits, and time and area closures, has been the result. These effort control management strategies have been largely ineffective, often encouraging inefficient and excessive use of effort and capital of existing vessels, and in some cases, promoting and subsidizing further entry of new vessels. . . . These "command-and-control" measures may achieve short-run stock improvements, but in the long-run they generally are not successful at reducing effort. Despite early recognition of the potential for overfishing in the United States, the actions taken to control harvests from U.S. waters have often been ineffective from the standpoint of both biological and economic sustainability. . . .

A majority of U.S. fisheries have been 'diagnosed' by the NMFS biologists as operating at or above long-term potential yield, or maximum sustainable yield: 83% of the U.S. fishery resources which have been assessed are classified as over- or fully utilized from a biological standpoint. . . . Since most fisheries are still characterized by open-access, it seems fairly safe to suggest that the number of U.S. fisheries operating near the efficient point of effort, or harvesting using least-cost methods, is quite small.

Continuing problems with developing effective fisheries management plans led in 1996 to the passage of the **Sustainable Fisheries Act of 1996.** This law is meant to give the regional councils more authority, as well as responsibility, to develop plans that will rehabilitate fisheries deemed to be overfished. However, the law also puts a temporary moratorium on the establishment of new incentive-based management systems. To understand the impact of this, we must now focus on the basic bioeconomics of fisheries management.

MODELING A FISHERY

In this section we develop a simple **bioeconomic model** for analyzing both positive and normative questions about exploiting a fishery. A bioeconomic approach means that it combines two elements: the **biology** of fisheries growth and decline and the behavioral consequences that flow from **economic decisions** made by humans.

The Biological Growth Function

Consider a single **fishery.** By "fishery" we mean a collection of fish that inhabit a reasonably well delimited section of marine habitat. It might be fish of a single species (e.g., oysters in Chesapeake Bay) or fish of multiple, but related, species (e.g., all groundfish on Georges Bank off Cape Cod). At any given time the fishery consists of many individuals of different ages and sizes. To simplify this, we measure the total size of the fish stock in terms of **biomass,** essentially the aggregate weight of all the individuals of which the fishery is composed. The size of a fishery biomass is determined by many factors, not just the amount of fishing effort that is expended on it. Predator and prey factors, annual fecundity, ocean currents, food supply, water qualities, disease, and other factors play a role. There are few fisheries in the world where these factors are clearly understood. Fisheries biologists continue to pursue research into the complicated population dynamics of these situations.

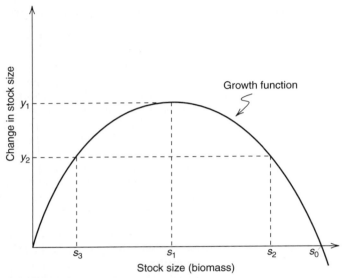

FIGURE 13-3
The Logistic Model of Population Growth for a Fishery

For the moment, however, we are going to set aside all these complex factors and focus on the all-important relationship between the **size** of the fishery biomass and the **growth** of that biomass. There are two major natural growth factors: increases in the number of individuals through processes of reproduction, and increases in the sizes (weights) of individuals through maturation. There are also two major forces working in the opposite direction: losses from predation and food scarcities and losses from natural mortality, especially old age.

At relatively small biomass levels the forces of reproduction and growth may be expected to dominate: With ecosystem abundance, high rates of reproduction are associated with rapid rates of growth of the biomass. But this obviously cannot continue indefinitely. As the size of the biomass gets relatively large, food scarcities would start to take their toll. So at some point we can expect a natural equilibrium to assert itself between the factors of growth and reduction. In this way a natural population size would be established.

This reasoning has given rise to the famous **logistic model** of population growth, first proposed by P. F. Verhulst in 1938.[2] It is pictured in Figure 13-3. The size of the biomass is indexed on the horizontal axis, and the increment, or change, in that biomass during a period of time such as a year is shown on

[2] P. F. Verhulst, "Notice sur la loi que la population suit dans son accroissement," *Correspondance Mathématique et Physique*, Vol. 10, 1938, pp. 113–121.

the vertical axis. The inverted U-shaped function starts at the origin—no fish, no increment. At higher stocks the increment is larger, reaching a maximum at a stock size of s_1. At larger stock sizes the increment is still positive but less than the maximum primarily because of the increased scarcities of food and space that the larger stocks imply. At a stock size of s_0, the different factors affecting stock size are all in balance, so that there is no increment. Stock size s_0 is thus a natural equilibrium, in the sense that this is the stock that would result if the population were left to itself and ecological factors were constant. At stock sizes above s_0, biological forces would be at work that would actually lead to negative increments, that is, to reductions in the size of the fishery biomass.

The logistic curve can be interpreted as a type of **sustained yield** curve, where by "yield" we mean a certain amount of the biomass harvested and therefore removed each year. For example, at a biomass size of s_2, the growth increment is equal to y_2 pounds, on the vertical axis. Thus if, at this stock size, y_2 pounds of fish were harvested each year, the yield would exactly match the growth increment and the size of the stock would be unchanged. This underlines an important point: There is not just one sustainable stock size in this situation. Any stock size is sustainable if the yield exactly matches the natural increment in the biomass. Note that the yield y_2 is also consistent with a stock size of s_3. But this pair, s_3 and y_2, is an unstable pair in the following sense. Suppose, with the yield kept at y_2, the stock size temporarily increased above s_3. Then the natural increment would exceed the yield, and the stock would be larger next year. So if the yield was held at y_2, the stock would slowly grow to size s_2, which is a stable situation, in the sense that short-run deviations of the stock above or below s_2 would be self-correcting.

But note also another possible outcome. Suppose, with a stock of s_3 and a yield of y_2, there was a short-run diminution in the size of the biomass, because of, say, temporary food shortages. If the yield or total catch is held at the level y_2, it will exceed the natural increment, driving the stock lower. If the yield continues at y_2, the biomass will eventually be driven to zero; the fishery will be wiped out.

From this analysis we can conclude that any yield equal to or less than y_1 is sustainable—that is, it can be continued indefinitely with a stable, sustainable stock size lying between s_1 and s_0. Any total catch over y_1 cannot be sustainable, because this would be greater than the maximum growth increment of which the fishery is capable.

The Effort-Yield Function

Now it is time to bring human behavior into the model. The "yield" referred to in the last section is actually a quantity of fish assumed to be harvested from the fishery, but this yield can come about only when human effort is given to the task. **Harvesting effort** refers to the economic resources devoted to catching fish; this includes capital goods (e.g., boats and gear), labor (captains and deckhands), and materials and energy. To simplify the graphics, we want to convert these resources to a single dimension. Perhaps the easiest way to do this is to think in terms of a standardized fishing boat, of a certain size, with a certain size crew and set of fishing gear. Then we can speak of larger or smaller amounts of human effort in terms of the number of days spent fishing by boats of the standard type. We make this assumption in order to proceed with our simple model. In the real world, of course, there can be substantial differences among boats on a fishery, in terms of size, equipment, the skills of people on them, and so on. We abstract from these differences here.

With this simplification, a typical **effort-yield curve** is depicted in Figure 13-4. It is important to keep in mind that this is a **sustained-yield** relationship. For example, an effort level of e_2 is associated with a sustained yield of y_2. This means that if effort level e_2 is applied each year on a permanent basis, the permanent (i.e., sustained) yield that will result is y_2. Yields may be different in the short run as adjustments are occurring, but eventually they will settle down to y_2.

The reasoning behind the inverted U-shape of the effort-yield relationship is because of the linkage between effort levels and the size of the stock. At a zero level of effort, the fishery will adjust to its natural size (level s_0 in Figure 13-3). As effort increases, the higher yields taken off the fishery result in the maintenance of small stock sizes; at an effort level of e_m, the sustained yield reaches its maximum point. At still higher effort levels, stock levels become re-

FIGURE 13-4
Effort-Yield Curve for a Fishery

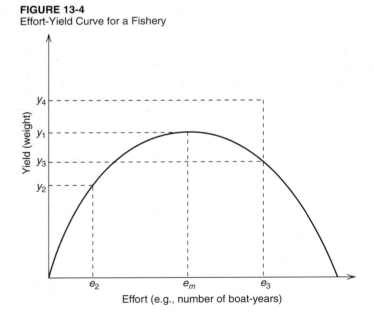

Effort (e.g., number of boat-years)

duced (we are on the rising portion of the graph in Figure 13-3). At a very high effort level, the stock would be driven to zero.

It is again important to keep in mind that the model shows **sustained yields,** that is, yields that would result if the indicated effort level is applied **continuously** and the stock has had time to adjust to these effort levels. It is possible, in the short run, to have yields that are not on the effort-yield curve, for example a yield of y_4 at effort level e_3. But this is not sustainable. A high short-term yield like this will drive the stock down, and the yield obtainable with this effort level will fall, in the long run, to y_3.

Maximum Sustained Yield

All the yields traced out by the effort-yield curve are biologically sustainable. An effort level of e_m produces the **maximum sustained yield** (MSY) from this fishery.[3] This is the maximum quantity of harvest that can be realized in the long run, that is, on a sustainable basis. Maximum sustained yield is often regarded as the best target to aim for in exploiting renewable resources such as a fishery. Its appeal is based on the fact that this is the maximum biological yield that the fishery is capable of producing. When humans are brought in, however, this conclusion does not necessarily follow, because social efficiency, the effort level that maximizes the net benefits of the fishery, requires that the consequences of alternative effort levels be expressed in value terms.

EFFICIENT RATES OF EFFORT

To explore economic efficiency, we must determine values for both the harvested fish and the effort that goes into catching them. Let us make the assumption that the harvested fish are sold on a market, at a given and constant price, and that this price represents the full social value of the fish. We also assume that each unit of effort has a given, and constant, opportunity cost. These assumptions allow us to construct the revenue and cost functions depicted in Figure 13-5. The total revenue curve is the effort yield curve of Figure 13-4 multiplied by the unit price of the harvested fish. Thus it preserves the inverted U shape of that relationship. The total cost curve is simply a straight line starting at the origin and rising to the right at a slope that represents the opportunity costs of a unit of effort. The higher this opportunity cost, the steeper the total cost relationship. The **net income** corresponding to any effort level, which equals net social benefits in this simple model, is given by the distance between total revenue and total cost. The effort level at which this distance is maximized is e^*, and net benefits at this point are equal to

---

[3] Recently, the National Marine Fisheries Service (a part of the National Oceanographic and Atmospheric Administration), which is the federal agency responsible for fisheries policies, has started to call this yield the **long-term potential yield** (LTPY).

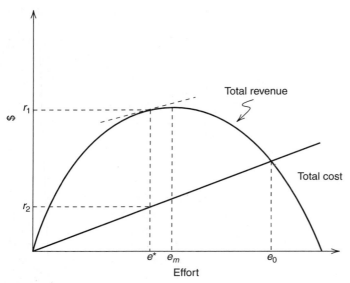

FIGURE 13-5
Efficient Harvest Level for a Fishery

$(r_1 - r_2)$.[4] It is easy to see that at any other effort level net benefits—the distance between the two curves—would be smaller than at e^*.

In particular, the net benefits produced at the point of maximum sustained yield (effort level e_m) are lower than at e_1. The reason is that, although the yields are indeed higher at e_m than at e^*, the extra costs of harvest are even greater, so the net revenues are lower. This shows that the point of maximum sustained yield in a physical, or biological, sense is not necessarily the point of maximum net social benefits in an economic sense. In fact economic efficiency implies a lower effort level, and therefore a higher permanent stock level, than does maximum sustained yield.

To explain an important point about the value of the fishery, suppose this fishery had a single owner. The annual net income of this person would be an amount equal to $r_1 - r_2$ in Figure 13-5. This value is in effect produced by the fishery; if this owner were to sell the fishery to another person, this annual net income would be the determinant of the price at which the fishery would sell. The annual return realized in this fashion is called the **annual resource rent** produced by the fishery. As we have seen before, a **natural resource rent** is the net value of a resource, prior to extraction, that is, its value **in situ.** Efficiency in natural resource use, therefore, implies using resources in such a way as to maximize their in situ value, or rent. In the case of our fishery the rent-maximizing level of effort is e^*.

[4] The way this is found is by drawing a line tangent to the total revenue curve with the same slope as the total cost curve. In the figure it is shown as a dotted line. The tangency point occurs at an effort level of e^*.

THE PROBLEM OF OPEN ACCESS

The next question to ask is whether, in the real world, effort levels on fisheries would tend to points like e^* in Figure 13-5. To answer this question we have to consider the incentive aspects of the situation, which get us into the question of how the property rights to the resource are held. In the real world, rights to ocean fisheries are typically not held by single owners or even, at least until recently, by defined groups of individuals. Rather, fisheries have historically been subject to **open-access** rules: Anybody who has wanted to buy or build a boat and go fishing essentially had the "right" to do so. To consider the incentive implications of this, suppose there is an open-access fishery in which the harvesting effort level is currently at e_1 (Figure 13-5). Consider the logic of one more fisher who is contemplating whether to get a boat and start harvesting from this fishery. Open access means that she need not get permission from anybody to do this, nor must she pay anybody for the right to engage in fishing. The only cost is the cost of buying the boat and gear, which are the standard costs reflected in the total cost curve of the model. Since effort is currently at e^*, she could be expected to compare this cost with anticipated revenues. At e^*, average revenues per unit of effort (per boat, for example) exceed average cost. Thus there are apparently profits to be made by any individual entering the fishery. Despite the fact that e^* is the efficient level of effort from the standpoint of society, there are still incentives for additional fishers to devote greater effort to harvesting from the fishery.

In fact this incentive in the open-access situation continues to exist as long as total revenue exceeds total cost (because average revenue exceeds average cost in this situation). The upshot is that entry will continue to occur until total effort has grown to e_0 in Figure 13-5. At this point total revenue equals total costs, and so the incentive for further entry has disappeared. Note also that all **resource rent** has disappeared at effort level e_0. At this level of effort the fishery is not producing positive net benefits. The resource rents have in effect been **dissipated** by excess entry and effort levels applied to the fishery.

The open-access condition of the fishery has produced substantially higher effort levels (and therefore substantially smaller stock levels) than is socially efficient. This situation is made much worse if **technological change** occurs so as to reduce the unit costs of harvesting effort. Diagrammatically, this implies a less steep total cost curve in the figure, which will make open-access levels of effort go even higher.

This is the basic incentive situation that historically has characterized most saltwater fisheries and many freshwater resources. It is accurate to say that most approaches to public fisheries management have been attempts to rectify the overharvesting implications of open access. Until recently, these management efforts were based for the most part on trying to regulate directly the performance of people harvesting particular fisheries. More recently attention has focused on changing the property rights aspects of these situations so as to alter the basic incentives facing harvesters.

APPROACHES TO FISHERIES MANAGEMENT

Throughout the world countries have been struggling in the last few decades to overcome the problems caused by open access in marine fisheries. Some of these efforts have already been successful, while many are still evolving in ways that may lead both to the restoration of depleted fish stocks and their efficient harvesting. A major factor has been the gradual change in attitudes, away from the long-standing notion that the ocean was a resource of unlimited abundance that ought to be freely available and toward one that recognizes the need for restraint if fisheries are to be preserved.

Fisheries regulations have, in general, progressed through a series of stages, starting first with modest regulatory moves and finally ending up, more recently, with more fundamental shifts in the property rights systems applicable to fisheries.

Restricting Access—First Steps

Open access means, very simply and in practical terms, that there are too many fishers, and fishing boats, exploiting a fishery. The natural tendency for people faced with this type of situation is to try and identify some means by which entry to the fisheries can be limited. Anthropologists and historians have found that, for centuries, localized groups of people have sought to define and defend territorial rights to fisheries, essentially by excluding outsiders from the resource. Informal territorial use rights in fisheries (**TURFs**) have been organized around particular geographical areas that make it possible to set boundaries and exclude would-be encroachers.[5] Sedentary species (clams, oysters, mussels) lend themselves relatively well to this approach because particular bays, lagoons, or coral reefs can be defended. A well-known example in a semisedentary species is the harbor gangs of Maine. These are groups of lobster fishers centered on particular bays who have pursued well-organized, but extralegal, efforts to exclude outsiders from fishing in the areas they control.[6]

But under some conditions TURFs may also be useful for migratory species. A TURF is not resource-specific as much as it is site-specific. So a species that migrated along a shoreline could be exploited by a TURF that controlled access for a certain distance along the shoreline. This might not be effective in controlling overfishing of the species because it doesn't offer control of access to the stock elsewhere in its migration journey.

The essential logic of the TURF (i.e., exclusion of outsiders) has recently been pursued worldwide at the level of the nation. As of the 1950s, most countries were claiming national jurisdiction over waters and resources that were

---

[5] See Francis T. Christy, Jr., "Territorial Use Rights in Marine Fisheries: Definitions and Conditions," Food and Agriculture Organization, Rome, Technical Paper No. 227, 1982.

[6] See Chapter 7.

within 3 miles (in a few cases 12 miles) from shore based on the long history of maritime custom. This meant that the majority of the productive fisheries of the world were situated on the "high seas," beyond effective political and management control. Large foreign fleets could exploit fisheries that many countries regarded as being essentially in their home waters. Attempts were made to deal with the problem through international negotiations and agreements. The International Fisheries Convention of 1946 targeted the northeastern Atlantic. The International Commission for North-West Atlantic Fisheries was established in 1949. During the 1960s a number of new regulatory bodies and conventions were formed, covering more than 80 countries and most of the world's oceans. But these international efforts were relatively ineffective at stopping overfishing, primarily because of marked differences among countries in terms of fishing technology and costs, opinions about fish stocks, and so on.

Thus the 1960s and early 1970s saw a push toward **extended jurisdiction,** essentially a state of affairs in which countries claimed and enforced offshore limits of 200 miles. This effectively nationalized, or put under the jurisdiction of national authorities of coastal countries, about 95 percent of the world's productive fisheries. In effect this might be thought of as a move toward national TURFs. But TURF will be successful only to the extent that it develops the institutional capacities with which to regulate or manage the affected fisheries within the TURF. In fact, in large countries such as the United States, the 200-mile zone is still subject to problems of open access and overfishing because of ineffective management institutions. In smaller countries, such as Iceland, authorities have been more successful at instituting effective fisheries management programs within their 200-mile exclusion zone.

Regulating Fishing Practices

The dominant approach in fishery regulation has been command-and-control types of restrictions on the fishing practices, in the hope that it could be made less productive and therefore less devastating on stocks of fish. These restraints included such measures as closing certain areas, limiting the number of days of fishing, prohibiting fine-mesh nets in order to target larger fish, restricting the size and horsepower of fishing boats, and so on.

Figure 13-6 shows a way of analyzing this approach. What regulations of this type do, essentially, is to raise the cost of fishing. By restricting certain inputs, say, the type of net that may be used, the effect is to make it more costly to catch a given quantity of fish. In our standard fisheries model, this rotates the total cost curve upward, giving it a steeper slope. If TC_1 is the original total cost curve, the new curve resulting from a regulation of this type would be something like TC_2. Now open access, instead of leading to e_0 units of effort on the fishery, would produce only e_m units of effort. This is approximately equal to the maximum sustained yield level of effort. A somewhat larger increase in costs, produced by somewhat more restrictive regulations, would shift up

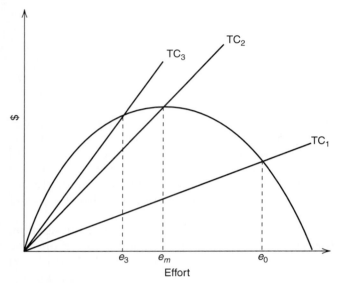

FIGURE 13-6
Effects of Fishing Regulations

total costs even more, say, to TC_3, moving the open-access level of effort to e_3, which is close to the original efficient effort level.

There are a couple of major problems with this type of approach. First and foremost is that, although it is possible to reduce effort levels and therefore increase stocks, and ultimately yields, in this way, it is being done by making fishing much more costly than it needs to be. Economic efficiency requires more than just arriving at the optimal yield and fish stock, it also requires that this yield be achieved with the minimum expenditure of scarce resources, that is, at minimum opportunity cost.

The second disadvantage of this type of direct control on fishing practices is that it can never be complete. When some parts of the fishing enterprise are constrained, fishers will attempt to expand in directions that are uncontrolled. Suppose, for example, authorities place a limit on the number of boats that may be used on a fishery. Fishers now have the incentive to build larger boats to increase their harvests. Suppose authorities step in and place an upper limit on boat length. Fishers now may shift to boats with larger engines. A limitation on horsepower may lead them to increase the number of trips they make each year. And so on.[7]

---

[7] Another potential problem, which our simple model does not illustrate, is where tighter regulations in one fishery lead fishers to shift and put added pressure on different fisheries.

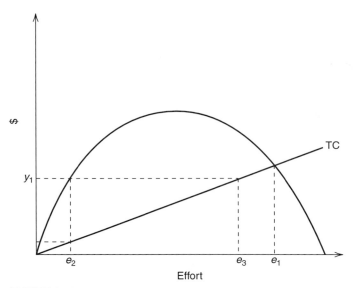

FIGURE 13-7
Catch Limits

Catch Limits

Another common regulatory approach is for authorities to establish upper limits on the quantity of fish that may be taken from particular fisheries. These are usually called TACs, for **total allowable catch** (or sometimes **total catch quotas**). TACs appear to give authorities a means of closely controlling yields. They simply establish a TAC, monitor incoming catches, and when the limit is reached, close the fishery. Apart from the difficulties in monitoring and enforcing this kind of limit, the major problem with it is shown in Figure 13-7. The open-access level of effort is e_1, which authorities regard as leading to diminished stocks. They therefore establish an upper limit on catch of y_1 (although there is a monetary scale on the vertical axis, it can readily be translated into quantity of fish by dividing by the unit price of fish). The y_1 level is below the efficient yield, but perhaps the thought is that it will be set at this level for some time to allow stocks to rejuvenate.

The minimum effort to harvest a yield of y_1 is e_2. Suppose this effort level was somehow temporarily established. At that point, there are rents being earned by fishers, and this will attract additional resources into the fishery. A common phenomenon that illustrates this is the **derby fishery.** Although the TAC has been set, no quotas have been set for individual fishers. Thus individuals will have the incentive to increase their **share** of the TAC. The advantage goes to the fishers who can get out on the fishery first with the greatest fishing power. So the effort level will get pushed to the right, as fishers do whatever it takes—bigger boats, engines, crews, and nets—to get bigger shares of the TAC before the fishery is closed down. In fact if the TAC is set permanently at y_1, the effort level will eventually increase to e_3, close to the open-access situation.

While setting catch quotas would seem to be a very specific and effective way to halt overfishing, trying to use them in fisheries where both biology and economic relationships are complex and imperfectly known can encounter a tangle of difficulties, as the excerpt in Exhibit 13-1 describes in the case of an important New England fishery.

Individual Transferable Quotas (ITQs)

The problem with these regulatory approaches is that they do not address the fundamental problem, which is that the value represented by the fishery resource is left open to capture by anybody who feels like trying. If rents are temporarily positive in a fishery, nothing stops new entrants from trying to appropriate some of them. It is this process that drives the effort level upward, eventually to e_2, and the rent to zero. Setting TACs, and then dividing them up into quotas for individual fishers, partly solves the problem, as it reduces the incentive for a "race to fish." But individual catch quotas can lock in inefficiencies and inequities stemming from the way they are originally determined. The last all-important step is to make the quotas transferable, hence the name **individual transferable quotas,** or ITQs. The approach has caught on in many fisheries around the world, as regulatory authorities seek to achieve fish harvesting levels and methods that are both efficient and sustainable.

To establish an effective ITQ, authorities must accomplish the following:

1 Establish TACs that are both economically and biologically meaningful.
2 Divide the TAC into a number of individual catch limits, or catch quotas, to be allocated to participants in the fishery.
3 Allow these individual quotas to be bought and sold, and keep track of who owns how many.
4 Enforce the catch quotas, so that fishers cannot harvest and sell quantities of fish in excess of their quota holdings.
5 Monitor the performance of the ITQ market to spot and manage problems related to concentrated ownership, community impacts, and biological uncertainties.

Step number one is easy to understand, but may be a lot harder to implement than might first be thought. Clearly some limitation on total catch is necessary if open-access conditions have led to economic and/or biological overfishing. But setting a TAC reasonably accurately requires both biological and economic information that may not be available. This is especially true if, as is normally the case, stocks fluctuate from year to year because of factors not related to fishing pressure. We discuss below some issues related to fisheries management in cases of great uncertainty.

EXHIBIT 13-1

PROBLEMS IN SETTING TACs

It is believed that there are two fairly distinct stocks of yellowtail and cod, but only one stock of haddock. The two stocks of yellowtail are thought to be located east and west of 69° west longitude, while the two stocks of cod are found in the Gulf of Maine and on Georges Bank respectively.

The fleet that harvests these three species comes mostly from New England and it also harvests other species during certain parts of the year. Because of the biological relationships between these species, as well as certain economic phenomena, this particular fishery is perhaps one of the most difficult and challenging to manage.

The plan for cod, haddock, and yellowtail was initiated in 1977 and established a total quota for each of the stocks of fish. Fishing licenses were required, but they were easily available and there was no moratorium on entry as there was in the surf clam and ocean quahog fishery. It was soon discovered that with the existing fleet and the many new entrants, the annual quota would be harvested very early in the year. This infuriated fishermen. In the following year the quota was caught early in the year but because absolute closure of the fishery would cause hardships for the industry, the council adopted a policy which effectively turned back the clock and started the fishing year and quota over again. While this may have protected employment in the short run, if continually repeated it would have serious consequences on the long-run productivity of the fishery.

Eventually the quarterly quotas were further subdivided by vessel size, and other stipulations were introduced which limited catch per boat trip. These limits were particularly wasteful of resources since boats had to return to port before they would normally have done so and hence wasted fuel and other resources. These allocation methods were not enough to subdue the loud voices heard at most council meetings concerning the perceived inequities of the plan. Larger, new boats needed substantial catches in order to pay their mortgages; smaller boats felt unable to get a fair share of the total quota since they could not fish in stormy weather. The quarterly quota allocation by vessel size did not solve either of these problems since, if the smaller boats and fixed gear vessels did not harvest their allocation, it was given to the larger boat categories rather than reserved for the following quarter. Trip limits based on the number of crew members were then instituted, presumably to allow the larger boats to catch more. The effect of doing so was predictable. Many boats increased the size of their crews in order to increase their allowable catch.

The system deteriorated still further. Toward the end of a quarter, it was possible for small boats to be forbidden to fish for yellowtail flounder west of the 69° meridian because their share of that quarterly quota was used up, but permitted to harvest them east of that line. At the same time, medium boats might be forbidden to fish for flounder on either side of the line while big boats could fish anywhere for flounder. The rules for cod and haddock, which are caught in the same nets, could be different. Vessels were subject to different rules if they fished in state waters before or after fishing beyond the 3-mile line. Since it was impossible to tell where a fish was caught, enforcement was all but impossible. Finally, complaints led to changes in both total quotas and the rules to enforce them. Neither fisherman nor regulator knew what was going on.

This excerpt explains the difficulties encountered by the New England Fisheries Council in establishing catch quotas for cod, haddock, and yellowtail flounder caught off New England.

Source: Lee G. Anderson, "Marine Fisheries," in Paul R. Portney (ed.), *Current Issues in Natural Resource Policy*, Johns Hopkins Press for Resources for the Future, Baltimore, Chapter 5, 1982, pp. 173–175. Copyright © 1982 by Johns Hopkins Press.

The division of the total quota into individual quotas is the next step, and obviously is one that will be controversial in most cases. The quotas will eventually be valuable property rights. Every participant will prefer to have more rather than less, so some acceptable means must be found for their distribution. They might be auctioned off, or given away on some criterion, for example, past production (measured on some basis) or number of boats. Exhibit 13-2 discusses how an ITQ system was established for a fishery off the east coast of the United States and how the quotas were first distributed.

Step three is inherent in the quota system itself. But monitoring all quota transactions will require a good accounting system, especially if the number of present participants is large. In a smoothly functioning market, quotas will not

---

EXHIBIT 13-2

ITQs IN THE ATLANTIC SURF CLAM FISHERY

Surf clams are large, hard-shell clams harvested along coastal locations. The mid-Atlantic fishery lies off the shores of New Jersey, Maryland, Virginia, and the Carolinas. Prior to 1977 this fishery was regulated by the individual states, but there were problems in coordinating efforts. For example, the Virginia portion collapsed in the early 1970's, so fishing pressure shifted to New Jersey, prompting a closure there in 1976.

The surf clam offshore fishery was brought under federal management in 1977, when it was characterized by excessive effort levels and low yields. The first federal management effort consisted of a vessel moratorium program, an annual total catch quota, a limitation of vessel fishing hours, catch log books and vessel permits. Other measures such as minimum clam sizes were added in later years. Under the moratorium, only vessels that had fished for clams between November 1976 and November 1977 could take part in the fishery. Special provisions were added for qualifying newly constructed boats.

The moratorium program eventually became an administrative nightmare. Although the overall harvest was under reasonable control, continued efforts by fishers to expand effort led to gross inefficiencies. Allowable fishing hours were gradually reduced in response to continuous increases

in vessel fishing power. By 1990 a boat was permitted to fish just six hours a week.

These conditions led the Mid-Atlantic Fishery Management Council in 1990 to shift to an ITQ system. Initial ITQ shares were issued to fishers on the basis of a formula of vessel historical catch and vessel size. Initial shares were allocated to 67 vessel owners. Most other regulations were dropped.

Within two years the number of vessels on this fishery dropped by 54 percent. The fishing time per vessel increased from 154 hours a year to 380 hours a year. The average catch per vessel increased by 96 percent in the first two years of the program. Thus the total catch increased as fishing effort declined.

ITQs are not without their problems, of course. One that has developed in this case is the concentration of quota holdings. To control the flow of their raw product supply, onshore clam processing companies have sought to expand their ownership of quota permits. It remains to be seen how important this problem becomes.

Source: Organization for Economic Cooperation and Development, *Towards Sustainable Fisheries, Economic Aspects of the Management of Living Marine Resources*, OECD, Paris, 1997, pp. 264–266.

only be bought and sold outright, but leased, or perhaps loaned, in varying amounts for varying periods of time. Step four calls on the same type of monitoring and enforcing efforts that any kind of TAC and quota system requires. As mentioned earlier, enforcement is not something that just happens automatically when a regulation is promulgated. Enforcement activities have to be designed and funded with enough resources to achieve acceptable levels of compliance. Enforcing fishery regulations is hard because fishing is done in places away from easy scrutiny, and in many cases it is fairly easy for fishers to offload "hot" fish in ways that escape surveillance. One of the major advantages of ITQs is that it can make unnecessary the kinds of detailed gear and performance restrictions that are inherently hard to monitor and enforce.

Step five is sometimes not given adequate attention. The ITQ system works by creating a new property right and a market on which that property right may be traded. It is virtually impossible to predict all of the important problems that novel institutions like this will encounter. Clear and accurate data on their operation is essential. This is especially so because one of the implications of establishing tradable quotas in a fishery is that there is no longer a tendency for the natural resource rent to be **dissipated.** This value, which is squandered under open-access conditions, will accrue, at least initially, to those who possess the fishing rights. There are many who feel that private appropriation of these values is in conflict with the fact that its source is a resource essentially supplied by nature herself. And so the issue of who ends up with the resource rents can become an important point of conflict.[8]

UNCERTAINTY AND FISHERIES MANAGEMENT

In the analyses of the previous section we implicitly assumed that the population biology of the affected fisheries was reasonably clear; regulators were assumed to have accurate knowledge of the stock-yield and effort-yield curves. A major problem with fisheries management in the real world, however, is that knowledge of these relationships is highly uncertain. One source of uncertainty is lack of complete biological and yield data, both current and historical, on the fishery, including landings and factors that would affect the stock size. Important economic information may also be missing, such as accurate data on fishing costs and likely future changes in fishing technology. Biological variability is a major problem. Natural variability in ecological variables (e.g., ocean temperature, predators) can make it difficult to identify the fish stocks accurately, not to mention the fact that the underlying biological models used for the purpose may not be accurate.

---

[8] In Iceland there is pressure on public authorities to tax away some of the resource rents from the rights holders: to have them pay, in a sense, for the right to fish. For the most part, this is a **distributional issue,** not an efficiency issue. If the efficient level of effort is being applied to the fishery, the resource rent could be taxed away, in part at least, without inducing a change in this effort level.

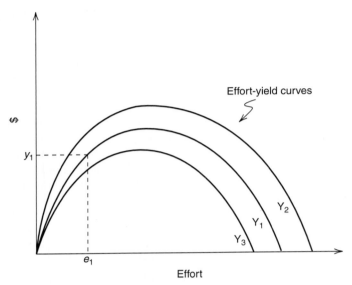

FIGURE 13-8
A Precautionary Approach in the Face of Uncertainty

When there are large uncertainties, fisheries management authorities may want to adopt rules that reflect this fact. Consider Figure 13-8. Suppose that biologists believe the most likely effort-yield curve is Y_1, but because of uncertainties in their knowledge of the fishery, there is a fairly strong probability that it could be as high as Y_2 or as low as Y_3.

Suppose the authorities establish a TAC of y_1, setting up an ITQ system so that the effort level is e_1. If the actual effort-yield curve is equal to Y_2, or anywhere else above Y_1, the fish stock will either maintain its size or even grow. But suppose the actual effort-yield curve is Y_3. In this case the harvest level y_1 is not sustainable; at effort level e_1 the sustainable harvest rate is y_2. With effort at e_1 and harvests (temporarily) at y_1, something has to give. If the effort level is maintained, stocks will decline and harvest levels will gradually diminish to the sustainable level y_2. But a more likely scenario, perhaps, is that fishers will increase effort levels as they try to maintain the permitted harvest level of y_1. If this were to happen, stocks could be driven to a precariously low level. The way out of this dilemma is for authorities to establish a lower quota level in the first place, commensurate with their uncertainty about the true bioeconomic relationships of the fishery.

SUMMARY

Ocean (and freshwater) fisheries are renewable resources, which require **bioeconomic models** for understanding and effective management. Such models combine both the biology of the resource and the economics of human behavior.

The fish biomass **growth function** shows the increment to the stock of fish as a function of the size of that stock. After converting this into an **effort-yield** curve, we were able to analyze the effects of open access on **rent dissipation** in the fishery and the effectiveness of different types of fishery regulation. In many historical situations, TURFs (territorial use rights in fisheries) have been developed in an attempt to limit access to certain individuals, but these may be ineffective in the face of rising demand and technical change in fishing. Most fishery regulations historically have been based on **command-and-control** approaches, especially gear restrictions and **catch quotas** (total allowable catch, or TACs). These regulations do nothing to solve the rent dissipation problem of the fishery. In more recent years some countries have moved in the direction of incentive-based regulations, especially **individual transferable quotas.**

KEY TERMS

Bioeconomic model	TURFs (territorial use rights in fisheries)
Open access	Extended jurisdiction
Maximum sustained yield	Magnuson Act
Effort-yield curve	TAC (total allowable catch)
Rent dissipation	ITQs (individual transferable quotas)
Natural resource rents	Derby fishery

QUESTIONS FOR FURTHER DISCUSSION

1 What would the biological growth curve look like if there exists a critical stock size below which growth rates become negative and the stock evolves to zero?
2 What would be the efficiency and equity implications of granting a fishery to one individual as a sole owner?
3 By decreasing effort, fishers can often catch more fish. Explain this.
4 Why is there a difference between the maximum sustained yield and the economically efficient sustained yield?
5 What other natural resources are like a fishery, in the sense that there are many different possible levels of steady-state stock among which one may be identified as economically efficient? (A steady state is simply one that persists over a long period of time. The optimal stock is a steady-state stock, but, as the question implies, not all steady-state stocks are efficient.)
6 What are some of the problems that might be anticipated in moving from a temporary, short-run yield to a long-run, sustainable yield?

USEFUL WEB SITES

The National Oceanic and Atmospheric Administration (NOAA) maintains a number of relevant sites:

- National Marine Fisheries Service (http://www.nmfs.gov)
- The Seagrant program in cooperation with the states (http://www.nsgo. seagrant.org)

- Regional fisheries management councils, for example, North Pacific Fishery Management Council (http://www.fakr.noaa.gov/npfmc/default/htm) and Mid-Atlantic Fishery Management Council (http://www.mafmc.org)

Various internationally oriented agencies have fisheries programs:

- Fish Net of the World Bank Group (http://www.worldbank.org), under "development topics"
- Food and Agriculture Organization of the United Nations (http://www. fao.org)

Numerous public interest groups focus on fisheries:

- American Fisheries Society (http://www.fisheries.org)
- Sustainable Fisheries Foundation (http://www.wolfe.net/~csteward/)

SELECTED READINGS

Anderson, Lee G.: *The Economics of Fisheries Management,* revised and enlarged edition, Johns Hopkins Press, Baltimore, 1986.

Batkin, Kirsten M.: "New Zealand's Quota Management System: A Solution to the United States' Federal Fisheries Management Crisis?" *Natural Resources Journal,* 36(4), Fall 1996, pp. 855–880.

Christy, Francis T., Jr., and Anthony Scott: *The Common Wealth in Ocean Fisheries: Some Problems of Growth and Economic Allocation,* Johns Hopkins University Press, Baltimore, 1965.

Crutchfield, James A., and Giulio Pontecorvo: *The Pacific Salmon Fisheries: A Study of Irrational Conservation,* Johns Hopkins University Press, Baltimore, 1969.

Doeringer, Peter B., and David G. Terkla: *Troubled Waters: Economic Structures, Regulatory Reform, and Fisheries Trade,* University of Toronto Press, Toronto, 1996.

Gordon, H. S.: "The Economic Theory of a Common-Property Resource: The Fishery," *Journal of Political Economy,* Vol. 62, 1954, pp. 124–142.

Iudicello, Suzanne, Michael Weber, and Robert Wieland, *Fish, Markets, and Fishermen: The Economics of Overfishing.* Island Press, Washington, DC, 1999.

National Marine Fisheries Service: *Our Living Oceans, The Economic Status of U.S. Fisheries, 1996,* NMFS, Washington, DC, 1997.

National Research Council, Committee to Review Individual Fishing Quotas: *Sharing the Fish: Toward a National Policy on Individual Fishing Quotas,* National Academy Press, Washington, DC, 1999.

OECD: *Towards Sustainable Fisheries, Economic Aspects of the Management of Living Marine Resources,* OECD, Paris, 1997.

Pontecorvo, Giulio (ed.): *The New Order of the Oceans: The Advent of a Managed Environment,* Columbia University Press, New York, 1986.

Scott, Anthony: "Development of Property in the Fishery," *Marine Resource Economics,* Vol. 5, 1988, pp. 289–311.

CHAPTER 14

LAND ECONOMICS

Land is the ubiquitous natural resource. Human beings are land-dwelling creatures; for them land is both a **spatial resource,** providing space to live, work, travel, and play, and a **productive resource** from which they draw their sustenance of food, fiber, and other materials. This chapter focuses on some basic **land economics,** which draws on economic principles to examine and understand human decisions about land use.

Table 14-1 shows some of the major land-use categories and how the amounts of land devoted to these uses in the contiguous United States have changed over the last five decades. As one would expect, urban land has increased by almost 300 percent during this period, and land devoted to transportation has increased by about 10 percent. As a percent of total land, these two uses (urban and transportation) represented about 2 percent of the total in 1945 and 4.4 percent of the total in 1992. This is a national (in the contiguous United States sense) average, and does not reflect regional variation. The percentage would be much lower in the mountain states and much higher in the northeastern states, for example. The total amount of agricultural cropland in 1992 was quite close to the figure for 1945. Grazing land (excluding grazing land in forests) declined by about 11 percent during the period. Total forest use land declined during the period, but trends were very different for forest grazing land (a 57 percent decrease from 1947 to 1992) and forest land not grazed (a 61 percent increase during this period). Land devoted to recreation

TABLE 14-1
MAJOR USES OF LAND IN THE CONTIGUOUS 48 STATES, 1945–1992 (MILLION ACRES)

Land use*	1945		1954		1964		1974		1982		1992	
	m.a.	%	m.a.	%	m.a.	%	m.a.	%	m.a.	%	m.a.	%
Urban land	15.0	0.8	18.6	1.0	29.2	1.5	34.6	1.8	49.6	2.6	58.0	3.0
Transportation	22.6	1.2	24.5	1.3	25.8	1.4	26.0	1.4	26.4	1.4	24.8	1.3
Recreation and wildlife areas	22.6	1.2	27.5	1.4	49.7	2.6	56.9	3.0	71.1	3.8	86.9	4.5
National defense areas	24.8	1.3	27.4	1.4	29.3	1.5	22.4	1.2	21.8	1.4	18.6	1.0
Farmland												
Cropland†	450.7	23.7	465.3	24.4	443.8	23.3	464.7	24.5	468.9	24.7	459.7	24.3
Pasture and rnage	659.5	34.6	632.4	33.2	636.5	33.5	595.2	31.4	594.3	31.3	589.0	31.1
Miscellaneous farmland	15.1	0.8	12.2	0.1	10.5	0.5	8.0	0.4	8.0	0.4	6.2	0.3
Forest-use land‡												
Forest land grazed	345.0	18.1	301.3	15.8	223.8	11.8	178.9	9.4	157.5	8.3	145.0	7.6
Forest land not grazed	256.7	13.5	314.1	16.5	388.0	20.4	419.6	22.1	409.7	21.6	413.7	21.8
Miscellaneous other land§	93.4	4.9	80.5	4.2	63.0	3.3	90.6	4.8	88.5	4.6	92.4	4.8
Total	1,905.4	100.0	1,903.8	100.0	1,899.6	100.0	1,897.0	100.0	1,895.7	100.0	1,894.1	100.0

*Distributions may not add to totals because of rounding.
†Includes cropland harvested, crop failure land, cultivated summer fallow, cropland used for pasture, and idle cropland.
‡Land that is normally used for forestry purposes.
§Includes cemeteries, golf courses, deserts, wetlands, and miscellaneous uses not included elsewhere.
Source: U.S. Department of Agriculture, Economic Research Service, Agricultural Resources and Environmental Indicators, 1996–1997, Washington, DC, ERS Handbook No. 712, July 1997, p. 3.

and wildlife areas increased by 285 percent during this time and is today roughly the same in total (87 million acres) as urban and transportation land (83 million acres).

Within some of these broad categories and trends there have been some very substantial changes. In forest lands, for example, especially publicly owned forest land, there has been a very substantial dropoff recently in timbering and grazing activity and a rapid rise in recreational use. The growth in land area devoted to urban uses testifies to the trend in **urban decentralization** (sprawl), but in recent decades the nature of this trend has also changed. Decentralized **employment subcenters** and **edge cities** have appeared, which will impact on the nature of sprawl and its implications for land-use changes in the future.

The rest of the chapter takes two directions. First, we introduce some conceptual ideas about land values, efficient land use, and the workings of the land market. Then we discuss a number of specific problems in land use applying, insofar as we can, the principles of land-use economics to these issues. A list of important contemporary land-use problems would include the following:

1 **Urban sprawl** There is widespread concern in the United States, and much commentary, about the spread of suburban areas out into areas that were once farmland and forest. Is this loose, decentralized, spread-out pattern of urban/suburban growth the best? Should it be discouraged, encouraged?

2 **Resource preservation** Some of the land subject to strong development pressure has unique ecological values. Wetlands, for example, are tied into basic hydrological systems; scenic lands are well suited to public parks. How are the values of these lands to be recognized, and what steps are appropriate for their protection?

3 **Implications of land-use regulations** Public regulations to affect land use are common throughout the country, and pressure is strong to tighten these regulations to ensure certain land-use patterns. But the benefits and costs of these regulations often (usually) fall on different people. What is the efficient and fair action for society to take in cases like this?

4 **New types of regulations** Traditional land-use control regulations have been based on the police power that the Constitution gives communities to make decisions. Might other types of land-use policies give better results?

SOCIAL EFFICIENCY IN LAND USE

The first question to consider is what do we mean by a pattern of land use that is **socially efficient**? In a given region, such as a community or river basin, there is a large number of "parcels" of land. For example, if we define a parcel as equal to an acre, then the number of parcels is equal to total acreage. Any acre can be put to many purposes: such as agriculture, residential, industrial, commercial, and parks. And within each broad category there are many subcategories, single-family vs. multiple-family homes, small office buildings, light vs. heavy industry, and so on. Any particular use, located on any given acre of land, will produce a stream of net benefits extending into the future. The net social benefits produced by an acre of land is usually called rent or, more appropriately, **land rent.** The rent on a piece of land devoted to any use represents the benefits produced by that use, minus all the other nonland costs of producing these benefits. Suppose an acre of land, if used to grow potatoes, could produce $1,000 of potatoes annually at a cost (fertilizer, seed, labor, etc.) of $600. Then the annual rent this acre would produce in potato production would be $400. Suppose that if a single-family dwelling were built on the acre, it would produce annual housing services of $4,800, at a cost (operating plus annualized capital costs) of $3,900. Then the rent the acre would produce if devoted to houses would be $900 per year.

A socially efficient land-use pattern in a region is one in which each acre of land in the region is devoted to the one use that yields the maximum land rent on that acre. Since each acre is producing its maximum rent, social efficiency obviously implies that **aggregate land rent** in the whole region is at a maximum.

If all parcels of land were exactly the same, it would not matter what uses were made of each one. The interesting thing about the land resource, however, is that every land parcel is by definition unique. In any real-world setting, land will differ according to geological and hydrological characteristics. Certain acreage may be capable of producing greater agricultural rents, some acres may have a scenic view, some acreage may have topographical features that make any sort of structures very costly to build, and so on. **Productivity** differences such as these will produce differences in land rents according to the different types of uses to which the land is put. All land parcels must also be unique in terms of **location,** since no two acres can occupy the same spot. This is important because the benefits produced by a piece of land will normally depend on its location with respect to land that has complementary, or competitive, uses. The rents produced by land devoted to housing will depend on how close the land is to employment opportunities; the value of land devoted to commercial purposes will depend on the geographical location of the land in relation to other enterprises that provide essential inputs; and so on.

Compounding the problem of identifying the distribution of land uses that maximizes overall land rents is the abundant network of environmental and natural resource interrelationships that affect net benefits of nearby parcels of land. A factory built next to a group of houses may produce effects (smoke, scenic disruption) that reduce the value of the housing services, and therefore of the land rents, of these neighboring lots. Land devoted to a highway will often have impacts (noise, dust) that affect the rents of nearby land. Agricultural practices can affect neighboring land both negatively (dust, smells, contamination of groundwater) and positively (scenic values). These impacts are often what we think of as external costs and benefits, though whether they are really external or not depends on ownership factors—how property rights are distributed.

How much rent a piece of land in a particular use produces and how this rent is **distributed** among different parties are two different issues. Suppose I own a small factory and my net profits, after deducting all **nonland costs** (including the opportunity cost of my own skills and time) are $5,000. Suppose the town in which I am located charges me $1,000 per year to lease the land on which the factory sits. Then the land rent of $5,000 ends up partly ($4,000 of it) in my pocket, and partly ($1,000 of it) in the coffers of the community. Besides taxes, the distribution of land rent depends also on the state of **competition** in the various markets in which parcels of land are traded.

LAND MARKETS AND PRICES

Even in a relatively small region, the number and heterogeneity of parcels and the number of different uses to which each parcel could be put mean that the number of different ways of distributing these uses among the parcels will be extraordinarily high. How should we (i.e., society) seek to find the one land-use pattern that maximizes land rents? In the United States, as in most other countries, we rely on a **private land market** to do most of the work of determining what uses of land are located on which parcels of land. The private land market works the way all markets do: Buyers and sellers agree on the terms by which land, or sometimes just the services of land, will be transferred between them. The most important aspect of the transaction is what the price will be, because it is the price that reflects all the thousands of factors that go into determining the usefulness and desirability of using a particular piece of land for a particular purpose.

Consider a parcel of land devoted in perpetuity (or at least for a very long time) to a particular use, say, a house, or a small office building, or a public park. The use in question will generate a stream of **annual net benefits,** or annual land rents. The present value of this stream of annual rents can be written explicitly as

$$PV_R = R_0 + \frac{R_1}{1 + r} + \frac{R_2}{(1 + r)^2} + \frac{R_3}{(1 + r)^3} + \dots$$

where R stands for annual rent and r is the discount rate. If the R's in the numerator are all the same, this sum equals R/r. Each different use of the land would generate a different PV_R. In a completely free, competitive land market, the **market price** of a parcel of land will be equal to the highest of all the different possible PV_R's associated with the different ways that the land could be used.

The reason for this is that in the bids and offers of buyers and sellers in the land market, all the potential net benefits associated with owning a piece of land will be **capitalized** into its price. Suppose, for example, a piece of land is currently used for farming, and in this use it has a value of $5,000 per acre (i.e., the present value of rents when the land is used for agriculture is $5,000). Now suppose that, because of the growth of a nearby town, the land could potentially produce a stream of rents (as house lots) with a present value of $12,000.

If there is a competitive land market, the market price for this (and similarly situated) land will increase to $12,000, even though it is still used for farming. This is because the price will be bid upward to reflect the potential rents the land could produce, not what they happen to be producing in the short run.

Thus, all changes in the net benefits producible by a parcel of land, as long as these will accrue to the owner of that land, will get capitalized into its price. For example, suppose in an urban area steps are taken by pollution control authorities to reduce the level of air pollution. There is no direct market for clean air; people do not literally buy and sell quantities of clean air. But if cleaning up the air in the community adds $85 per year to the net benefits of living in a house there, the prices of land on which to build houses, or of land on which houses already exist, will increase to reflect the capitalized value of these new net benefits. The land prices, in other words, will increase by an amount[1] equal to

$$85 + \frac{85}{1+r} + \frac{85}{(1+r)^2} + \frac{85}{(1+r)^3} + \ldots = \frac{85}{r}$$

There are several provisos to the idea that land prices will reflect land rents. One has to do with **land taxes.** Virtually every community in the country raises a portion of its revenues through land taxes; in many cases this is by far the largest source of funds. The part of land rents that is paid in taxes will not be capitalized into its price, since these rents are not ending up in the pockets of the buyers and sellers in the private land market. Thus, communities have sometimes attempted to use differential tax rates to affect land rents and the uses to which land is put within their borders.

The other proviso is that land prices will not necessarily reflect all the net benefits associated with the use of the land. Land prices will adjust to reflect (i.e., "capitalize") all net benefits that accrue to the user of the land. But if some net benefits accrue to others, they will not be so capitalized. The best example of this is certain environmental impacts that particular land uses may have. Suppose, for example, that a certain large parcel of land is expected to be used for building a number of single-family dwellings. The price of land in this parcel will reflect all the benefits and costs that will accrue to those who end up living in the houses: amenity values (perhaps the land is close to a public park), value of time in commuting (perhaps it is near a rail commuting line), value of time to the nearest grocery store, and so on. But suppose the land is also a strategic piece of watershed and building houses on it will impact negatively (i.e., inflict costs) on others who live downstream from the

---

[1] This is based on the standard relationship for equal annual payoffs over an indefinitely long period of time:

$$\sum_{t=0}^{\infty} \frac{M_t}{(1+r)^t} = \frac{M}{r}$$

new development. These are external costs. Were they to be capitalized into the prices of the land in question, these prices would be lower (because net benefits are lowered). But because they are external costs, they will not be so capitalized. In cases like this, normal market prices of land will not accurately reflect all the social benefits and costs arising from the uses creating the externalities. By the same token, the prices of land in the proposed development may be affected by external costs and/or benefits flowing in from elsewhere. If a factory is built next to this land, for example, land prices will be pushed down because of the external costs stemming from this source.

PUBLIC POLICIES AND LAND USE

Land markets work through the private interactions of individual buyers and sellers. Groups of people, especially groups working through their governmental institutions, can affect the way land is used. We provide first a brief catalog of these means, and then set up a simple example to illustrate each one:

1 **Working through land markets:** Both public and private groups (as well as individuals, for that matter) can simply work through the **private land market;** buying, selling, exchanging, or otherwise engaging in voluntary transactions that affect the way land is used.

2 **Eminent domain:** The power of **eminent domain** essentially means the power that recognized political authorities have to condemn property for a public purpose. Condemnation involves the forced appropriation of property, and must be accompanied by **fair compensation.** This is a power possessed by federal and state governments, and usually delegated by them to local governments and to some quasi-governmental organizations, such as electric companies.

3 **Police power:** The **police power** means the power that governmental authorities have to regulate the behavior of citizens so as to ensure the health, welfare, safety, and morals of the public. This is a power of local governments, not the federal government. Police power regulations include **zoning regulations, subdivision controls** (e.g., minimum lot-size requirements), **building codes,** and **environmental regulations** (e.g., wetlands protection regulations). Whenever these police power tools are applied, the ongoing question in particular circumstances is whether they represent valid exercises of a community's right to govern itself, or "takings" of private property that are forbidden by the U.S. Constitution unless compensation is paid.

4 **Taxes:** Governments have the power to tax, and **property taxes** are an important source of tax revenues. But beyond their revenue-raising capacity, they may also be applied in such a way as to encourage or discourage certain types of land use.

The easiest way to illustrate the strengths and weaknesses of these policy approaches is to apply them to a simple example. Suppose there is a parcel of

TABLE 14-2
LAND RENTS AND PRICES
FOR ALTERNATIVE LAND USES

Land use	Farmer	Society
	Annual land rents per acre ($)	
Agricultural	200	600
House lots	400	400
	Land price per acre ($)*	
Agricultural	4,000	12,000
House lots	8,000	8,000

*The present value of a perpetual stream of rents is equal to $PV = R/r$, where R is the rent and r is the discount rate. The numbers in the table were discounted at 5 percent.

land that is currently owned by a farmer and used to raise crops. Suppose, however, that suburban growth is encroaching into the region and that the land is also valuable as a site for a housing development. Suppose, further, that if the land is used for farming purposes, it produces substantial net benefits from two other sources besides the crop production: scenic values and wildlife protection values. These last two types of net benefits accrue to members of the broader community, however, not simply to the farmer herself.

The numbers are illustrated in Table 14-2. It shows annual flows of net benefits per acre, together with the price per acre of land if these net benefits are fully capitalized, in this case at 5 percent. Actual land prices, however, will represent only those parts of land rents that accrue to the user of the land in question. The scenic and wildlife benefits are **external** to the land user.[2] These two types of resource services are also **public goods.** Thus, land prices will not reflect these sources of value produced by the land when it is used for agricultural purposes. The farmer can maximize her wealth by converting the land from agriculture to house lots. Since land prices reflect private rent flow in these two uses, the farmer can do this simply by selling the land to a developer. Assuming competition in this market, the selling price would be $8,000 per acre, which is twice what the land would sell for if it were to be used as a farm.[3]

---

[2] In actual situations, of course, the farmer would also likely accrue a small portion of these benefits. In Florida, for example, some ranchers receive satisfaction knowing that the Florida panther inhabits their ranches. The vast bulk of the benefits, however, are external.

[3] Of course, the market may not be competitive. There may be relatively few developers to compete with one another; for example, the farmer may not have a good idea of what house lots are being sold for. This simply means that the price agreed upon by farmer and developer will lie somewhere between $4,000 and $8,000. Some of the stream of discounted rents, in other words, will end up in the bank accounts of the developer. The $8,000 is assumed to reflect the costs it would take to convert the land and build the houses; in other words, it is based on the net returns from houses.

From the community's standpoint the maximum net benefits, or land rent, are achieved if the land is kept in agricultural uses. We are assuming, of course, that these scenic and wildlife values are known. Net benefits accruing as incomes to land users are relatively easy to measure, because they will be capitalized into land prices. But the external values will not, so other means would have to be found for estimating them. Suppose, now, that the community wishes to take steps to make sure that the land remains in agricultural use. We now consider the different ways it has of trying to achieve this.

Working through the Market

The first apparent option is for the community simply to purchase land. Of course, this might forestall the housing development, but may not preserve agriculture. Some additional steps might be needed for this, say, a lease back to the farmer so that she could continue farming the land. The advantage of this approach is that the price the community is willing to pay probably would bear some relation to the net benefits accruing to the community members from the scenic and wildlife preservation functions. On the other hand, there are the public good, free-rider problems, as mentioned above.

If the community does not purchase the land, it perhaps could be purchased by a private group. In the United States and many other countries, there are many private **conservancy groups,** whose objective is to operate in the land market to preserve ecologically sensitive land. Deriving the bulk of their funds from members' contributions, these groups then seek to purchase land areas that, in our terminology, produce substantial values in the form of ecological services; see the discussion of Exhibit 14-1.

Land preservation through purchase can often be achieved if communities or other groups purchase only partial rights from the landowner. They might purchase from the farmer only the right to develop the land, not the entire **fee simple** ownership of the land.[4] In our example, the **development right** alone is worth $4,000 per acre to the farmer. The land without this right attached to it is still worth $4,000 for agricultural purposes. So the community could forestall development by purchasing the development right for $4,000 an acre rather than the entire fee simple right for $8,000 per acre.[5]

There is another way that the private market might provide a solution to this land-use problem. If a market existed, or could be brought into being, that would allow the farmer to receive some or all of the scenic/wildlife values as revenue, then their own private wealth-maximizing decisions could

---

[4] Fee simple is a legal term meaning the entire set of use rights of a piece of land.

[5] There is a substantial caveat here. The community's ultimate objective is to preserve agriculture. Buying the development right will forestall development, but this is not the same as preserving agriculture. If at some future time the net income from farming becomes too low, the land may be abandoned rather than farmed. Of course it may still produce some benefits as abandoned land.

EXHIBIT 14-1

USING THE MARKET TO PROTECT ECOLOGICALLY SENSITIVE LAND

One way to protect ecologically sensitive land is to make use of the land market. The most straightforward way of doing this is to purchase land that has high ecological values and hold it in preservation status. This is what conservancy organizations do.

On the national level in the United States, the **Nature Conservancy,** the **American Land Conservancy,** and the **American Farmland Trust** have active programs through which land is acquired. There are many state-level conservancy organizations (often called **land trusts**) and a great abundance of local groups who work in this way. Altogether there are probably thousands of organizations in the United States that attempt to work through the land market to protect ecologically sensitive land. They may buy land outright, purchase development rights or easements, engage in land swaps, or use other means.

Some federal agencies have also used the market to protect land. The U.S. Forest Service, for example, has an active **land swap program.** The agency and other federal natural resource agencies do not have ample funds to buy land outright, but they have been able to acquire environmentally important acreage, paying for it by swapping other land currently in their ownership inventory. The accompanying tabulation shows the number of acres involved.

Source: U.S. Department of Agriculture, Washington,DC, various years.

---

lead them voluntarily to maintain the land in agriculture. Perhaps the wildlife situation is such that hunters, fishers, or wildlife watchers would be willing to pay to have access to the wildlife resources of the farm.[6] Perhaps tourists would be willing to pay to be close to, or to participate in, actual farm operations. In some cases there may be substantial potential for market revenues of this type.

Eminent Domain

The right of **eminent domain** means the right to condemn property and acquire it for a public purpose. The legal rules of eminent domain require that the landowner be paid **just compensation** for the land. Eminent domain is used primarily to obtain land that is to be devoted to a specific and concrete public purpose, such as a highway, a powerline right of way, or a reservoir. These are essentially public facilities required for the production of what most people would regard as essential services in the modern world. Eminent domain might also be used to acquire land for a public park; in this case it is amenity services that are being produced. In our example, questions would come up as to whether amenity and wildlife values represent public purposes that would justify land condemnation.

---

[6] In the western United States, and in some European countries, private landowners in some cases can generate revenues by selling rights to fish in streams and rivers passing through their lands, or hunting rights for game animals on these lands.

Although condemnation might not be legal in our case, we can use the example to illustrate a major problem in eminent domain cases: the problem of what is **just compensation**. Courts usually define this to mean **fair market value**. This sounds quite specific, but problems can easily appear in trying to apply the idea. Which market is appropriate? The market governing the land's current use? In our example the price of agricultural land is $4,000 an acre. Or should the price be the market for a different use? In our case the market price of the land as a housing development is $8,000 an acre. Or should it be a market price adjusted for amenity values that may exist even though they don't show up in standard market prices? In this case the fair price might be something approaching $12,000 an acre.

Another issue in determining just compensation is that current owners may attach personal values to a property that exceed its current market price. Suppose the farmer in our case is one of a long line of mothers and daughters who have been born, have lived, and have died on this farm, and who have an attachment to it in excess of its current market price. The market price is, after all, a number applying to average sale prices of similar properties over some recent time period. The current owner may value it more highly than this, for any number of personal reasons. Is the market price fair in this case?[7]

Police Power

Communities have the constitutional right to exercise the **police power** to ensure conditions that promote public health, welfare, and morals. For example, they can establish speed limits, or require homeowners to fence swimming pools and keep their property picked up, or mandate local factories to avoid conditions that damage public health, and so on. They also have certain powers to regulate the way land is used. The most basic right that communities have under the police power is the power to designate the types of uses to which specific parcels of land may be put. The way this is done is through **zoning ordinances.** A typical zoning ordinance divides a community into zones or districts, and designates the types of uses that are permitted in each zone. A typical zoning plan, for example, would designate zones for single-family dwellings, multiple-family dwellings, light commercial, industrial, and so on.

The basic principle behind zoning is to regulate externalities. Certain uses, if located next to other types of uses, are likely to create external costs that would devalue the affected properties. Thus, a factory constructed in a residential area would be expected to inflict external costs in the form of noise, unsightliness, and congestion.

---

[7] Of course, if the farmer attached such a high value to the farm they might not be tempted to sell it to a developer. But the community may not have a very good idea about the strength of these values. Many farms that have been in families for generations have ended up in houses.

The biggest problem with zoning plans is that they do not address the underlying economic incentives of the situation. Suppose that the farm in our example is placed in an agricultural zone. This does nothing to change the fact that the farmer could realize a substantial increase in wealth if she could get permission to sell the farm to a developer. She could perhaps take the town to court over the zoning plan. More likely she would appeal the zoning designation, asking the local **zoning board of appeals** for a **variance** that would allow the sale to proceed despite the zoning plan. Even though the potential gain from getting a variance might be modest today, in a number of years it could be much greater if the demand for houses continues to grow.

Communities may also use the police power to make specific regulations governing the use of land within their boundaries. Many communities in the United States, for example, have laws that allow a local **conservation commission** to deny a building permit for any structure that would adversely affect wetlands or other ecologically sensitive lands. Most communities also have **planning boards,** which can legally enforce subdivision regulations, such as requirements for streets, sidewalks, and sewers. The regulatory approach to land-use control involves an ongoing struggle between two ideas: the **rights and responsibilities of communities** to encourage conditions that are conducive to the public welfare, and the **rights and freedoms of private individuals** to use and enjoy their property in ways they see fit, without hindrance from political authorities. The struggle has seen a long series of court battles and legal pronouncements that have evolved over time as people have changed and as the problems faced by communities have changed. The conflict centers on the **takings clause** of the U.S. Constitution, and it is of sufficient importance that we devote a section to it later in this chapter.

For now, however, we return to our simple land-use example and consider the last type of policy approach that a community might take to affect land use.

Land Taxation

Communities typically levy **property taxes** to raise government revenues. Taxes affect the flows of the net benefits landowners receive from land in particular uses, so taxes can also affect the incentive landowners have for choosing one use over another. Property taxes are usually set at some proportion of the **appraised value** of a property. The appraised value, in turn, is usually based on the supposed market value of the properties. It is "supposed" because for properties not on the market, which includes most of them, a market value will have to be estimated by comparing them with properties that have recently been traded.

Property taxation strategies are often used on the rural/urban fringe, where the problem is the conversion of land, usually from agricultural uses to domestic uses. One technique that has been employed by many communities is "use-value taxation." Suppose the community in our example is seeking to keep the farm in agriculture. If the farmland is taxed at its market value, this would presumably mean basing the tax on what it would expect to sell for if it were devoted to a housing development. In the example this is $8,000 per acre. A way of reducing the tax burden of the farmer, and thus supposedly making it easier for her to continue the farm is to base the tax on its value in current use, or use value. This would be $4,000 per acre, which would imply a tax bill only half as large as if the tax were based on market value.

If land prices are rising rapidly on the rural/urban frontier, the modest effect on farm net income implied by use-value taxation may not be sufficient to outweigh the potential wealth gain that land sale and conversion to houses would produce. Another drawback of some use-value taxation programs has been that by reducing the costs of holding land prior to actually developing it, it can increase the incentive for developers to purchase agricultural land and target it for eventual development. The tax program essentially reduces the developer's cost of holding the land. To reduce this incentive many use-value tax programs require land developers to repay back taxes that were saved by holding the land in agriculture. But the financial penalty of this type of procedure, especially in the face of briskly rising land prices, may not be strong enough to reduce the overall incentives of the practice.

LAND-USE ECONOMICS AND THE "TAKINGS" ISSUE

The fifth amendment to the U.S. Constitution contains the following language: "No person shall be . . . deprived of life, liberty, or property, without due process of law; nor shall private property be taken for a public use, without just compensation." It is clear that this language authorizes governments to take title to private property, provided that it be for the **public purpose** and that it be accompanied by **just compensation.** Eminent domain cases of this type usually involve physical takings, where land, in other words, is taken for the construction of a school, or road, or reservoir. We discussed above the issue of defining **just compensation.** In a number of recent instances of the community exercise of their police powers, however, landowners have argued that the **regulations** have the effect of taking their property, even though there may be no physical invasion of the property. If they are takings, then the Constitution requires that there be a clear public purpose and that the landowners be compensated. In the absence of the compensation, the regulations would be regarded as an unconstitutional taking of private property.

The "takings" issue raises the following question: Under what conditions will a local land-use regulation amount, in effect, to an unconstitutional taking of private property and require, as a result, either just compensation for the effects of the regulation or a rescinding of the regulation by the authority that issued it. Property rights proponents, who wish the language to be interpreted strictly, take the position that any regulation that reduces the value of a property right ought to be considered a taking. Advocates of more active public regulation take the position that communities ought to have leeway to enforce a wide range of regulations for the public good without having to face the financial burden of paying compensation to affected landowners.

Thoughts and opinions on the interpretation of the takings clause have gone back and forth over the decades and centuries. The final arbiter has been the U.S. Supreme Court, which over the years has rendered many decisions on takings cases. The content of these decisions has reflected both the nature of the cases and the jurisprudential views of changing members of the Court. The most recent case on the takings issue was the **Lucas decision** relative to a conflict in a coastal region of South Carolina.[8] Going into the case, there was reasonably widespread agreement with the view that public regulation via the police power is warranted as long as it does not go "too far," but if a regulation does go beyond some point, it constitutes a taking. The question is, where is that point.

Mr. Lucas had purchased two beachfront lots in 1986, for $975,000. Nearby lots had already been developed with condominiums, and he fully expected to be able to build similar structures on his lots. The lots were not in any publicly recognized critical area, and therefore a permit to develop was not required. Two years later, however, the South Carolina legislature passed the Beachfront Management Act, which effectively prohibited the construction of any occupiable improvements on the lots in question. Lucas sued, on grounds that the regulations effectively denied him all economically valuable use of the lots. The trial court in South Carolina agreed, but the South Carolina Supreme Court reversed, on the grounds that no compensation was required for regulations meant to prevent serious harm to the public.

The U.S. Supreme Court, however, reversed the South Carolina decision, taking the position that the regulation did in fact constitute a taking. The Court based this decision on several grounds:

1 That the regulation essentially deprived Lucas of the entire economic value of the property, that is, that it rendered the land essentially valueless to Lucas
2 That when Lucas purchased the property, there was no prohibition in place, and that, while normal land transactions must be concluded in the light of some possible future regulatory constraints on the land, Lucas had no good reason in this case to expect that the subsequent regulation would render the land totally valueless to him
3 That the Beach-front Management Act was overly vague in terms of the specific social harms it was attempting to avoid and the general types of land-use prohibitions that were necessary to accomplish this

The takings issue will continue to be politically and jurisprudentially controversial in the future. It is a major line of collision between the rights of individuals to be free of outside political interference and the rights of communities to constrain individual behavior in the name of the public good.

---

[8] *Lucas v. South Carolina Coastal Council*, 505 U.S. 1003, 1992.

LAND RENT AND PRICE GRADIENTS

We have discussed how the prices of land ultimately are determined by the maximum potential land rents flowing from parcels of land devoted to particular uses. This also implies that the uses to which land will be put in practice will be related to the prices of land. So by looking at spatial patterns of land rents and land prices, we can (usually) understand land-use patterns as they actually have developed or as they are likely to develop in the future. One common application of this idea is understanding the typical ways that cities develop spatially. Suppose we identify three potential uses of land in a region: commercial (office buildings, small factories), residential (single-family homes) and agricultural. And suppose we consider the capitalized land rents that a parcel of land would produce in each of these uses, as a function of the **distance** of the parcel from the center of the city.

Take commercial uses first. We would normally expect that the net return to land used for commercial purposes would be much higher in the center of town than farther out. If we assumed, for illustrative purposes, that we had a city surrounded by land of more or less equal geographical characteristics, we might expect a commercial **rent gradient** like that labeled as CRG in Figure 14-1. Commercial land rents are highest in the downtown area, where costs of business are reduced by the closeness among buyers and sellers, where communications are the quickest, and where distance to shipping nodes is the least. As the distance from downtown increases, potential commercial land rents fall because of the weakening of these factors, sometimes called **agglomeration economies.** So CRG is downward-sloping and rather steep.

FIGURE 14-1
Commercial, Domestic, and Agricultural Rent Gradients, and the Spatial Pattern of Economic Activity

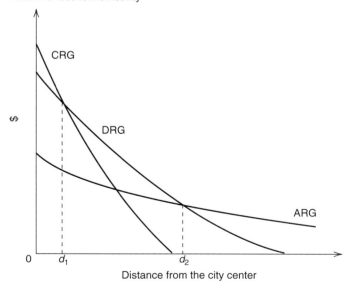

Distance from the city center

The DRG function shows potential land rents from land devoted to housing. These are also highest in town and decline with distance, primarily because of transportation costs and their impact on commuting costs. But the domestic rent gradient starts at a lower level and declines less rapidly than CRG with distance. Similarly, ARG (the agricultural rent gradient) is highest close in and declines with distance, again for reasons of higher transportation costs. But this is the flattest of these rent gradients; it starts rather low and declines only slowly with distance.

The critical distances are the points where the rent gradients cross. At a distance of d_1, the rents from commercial and domestic parcels are the same. On land closer to downtown than this, commercial rents exceed domestic rents. Similarly, at d_2, ARG = DRG and parcels closer to town are characterized by the fact that rents from land devoted to housing exceed rents of land devoted to agriculture.

If these are accurate depictions of the three rent gradients, we can now predict that the land-use pattern around the city will be the following: From the center to a distance of d_1, land will be devoted primarily to commercial uses. At d_1, the dominant land use will change to houses. The housing zone will extend from d_1 to d_2. At d_2 we will have the **urban/rural fringe,** the point where housing developments stop and agricultural uses begin.

This is a typical urban/rural land-use pattern in and around many cities. These rent gradients create a **land price** gradient, that is, a spatial profile of market prices of land that consists essentially of the maximal portions of each of the underlying rent gradients. From the center to distance d_1, prices would reflect CRG; between d_1 and d_2, land prices would reflect DRG; and from d_2 outward, prices would reflect ARG.

Rent gradients and land price gradients in the real world, however, are never as smooth as those depicted in the figure. Nor are the boundaries between land-use types as sharp and clear as those depicted at d_1 and d_2. Geographical factors such as hills and bodies of water intervene, highway patterns can create irregular patterns of travel cost, and so on. But the basic pattern is accurate. By considering how changes in the underlying factors give rent gradients their basic shapes, we can get an understanding of how they will affect overall land-use patterns in and around urban areas.

THE ECONOMICS OF URBAN SPRAWL

We can use some of these insights to investigate the phenomenon of **urban sprawl.** Sprawl is usually used in a negative sense, as something that is not desirable. From the previous discussion we have seen that there is a natural tendency in any urban area to progress from high-price, high-density commercial use in the city center to low-density, lower-priced lands in the suburbs, with a transition to agriculture on the urban/rural fringe. Sprawl refers essentially to a situation in which the housing rental/land-price gradient has an overly shallow slope such that the entire urban area spreads over a very large region and the rural fringe is pushed out a long way into agricultural areas.

This leads to the conversion of large amounts of increasingly remote agricultural and forest land, with the natural resource consequences this implies.

The visual manifestation of urban sprawl is the construction of low-density suburban housing developments on the fringe. Sometimes there is **leapfrogging,** as developers go out somewhat past the current fringe to build houses, with the land areas over which they have vaulted being left to fill in later with additional developments. Very often, also, open land outside the current fringe will be purchased and held for future development well in advance of planned construction times. This can induce pronounced changes in the ways these close-in rural lands are used. Land in the "holding mode" may not be devoted to particularly productive land uses, so that when the time comes to convert the land to houses, there is no especially strong sense of losing any important natural resource values.

In many places, sprawl has been accentuated in recent years in the development of edge centers, that is, secondary centers of high-density commercial development that have materialized some distance out from the center of the large, parent urban district. These edge developments can cast out new higher land-price gradients into the underdeveloped lands lying beyond the old urban/rural fringe, thus increasing the development pressure on these lands.

What is the efficient level of sprawl? Clearly, sprawl can be managed with vigorous-enough public policies. In Great Britain, for example, sprawl has been more closely controlled with public regulation, so many towns have relatively high density development right up to the rural fringe, which tends to be much more sharply defined as compared to the typical case in the United States.

Sprawl, however, represents a trade-off. On the one hand are the lost natural resource values of the land that comes under urban pressure, as well as the added costs (e.g., transportation costs) of living and working in a geographically dispersed urban/suburban pattern. On the other hand are the benefits accruing to people who are able to live in a way that the majority of them apparently want, which is in a single-family house with a reasonably sized lot around it. Of course, if people did not wish to live in this fashion, but preferred living at high density near city centers, sprawl might not be a problem. The qualifier "might" is necessary because land-use patterns are a direct reflection of housing preferences only if the prices they face are competitively determined, are not affected by unpriced external costs or benefits, and are not subsidized. In urban and suburban regions of the United States, and in many other parts of the world, externalities and subsidies are rampant. The net effect of these may be to encourage urban growth that spreads too rapidly.

A major factor behind sprawl is transportation costs, especially the costs of automobile commuting. Road access is typically unpriced in the United States. While there are some toll roads, most are not, so the cost of driving an extra mile includes only car operating costs and the cost of the time of the people in the car. Because of this, the marginal cost of commuting, that is, the cost of commuting the marginal mile, are below social marginal costs. The effect is to encourage people to commute longer distances than are socially efficient. It is possible that subsidies to home buyers have the same effect. Because of the way that federal and state tax laws are written, tax liabilities may be lowered for those people who have home mortgages. The effect of this may be to lower the **effective price** of homes in the suburbs, thereby increasing the quantity demanded of them and encouraging suburban sprawl.

LAND MANAGEMENT ISSUES ON THE URBAN/RURAL FRINGE

Nowhere is there a more complex and vigorous struggle about the way a natural resource is to be used than on the expanding fringe areas that mark the advance of urban/suburban settlement into surrounding rural/agricultural areas. Colliding interests are the norm: developers, homeowners, farmers and other landowners, environmental interests, economic development interests, transportation groups, community groups, and diverse public agencies are some of the people and organizations normally involved, each with their own views about how land in general, and certain parcels in particular, should be used.

Over the years communities and groups have developed a substantial arsenal of means that can be used to affect land conversion. The main ones are listed in Exhibit 14-2. They vary from classic zoning ordinances to individual contracts between towns and developers to third-party actions (e.g., action by nonprofit environmental groups). The political/demographic/economic complexity of these cases makes it hard to see clearly the major cause-and-effect relationships that are involved. From our standpoint perhaps our biggest interest is in understanding how these various development practices and regulations affect the natural resource and environmental endowments of the urban/rural fringe.

One way in which zoning regulations are used in **edge communities** is to establish **density limits** for development. This can be done through **large-lot zoning,** requiring that all house lots must have a minimum total acreage. Or it might be through establishing explicit limits on development in terms of the number of housing units allowed on developed parcels. The normal justification given for density limitations is to ensure that overall population growth is kept at a moderate pace, that new homes are of the sort that will maintain or lift average property values in the community, and that it will preserve a substantial amount of natural coverage of the land, such as woodlands, wetlands, and open areas.

The problem that immediately suggests itself is the potential perverse impacts of this approach. Consider the total fringe area of a specific community. The following simple relationship holds:

$$\begin{array}{ccc} \text{Total acres} & \text{Number of} & \text{Acres used} \\ \text{developed} = \text{new houses} \times \text{per new house} \\ \text{(A)} & \text{(NH)} & \text{(A/NH)} \end{array}$$

EXHIBIT 14-2

METHODS USED BY COMMUNITIES TO CONTROL LAND DEVELOPMENT

Throughout the United States and in other countries communities have many ways of controlling and shaping the quantity and quality of land development within their boundaries. Some of these are the following:

- **Zoning regulations:** This is the most common approach, usually supplemented with other means. Zoning can be used to restrict the amount and density of development, by specifying minimum lot sizes, maximum structure sizes, and other development features.
- **Tax relief, or public grants:** Monies for nonprofit organizations that purchase ecologically sensitive fringe lands and manage them in ways that preserve environmental values. The generic name for this type of organization is **conservation trust.**
- **Impact fees:** Fees must be paid by developers to proceed with a project. These fees are usually justified by the added costs the community will experience (such as schools and roads) as a result of the development. Impact fees have gained greater importance in some

states where traditional property taxes have been limited by law.

- **Contract zoning:** In return for rezoning a development tract, developers are required to proceed in specified ways regarding number and layout of units, road and sewer construction, and so on.
- **Public/private contracts:** These contracts are concluded between public authorities and landowners in fringe areas whereby the latter, in return for annual payments, agree to adopt environmentally sensitive land management practices.
- **Outright land acquisition by public agencies:** Objectives are to conserve sensitive natural resources. Acquisition can be the full transfer of fee simple ownership or a partial rights transfer such as purchase of development rights in cases where some private use is compatible with ecological preservation.
- **Land-use covenants:** Groups of propinquitous landowners agree to rewrite their land deeds so that they, and any future owners of the affected properties, are enjoined from engaging in certain types of land uses or management practices.

Rules that establish maximum densities in particular communities are, in effect, increasing A/NH. For a given NH, therefore, this works so as to increase A, the term on the left. When individual communities seek to limit development densities within their borders, it tends to work in the direction of increasing the total amount of land that is converted on the fringe; that is, it tends to encourage suburban sprawl.

Most of the development and density control measures undertaken on the suburban fringe in the past have been aimed at supporting property values. In essence, communities have sought to control the development process so as to ensure that **property values** have been maximized. Some conflicts have involved **natural resource preservation** issues, for example, making sure that development does not impinge on watersheds that nourish important surface or groundwater resources.

In recent years a new motive has been added to the mix, that of **preserving the habitats** of important species of plants and animals. Austin, Texas, has experienced phenomenal growth and suburban expansion in recent decades. In the early 1980s, the U.S. Fish and Wildlife Service placed on the official list of endangered species the black-capped vireo, a small bird that was once fairly extensive in the western United States but now is confined to a few small areas in Oklahoma and Texas. Planned new large housing developments in Austin had the potential of encroaching on vireo habitat situated on the (then) outskirts of the city. After a great deal of conflict and political struggle, a plan was adopted to alter normal development processes to preserve some portions of vireo habitat. This and similar cases led the U.S. Congress in 1982 to alter the Endangered Species Act to provide for a way of trying to reconcile the incentives of developers and the desire for habitat preservation to protect endangered species.[9] The law calls for the development of **habitat conservation plans,** which basically are a vehicle for developing specific development plans that will provide some degree of protection for affected species at a moderate cost in terms of the altered plans required of developers.

Another type of land-use issue that has been at the forefront in the last few decades is the **protection of wetlands.** Wetlands, in a variety of forms, are found throughout the country. Locally, they may be called swamps, bogs, potholes, marshes, fens, or some other name. They provide a number of valuable hydrological and biological services, the exact nature and extent of which varies according to their location, size, and relationship to adjacent land and water areas.

LAND USE IN UNCERTAIN ENVIRONMENTS

In the example discussed above, we assumed that there were two alternative land uses (farming and a housing development) and that the annual rents flowing from each were **known with certainty.** In the real world, this is usually not the case. Not only are there economic variables that cause land rents to vary from year to year (e.g., the fluctuating price of agricultural crops), but nature itself can cause rents to vary. Homes built in floodplains, or along seashores, are subject to storms and flooding; land in seismically active regions is subject to earthquake damage; droughts, hurricanes, and wildfires can have their impacts. The main questions here are: (1) how do uncertainties of this type affect efficient land use patterns, and (2) do normal private markets function efficiently when uncertainties of this type are important?

Suppose there is a parcel of land on which one might build a house. In an average year, the benefits of living in this house in this particular location would be, say, $1,400, and the costs (including capital costs[10] plus operating costs) would be $600. Net benefits would be $800, which, capitalized at 5 percent, would yield a value of $16,000. In a competitive market, the price of this parcel would be equal to these capitalized rents.

---

[9] For a discussion of this case see Charles C. Mann and Mark L. Plummer, *Noah's Choice,* Knopf, New York, 1995, pp. 175–211.

[10] Annual capital costs are the annualized amount of construction costs.

Now suppose this were actually beachfront property. This kind of property is frequently subject to storm damage, such as from the high winds and waves kicked up by hurricanes along the eastern coast of the United States. Let us assume that in this situation there is a 10 percent chance that the house will be completely destroyed. Thus, we have the following situation:

	No storm (90% chance)	Storm (10% chance)
Benefits	1,400	0
Costs (operating)	600	600
Net benefits	800	−600

Now we can calculate the expected value of **net benefits,** which is what average net benefits would be over a very long string of years, 10 percent of which have storms. The expected value of net benefits equals:

$$800 \times 0.9 + (-600) \times 0.1 = \$660$$

and the capitalized value of this at 5 percent is $13,200.

If market participants react to risk in a straightforward fashion, we would expect the market price of this property to be reduced because of the likelihood of periodic storm damage. Suppose an insurance company now steps in and offers storm insurance, at **actuarially accurate rates,** that is, at premium rates that accurately reflect annual expected losses. The insurance covers the lost benefits in the case of a storm-caused destruction of the house. Thus, the insurance company's losses will be $1,400 × 0.1 = $140. Suppose this much is charged as an insurance premium to the homeowner. Their situation is now:

	Annual
Benefits	1,400
Costs (operating plus insurance premium)	740
Net benefits	660

which, again, capitalizes to a value of $13,200. The presence of the insurance, in other words, does not change land prices, but only the distribution of net benefits flowing from the use of the land.

Why, then, do people build houses right next to the San Andreas fault in California,[11] or on low-lying coastal lands in the east, or on floodplains? A major reason is simply that the benefits associated with living in these locations outweighs the costs, even when the costs include risks associated with

---

[11] The San Andreas fault runs near San Francisco, and is the source of the great San Francisco earthquake and fire early in the twentieth century. Seismologists have predicted, for a number of years now, that a new major earthquake is likely in the vicinity of this fault.

natural events. Another reason is that special public programs serve to reduce the effective costs of these events, thereby leading people to make riskier decisions. A good example of this is the program of **federally subsidized flood insurance.** For people living in areas prone to flood damage, this program provides insurance against such losses at relatively modest premium rates, rates that are below those which would prevail if they were set on the basis of real expected damages. In other words, they are sold at rates below cost, with the general taxpayer covering the difference. The impact of this is that net benefits, or land rents, will rise by an amount equal to the value of the subsidy.

Suppose, in the example above, federal flood insurance were available at a cost of only one-quarter of the actuarially sound price. Since the latter is $140, the government price is assumed to be $35 per year. Now the net benefits to the homeowner for a typical year are the following:

	Annual
Benefits	$1,400
Costs	635
Net benefits	765

and the capitalized value of a net benefit stream of this amount is $15,300. The subsidized insurance, in other words, lifts land prices, and will lead people to use land in a way that is socially inefficient.

This type of problem is an ongoing feature of publicly provided flood insurance. Of course, it is a characteristic of any public program that lowers the cost of **foreseeable risk.** Federal disaster relief is often used to lower the burden to people of natural disasters. There are powerful humanitarian motives behind this program. But if the relief serves basically to lower the cost to people of predictable disasters, it may actually lead to higher losses in the future, as people persist in making decisions that are overly risky. Only if the disaster relief is forthcoming for truly unpredictable natural events will it not tend to produce these perverse results.

MANAGING PUBLIC LANDS

So far in this chapter the major focus has been on private land markets, how they operate and how they might be managed to move toward socially efficient land-use patterns. Another important set of land-use issues in the United States, as well as many other countries of the world, revolves around how publicly owned land should be used. In the United States, 29 percent of the total land area is actually owned by the federal government. State and local governments also own a substantial amount of land. These land areas vary from spectacular natural wonders to barren wasteland, but many of them are under demand for their natural resources. Because they are publicly owned lands, however, these demands are normally not mediated through the private market, but are managed through the decisions of public agencies of various types. Thus the expression of the demands and the decisions about the uses to which public lands will be put are part of a lively political process in which groups contend for influence and try to shift the uses of the public lands in directions that are congenial to their own interests.

The number of different activities pursued by visitors to public lands is very long: hiking and camping (day, overnight, and wilderness), animal watching and sightseeing, hunting (big game, small game) and fishing, timbering, mining, snowmobiling and use of all-terrain vehicles, boating of all types, livestock grazing, scientific study, and others. Conflicts arise because these activities often are not compatible with one another. Cutting timber may interfere with sightseeing and camping, white-water boating may conflict with fishing, wilderness hiking is not compatible with all-terrain vehicles, and so on. The way public agencies typically deal with these conflicts is to specify a list of permitted activities for the areas under their management. This is usually done as part of their legislative and administrative "charter," with a certain amount of local variation tailored to the features of particular sites. Exhibit 14-3 presents information on the range of permitted activities in the areas managed by the four major federal land management agencies: the National Park Service (NPS), National Forest Service (NFS), Bureau of Land Management (BLM), and the Fish and Wildlife Service (FWS). Material relevant to the activities managed by these agencies is located in other chapters: Chapters 18 and 19 for the FWS, Chapter 17 for the NPS, and Chapter 12 for the NFS. We discuss some simple conceptual issues here.

When a range of permitted activities is specified in general enabling laws, local managers' decisions are already constrained to some extent. Significant problems can still exist, however, in terms of whether the activities that are permitted should be pursued together throughout an area or whether managers should identify separate nonintersecting portions of the land for the pursuit of each activity by itself.[12] Suppose there are two activities that might be pursued on a given land area. Should both be allowed over the whole area, or should it be divided, with one activity allowed on one part and the other on the other part? The relevant comparison would seem to be straightforward: the sum of the net benefits of the separate areas compared to the net benefits of the two activities when they are pursued together over the larger area. Two primary factors would determine the outcome of this comparison: (1) the nature of the interaction between the activities and (2) the variation in the quality of the area that makes some parts of it more suitable to one activity than to the other.

---

[12] In the policy world the doctrine of mixing uses is called **multiple use.** The idea is set out in the Multiple-Use Sustained Yield Act of 1960.

EXHIBIT 14-3

PUBLIC LANDS MANAGED BY FEDERAL AGENCIES IN THE UNITED STATES

Four federal agencies administer most of the 657 million acres of federal land (29% of the land in the United States): the National Park Service (NPS), the Fish and Wildlife Service (FWS), and the Bureau of Land Management (BLM) in the Department of the Interior, and the Forest Service (FS) in the Department of Agriculture. The majority of the federal lands (92%) are in 12 western states, and the federal government owns more than half of the land in those states (54%, ranging from 27% in Washington to 83% in Nevada).

The National Park System

The National Park Service (NPS) manages 77 million acres in the 378 units of the National Park System (also NPS). NPS has many diverse categories for its units, with 20 different designations. The largest units are the national parks, preserves, and monuments.

National Parks. Fishing is allowed in most national parks, but hunting and resource development activities (e.g., mineral extraction and timber harvesting) generally are prohibited unless grandfathered or expressly permitted in the park's authorizing legislation.

National Preserves. Management of national preserves is generally similar to that of national parks, but typically allow not only fishing and other recreation allowed in the parks, but also hunting and mineral extraction, as long as the natural values for which the preserve was established are not jeopardized.

National Monuments. Permitted and prohibited uses in national monuments are largely the same as in the national parks: many recreation uses are allowed, although hunting may be restricted or forbidden. Wood cuffing and most commercial activities are usually curtailed (but mineral extraction may be allowed). . . .

In addition to these categories, the NPS has numerous other designations, including: national battlefields, historic sites, national seashores and lakeshores, and more. The NPS also administers 19 national recreation areas (NRAs), while 19 are administered by the FS, one by the BLM, and one by the Tennessee Valley Authority. . . . Recreation is the dominant use, but other uses may be allowed in NRAs including recovery of timber or mineral resources, livestock grazing, watershed protection, and resource preservation as long as these uses are compatible with the primary purpose for which the area was set aside.

The National Wildlife Refuge System

The Fish and Wildlife Service (FWS) manages 93 million acres in 512 national wildlife refuges, 198 waterfowl production areas, 50 wildlife coordination areas, and 114 other sites.

The National Wildife Refuge System Administration Act of 1966 and the National Wildlife Refuge System Improvement Act of 1997 direct the FWS to administer the System primarily to conserve and enhance fish and wildlife and their habitats. Only uses compatible with these gen-

The activities could vary from compatible to antagonistic. Limited clear-cutting of timber may be quite compatible with small-game hunting (because it creates animal-attracting edges) and not at all with big-game hunting. All-terrain vehicles may be incompatible with most other activities (except perhaps forestry and mining), so separate areas for this type of activity may be called for. Snowmobiling and cross-country skiing are likely to be antagonistic,

---

EXHIBIT 14-3—*Continued*

PUBLIC LANDS MANAGED BY FEDERAL AGENCIES IN THE UNITED STATES

eral purposes, and with any specific individual purposes set out for each refuge, are permitted. For example, grazing and mineral activities are permitted in certain refuges and under certain circumstances; hunting, fishing, and other recreational uses generally are permitted in wildlife refuges.

The Public Lands [Bureau of Land Management]

The BLM administers 264 million acres concentrated in 11 western states: Alaska, Arizona, California, Colorado, Idaho, Montana, Nevada, New Mexico, Oregon, Utah, and Wyoming. . . .

BLM manages the public lands for sustained yields of multiple uses livestock grazing, outdoor recreation, wood production, water supply, wildlife and fish habitats, and wilderness; mineral extraction also is allowed. . . .

The National Forest System

The Forest Service (FS) manages the 192 million-acre National Forest System (NFS), consisting of 155 national forests, 20 national grasslands, and 112 other areas. NFS lands are concentrated in the West, but the FS manages more than half of all federal land in the East.

Congress has provided uniform, general management guidance for most NFS lands. As with the public lands, NFS lands generally are administered for sustained yields of multiple uses. . . .

Special Systems

Three special management systems have been created to protect particular features or characteristics: the National Wilderness Preservation System, the National Trails System, and the National Wild and Scenic Rivers System.

The Wilderness Act defines the purpose of wilderness as "devoted to the public purposes of recreational, scenic, scientific, educational, conservation, and historical use." The Act generally prohibits commercial activities (e.g., timber harvesting), motorized access or mechanical transport, and permanent roads, structures, and facilities in wilderness areas. . . .

National trails are administered by the FS, NPS, and BLM, many in cooperation with appropriate state and local authorities. Most recreation uses are permitted, as are other uses or facilities that do not substantially interfere with the nature and purposes of the trail. Motorized vehicles generally are prohibited on System trails.

National Wild and Scenic Rivers System. . . . To date, 155 rivers totaling 10,896 miles have been included in the National Wild and Scenic Rivers System.

The principal protection of the wild and scenic river designation is the prohibition of water resource projects which may divert or hinder the flow of the river. Management of permitted use varies with the class of the designated river.

Source: Excerpted from Ross W. Gorte, *Federal Land and Resource Management: A Primer,* Congressional Research Service, RS 20002, December 22, 1998, Washington, DC.

---

while fishing and day or overnight camping would be much less so. We are speaking here essentially of the nature and extent of external costs that different activities inflict on one another. Separate facilities are called for when the external costs of combined usage outweigh the direct benefits of the activities arising from allowing them over a wider area. Research is required if these externalities and benefits are going to be estimated with any degree of accuracy.

The other important factor affecting the desirability of mixing or separating activities is variations in the qualitative characteristics of the land itself. Some portions of a national park may clearly be better suited to sightseeing, and some to remote hiking and camping. Certain areas may lend themselves to forestry, or livestock grazing, whereas others do not. As with most other variables, the adaptability of an area to specific activities is not a yes-no situation but rather a more or less. This puts a premium on gaining knowledge about the relationships between site characteristics and the benefits that accrue to people using them for different activities.

SUMMARY

Land is the ultimate resource in the sense that it is the surface of the earth on which the activities of humans and of nonhuman organisms are concentrated. Land is an important resource in two senses: in terms of its physical properties and the ecosystem functions it supplies and in terms of its role in the spatial distribution of human activities. Efficient patterns of land use are those which maximize the net benefits of the activities distributed over its surface. Land prices are the **capitalized values** of net benefits, or land rents. Land prices will be affected both by physical and locational aspects of land parcels, and by taxes and external benefits and costs that flow among the uses to which different parcels may be put. The **land rent/price gradient** is a way of showing the structure of land prices in and around an urban area; it is useful in studying decisions involving open-space preservation and the impacts of land-use controls. Public methods to control land-use patterns include **outright purchase, eminent domain,** and the **police power;** the latter includes such approaches as **zoning, subdivision controls,** and **environmental regulations.** A major ongoing issue in the exercise of the police power to shape land use has been the **takings** issue. Public policy can also have an impact on land use by affecting the probabilities of loss and the degree of risk from such things as floods, earthquakes, and storms. The chapter concluded with a brief discussion of management issues on public lands.

KEY TERMS

Urban sprawl	Takings
Land rent	Just compensation
Land prices	Zoning
Externalities	Fee simple
Land taxes	Development rights
Land market	Rent/price gradient
Eminent domain	Leapfrogging
Police power	Uncertainty and land prices

QUESTIONS FOR FURTHER DISCUSSION

1 Suppose the town allows me to operate a small ferry from a point of land in the town to a small island not far away. My operating costs are $50,000 per year, and my total revenue is $62,000 per year on average. Is the $12,000 difference a land rent? The land in question is the site where the ferry dock is located.

2 A piece of land has a market value of $2,000 if used for agricultural purposes. A land "speculator" buys some of the land, paying $3,000 an acre. Five years later she sells it to a house builder for $7,000 an acre. The builder builds a house for $50,000 and sells it (and the land on which it sits) to a homeowner 2 years later for $68,000. Assuming the land market and housing market are both competitive and that there was no inflation during all of this, what's the total land rent in houses, and how was that rent distributed among farmer, speculator, builder, and homeowner?

3 A community enacts a regulation that keeps people from building houses within 500 yards of the top of any hill in town. The stated purpose of the law is to protect the scenic quality of the town. Do you think this regulation amounts to an unconstitutional taking of private property?

4 How would the rent gradient of a city change if a new four-lane expressway were built from the middle of the city out to the next city, which is 100 miles away?

5 How do interest rate changes affect land prices?

USEFUL WEB SITES

Maps on land use, land resources, and characteristics:

- Earth Resources Observation System (EROS) of the U.S. Geological Survey (http://edcwww.cr.usgs.gov/eros-home.html)

Land-use and natural resource problems in North America and around the globe focusing on sustainability, social conflict, and political economy:

- University of Wisconsin Land Tenure Center (http://www.wisc.edu/ltc)

Using the market to accomplish land preservation:

- Nature Conservancy (http://www.tnc.org)

Public interest groups focusing especially on the use and abuse of public lands:

- Sierra Club (http://www.sierraclub.org)
- Wilderness Society (http://www.wilderness.org)
- Friends of the Earth (http://www.foe.org)

President Clinton's Council on Sustainable Development was transferred into the Department of Energy and became the U.S. Center of Excellence for Sustainable Development, with a lot of attention focused on land-use issues and the consequences of sprawl (http://www.sustainable.doe.gov).

For wetlands laws, check out the publications on this topic by the Congressional Research Service, available through the National Institution for the Environment (http://www.cnie.org/nle/crswet.html).

SELECTED READINGS

Babcock, Richard F., and Charles L. Siemon: *The Zoning Game Revisited,* Oelgeschlager, Gunn and Hahn for Lincoln Institute of Land Policy, Boston, 1985.

Barlowe, Raleigh: *Land Resource Economics, The Economics of Real Estate,* 4th ed., Prentice-Hall, Englewood Cliffs, NJ, 1986.

Ellickson, Robert C.: "Suburban Growth Controls: An Economic and Legal Analysis," *Yale Law Journal,* 86, January 1977, pp. 385–511.

Epstein, Richard A.: *Takings: Private Property and the Power of Eminent Domain,* Harvard University Press, Cambridge, MA, 1985.

Fischel, William A.: *Do Growth Controls Matter?* Lincoln Institute of Land Policy, Cambridge, MA, 1990.

Fischel, William A.: *The Economics of Zoning Laws,* Johns Hopkins University Press, Baltimore, 1985.

Fischel, William A.: "Zoning and the Urban Environment," in Daniel W. Bromley (ed.), *The Handbook of Environmental Economics,* Blackwell, Cambridge, MA, 1995, pp. 61–88.

Heimlich, Ralph E. (ed.): *Land Use Transition in Urbanizing Areas,* The Farm Foundation, Washington, DC, 1989.

Miceli, Thomas J., and Kathleen Segerson: *Compensation for Regulatory Takings: An Economic Analysis with Applications,* TAI Press, Greenwich, CT, 1996.

Mills, Edwin S., and Bruce W. Hamilton: *Urban Economics,* 4th ed., Scott, Foresman, Glenview, IL, 1989.

Santos, José Manuel L.: *The Economic Valuation of Landscape Change: Theory and Policies for Land Use and Conservation,* Elgar, Cheltenham, England, and Northampton, MA, 1998.

CHAPTER 15

WATER RESOURCES

Water resources are critical to human development. Water is a biological necessity for human existence, like air. But the importance of water resources extends far beyond this—to public health, economic development, and the health of ecosystems.

Most of the water on earth is salty. Throughout history this has not been available for human consumption, but recent developments in desalination technology and increases in the scarcity of freshwater have turned many communities toward the ocean for freshwater supplies. Much of the global supply of freshwater is more or less locked up in glaciers, ice caps, and elsewhere. This means that freshwater supplies for humans and ecosystems must come from the relatively small amounts that run off as **surface water,** or are contained in accessible **groundwater** aquifers.

If all freshwater supplies were spread perfectly evenly about the globe, there would be few water shortages. But, of course, they are not. Some regions enjoy a plentiful supply, whereas others face extreme scarcity. In the United States there is great variation in natural freshwater supplies. In general, the eastern half of the country is humid and reasonably well watered, while the western half is arid or semiarid where rainfall and runoff are restricted.

WATER USE IN THE UNITED STATES

Tables 15-1 and 15-2 give some detail about how water is used in the United States. The data are for 1990, but relative use patterns do not change markedly in the short run, and so they are still reasonably accurate for getting a picture of current utilization. Total withdrawals for 1990 were estimated at 408 million gallons per day of which 327 million, or 80 percent, came from surface water and the rest from groundwater sources. For coastal states a substantial portion of surface water withdrawals is of salt water used for industrial cooling purposes, especially electricity generating plants. In 1990 water withdrawals per capita were estimated at 1,340 gallons per day. There was considerable variation among the regions, from the smallest, the 370 gallons per day of New England, to the 11,300 of the Upper Colorado region. This great variation in per capita consumption is explained in large part by the use of water in industrial and agricultural purposes.

TABLE 15-1
WATER WITHDRAWALS, BY REGION, UNITED STATES, 1990*

Region	Groundwater (millions of gallons/day)	Surface water (millions of gallons/day)	Freshwater per capita (gallons/day)
New England	694	13,200	370
Mid Atlantic	2,640	44,900	508
South Atlantic–Gulf	7,120	37,100	962
Great Lakes	1,220	31,200	1,510
Ohio	2,670	27,800	1,390
Tennessee	305	8,900	2,350
Upper Mississippi	2,630	18,200	977
Lower Mississippi	8,340	10,800	2,510
Souris-Red-Rainy	130	166	439
Missouri Basin	8,530	29,000	3,730
Arkansas-White-Red	7,710	7,990	1,870
Texas-Gulf	5,880	12,600	886
Rio Grande	2,180	3,850	2,690
Upper Colorado	155	6,950	11,300
Lower Colorado	3,080	4,670	1,630
Great Basin	1,990	5,320	3,300
Pacific Northwest	9,780	26,500	4,070
California	14,700	32,400	1,200
Alaska	112	529	517
Hawaii	590	2,150	1,070
Total	80,440	323,960	1,340

*Figures may not add to totals because of independent rounding. Totals include fresh and saline.
   Source: Solley, Wayne B., Robert R. Pierce, and Howard A. Perlman, "Estimated Use of Water in the United States," *U.S. Geological Survey Circular 1081,* Government Printing Office, Washington, DC, 1993.

About 11 percent of the total freshwater withdrawn in the United States was used for public water supply systems (see Table 15-2). Much of the rest was essentially water that was **self-supplied** by users, some for domestic purposes but most for industry and agriculture. There is a lot of interregional variation in this percentage. For example, commercial and industrial withdrawals are much more important in the East than in the West.

Irrigation withdrawals are predominantly a western phenomenon. It needs to be emphasized that these are **water withdrawals;** that is, it is water that is taken out of the lakes and streams that make up the natural water system. A substantial amount of this water is returned through runoff or wastewater. Amounts that are not directly returned are called **water consumption.**

These aggregate withdrawal data do not immediately reveal the extent of water resource problems in the country. For the public at large, the perception of water problems probably tends to wax and wane according to hydrological

TABLE 15-2

TOTAL WATER WITHDRAWALS BY WATER-USE CATEGORY, BY WATER-USE REGION, 1990* (MILLION OF GALLONS/DAY)

Region	Public supply	Domestic	Commercial and industrial	Agriculture	Other[†]	Total
New England	1,400	169	680	128	11,510	13,890
Mid Atlantic	5,980	396	3,333	297	37,617	47,600
South Atlantic–Gulf	4,850	659	3,038	7,260	30,846	44,200
Great Lakes	4,340	283	4,298	382	23,057	32,411
Ohio	2,530	360	2,459	200	24,922	30,422
Tennessee	511	56	1,246	228	7,162	9,200
Upper Mississippi	1,890	371	1,227	661	16,658	20,804
Lower Mississippi	1,040	90	2,779	8,450	6,740	19,120
Souris-Red-Rainy	72	22	49	119	34	295
Missouri Basin	1,620	139	210	25,215	10,316	37,537
Arkansas-White-Red	1,400	118	533	8,749	4,895	15,691
Texas-Gulf	2,520	79	2,258	5,256	8,389	18,510
Rio Grande	533	23	32	5,323	123	6,039
Upper Colorado	118	10	11	6,707	256	7,108
Lower Colorado	1,070	39	203	6,158	280	7,751
Great Basin	610	15	124	6,337	224	7,312
Pacific Northwest	1,580	220	1,784	32,420	370	36,336
California	5,750	313	426	28,705	11,978	47,100
Alaska	92	7	129	1	413	641
Hawaii	238	10	84	762	1,646	2,740
Total	38,089	3,382	13,577	141,351	197,884	405,195

*Figures may not add to totals because of independent rounding. Totals include fresh and saline.
†Principally mining and thermoelectric.
Source: Solley, Wayne B., Robert R. Pierce, and Howard A. Perlman, "Estimated Use of Water in the United States," *U.S. Geological Survey Circular 1081,* Government Printing Office, Washington, D.C., 1993.

factors. In the East, the last major drought was several decades ago, so today there is perhaps a somewhat relaxed attitude about water supply issues. In the arid West, where urban population growth has led to the construction of massive water supply systems[1] and where a major drought has occurred more recently, water problems are always higher up on the public agenda.

Important contemporary water resource problems in the United State include the following:

1 In the East, there is a continuing need for the effective management of large water systems, public and private, to adapt to the demands of growing urban and suburban populations.
2 Throughout the country, but especially in the eastern half, there is the growing appreciation of the importance of coastal and inland **wetlands,** for the effective functioning of the entire water system, both surface and subsurface. Demands for land for commercial, domestic, and agricultural purposes are putting greater stress on these wetland areas, and so their management and preservation has become a major water resource issue.
3 There are growing scarcities of water from many **groundwater aquifers** used heavily for freshwater supplies. In the East, many aquifers have been contaminated from chemicals or from saltwater intrusion. In the West, many large aquifers have been exploited at rates far in excess of recharge rates. In these cases, municipalities and water supply organizations have been forced to turn to alternative freshwater supplies. Decisions need to be made about managing existing aquifers, especially to coordinate groundwater and surface water withdrawals.
4 In the West, rapidly growing urban areas are searching for new sources of water to support the populations. One possible source is to **transfer water** that would normally go to agricultural irrigation. Water transfers of this type and magnitude have enormous legal, economic, and social ramifications.
5 Throughout the country, demands are growing for **instream water services,** like boating, fishing, ecosystem protection, and scenic values. The question is how to balance these with traditional demands for water withdrawals.

In this chapter we examine some of the economic analytics that can be used to advance our understanding of some of these problems.

WATER LAW IN THE UNITED STATES

We have stressed many times the importance of **natural resource law** in shaping the way resources are utilized and developed. **Water law** is a prime example. Water is given by nature in certain quantities at certain locations and at certain times. How it is ultimately developed and used is critically affected by

---

[1] The Central Valley Project in California and the Central Arizona Project are the major examples.

the status of the law regarding who has the legal right of ownership, or of utilization. Water law has evolved and changed in extent and complexity in response to the demographic, technological, and geographical changes that have occurred over the last 350 years in the country.

Surface Water

When the first European settlers organized their farms and communities along the northeast coast in the seventeenth century, they found hydrological patterns quite similar to those with which they were familiar. The lands were well watered in general, and there was an abundance of streams, lakes, and rivers. Being at the time subjects of the English Crown, they naturally brought and applied English legal doctrine to these water resources. In this doctrine, the rights to the use of water (other than for irrigation, which was a right reserved to the government) belonged to those people who owned the banks of the streams or lakes in question. This was known as **riparian water rights,** a word stemming from the Latin word *riparius,* meaning "situated on the banks of a natural watercourse or body of water." As described in the following extract,[2] each riparian landowner had the rights to a reasonable use of the water in the stream; no one of them could use the water in such a way as to materially damage other riparians, although "reasonable" withdrawals and use were allowed.

> Though definition of "reasonable" uses could be difficult, other features of the reasonable-use riparian doctrine are quite clear. Only riparian landowners have rights to the use of water. Owners of nonriparian lands and any others wishing to preserve free-flowing waters do not have any legal rights to the water. As the water right is a consequence of land ownership rather than a separate piece of property, the right is not lost simply because it has not been exercised. The relationship among riparian landowners is one of parity rather than priority, and the doctrine allows the entry and accommodation of new water users. Water rights are relative rather than absolute. The possibility that existing landowners may develop new water uses, or that new water users may be added to a stream, means that riparian rights do not attach to a fixed amount of water. And uses that are reasonable under existing circumstances may become unreasonable as new uses are initiated or conditions change, so that riparian rights for specific water uses may not be secure in situations in which there is not enough water to accommodate all desired uses.

When settlers ventured into the western part of what was to become the United States, they found that climate and hydrology were very different from those of the East. In particular, water was much more scarce and consequently the climate much more arid. At first some of the new western states tried to adopt riparian water law, but it became clear very shortly that a legal doctrine suited for humid water-abundant regions would not work in cases of relative water scarcity.

---

[2] David M. Gillilan and Thomas C. Brown, *Instream Flow Protection,* Island Press, Washington, DC, 1997, p. 15.

An example will illustrate the problem. Suppose a rancher named Smith had moved into Colorado in the mid-nineteenth century and started a live-stock operation, pursuant to which he diverted water from a local stream to irrigate some hay land. Because of the general arid conditions, the stream was not large, so the diversion took a relatively large share of the water in the stream during hay growing season. Now Farmer Jones moves into an area downstream from Smith and attempts to begin a ranching operation similar to Smith's. To do this he must have irrigation water. But most of the water in the stream is already being used. If the water law of the area was a riparian-type law, Jones, being a riparian landowner, would have some rights to the water of the stream, and Smith would have to adjust his use so that both shared the available water in some reasonable proportion.

If this same system were applied to new settlers as they continued to locate downstream, the end result would be inadequate water for everybody. The riparian laws would make it impossible for any one of the ranchers to have an operation sufficiently large to be efficient, given the arid conditions of the region. Because of this general kind of problem, a new type of water law developed in many parts of the western United States—the law of **prior appropriation.**

Prior appropriation essentially gives water rights to the first person who appropriates it and makes beneficial use of it. It is sometimes called "first in time, first in right." While riparian water law tends to see water rights holders as equal in status, prior appropriation creates priorities, such that first users have rights that take precedence over those coming later. So rancher Smith, being the first to divert water for irrigation, would have the **senior** water right in this case, that is, the absolute right to all the water needed to irrigate his hay. Those coming later would have **junior** rights, meaning that they could gain rights over that portion of the water not used by Smith. Appropriation water rights are also "use it or lose it" rights. The right exists only so long as the water is actually used; if use stops, the right is lost.

Most of the small- and medium-sized rivers in the West were fully appropriated by the end of the nineteenth century. The result was a widespread system of privately built diversion ditches, small impoundments, irrigation works, and the like. During the first two-thirds of the twentieth century, the federal government sponsored a massive construction program of large dams and canals, primarily for irrigation purposes. This action got the federal government thoroughly involved with western water issues. In recent years the huge growth of urban population centers in parts of the West have led most states to get actively involved in managing their water systems. Thus in some areas the trend is toward **administered systems,** in which public agencies are more actively involved in regulating surface water use and in making the trade-off decisions this implies.[3] And with increasing emphasis on maintaining maximum instream flows, the trend is toward a kind of riparian approach in which the rivers must be managed so as to balance competing interests.

---

[3] It's interesting to recall that one of the earliest large western water systems was an administered system. This was the one developed by Mormons in nineteenth-century Utah.

Groundwater

The law of groundwater resources is different from, but related to, surface water rights. Groundwater is extracted from underground **aquifers,** the geo-hydrological characteristics of which vary widely. They range enormously in size, some being small and local and others very large interstate formations. Some aquifers have very slow **recharge rates,** whereas others have more rapid rates; some recharge rates are steady, others vary greatly from year to year. In many cases they are hydrologically interconnected to surface water resources, recharging from, and discharging to, water in streams and lakes.

Early English groundwater law, which provided the foundation for early American law, conferred the rights of absolute ownership on those who held surface rights over an aquifer. Essentially this allowed any landowner to pump as much as they wished out of the aquifer without regard to any impact this might have on other landowners who might be extracting water from the same aquifer. Assuming a limited size, and a small recharge rate, this puts groundwater resources in the category of **open-access resources,** which we have discussed from a conceptual standpoint in Chapter 6. We explored there how open-access resources would tend to get overexploited because of the "use it or lose it" incentives facing those who are utilizing the resources. Or, more technically, because of the **open-access externalities** that individual resource users will inflict upon one another. In effect, when one person or group of people pump water without restriction from a groundwater aquifer, it can adversely affect the water supply available to others using the same aquifer. In the West, groundwater law developed in a way consistent with **prior appropriation.** Senior rights to specific quantities could be claimed by the first to exploit the resource, and, subject to limitation, these could be defended against subsequent claimants.

The conflicts these doctrines have produced in situations of ever-increasing demand have led to change. In the eastern United States the idea of **reasonable use** is important. This says that any overlying landowner is allowed to make reasonable use of water from the aquifer. This rules out uses that might be regarded as wasteful or excessive, as well as transfers to nonoverlying landowners. More recently some eastern states have moved toward outright systems of **withdrawal permits.** These involve public agencies issuing permits to water withdrawers that specify maximum quantities of water that may be withdrawn. Many western states have also moved toward more administered groundwater systems. Through the specification of groundwater management areas a state or regional agency may be empowered to set and enforce rules, such as permit requirements, well spacing requirements, well construction standards, allocation preferences, limited pumping rates, restrictions on place of use, and water use monitoring and reporting.[4]

---

[4] Jean A. Bowman, "Groundwater Management Areas in the United States," *Journal of Water Resource Planning and Management,* Vol. 116, 1990, pp. 484–502.

WATER PRICING

Fundamental to the delivery of any good or service, and its distribution among users, is the way its **price is determined.** In a market economy, the expectation is that buyers and sellers will interact and trade, and out of this will come the prices of the items traded, which will shift up or down through time as supply and demand factors change. If there are reasonable levels of competition among buyers and among sellers, well-defined property rights, and few important externalities, the established prices will be efficient and the quantities traded will be the ones that are socially efficient. That is how it works in principle and sometimes in practice. But in the real world any number of factors can upset this process. Some of these are technical, such as the way users are jointly related when they are hooked up to a single water system. Others are political in nature, brought on by the fact that public authorities often intervene in markets for one reason or another.

Water is a good example of the latter. Water is usually thought of as something special, with qualities that make it different from "normal" commodities. One can get along without many goods, but one cannot get along without water for very long. And most people have few alternatives when it comes to water; they either hook up to the same system everybody else is on, or go without. Nor is it possible to run a modern public sanitation system without copious amounts of water. All of which tend to give water a special status in the eyes of consumers and political authorities. One implication of this is that, over the years, politicians and other public authorities have had a lot to say about how water has been priced. This obviously has had enormous implications for the way water has been used and on the demand for expansion in water supply systems.

Average Cost Pricing

Most domestic water in the United States is supplied by **public water supply companies.** These are entities who essentially function as public utilities, holding monopoly positions within communities and subject to the oversight of public advisory boards or commissions. It is the pricing ideas of these groups that have usually determined the actual prices that water supply companies have set. Among the general public, and especially among public administrators, the belief is widespread that the basic reason for having prices at all is to cover the costs of production. For those in charge of water and other public utilities this belief leads to a **cost-based pricing rule:** Set prices so that revenues cover costs. Revenues should not fall short of costs, because if they do, losses presumably have to be made up some other way, for example, from general tax revenues. Nor should revenues exceed costs, because this implies profits, which are thought to be inappropriate for public enterprises. This type of reasoning has historically led to what is called **average-cost pricing.** The total costs of delivering water are divided by the total quantity of water delivered, and the unit water price set accordingly.

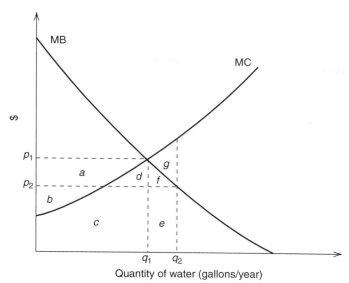

FIGURE 15-1
Marginal and Average Cost Pricing

The efficiency implications of average-cost pricing are easy to see. Figure 15-1 shows a supply and demand curve for water for a community water supply system. MB is the marginal benefits function, while MC is the long-run marginal cost function based on the costs of delivering water. Note that the demand curve for water is drawn as downward-sloping to the right, just like any other good or service. Water is necessary for life, in particular the 2 or 3 gallons per day that are a biological requirement. But considering the large quantities consumed by the average person in the developed world, it is in fact an economic good. The water consumption of an average U.S. household is several hundred gallons per day, which means that, at the margin, it is being used for many purposes well beyond the biological maintenance of life. This is why, in the normal range of prices, water may be regarded as a normal economic good.

Given the basic relationships of Figure 15-1 the efficient quantity of water is q_1 gallons per year, and the market-clearing price for this is p_1 per gallon. Suppose the water company charges this price. Total costs of water supply are an amount equal to the area $c + d$. But total revenue is equal to price times quantity, or the rectangle $a + b + c + d$, which clearly exceeds the amount $c + d$. So if the utility sets its price this way, it will be running a profit, in both appearance and fact. To avoid profits, therefore, utilities usually price below marginal cost, for example, something like p_2 in the figure.[5] By setting the

---

[5] This is sometimes called **average-cost pricing,** as opposed to **marginal cost pricing.**

price in this way, it can find the point where total cost $(c + d + e + f + g)$ is equal to total revenue $(b + c + e)$. But a price like p_2 is not efficient. The amount of water demanded at that price is q_2, and if the utility produces at this level, there will be a discrepancy between marginal cost and marginal benefits; the latter will be below the former. The utility will be producing some water for which the marginal valuation of consumers is lower than the marginal costs of production.[6]

Declining Block Pricing

A practice in which many water companies have historically engaged is **declining block pricing.** Under this pricing scheme, consumers pay a relatively high price for some initial quantity of water, up to some maximum, and then pay lower prices for quantities in excess of this level. There may be several declining blocks, as pictured in Figure 15-2. For any quantity at or below q_1 gallons per month, the consumer pays a price of p_1. For a quantity of q_1 or more but less than q_2, the price drops to p_2, and for quantities of q_2 or greater, the price drops to p_3.

The justification normally given for declining block pricing is that the cost per gallon of water delivered to large consumers is lower than the costs per gallon of getting water to smaller consumers. This is frequently thought of as being related to the costs of hooking up users to a public system; smaller hookups (using, say, smaller pipe and smaller ditches) may cost less than larger hookups, but they may cost more per gallon of water delivered. Whether this is true or not of course depends on how the system is laid out relative to topography and the location of the water supply, and will presumably differ from system to system and case to case. An even stronger element of justification for declining block pricing historically has been that it offers an economic advantage to commercial and industrial (i.e., large) water users. States and communities interested in economic development—and most of them are—have seen declining block pricing as a way of offering economic aid and support to water-using firms and organizations.

From an economic standpoint, declining block pricing has two major limitations. First, it tends to encourage water use. If the price of something gets lower the more of that something one consumes, incentives to conserve are weakened; in fact, it produces incentives to expand water consumption to take advantage of lower prices. This may not be a particularly important problem in water surplus situations, but when water is becoming increasingly scarce, as it is almost everywhere, this type of an incentive structure is unfortunate.

---

[6] This example is based on the assumption that the marginal cost of water is increasing. If it is decreasing, then pricing at marginal cost will lead to losses. One of the problems at the end of the chapter deals with this case.

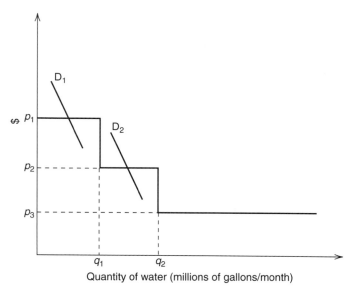

FIGURE 15-2
Declining Block Pricing for Water

From a slightly more technical standpoint, declining block pricing is also likely to upset the conditions for economic efficiency. Suppose, in the situation pictured in Figure 15-2, that there are two water users, one with the demand curve labeled D_1 and the other with D_2. The D_2 consumer will end up consuming more water than the D_1 consumer and will be on the second block price for water. This means that the price paid for one more gallon of water (the "marginal" gallon) will be higher for the D_1 consumer (it will be p_1) than the marginal price paid for the D_2 consumer (which will be p_2). But to have two consumers paying different prices for the same commodity is a violation of standard efficiency conditions, unless of course the two consumers differ in terms of the costs of delivering water to them. To see this, note what would happen if a gallon of water were reallocated from the D_2 consumer to the D_1 consumer. The former would lose something that has a marginal valuation of p_2, and the latter would gain something with a marginal valuation of p_1. Since $p_1 > p_2$, the total value of the water has been increased, simply by reallocating a small quantity from one user to another.

Declining block pricing, then, unless it is matched to real decreases in water delivery costs, is likely to violate one of the principal tenets of economic efficiency, which is that all users should pay the same price for the item in question. This, and the effect on conservation mentioned above, are the reasons that declining block pricing is being looked on with increasing disfavor by water authorities.

INVESTING IN WATER SUPPLY SYSTEMS

The discussion of how **existing water supplies** are allocated—especially how water is priced—can give us some very interesting insights into the ways water is used and misused and into the efficiency and equity implications of changing water utilization practices. Throughout the country, however, communities and water supply companies are faced with a whole range of **investment decisions** related to the overall **size or capacities** of their systems. These situations might include, for example:

1 Investments to protect existing water supplies (e.g., a community has to decide whether to buy land in the watershed area around its reservoirs so that development on these lands will not threaten water qualities and quantities in the reservoir)
2 Shifts from one type of water supply source to another (e.g., a coastal community faced with saltwater intrusion into its groundwater supply considers whether to switch to a desalination plan)
3 Investments in the existing system that have the effect of increasing system capacity (e.g., a community may decide to replace some of the existing water mains to reduce leakage)
4 Expansions of the existing system (e.g., a community has to decide whether to build an additional reservoir or new water canals to another surface water source in order to increase the capacity of its total water supply system)

All these situations call for **investment-type decisions,** that is, decisions in which most of the costs occur today or in the near future whereas most of the benefits are in terms of future consumption values—often very distant ones. Cases like this require techniques that we have discussed earlier for making decisions that have future consequences: some way of predicting accurately what future costs and benefits will be, and the discounting of future values so that all investment costs and benefits are in terms of **present values.**

But in reality it is not really possible to separate the water pricing problem from the water system investment problem. Investments affect future supplies, and prices will affect future demands and thus the balance between demand and supply. Consider Figure 15-3. Suppose that at the present time the water demand curve for the community in question is D_1 and the price of water is currently p_1. This means that the quantity of water demanded is q_1. Suppose that this quantity q_1 is also equal to the present capacity of the water system. Thus there is a balanced situation, with neither excess demand nor excess supply in the system.

Suppose also the community believes that because of anticipated economic and demographic growth, future water demand will also grow. For purposes of illustration, suppose that in 10 years the water demand curve is expected to be D_2. The community must now give thought to its water supply system. If it does nothing, and the new population materializes anyway, there will be ex-

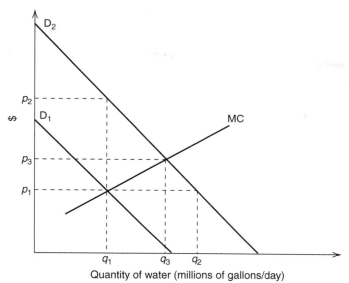

FIGURE 15-3
Pricing and the Addition of Capacity to a Water Supply System

cess demand at the old water price of p_1. At that price, with demand curve D_2, the quantity demanded of water is q_2, which is substantially in excess of the capacity of the current system at q_1. The excess demand could be wiped out if the price were raised to p_2, because even with the expanded demand, the quantity demanded at this higher price would not exceed the capacity of the current system.

It's unlikely that water planners would countenance such an increase in water price, however. Not only would consumers have to pay much higher prices, but the water utility or company would probably be making sizable profits in that situation. More than likely, the planners would think in terms of adding capacity to the system by investing in additional water supplies (enlarging a reservoir, adding a new reservoir, or perhaps drilling additional wells). Here is where price comes in. If the planners seek to maintain the current price of water, they will need an increment to capacity of $q_2 - q_1$ million gallons per day, because at a price of p_1, quantity demanded with the higher demand curve is q_2 million gallons per day. If future prices are somewhere above p_1 but below p_2, then the increment in capacity could be somewhere greater than zero but less than $q_2 - q_1$. What's the right course of action?

There are several ways of answering this question. From the standpoint of economic efficiency, however, the answer depends on how much it will cost to increase the capacity of the system. In technical terms, it depends on the shape of the long-run marginal cost curve (i.e., the supply curve) for water. Suppose this is horizontal, in other words the system can be expanded in such a way that the costs (capital costs plus operating costs) of delivering the water are constant. Then, indeed, the efficient system increment is equal to $q_2 - q_1$, and the efficient price of water would remain at p_1.

But suppose the long-run marginal costs of added capacity are upward-sloping, such as is depicted in the curve labeled MC that goes through the original price-quantity combination p_1, q_1. This would be the case, for example, if it becomes increasingly costly to add capacity. We would probably expect this to be the case, especially in arid or semiarid conditions. Cities may find that they have to reach out farther to get additional water supplies, or they may have to bid additional water supplies away from other users at higher prices than they are currently paying. Even in relatively humid areas, marginal costs may increase if people have to turn to increasingly costly sources of water. With rising marginal costs, the efficient course of action is some combination of higher price and added quantity. With the MC curve as depicted in Figure 15-3, the efficient course of action would be to increase system capacity to q_3 and raise the price of water to users to p_3.

WATER RIGHTS TRANSFERS AND MARKETS

In Los Angeles the going price for an acre-foot[7] of untreated water in the metropolitan water supply system is about \$350.[8] In the nearby Imperial Valley, farmers are paying around \$14 for an acre-foot of irrigation water. The cost of getting an acre-foot of water from the Imperial Valley to Los Angeles is substantially lower than the price difference, since they are connected to the same system of large water transport canals in southern California. The reason for the discrepancy is that the farmers of the Imperial Valley have been successful historically at acquiring water rights, largely rights to water from the Colorado River.[9] Los Angeles, on the other hand, has struggled through the years to obtain additional water supplies to keep up with their exploding population. They have had to reach into northern California and elsewhere to obtain these supplies, which has made them very expensive.

Figure 15-4 depicts this situation graphically. There are two demand curves: D_c is the demand for water in the city, and D_i is the demand for water by agricultural irrigators. For reasons of the historical development of water rights, q_i is the quantity of water available to irrigators and q_c is the total quantity available to people in the city. The market clearing prices for these two quantities, given the demand curves, are, respectively, p_i and p_c. The price for irrigation water is far below that for urban uses. In a smoothly adjusting **market economy,** this condition would be something of an anomaly. In principle, the presence of potential **gains from trade** would lead to adjustments where

---

[7] An acre-foot is a quantity of water that would cover one acre of level ground to a depth of one foot. It amounts to about 326,000 gallons.

[8] Metropolitan Water District, Press Release, January 12, 1999.

[9] These water rights may be held by farmers individually or often by irrigation district organizations, groups who manage regional systems of canals and small impoundments to supply irrigation water to the region's farmers.

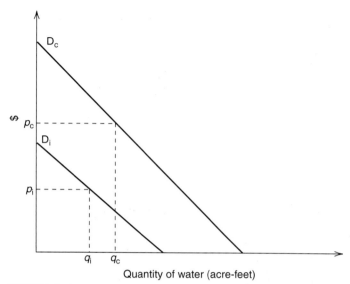

FIGURE 15-4
Water Rights and Water Prices

resources shift out of the relatively low valued uses and into the higher-valued uses. This is the process that economic markets are supposed to facilitate, with the result that the overall social value of the resources is maximized.

Water Transfers

In the world of water resources, large differences in water prices among users is fairly strong evidence that this normal adjustment process has not worked. Figure 15-5 shows two water demand functions. The one on the left is that for municipal and industrial (M&I) water used in an urban area. The one on the right is that for water used in irrigation in the nearby farming area. Let us suppose that the cost per acre-foot of delivering water to the two uses is exactly the same. Because of the way water rights have been allocated in the past, the city is currently consuming q_1 acre-feet of water while irrigators are applying q_4 acre-feet of water to farms.[10] The marginal value of water for M&I purposes is p_1, whereas that for irrigation water is p_3. These are clearly very different. If we reallocated just 1 acre-foot of water from agriculture to M&I, we would have a gain of p_1 in the latter and a loss of p_3 in the former, hence an overall net gain of $p_1 - p_3$. In this figure some illustrative dollar numbers have been

---

[10] In most real-world settings, of course, the situation will be much more complicated. Production and delivery costs may differ between the two uses, for example. Or some of the water applied to farms may run off and provide some of the water withdrawn downstream for M&I purposes. We are using this very simple illustration to get the basic point across about the efficiency gains from water transfers.

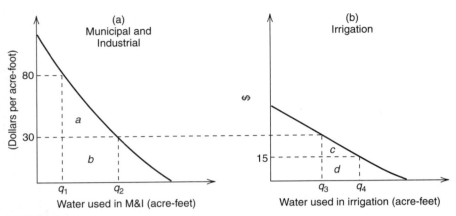

FIGURE 15-5
Mutual Gains from Trading Water Rights

put on the vertical axis to help in understanding the problem. The marginal value of water for M&I is currently $80 per acre-foot. That for agriculture is $15. Gains from trade clearly exist. If an acre-foot of water is reallocated from agriculture to M&I, the net gain is $65 (the $80 gain in M&I minus the $15 loss in agriculture). As long as these marginal valuations differ, reallocations will continue to have positive net benefits. Thus, the total gain would be maxi-mized by reallocating to the point where the marginal valuations are equal, which is at a price of $30 in the figure. At that point, q_2 acre-feet would be going to M&I and q_3 to irrigation. The total net gain from the reallocation would be $(a + b) - (c + d)$.

Suppose we have a situation like this in the real world. Should the water transfer be allowed, in whole or in part? Should it be facilitated somehow through public action? If so, how? If the commodity we were talking about were potatoes, we probably wouldn't spend much time worrying about it, be-cause we would expect the flow of potatoes around the market to adjust to price discrepancies like this. But water may be different. Or is it? Historically, nobody has worried about potato rights, but water rights have long been something to fight over. (See, for example, Exhibit 15-1.) If water is reallocated among users, and perhaps shipped from one location to another, the potential economic impacts could be far reaching. Consider the question of how the transfer is to be made. In keeping with the earlier distinctions we made be-tween different types of policy approaches,[11] there are two basic ways of doing this: an **administrative action** by a public regulatory agency or **transactions on a market for water rights.**

An administered shift in water rights would be carried out by having a public agency, such as a state department of water resources, reduce one party's water rights and confer these rights on another party. This would be

[11] See Chapter 7.

EXHIBIT 15-1

WHERE WATER IS POWER, THE BALANCE SHIFTS

Timothy Egan

PYRAMID LAKE, Nev., Nov. 26—Over the last century, the American West was remade with exclamation points. Free Land! Unlimited Water! No Chance of Failure! So went the trumpeting in the dust as the Federal Government tried to build an oasis civilization in the driest part of the United States.

Now, a major corrective is under way as the Government tries to undo some of what billions of tax dollars have done. More than ever, water still shapes destiny, but it is changing hands now, without bands blaring, cameras rolling or fliers promising riches.

And the exchange in power is no less dramatic. From the Colorado River to California's Central Valley, water from the subsidized farms and playgrounds created by Government irrigation is being diverted to nearly extinct fish and wildlife, long-forgotten Indian tribes and cities that barely existed when the big dams and canals were built.

Perhaps the most significant of the efforts to alter the balance of power in the arid lands is taking place here on the Truckee River in northern Nevada, site of the nation's first major Federal irrigation project, and one of the most fought-over streams in the country.

Flowing out of Lake Tahoe on the California-Nevada border, the Truckee runs down the east slope of the mountains, trickles through fast-growing Reno, is diverted to farmers in the desert and ends its 105-mile ride at Pyramid Lake, where Paiute Indians have lived for at least a thousand years.

Until recently, most of the river's water was siphoned off to alfalfa farms and cattle ranches created by Government enticement 80 years ago in the middle of the high desert east of Reno. Now, the Government is buying back much of that water and giving it to the Pyramid Lake Paiute Indians, to projects to restore fish runs and once-bounteous wetlands, and to new communities in Nevada, the fastest-growing state in the nation.

The farmers feel betrayed, comparing the Government to the mob. Indians say they are getting some measure of repayment for lost water that caused the biggest natural lake in Nevada to fall by 80 feet, killed off a species of cutthroat trout and drained one of the nation's first wildlife refuges. And the city of Reno, given a guarantee of future water as long as it learns to conserve and clean the water it uses, is no longer talking about withering up. . . .

Many of the changes were started in the Bush Administration, but are being enacted, with buyouts, closing of dams and river restoration, during the Clinton Presidency. And just as it was when the Federal Government set out to dam, divert or straighten the major rivers of the West at the start of the century, there are clear winners and losers. . . .

The biggest losers will be the biggest water users—the irrigated farms in the desert.

"About 45 miles from the irrigated desert farmland, on the Paiute Indian Reservation, the tribe that was nearly wiped out by the diversions of the earlier part of the century has rebounded somewhat. There are new fish hatcheries for the cui-ui, a Pleistocene-era fish that was the foundation of the Paiute diet, and for a different strain of Lahontan cutthroat that has been reintroduced into the lake.

done by fiat, after ascertaining that the shift is in the **public interest** and using standard **regulatory enforcement procedures** to make sure that the change goes through. Changes of this type, especially large-scale shifts among different types of users (e.g., farmers vs. urban dwellers), usually spark energetic legal and political struggles that pit one side and its allies against the other side and its allies. The outcome would probably depend as much or more on the political strengths and abilities of the participants as on the economic values (benefits and costs) of the proposed transfer.

The other way to effect the transfer is through transactions on a market for water rights. Market transactions occur because willing sellers meet willing buyers and trade something of value at a price agreed to by both participants. The buyers gain an amount $(a + b)$ from purchasing $q_2 - q_1$ of additional water in Figure 15-5. The sellers lose an amount equal to $(c + d)$. It's possible to find a price per acre-foot that, when multiplied by $q_2 - q_1$, the quantity traded, will allow both participants to gain from the trade. It will be lower than the gain experienced by the buyer, and higher than the loss of the seller.

Water Markets

In the arid western United States, urban populations continue to grow, state and regional economies move increasingly away from agriculture, and the ability to meet new water demands by developing new sources of supply continues to diminish—hence the interest in **transferring existing water** supplies among users to foster its efficient utilization. But as these economies become more and more complex, it becomes increasingly difficult for a public water management agency to be aware of all the efficiency-enhancing transfers that might be concluded or to be able to carry out these transfers without continuous political conflict and turmoil. In recent years, interest has grown in moving away from **administered transfers** of water rights and toward greater reliance on **water rights markets** to foster the kinds of transfers depicted in Figure 15-5. A water market would function analogously to markets in other types of goods and services: Willing sellers and buyers, individuals or groups, would be able to conclude private agreements to transfer given quantities of water at agreed-upon prices. As with any market there would have to be rules and regulations covering these transactions. And this is a point of great controversy: Should the rules be set so that there are few limits on permissible water transactions? Or should public water agencies have direct oversight and control over all transactions? We return to this issue below.

Local water markets, for example neighboring irrigators trading small amounts of water among themselves, have existed for a long time. Even some large-scale transactions were carried out many years ago. The notorious Owens Valley case, where the city of Los Angeles secretly bought up agricultural land in the Owens Valley so that the attached water rights could be transferred to the city, took place in the 1920s.[12] But the 1980s saw a very substantial increase in transactions involving large amounts of water, transported longer distances, between different types of users.

---

[12] This incident was featured in the film *Chinatown*.

EXHIBIT 15-2

FUNCTIONING WATER MARKETS

The Colorado Front Range consists of an area about 30–40 miles wide and stretching north to south just east of the Rocky Mountains. It contains the large cities of Denver and Colorado Springs and surrounding suburban developments. Very large scale water supply systems have been built so that people living in this area could reach out and import supplies of water to support economic and demographic growth. In the northern part of the area is the Northern Colorado Water Conservancy District, which integrates the activities of dozens of different water service organizations operating canals, storage reservoirs, pumping facilities, and water treatment plants. One of these organizations is the North Poudre Irrigation Company (NPIC). This company issued 10,000 original shares of stock, each share of which entitled the owner to 6 acre-feet of water per year. There is a well-developed market for these shares, and they may easily be bought and sold. Shareholders may divide their shares into quarter shares, each representing about 1.5 acre-feet of water, in order to buy and sell smaller quantities of water. The rights are rather widely distributed among a variety of municipal/industrial, rural domestic, and agricultural water users. Prices of the shares (per acre-foot of water) were around $200 in the early 1960s, gradually rose to well over $1,000 in the late 1970s, and have since declined somewhat as alternative water sources have come on line. Although NPIC water rights are highly marketable, there is a limit on the service area in which trades can be freely made. Sales of rights out of the service area may be done only after satisfying certain legal requirements.

In Colorado, cities along the Front Range (Denver, Colorado Springs, and Fort Collins) purchased agricultural water rights to satisfy increasing urban demands. Prices in the 1980s ranged from $1,000 to $5,000 per acre-foot of water (see Exhibit 15-2). In Arizona, the cities of Tucson and Phoenix purchased "water ranches," agricultural lands that came with attached water rights. These sold for more than $1,500 per acre-foot in the 1980s. Albuquerque paid over $1,000 per acre-foot for agricultural water rights. In Nevada, developers and municipal water providers bought irrigation water rights in the 1980s for between $2,000 and $3,000 an acre-foot. During that decade Salt Lake City bought irrigation water rights, paying between $160 to $250 per acre-foot. These lower prices reflect the more water-abundant conditions of that area compared to the very arid southwestern states.[13]

Interest is still strong in expanding the scope for water markets in the future. In California, where the presence of huge state and federal water projects has historically tended to make it difficult to transfer water rights, a new federal law facilitates the development of water markets. The Central Valley Improvement Act of 1992 allows individuals or districts who receive water from the Central Valley Project (CVP) to sell some or all of their allocations to any beneficial use within or outside the CVP area.[14]

[13] Bonnie Colby Saliba and David B. Bush, *Water Markets in Theory and Practice*, Westview Press, Boulder, CO, 1987.
[14] Marcia Weinberg, "Federal Water Policy Reform: Implications for Irrigated Farms in California," *Contemporary Economic Policy*, Vol. XV, April 1997, pp. 63–73.

Conditions for Social Efficiency in Water Markets

Although many people advocate increasing the role of markets in allocating the water resource, many also remain skeptical about the ability of unfettered water markets to attain economic efficiency in the full social sense. And there are also many in the middle, who think that water markets will be an improvement over past practices but that these markets will have to be carefully guided by responsible public agencies. To help answer this question we must first look at the requirements that have to be met if markets are to function in a way that is socially efficient. We can then consider whether these factors are likely to hold in the real world. There are two types of requirements, one on the **nature of the water rights** themselves, and the other on the **structure of the markets** on which these rights are traded.[15]

For markets to perform well, property rights in water have to be **clearly defined, reasonably complete, secure, and transferable.** "Clearly defined" means that there is no ambiguity about the nature of the right that is owned. Suppose I am the owner of some water rights and according to current law my rights are subject to the use of the water for beneficial purposes on my farm. There is a drought, and my neighbor would like to lease some of these rights temporarily to get through it. I am able to take steps to conserve on my water use and apparently free up some of the water to lease to my neighbor. But suppose I fear that if I lease some of the water, the authorities might take this as evidence that I had more water than I needed in the first place and they therefore might confiscate some of these water rights. Because of this **uncertainty** I might refrain from leasing the water, despite the fact that it would be an efficiency-enhancing transaction.[16] Uncertainties as to what is actually owned when one owns a water right clearly will make it very difficult for these rights to be exchanged on markets.

By "**reasonably complete**" is meant that water rights must not be so narrowly defined that the opportunities for exchange are unduly restricted. For purposes of illustration take an unrealistic example. Suppose you have water rights and you use this water to irrigate your large fields of cantaloupes. Suppose that the water management agency in the area enacts a rule saying that water rights are freely transferable as long as the water is used only for the irrigation of cantaloupes. This has the effect of substantially narrowing the potential for efficiency-improving transactions, because it rules out all but one kind of potential participant. At the same time, this criterion says "reasonably." Some limitations on what water may be used for may be useful in most

---

[15] In Chapter 7 we discussed the use of property rights systems to solve natural resource allocation problems and considered the features that property rights and markets would have to have if they were to function efficiently. It is worth reiterating some of these ideas here, in the specific context of water markets.

[16] This is in fact a major problem in many states. See Charles W. Howe, "Increasing Efficiency in Water Markets: Examples from the Western United States," in Terry L. Anderson and Peter J. Hills (eds.), *Water Marketing, The Next Generation*, Rowman and Littlefield, Lanham, MD, 1997, pp. 79–99.

cases. For example, it would be appropriate to limit a water transfer if it seemed destined to contaminate a large ecosystem.

Property rights have to be **secure** if markets are to function well. They have to be defendable, at a reasonable cost, from would-be encroachers or appropriators. Suppose I want to purchase the right to withdraw a certain amount of water from a nearby river. I would certainly not be willing to pay for it if I had no way of stopping upstream people from pumping "my" water in times of low flow. Usually this means having a functioning legal system with courts and police. It also means that I need a way of knowing about upstream withdrawals—of monitoring the situation so I can tell when my water rights have been encroached upon. Finally, it goes without saying that markets cannot function at all if water rights are not **transferable.** This goes to the very heart of the matter, because it is the transferring of water from one person to another that produces the efficiency gains.

The other type of requirements for efficient water rights markets is in the **structure of the markets** themselves. Markets work on the basis of **price signals.** If prices go up, it is a signal that demand is increasing relative to supply (or supply has decreased relative to demand); if prices go down, the opposite is true. For markets to function well, knowledge of prices must be widespread (i.e., no secret deals), and there must be **competition** among and between buyers and sellers. To have competition there must be a relatively large number of participants on both sides of the market. What "relatively large" means varies from case to case, but it's clear that at the present time many, if not most, water rights transactions are being worked out among a small number of participants. The current battle to buy and sell water rights from the Colorado River, for example, is not occurring in a competitive water market, but rather through negotiations among the small number of states who have the basic rights to the water of the Colorado River.

Another primary requirement is that markets have to be **complete.** Completeness has two components, completeness in the sense that all affected parties have the right to participate in the market and completeness in the sense that all impacts forthcoming from a water transfer are tradable on a market. Suppose I am a farmer who irrigates crops by withdrawing water from a nearby stream. Some of this water runs off and back into the stream; this return flow is used downstream by another farmer. Suppose now a nearby city comes to me and offers to buy my entitlement. They want to build a canal from my property to the city water treatment plant, whence the water will enter the city water mains. Suppose the water is worth $25 per acre-foot to me, and the city will pay me $50 per acre-foot for it. Can we conclude that such a transaction would be socially efficient?

The obvious potential problem with this is the impact on the downstream farmer who uses the return flow. If the return flow is disrupted, that person loses something of value. The only way we can be assured that the original transaction is socially efficient is if the downstream farmer has the legal right to the return flow and has no restrictions on his participation in the market. In that case the city will also have to conclude an agreement with him, buying, for an agreed-upon price, the rights to the return flow. In water market discussions, impacts like this are often called **third-party effects.** A third party is a party other than the buyer and seller who is affected directly by the water rights transfer concluded by the buyer and seller. A third party is essentially a nonparticipant. If the rules of the market permit the participation by people in this case, they are no longer third parties.

The other type of market completeness is that all the impacts of a water rights transfer be potentially tradable on a market. Suppose that the return flow, in the above example, supports ecosystem values in the stream below the farmer-irrigator. These values are in terms, say, of habitat protection for certain plants and animals. Without the irrigation return flow, a number of these biological populations would be damaged and perhaps destroyed. The difference between this and a downstream irrigator with rights to the return flow is that there is no well-developed market on which these particular third parties, namely endangered animal and plant species, can be represented. The main problem is that ecosystem protection like this is in the nature of a **public good,**[17] and private markets are not particularly good at representing the values of goods of this type.

Conditions in the real world never match the conditions of economics textbooks. Such problems as competitive "thinness" (i.e., too few participants to foster brisk competition), and third-party representation will be around for a long time. The real question is not whether markets do a perfect job of allocating water efficiently, but whether they are capable of doing a better job than has been done over the years by traditional water managing institutions. Many people think the markets can do a better job, provided that we strike the right balance between letting the inherent power of markets work its influence and exercising some degree of public control over how the markets function.

INSTREAM FLOW PROTECTION

Historically most conflicts about water rights and utilization centered on water withdrawals, where water was physically removed from stream or lake for irrigation, mining operations, manufacturing needs, and so on. Many rivers, especially in the West but even in the East as well, have reached points where most of the water is fully used or appropriated, leaving very low instream flows, especially in the drier seasons of the year. In recent decades, however, the values produced by water that is left in its natural location have become much more obvious and important. Thus there has been a growing demand for the protection of **instream flows.** Instream flows protect the estuarine environment and its ecological and aesthetic values. They are also the basis for a large and growing segment of the outdoor recreation market: fishing, white-water and flat-water sports, hiking and camping, bird watching, and so on.

The legal status of instream flow water rights varies from state to state. In most cases the major players in protecting instream flows are public water

---

[17] For a discussion of public goods, see Chapter 6.

management agencies, and so groups and individuals who seek to increase instream flow have to work within the political process in which these agencies are embedded. A natural extension of the water rights marketing concept would be to allow individuals or groups to buy instream water rights. Naturally, traditional water withdrawers are quite reluctant to move in this direction, as it could lead to major shifts in the way water is managed.

Optimal Instream Flows

How much water should be left in a stream? It is easy to think about this conceptually, though difficult to determine very precisely in practice. Figure 15-6 shows the benefits and costs of instream water flows, and how these benefits and costs change as flows change. The curve labeled B shows benefits, starting to the right of the origin. Some minimal amount of water is necessary before any benefits appear at all. The function increases, reaches a maximum at a_1, and then begins to decline, because still larger flows actually reduce most instream values. This is an illustrative benefits function shape; the actual shape would of course vary from one real-world situation to another.

The cost relationship is labeled C; it rises to the right and becomes increasingly steep. The primary costs of instream flows are the values of forgone water withdrawals. Since the values of different types of withdrawals (e.g., agriculture vs. urban) differ, the cost curve is drawn under the assumption that it captures the most valuable forgone alternative use. The instream flow that maximizes total benefits is not the one that maximizes net benefits; the former is a_1 and the latter is a^*. The reason for the discrepancy is that costs are

FIGURE 15-6
Benefits and Costs of Instream Water Flows

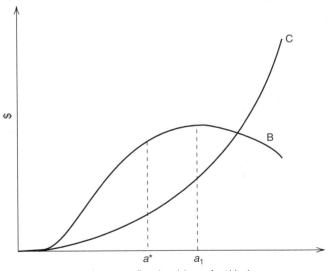

Instream flow level (acre-feet/day)

taken into account in one case but not in the other. Note that at a^*, marginal benefits (the slope of the B curve) are equal to marginal costs (the slope of the C curve).

There is a certain amount of ambiguity in this model, since it is so simple. The horizontal axis indexes quantity of water per day. But most rivers and streams, unless they can be completely controlled through upstream impoundments, have flows that fluctuate from day to day and season to season. So we might think of the horizontal axis as measuring the mean value of instream flow over a year's time. On any single day the flow might be somewhat, or perhaps substantially, below the average. And this would affect the benefits and costs produced by the river over the course of the year. In other words, you could have two rivers, each with the same average instream flow but with very different variation about the mean. In this case benefits and costs would likely be different between the two.

An interesting question is, how sensitive are net benefits to changes in stream flow? If flow is not at a^* but above or below it a certain amount, will this substantially affect net benefits? The answer to this is reflected in the shapes, especially the curvature, of the benefit and cost curves. If the curvature is low in both cases, then any flow rate around a^* will be almost as good as any other. If the relationships are very curved, then the opposite is true, and a flow of exactly a^* is required to ensure maximum net benefits.

While the logic of Figure 15-6 is straightforward and clear, its application in any particular real-world case is going to be difficult. One problem is just getting the necessary data to determine the relationships; data are required on both benefits and costs. Another major problem is that very often there is more than just one type of instream benefit, and the best flow rates may very well differ among the benefit types. The flow rate that is best for maintaining a trout fishery, for example, may be very different from the best flow rate for maintaining white-water rafting activity. Exhibit 15-3 discusses a problem of this type for a river in New Mexico.

SUMMARY

In the United States, water is relatively abundant in the East and scarce in the West. The historical laws covering the right to make water withdrawals have differed between the two regions, with **riparian** law in the East and the **prior appropriations** doctrine predominating in the West. Both systems are giving way in modern times to more administered systems, in which public agencies are responsible for managing water systems and proceed to adopt rules for the purpose. Most water supply systems are handled by publicly owned companies or private companies subject to public oversight. A fundamental decision to be made by these companies is how water is to be priced. **Pricing decisions** are usually undertaken with the objective of covering costs, which frequently leads agencies toward average-cost pricing. If marginal cost curves are upward-sloping, this will lead to prices that are too low on efficiency grounds. Water pricing decisions are related also to decisions about expanding the

EXHIBIT 15-3

MANAGING INSTREAM FLOWS: THE RIO CHAMA[1]

The Rio Chama is in northern New Mexico. It is a tributary of the Rio Grande, and is heavily used for agricultural and municipal purposes. It is also heavily used for recreational purposes. In managing the flow of the river, priority has to be given to certain downstream water rights holders. But it is also possible to vary somewhat the releases of water from El Vado Reservoir upstream. This brings up the thorny question of how much water should be released in relation to the various services supplied by the instream flows.

A study team examined the situation carefully, identifying the major instream purposes and stream flows that were conducive to these purposes. These are shown in the accompanying tabulation. Note that there are a number of potential conflicts. Most clearly, white-water boating calls for substantially greater releases (800–1,000 cubic feet per second, or cfs) than any other use. Some of these, like aesthetic values, would be compatible with these large releases while others, such as scenic (essentially flat-water) boating would not. The optimal releases for fishing (400 cfs during the winter) are in conflict with bald eagle habitat, and so on.

Since there can be only one release schedule, how are these conflicts to be resolved? One way might be to try to estimate the economic values of these alternative river services, in terms of willingness to pay. This would be relatively easy for example, for white-water boating and fishing, but very difficult for such services as general habitat

maintenance and the protection of bald eagles in this region.

FLOWS NECESSARY TO SUPPORT DESIGNATED RESOURCE VALUES IN THE RIO CHAMA

Resource/flow magnitude and timing
Fish habitat (brown trout)
150–700 cfs, October 15–March 31
(400 cfs optimum)
150–300 cfs, April 1–August 31
(200 cfs optimum)
75–300 cfs, September 1–October 14
(200 cfs optimum)
Macroinvertebrates
185 cfs minimum
Scenic/aesthetic
40 cfs minimum
White-water rafting
800–1,000 cfs
Scenic boating
500–600 cfs
Fishing
150-300 cfs
Riparian (maintenance flow)
185 cfs, April 1–September 30
Riparian (regeneration flow)
5,000 cfs at least one day every 5–10 years, between May 15 and June 15
Bald eagles
150–250 cfs, December 1 to March 1

[1]This example is taken from David M. Gillilan and Thomas C. Brown, *Instream Flow Protection*, Island Press, Washington, DC., 1997, pp. 87–94.

capacity of existing systems. In the West, the most important water resource issue at the present time is the use of **water markets** to reallocate water among users, especially between agricultural and municipal users. There are many questions about the extent to which these markets can work efficiently and fairly and about the appropriate role of public agencies in overseeing their operation. In the future the role of markets in allocating water will undoubtedly increase. One major change to which they will have to adapt is the rapidly rising values placed on the maintenance of **instream water flows.**

KEY TERMS

Surface water
Groundwater
Water withdrawals/consumption
Riparian water rights
Prior appropriation water rights
Administered water systems
Average-cost pricing

Declining block pricing
Investment in water supply systems
Water rights transfers
Water markets
Third-party effects
Instream flow protection

QUESTIONS FOR FURTHER DISCUSSION

1 Show that if the marginal costs of water supply are downward-sloping, then pricing so that marginal cost equals marginal willingness to pay will mean that the water company will experience losses. How might these losses be made up?

2 If water is a "necessity for the maintenance of human life," how can it be rational to price it the same way we would any economic good or service?

3 What are some of the potential "third-party effects" in the large-scale transferring of water rights from agricultural to urban areas?

4 What are some of the problems that a public agency might face in trying to provide oversight and guidance for water markets?

5 The eastern part of the United States has much more abundant water than the West. But per capita water consumption in the West is higher than that of the East. Why?

USEFUL WEB SITES

Information on the major federal water resource agencies:

- Bureau of Reclamation (http://www.usbr.gov)
- U.S. Army Corps of Engineers (http://www.usace.army.mil); a faster way into this material is (http://www.nap.usace.army.mil/sb/flood.htm)
- Natural Resources Conservation Service (USDA) (http://nrcs.usda.gov)
- Another federal site is the water resources division of the U.S. Geological Survey (http://www.er.usgs.gov), primarily involved with water resources states reports and data

Many state universities have water resource research institutes and centers, such as:

- Oregon (http://www.orst.edu/dept/owrri)
- Texas (http://www.twri,tamu.edu)
- California (http://endeavor.des.ucdavis.edu/cara)

There are many water-oriented public interest groups:

- American Rivers (http://amrivers.org)
- North American Lake Management Society (http://www.nalms.org)

Australia has a good site that discusses transferable water entitlements:

- Environment Australia Online (http://www.environment.gov.au), in its publication "Evaluation of Findings—Environmental Incentives"
- Bureau of Land Management, Clean Water Action Plan (http://www.blm.gov/nhp/whatwedo/cwap)

REFERENCES

Anderson, Terry L., and Peter J. Hill (eds.): *Water Marketing—The Next Generation*, Rowman and Littlefield, Lanham, MD, 1997.

Bates, Sarah F., David H. Getches, Lawrence J. Macdonnell, and Charles F. Wilkinson: *Searching Out the Headwaters: Change and Rediscovery in Western Water Policy*, Island Press, Covelo, CA, 1993.

Beck, Robert F.: "The Movement in the United States to Restoration and Creation of Wetlands," *Natural Resources Journal*, 34 (4), Fall 1994, pp. 781–822.

Brajer, W., A. Church, R. Cummings, and P. Fanal: "The Strengths and Weaknesses of Water Markets as They Affect Water Scarcity and Sovereignty Interests in the West," *Natural Resources Journal*, Vol. 29, Spring 1989, pp. 489–509.

Colby, Bonnie G.: "Regulation, Imperfect Markets, and Transaction Costs: The Elusive Quest for Efficiency in Water Allocation," in Daniel W. Bromley (ed.): *The Handbook of Environmental Economics*, Blackwell, Oxford, England, 1995, pp. 475–502.

Easter, K., and M. Rosegrant (eds.): *Markets for Water, Potential and Performance*, Kluwer Academic, Dordrecht, Netherlands, 1998

Frederick, Kenneth D.: "Water Supplies," in Paul R. Portney (ed.), *Current Issues in Natural Resource Policy*, Johns Hopkins Press for Resources for the Future, Washington, DC, 1982, pp. 216–252.

Gleick, Peter H.: *The World's Water, 1998–1999*, Island Press, Covelo, CA, 1998.

Haddad, Brent M.: *Rivers of Gold: Designing Markets to Allocate Water in California*, Island Press, Washington, DC, 2000

Merrett, Stephen: *Introduction to the Economics of Water Resources: An International Perspective*, Rowman and Littlefield, Lanham, MD, 1997.

Moore, Michael R., Aimee Mulville, and Marcia Weinberg: "Water Allocation in the American West: Endangered Fish versus Irrigated Agriculture," *Natural Resources Journal*, 36 (2), Spring 1996, pp. 319–357.

Naeser, Robert Benjamin, and Mark Griffin Smith: "Playing with Borrowed Water: Conflicts over Instream Flows on the Upper Arkansas River," *Natural Resources Journal*, 35 (1), Winter 1995, pp. 93–110.

National Research Council: *Water Transfers in the West, Efficiency, Equity and the Environment*, National Academy Press, Washington, DC, 1992.

Reisner, Marc: *Cadillac Desert: The American West and Its Disappearing Water*, Penguin Books, New York, 1993.

Saliba, B. C., and D. B. Bush: *Water Markets in Theory and Practice: Market Transfers, Water Values and Public Policy*, Westview Press, Boulder, CO, 1987.

Schmandt, J., E. T. Smerdon, and J. Clarkson: *State Water Policies: A Study of Six States*, Praeger, New York, 1988.

Spulber, Nicolas, and Asghan Sabbaghi: *Economics of Water Resources: From Regulation to Privatization*, Kluwer, Boston, 1998.

CHAPTER 16

ECONOMICS OF
AGRICULTURE

Human beings have walked the earth for about 2 million years. A very short time ago, in comparative terms, they invented agriculture, the purposeful cultivation of domesticated plants and animals. Today agriculture is fundamental to the continued existence and welfare of the global population. It is a prime natural resource–using sector, requiring inputs of land, water, air, and biodiversity. The developed world has achieved, for the most part, tremendously productive agricultural systems, though there are questions about its long-run sustainability. The developing world is mixed: Some countries have achieved impressive gains in agricultural productivity, but many others have not. There is also a third group of countries facing a unique set of problems: formerly socialist countries who are trying to move away from centrally directed systems toward decentralized, owner-operated farm systems.

In this chapter we take up some of the important questions of agriculture in the contemporary world. Some of these problems are, at least conceptually, the same in the modern agricultural sectors of the developed world as they are in those of the developing or restructuring countries. Issues of **technological change,** the **management of soil productivity** over time, and the importance of analyzing **incentives** are problems everywhere. But for some countries, the issues are more complex. In the United States and most other developed countries there is relatively little controversy any more over the **distribution of agricultural land.** Furthermore, farmers in these countries usually (though not always) have adequate access to marketing, credit, and information services. This is not true of farmers in many developing countries. Countries in a state of transition from socialist to capitalist agricultural systems have some characteristics of both developed and developing countries. On the one hand their agriculture may be modern from a technological point of view; on the other hand the incentive problems and the need for large-scale restructuring of their agricultural sectors are more characteristic of problems faced by developing nations.

HISTORICAL CHANGES IN SUPPLY AND DEMAND

If we look at the recent history of agricultural production and food availability in the broadest possible way, we can understand it as an ongoing dynamic interaction between the forces that increase production and those that increase consumption. Some recent history in this respect, for major regions of the world, is shown in Figure 16-1. The top panel shows the path over the last 40 years of **total production,** in terms of indices developed by the Food and Agriculture Organization of the United Nations. The bottom panel shows the path of **per capita production** over this period. Several trends stand out. On the positive side there have been very substantial increases in total output over the last few decades in Asia. These have been high enough to offset the rapid population growth of many of these countries, so that per capita production has also increased rapidly in that part of the world. Total output in Latin America has also increased fast enough to offset population, as it has in Europe and North America.

On the down side are Africa and the countries of the former Soviet Union. In Africa, especially sub-Saharan agriculture, total food output has increased over the last several decades but not enough to match population growth; so per capita production has shown a marked decline. We revisit this situation in a later section on economic development and natural resources.[1] Another situation that stands out is the collapse of agricultural output, both total and per capita, in eastern Europe and the countries of the former Soviet Union. These are countries that moved strongly toward large-scale industrial agriculture during the post–World War II years and up to the dissolution of the Soviet Union in 1989. Since then they have worked, to a greater or lesser degree, toward a return to an owner-operator type of agricultural structure. This has led to tremendous dislocation and disruption of agricultural production and distribution in these countries, which accounts for their performance as pictured in Figure 16-1.

The most straightforward way to understand these data analytically is as an interplay over time of forces affecting **supply and demand** for food. This is depicted in Figure 16-2. A century ago, we can imagine, the United States was at a position like that labeled ①, which is the intersection of demand curve D_1

---

[1] See Chapters 20 and 21.

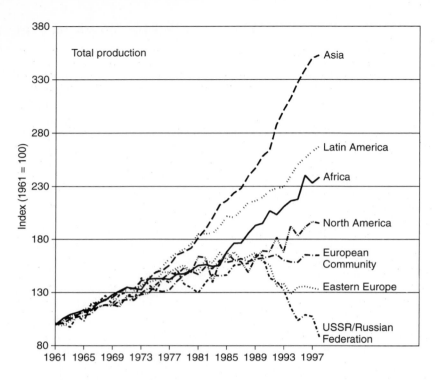

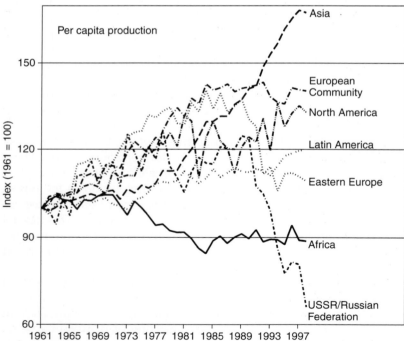

FIGURE 16-1
Food Production, Selected Regions, 1961–1998 (*Source:* Food and Agriculture
Organization of the United Nations, FAOSTAT Statistical Database, FAO, Rome, 1999.)

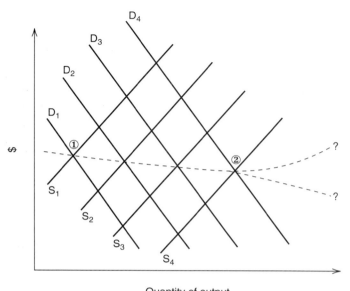

Quantity of output

FIGURE 16-2
Long-Run Demand and Supply Shifts in Agriculture

and supply curve S_1. Through the last century both demand and supply have shifted to the right. The most important factor behind the demand shifts has been demographic growth; more people demand more food. Factors pushing out the supply function are technological and institutional in nature: more productive biological stock, machinery, fertilizers, irrigation, business practices, and so on. The notable part is that technology has developed faster than population; thus supply shifts have outstripped demand shifts, food production has more than matched population growth, and prices have been pushed down.

Let us think of our current position as the one labeled ② in the figure. How will our future play out? Two possible tracks are identified. One is a continuation of the trend downward, perhaps with some slackening of the pace, but no reversal. The second is a track defined by a reversal of (recent) historical supply and demand changes, leading to reductions in output growth, falling agricultural output per person, and rising agricultural prices. Which course is the more likely? We are back to a problem mentioned in several previous chapters: Is it more appropriate to be optimistic about future technological/demographic developments, or to be pessimistic about these factors? Malthus set the tone of the debate 200 years ago. Population growth, he said, would inevitably outstrip productivity growth, leading to widespread famine.[2] It has not happened yet, but perhaps it will in the not-too-distant future. Or is there

[2] T. R. Malthus, *An Essay on Population,* London, 1978.

EXHIBIT 16-1

CONTRASTING STATEMENTS ON THE FUTURE OF AGRICULTURAL OUTPUT
AND FOOD SUPPLIES

A Bearish View

All key indicators of food security show a decline in recent years.

In 1996, the world grain harvest climbed to a record 1.87 billion tons, well above the previous record set in 1992. The 1997 world grain harvest was about the same, but since consumption rose, grain stocks dropped slightly, falling from 57 to 55 days of consumption.

Rising world grain prices may be the first global economic indicator to tell us that the world is on an economic and demographic path that is environmentally unsustainable. Over most of the last half-century, world grain prices have fallen, reflecting technological gains that have increased the overall efficiency of grain production.

Since 1993, however, the trend has been reversed. The world price of wheat climbed from a low of $3.97 per bushel in 1993 to $5.54 in 1996, a gain of 39 percent. During this same time, rice prices climbed by 30 percent and corn was up by 58 percent. The price of each of the grains reached either its all-time low or close to it in 1993, and all three have risen since then. While three years do not make a new long-term trend, this rise is what would be expected with strong continuing growth in demand and slower growth in production.

Source: Lester R. Brown, *State of the World, 1998,* World Resources Institute, Washington, DC, 1999, pp. 16–17.

A Bullish View

Over the next quarter century, the world's supply of food will grow somewhat more rapidly than will the demand for it, leading to lower real prices of food. Thus, the trend of food prices, as measured by grain prices, is likely to continue the trend of the current century, though at a slower rate of decline.[1] The remarkable reduction in the international price of grain that has occurred in this century is given all too little emphasis in discussions of the world food situation, certainly so in the discussions of the food pessimists.

I am confident that the real per capita incomes of the majority of the population in the developing countries will continue to increase, contributing to an improvement in food security. Finally, I believe that, with the changes in agricultural policies in the major industrial countries, world trade in farm products, especially grains, will be further liberal-

ized in the future. In addition, more and more developing countries are reducing barriers to trade, thus increasing access to world food supplies. Thus, all the broad trends point to an improvement in world food security and a reduction in the number of persons adversely affected by both long-term or short-term inadequate access to food.

[1]Not everyone agrees that real grain or food prices will decline. Two recent studies conclude that real grain or food prices will increase. The studies are the OECD's *The Agricultural Outlook 1998-2003* and Luther Tweeten's recent study of global food supply and demand balance. The OECD study projects international price increases between 1997 and 2003 of 17% for wheat and 7% for corn. Tweeten is quite bullish for food prices, projecting an annual rate of price increase of more than 1.2% for the next two decades.
Source: D. Gale Johnson, "Food Security and World Trade Prospects," *American Journal of Agricultural Economics,* 80(5), 1998, p. 941.

something about the tendency of population growth to moderate, and the ability of human ingenuity to increase agricultural productivity, that will forestall this dismal forecast, perhaps forever? Opinions remain divided, as indicated by the contrasting statements in Exhibit 16-1.

It is not the direct objective of this chapter to delve into major issues of food demand and the ability of agricultural sectors to meet that demand. Our goal is, rather, to look at some of the important issues related to how agricultural systems impact the quantity and quality of the natural resource base. Obviously, these issues are related. Efforts to expand agricultural production lead to intensified methods of production, which have resource impacts. Institutional systems that create perverse or weak incentives for agricultural decision makers can lead to decisions that impact natural resources in inefficient, unsustainable ways. Nevertheless, the focus here is on some of the specific resource-using decisions faced by farmers, examining how these decisions affect the resource base and how they are affected by the technological, organizational, and institutional situations in which they find themselves.

INCOME SUPPORT POLICIES IN AGRICULTURE

Agriculture in the developed world has attained high levels of productivity. It has also attained very high levels of attention and concern from politicians. From the brief discussion above, it is easy to understand the income pressure that farmers have been under. Rapid technological advance drives prices lower, which leads to increased competitive pressure for farmers and puts many of them out of business. The rapid shrinking of the farm sector has led to calls for political intervention. Thus over the last four or five decades almost all developed countries have pursued policies and regulations designed to give aid and support to their farmers. The ultimate aim of these programs has been to lift farm incomes above those which would prevail in competitive markets with no control over the rate of technological innovation.[3]

Table 16-1 shows some of the major approaches that policy makers have used to shift income toward agriculture. They have often been used in combination. Continued attempts have been made through the years to reduce the levels of public support going to farmers, but this has been hard to do, given the political realities of most countries.[4] There has been a trend, however, away from programs of supply restrictions, price supports, and input subsidies, toward programs of direct income payments.[5] One reason for this is a growing appreciation for the **economic distortions** that the earlier types of support programs produced. A distortion is where farmers shift their operations to take advantage of the particular provisions of public programs, introducing various types of biases that, within a wider market context, are inefficient and cost-ineffective. Many of these distortions have influenced the impacts of agriculture on the quantity and quality of the underlying natural resource base.

---

[3] This is not true of some countries of the developing world, which have sought to drain income out of agriculture for use elsewhere.

[4] Over half of the budget of the European Union goes for the support of farmers in the member states. It has proved impossible to reduce these support levels in any significant amount.

[5] Organization for Economic Cooperation and Development, Environmental Effects of Reforming Agricultural Policies, OECD, Paris, 1998.

TABLE 16-1
TYPES OF INCOME SUPPORT PROGRAMS THAT HAVE BEEN USED
TO BENEFIT FARMERS

- **Price supports.**   Since technical change tends to drive agricultural product prices lower, some programs have been put in place that essentially guarantee certain minimum prices. This can be accomplished in several ways, such as price-based loans or payments to farmers and public purchase of farm commodities.
- **Supply restrictions.**   Restrictions on total output, or on the use of certain inputs, in an attempt to lower the supply of farm output so that prices will be higher. In the United States the primary restriction of this type has been acreage restrictions.
- **Direct income payments.**   Farmers are offered direct payments from the public treasury to bring their incomes up. Payments may be tied to certain parameters (e.g., payments related to size of the farm), or be designed to lift income by certain amounts.
- **Input subsidies.**   Costs of selected farm inputs are subsidized so that their effective prices to farmers are lowered. An example is the provision of large quantities of irrigation water at below-market prices.
- **Structural adjustment payments.**   Farmers are helped financially in making certain operational changes, such as putting some land aside into a conservation reservation, shifting to a new crop, or engaging in certain environmental practices.

Acreage Restrictions and Intensification

In the United States during the 1950s Congress sought to support farm incomes by instituting minimum prices for certain agricultural commodities such as corn, wheat, and cotton. The result was predictable: To take advantage of these price supports farmers boosted their outputs. But this led to crop surpluses: crops that could not be sold at the support level prices. This in turn led to a system of acreage restrictions. For each farmer the U.S. Department of Agriculture identified a certain number of acres, called their **acreage allotment.** Crops grown on the allotment qualified for the support price. Any crop grown on nonallotment acreage was not supported—it might have been actually penalized under some circumstances. These allotment restrictions had the predictable effect.

The total output of a crop farmer can be broken down in the following way:

$$\begin{array}{ccc} \text{Total} & \text{Total acres} & \text{Yields} \\ \text{output} = & \text{harvested} & \times \text{ per acre} \\ \text{(TO)} & \text{(A)} & \text{(TO/A)} \end{array}$$

The allotment programs sought to control total output by controlling the total acreage harvested. Farmers responded by putting their energies into increasing yields per acre. This is what is meant by the **intensification** of agricultural production. Intensification of this sort has many forms: more fertilizers and pesticides, more use of machinery, adoption of high-yield crop strains, more irrigation water use, and so on. Thus farmers have had the incentive to move toward a low-acreage, high-intensification system, as compared to a higher-acreage, lower-intensification system that would have resulted if the acreage allotment system had not been put in place.

The relatively simple acreage restriction programs of the 1950s have become increasingly complicated over the intervening decades, as Exhibit 16-2 makes clear. Today it is virtually impossible to tell what modern agriculture would look like if all these income support programs had never been put in

---

EXHIBIT 16-2

CURRENT CROPLAND PROGRAMS AND DEFINITIONS IN THE UNITED STATES

Conservation Reserve Program (CRP) was designed to voluntarily retire from crop production about 40 million acres of highly erodible or environmentally sensitive cropland for 10–15 years. In exchange, participating producers receive annual rental payments up to $50,000 and 50 percent cost-share assistance for establishing vegetative cover on the land. The Federal Agriculture Improvement and Reform Act (1996 Farm Act) of 1996 limited CRP enrollment to 36.4 million acres.

Acreage Reduction Program (ARP) was a voluntary land retirement program in which farmers reduced their planted acreage of a program crop by a specified proportion of that crop's acreage base to become eligible for deficiency payments, loan programs, and other USDA commodity program benefits. Crops under this program included corn, sorghum, oats, barley, wheat, cotton, and rice. The 1996 Farm Act eliminated the authority of USDA to implement an annual ARP.

0/85-92 Provision, an optional, Federal acreage diversion program, allowed wheat and feedgrain producers to devote all or a portion of their permitted acreage to conservation uses or to a minor oilseed crop, sesame, or crambe and, under some conditions, receive deficiency payments. At least 8 but no more than 15 percent of the producer's maximum payment acres had to be maintained in conserving uses or other allowable crop use. Eliminated by the 1996 Farm Act.

50/85-92 Provision, an optional, Federal acreage diversion program, allowed upland cotton and rice producers to underplant their permitted acreage and, under some conditions, receive deficiency payments on part of the underplanted acreage.

At least 50 percent of the crop's maximum payment acreage had to be planted. An additional 8 percent but no more than 15 percent had to be designated for conserving use. Minor oilseeds could not be planted on the 50/92 conservation-use acres, but sesame or crambe could be planted, with producers still qualifying for deficiency payments. Eliminated by the 1996 Farm Act.

Crop acreage base, for 1995 wheat and feedgrains, was the average of the acreage planted and considered planted to each program crop in the 5-year period, 1990–94. For upland cotton and rice, the crop acreage base in 1995 was the average acreage planted and considered planted for 1992–94, with no adjustment for years with zero planted or considered planted acreage. The 1996 Farm Act used crop acreage base only in determining eligible production flexibility contract acreage.

Deficiency payments were payments made to farmers who participated in feedgrain (corn, sorghum, oats, or barley), wheat, rice, or upland cotton programs up to 1996. The payment rate per unit crop production was based on the difference between a target price and the market price or loan rate, whichever difference was less. The total payment a farm received was the payment rate multiplied by the eligible production. Eliminated by the 1996 Farm Act and replaced by production flexibility contract payments in 1996.

Production flexibility contract payments are authorized under provisions of the 1996 Farm Act as a replacement for deficiency payments, and cover the 1996 through 2002 crops of wheat, feedgrains, upland cotton, and rice of landowners or producers with eligible cropland. In ex-

(continued)

EXHIBIT 16-2—Continued

CURRENT CROPLAND PROGRAMS AND DEFINITIONS IN THE UNITED STATES

change for a series of annual contract payments for the 7-year period based on a predetermined total dollar amount for each year, the owner or producer agrees to comply with specified conservation requirements concerning the use of highly erodible cropland and wetlands; to comply with planting flexibility requirements of the Act; and to use contract acreage for agricultural or related activities, not for nonagricultural commercial or industrial use.

Production flexibility contract acreage is equal to a farm's crop acreage base for 1996 calculated under the provi-

sions of the previous farm program, plus any returning CRP base acreage and less any new CRP acreage enrollment. A landowner or producer can enroll less than the maximum eligible acreage. In 1996, contracted acreage totaled just over 207.5 million acres, 98.8 percent of the eligible 210.2 million acres (USDA, FSA, 1996).

Source: U.S. Department of Agriculture, Economic Research Service, "Agricultural Resources and Environmental Indicators, 1996–97," *Agricultural Handbook No. 712*, Washington, DC, 1997, p. 12.

---

place or if the program had been kept very simple and with a minimum of distorting effects. With the more recent growth of public concern about natural and environmental resources, there is increasing concern about the distorted way in which modern agriculture has developed and a growing emphasis on moving toward income support methods that are less distorting. Among many developed countries, for example, there is a perceptible movement away from programs such as acreage restriction toward direct income payments. In theory these should reduce the distortions that characterize modern agriculture.

WETLANDS CONSERVATION

From an analytical perspective it will be much more fruitful for us to look at specific aspects of the agriculture/natural resource connection. One such problem, for example, is the conversion of wetlands, through drainage and/or filling, into cropland. Until quite recently the draining and filling of wetlands for agricultural purposes was not regarded as a negative action, except in extreme circumstances. It was usually thought of as a case of taking an asset of low or modest value (a wetland) and converting it to an asset of much higher value (productive agricultural land). Today we know that this is not right. We now understand that wetlands are of much higher value than originally thought for a variety of reasons, including their strategic role in hydrological systems and their value in terms of wildlife habitat. But it has taken a while to change the agricultural support laws to reduce the incentives that farmers have to convert wetlands.

Between 1954 and 1974 the average number of acres of wetland converted to agricultural production in the United States was 593,000 acres per year.

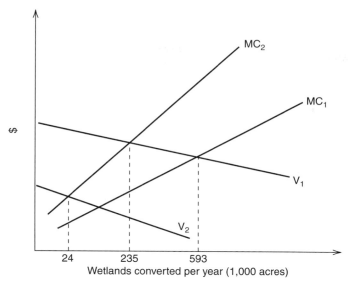

FIGURE 16-3
Reducing the Incentive to Convert Wetlands to Agricultural Use

During the next decade conversion of wetlands fell to an average of about 446,000 per year.[6] The reasons for this may relate to provisions of the Clean Water Act of 1977, which contained provisions for the regulation of wetland drainage and filling. Consider Figure 16-3: The horizontal axis contains a scale representing the number of acres of wetland converted per year. The incentive to convert wetlands is the value of agricultural production that can be produced on the converted land.[7] The curve labeled V_1 shows the marginal private value of converted land at the beginning (i.e., before 1974). This marginal value decreases as more and more land is converted. The curve labeled MC_1 shows the marginal private cost of converting wetland acreage; this is shown as a rising function.

At the beginning, the profit maximizing number of wetland acres converted to agriculture is given by the intersection of V_1 and MC_1. This is shown as 593,000, corresponding to the number given above for annual conversions during the period 1954–1974. The Clean Water Act (CWA) of 1977 made it more difficult (costly) to convert wetlands, by introducing specific procedures that

---

[6] Roger Claasen et al., "Estimating the Effects of Relaxing Agricultural Land Use Restrictions: Wetland Delineation in the Swampbuster Program," *Review of Agricultural Economics*, 20 (2), Fall/Winter 1998, p. 391.

[7] It may seem paradoxical that at the same time that authorities are trying to introduce programs to get farmers to reduce agricultural acreage, there might also be incentives to create new agricultural acreage by draining wetlands. But in such a complex program, it is easy for one element to be working in a direction opposite to that of other elements.

had to be followed. A way of expressing this is as an upward shift in conversion costs to MC_2. Thus during the period after the CWA, conversions dropped to 235,000 acres per year (the intersection of MC_2 and V_1). The next step taken by Congress was to try to reduce the incentives inherent in the agricultural support programs to convert wetlands. To the extent that such programs increase the returns per acre that can be obtained from farming, they would clearly provide an incentive to expand the acreage in farms, although other parts of the program may be working in the opposite direction. The answer was to add the **swampbuster** provision in the 1985 general agricultural act. This law makes farmers ineligible for general crop support programs on that part of their harvest grown on converted wetlands. The impact is to reduce the value of income that farmers can obtain on converted wetland, which means a shift backward in the value function from V_1 to V_2. Now the relevant intersection is that between V_2 and MC_2, giving a reduction in acres converted to an average of 24,000 per year, which is what the actual rate was from 1982 to 1992.

While this analysis seems clear, at least conceptually, it is more difficult to apply it in practice because during the time periods indicated there were many other changes happening besides the provisions targeting wetlands. A general rise, or fall, in agricultural prices will also shift the V functions in Figure 16-3, as might happen also when other parts of agricultural policies and regulations are changed. For example, changes in farm income tax laws might shift these relationships around. In the early 1990s attempts were made by some political interests to weaken certain portions of the regulations applying to wetlands conversion (by changing, for example, the definition of what is a wetland).[8] Thus, it is an important policy issue whether past policy changes were responsible for the reduction in wetlands conversion rates or whether other factors were responsible. This illustrates the difficulty in trying to understand the complex world of agricultural policy and the impacts it has had on the natural resource base.

ECONOMICS OF PESTICIDE RESISTANCE

Modern agriculture, and increasingly the agriculture of the developing world, is characterized by the use of relatively large amounts of chemical inputs, particularly fertilizers and pesticides. In 1940 U.S. farmers spent $44 million on pesticides; in 1996 this number grew to $8.3 billion. Aggregate pesticide application rates (quantity applied per acre) increased until around the years 1981–1982, and since then have declined moderately. A large part of the

---

[8] The way this was attempted is revealing. There is clearly a smooth continuum from the driest to the wettest acreage. To identify a wetland, one must choose some discrete criterion so that one can draw the line somewhere. The original swampbuster regulation defined "wetlands" as those lands which are typically inundated (ponded or flooded) for 15 consecutive days during the growing season. The proposal was to change this 15-day period to 21 days. This adjustment would have meant that much of the land defined as wetland under the 15-day rule would not be classified as wetland under the 21-day criterion.

reason for the decline is that pesticides quality (potency, toxicity, and persistence) has increased, thus leading to a decline in quantity. There are wide differences of opinion on such basic questions as the way public regulation has affected pesticide use, the economic benefits to farmers of using pesticides, and the specific environmental implications of pesticide use practices.[9]

Pesticide use has usually been thought of as an environmental problem, especially as regards ecosystem contamination and human health impacts. But it also has important production ramifications. One of these is the problem of increased pest resistance stemming from the overuse of pesticides. Organisms evolve in directions related to the conditions of their environment. Higher pesticide levels create conditions leading to the evolution of organisms with greater resistance to the pesticides. Over time pesticide use can lead to greater pest resistance, which motivates higher levels of pesticide use, which spurs further resistance, and so on. Why would not a rational farmer, realizing that elevated levels of pesticide use will lead to greater pest resistance, reduce his use of the substances so as to lower the likelihood of that happening? We have here an interesting and important problem of shaping incentives so as to harmonize individual behavior with the welfare of society.

To explore this, consider a simple example. Suppose there is a certain relatively small geographical region, for example, a particular valley, with several dozen farms, all growing the same crop, say, corn. The corn is attacked by a certain pest, which lowers yields and reduces incomes of the farmers in the region. Let us assume that the region is biologically distinct, in the sense that the pest population here is relatively independent of outside influences. Farmers use a particular pesticide to control the pest. The pesticide is quite effective, but there is a hitch. At high pesticide use levels, the pests will develop a resistance that makes the chemical less effective. This decreases yields and lowers returns. If all farmers use low pesticide levels, resistance does not occur. The problem this presents is the following: Although the level of pest resistance in the region is determined by the **aggregate quantity of pesticide** used there, individual farmers have control only over the quantity of pesticide they apply themselves.

We now present some illustrative numbers to show how this shapes the **incentives** faced by individual farmers. The numbers do not correspond to any real-world situation, but they do show the relative levels of returns that would result from different courses of action, which is enough to explore the incentives inherent in this type of situation. We focus, then, on the returns available to one typical farmer in the valley. To simplify even further, suppose the farmer is faced with just two choices: to use pesticides in a small quantity or to

[9] Some of these are reviewed in Jorge Fernandez-Cornejo, Sharon Jans, and Mark Smith, "Issues in the Economics of Pesticide Use in Agriculture: A Review of the Empirical Evidence," *Review of Agricultural Economics*, 20(2), Fall/Winter 1998, pp. 462–488.

use them in a large quantity. The incomes he would receive from each of these two strategies is shown in the following tabulation:

		Other farmers	
		Low usage	High usage
Farmer A	Low usage	$10	$5
	High usage	$15	$7

Note that the incomes to our farmer (Farmer A) depend on what the other farmers choose to do. That seems reasonable because the evolution of pesticide resistance is a valleywide phenomenon, linked to overall usage rates, not just the rates on one farm. Thus the returns to farmer A will depend in part on pesticide levels used by other farmers.

Suppose the farmer were to choose a low pesticide use rate. If others also use a low rate, the farmer will have a "payoff" of $10, whereas if other farmers use a high rate, the return will be only $5. This seems reasonable. If everyone sticks to a low use rate, resistance is slow, losses to pests are relatively low, and incomes relatively high. But if all other farmers choose high application levels, resistance is high and farmer A suffers from being the only one who refrains from the higher use; he uses low pesticide levels in a high resistance situation.

Suppose instead that the farmer chooses a high application level. If everyone uses a high level, the farmer's income will be $7. Large applications imply high resistance, lower yields, and therefore lower returns than if everybody were to keep their applications low. On the other hand, if all others use low pesticide levels, farmer A would get a high return ($15) from using a high level, because the pests will have low resistance, and so with high application levels he will get rid of them all.

Note carefully how this affects the incentives facing our farmer. Regardless of what the other farmers do, farmer A is better off choosing a high application level. If other farmers choose low application levels, farmer A will have the highest returns if he applies at the high level. This strategy is also the best one if others use the high pesticide levels. The high application level is individually best under both circumstances. But if this is the incentive situation facing farmer A, it is also the incentive situation facing each of the other farmers. Thus, we are brought to the following conclusion: Although individual farmers can be presumed to act rationally in terms of selecting the strategy that has the highest expected payoff for themselves, the overall result will be an outcome in which everyone has lower incomes. The individual payoff to the self-interest decision situation is $7, even though they could each get a payoff of $10 if somehow they would all use the lower rate.

We have seen this dilemma many times before in earlier chapters. **Open-access resources** present problems of this type. Users of the resource, in making their own individual decisions about whether and how much to use it, contribute to an outcome in which the resource is overused in the aggregate. In the pesticide case we also have a type of open-access resource that gets overused. The resource in this case is the **susceptibility** of the pest to the pesticide. This quality of susceptibility is in fact a valuable resource which can be significantly degraded and lost if overall pesticide use is too high. The **open-access externality** in this case stems from the fact that if an individual farmer chooses a high application level, the effects, in terms of its contribution toward increasing pesticide resistance, will be felt by him and by all the other farmers in the valley.[10]

Another revealing way of looking at this is with the concept of **public goods.** These are goods or services that, when made available for one person, automatically become available to others. There is no way of excluding others from enjoying the benefits of the good or service. Suppose every farmer is applying pesticides at the higher level. Why wouldn't individual farmers voluntarily reduce their pesticide usage? Because the impacts of individual cutbacks of this type are public goods; the benefits they produce, in terms of a small reduction in resistance, accrue equally to all farmers in the region, not just to the individual who makes the cutback. As we saw earlier, public goods will tend to be undersupplied by individual actions of this type. Thus cutbacks in individual pesticide use will be undersupplied, which is the same as saying that the overall level of pesticide application will be higher than the socially efficient level.

To achieve socially efficient levels of aggregate pesticide use, some means must be found to get all farmers (or a significant fraction of them) to use the lower pesticide application rates and to refrain from trying to take advantage of this situation by opportunistically shifting to higher levels. There are several ways of doing this: One is to sponsor an agreement among the farmers themselves to use lower application levels. This could be a **voluntary agreement,** if it were possible to get wide-enough participation through this means. Perhaps if a voluntary agreement could be developed among 90 percent of the farmers, aggregate pesticide use could be controlled enough to preserve pest susceptibility at high levels. Perhaps some way could be found by the participating farmers to sanction those who refuse to join the agreement, such as by controlling some other part of the overall process (e.g., the town grain elevator could refuse to accept grain from farmers who are not part of the pesticide program).

Of course **direct public regulation** is also an option. A regulation requiring lower pesticide use levels would have to be enacted by a political body with the appropriate jurisdiction (local, regional, or state), and this would then have to be enforced through such techniques as self-reporting by farmers, surveillance, and examination of pesticide purchase records. One problem with regulations of this type (and with voluntary agreements) is that the incentives are still strong for farmers individually to apply the higher levels, in this case surreptitiously. How often this happens will depend in large part on the effectiveness of the enforcement of the regulation or agreement.

---

[10] The growing resistance of bacteria to antibiotics is exactly the same phenomenon as this, and explains why antibiotics continue to be overused despite the problem.

Another way of controlling individual pesticide use is through an incentive program such as a **tax on pesticide use.** The tax would have to be sufficient to lower the high usage return rates of the tabulation above to levels that are below the return rates for low usage levels. Since it is probably not feasible to tax each unit (pound or gallon) of the pesticide as it is applied, a tax here would probably have to be placed on the quantity of pesticide purchased. In effect the idea is to make the pesticide expensive enough that farmers will choose the low use levels automatically.

THE ECONOMICS OF MONOCULTURE

Modern agriculture has often been described as involving a system of **monoculture.** This means several things. First, a very large proportion of the human food supply comes from a small number of crops. In particular, corn, wheat, rice, and potatoes account for a very large proportion of the total calories consumed by human beings, either directly or through the animals they support (especially corn). Many other crops, which potentially could supply important amounts of nutrition, have been overlooked or undeveloped.[11] Monoculture also refers to reduced **genetic diversity** within specific crops. The genetic makeup of crops determines their characteristics, such as potential yield, growth rate, and degree of resistance to diseases and pests. Most modern agriculture is based on a limited number of crop strains that have been developed through techniques of plant breeding and development, including the classical techniques of controlled growth and selection and more recently advances in **biotechnology.**

Preserving genetic diversity on the farm involves two phenomena: (1) developing new cultivars that have desirable genotypes and (2) getting farmers to grow a diverse portfolio of cultivars.[12] We focus on the second of these. Plant breeding has contributed to the development of new cultivars that have substantially higher potential yields than the older ones. The concern, however, is that through this breeding and adoption program we will lose **genetic diversity.** If there is a widespread shift to newly developed varieties, which are genetically uniform within themselves, we end up with a situation in which a large proportion of the crop may be susceptible to a particular disease or pest. Widespread crop failure could then result. The way to reduce this risk is to develop cultivars of the crop that are genetically different, especially in terms of the genes that confer resistance to certain important diseases, present or future; and then have farmers adopt and grow a reasonably broad portfolio of cultivars rather than only one or two. With a broad portfolio in use, the loss

---

[11] See, for example, the discussion in Edward O. Wilson, *The Diversity of Life*, Harvard University Press, Cambridge, MA, 1992, pp. 287–298.

[12] A variety, or "cultivar," is a subset of a species consisting of a group of cultivated plants having a clearly distinguished set of characteristics that are retained when the plant is reproduced.

of any one cultivar through disease can most easily be compensated for by shifting to other available cultivars that do not have the same susceptibility.

Note that this is a diversity problem, not a problem dealing with classic negative externalities from the choice of specific cultivars. If cultivar A is regarded as having undesirable properties (perhaps it is insufficiently disease-resistant), its use could presumably be stopped with a simple regulation—assuming it could be enforced. But for diversity to prevail there must be a collection of cultivars available for farmers to choose among. This "collection" cannot consist of one approved cultivar, no matter how good it appears, because its exclusive adoption by all farmers puts us back in a condition of strict monoculture, which could easily be invaded by an evolving pathogen.

If public authorities rule out, by regulation, all unsatisfactory cultivars, how is it possible to get farmers to choose a diverse portfolio from among the group of cultivars that are approved? It seems highly unlikely that individual farm production portfolios could be identified and enforced by public authorities. This is why we must understand how farms choose these portfolios and how they may be influenced to choose more diverse portfolios. One way of thinking about this is in terms of the private and public benefits of the portfolio choices made by individual farmers. Suppose a number of cultivars are available for farmers to choose among. These cultivars vary in terms of their (disease-free) yields and of their resistance to a certain disease. Left to themselves, farmers will choose a portfolio of cultivars that maximizes their expected net incomes.[13] They probably will not choose the single cultivar with the highest disease-free yield, because this would expose them to an unacceptable level of risk. By also growing some cultivars with lower yield but also lower risks of loss, they can actually increase their expected long-run net income.

But there may be additional, external benefits from choosing a diverse portfolio of cultivars. A larger portfolio will lower not only individual risks, but also the risks to neighboring farmers. Diseases tend to spread beyond the borders of the fields where they first break out. Thus when one farmer lowers his risk, the risk to nearby farms will also be lower. What this implies is that some portion of the total social benefits from a larger portfolio of cultivars will accrue as **external** benefits. And, as we have mentioned many times throughout the book, when an activity produces external benefits, private decision makers—left to themselves—will tend to undersupply the service, relative to levels that maximize social benefits. Thus farmers, in the situation described above, will tend to select portfolios of cultivars that are less diverse than those called for by the criterion of social efficiency.

From an incentive point of view, the problem is that the external benefits produced by farmers who might choose a diverse cultivar portfolio normally

---

[13] To review the concept of **expected values,** see Chapter 8.

do not accrue to them. Nor does there seem to be any strictly private market arrangement that could be set up to accomplish this. Perhaps some type of public subsidy program is the answer: The subsidy could be linked to the number of cultivars a farmer grows. One way of administering the subsidy would be to offer price rebates on the purchase price of cultivars that farmers might not choose under normal circumstances.

THE ECONOMICS OF SOIL PRODUCTIVITY

Another major problem facing farmers is the management of **soil productivity.** The productivity of soil is simply its power to produce crops in useful quantities, and is related to the physical and chemical characteristics of the soil itself together with the hydrological and meteorological systems in which it is situated. Loss of soil productivity has been a continuing concern around the world. In developed economies, the main issue tends to be the long-run effects of modern agriculture on soil productivity. In developing economies, however, there is more concern about farmer incentives and the potential for "extracting" productivity to achieve short-run gains by farmers who are nearer subsistence levels of living.

Problems of soil fertility have frequently been discussed within the framework of **sustainability.** Agricultural practices are "sustainable," according to this view, as long as they do not lead to diminished soil productivity over the long run. This perspective is useful in that it leads us to be especially watchful for practices that may undermine soil productivity irreversibly in the long run. But it is not an adequate concept for addressing the decisions that need to be made by farmers in actually managing their soil productivity. These decisions are **investment decisions;** they involve actions that reduce current incomes in return for higher incomes in the future. A sustainability perspective leads us to think of doing whatever it takes to hold the line against soil productivity loss. An investment perspective leads us to ask what constellation of actions leads to the **efficient level of productivity.** Furthermore, it is useful to think of soil productivity as a **renewable resource,** so that it makes sense to look for a **steady-state** usage pattern, that is, a level of soil fertility that is managed at a **constant level** through time. A constant level of productivity presumably satisfies the sustainability criterion; it satisfies the efficiency criterion only if this constant level of productivity is also the correct level in efficiency terms.

An Efficient Steady State

Think back to Chapter 2, where we discussed the basic features of different types of natural resources, in terms of a simple accounting equation:

$$S_1 = S_0 - Q + \Delta S$$

Let S_0 and S_1 now refer to soil productivity, the former being the productivity at the beginning of the year, and the latter being the productivity at the end of the year after all production operations have been concluded. A steady-state, or sustainable, situation is defined as $S_1 = S_0$, which obviously implies that $Q = \Delta S$. In this case, Q refers to the amount of soil productivity that is extracted from the soil during production, and ΔS refers to the amount of productivity added. In agricultural use, Q is determined by such things as choice of crops and cultivation techniques. Some crops, for example, are more demanding of soil nutrients than others; some crops can help replenish certain soil qualities, and so on. Traditional plowing and harrowing can expose soil to substantial wind erosion; practices such as no-till or low-till cultivation can substantially reduce soil loss.

The term ΔS refers to the productivity that is returned to the soil during the growing season. This can occur in a variety of ways. Productivity may naturally replenish itself through geological and hydrological processes. Land in floodplains is subject to replenishment during spring flooding. Weathering processes and the decay of vegetation can add to the depth of topsoil, and hence to its productivity. Productivity can also be added by direct human action. Terracing can actually lift soil productivity permanently above its "natural" state; contour plowing can prevent soil erosion; fertilizers and cover crops can replenish nutrients; and so on. $Q = \Delta S$ means, therefore, that steps are undertaken to put productivity back into the soil equal to that which was taken out.

But the condition $\Delta S = Q$ is a condition for the steady state in terms of soil productivity. It does not tell us **which** steady state is the most efficient. In the absence of any externalities, the most efficient productivity level is that which leads to a maximum of net incomes accruing to farmers. We can envisage a relationship between maintained soil productivity and net farm incomes as pictured in Figure 16-4. The inverted U shape comes about for the following reasons. At low productivities, agricultural output is also low, so although it may not cost much to maintain productivity at this level, net farm incomes are low. At high soil productivities, total output will be large but the costs of replenishing the productivity "drawdown" will be very high, leading again to low net incomes. At an intermediate level of maintained soil productivity, indicated as s^* in the figure, net farm income is maximized.

Note several things. It is certainly not efficient to try to maintain soil productivity at a maximum, whatever that means. In effect there is no maximum. Productivity could always be increased with the right management practices, no matter how high it is to begin with. The appropriate action is not to try to maintain some maximum productivity, but to maintain the efficient level of soil productivity. Note also that nothing has been said about the **initial level** of soil productivity. If the initial condition is to the left of s^*, it would imply a buildup of steady-state productivity, through such means as terracing, irrigation, or soil amendments. In this way agricultural land productivity as it is

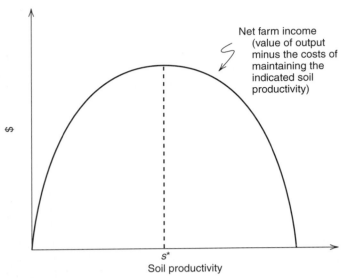

FIGURE 16-4
Efficient Steady-State Soil Productivity

currently maintained may exceed the productivity that the land originally possessed. If the initial level of productivity is to the right of s^* on the other hand, some **disinvestment** in productivity may be called for.

SUMMARY

There is widespread concern, but by no means widespread agreement, about the ability of modern agriculture to feed the ever-higher levels of world population. Problems tend to be different among countries, particularly among developed, developing, and transitional economies. A prime source of concern is the impact of modern agriculture on the quantity and quality of the natural resource base on which it depends. Agriculture in the developed world is normally heavily **subsidized for political reasons.** These public programs are normally very complex and have introduced many **distortions** into the agricultural production system. For example, acreage restrictions in the 1950s and 1960s undoubtedly led to the development of an **intensive agriculture** and vigorous efforts to increase per-acre yields. It is, however, virtually impossible to know what modern agriculture would look like if many of these programs were stopped. It is perhaps more instructive to focus on particular agricultural decisions and practices in order to understand the forces that shape them and how they might respond to change. In the chapter we looked at the problem of **wetlands preservation,** the use of **pesticides** in situations where **pest tolerance** may increase, the management of **soil productivity,** and decisions surrounding the system of **monoculture.**

KEY TERMS

Agricultural supply and demand
  shifts
Income support policies
Acreage restrictions (allotments)
Intensification of production
Wetlands conversion and conservation
Pesticide resistance

Open-access externalities
Voluntary agreements
Monoculture
Biotechnology
Genetic diversity
Sustainability
Steady-state soil productivity

QUESTIONS FOR FURTHER DISCUSSION

1 How does the economics of managing pesticide resistance resemble the economics of fisheries management?
2 In Figure 16-1, what difference would the steepness of the supply and demand curves make for the way prices of agricultural commodities change through time?
3 In establishing the efficient steady-state level of soil productivity, what role would the interest rate play?
4 What relationship do you see between the decisions by farmers on what portfolio of cultivars they grow and compulsory auto insurance laws?
5 The problem of reducing pesticide use to avoid the growth of pest resistance is actually a public good problem. What is the nature of the public good in this case? The cultivar choice problem can also be explained in these terms. What is the public good in this case?
6 How have government programs to support agricultural incomes in general led to an increase in monoculture, that is, a reduction in crop and animal diversity?

USEFUL WEB SITES

Studies of agricultural markets and agricultural support programs in the United States:

- U.S. Department of Agriculture, Economic Research Service (http://www.econ.ag.gov)
- Agricultural Research Service (http://www.ars.usda.gov)
- Natural Resources Conservation Service (http://nrcs.usda.gov)

For international material:

- Food and Agriculture Organization of the United Nations (http://www.fao.org)

Many state universities have departments of agricultural economics that sponsor research on a wide range of topics in agriculture; see especially their publications lists, including

- University of Wisconsin (http://www.aae.wisc.edu)
- University of Wyoming (http://www.uwyo.edu/ag/agecon)
- Cornell University (http://www.cals.cornell.edu/dept/arme)

SELECTED READINGS

Brown, L. R.: *Who Will Feed China?* W. W. Norton, New York, 1995.

Carlson, Gerald A., David Zilberman, and John A. Miranowski: *Agricultural and Environmental Resource Economics*, Oxford University Press, New York, 1993.

Center for Agricultural and Rural Development: *Food Security: New Solutions for the 21st Century*, Iowa State University Press, Ames, IA, 1998.

Cochrane, Willard W.: *The Development of American Agriculture, A Historical Analysis*, 2nd ed., University of Minnesota Press, Minneapolis, 1993.

Heisey, Paul W., et al.: "Wheat Rusts and the Costs of Genetic Diversity in the Punjab of Pakistan," *American Journal of Agricultural Economics*, 79(3), August 1997, pp. 726–737.

McConnell, Kenneth E.: "An Economic Model of Soil Conservation," *American Journal of Agricultural Economics*, Vol. 65, 1983, pp. 83–89.

Mitchell, D. O., M. R. Ingco, and R. C. Duncan: *The World Food Outlook*, Cambridge University Press, Cambridge, England, 1997.

Moyer, H. Wayne, and Timothy E. Josling: *Agricultural Policy Reform. Politics and Process in the E.C. and the U.S.A.*, Iowa State University Press, Ames, IA, 1990.

Robertson, Thyrele, Burton C. English, and Robert R. Alexander: *Evaluating Natural Resources in Agriculture*, Iowa State University Press, Ames, IA, 1997.

Seitz, Wesley D., Gerald C. Nelson, and Harold G. Halcrow: *Economics of Resources, Agriculture and Food*, McGraw-Hill, New York, 1994.

CHAPTER 17

ECONOMICS OF
OUTDOOR RECREATION

In this chapter we examine a number of issues in the economics of outdoor recreation. "Outdoor recreation" in its most general sense involves all kinds of activities, from sitting in the backyard watching birds to deep-wilderness winter backpacking. We are primarily interested in outdoor recreation activities that are **resource-intensive,** that make use, in other words, of forests, grasslands, lakes, and rivers. No clear dividing line separates the activities that are resource-intensive and those that are not. But we do recognize that some, such as picnicking in a national or state park, are closely related to the quality of the natural resources with which visitors interact. Others, such as golf and jogging, do not place direct demands on natural resources, though they must use resources to some extent—land for golf courses and roads for jogging.

Outdoor recreation in many developed countries has grown rapidly in the latter part of the twentieth century. Table 17-1 presents some recent data for the United States on the number of people who participated in different types of outdoor recreation, and the changes between the years 1982–1983 and 1994–1995. Remember that between those two periods of time, the total population of the United States increased by about 14 percent, and so one can see which particular activities involved increases in both total participation and the rate of participation. Note the relatively large increases in bird watching, hiking, backpacking, and camping and the declines in fishing and hunting. To some extent we may be seeing here the impacts of the environmental move-

TABLE 17-1

PARTICIPATION IN OUTDOOR RECREATIONAL ACTIVITIES, 1982–1983 AND 1994–1995

	Number participating (millions)		Percent change 1982–1983 to 1994–1995
	1982–1983	1994–1995	
Walking	93.6	133.6	42.7
Bird watching	21.2	54.1	155.2
Sightseeing	81.3	113.4	39.5
Attending outdoor sports event	70.7	95.2	34.7
Hiking	24.7	47.7	93.1
Swimming (nonpool)	56.5	78.1	38.2
Picnicking	84.8	98.4	16.0
Motor boating	33.6	46.9	39.6
Swimming (pool)	76.0	88.5	16.4
Camping (developed area)	30.0	41.5	38.3
Camping (any)	42.4	53.7	26.7
Boating	49.5	60.1	21.4
Camping (primitive area)	17.7	28.0	58.2
Off-road driving	19.4	27.8	43.3
Outdoor team sports	42.4	49.5	16.7
Golf	23.0	29.6	28.7
Running, jogging	45.9	52.5	14.4
Backpacking	8.8	15.2	72.7
Downhill skiing	10.6	16.8	58.5
Sledding	17.7	20.4	15.3
Water skiing	15.9	17.8	11.9
Snowmobiling	5.3	7.0	32.1
Cross-country skiing	5.3	6.6	24.5
Bicycling	56.5	57.4	1.6
Ice skating	10.6	10.4	−1.9
Sailing	10.6	9.6	−9.4
Horseback riding	15.9	14.2	−10.7
Fishing	60.1	58.3	−3.0
Hunting	21.2	18.8	−11.3
Attending outdoor concert	44.2	41.5	−6.1
Tennis	30.0	21.2	−29.3

Note: Number of persons aged 16 or older participating in selected outdoor recreational activities, numerical and percent change in number of participants, 1982–1983 and 1994–1995; ranked by numerical change.

Source: USDA Forest Service, 1982–1983 Nationwide Recreation Survey and 1994–1995 National Survey on Recreation and the Environment, as reported in Alison Stein Wellner, *Americans at Play: Demographics of Outdoor Recreation and Travel*, New Strategist Publication, Ithaca, NY, p. 3.

ment, which has tended to put greater emphasis on nonconsumptive uses of resources rather than the traditional consumptive uses.

A major impetus for the development of a separate economics of outdoor recreation is the fact that, traditionally, much of the supply of outdoor recreation resources has been a public function, through national and state parks and forests and through the water resources made available with the building

of large federally subsidized dams. Public authorities who control these resources need guidance for their decisions. In recent decades there has also developed a thriving private market in outdoor recreation, from ski resorts to
privately provided hunting and fishing, to whale watching and scuba diving
resorts. So the economics of outdoor recreation now includes questions about
managing public reservations, the appropriate roles of public and private initiatives, and the management problems facing private firms operating in this
space.

THE DEMAND FOR OUTDOOR RECREATION

Several different perspectives are important in studying the demand for outdoor recreation. One is to estimate the demand for a certain type of outdoor
recreation activity among a defined group of people. Suppose we are a California company dealing in camping equipment. Our interest would be in
knowing how the demand for backpacking by the residents of California (or
the country, if we were selling by mail-order, or online) could be expected to
grow over the next decade. We would want to estimate the impacts of anticipated growth in population and incomes, and of other factors we thought
might be important in determining how many people might be expected to
engage in this activity. We might then want to determine the implications of
this demand growth for the growth in demand for the specific products we expect to sell. This perspective would also be of interest to the private individuals and public agencies whose objectives are to supply the parks and areas in
which backpackers pursue their recreational activity.

Another perspective is what we might call the **facilities management** viewpoint. Suppose we are in charge of a particular park, current or proposed. Our
need would be to develop an understanding of the demand curve facing our
single facility, which is affected by population, incomes, transportation services, and the presence of other competing or complementary areas. A demand curve of this type is drawn in Figure 17-1. The horizontal axis has an
index of **visitor-days,** defined as the total number of day-long visits (e.g., two
half-day visits make one visitor-day). Note that this is probably a great simplification. Many parks produce a multiplicity of recreational services: day trips;
overnight, or longer visits; active recreational visits; sightseeing visits; and so
on. But to have a tractable analysis, we must boil these down to a single "output" variable—thus the choice of visitor-days. The vertical axis has a monetary index, which will be used to measure the entrance price to visit the park.
In many cases no entrance fee is charged. Of course, there still are other costs
of visiting the park, namely, the travel costs of getting there. In this sense it is
no different from any good or service; even to buy a cantaloupe, one has to
drive to the store. But travel costs usually loom much larger in visiting parks
since they are usually a considerable distance from visitors' points of origin.
The price indexed on the vertical axis, however, is the admission price visitors
must pay to enter the park.

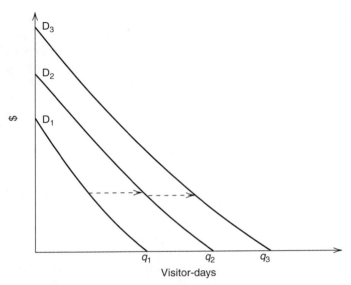

FIGURE 17-1
Demand Curves for an Imaginary Public Park

Figure 17-1 shows a series of demand curves, each pertaining to a different time period. These are **aggregate demand curves,** arrived at by summing together the individual demand curves of visitors to the park. We can assume that D_1 is the demand curve for some past year, say, 10 years ago, and that D_2 is the demand curve for the current period. Thus, D_3 is the **expected demand curve** for a future period, perhaps one that is for 10 years in the future. What are the factors behind this shifting demand curve? One of the major ones is **population growth.** Another is **income growth.** A third factor, actually a set of factors, is the cost of travel. **Transportation improvements** (e.g., building a new access road, or linking it to the interstate system), or drops in the **price of gas,** have the effect of shifting the demand curve to the right. And we must not forget the **taste and preference** factor; over time people learn more about outdoor recreation and come to appreciate it as a valuable source of psychic benefits in an increasingly urbanized society.

It is easy to hypothesize the existence of demand curves such as these, but difficult to estimate them in fact. It is especially difficult to measure how they have shifted over time. In the open-access experience of most public parks, detailed studies of demand have not been a high priority. This is changing, as crowds have increased and interest grows in managing the access to, and use of, outdoor recreation facilities. In addition, economists have been successful in developing methods for estimating recreation demand functions, like the travel cost method discussed in Chapter 9.

Efficient Visitation Rates

In keeping with the idea used throughout the book, the **socially efficient visitation rate** is the rate that maximizes net benefits to society. If entrance fees are zero, the actual and expected number of visitor-days will be those shown as the sequence q_1, q_2, and q_3 in Figure 17-1. The first of these is a historical number, pertaining to 10 years ago, the second shows visitor days this year, while q_3 shows the expected visitor-days 10 years into the future. There are two reasons for thinking that these do not represent socially efficient visitation rates. First, the costs of operating and maintaining the park are not being recovered through admission fees. These costs are covered through some other means, perhaps through expenditures of tax moneys collected from the citizenry of the relevant political district. In this case there is a disconnect between the people using the park and the people paying for it, so there is no reason to suspect that the willingness to pay of the marginal user corresponds to the marginal cost of accommodating that visitor. This is a requirement for efficiency, as we saw back in Chapter 5.

The second reason for thinking that q_1, q_2, and q_3 are not socially efficient is the presence of **congestion externalities.** If admission prices are zero, we have a situation essentially of **open access.** Open access, as we saw in Chapter 6, will normally lead to use rates that exceed socially efficient levels. In that earlier chapter we used the example of an open-access beach to show how congestion externalities arise. That example is perfectly illustrative of the situation facing open-access parks except that, in the latter, congestion externalities are likely to be even more important because activities such as backpacking are usually undertaken in the name of solitude, or at least a very low intensity level of activity.[1]

The quantities q_1, q_2, and q_3 of Figure 17-1 show an increase in the open-access use levels of this park. Congestion externalities would tend to increase as the demand curve shifts outward, and eventually, once visitation became very high, might choke off any further increases in visitation despite increases in population and other factors. This point has perhaps been reached in some national parks, when summertime visitor rates can be so high that physical capacities are reached. But in many other parks where visitation is less than what perhaps could be physically accommodated, questions have arisen regarding what the "optimal" visitation is and how it should be achieved.

---

[1] In many of the contingent valuation studies of willingness to pay for backpacking experiences, the likelihood of meeting other backpackers strongly affects the valuations expressed by respondents. One of the early examples is reported in Charles J. Cicchetti and V. Kerry Smith, "Congestion, Quality Deterioration and Optimal Use: Wilderness Recreation in the Spanish Peaks Primitive Area," *Social Science Research,* Vol. 2, 1973, pp. 15–30. See Chapter 9 for a discussion of contingent valuation analysis.

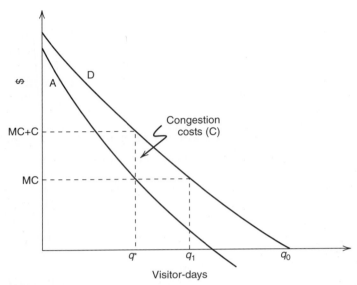

FIGURE 17-2
Socially Efficient Visitation Rates

To examine this question more closely, consider the model in Figure 17-2. The curve labeled D is the normal market demand curve for visits to a public park. The point where this curve hits the horizontal axis (q_0) gives the **open-access** level of visitation, that is, the level that would pertain if no entrance fees are charged. Now suppose the marginal costs of operating the park are constant at a level of MC. If a price were charged equal to this amount, visitation would go to q_1 visitor-days per year. This is not necessarily the efficient level of usage, and the reason is that the curve D does not take congestion effects into account.

When the rate of visitation increases at a public park, the new visitors may cause congestion that lowers the value of the visitation experience not only for them but also for people who are already there. The nature of the congestion costs will vary from place to place. If it's a wilderness area, congestion is connected to meeting other people on the trail. If it's a ski hill, congestion is having to dodge other skiers on the slopes. If it's a picnic area, congestion means having all the good sites taken and having to put up with the sight and noise of neighboring groups. Ordinary demand curves do not account for these congestion effects because they are based on the willingness to pay of the **marginal user.** What we need is a demand curve **net of congestion effects,** that is, a curve that shows the marginal willingness to pay of the marginal user **minus** the congestion costs of existing users. These costs are essentially a reduction in the value of their visits caused by the entry of additional visitors. A demand curve adjusted for the congestion effects is shown as curve A in Figure 17-2.

The height of D shows the willingness to pay of the marginal user; the height of A shows this marginal willingness to pay minus the congestion costs inflicted by the marginal user on existing users.

We now have a way of identifying the socially efficient use rate—it is q^*. But the curve D is the one that shows how visitation would vary with changes in the entrance fee. Thus, if we want to put into place a fee that will lead to a use rate of q^*, the fee must be equal to standard marginal costs (MC) plus congestion costs (C). This is shown as MC + C in the figure.

RATIONING USE

Open access in many public parks and recreation areas has led to overuse, congestion, and often to the degradation of natural resources in the areas. In effect, open access leads to use rates like q_0 in Figure 17-2. This leads naturally to the question of how managers can limit visitation rates to something more consistent with the implications of social efficiency. **Rationing use** means finding some way to exclude certain of those who would have visited if open-access conditions had continued. It perhaps needs emphasis that rationing use makes sense only in terms of the efficiency criterion we are employing. If the objective at the park is simply to have as many visitors as possible, regardless of the quality of the visits, and if revenue collection is neither necessary nor sought, then uncontrolled access is "optimal." The actual trend in the real world, however, is away from this.

The following list describes the various methods available to a managing agency for rationing visitation:

1 Limit entry to those people who meet some prespecified characteristic(s). For example, many communities limit entry to the town beach solely to town residents.
2 First-come, first-served. Determine the visitation level one wants, then admit on a first-arrival basis; when the desired visitation level has been reached, close the entry point(s).
3 Charge an entrance fee sufficiently high that visitation is equal to q^*.

The first two of these are **nonprice rationing procedures.** They could also be used in combination (admit only town residents up to some maximum). Nonprice approaches are usually undertaken in the name of an **equity objective,** for example "all town residents should have equal access," or "the national parks should be open to all." Nonprice systems normally involve some amount of wealth distribution. If the costs of operating the parks are not covered by visitors themselves, they must be through some other means, for example general tax revenues. This means that there will undoubtedly be people who help pay for the parks but do not enjoy their services. Some of this might be justified if it is determined that nonuse, or passive, values produced by outdoor recreation parks and areas are widespread and significant.

Rationing by Price

Entry fees to ration use have not been commonly used historically, except in private resource-based ventures such as ski hills. Thus, the provision of public parks and reservations has been seen as an important part of civic life and cultural identity, an activity that ought to be outside the market. This view is changing, however, under a number of influences. One is that admission fees may be a more appropriate and effective way of raising revenues to support the maintenance of park areas. Another is the rise of **ecotourism** as a potential revenue producer for developing countries, as well as for communities everywhere who are looking for ways to support public services. A third factor is that privately produced outdoor recreation is a fast-growing sector, and in this case entry fees are an integral part of the system. Finally, there is perhaps a growing appreciation of the fact that entry fees and the revenue they produce can provide a justification for expanding the system of parks and reservations in terms of both quantity and quality. The incentive for protecting resources is increased if that protection also yields a revenue flow. Perhaps one additional factor is the realization that access is already rationed by price to a very large extent, except that the price is in the form of travel costs. Those people who can afford the time and money to visit national parks and forests are the people who visit; those who cannot afford it do not.[2]

A number of U.S. federal agencies have recently been authorized to investigate the feasibility and effects of charging entrance fees at areas they manage. Exhibit 17-1 is an excerpt from the 1997 annual report to the U.S. Congress on progress being made under the program. In the demonstration program a variety of fees are being explored: fees per person; fees per carload of people; daily fees; annual fees; and so on. You can perhaps appreciate from reading the material in the exhibit that the primary justification for admission fees, in the eyes of the participating agencies, is to recover revenues so that more money can be put into developing, maintaining, and operating the sites. As we have seen above, this rationale will lead to entrance fees that are too low for social efficiency if congestion is involved, and may also be too low to protect ecosystems in the reservations from excessive wear and tear by visitors. Although fees do indeed create a revenue flow, their primary justification is to ration the use of an asset that is scarce and to ensure that people who visit the parks value the experience more highly than people who do not visit.

Pricing and Total Revenue

But since a major rationale for entry fees in practice is to raise revenue, it will be useful to clarify the connection between price changes and revenue

---

[2] This is not to say, however, that all opposition to entrance fees has disappeared. See Aldo Leopold, Wilderness Research Institute, "Societal Response to Recreation Fees on Public Lands," paper given at a conference on May 27–31, 1998, University of Missouri–Columbia (available at www.fs.fed.us/research/rvur/wilderness/recreation_fees.htm).

EXHIBIT 17-1

RECREATIONAL FEE DEMONSTRATION PROGRAM

Congress authorized the Recreational Fee Demonstration Program to begin on October 1, 1995 and to end on September 30, 1998, and later extended the program for an additional year. The program authorizes the National Park Service, Bureau of Land Management, U.S. Fish and Wildlife Service, and USDA Forest Service to implement and test new fees across the geographic and programmatic spectrum of sites that they manage. Importantly, the program allows the participating agencies to retain all of the demonstration project revenues, and to retain at least 80 percent of the revenues at the sites where they are collected. These revenues yield substantial benefits because they provide on-the-ground improvements at local recreation sites.

As of September 30, 1997, there were 97 National Park Service demonstration projects, ten Bureau of Land Management projects, 61 U.S. Fish and Wildlife Service projects, and 40 USDA Forest Service projects. The agencies collected $138,775 thousand in revenues from all recreation fee sources during the first year of the program at Recreational Fee Demonstration Program sites. This represents an increase of $53,493, or 61 percent, from revenues the previous year, a gain that is attributable to the Recreational Fee Demonstration Program. It is clear that substantial gains can be made generating revenues from recreation sites.

As a result of the Recreational Fee Demonstration Program, the agencies are beginning to apply the revenues to backlogged projects and to improving public services on the fee demonstration sites. The National Park Service is using the new revenues to reduce backlog needs in maintenance, infrastructure, and resource management, as identified in the Department of the Interior's ongoing efforts to establish clearer priorities. The U.S. Fish and Wildlife Service is using the revenues to improve visitor services and facilities, such as boat docks and ramps, auto tour routes, information kiosks, exhibits, signs, brochures, and trail guides. The Bureau of Land Management is using the revenues to improve campgrounds, parking areas, visitor services, site access, safety and health services, and environmental protection. The USDA Forest Service is using fee demonstration funds to provide quality recreation settings, reduce maintenance backlogs, and provide enhanced public services.

Public acceptance of the program has been generally high. There has been strong public support for retaining fee revenues at the site to improve visitor services and not return revenues to the United States Treasury. In a National Park Service survey of visitors, 85 percent indicated that they were either satisfied with the fees they paid or thought the fees were too low. In a USDA Forest Service survey, 64 percent agreed with the statement that the opportunities and services they experienced were at least equal to the fee they paid. Visitation to the fee demonstration sites does not appear to have been significantly affected, either positively or negatively, by the new fees.

The flexibility provided to the agencies has resulted in innovative approaches to fee collection, and a high level of responsiveness to the public in the design and implementation of fee programs. The ability to retain funds for visitor improvements at the site has given agency personnel a strong incentive to work with the public on revenue generation, and is the source of public support to the fee program. It is important that future fee programs contain these agency and public incentives, and that they provide flexibility to tailor fee programs to specific needs and situations and to address revenue inequities.

Source: National Park Service, Recreational Fee Demonstration Program, Annual Report to Congress, Executive Summary, 1997, USNPS, Washington, DC, undated.

changes. For any given price there will be an associated quantity, as given by the demand function. Increases in price will lead to decreases in quantity and vice versa. Since total revenue is simply price times quantity, an increase in price by a certain amount can lead to increases or decreases in total revenue, depending on how much quantity changes. Consider Figure 17-3, which represents the demand curve of an imaginary public park. At a fee of $12 per day, visitation will average 180, thus the total revenue, indicated by rectangle $b + c$, is $2,160. At a price of $14, visitation drops to 160, and total revenue (area $a + b$) increases to $2,240. Had quantity decreased by more in response to the higher price, total revenue could have decreased. If the demand curve was flatter, for example, so quantity decreased to 140 visitor-days, the new total revenue would have been $1,960, a decrease.

The critical parameter of a demand function, which determines whether total revenues increase or decrease (and how much) when prices change, is the **price elasticity of demand** (E_p). It is defined as:

$$E_p = \frac{\text{Percentage change in quantity}}{\text{Percentage change in price}}$$

and we use the following terminology:

   if $E_p = -1$, we have unitary elasticity
   if $E_p < -1$, we have a **relatively elastic** demand curve
   if $-1 < E_p < 0$, we have a **relatively inelastic** demand curve

FIGURE 17-3
Price Changes and Total Revenue

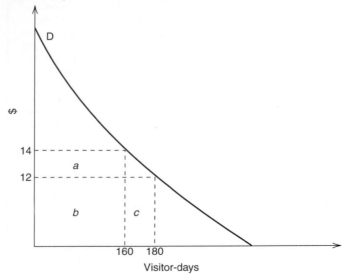

Note that when $E_p = -1$, the percentage change in quantity is exactly the same as the percentage change in price, and since total revenue is equal to price times quantity, it would not change in this case when price changes. On the other hand, if the demand curve is inelastic, quantity changes (in percentage terms) are lower than price changes, so total revenue will increase if price increases and will fall if price decreases. It is just the opposite when the E_p is elastic; in this case quantity increases (in percentage terms) exceed price changes, hence total revenue will go up with price decreases and down with price increases. So in Figure 17-3, the demand curve was relatively inelastic between prices of $12 and $14; total revenue increased when the price increased.

Panel (a) of Figure 17-4 shows three demand curves, differing in terms of their height and slope. Their shapes are derived both from the nature of the resource involved and the economics and demographics of the relevant population of demanders. Panel (b) of the figure shows the relationship between price and total revenue for each demand curve. In each case they are inelastic at low prices, thus total revenue increases as price increases. Each also reaches a point where the elasticity becomes unitary, except it is at a different point (a different price) in each case. These points are where the total revenue curves in the diagram reach their maximum levels. At prices higher than this, the demand curves become elastic, which explains why total revenue declines as prices continue to increase. Exhibit 17-2 discusses a research project that was undertaken to investigate the demand for visitation at three national parks in Costa Rica and the consequences of setting entrance fees at different levels. The researchers estimated, among other things, the level of entrance fees in the three cases that would maximize park revenues.

It should be emphasized that maximizing total revenue is not necessarily recommended as an appropriate strategy for national parks, forests, and other reservations. Social efficiency calls for maximizing net benefits, and the price-visitation combination that maximizes net benefits may not be the same as the one that maximizes simply total revenue. One major reason for this discrepancy is that environmental costs are included when determining social efficiency. They may or may not affect revenues in a consistent way. If willingness to pay by visitors is correlated strongly with the environmental quality of the sites, such that environmental damage impacts the individual demand functions, then damage may be fully reflected in revenue losses. But visitors may not necessarily be sensitive to all types of ecological disruption, so willingness to pay may not be an accurate reflection of the ecological status of the park or reservation.

Another important factor in pricing park access is that parks and reservations normally exist as **systems;** states have multiple parks that they wish to manage in a coordinated fashion, as does the federal government with its network of national parks, forests, and monuments. In these cases it probably will not be appropriate to price each one independently in an attempt to maximize its own total revenues. Prices at the various reservations have to be established in a coordinated fashion, taking into account the demand interrelationships among them.

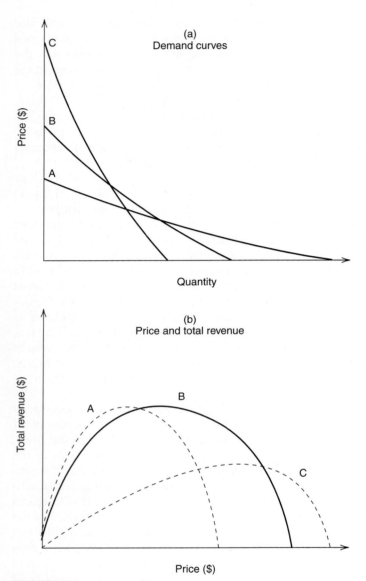

FIGURE 17-4
The Relationship between Price and Total Revenue for Three Different
Demand Curves

EXHIBIT 17-2

PRICING NATIONAL PARK ACCESS IN COSTA RICA

Costa Rica has developed an extensive series of national parks, which are visited by large numbers of tourists each year. Earnings from ecotourism have become the country's largest single source of foreign exchange in recent years. Tourism is not distributed evenly among the country's parks. The three parks discussed below account for approximately two-thirds of foreign tourists visits in recent years. Until 1994, modest entrance fees were charged at these parks. On September 1 of that year fees for foreign visitors were increased by 1,100 percent, from 200 colones ($1.25 U.S.) to 2,400 colones ($15 U.S.). Fees for residents remained at 200 colones. This abrupt increase led to controversy between local groups and tourism operators and the rate setting authorities, and to questions about what entrance fees were appropriate. A group of researchers undertook to examine the pricing situation, in particular to estimate the important features of the demand functions of ecotourists for visits to the three most heavily visited parks. Some of the results they obtained are as follows:

	Park		
	Volcán Irazú	Volcán Poás	Manuel Antonio
Actual fee paid	$12.28	$9.85	$9.56
Average length of visit (days)	1.00	1.00	1.45
Maximum willingness to pay for a visit	21.75	21.60	24.90
Fee that visitors felt would be "appropriate"	6.48	6.77	7.37
Price elasticity of demand	−1.05	−2.87	−.96
Actual total revenues 1994–1995	427,307	669,940	431,371
Revenue-maximizing entry fee	7.06	9.28	13.59
Projected total revenues if revenue-maximizing entry fee had been used	$1,372,844	$ 675,447	$518,187

There are a number of interesting things about these results. Note that the price elasticities of demand are quite different for the three parks. In two of them the elasticity is near unity, while at the third demand is quite elastic. Note also that at one park the actual admission price was quite close to the revenue-maximizing one, at one park it was well below the revenue-maximizing price, and at the other the actual price was well above the revenue-maximizing price. By comparing the actual with projected revenues you can see how much additional revenue can sometimes be obtained with the appropriate price. It needs to be kept in mind, however, that revenue maximization is not necessarily the most appropriate goal for park managers to pursue.

Source: Lisa C. Chase, David R. Lee, William D. Schulze, and Deborah J. Anderson, "Ecotourism Demand and Differential Pricing of National Park Access in Costa Rica," *Land Economics,* 74(4), November 1998, pp. 466–482.

Differential Pricing

The real world, however, is obviously more complicated than the simple model above implies. One way it is much more complicated is that not all users or visitors are necessarily alike in terms of characteristics that affect their willingness to pay. This brings up the question of when it is justified, for efficiency and/or equity terms, to establish different prices for different users. Consider the following:

- Given the normal constraints on time and the extent of the normal workweek, the willingness to pay on weekends will often be higher than that on weekdays, especially for the less remote areas. Is it efficient and fair to charge different prices on weekends than on weekdays?
- Very often the same park or forest will accommodate visitors who engage in different activities, for example, some people are interested in backpacking and solitude, while others want easier access and are less in search of a "pure" wilderness experience. Is it efficient and/or equitable to charge different rates to people in the two groups?
- There are two public parks, alike in every way in terms of environmental values. But one is relatively close to an urban area and one is far away. Is it efficient and/or equitable to charge different entrance fees at these two parks?

Questions like these can get quite complex. We now try to develop some reasonably simple principles to help in thinking about the issues. Consider Figure 17-5. This applies to a situation where there are two types of users of a park. One group has a demand curve labeled D_1, and the other has demand curve D_2. Note that the latter is steeper than the former; perhaps these are rock climbers, who have a relatively inelastic demand for this area, whereas the more elastic D_1 is the demand of day picnickers in the park. The **aggregate demand curve,** labeled D_t, is the horizontal summation of D_1 and D_2.

MC is the marginal cost curve, drawn horizontally on the assumption that the marginal cost of servicing all visitors is constant and the same for each visitor type. Let us assume that there are no congestion problems. Overall social efficiency requires that aggregate marginal willingness to pay be equal to marginal cost. The single price that will lead to this is to set price equal to marginal cost ($p = MC$) for both sorts of users. Total visitor-days will then be q_t, and the visitor-days of each type will be q_1 and q_2. Note that total revenue taken in will just equal total costs (the area $d + e + f + g + h$). Of this total revenue, $d + e + f$ is paid by group 1 and d is paid by group 2. Net benefits accruing to group 1 are $b + c$; those going to group 2 are equal to $a + b$. Total net benefits are maximized (i.e., we achieve social efficiency) when the same price is charged to each type of user. Suppose we didn't; suppose we charged $10 a day to type 1 visitors and $5 a day to type 2 visitors. This means that the marginal type 1 visitor valued the visit at $10 while the marginal type 2 visitor valued it at $5. It is not socially efficient to let the former in but keep the latter out. Thus, as long as the

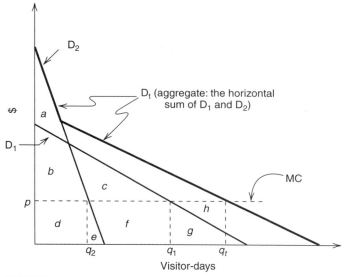

FIGURE 17-5
Efficient Pricing When There Are Two Classes of Visitors

marginal costs of servicing individuals in the two groups is the same, there is no efficiency justification for charging different entrance fees.[3]

The obverse of this is also true, however. If the marginal costs of servicing people in the two groups are different, efficiency requires that they be charged different prices. In particular, prices should be higher to the group with the highest marginal cost, and lower to the group with the lower marginal cost. The rule: Set $p = MC$ for each subgroup of users will achieve this result. An example might be that rock climbers require higher costs than picnickers because of the need for closer supervision, stand-by rescue and medical equipment, and so on.

An example where there is a cost difference is when congestion costs differ from one time period to another. Many parks have capacity limits, either hard limits like a certain number of campsites or visitation levels where congestion externalities begin to take hold. Consider a very simple case of a park with a certain number of picnic sites, indicated as q_0 in Figure 17-6. Suppose that the marginal costs of servicing the sites is quite low, set at the level MC in the figure. There are two demand curves: D_1 pertains to weekday visitors, and D_2 is

---

[3] If the park agency were out to maximize revenues, on the other hand, it would probably want to differentiate prices. By charging higher prices to the group with inelastic demand, its revenues here would increase. By charging lower prices to the elastic-demand group, it would also increase revenues from this source. This is what airlines do. Business travelers are group 2, "recreational" travelers are group 1. This practice is called **price discrimination.**

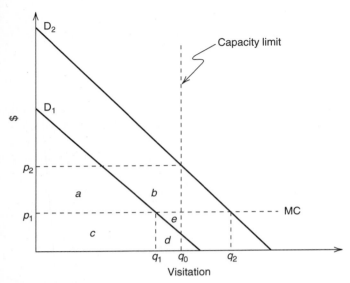

FIGURE 17-6
Peak Load Park Pricing

for weekend visitors. The latter is well outside the former because of the greater time availability that people have on weekends. Efficiency in this case requires two prices. During the week, set p = MC. In this case the average weekday visitation will be q_1. But this price will not do for weekends, because the quantity demanded at this price on weekends will far exceed the capacity of the park (that is, $q_2 > q_0$).

Parks might be under political pressure to charge the same rates during the weekend that they do on weekdays. In this case some type of nonprice rationing would be required to limit the weekend use and to avoid situations where people without campsites tie up the park by milling around looking for an open picnic site. Furthermore, if the price p_1 (= MC) were set on weekends, we would have no guarantee that people ending up with picnic sites would be those who valued them the most highly. They could be simply the luckiest, or the first ones to show up in the morning. Thus, to ensure a maximum of net benefits, we set p_1 = MC during the week, and p_2 during the weekends. You can see immediately that there is an extra element in this model. On weekends, total costs are equal to $c + d + e$, while total revenue from entrance fees is equal to $a + b + c + d + e$; the park is making a profit of $a + b$. In effect, this is a redistribution of income from the weekend park visitors to whoever ends up with these revenues, perhaps the general taxpayer if they go into a general account of some political entity. But this creates even an added wrinkle. Suppose the park agency is under a political directive to operate as a **nonprofit.** Then it would have to resort to some means to avoid making the profit ($a + b$). There are two possibilities. One is to charge p_1 on the weekends but resort also to nonprice rationing, as mentioned above. Another is to inflate costs until they match revenues. By "inflate" we mean undertaking expenses that are not really needed to maintain the park at an acceptable level.

Pricing to Cover Fixed Operating Costs

Let us look at one last pricing issue. The examples in the previous section all had constant marginal cost curves at some level. This means that we were assuming that total costs increased linearly with the number of visitors; each new visitor increased costs by exactly the same amount. But this is probably not an accurate assumption in some cases. Very often the operating costs of a public park will be somewhat fixed in nature. To operate the park at all involves certain staffing and other costs, and these costs don't necessarily vary smoothly with the number of visitors that show up. Another way to say this is that, once the park is open and operating with the normal staff and supply costs, the **marginal cost** of accommodating an extra visitor is quite low, perhaps even zero in some cases. This is so at least up until the point where congestion begins, after which there are positive congestion costs.

Consider the case of zero marginal costs. Efficiency says to set price equal to marginal cost, and so here the entrance fee would be set at zero. But in this case, revenues are also zero, and the park is unable to cover its costs. What to do? In cases like this it may be useful to move in the direction of a **two-part price** system. In this kind of system the total visitation fee is broken into two parts, one part that is based on **current marginal visitation cost** (which in the example is zero), and the other part a **one-time-only seasonal payment** that gives individual visitors the right to have access whenever and however many times they choose throughout the year. The price of the seasonal pass is set (as closely as possible) so that it recovers the fixed operating costs of the park. For a person who visits the park just one time throughout the season, of course, the prices of the two permits meld into a single payment; it is only with multiple visits that the two prices become distinct.

ECOTOURISM

Tourists are a ubiquitous part of the modern world. **Ecotourists** are those whose visits are linked in some fashion to natural or environmental resources; the term covers essentially the same activities—touring, observing, participating—that we have discussed under the older term "outdoor recreation." Ecotourism can clearly be domestic, but perhaps has a stronger connotation of international travel, especially travel from countries of the developed world to visit the unique natural resource endowments of the countries in the developing world. Ecotourism is seen by people in some locales as a key element for stimulating economic development. On the level of incentives, it can elevate the value of natural assets that previously were outside the market, which may lead people to put greater stress on their conservation. If, through ecotourism, resources worthy of conservation can be increased in market value, then there will be less incentive for them to be deforested, converted to pasture or cultivation agriculture, or otherwise disrupted. Ecotourism has a number of important bioeconomic aspects.

Demand Estimation and Management

Many of the concepts discussed earlier in this chapter, on demand estimation, revenue generation, and pricing issues, are directly applicable to ecotourism. If prices, such as park entrance fees or wildlife tour fees, are to be used to raise revenue, or to protect sensitive resources from overuse, then knowledge of the relevant demand functions is useful and important. Private firms in the ecotourism industry have faced this problem all along and have presumably developed the necessary knowledge as a condition of staying in business. But the problem is relatively new within the public sector. Questions about access rights have traditionally been dealt with politically, which is where pricing decisions will be addressed, at least initially. The situation is complex because countries are making many different types of resource reservations, with important differences among them in terms of type of resources, objectives, and clientele. The list in Table 17-2 gives some idea of these differences for developing countries. Developed countries also normally have systems of national parks, wildlife refuges, and wilderness areas.

Biological Impacts

There is a great deal of very legitimate concern that opening up resources to tourist impacts, especially resources that are ecologically sensitive, could lead to their long-run diminishment in terms of quantity and/or quality. A strong desire to generate revenues could motivate visitation rates that are too high, relative to some longer-run "sustainable" level. Or investment in infrastructure such as roads could open up resources that before had been protected by their remoteness. The concept of **sustainable ecotourism** has been suggested as the relevant guide for action.[4] This is certainly appropriate in the sense of making sure that ecological resources are not permanently damaged by tourism activities. But most ecotourism activities are connected with biological resources, and the question comes up, as it has repeatedly throughout the book, as to what the efficient stock of a resource is when used as an ecotourism resource. Virtually any level of tourism will affect the quantity/quality of a resource. The appropriate quantity and quality of a natural resource open to ecotourism will undoubtedly be different from what it would

---

[4] See, for example, Erlet Cater and Gwen Lowman, (eds.), *Ecotourism, A Sustainable Option?* Wiley, Chichester, England, 1994.

TABLE 17-2
CATEGORIES AND MANAGEMENT OBJECTIVES OF PROTECTED AREAS

1 **Scientific reserve/strict nature reserve**: To protect nature and maintain natural processes in an undisturbed state in order to have ecologically representative examples of the natural environment available for scientific study, environmental monitoring and education, and the maintenance of genetic resources in a dynamic and evolutionary state. *Examples* include the Yala Strict Nature Reserve in Sri Lanka, the island of Barro Colorado in Panama, and the Gombe Stream National Park in Tanzania.

2 **National park:** To protect relatively large natural and scenic areas of national or international significance for scientific, educational, and recreational use, under management by the highest competent authority of a nation. *Examples* include the Royal Chitwan National Park in Nepal, the Etosha National Park in Namibia, the Iguazu National Parks in Argentina and Brazil, and Volcan Poas National Park in Costa Rica.

3 **Natural monument/natural landmark:** To protect and preserve nationally significant natural features because of their special interest or unique characteristics. *Good examples* include Angkor Wat National Park in Kampuchea, the Petrified Forests Nature Monument in Argentina, and Gedi National Monument in Kenya.

4 **Managed nature reserve/wildlife sanctuary:** To ensure the natural conditions necessary to protect nationally significant species, groups of species, biotic communities, or physical features of the environment when these require specific human manipulation for their perpetuation.* *Examples* include Manas Wildlife Sanctuary in India. Most of the national reserves in Kenya also fall in this category, as do the biotope reserves in Guatemala.

5 **Protected landscapes:** To maintain nationally significant natural landscapes characteristic of the harmonious interaction of man and land, while providing opportunities for public enjoyment through recreation and tourism within the normal lifestyle and economic activity of these areas. *Examples* include Pululahua Geobotanical Reserve in Ecuador and Machu Picchu Historic Sanctuary in Peru. The national parks of England are also classified under this category.

6 **Resource reserve:** To protect the natural resources of the area for future use and to prevent or contain development activities that could affect the resource pending the establishment of objectives based on appropriate knowledge and planning. *Few countries* have yet applied this category, but several resource reserves exist in Kenya, including Kora and South Turkana National Reserves. Other examples include Brazil's Forest Reserves, and Tahuamanu Protected Forest, Bolivia.

7 **Natural biotic area/anthropological reserve:** To allow the way of life of societies living in harmony with the environment to continue undisturbed by modern technology. *The Gunung Lorentz Nature Reserve* of Indonesia, Xingu Indigenous Park of Brazil, and Central Kalahari Game Reserve of Botswana are all occupied by indigenous people and are classified as Category 7 areas. Many protected areas in the South Pacific islands also fall into this category.

8 **Multiple-use management area/managed resource area:** To provide for the sustained production of water, timber, wildlife, pasture, and outdoor recreation, with the conservation of nature primarily orientated to the support of the economic activities (although specific zones can also be designed within these areas to achieve specific conservation objectives). T*he most famous* example is the Ngorongoro Conservation Area of Tanzania. Other examples are the Kutai National Park of Indonesia, Jamari and Tapajos National Forests of Brazil, and Von Humboldt National Forest of Peru.

*To this list should be added marine reserves such as the one located in the Galapagas.
   Sources: International Union for the Conservation of Nature (IUCN), "Categories, Objectives, and Criteria for Protected Areas," in J. A. McNeely and K. R. Miller (eds.), *National Parks, Conservation and Development*, Smithsonian Institution Press, Washington, DC, 1984; J. Mackinnon et al., *Managing Protected Areas in the Tropics*, IUCN, Gland, Switzerland, 1986; as cited in Gardner Brown, "Wildlife in Developing Countries," in Partha Dasgupta and Karl-Gören Mäler, *The Environment and Emerging Development Issues*, Vol. 2, Clarendon Press, Oxford, England, 1997, p. 562.

be if there were no ecotourism. And the difference will hinge on the trade-off between the values of the biological impacts and the economic values associated with the ecotourism. Furthermore, many ecotourism projects have been undertaken with the notion of providing a stimulus to economic development, which might become less resource-dependent in the future if it is successful. This raises the possibility that the optimal stock of an ecotourist resource is not steady state, at least not yet. Rather, development may call for relatively heavy use in the short run and lower rates of use in the long run.

Institutional Issues

There are a range of institutional questions involved in the social management of ecotourism. One of the most important is the balance that should be struck between public sector and private sector. In many countries federal or regional governments are directly involved, for example, in managing access to national parks and wildlife refuges. In some cases (e.g., wildlife in Africa), private companies have formed to operate ecotourism activities in a market setting. In some cases units of local government function to some extent like private firms in managing local ecotourism.[5]

The institutional arrangements that are best in any specific case presumably depend on the details of that case—resource involved and political and economic attributes of the countries. Some general principles may be possible, however. Ecotourism is based on market principles, in which supply must be directed at the demand, in this case the demands of ecotourists. Not all resources that are valuable in some biological sense will be valuable to tourists in a market sense. It is clearly important that economically popular resources not be favored to the detriment of unpopular, but ecologically important, resources. When decisions are located in the private sector, that is, with private ecotourist firms, this problem comes under the heading of **external costs.** When decisions are made in the public sector, that is, by public agencies responsible for ecotourist resources, decisions may be made by reference to the narrow political interests of those who have the power, to the exclusion of other values that may be important in a wider social context.

The distribution of resource rents is also an important dimension of the institutional question. If ecotourism is undertaken in the name of economic development, it clearly makes a difference who accumulates the resulting rents. If they go to the state, they will be used for purposes that state planners and politicians deem to be important. If they go to individuals locally, they are likely to be spent on entirely different goods and services. We will have more to say about this in Chapter 20, when discussing natural resources and economic growth. The distribution of resource rents is important also for another

---

[5] The well-known Campfire (Communal Areas Management Program for Indigenous Resources) program in Africa allows local communities, functioning collectively, to profit by selling access to local wildlife resources to safari operators.

reason. The motivation for many ecotourism projects is to provide incentives to conserve the resources in question as mentioned above. If this is to be successful, the rents must go, in large part at least, to those of the local population who have the power to conserve the resource. For example, the most effective way to stop poaching, or deforestation, by local people of public ecotourist reservations, may be to direct some of the rents to these people.

SUMMARY

In this chapter we focused on important issues in the economics of **outdoor recreation.** Many of these issues are connected to an understanding of the **demand curves** people have for outdoor recreation in general and for specific recreation sites. We looked at the general question of **efficient visitation rates** at a public park and brought in the problem of congestion externalities. A major part of the chapter dealt with the problem of how to **ration** use of public parks, which is becoming a much more difficult problem as populations and incomes grow. We considered **nonprice rationing** schemes and the use of **entry fees** to ration visitation. We looked at the relation of **prices** and **total revenues,** which hinges on the value of the **price elasticity of demand,** and also at questions of **differential pricing** and problems of pricing when marginal short-run visitation costs are very low, perhaps zero, but annual fixed costs must be covered. Lastly, the chapter discussed **ecotourism,** including **price policy, biological impacts,** and the disposition of **rents** from ecotourism projects.

KEY TERMS

Outdoor recreation demand function	Price elasticity of demand
Congestion externalities	Inelastic demand
Efficient visitation rates	Elastic demand
Rationing use	Price charges and total revenue
Nonprice rationing	Differential pricing
Rationing through price	Peak load pricing
Ecotourism	Pricing to cover fixed costs

QUESTIONS FOR FURTHER DISCUSSION

1 Suppose the demand curve for a public park is $Q = 80 - 2p$, where Q is the number of visitor-days and p is the entry price. The marginal cost of operating the park is $MC = 10$.
   a What is the efficient level of entrance fee and the number of visitors at this fee level (assume no congestion problems)?
   b At the price/quantity combination of (*a*), what is the price elasticity of demand for park visitation? (To find this, take a small change in price, say, $1. Figure out the elasticity with the change in quantity that would result from this price change. The percentage change in price and quantity will be different depending on

whether the price has gone up by one dollar or down by one dollar. Take the average of the two estimates.)

   c What is the price-quantity combination that will maximize revenues, and what is the price elasticity of demand at this point on the demand curve?

2 If one rations the use of a public park with an entrance fee, we know that each of the users of the park will value that visit at a level equal to or above the fee. If we ration by "first-come, first-served," what do we know about the visitors?

3 We talked earlier (see Chapter 9) about measuring demand curves. How might we proceed if we wanted to measure congestion externalities associated with various outdoor recreation activities?

4 One reason for levying entrance fees at public parks is to generate revenues to help cover costs. What are the other reasons?

5 Suppose a natural resource area is set aside and designated as a scientific preserve, to be open to scientists who are studying, for example, species diversity issues. Should scientists be charged for access to the area?

6 You have built a number of blinds that can be used to hunt or observe the migrating Canada geese in a spot on the main flyway. You have to establish a price to charge people for using the blinds. What considerations would go into determining this price?

USEFUL WEB SITES

Information on national parks, visitation data, and forecasts, as well as impact data on local communities:

- National Park Service, Public Use Statistics Office (http://www.aqd.nps. gov/stats)

Other federal agencies are also relevant:

- U.S. Forest Service, information on fee demonstration programs (http://www.fs.fed.us/recreation/fee_demo/fee_intro.shtml)

For a proposal to establish a Center for the Economic Study of the National Parks:

- Resources for the Future (http://www.rff.org)

Information on national parks in other countries:

- Costa Rica (http://www.gemlab.ukans.edu/cr)

Relevant public interest groups:

- National Parks and Conservation Association (http://www.npca.org)
- Wilderness Society (http://www.wilderness.org)

General information on outdoor recreation and ecotourism:

- Great Outdoor Recreation Pages (http://www.gorp.com)
- Ecotourism Society ((http://www.ecotourism.org)

SELECTED READINGS

Chicchetti, Charles J., and V. Kerry Smith: *The Costs of Congestion: An Econometric Analysis of Wilderness Experience,* Ballinger, Cambridge, MA, 1976.

Clawson, Marion: "Methods of Measuring the Demand for and Value of Outdoor Recreation," in Wallace E. Oates, (ed.), *The Economics of the Environment,* Elgar, Aldershot, England, 1992, pp. 301–336.

Clawson, Marion, and Jack L. Knetsch: *Economics of Outdoor Recreation,* Johns Hopkins Press for Resources for the Future, Baltimore, 1966.

Fisher, Anthony C., and John V. Krutilla: "Determination of Optimal Capacity of Resource-Based Recreation Facility," *Natural Resource Journal,* Vol. 12, 1972, pp. 417–444.

France, Lesley, (ed.): *Sustainable Tourism,* Earthscan, London, 1997.

Langholz, J.: "Economics, Objectives, and Success of Private Nature Reserves in Sub-Saharan Africa and Latin America," *Conservation Biology,* Vol. 10, 1996, pp. 271–280.

Leuschner, W. A., P. A. Cook, and J. W. Roggenbuck: "A Comparative Analysis for Wilderness User Fee Policy," *Journal of Leisure Research,* Vol. 19, 1987, pp. 101–114.

Lindberg, Kreg, and Richard M. Huber, Jr.: "Economic Issues in Ecotourism Management," in Kreg Lindberg and Donald E. Hawkins (eds.), *Ecotourism, A Guide for Planners and Managers,* The Ecotourism Society, North Bennington, VT, 1993, pp. 82–115.

McConnell, Kenneth E.: "The Economics of Outdoor Recreation," in Allen V. Kneese and James L. Sweeny (eds.), *Handbook of Natural Resource and Energy Economics,* Vol. 2, North-Holland, Amsterdam, 1985, pp. 677–722.

More, Thomas A., Daniel L. Dustin, and Richard C. Knopf: "Behavioral Consequences of Campground User Fees," *Journal of Park and Recreation Administration,* 14 (1), Spring 1996, pp. 81–93.

Munasinghe, M., and J. McNeely: "Protected Area Economics and Policy: Linking Conservation and Sustainable Development," World Bank, Washington, DC, 1994.

Mungatana, E. D., and S. Navrud: "Environmental Valuation in Developing Countries: The Recreational Value of Wildlife Viewing," *Ecological Economics,* Vol. 11, 1994, pp. 135–151.

Rosenthal, D. H., J. B. Loomis, and G. L. Peterson: "Pricing for Efficiency and Revenue in Public Recreation Areas," *Journal of Leisure Research,* Vol. 16, 1984, pp. 195–208.

Walsh, R. G.: *Recreation Economic Decisions: Comparing Benefits and Costs,* Venture Publishing Company, State College, PA, 1986.

Wilman, E. A.: "Pricing Policies for Outdoor Recreation," *Land Economics,* Vol. 64, August 1988, pp. 234–241.

CHAPTER 18

THE ECONOMICS OF WILDLIFE MANAGEMENT

The various impacts of human beings on wildlife resources have become more frequent and more contentious in recent years. Continued demographic and economic growth has brought human work and dwelling places more directly into conflict with wild animals and plants. At the same time, these resources are becoming more highly valued, for preserving ecosystem integrity, for providing unconventional inputs for human societies, and as sources of direct enjoyment for an increasingly urbanized population. On a more philosophical level, preservation of wildlife has to some extent become a rallying cry for those who believe it important that modern humans seek to reestablish their roots in the workings of the natural world.

Wildlife, in its most general sense, refers to living, nonhuman organisms that have not been domesticated. The line between what is domesticated and what is not is sometimes a little fuzzy, but for present purposes we don't have to be too precise. We have dealt with several important categories of wildlife in other chapters, in particular marine, forest, and diversity resources.[1] In this chapter we deal with wildlife issues from a somewhat different perspective, in particular those cases where the value of wildlife is not solely a function of its harvested value, but rather of the contributing role it

[1] Each of these has wild and domesticated parts; aquaculture is the domesticated part of fisheries; commercial tree farms are the domesticated part of forestry; conventional plant breeding may be the domesticated part of diversity.

plays in various wildlife-related activities pursued by humans. This includes, for example, sport hunting and animal watching. Defined broadly, it could also include situations in which what is involved are **existence values,** that is, the values to humans of knowing that certain wildlife are present, usually in adequate numbers, in a given area.

The chapter begins with a discussion of some basic questions concerning wildlife ecology, economic institutions, and public policy. It then treats a number of important wildlife-related issues: hunting, animal watching, predator control, and the control of wildlife markets. Several other wildlife problems are treated in other chapters: land-use restrictions and habitat control in the chapter on land economics, and endangered species protection in the chapter on the economics of diversity preservation.

WILDLIFE ECOLOGY AND HUMAN INSTITUTIONS

We saw in Chapter 12 that fisheries economics and policy essentially involved bringing together the ecology of fish populations with the economic incentive of human decision makers. Wildlife economics requires the same approach. In this case, however, the interaction of the two—ecology and human institutions—may be more complicated, because of wider variations in the animals and ecological niches in which they are found, the closer physical proximity that exists between terrestrial animals and humans, and the more complicated array of human motivations that characterizes noncommercial situations.

Population Growth Curves

Regardless of what the objective of wildlife management is—hunting, ecotourism, predator control—the critical relationship is the growth dynamics of the wildlife population of interest. A population will increase, decrease, or remain constant, depending on a host of factors such as food availability, sex ratios, fecundity and mortality rates, and predation pressure. In 1942 Arthur Einarsen studied the way a population of pheasants grew after the species was introduced onto a previously uninhabited (by pheasants) island.[2] What he found is pictured in panel (a) of Figure 18-1. For the first few years population increases were modest, but then the rate of change started to get much larger. In 1941 the increment reached its maximum, and the next year it was lower. Assuming a continuance of this trend, it was expected that at some point, perhaps around 1946, the population of pheasants would meet its maximum, or the **carrying capacity** for the habitat. After that the curve would flatten out, signifying no further increase.

---

[2] Arthur S. Einarsen, "Specific Results from Ring-Necked Pheasant Studies in the Pacific Northwest," Transactions, Seventh N.A. Wildlife Conference, 1942, pp. 130–138.

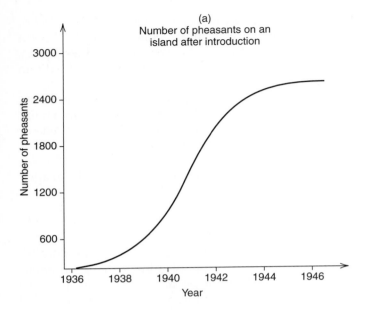

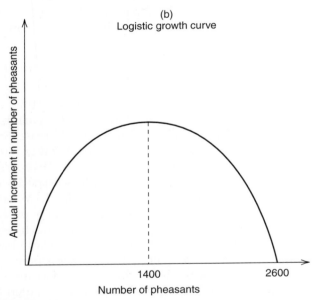

FIGURE 18-1
Growth of a Pheasant Population (*Data Source:* Arthur S. Einarsen,
"Specific Results from Ring-Necked Pheasant Studies in the Pacific
Northwest," Transactions, Seventh N.A. Wildlife Conference, 1942,
pp. 130–138.)

What he was seeing in this case was apparently a phenomenon following a **logistic growth curve,** a relationship we first encountered in Chapter 13. It is an inverted U curve showing how the growth increment to a population is related to the size of that population. A logistic curve is depicted in panel (b) of Figure 18-1. The annual increment of small populations is relatively low; it reaches a maximum at a population size of about 1,400 pheasants and then drops to zero at a population of about 2,600. Not all wild animals behave according to simple logistic models like this, but despite its simplicity it summarizes the basic population dynamics for many of them, as far as is known. Carrying capacity in this case is at about 2,600 animals, while 1,400 is the stock size that defines **maximum sustained yield,** the maximum quantity of the wildlife in question that could be harvested on a **sustainable** basis.

Several important points must be made here. The first is that, although 1,400 is the population level that gives the maximum sustained yield, this strictly biological point of reference is not necessarily the stock that is optimal from a social standpoint. We saw in the case of the fishery that the commercial aspects of the problem—the market values of the fish and the costs of harvest—led to an economic optimum different from the biological point of maximum sustained yield. If we consider wildlife more broadly, we have to allow for the possibility that there are other sources of value, for example, value for **recreational hunting,** or for **ecotourism** (wildlife viewing), value for purposes of **biological diversity,** or simply **existence value.** These other sources of value could make it even more difficult to identify a socially optimal wildlife stock in any particular case.

The other point to be made is about uncertainty, especially when we lack a very clear idea of what the growth curve looks like. Theoretically, if the growth function for any animal population were well known, it could be used to establish optimal harvest policies. The problem is that, in the real world, so many factors are at work that it may be very difficult, even with diligent research, to identify a simple relationship between stock size and the increment to that stock. Exhibit 18-1 illustrates this in the case of the wild turkey. The upshot is that management of many, if not most, wildlife populations will have to proceed in the face of great uncertainty about underlying growth dynamics.

Human Institutions and Values

The other side of the wildlife management and conservation issue is the array of human institutions and values that have shaped the historical development of wildlife law and management practices. Chief among the former is the institution of **property rights.** Terrestrial wildlife is just that; it exists on or close to the land surface. Property rights in land, therefore, have critical implications for the ways human beings have related to wildlife populations.

The dominant landowning tradition in the United States is private property. Landowners have the legal right to devote their land to any lawful purpose

EXHIBIT 18-1

DIFFICULTIES IN DETERMINING WILDLIFE GROWTH RELATIONSHIPS:
THE WILD TURKEY

Hunting regulations were set cautiously after wild turkeys (*Meleagris gallopavo*) were re-established successfully in much of the United States. Weaver and Mosby (1979) analyzed the effects of varying season lengths and bag limits by comparing population data for turkey flocks in two areas of Virginia. In a study area in the Central Mountains, the turkey population was estimated at 19,600 in 1963 and 29,400 in 1976, representing a gain of 50 percent. In an area of the Eastern Piedmont, turkeys numbered 20,700 in 1963, but the population declined by more than 13 percent to 18,100 birds in 1976. The harvest generally increased in the Central Mountain population; the average kill of 1,126 birds per year for 1959–62 increased to 1,794 for 1964–1968 and reached an average of 2,271 turkeys per year for 1969–1976. Conversely, harvests in the Eastern Piedmont declined from an average of 1,075 birds for 1951–1962 to 379 turkeys per year for 1971–1976. The results show that a reduction of the harvest to levels of about 2–3 percent of the autumn population did not halt a decline of turkeys in the Eastern Piedmont. Conversely, harvests of 8 to 10 percent did not prevent steady growth in the Central Mountain population. Therefore, hunting was not a factor causing a decline or preventing an increase, respectively, in these turkey populations.

Turkey populations in good habitat may prove resilient to large reductions. Rush (1973) described the effects of live trapping and removing turkeys for stocking in other areas. No detectable decline in the resident population could be detected, even though 38 to 43 percent of the autumn population of 350 to 400 birds was removed each year during a 10-year period. Turkey numbers in Michigan have continued growing concurrently with increased harvests of gobblers.

One might ask, if turkeys can withstand heavy hunting pressure, why were they so scarce 50 years ago? Factors apart from hunting apparently play a major role in determining turkey numbers, especially habitat conditions, disease, and weather. Therefore, beyond adjusting harvest rates, a full range of ecological conditions must be addressed in the management of wild turkeys.

Source: Eric G. Bolen and William L. Robinson, *Wildlife Ecology and Management,* Prentice Hall, Englewood Cliffs, NJ, 1995, pp. 177–178. Data are from J. K. Weaver and H. S. Mosby, "Influence of Hunting Regulations on Virginia Wild Turkey Populations," *Journal of Wildlife Management,* Vol. 43, 1979, pp. 128–135, and G. Rush, "The Hen-Brood Release as a Restoration Technique," in G. C. Sanderson and H. C. Schultz (eds.), *Wild Turkey Management: Current Problems and Programs,* University of Missouri Press, 1973.

they wish and to exclude trespassers, that is, those who enter without permission. The law governing the wildlife resource itself has evolved in a different direction.[3] Ownership of wildlife, in the sense of having the rights and responsibilities of its management, has become vested within political bodies, especially the state governments and more recently with the federal government. Why this has happened can be seen by looking at the simple schematic in Figure 18-2. The shaded areas in the figure represent the habitat of a particular

---

[3] Numerous books deal in whole or in part with wildlife law in the United States and elsewhere. A number of these references are listed at the end of the chapter.

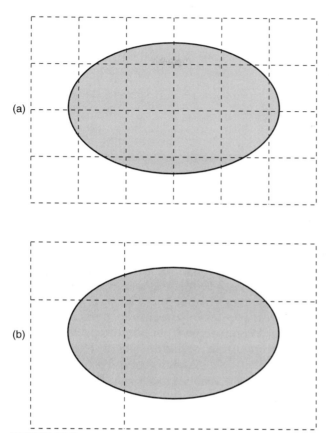

FIGURE 18-2
Schematic Representation of Wildlife Population Habitat as
Compared to Property Boundaries

population of wildlife, perhaps a certain animal, or a plant of some distinct species. The dashed lines represent property boundaries as they have developed among the holdings of a number of private owners. Naturally, these are highly artificial; in the real world, boundaries and habitats take on all sorts of complicated shapes. But the simplicity will allow us to see the concept clearly.

Panel (a) depicts a situation where the habitat of this population is broken up into many different property holdings. Put the opposite way, any one piece of property contains only a relatively small portion of the total habitat. Panel (b) is different in two senses. First, the number of property holdings is smaller, in this case just four; second, just one property holding, the one in the southeast, contains the majority of the habitat. Panel (a) typifies the situation in early America: small land holdings relative to the geographic spread of wildlife habitats. In such situations it is useless to expect individual landowners, acting on their own, to engage in efficient wildlife conservation and management activities; each one owns such a small part of the overall habitat that uncoordinated efforts would likely be fruitless. Effective wildlife management in this case calls for one of the following alternatives:

1 Coordinated action among the landowners achieved by agreement among themselves
2 Action by some higher political body that has the power to make and enforce wildlife-related regulations

The first of these may be difficult, depending on circumstances. The costs of trying to reach and enforce an agreement among landowners are called **"transactions costs."** Factors that lead to high transactions costs in cases like this are the relatively large number of landowners, the possibility of **free riding,**[4] and the fact that not all landowners are likely to have the same views about the value and role of the wildlife in question.

In the United States, this state of affairs has led historically to two outcomes. One is that wildlife has tended to be treated as an **open-access resource.** Landowners individually had no particularly strong incentives to conserve wildlife, and so hunters and harvesters essentially had the freedom at the beginning to take the wildlife without limit. This had the predictable effects, namely overharvesting and diminution of wildlife stocks. This led to the second outcome, which is that wildlife law in America evolved historically in the direction of giving authority and responsibility over wildlife stocks to the various states. Thus, it is essentially state wildlife authorities who have primary jurisdiction over the wildlife resource. Individual landholders may take steps to exclude hunters and other harvesters from their properties, but they do not have direct jurisdiction over the wildlife on their property, in the sense of being able to enforce their own rules for hunting or otherwise harvesting it.

The historical wildlife situation in England, where much of U.S. law originated, was more like panel (b) of Figure 18-2. Private holdings were in general much bigger there, in relation to typical wildlife habitats. Thus, the transactions costs of private wildlife management were relatively modest, and for this reason wildlife law in the United Kingdom came to be based on private ownership. That is, individual landowners are also endowed with property rights over the wildlife that inhabits their property.

Public Landownership and Management

There is a third way of dealing with the landownership problem: maintain or convert the land to public ownership, and then designate a public agency to

---

[4] To review the concept of free riding see Chapter 6.

manage the wildlife resources. Chapter 14, on land economics, contains information on the extent of public lands in the United States. Table 18-1 shows the federal agencies that are heavily involved in wildlife management. State agencies also oversee wildlife resources on state-owned land.

In a very general way there are two types of public lands on which wildlife issues are important: A variety of public areas, such as national and local parks, forests, wilderness areas, and the like, have been established for a variety of purposes, of which wildlife may be one; and there are public lands, such as wildlife refuges, which have been set aside specifically for the purpose of protecting wildlife resources. At the national level the latter is the National Wildlife Refuge System, which has grown to over 92 million acres of land and water since its inception in 1924.

Despite the fact that the primary purpose of wildlife refuges is to preserve the conditions that foster the health and welfare of wildlife species, refuge management frequently confronts the same type of question that comes up on other types of public preserves: whether, and to what extent, other objectives besides wildlife preservation should be pursued within the wildlife refuges. For example, a number of refuges allow cattle grazing, which is managed by the U.S. Fish and Wildlife Service through a system of grazing permits. Many refuges allow hunting, some allow timber cutting or mining. The basic question in these cases is how much of the non-wildlife-related activity to allow on the refuges.

The relevant laws on this issue[5] state essentially that the refuges may be used for other purposes as long as these are "compatible" with the major purposes for which the refuges were established. Conflicts about what is and what is not compatible are sure to increase in the future both because people are placing higher values on wildlife preservation as a goal, because population and economic growth will increase the pressure on refuge resources, and because of underfunding of the refuge maintenance and management operations.

THE ECONOMICS OF SPORT HUNTING

In colonial America commercial harvesting of terrestrial wildlife was an important source of food and materials (like deerskins and beaver pelts). In the marine world this continues to be true. The colonials found early that, with open access to wildlife stocks, commercial exploitation of wild animals could lead very quickly to stock reductions and scarcities. Their first response was to institute closed seasons and other regulations. Eventually, the states passed laws prohibiting the commercial sale of most wild animals. But although commercial hunting declined, sport, or recreational, hunting grew as a popular pastime in the United States and elsewhere.

---

[5] Primarily the National Wildlife Refuge System Administration Act of 1966, as amended.

TABLE 18-1
PARTIAL LISTING OF FEDERAL AGENCIES HAVING RESPONSIBILITIES
FOR WILDLIFE MANAGEMENT

Cabinet-level department	Agency name	Activities and responsibilities for wildlife
Interior*	U.S. Fish and Wildlife Service	Leading agency for conservation of migratory birds, certain mammals, and sport fishes; manages refuges and hatcheries; coordinates endangered species programs; administers federal aid to states; negotiates international agreements; works primarily from regional offices.
	National Park Service	Research and management of wildlife on national parks and monuments; coordinates Wild and Scenic Rivers System.
	Bureau of Land Management	Leading agency for managing lands in the public domain, primarily in western states; supervises multiple use, including wildlife, grazing, mining, recreation, timber, and watershed; about 55 percent of all federal lands are under Bureau of Land Management.
	Bureau of Indian Affairs	Trust for grazing, timber, water, and other resource management, including wildlife.
	Bureau of Reclamation	Leads programs for water development in western states; wildlife management and recreation considered in reclamation projects.
Agriculture†	Forest Service	Administers national forests and grasslands and wildlife thereon; research and management of all forest resources; fire protection and timber harvests are major concerns; regional experiment stations are activity centers.

In 1996 there was a total of 39.7 million participants in hunting and fishing activities in the United States (Table 18-2). The most popular activity was freshwater fishing, followed by big game hunting. Total expenditures on hunting activities in 1996 were estimated at about $72 billion. The total number of people participating in animal watching in that year was estimated at about 63 million, with $29 billion of related expenditures. Residential animal watching had three times the number of participants in nonresidential animal watching.[6]

We dealt with commercial hunting in effect, when we looked at marine resource economics in Chapter 13. The models we used there would carry over to terrestrial commercial hunting, for example, the trapping of animals for fur. The value of the harvested product in this case is established on a market, sim-

---

[6] Residential animal watching is defined as an activity that takes place within 1 mile of home.

TABLE 18-1—*Continued*
PARTIAL LISTING OF FEDERAL AGENCIES HAVING RESPONSIBILITIES
FOR WILDLIFE MANAGEMENT

Cabinet-level department	Agency name	Activities and responsibilities for wildlife
Agriculture†	Soil Conservation Service	Publishes soil surveys; provides data and technical assistance for soil and water conservation; no research activities; funds small watershed projects and assists with habitat development on private lands; works primarily with organized districts.
Commerce‡	National Marine Fisheries Service	Provides management, research, and other services for living marine resources, including mammals and invertebrates as well as marine fishes; lead agency in managing offshore development as component of National Oceanic and Atmospheric Administration.
Defense§	Army Corps of Engineers	Major responsibilities for dredging, stream stabilization, and other developments of navigable rivers and coastal wetlands; issues dredge and fill permits authorized by Section 404 of the Clean Water Act.

Source: National Wildlife Federation (1987) as reported in Eric G. Bolen and William L. Robinson, *Wildlife Ecology and Management,* 3rd ed., Prentice-Hall, Englewood Cliffs, NJ, 1995, p. 477.
*Other Department of Interior agencies in one way or another involved with wildlife management include: Bureau of Mines, U.S. Geological Survey, Office of Surface Mines, and the Office of Water Research and Technology.
†Other Department of Agriculture agencies with wildlife-related activities include Animal and Plant Health Inspection Service, Agricultural Stabilization and Conservation Service, and Economic Research Service.
‡Other Department of Commerce agencies with wildlife-related activities include the Office of Coastal Zone Management and the National Sea Grant College program; both are components of the National Oceanic and Atmospheric Administration.
§Other Department of Defense agencies (e.g., Department of the Air Force) also manage wildlife and other natural resources on military lands.

ilar to the market price of fish. Recreational hunting has the added factor that its value is related not only to the wildlife harvested, but also to the satisfaction derived from engaging in the activity itself. In fact, in many cases the greater part of the value of hunting may stem from engaging in the activity rather than in the number of wildlife harvested.

Conceptually, however, we can approach it in a similar way. In Figure 18-3, panel (a) represents the **growth relationship** of the wildlife being hunted. It has the standard U-shaped relationship between the stock level and the annual growth increment, thus s_0 is the stock level that would result in the long run if the animal (or plant) were not hunted. Any stock level lower than s_0 can be maintained indefinitely if the appropriate corresponding harvest level is correctly maintained.

TABLE 18-2
PARTICIPATION AND EXPENDITURES IN WILDLIFE-RELATED ACTIVITIES, 1996

	Number of participants (millions)	Expenditures ($ billion)
Sport fishing		
Freshwater	29.7	
Saltwater	9.4	
Sport hunting		
Big game	11.3	
Small game	6.9	
Migratory birds	3.1	
Other	1.5	
Total fishing and hunting*	39.7	71.9
Wildlife watching		
Residential	60.8	
Nonresidential	23.7	
Total wildlife watching*	62.9	29.2

*Totals do not equal the simple sum of constituent activities because people may engage in multiple activities.
Source: U.S. Fish and Wildlife Service, National Survey of Fishing, Hunting and Wildlife Associated Recreation, 1996.

An **effort-benefits** function for **recreational hunting** is shown in panel (b) of Figure 18-3. It is drawn to reflect the fact that people obtain benefits from the activity of hunting, not solely from the number of animals taken. By contrast, the figure also shows an **effort-revenue** function that would pertain if this were a strictly commercial harvest. In that case the value is tied directly to the number of animals harvested, which is the assumption used before to model a commercial fishery.[7] Note that the effort-benefits function and the effort-revenue function have the same end points; in the long run, hunters will not get benefits from hunting if success rates are always zero. But it is skewed to the right somewhat, because benefits arise from both the catch and the activity.

Figure 18-4 shows the effort-benefits function in combination with the function representing the costs of hunting; the former is labeled EB and the latter TC. The TC function is drawn under the assumption that each hunting day has the same cost. The open-access hunting level is e_1, which is very close to the zero-catch level of e_0. The latter is the effort level that drives the stock to, or near, extinction. The reason why open access would tend to be this close to the extinction point is, to repeat, the fact that hunters get benefits from the activity itself, not just from the catch. Because of excess effort levels, no net benefits are being produced by this particular wildlife population at effort level e_1. Total costs are high enough that they exactly equal total benefits. The effort level that maximizes net benefits, on the other hand, is e^*. This is the level where the

[7] See Chapter 13.

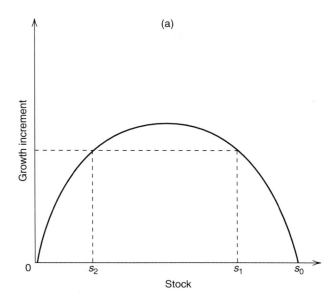

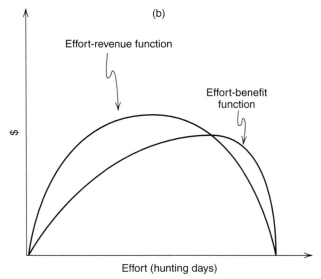

FIGURE 18-3
Stock-Growth and Effort-Benefits Functions for Recreational
Hunting

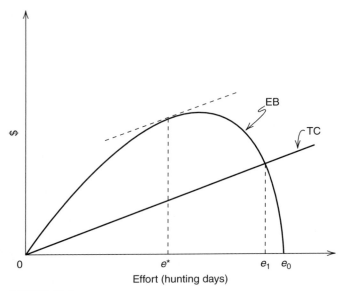

FIGURE 18-4
Efficient and Open-Access Hunting Levels

slope of the marginal cost curve (marginal cost) is equal to the slope of the EB curve (marginal benefits). Note that the efficient point involves lower levels of hunting but higher benefits than the open-access effort level.

High effort levels associated with open access suggest that some way is needed to control effort or the catch rate. Historically, authorities have tried to do this through command-and-control regulations. **Closed seasons** is one of these. The hope behind limiting the length of a hunting season, is that the number of hunting days will be reduced. How much this attains that objective, as opposed simply to compressing a given number of hunting days into a shorter time span, is an open question. In many places public authorities are using lotteries to control hunting effort. The state of Maine has a lottery to distribute moose hunting permits, as does Wyoming for distributing permits to hunt elk. Massachusetts uses a lottery to issue deer hunting permits for certain state-owned land.

Another common way of trying to reduce the impacts of open access is for public authorities to enforce **bag limits,** that is, a limitation on the number of wildlife that may be taken per trip or per year. A way of modeling this is to see it as a shift back in the effort-benefit function. By setting a bag limit, authorities attempt to reduce the benefits accruing to hunters on a typical hunting trip. In Figure 18-5, this is shown as a shift from the outer to the inner effort-benefit function (from EB_1 to EB_2). The open-access hunting level would move from e_1 to e_2. How much this changes depends on how much the effort-benefit function changes in response to the catch limitations. If the bulk of the benefits of hunting come from the activity rather than the size of the catch, the

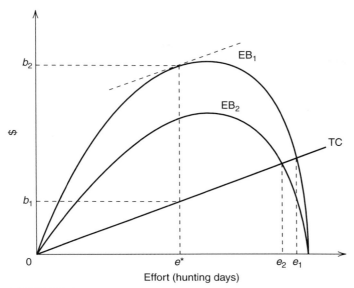

FIGURE 18-5
Policies for Controlling Hunting

relationship would not change much and the level of effort would not change much. The bag limit reduces the yield from a given number of hunting days. So though the effort level is reduced only modestly, the equilibrium size of the stock would increase. From an economic standpoint, however, the fact that there is open access, even with the bag limits, means that the effort level is still too high and net benefits are still zero. It is theoretically possible to lower the bag limit sufficient to shift the effort level back to e^*, even with open access. Net benefits would still be zero, however.

Private Ownership

Why doesn't the public wildlife management agency simply charge a price for access to the wildlife sufficiently high to shift effort levels back to e^*? State fish and game agencies typically sell hunting licenses or permits, but the prices of these are normally kept quite low for political reasons. Thus, hunting access is usually regulated through command-and-control regulations, such as bag limits, gear restrictions, and establishment of open seasons.

Private landowners, on the other hand, have the right to restrict access to their property. One possibility is to have landowners charge hunters for access and keep out those who are not willing to pay. If this could be done, and if the motives of these landowners were to maximize their net incomes, they would charge exactly the price that is needed to reduce effort to e^*. The economically efficient effort level e^* is the same effort level that would maximize the net incomes of the owners. The net income obtainable to the owners is an amount equal to $b_2 - b_1$.

With the population and income changes of recent decades, and with diminished stocks of many wildlife populations because of open-access problems, it is not surprising that privately provided hunting has started to become popular in the United States and elsewhere. It is widespread in the Southwest as well as on commercial timberland of the southern states.[8] A market for hunting big game on private land has also developed in many states of the American West and on a number of Native American reservations in the West. In this sense, the United States is catching up with Europe, where markets in privately provided hunting and fishing opportunities have existed for some time. Privatized hunting is also growing in Africa.

One important element of these markets is a factor we discussed above, the patterns of property rights in comparison with the location of the habitat for the game animals in question. Suppose there is a pattern similar to panel (a) of Figure 18-2. Here the bulk of the habitat is divided among a large number of landowners, each of whom owns only a small part of the total area. To privatize the hunting would require all the landowners to get together and agree on goals, procedures, and especially on how the total revenues would be shared among themselves. The transactions costs of doing this may simply be too high to overcome, especially if the projected revenues are not particularly great. If there is only a modest number of landowners, however, transactions cost may not be excessive. In some parts of the world new businesses have appeared whose specialty is contracting with a sufficient number of contiguous landowners to put together a large hunting territory, then managing the territory as a private hunting preserve.

The reservation of land for market-regulated hunting of wild, free-ranging animals blends into what can be called **game ranching,** where active management steps are undertaken to enhance the value of the wildlife stock. Such management practices as supplementary feeding, selective culling, and predator control may be used to increase the value of the stock of game animals. Of course to do these things effectively, it is important that the firms or agencies doing the managing have control over most of the habitat of the target wildlife.

The models used above are extremely simple and unrealistic in many ways. We use them simply to explore some of the basic aspects of recreational hunting. One factor that is common in the real world, but overlooked here, is that there will usually be other wildlife species, both plant and animal, that interact with the species being hunted. These other species may also be hunted, or perhaps are valuable in other ways, say, for habitat control or animal watching. The relevant effort-benefits function now becomes much more complex, because a relationship that contained all social benefits associated with hunting this species would have to take into account all these other impacts. This can be a problem in both publicly and privately provided hunting arrangements.

---

[8] Robert K. Davis, "A New Paradigm in Wildlife Conservation: Using Markets to Produce Big Game Hunting," in Terry L. Anderson and Peter J. Hill (eds.), *Wildlife in the Marketplace,* Rowmand and Littlefield Publishers, 1995, pp. 109–125.

WILDLIFE IN SUBURBAN AREAS

In most parts of the world urban areas are growing both demographically and in terms of area. For the most part it is a process of **suburbanization,** in which growth occurs on the fringes of expanding urban areas, to satisfy peoples' demands for single-family dwellings with an attached amount of surrounding space. Thus the common phenomenon of low-density housing developments spreading slowly, or sometimes rapidly, into lands that were previously uninhabited or used for farms. One effect of this has been to bring people into contact with the wildlife that were living on the suburban fringe. Coupled with this is the fact that in some parts of the country, such as the Northeast, changes in rural landscapes (e.g., the abandonment of farms) has allowed the reestablishment of some species in areas from which they previously had been pushed out. This has added to the likelihood of human/animal contacts as suburban development spreads.

There are two major dimensions of this phenomenon: (1) the biology, ecology, and population dynamics of the particular animal species at issue and (2) the human demography and attitudes that determine the social benefits and costs of animal populations in the suburbs. In extremely simple terms, we have pictured these two dimensions in Figure 18-6. Panel (a) shows the standard model of population growth. It says essentially that if nothing is done with respect to managing the particular animal in question, its population will settle at something around k_0. Population levels lower than this can be realized, but only if some amount of harvesting or stock reduction is pursued. To keep the population at a level of k^*, for example, would require that Δk^* of the animals be removed each year.

The population level k^* is chosen for a reason, as we can see by looking at panel (b) of the figure. This schematic presents the marginal benefits (marginal willingness to pay) by suburbanites at different stock levels and also the marginal costs associated with different population levels of the animal in question. The benefit function (labeled MWTP) summarizes peoples' attitudes about wildlife. It shows that they place a high initial value on this animal and that the value of a marginal animal declines as the animal population gets larger. This value is based on such factors as **existence value, hunting value,** or **viewing value.** The relationship—its height and shape—clearly will depend on the particular animal involved (deer vs. skunks, for example) and the size and characteristics of the human population involved.[9]

---

[9] For any species there may be indirect sources of value. These are animals (and it could also apply to plants) that are not particularly valuable to humans in themselves, but either support or diminish other species that are so valued. Mice may not be particularly desirable themselves, but they may be highly valued because they support other animals, such as foxes and hawks. In such cases the social value that is inherent in marginal willingness to pay is a **derived value.** The social value of the species is derived from the social value of the supported species that is essentially transmitted through the biological linkages connecting the different species in a particular ecosystem.

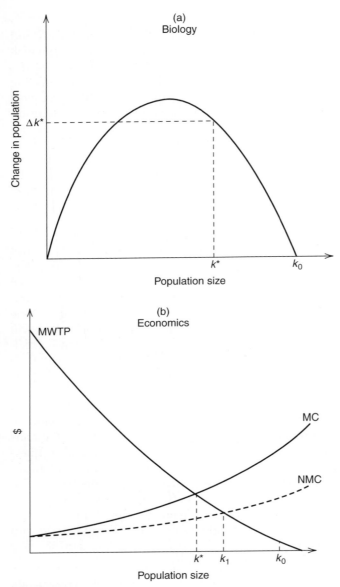

FIGURE 18-6
Wildlife in Suburban Areas

The marginal cost curve (labeled MC) shows the social costs of this stock of wildlife. Costs could arise from several factors. The animals could bring about changes in the ecosystem sufficient to produce costs for humans. A case of this, for example, is changes to a surface water system produced by beaver dams. Health costs may occur in some cases, such as threats of lyme disease from tick-carrying deer and rabbits. A major cause of damage in some regions is collisions between animals and automobiles. Physical threats to pets and children may be at issue, or perhaps damage to agricultural crops. Whatever the source of the costs, the MC curve is meant to encompass all the relevant ones present in the case at issue. On the basis of the marginal benefit and marginal cost curves indicated, the efficient animal population size is k^*. This is substantially below the nonintervention level of k_0, but in different circumstances and with different animals, of course, the relationship of these two stock levels could be quite different.

As it stands, the analysis says nothing about the actual costs of managing the animal stock, of removing a portion of the animal population if that is what is called for. This can be a contentious issue in itself, because many people and groups are committed to their views of humane treatment of animals, which may rule out certain approaches to animal removal. One way of modeling this is by deducting removal costs from the MC curve pictured. As a community moves to a lower population size, it does not experience a savings in cost indicated by the original MC curve, but by this amount minus the control costs. This would yield a **net MC curve** (labeled NMC), which is sketched in the figure as a dashed line under the MC curve. The new dashed marginal cost curve intersects the MWTP curve at k_1, which is to the right of k^*, indicating that when control costs are included, the efficient population size of the animal would be somewhat larger than when these costs are not taken into account. Exactly what these removal costs are is open to question. Certainly they include the opportunity costs of reducing the stock size. Exhibit 18-2 contains a newspaper account of a company organized to reduce the size of deer herds in suburban communities.

DISTRIBUTIONAL ISSUES IN RESTORATION AND PREDATOR CONTROL

In the analysis of the previous section we were assuming that members of a particular suburban community were both recipients of benefits and the bearers of costs associated with wildlife control. In many wildlife management programs, however, there is a major difference between groups of interested people: some groups being primarily beneficiaries and others being primarily bearers of cost.

In Minnesota the reestablishment of the gray wolf has been quite successful; as of 1998 there were well over 2,000 individuals in the state, and steps were being taken to delist the animal as an endangered species. This program is quite similar in concept to many other wildlife restoration programs. It confers existence value benefits on a widely dispersed group of people, both inside and outside of the state. And it leads to substantial costs for a relatively small group, in this case ranchers and farmers who experience depredation of their domestic livestock. Many cases involving the endangered species fit this type of pattern: diffuse benefits, concentrated costs.

The basic structure of the problem is depicted in Figure 18-7. The horizontal axis measures the stock size of an animal in a particular community, while the vertical axis contains a monetary scale. People who receive benefits from this stock are divided into two groups, a local group and everybody else. The local

EXHIBIT 18-2

SHARPSHOOTER AND ASSOCIATE KILL 50 DEER IN TOWN CULL

Don Ward

DUNE ACRES, Ind.—A professional sharpshooter and his associate killed 50 deer over the past week in the state's first municipal deer cull.

But additional deer kills probably will be considered necessary in future years to control the size of the herd, reduce vegetation damage and improve drivers' safety.

"We barely made a dent in our deer population, but at least we got through it. And maybe we set a precedent for other towns in Indiana, so they won't have to go through the legal expense of sorting it all out in court," said Town Council President Yolanda Stemer.

So far, no other towns have approached the Indiana Department of Natural Resources about conducting a deer kill, said spokesman Stephen Sellers.

The privately owned Hayes Arboretum in Richmond conducts an annual deer kill to protect the 179 plant species in the 355-acre nature preserve. And in 1994, Northern Indiana Public Service Co. employed the same sharpshooter used by Dune Acres, Anthony DiNicola of White Buffalo Inc., to thin the deer herd at a generating station in Wheatfield.

And the Department of Natural Resources itself has used supervised hunts in recent years to thin the deer population at several Indiana state parks.

Sellers said natural resources agency studies have shown a significant reduction in deer populations at those parks.

"We want a balance to be able to see deer and to hunt deer, but also to minimize the damage to crops and vegetation, and to reduce the number of accidents with vehicles," Sellers said.

Dune Acres might be breaking ground in Indiana, but it is hardly the nation's first city or town to do so.

For instance, DiNicola recently returned from Eden Prairie, Minn., an affluent Minneapolis suburb, where he killed 160 deer in two weeks.

The Pittsburgh suburb of Fox Chapel, meanwhile, has been using bow hunters to thin its deer herd because of the community's dense population.

But after killing 300 deer in three years, the town still had made only a small dent in its deer population. Despite protest, town officials planned to continue the program for at least six more years.

In nearby Illinois, some Chicago suburbs have been conducting their own deer culls for years using their own trained shooters, most of whom use guns and spotlights.

Officials in DuPage County, Ill., however, started killing deer in 1992 using a controversial method: catching deer with a net and then killing them with a bolt gun. After much opposition by animal rights groups, the county resorted to guns and spotlights.

"After five years of culling deer, we're just now getting the numbers down to where we want," said DuPage County Board member Patricia Bellock. "You have to stay at it for several years until a faster method comes along, especially because of the fact the deer give birth to two or three fawns at a time."

At Dune Acres, working without the aid of gun silencers and spotlights, DiNicola and an associate used .223-caliber bolt-action rifles and military-style night vision scopes to spot and kill deer. Accompanied at all times by Department of Natural Resources officials, the two fired from the back of a truck as it stopped at a dozen sites previously baited with corn.

The method was considered the best—and the quickest—by Town Council members.

"There's no sport or hunt in this," said Stemer. "It's the most efficient, humane solution to the problem."

Source: The Indianapolis Star, March 2, 1998. Reprinted by permission.

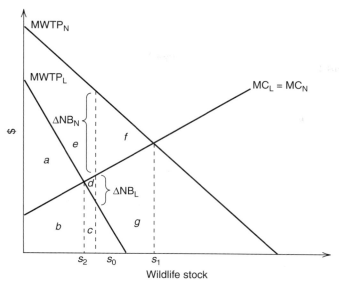

FIGURE 18-7
Wildlife Restoration

group consists of people who live in the vicinity of the animal community; $MWTP_L$ depicts the benefits this group receives from this wildlife. It could be expected to contain both market-type benefits (stemming from, for example, net revenues from animal spotting businesses) and nonmarket benefits. Ranchers in Florida whose livestock may be threatened by the Florida panther also appear to gain some satisfaction from knowing that panthers inhabit their lands.[10]

$MWTP_N$ represents the valuation of this animal by all nonlocals. We would suppose that this is primarily existence value, though some will be viewing value also by people who visit the area. Both MWTP curves are of traditional shape, that is, downward-sloping to the right.

The curve labeled $MC_L = MC_N$ represents two marginal cost curves—the marginal cost curve for the locals is assumed to be the same as for the nonlocals. Remember these are aggregate marginal cost curves for the two groups. Thus, although the damage per person is undoubtedly higher among the local group, there are fewer of them. And although the costs per person (e.g., in terms, say, of lost hunting values) are much lower for outsiders, there are far more of them than there are locals. Thus, the two marginal cost curves have been drawn as the same. The reason for this is to keep the graph relatively uncluttered.

The model shows a substantial discrepancy between the stock levels that are efficient from the standpoint of the local community and from the standpoint of the nonlocal group. These are, respectively, s_2 and s_1. The overall social efficiency level would lie between these two points. If current stock levels

[10] David S. Maehr, *The Florida Panther, Life and Death of a Vanishing Carnivore*, Island Press, Washington, DC, 1997.

were to the left of s_2 or to the right of s_1, there would be agreement between locals and nonlocals for building up the stock with a restoration program in the first case, and for reducing the stock in the second case.

But there would be conflicts for any stock level between s_2 and s_1. Suppose the actual stock level was s_0. Locals would be improved (i.e., their net benefits would increase) by a move to the left, whereas nonlocals would be improved by a move to the right. It's possible to determine the gains and losses from the diagram. For a small increase in the stock at s_0, nonlocals would experience a gain equal to the distance between $MWTP_N$ and MC_N, shown as the distance ΔNB_N (for change in net benefits to the nonlocal group). Locals would experience a reduction in net benefits equal to ΔNB_L. Since $\Delta NB_N > \Delta NB_L$, overall social efficiency would call for an increase in the stock size. As the stock size increases, ΔNB_N would diminish and ΔNB_L would increase, and at some stock size they would come into balance. This would identify the socially efficient size of the animal population.

How different s_0 and s_1 are, and how much adjustment of the actual stock would be required, and how much difference there is between net benefits to the two different groups, obviously depends, at least conceptually, on the shapes and slopes of the different curves. Even though we don't know them exactly, they can still be used to help us think about cases of wildlife management. In Alaska in recent years, state officials planned a wolf control project to reduce depredation of the state elk herds. In effect, their planning was done in accordance with the $MWTP_L$ and MC_L curves, as depicted in the figure, with little recognition that there might be a $MWTP_N$ curve well to the right, representing the values of people in the rest of the country for the existence of wolves in Alaska. After a notable political backlash from this nonlocal group, the Alaskan authorities were essentially forced to return to the drawing board and develop new plans.

Another idea that presents itself just from the logic of the diagram is the possibility of compensation. Suppose the initial population is at s_0. For a small increase in the stock size, $\Delta NB_N > \Delta NB_L$, implying that compensation could be paid by the nonlocals to the locals to cover their loss in net benefits and still leave positive net benefits for the nonlocals. In fact, compensation could be used to reduce the political opposition that locals might express for the program. In the Minnesota restoration program, for example, compensation is paid to ranchers for livestock killed by the wolves.

These are abstract notions, however, until they can be filled in with actual numbers from surveys or other types of economic analyses. An illustration is available from a recent national survey to assess the net benefits stemming from the reestablishment of wolves in Yellowstone National Park.[11] The researchers surveyed 335 local people (defined as people who lived in the three-

---

[11] See John W. Duffield and Chris J. Neher, "Economics of Wolf Recovery in Yellowstone National Park," Transactions of the Sixty-First North American Wildlife and Natural Resource Conference, 1996, pp. 285–292.

TABLE 18-3

BENEFITS AND COSTS TO LOCAL AND NONLOCAL PEOPLE FROM WOLF RESTORATION IN YELLOWSTONE NATIONAL PARK

	Local	Nonlocal	Total
Mean WTP* of supporters	$20.50	$8.92	
Mean WTP of nonsupporters	$10.80	$1.52	
Estimated number of supporters	391,204	50,152,416	50,543,620
Estimated number of nonsupporters	340,522	25,774,280	26,114,802
Total WTP of supporters†	$160,553	$8,956,130	$9,116,683
Total WTP of nonsupporters†	$68,718	$784,322	$853,040
Net benefits	$91,835	$8,171,808	$8,263,643

*WTP = willingness to pay.
†These numbers are calculated by assuming a perpetual income stream, discounted at 7 percent, that gave a present value equal to the one-time payments that respondents indicated as their willingness to pay. They are also adjusted to reflect an estimate that **actual willingness to pay** is only 28.6 percent of **stated willingness to pay;** this is based on the researchers' previous work on the relationship between stated and actual WTP.
   Source: John W. Duffield and Chris J. Neher, "Economics of Wolf Recovery in Yellowstone National Park," Transactions of the Sixty-First North American Wildlife and Natural Resource Conference, 1996, pp. 285-292.

state region of Wyoming, Montana, and Idaho) and 313 nonlocal individuals, asking them willingness-to-pay–type questions for wolf restoration in Yellowstone. The mean response levels of the surveyed individuals were then blown up to regional and national dimensions by using state and national population numbers. The results are shown in Table 18-3.

The respondents were broken into supporters and nonsupporters of the wolf restoration. If we assume that the willingness to pay by supporters represents benefits, and willingness to pay by nonsupporters[12] represents costs,[13] then we can interpret these numbers in terms of the areas shown in Figure 18-7. Benefits to locals ($a + b + c$ in the diagram) are $160,553, and their costs ($b + c + d$) are $68,718, leaving net benefits of $91,835. For nonlocals, benefits ($a + b + c + d + e + f + g$) equal $8,956,130, while costs ($b + c + d + g$) are $784,322, leaving a net of $8,171,808. Note, again, how much more the net benefits are for nonlocals as compared to locals. The reason for this is that the total number of nonlocals essentially swamps the number of locals, and so the net benefits to nonlocals is the most important determinant of overall net benefits. Note further, however, that net benefits to nonlocals are at least positive.

PUBLIC POLICY AND WILDLIFE MARKETS

The harvesting of wildlife, as well as much of the nonconsumptive appreciation of wildlife, is usually governed by, or influenced by, what happens in

[12] This is the willingness to pay by nonsupporters to have the restoration stopped or abandoned.
   [13] This basically assumes that no individuals will experience both benefits and costs from the restoration.

markets. This is clearly true of commercial harvesting. But it is increasingly true of noncommercial activities. The commercial packaging of sport hunting and fishing on private lands is a growing activity, as is ecotourism. What is more, illegal markets often thrive in places where conservation regulations cannot be enforced with vigor. This means in many cases that we must look to the operation of those legal and illegal markets for an understanding of the forces that are pushing toward or away from conservation. An understanding of these markets can give us valuable perspective on how best to conserve wildlife resources in ways that are efficient and equitable.

To illustrate this let us look at two elements of African wildlife, the elephant and the black rhinoceros.[14] Several decades ago these animals were widely hunted for elephant ivory and rhino horn, which had high value in world markets. But growing scarcities of the animals led to concern about their long-run survival prospects. Conservation groups such as the World Wildlife Fund and the International Union for the Conservation of Nature were instrumental in getting a ban on rhino horn (1977) and later on elephant ivory (1989). The bans were carried out under the Convention on International Trade in Endangered Species.

The reason for the market ban was to take away the incentives for hunters to kill these animals for their horn and ivory. In fact, the ban on ivory has been quite successful, leading to substantial increases in elephant numbers and greatly reduced concern for their long-run survival.[15] The rhino horn ban, however, has been a disaster for the black rhino. Illegal rhino hunting ("poaching") has continued and even grown in intensity, enforcement has been insufficient, and black rhino populations have continued a precipitous decline.

The question is: Why the difference? Why has the ban worked with one animal and not with the other? The reason is that there are big differences between the factors affecting the supply and demand for ivory and those affecting rhino horn. The differences can be seen in Figure 18-8. Panel (a) shows very generally the situation in the ivory market, and panel (b) illustrates the horn market. Each model contains two supply (marginal cost) curves and two demand (marginal willingness-to-pay) curves. In each case, D_1 is the demand curve prior to the ban and D_2 is the demand curve after the ban. The bans, in other words, have the effect of reducing the demand for the products in world trade. Accompanying the bans are laws making it illegal to hunt the animals in question. This has the effect of raising the harvest marginal cost curves in the two cases, from the lower one, which is applicable before the ban, to the upper one, labeled S (poachers). The regulations against hunting, in other words, do not end the activity; they just make it somewhat more expensive be-

---

[14] The inspiration for this example comes from Gardner Brown and David Layton, "Saving Rhinos," paper given at the meetings of the Association of Environmental and Resource Economists, Annapolis, MD, June 1997.

[15] This is a judgment from the standpoint of the international community; from that of the African communities who might see elephants more as a potential source of economic wealth the judgment might be different.

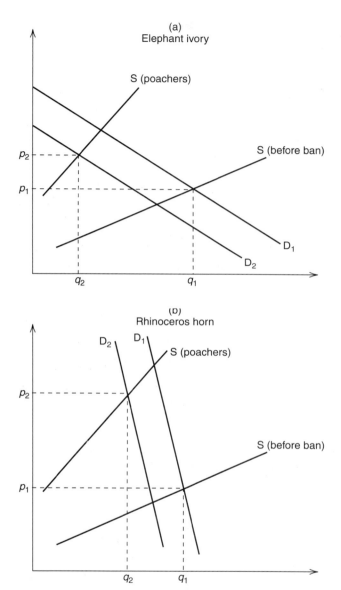

FIGURE 18-8
The Markets for Elephant Ivory and Rhinoceros Horn

cause of the possible costs of getting caught and punished; in effect, they shift up the supply functions.

The major underlying difference between the two markets is the slopes of the demand curves. In the ivory market it is relatively flat, whereas in the horn market it is quite steep. The basic reason for this is that there are relatively good substitutes for elephant ivory, but not for rhino horn. Ivory is used primarily for tourist carvings and for such specialty items as piano keys. These items have relatively good substitutes; in fact, an environmental group was instrumental in helping develop a plastic substitute for ivory piano keys. Good substitutes mean that the ivory demand curve will be relatively flat, because modest price increases will cause many consumers of ivory to shift to substitute materials. The major result that follows from this is that when the ivory ban is put in place, demand shifts back and supply shifts upward; the overall increase in market price is modest, but there is a large dropoff in quantity bought and sold. The ban, in other words, produces a substantial drop in quantity at a relatively small increase in price.

The rhino market is different. The demand for rhino horn comes mainly from its supposed medicinal value. In some Asian countries there are many medicinal recipes for which rhino horn is an essential ingredient; in effect it has no ready substitutes. The impact of this is that the market demand curve for rhino horn is quite steep. Increased prices do not lead to substantial decreases in quantity demanded. Thus, the ban on rhino horn will have a very different impact from the one on ivory. The rhino horn demand curve shifts back because of the ban, and the supply function shifts upward to the illegal poachers supply. There is a large increase in price for rhino horn, and a relatively small drop in quantity sold and bought. The ban does little, then, for reducing the quantities of rhino horn traded, so the rhino remains threatened by high rates of harvest.

The major lesson to get from this discussion is that simple attempts by regulators to intervene and change the way a market operates can have very different impacts, depending on the basic structure of supply and demand factors in those markets. This should be a cautionary note that market intervention, if it is to be at all successful, has to be done with good knowledge of the parameters of the markets affected, not only the primary market in which intervention is carried out, but also of markets for closely related goods and services.

SUMMARY

Wildlife management issues have become much more prominent in recent years. Increasing population growth has brought about greater contacts between humans and wildlife, and value changes among wealthier populations giving wildlife a higher priority in public decisions. To manage wildlife efficiently and effectively requires information from wildlife biologists combined with that from economics and other social perspectives. **Wildlife law** has developed in ways consistent with other dimensions of social change. In the United States, wildlife has been regarded as essentially an **open-access resource,** available to whoever gets there first. Open access, coupled with habitat loss, have led to substantial declines in many species of wildlife. This has led, among other things, to an expanded system of **wildlife refuges** here and elsewhere. It has also led to the growth of **private provision** of wildlife access, for hunting or viewing. The management of wildlife in **suburban** areas is becoming an increasing problem. **Wildlife restoration** and **predator control** programs have important distributional characteristics, usually consisting of benefits that are spread widely among a population and costs that are borne by a relatively small subgroup of the population. An investigation of several African wildlife restoration programs highlighted how important it is to have knowledge about the markets that one is trying to manage.

KEY TERMS

Wildlife biology	Suburbanization
Open-access resources	Recreational hunting
Private provision of wildlife benefits	Closed seasons
Distributional impacts of wildlife management programs	Bag limits
	Game ranching
Management of suburban wildlife	Existence, hunting, and viewing values

QUESTIONS FOR FURTHER DISCUSSION

1 If access to a hunting area is rationed by price, we can be sure that the level of visitation that results will maximize the social net benefits of the activity. If the same activity level is determined by lottery, however, we cannot be sure of this. Explain why not.
2 The bioeconomic models used in wildlife economics are based on biological growth processes. How would the basic model change in a case like recreational trout fishing where the replenishment process is one of stocking by humans?
3 In determining the optimal stock levels for suburban wildlife, whose preferences should count, everybody's or just the people living in the particular suburb under analysis?
4 Suppose an elk herd is to be managed for the benefits it produces for hunters. Would you expect that management decisions would be different if a public agency is in charge of the operation as compared to a private firm?
5 Apply the concept of price elasticity of demand, as discussed in Chapter 17, to the two elements of African wildlife, the elephant and the black rhinoceros.
6 For the situation depicted in Figure 18-4, the state is going to use a lottery to choose e^* hunters who will each be allowed to hunt one day. If the state wishes to maximize the amount of revenue it can obtain from this system, what price should it set for each permit?

USEFUL WEB SITES

The primary federal agency for wildlife resources:

• U.S. Fish and Wildlife Service in the Department of Interior (http://www.fws.gov)

Virtually all states have wildlife agencies, e.g.,

• Montana: Department of Fish, Wildlife, and Parks (http://www.fwp.state.mt)

- California: Department of Fish and Game (http://www.dfg.ca.gov)
- North Carolina: Wildlife Resources Commission (http://www.wildlife.state.nc)

Public interest groups provide useful information on policy issues and a wide range of wildlife populations:

- National Audubon Society (especially for birds) (http://www.audubon.org)
- World Wildlife Fund (http://www.wwf.org)
- National Fish and Wildlife Foundation (http://www.nfwf.org)

A number of organizations are devoted to specific species or populations, for example:

- Ducks Unlimited (http://www.ducks.org)

SELECTED READINGS

Anderson, Terry L., and Peter J. Hill (eds.): *Wildlife in the Marketplace*, Rowmand and Littlefield, Lanham, MD, 1995.

Brown, Gardner: "Wildlife in Developing Countries," in Partha Dasgupta and Karl-Göran Mäler, *The Environment and Emerging Development Issues*, Vol. 2, Clarendon Press, Oxford, England, 1997, pp. 555–573.

Decker, Daniel, and Gary Goff: *Valuing Wildlife: Economic and Social Perspectives*, Westview Press, Boulder, CO, 1987.

Dixon, John, and Paul Sherman: *Economics of Protected Areas: A New Look at Benefits and Costs*, Island Press, Washington, DC, 1990.

Eltringham, S. K.: *Wildlife Resources and Economic Development*, John Wiley, New York, 1984.

Hammack, Judd, and Gardner Brown: *Waterfowl and Wetlands: Toward Bioeconomic Analysis*, Johns Hopkins Press, Baltimore, 1974.

Jewell, Peter A., and Sidney Holt: *Problems in Management of Locally Abundant Wild Mammals*, Academic Press, New York, 1981.

McCullough, Dale R. (ed.): *Metapopulations and Wildlife Conservation*, Island Press, Covelo, CA, 1996.

Porter, Douglas R., and David A. Salvesen (eds.): *Collaborative Planning for Wetlands and Wildlife: Issues and Examples*, Island Press, Covelo, CA, 1995.

Tober, James A.: *Who Owns the Wildlife, The Political Economy of Wildlife in Nineteenth Century America*, Greenwood Press, Westport, CT, 1981.

Tober, James A.: *Wildlife and the Public Interest*, Praeger, New York, 1989.

CHAPTER **19**

THE ECONOMICS OF BIODIVERSITY PRESERVATION

Twenty years ago the word **biodiversity** did not exist. Now it is a household word and a major focus of research in biology and ecology.[1] It refers to the **variation** that exists at all levels of biological organization: variation among individuals in a species, among species in a community, among communities in an ecosystem, and among ecosystems themselves. This variation is critical to the continued existence of life itself, not only the lives of the millions of organisms that make up the biological world, but also the life of the top predator in that world, human beings.

The normal very long run cadence of biological existence is that species develop, exist for a few million years, and then disappear. Over the billions of years that life has existed on earth, therefore, almost all species that once existed have become extinct. But evolution is relentless and profuse. Thus at the present time more species are alive on earth than ever before. Why then should the disappearance of species, a major phenomenon within diversity change, be a problem today? It is a problem because we (humans) apparently have touched off a new and massive species die-off. In the prehistory of the world there have been other times when biodiversity disappeared in a major way. Paleontologists have identified five previous mass extinctions during

---

[1] It is the work of Edward O. Wilson that has done much to spread the concern about diversity loss and its consequences. See his award-winning book: *The Diversity of Life*, Harvard University Press, Cambridge, MA, 1992.

each of which there was a major, rapid spasm of species extinction. The last one, about 65 million years ago, killed off the dinosaurs and many marine and flying reptiles. What is new about today's decline is that it is not the working out of the consequences of some natural event like the striking of an asteroid that apparently caused the last one, but the result of massive human demographic growth and the technologies of economic maintenance and expansion that people are using. Although much of the popular press, as well as scientific attention, has focused on diversity among animals, diversity losses among plants is also a threat, as Exhibit 19-1 discusses.

What can economics say about diversity preservation? Many people think it can't, or shouldn't, have much to say on the subject. When the U.S. Congress enacted the original Endangered Species Act in 1973, it specifically forbade the bringing in of economic considerations into decisions about protecting specific species. And many biologists believe that economics, with its focus on the study of **trade-offs,** is not suitable, either analytically or morally, as a framework for studying biodiversity problems and making decisions about biodiversity resources.[2]

In this chapter we consider biodiversity protection and conservation using the analytical tools of economics. Usually in analyses of this type we start with concepts and principles, and then proceed to a discussion and evaluation of recent public policy initiatives. It might be interesting in the present case to reverse this order. Accordingly we will start off with a discussion of the U.S. Endangered Species Act. This will alert us to some of the difficulties that stand in the way of effective diversity preservation, which will then open the way for addressing some principles that might be applicable to this policy space.

THE ENDANGERED SPECIES ACT

The best-known effort in the United States to preserve biodiversity has been the **Endangered Species Act of 1973** (ESA). Several previous federal statutes had addressed species preservation.[3] Among other things, these forerunner acts authorized the federal government to purchase land for the preservation of threatened species and to preserve these habitats "insofar as practicable." This language in effect allowed the relevant public agencies to weigh the **expected benefits** of species protection with the **expected costs** of that protection.

The ESA was enacted in the early 1970s. That was a time of strong environmental activism at the federal level—a time when a number of other major environmental laws were passed. The spirit of that time among many political participants was that the environment needed massive new protection regardless of the cost. The ESA was written accordingly. It basically said that federal agencies were to protect endangered and threatened species at all costs,

---

[2] See, for example, many of the papers in E. O. Wilson (ed.), *Biodiversity,* National Academy Press, Washington, DC, 1988.

[3] In particular the 1916 National Park Services Act, the Endangered Species Preservation Act of 1966, and the Endangered Species Conservation Act of 1969.

EXHIBIT 19-1

1 OF 8 PLANT SPECIES AT RISK OF EXTINCTION

A 20-year worldwide study by scientists, conservation organizations, botanical gardens and museums claims that one out of eight plant species is at risk of extinction.

Titled the "Red List of Threatened Plants," the 800-plus page report stated that 12.5 percent, or 34,000, of the world's plant species are threatened.

Major studies were conducted in North America, Australia and Southern Africa, but coverage of the rest of Africa, Asia, the Caribbean and South America was fragmentary.

In the 200 countries studied, 33,798 species of the 270,000 vascular plants are considered at risk of extinction. Vascular plants include ferns, conifers and flowering plants.

Ninety-one percent of the species named are found in a single country.

In the United States, the most-studied country, the study indicated that 29 percent of the nation's 16,000 plant species are at risk of extinction.

The findings in the Red List should sound alarm bells around the world, said John C. Sawhill, president and CEO of the Nature Conservancy. He blamed loss of habitat and introduction of alien or non-native plant species as two main factors for the rapid loss of plant life.

David Bracket, chairman of the Species Survival Commission, said the numbers are staggering because they are the organisms on which humans depend for food, clothing and medicines.

Brian Parsons of the Holden Arboretum said that the Center for Plant Conservation figures agreed, indicating that 200 years of existence in this country have resulted in bringing slightly more than one-fourth of flora to the brink of extinction, but that most of these are in Hawaii and California.

These states have more diversity of plants and many that grow nowhere else in the country.

"Everyone's actions have an impact on the environment," Parsons said. "One in eight plants is threatened with extinction in the next 10 to 20 years. For every plant that goes extinct, 10 organisms will go extinct with it."

Cusick said that in Ohio, the northern wild monkshood and the Lakeside daisy are the rarest plants.

Ohio and the Midwest are examples of human development taking away habitats, Cusick said. "I think that there are few rare plants; there are rare habitats," he said. "If you have a habitat, you have a plant community."

"Eventually the most common habitat can become rare, if destroyed. Beech and maple forests are the most common, but it is hard to find a good-quality beech and maple forest because it is a limited resource."

Cusick believes the supply of white oaks will become critical in a few decades. "They are extensively used, and not a fast-growing species. There is a dearth of young oak trees."

Only two old growth oak forests are left in Ohio, Cusick said, one in Fulton County and one in Wayne County.

However, Jim Bissell of the Cleveland Museum of Natural History said that the work of museum staff and volunteers has resulted in some plants being reduced from high on the list of rarity to less threatened, as populations were found in more areas.

Source: The Plain Dealer, May 16, 1998.

notwithstanding any questions about the "practicability" of their actions. The law also says that the determination that a species is threatened or endangered is to be made strictly on grounds of biological science and that private individuals everywhere are prohibited from "taking" individuals from any species designated as endangered.

To gain protection, a species must be **listed** as "endangered" or "threatened." An individual, agency, or any other entity may propose a species for listing. After negotiating an involved process of data gathering, public hearings, and comments, the Secretary[4] may list the candidate species as endangered or threatened. When a species is listed, it is critical to specify the habitat, which is the geographical area that is essential for the survival of the species. The administering agencies, the U.S. Fish and Wildlife Service and the National Marine Fisheries Service, must then develop **recovery plans,** detailing the actions required to bring about the recovery of the listed species. Species residing in domestic or foreign lands and waters may also be listed.

The ESA has been controversial throughout its history and probably will continue to be so. Shortly before it became law, a small fish, the **snail darter,** was found in waters below the construction site of a new, large federally financed dam being constructed on the Little Tennessee River. Construction on the dam was halted by court order, the judge essentially saying that it really didn't matter how big and economically important the dam would be, or how small and apparently inconsequential the snail darter was, the clear language of the ESA required the protection of species—any species—at all costs. The subsequent fight in Congress and the U.S. Supreme Court led to the 1978 amendments to the ESA. They created a cabinet-level committee (nicknamed the **God Squad**), which can grant exemptions to the provisions of the ESA if the project:

1 is of regional or national significance
2 has no reasonable or prudent alternatives
3 is one that clearly outweighs the alternatives

Although the committee originally voted against the snail darter exemption, Congress did approve an exemption, and the dam project went forward.

Controversy and conflict over the Endangered Species Act have usually been conducted in absolutes and extremes, one side stressing the need to do whatever it takes to avoid ecosystem collapse, and the other side talking about economic collapse if the law is enforced. Although the original act precluded economic considerations in the actual listing decisions, one way they were smuggled in was in the language applying to the development of habitat protection plans. The Secretary of the Interior, in specifying a critical habitat for an endangered or threatened species, may take economic factors into account

---

[4] The actual criteria the Secretary of the Interior is supposed to use in listing an endangered species are: (1) present or threatened destruction of habitat, (2) overutilization of the species, (3) disease or predation, (4) the inadequacy of existing legislation, and (5) other natural or manmade factors.

and may, for example, exclude a particular region from designation as critical habitat if the benefits would outweigh the costs of so doing. This is not enough to mollify the critics of the ESA, however. What seems to have gradually become clear is that the main issue is not the total social cost of preserving endangered species, but how these costs are distributed. Although the benefits of the law are distributed widely throughout society, its costs are concentrated on a small but vocal minority. We return to this below.

In recent years efforts have also been under way to change the way the law is administered for another major reason. It has become clear that attacking the problem species by species may not be the best way of carrying out the intent behind the law. Rather, the focus should be on preserving strategic ecosystems as a whole. This, and the cost distribution problem mentioned above, has led the Clinton Administration to pursue more aggressively an idea called **habitat conservation plans** (HCPs) on private lands, where 80 percent of endangered species are to be found. These are voluntary, binding agreements between private landowners and public agencies. Landowners agree to undertake some conservation efforts on their properties, perhaps leaving large amounts undeveloped or particularly sensitive portions untouched. In return the agency agrees to let the landowner use some portion of the property, even if it leads to an **incidental taking** of some endangered or threatened species. The government further agrees to refrain from enforcing new regulations on the property throughout the life of the plan (perhaps several decades) even if new biological information later becomes available suggesting that further steps are needed to protect a species.

Needless to say, HCPs are controversial. Many in the environmental community feel that they won't provide sufficient species protection; many landowners are still leery of the idea of trying to conclude permanent agreements with highly politicized public agencies. And many ecologists are concerned that the system does not recognize the need for continued flexibility as more biological information becomes available and nature continues to respond in unpredictable ways, as it often does.

Has the ESA been effective? Table 19-1 shows a box score, as of mid-1997, of listed threatened and endangered species. A total of 1,664 species have been listed, of which 1,104 were domestic; 876 of these domestic species were listed as endangered, 228 as threatened. Of the 876 endangered domestic species, 539 were plants, 337 were animals. The relevant federal agencies have endangered species divisions that consider new listings, but budgetary limitations place a limit on the rate with which this can be accomplished. Of course the listing process has also become filled with political controversy over the years. Notice also from Table 19-1 that, of the 1,664 species listed as endangered or threatened, less than half (700) have recovery plans.

Beyond the simple box score of the listing numbers, have the listings made sense in terms of which particular species have been listed and which have not? The U.S. Fish and Wildlife Service has been criticized for being overly political in its listing decisions, but given the dearth of hard information on val-

TABLE 19-1
SPECIES LISTED AS ENDANGERED AND THREATENED AS OF JULY 31, 1997

	Endangered		Threatened			
Group	U.S.	Foreign	U.S.	Foreign	Total species	Species with plans
Mammals	57	251	7	16	331	39
Birds	75	178	15	6	274	72
Reptiles	14	65	18	14	111	30
Amphibians	9	8	7	1	25	11
Fishes	67	11	41	0	119	74
Snails	15	1	7	0	23	18
Clams	56	2	6	0	64	44
Crustaceans	15	0	3	0	18	6
Insects	24	4	9	0	37	21
Arachnids	5	0	0	0	5	4
Animals subtotal	337	520	113	37	1,007	319
Flowering plants	511	1	113	0	625	360
Conifers	2	0	0	2	4	1
Ferns and others	26	0	2	0	28	20
Plant subtotal	539	1	115	2	657	381
Grand total	876	521	228	39	1,664	700*

*There are 457 approved recovered plans—some plans cover more than one species, and some species have more than one plan.
Source: United States Fish and Wildlife Service, Division of Endangered Species, 1997, as cited in Gardner M. Brown, Jr., and Jason F. Shogren, "Economics of the Endangered Species Act," *Journal of Economic Perspectives*, 17(3), Summer 1998, p. 7.

ues, costs, and other factors weighing on these decisions, it's hard to see how they could be otherwise. Studies clearly seem to show that, other things equal, if an animal is a mammal or a bird, it has a better chance of being listed than if it is a reptile or an amphibian.[5] The term that has been invented to describe this bias is "**charismatic megafauna**," which refers to large, usually attractive species that for one reason or another capture the attention and affection of the public, like wolves, bald eagles, whooping cranes, and the like.

Despite this type of bias, can it be said that the Endangered Species Act has been effective? Views differ of course, often greatly, depending on what side of the political issue one happens to be on. Two economists[6] who have studied the law and its implementation offer the following assessment.

Measuring the effectiveness of the Act requires one to decide when to declare victory. Should it be when a listed species is taken off the list? When a declining trend

[5] See Andrew Metrick and Martin L. Weitzman, "Conflicts and Choices in Biodiversity Preservation," *Journal of Economic Perspectives*, 12(3), Summer 1998, pp. 21–34.
[6] Gardner M. Brown, Jr., and Jason F. Shogren, "Economics of the Endangered Species Act," *Journal of Economic Perspectives*, 17(3), Summer 1998, p. 10.

is reversed? When the rate of extinction is slowed? When critical habitat is protected so as to prevent species from declining to the point of being considered for listing? Although the answers to these questions are unclear and notwithstanding our pleasure from keeping favorite species like the bald eagle around, only one with modest expectations would give the Endangered Species Act a high performance rating.

Since the inception of the Act in 1973, 11 species of more than 1,000 listed have recovered and have been removed from the list, including the eastern states brown pelican, Utah's Rydberg milk-vetch, and the California gray whale. Species down listed to threatened from endangered include the Aleutian Canada goose, greenback cutthroat trout, Virginia round-leaf birch and bald eagle. According to the Environmental Defense Fund, less than 10 percent of the listed species have exhibited an improved status and the status of four times that amount is declining. For example, the population of Attwater's prairie-chicken, listed in 1967, has dropped to 42 in 1996 from 2,254 birds in 1975. The ratio of declining species to improving species is 1.5 to 1 on federal lands, and 9 to 1 on private lands.

Funding for the endangered species program of the Fish and Wildlife Service has failed to keep pace with the number of listed species, with the result that the real budget per species is 60 percent of its 1976 level. The Office of Endangered Species has inadequate funds to assay the status of about one-third of the listed species.

How the Endangered Species Act fares in the future will depend on the ebb and flow of political events in federal and state governments. Our job here must be to back away from the political controversies and consider the phenomenon as a problem of social choice. What factors determine the extent to which decisions made to protect endangered species will or will not advance overall social welfare? There are many who regard this as an overly "human-centric" approach to the problem. Drawing a line in the sand—"all species have a right to exist"—is heroic, but not the way real people live. As far as we know, humans are the only creatures on the globe that are blessed, or cursed, with the ability to make decisions by consciously looking at alternatives and choosing the one that is in some sense the best. How should we choose in this case?

THE NOAH PROBLEM

A good way of getting into this is to consider the **Noah problem.**[7] This is essentially a parable that can be used to focus on the core issues of biological diversity preservation and the factors to be considered when making preservation decisions. Noah has been told of the coming flood. He and his sons and daughters have constructed an ark which, though immense, is not unlimited in capacity.[8] They now select species of animals and plants to put in the ark.

[7] Not to be confused with the **Noah principle,** which has been put forth by David Ehrenfeld, a biologist, on the assumption that Noah had room enough for anything. It says that all species, without exception, should be protected at all costs, and especially without regard to human values. See D. W. Ehrenfeld, "The Conservation of Non Resources," *American Scientists*, Vol. 64, 1976, pp. 648–656.

[8] According to the Bible it is $300 \times 50 \times 30 = 450,000$ cubits^3, where a cubit is the length of the forearm to the tip of the middle finger, or about 18 inches. So the ark was about 1.5 million cubic feet, or roughly the size of a modern destroyer.

But there are simply too many species in total to put in the ark. One might conclude simply that a bigger ark is needed, but the same problem would arise because literally all the world's species cannot fit in an ark. Nor is post-poning the flood a practicable alternative, since this is out of Noah's hands.

The question is: Which species should Noah load onto the ark before bat-tening down the hatches? He could just take them first-come, first-served, or just select those which look cute and cuddly, as the U.S. Fish and Wildlife Ser-vice is accused of doing. Or he could use a more complicated **decision rule** to make the decision. Of all the species extant, he needs a means of deciding which should be allowed aboard and which should not. If his desire is to pick species so as to maximize social welfare in some sense, what criteria should he use for the selection? Of course, Noah's choice problem is analogous to soci-ety's problem in choosing species preservation programs. Consider the factors affecting the benefits and costs of including particular species. On the benefit side there are two types of factors:

1 The effects that including a species on the ark will have on its survival probability
2 The social value of the species, using whatever criteria are important for measuring social worth

On the cost side we have:

3 The social opportunity cost of including the species

Let us consider each of these factors.

Impacts on Survival

A critical first piece of information needed is **survival probabilities,** on and off the ark. In Noah's case we could perhaps assume that any species included on the ark will assuredly survive, while any species off the ark would just as assuredly disappear. The assumed survival probabilities, in other words, are 1.0 and 0, respectively. This is not an accurate reflection of reality, at least today. In real-world species protection programs survival probabilities are hardly ever at such extremes, rather they are intermediate, and the question becomes how much will they be increased by particular types of conservation programs or decreased by certain habitat-disrupting activities.

It's important to emphasize this perspective. If we are designing species conservation programs, we ought to consider survival (or alternatively, extinc-tion) probabilities **with and without** the programs. Suppose we have two species, A and B. If no efforts are made at preservation, species A has a 100-year survival probability of 30 percent (i.e., a 70 percent chance of becoming extinct during the next century), whereas for B the survival probability is 10 percent. Suppose we have $1 million to spend on just one preservation pro-gram (that is, Noah has room for just one more species on the ark). Which species should we spend it on? You might think that species B ought to be chosen, because it is the most highly endangered. But suppose the best-designed preservation programs in the two cases would increase survival probabilities to 90 percent for A and 20 percent for B. We can double the survival probability of B, but triple it for A. If we can only afford one program, which should it be?

Survival probabilities, with and without various types of preservation programs, are the province of biologists and ecologists. Enormous progress has been made in the understanding of biodiversity relationships and the population dynamics of some species. It's clearly too much to expect that survival probabilities soon will be available for a large number of the world's species. In fact, nobody knows with a high degree of accuracy yet how many species actually exist. So survival probabilities may be hard to come by, except for certain individual species that attract a lot of political and scientific interest, such as whooping cranes and spotted owls.

Having said this, however, we must stress that **some general notion** of survival probabilities, for individual species, or perhaps groups of species in a region, and the way they are impacted by human activities of different types, is important in trying to make reasonable decisions about diversity preservation. Noah can make the choice between A and B in two ways, by flipping a coin or by trying to reflect on the qualities of the two species and what inclusion or exclusion from the ark would mean for each of them.

The Benefits of Survival: Individual Species

What is the social value of a species? This is a controversial question. We could try to avoid it. Noah might try to make a decision on something other than species value, for example, by looking at species survival rates, as mentioned above. He would select the species for which the survival probability was increased the most by inclusion on the ark. With two similar species, this might be reasonable. But suppose species B is a domesticated animal used for an energy source, say, a horse, while species A is a nasty microorganism, such as the smallpox bacteria. Now it's unreasonable to treat them as equal in value. We could treat this strictly as a scientific exercise. Noah could admit species that in his judgment, as an ecologist, would contribute most to an ecosystem that functions in a certain way. But this would appear to smuggle human values into the problem, because Noah would be making decisions on the basis of his vision of a desirable world. Thus the logic of intelligent species diversity preservation requires that we consider the value of species, that is, the benefits that would flow from species preservation.

The value of a species can be broken down into two parts:

1 The value of a species in itself
   a Commercial, or market, value
   b Nonmarket value
2 The value of a species because of its relationship to other species.

The first of these is relatively easy to think about, at least conceptually, though it may be very difficult to measure in practice. There are certain obvious sources of value for particular wildlife species. Certain species have a commercial value when harvested, such as fish; or when linked to **ecotourism,** such as whale watching. Recreational use may also be consumptive or nonconsumptive, like hunting vs. bird watching. Among plants, certain wild species may have value because they have useful genes, which when transferred to commercial crops will impart desirable properties in terms of characteristics such as of disease resistance or growth rates. A much-emphasized source of commercial value is as a basis for pharmaceutical products. Examples of the latter are the rare rosy periwinkle, which is the source of an effective drug to treat leukemia, and the Pacific yew tree, which is the source of a drug to treat ovarian cancer. In 1996 the market for this cancer drug was estimated at about $1 billion.[9] It is relatively easy to measure the economic value of commercialized species, because people are registering their willingness to pay in organized markets, for food, medicines, and outdoor recreation.

But while numerous individual species have been discovered, ex post facto, to contain chemicals useful to humans, the real question in species preservation is how should we make decisions about the preservation of species with **unknown characteristics.** Here we run into a variant of what is called in economics the **diamond-water paradox.** Something that is very valuable in total need not be valuable on the margin. Water is necessary for life, both biologically and, in practical terms, for public health. Diamonds are not necessary in the same way; apart from a few industrial uses they are primarily devoted to jewelry. Yet diamond prices are very high while the price of a gallon of water is, in general, very low. Prices, in other words, do not seem to reflect the biological realities of the situation. The answer to this riddle is that prices are a reflection of **marginal value,** not **total value.** In graphical terms, marginal value is the height of the marginal willingness-to-pay curve at a point, whereas total value is the area under the curve up to that point. It's quite possible to have an item, like water, which has a relatively low marginal value but a very high total value. And vice versa, as in the case of diamonds.[10]

Let us apply this to the phenomenon of **species prospecting.** Suppose that we are looking for a particular chemical compound for a specific pharmaceuti-

---

[9] R. Norton, "Owls, Trees and Ovarian Cancer," *Fortune,* February 5, 1995, p. 49.

[10] The apparent counterparable to the diamond/water paradox is the airplane rivet story. Individual species extinctions are likened to pulling individual rivets out of an airplane. For a while nothing happens, because there is a redundancy in the number of rivets in the airplane. So the persons popping the rivets develop a false understanding of the value of the marginal rivet; since the airplane still flies, it must be true that the marginal rivet has no value. A point is reached, however, where one more popped rivet leads to a catastrophe. But airplanes are not nature. Airplanes are designed by humans, and one trade-off that is analyzed carefully is the number of rivets (strength) vs. weight (speed). The more rivets the stronger, but slower, the airplane, other things equal. It would be foolish to start popping rivets when you know the number of rivets is already optimized. It probably won't take many, as the histories of several air crashes have revealed. The fact that there are few redundant rivets in airplanes does not generalize to the natural world.

cal use and that once we have found it in one species, we won't have to look any further. We might call this the **needle-in-a-haystack** type of search. Now suppose that there are 1 million species and that we believe one of them contains the substance we are seeking. If it is found, it will generate benefits of $100 million per year. We are able to sample 100 species per year to see if they contain the substance having this quality. Obviously, the probability that we will find it this year is 100 in 1 million, or .0001. Suppose now that one of these 1 million species is in danger of going extinct this year. How much should we spend on trying to preserve this species? The value is $100 million times the probability that this species contains the required compound. If it is true that only one species has the material, this latter probability is 1 in 1 million. Hence the value of the one endangered species is $100. Note that this is a small fraction of the value of the substance once it is found. Suppose we have reason to think that there are about 10 species out of the total of 1 million that might contain the substance we seek. In this case the value of the threatened species is even smaller, because there are potential substitutes for it if it becomes extinct and if it contains the substance we are looking for.

These conclusions stem importantly from the assumption we made that species prospecting[11] is a needle-in-the-haystack phenomenon. But reality may be more complicated than this. If one species is found to have a desirable property, investigators might want to look at related species in the hope that they would also have useful characteristics—perhaps a substance which is the same as is contained in the first species but which in the related species is much less costly to obtain. It is as if finding one needle in the haystack strongly suggests that there may be other valuable needles in the general vicinity of the first one. In this case the probabilities discussed above are altered in a way that gives the marginal species greater value.

The fact that the marginal species has relatively modest value does not imply, however, that we can sit back and not worry about species loss. For one thing, the rate of species loss is important. If, as some predict, 20 percent of global species are lost in the next two decades,[12] this would be very much more than a marginal change. We come back to this theme below.

The other factor that has to be taken into account in valuing species is **nonuse,** particularly **existence,** value. People value knowing that species are preserved. They will be willing to pay for preservation programs even if there is no particular market value attached to the species. They will probably value particular species more than others; they are also likely to express an existence value for all species, without distinctions among them.

If, in the end, we could come up with a measure of the total (marginal) value, from all sources, for each species, Noah's course of action would be

[11] "Species prospecting" is the name given to the search for beneficial properties of wild species that might be useful, say, in agriculture or pharmaceuticals.
[12] Edward O. Wilson, *The Diversity of Life,* Harvard University Press, 1992, p. 278.

clear. Knowing these estimated values, he could then calculate the value per unit of space that each species would have on the ark (note that this allows for different space requirements for each species) and load the ones with the highest value, up to the point where the ark is filled. Analogously, a public agency could act so as to maximize the social value of species preservation, given the size of its budget.

The Diversity Benefits of Survival

That benefits flow from the preservation of individual species is undeniable; that benefits are different for different species is also probably true, though somewhat more controversial. But species diversity is essentially about **collections of species,** not individual species. So **diversity-related benefits** of a species come, in some fashion, from the contribution a species makes to the diversity of a collection of species. There are two questions to explore: (1) What are the benefits of diversity; for example, what is better about having a population with a diverse set of species rather than one that is relatively nondiverse, and (2) what contribution does an individual species make to the diversity of the population of which it is a member? We deal first with the value question.

Suppose you are stocking a first-aid kit. Right now it contains two items, bandages and aspirin. Your budget allows you to buy one additional item this year. What should it be? If you were quite sure that in the year to come the only medical problem you will encounter is little finger cuts, you might buy more small bandages. But you don't know this, in fact you realize that there are lots of different problems you may encounter and you don't know which ones will occur with certainty. Under the circumstances you might put a high value on diversity, that is, adding something to the first-aid kit that is different from what is already there, for example, an antiseptic cream to put on cuts and abrasions.

In species preservation the same principle may hold. There is value in preserving differences, or diversity, among species. Noah has already loaded species A, and now species B and C come along. Species B is quite similar to A, while species C is very different from A. Noah might want to load species C on the grounds that it will make the ark more diverse. We are speaking here of **insurance.** If the future is uncertain, as it always is, it is also uncertain what qualities will have the greatest value when that future arrives—hence, the value of preserving sets of species, or organisms, with diverse qualities. The diversity itself is a source of value.

Apart from the insurance value of preserving a diverse nature, there are good biological and ecological reasons for doing so. These are related to the role that diversity plays in maintaining the **health of natural ecosystems.** One important dimension of ecosystem health is **resilience.** An ecosystem is resilient to the extent that it will reestablish old ecological parameters after a major disturbance. A grassland experiences a severe drought over several years. It is resilient if the grassland reestablishes itself after the drought. There

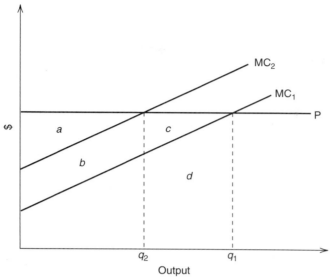

FIGURE 19-1
Cost Implications of Ecosystem Disruption and the Value of Resilience

are many aspects of resilience, for example, how fast the reestablishment occurs and how closely the new ecosystem resembles the old. But resilience
clearly is one of the factors that determines the ability of an ecosystem to de-
liver services of value to human beings.[13]

Exactly how diversity affects resilience is a complex biological question.
There are many dimensions of diversity and many dimensions of resilience.
This is a case where the question of economic valuation of resilience may be
easier than its biological aspects. Consider Figure 19-1. Suppose there is an
agricultural area that suffers some type of ecological disruption, perhaps an
act of nature, or perhaps an act by humans. One effect of this disruption is the
shifting of marginal costs of agricultural production upward, from MC_1 to
MC_2. In the face of constant prices (P) (assumed to keep the problem simple),
output and incomes decline, the former from q_1 to q_2, and the latter by an
amount equal to $b + c$ per year.[14] As long as the higher cost function prevails,
incomes are $b + c$ lower than they were before the disruption. The economic
face of resilience is the regaining of these net benefits as the ecosystem recovers its former parameters and productivity. The recovery trajectory could be
fast or slow, direct or circuitous, human-aided or not.

---

[13] C. S. Holling, D. W. Schindler, Brian W. Walker, and J. Roughgarden, "Biodiversity in the
Functioning of Ecosystems: An Ecological Synthesis," in Charles Perrings et al. (eds.), *Biodiversity
Loss, Economic and Ecological Issues*, Cambridge University Press, Cambridge, England, p. 54.
[14] Revenue decreases by $c + d$, whereas costs decrease by $d − b$; the net change is therefore $b + c$.

COST-EFFECTIVE BIODIVERSITY PRESERVATION

Credible estimates of the social value of biodiversity are very difficult to produce, even though we all recognize that the values exist. This suggests that we fall back to the perspective of **cost effectiveness.** Cost-effectiveness analysis would take a physical measure of diversity and then try to figure out the maximum amount of that measure that could be obtained with a given budget or cost or, equivalently, the minimum cost of achieving a given amount of diversity as expressed by the diversity measure we have chosen. The Noah problem can be cast in this form. The "budget" in this case is simply the size of the ark; given this, the goal is to maximize the amount of diversity among the animals that are loaded.

To give this problem a measure of concreteness, let us deal with the issue of habitat protection. Preserving habitats is not the only way of protecting species; such activities as the control of legal or illegal hunting, the control of animal predators, and raise-and-release programs can also be effective. But habitat protection is clearly the prime strategy in most cases. And this brings up the following type of question: On the assumption that there is a limit on the resources that can be devoted to habitat protection and that there are many candidate sites for protection, which particular sites should be chosen? This is known as the **optimal reserve site selection problem.** The nature of the problem is easy to see. Suppose there are 100 candidate sites and we can only preserve 10 of them. There are in fact 17.3 trillion different sets of 10 sites that can be drawn from a total of 100. Some way must be found to determine the best 10 sites, in terms of their contribution to diversity conservation.

Hot Spots

Diversity is sometimes equated with simply the **number of species** present in a collection; that situation is more diverse the larger the number of species it contains.[15] By this criterion Noah would be correct simply to maximize the total number of species loaded onto the ark. This would lead to questionable results, because it would mean that species taking up less room would be favored; large animals and plants would be less valuable. Noah could maximize his plan by loading mostly microorganisms.

The idea of **species hot spots** is based primarily on species numbers. Hot spots are identified as regions containing relatively large numbers of species in small areas. Myers, for example, has listed 18 hot spots around the globe; collectively they occupy about 0.5 percent of the earth's surface, but he estimates that they contain about 20 percent of all extant species.[16] The biggest

---

[15] We are speaking of species diversity, but the same principle could hold at any level: the number of different individuals within a given species, of ecosystems within a geographical area, and so on.

[16] Norman Myers, "The Biodiversity Challenge—Expanded Hot Spot Analysis," *Environmentalist*, 10(4), 1990, pp. 243–256.

TABLE 19-2
EXAMPLE SHOWING THE FAILURE OF THE HOT SPOTS APPROACH

	Potential reserve sites			
	A	B	C	D
Species present	1	1	1	3
	2	2	2	4
	3	3	5	6
	4	4		

advantage in using number of species as an index of diversity is that it is simple. It implies a very straightforward action plan; if you want to conserve diversity, save as many species as possible, with one species as good as any other. But a simple rule like this may not give the best results. Consider Table 19-2.[17] This shows the species present in four candidate reserve sites A, B, C, and D. There are 6 species in total. Sites A and B contain species 1, 2, 3, and 4. Site C contains species 1, 2, and 5, and site D contains species 3, 4, and 6. Suppose the sites are all equal in terms of the costs of preservation. If we follow a simple hot spots approach, we would preserve sites A and B. The optimal set of sites, however, consists of sites C and D. The latter have fewer but more unique species, whereas sites A and B have more species, but they are the same for both sites. Instead of a simple hot spot rule, therefore, it would be better to have a rule that adds sites based not only on the number of species but also on their uniqueness.

A modified hot spot approach is possible. One that has been tried, for example, is nicknamed the "greedy algorithm."[18] Select first the site that has the greatest number of species. Then select sites sequentially that add the greatest number of additional species to those already represented. Although this procedure usually works fairly well, it does not guarantee that the selected sites in aggregate will preserve the greatest number of sites. In Table 19-2, for example, this algorithm would end up with either site A or site B in combination with either site C or site D.

Sites can also differ in terms of the relative abundance of species, which may be important to take into account. Suppose one area has 5 species, each of which has 20 percent of the total individuals in the area, whereas another area also has 5 species but 1 accounts for almost all the individuals and the others have only 1 individual in each. Ecologists have developed the notion of **species abundance,** in which not only the presence or absence of a species is recorded but also its relative abundance, expressed as the proportion of total

---

[17] This example is taken from Stephen Polasky and Andrew R. Solow, "Conserving Biological Diversity with Scarce Resources," Marine Policy Center Woods Hole Oceanographic Institution, April 1997.

[18] An algorithm is a mathematical procedure that one follows, like a recipe, to solve particular numerical problems.

individuals in the area belonging to this particular species.[19] One way of constructing a diversity index from these abundance proportions is:

$$D = \frac{1}{\sum p_i^2}$$

where D = the index
   p_i = the proportion of the ith species in the area under study

If there are 5 species and each is equally abundant (i.e., each species accounts for 20 percent of the total individuals in the sample), this index gives simply the total number of species, 5. But the number drops if the distribution is skewed, that is, if one species represents a disproportionately large share of the individuals in the sample. A measure like this may be useful for some purposes, but it might be misleading in certain cases. On the one hand, it may not decrease much at all if a species that is very low in abundance becomes extinct. And if an extinction is accompanied by a reshuffling of the abundance of the remaining species, the index actually could go up. This might run counter to most people's notion of diversity, which is tied up closely to specific extinctions.

Scientists have looked beyond indexes like D above to develop measures that would better represent the diversity of a set of species and, thus, the loss in diversity when one or more of the species goes extinct. The main requirement of a better index is that it be based on some notion of the **relative importance** of different species in an area. For example, if the extinction of one species will affect the survival probabilities of many other species in the area, but not vice versa, then the extinction of that species may be regarded as more important than the extinction of one of the other species.

Another important feature of a single species is its **genetic distinctiveness.** Suppose, for example, that a region contains 5 species of a certain genus of beetles. Suppose, further, that we have examined the genetic makeup of each species and determined how unique each is, in the sense of containing genes that the other species do not. We could measure how closely the species are related to one another in terms of the complement of genes they carry, and then develop an index of diversity based on these relationships. An index of this sort would show a big drop if a species became extinct that had no close genetic relatives, but it would show only a small drop if a species with a close genetic relative goes extinct. Suppose we are unsure which particular genetic characteristics might be valuable in the future, for example, in providing material for advanced medicines. Then we might want to adopt a strategy of pre-

---

[19] See, for example, Robert E. Ricklefs, *The Economy of Nature*, 4th ed., W. H. Freeman, New York, 1997, p. 516.

EXHIBIT 19-2

COST-EFFECTIVE BIODIVERSITY PRESERVATION

There are 15 species of wild cranes in the world. If the United Nations, for example, were to have a sum of money to devote to crane preservation, which species should it target? Martin Weitzman, of MIT, developed a theoretical approach to diversity preservation and applied it to this problem. The first type of information needed was extinction probabilities, the probabilities that the species will become extinct at some time in the next 50 years, given no additional preservation efforts. The probabilities, shown in the tabulation, are estimates made on the basis of several factors—most especially the pressures on the habitats and flyways used by the different species.

Crane species produce direct use values, such as those for bird watchers and hunters. The North American whooping crane, for example, is the basis of a substantial tourist business. But suppose we wish also to take diversity into account. Suppose we wish to direct our preservation budget so as to encourage the preservation of genetic diversity among them. Cranes have been well studied among biologists, and Weitzman was able to get data on the DNA of the 15 species. In particular he was able to calculate the genetic distances among the species based on certain dis-

similarities in their DNA. Preserving diversity in this case, therefore, amounted to preserving species that have the most dissimilar DNA. From the DNA he was able to estimate the impacts on overall crane diversity of improving the survival probability of each. These are also shown in the tabulation. Note, for example, that although the Siberian and whooping cranes have about the same extinction probabilities, preserving the former would have a much greater impact on overall crane diversity than would preserving the latter.

The next logical step in this kind of analysis would be to introduce cost estimates of preserving the different species of cranes. These would undoubtedly be very different because the cranes exist in very different locales and migrate over very different regions. But cost data of this type are almost impossible to get at the present time (the author of the study rightly concludes that gathering cost data of this type should be a high priority of environmental research).

Even without cost data, however, some interesting conclusions are revealed. The Siberian crane is in a class by itself. Not only does it have a high extinction probability, but it has no close genetic relatives

(continued)

serving as broad a collection of genetic material as possible. So the loss of a species with more unique genes would be counted as a bigger loss of diversity than one with genes common to many of the species. Exhibit 19-2 discusses a study of this type, in which the focus was on wild cranes.

The analytical and data problems of reserve site selection will continue to need the work of scientists, but practical steps will be taken by groups and agencies who are facing the problem now. The Nature Conservancy, a national organization that raises money to buy and conserve sensitive resource areas, has developed a ranking system for guiding their decisions about sites to purchase.[20] Two main types of information are used: the biodiversity

---

[20] As a part of its Natural Heritage Program.

EXHIBIT 19-2—Continued

COST-EFFECTIVE BIODIVERSITY PRESERVATION

among other crane species. The sandhill crane, on the other hand, is quite secure (very low extinction probability). Yet there is a greater payoff in diversity preservation from making the sandhill even more se-

cure, than one would get in any other species, even the threatened whooper. This is because the sandhill has no close genetic relatives, while the whooping crane has several.

Crane Information

Common name	Scientific name	Geographical range	Extinction probability	Diversity Impact
Black crowned	*Balearica pavonina*	Central Africa	0.19	8.7
Grey crowned	*Balearica regulorum*	South-East Africa	0.06	14.1
Demoiselle	*Anthropoides virgo*	Central Asia	0.02	7.0
Blue	*Anthropoides paradisea*	South Africa	0.10	4.8
Wattled	*Bugeranus carunculatus*	South-East Africa	0.23	7.8
Siberian	*Grus leucogeranus*	Asia	0.35	10.3
Sandhill	*Grus canadensis*	North America	0.01	11.1
Sarus	*Grus antigone*	South-East Asia	0.05	4.7
Brolga	*Grus rubicunda*	Australia	0.04	6.5
White-naped	*Grus vipio*	East Asia	0.21	9.2
Eurasian	*Grus grus*	Europe, Asia	0.02	1.3
Hooded	*Grus monachus*	East Asia	0.17	1.4
Whooping	*Grus americana*	North America	0.35	4.5
Black-necked	*Grus nigricollis*	Himalayan Asia	0.16	5.8
Red-crowned	*Grus japonensis*	East Asia	0.29	2.9

Source: Martin L. Weitzman, "What to Preserve? An Application of Diversity Theory to Crane Conservation," *Quarterly Journal of Economics*, Vol. 108, February 1993, p. 161.

---

present at a site, and the probabilities that the biodiversity would survive if the site were protected. Thus, a prospective site gets a higher ranking (higher priority for purchase) if it contains a large number of species or other diversity attributes and/or if the survival probabilities of the species would be greatly improved if the site were protected. A site that meets both criteria would, of course, come out with a very high priority for purchase and protection. The United States Fish and Wildlife Service has developed a system, called **Gap Analysis** (GA), to give more scientific backing to its habitat preservation programs. GA makes use of a variety of techniques (satellite mapping, on-site evaluations) to locate areas of biodiversity, especially in relation to areas currently in public ownership or under some existing type of habitat preservation. Those areas found to contain high-biodiversity resources but not covered by current land preservation programs are given high priority for protection.

COSTS OF DIVERSITY PROTECTION

We have mentioned several times that rational diversity preservation must take preservation costs into account. It is worth addressing this in more detail, particularly since there are many people—for example, the political representatives who passed the Endangered Species Act—who think otherwise. It is easy enough to see the logic of considering costs. Suppose there are three potential reserves that might be protected, that each has the same value in terms of whatever index of diversity is used, but that there are different costs associated with preserving them. In particular, suppose the costs are $100, $60, and $40, respectively, for the three sites. It is obvious that if we have a total budget of $100, we can preserve far more diversity by saving the last two sites, since with our budget we can afford both of them, than if we put our whole budget into preserving just the first of the sites. Consideration of costs will inevitably push us toward sites that, other things equal, are less expensive to preserve.

The social costs of preservation consist of two major parts: (1) the **social values** that are lost when restrictions are put on the use of the designated habitat sites, and (2) the **direct costs** of managing the sites once the restrictions have been introduced. Most of the lost social values are the lost values of production of commodities and services that preservation no longer allows. For example, this could be the lost value of timber production, agricultural output, or recreational values for activities that are incompatible with preservation. If the land is currently in private ownership and there is an active land market, these opportunity costs may be reasonably well estimated by looking at the changes in property prices before and after the restrictions are put in place. This brings up an important point when public purchase of habitat is involved. If the public agency purchases land outright for inclusion in a habitat preserve, it will presumably have to pay the full market price for the land in question. This is the **cash cost** of the acquisition. If externalities are associated with the private land use, the cash land cost may have to be adjusted to get the true social opportunity cost of the acquisition.

Economic Incentives and Habitat Preservation

Habitat preservation is clearly the key to biodiversity preservation. On public lands key players are the relevant public agencies, which will have to include biodiversity preservation along with whatever other objectives history or the political process has given them. But most endangered species, and by extension biodiversity, are on private land. So a critical question is what kind of public regulation or institutions, if any, are appropriate to achieve efficient levels of biodiversity preservation on private lands.

Consider Figure 19-2, which represents the cost-and-revenue situation of a single farmer. The horizontal axis shows the quantity of farm output produced, which is sold by the farmer at a price of p. The farmer's private marginal cost curve is labeled MC_p. This producer would maximize net income at

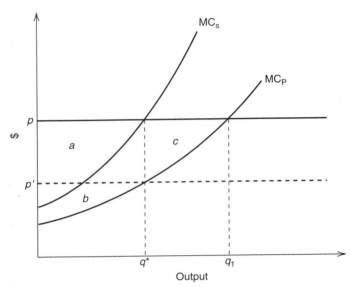

FIGURE 19-2
Analysis of Policies to Protect Endangered Species Habitat

an output rate of q_1 since this is where the private marginal cost curve intersects the price line.

Suppose that, starting with this situation, biologists discover certain threatened or endangered species on the farmer's property. Suppose also that it has
been possible to value the amount of habitat destruction that the farming operation causes and to relate this damage to the quantity of farm output. This is
a heroic assumption in the practical world, but it will allow us to explore the
conceptual aspects of the problem. This gives us a new social marginal cost
curve, labeled MC_s, which encompasses both MC_p and the habitat damage.

The output level q_1 exceeds the socially efficient output q^*. Let us consider
the different ways of getting output reduced to this lower rate. If we think
generally in the tradition of the Endangered Species Act, the first idea that
would come to mind is simply to pass a law requiring that output be reduced
to q^*. This is the traditional **command-and-control** approach, with enforcement carried out by our standard regulatory institutions. But although this approach conforms with tradition, it does not address the incentive aspects of
the situation. At q^* the farmer will have a strong incentive to increase output,
because the output price is so much higher than private marginal production
costs at that point. Prior to the regulation, the farmer's net income was $a + b +$
c, whereas afterward (assuming complete compliance) it is $a + b$, meaning that
income at q^* is c less than it would be at q_1. This shows the source of the perverse incentives that have in some cases worked against the effectiveness of
the Endangered Species Act. If the particular endangered species were not
found on the farm, the regulation would not be in force and the income of the

farmer would be the full $a + b + c$. It is essentially worth c to the farmer to be rid of the organism(s) in question, assuming that she gets no benefit herself from these species. This may be enough to motivate the farmer to get rid of the species before they are discovered publicly.[21]

Observers of the ESA have pointed out for some time that although its benefits may be widely distributed throughout society, its costs are concentrated on those private parties unlucky enough to own land that is the habitat of endangered species, such as the farmer whose situation is depicted in Figure 19-2. What is at issue, then, is not necessarily whether total benefits exceed total costs, but how the costs and benefits are distributed. A plan that has positive net benefits overall may nevertheless be vigorously opposed by some people or groups if they end up bearing a disproportionate amount of the costs. One can approach this at two levels: One can argue about who really owns endangered species or who has what rights. Or one can simply treat it as a practical problem that is reducing the effectiveness of the ESA. If we were to take the latter course, it would suggest that the landowner depicted in the figure be **compensated,** in whole or in part, for the lost income caused by the regulation.[22]

Compensatory payment programs of this type are quite common in some countries (see Exhibit 19-3). In general they take the form of contractual agreements between landowners and public agencies to refrain from certain practices or otherwise change their operating procedures, in return for a payment. The exact terms of the contract, as to its amount and the activities it affects, have to be worked out on a case-by-case basis. There is real promise in this type of approach. At the same time, we must recognize the problems that have to be solved if they are to be effective, for example: (1) paying landowners for actions they might have taken voluntarily, (2) agreeing on the size of the payment, and (3) monitoring to make sure landowners in fact act in accordance with the agreements.

Another possibility for addressing this problem is to develop a **market** for the services of the endangered species, so that its conservation by landowners and others would have a commercial rationale, that is, so the compensation to the landowner will come through revenues on the market. Perhaps the endangered species involved have **ecotourism** value in the sense that people are willing to pay the landowner for opportunities to observe or photograph the organism. Or perhaps it is a plant that has possible medicinal value, which a pharmaceutical company is willing to pay the landowner to conserve. Assume that these species values are directly related to the quantity of agricultural output. In the model, this change would imply a new price line. The

---

[21] See, for example, the cases discussed by Charles C. Mann and Mark L. Plummer, *Noah's Choice, The Future of Endangered Species,* Knopf, New York, 1995.

[22] This is not a new proposal. The 1930 American Game Policy, a public statement developed by a committee of experts under the direction of Aldo Leopold contained a section on "Inducements to Landowners." It suggested subsidies to rural landowners to provide wildlife habitat and hunting access. See Wildlife Management Institute, The North American Wildlife Policy 1973, WMI, Washington, DC, 1978, p. 39.

EXHIBIT 19-3

EXAMPLES OF COMPENSATION PROGRAMS FOR LANDOWNER ACTIVITIES AIMED AT DIVERSITY CONSERVATION

Sweden

The Nature Conservation and Agricultural Landscape Fund and the Landscape Preservation Fund aim to encourage the reduction in the area of land under cultivation, outside of protected areas. The goal is to create possibilities for alternative uses of 500,000 ha* of agricultural land. Currently, some 15 percent of all farmers are enrolled in the funds. Although set up for general nature conservation, biodiversity as an objective has become more central over time. The funds are available at a national level, and are administered through the County Administrative Boards, often with close liaison with local farmers' associations and other interested organizations. Both funds are thought to be effective; they operate through annual payments based on agreements with farmers, typically for a 5-year span. Priorities for allocation of funds are based on conservation plans, prepared by the county administrative boards. Payment rates are differentiated according to landscape types, and are set with regard to the estimated societal value of landscape/wildlife improvements, rather than opportunity costs to farmers.

Austria

The Lower Austria Landscape Fund, set up in 1993, is targeted on landscape rather than biodiversity, but includes conservation outside protected areas, restoration of damaged ecosystems, protection of rare and endangered species and support to environmentally sound practices in areas used for agriculture and forestry. The target groups are farmers and foresters, and the program is implemented through local NGOs [nongovernmental organizations] and private organizations which design the projects for support. This approach has minimized the need for additional bureaucracy. The funds are used either within private contracts to compensate for landscape protection measures, or as grants for the establishment of "new" biotopes or ecosystems. A condition of payment is that the existence of the new biotopes must be guaranteed for 20 years.

Switzerland

The Ecological Compensation Program was introduced in 1993 and aims to convert 12 percent of the country's cultivated area to ecological zones. The program offers payments to farmers for maintaining or establishing various types of natural landscapes. An objective is to arrest the disappearance of species in the country. There is a scale of rates for financial support which depends on the type of land, and conditions for management of the land are set down. There has been extensive consultation with agricultural organizations, environmental groups, and federal offices. The program is run at a federal level, but administration and monitoring are delegated to the cantons. Although it is too early to judge the effectiveness of the incentive, the response has been striking—since 1993, 47,000 ha have benefited (about 4 percent of agricultural area). Noted program difficulties include defining ecological criteria, and the precision of methods for calculating eligible surfaces.

*"ha" stands for hectare.
Source: Organization for Economic Cooperation and Development, *Saving Biological Diversity, Economic Incentives,* OECD, Paris, 1996, p. 94.

price for the agricultural crop is p, but since each unit of this output would cause a loss in market value of the endangered species of some constant amount, the new effective output price is now p', which is p minus the species value (in other words, $p - p'$ is the value of the endangered species, expressed as a function of agricultural output). In this case the normal profit maximizing incentive of the landowner would lead them to reduce agricultural output to the socially efficient level, that is, to undertake a socially efficient amount of species conservation.

How feasible is it to create markets in order to produce this kind of incentive effect? The ecotourism market appears to be the most promising. One problem with ecotourism is that, in the animal world, it frequently focuses on large, popular animals. Many animals, on the other hand, are pests to humans, for which willingness to pay may actually work in the wrong direction. Furthermore, the millions of small animals such as insects, or even microscopic animals such as bacteria, are not likely to be attractive enough to support tourist enterprises of any size, except in isolated instances.

SUMMARY

Biodiversity refers to the variation that exists at all levels of biological organization: individual, species, and ecosystems. Efforts to understand and preserve biological diversity have become a major focus within natural resources analysis and policy. In the United States much of that focus has been on the **Endangered Species Act,** which has been politically controversial and modestly successful in terms of conservation. From a conceptual standpoint, we presented the **Noah problem,** which is the issue of which species to include in the ark when space is limited. The answer to this depends on the value of individual species, on the relation of the species to others in terms of its contribution to biological diversity, and on the **value** of the diversity. Since the latter element is extremely hard to measure, effort has instead been devoted to **cost-effective** diversity preservation, that is, maximizing diversity preservation for a given expenditure of resources. This depends critically on the definitions that are used to express diversity, as well as on **extinction probabilities** and **preservation costs.** In practical terms, diversity preservation means **habitat preservation.** This brought up the problems of optimal reserve site selection and the use of **incentives** to help protect sites in private ownership.

KEY TERMS

Biodiversity resources
Endangered Species Act
Habitat conservation plans
Charismatic megafauna
Noah problem
Survival probabilities
Diamond water paradox
Reserve site selection

Species hot spots
Species abundance
Incentive-based habitat protection
Gap analysis
Greedy algorithm
Incidental taking
Preservation costs

QUESTIONS FOR FURTHER DISCUSSION

1 What is the difference between endangered species preservation and species diversity preservation?
2 What are the different ways that "success" under the Endangered Species Act might be measured?
3 What is the difference between describing the Noah problem as a benefit-cost problem and as a cost-effectiveness problem?
4 There are 10 small balls of equal size, but different color, in one urn, and 10 balls of the same color, but unequal size, in another. Which collection is more diverse?
5 A farmer is to be offered, on a take-it-or-leave-it basis, a sum of money as compensation for taking certain actions to preserve an endangered species of wildlife on the farm. How might you determine the minimum offer that could be made and still have the farmer accept the agreement?

USEFUL WEB SITES

For economic studies of various facets of biodiversity preservation:

- Resources for the Future (http://www.rff.org)
- World Resources Institute, biodiversity program (http://www.wri.org/biodiv)

For information, including country summaries, of activity under the International Convention on Trade in Endangered Species:

- Wildnet Africa (http://www.wildnetafrica.co.za/cites/index.html)

For information developing economic incentives for biodiversity preservation:

- International Union of Conservation of Native and Natural Resources, Economics of Biodiversity (http://www.economics.iven.org)

Other sites:

- The Audubon Institute (http://www.auduboninstitute.org)
- Natural Resources Institute (http://www.nri.org)

SELECTED READINGS

Barbier, E. (ed.): *Economics and Ecology: New Frontiers and Sustainable Development,* Chapman and Hall, London, 1993.
Colinvaux, P.: *Ecology,* 2nd ed., Wiley, New York, 1993.
Edwards, Victoria: *Dealing in Diversity: America's Market for Nature Conservation,* Cambridge University Press, Cambridge, England, 1995.
Houch, Oliver A.: "The Endangered Species Act and Its Implementation by the U.S. Department of Interior and Commerce," 64 *Colorado Law Review,* 227, 1993.
Jakobsson, Kristin M., and Andrew K. Dragun: *Contingent Valuation and Endangered Species,* Island Press, Northampton, MA, 1996.
Mann, Charles C., and Mark L. Plummer: *Noah's Choice, The Future of Endangered Species,* Knopf, New York, 1995.

Montgomery, Claire, and Gardner Brown: "Economics of Species Preservation: The Spotted Owl Case," *Contemporary Policy Issues,* April 1992, pp. 1–12.

Moran, Dominic, and David Pearce: "The Economics of Biodiversity," in Henk Folmer and Tom Tietenberg (eds.), *The International Yearbook of Environmental and Resource Economics 1997/1998,* Edward Elgar, Cheltenham, England, 1997, pp. 82–113.

Organization for Economic Cooperation and Development: *Saving Biological Diversity, Economic Incentives,* OECD, Paris, 1996.

Orians, G., G. Brown, W. Kunin, and J. Swierzbinski (eds.): *The Preservation and Valuation of Biological Resources,* University of Washington Press, Seattle, WA, 1990.

Pearce, David, and Dominic Moran: *The Economic Value of Biodiversity,* Earthscan Publications, London, 1994.

Perrings, C. A., K.-C. Mäler, C. Folke, C. S. Holling, and B.-O. Jansson, (eds.): *Biodiversity Loss: Ecological and Economic Issues,* Cambridge University Press, Cambridge, England, 1995.

Raffiee, K., Y. Luo, and S. Song: "The Economic Costs of Species Preservation: The Northwestern Nevada Cui-ui," *Review of Regional Studies,* 27(3), Winter 1997, pp. 277–295.

Randall, Alan: "The Value of Biodiversity," *Ambio,* 20(2), April 1991 pp. 64–68.

Shogren, Jason F. (ed.): *Private Property and the Endangered Species Act: Saving Habitats, Protecting Homes,* University of Texas Press, Austin, 1998.

Souder, Jon A.: "Chasing Armadillos down Yellow Lines: Economics in the Endangered Species Act," *Natural Resources Journal,* 33(4), Fall 1993, pp. 1077–1094.

Swanson, Timothy M. (ed.): *The Economics and Ecology of Biodiversity Decline: The Forces Driving Global Change,* Cambridge University Press, Cambridge, England, 1995.

Vane Wright, R. I., C. J. Humphries, and P. H. Williams: "What to Protect? Systematics and the Agony of Choice," *Biological Conservation,* Vol. 55, 1991, pp. 235–254.

NATURAL RESOURCES IN DEVELOPING COUNTRIES

This last section consists of two chapters dealing with the management and utilization of natural resources in **developing countries.** If current trends continue, the world in a few decades will be divided so that only about 10 percent of its human population will reside in economies that have achieved high levels of per capita wealth, while 90 percent will be in relatively poor countries where per capita wealth levels are an order of magnitude lower. Thus, a large share of the earth's natural resources will be utilized in these economic settings. It's important, then, to look at some of the major natural resource issues facing these countries. The next chapter deals with the question of the role of natural resources in economic growth. The last chapter looks at a number of resource-use situations in developing countries from the standpoint of the incentives facing individual resource users.

CHAPTER 20

NATURAL RESOURCES
AND ECONOMIC GROWTH

The people of the world, and the nations they form, are highly diverse. At present there are about 193 countries or recognized national political units in the world, and they vary enormously in almost every dimension: economic, social, demographic, and political. They are also diverse in their natural resource endowments, in terms of the type, quantity, and quality of resources within their borders. In this chapter we take a brief look at a huge subject: the role of natural resources in those countries of the world where there is special emphasis on **economic growth and development.**[1]

It has become customary to sort the countries of the world into several categories. The **developed countries** are those which have made successful transitions to industrial and postindustrial economies, with relatively slow demographic growth and relatively high levels of social welfare, and where the primary focus is on continued economic growth to match, at least, population growth. In the **developing world,** on the other hand, growth in per capita income and wealth have tended to lag behind those achieved in the advanced economies. Table 20-1 presents relevant data for certain broad demographic re-

---

[1] A distinction is sometimes made between **economic growth** and **economic development;** the former refers to increases in income and wealth per capita, whereas the latter also includes other social changes that accompany growth such as developments in education and health care, and demographic factors that moderate population growth. For our purposes we need not dwell on this distinction.

TABLE 20-1
POPULATION, ECONOMIC INDICATORS, AND HEALTH INDICATORS BY DEMOGRAPHIC
REGION, 1975–1990

Region	Population 1990 (millions)	Income per capita		Child mortality*		Life expectancy at birth (years)	
		Dollars 1990	Growth rate 1975–1990 (percent per year)	1975	1990	1975	1990
Sub-Saharan Africa	510	510	−1.0	212	175	48	52
India	850	360	2.5	195	127	53	58
China	1,134	370	7.4	85	43	56	69
Other Asia and islands	683	1,320	4.6	135	97	56	62
Latin America and the Caribbean	444	2,190	−0.1	104	60	62	70
Middle Eastern crescent	503	1,720	−1.3	174	111	52	61
Formerly socialist economies of Europe (FSE)	346	2,850	0.5	36	22	70	72
Established market economies (EME)	798	19,900	2.2	21	11	73	76
Demographically developing group†	4,123	900	3.0	152	106	56	63
Total FSE and EME	1,144	14,690	1.7	25	15	72	75
Total world	5,267	4,000	1.2	135	96	60	65

*Child mortality is the probability of dying between birth and age 5, expressed per 1,000 live births; life expectancy at birth is the average number of years that a person would expect to live at the prevailing age-specific mortality rates.
†Includes the countries of the demographic regions: Sub-Saharan Africa, India, China, other Asia and islands, Latin America and the Caribbean, and Middle Eastern crescent.
Source: The World Resources Institute, World Resources, 1998–99, Oxford University Press, New York, 1998, p. 2.

gions of the world. Note, in particular, that in 1990 the developing world (called in the table the "demographically developing group") contained almost 80 percent of the world's population. It's anticipated that this will increase to 90 percent by the middle of the next century.[2] Of course, these regional aggregates hide the experiences of different countries. Some individual countries have been quite successful in laying the institutional and social groundwork for economic growth. In others income growth has been almost nonexistent in recent years, and the political and social changes needed in order to produce economic development have been delayed. Within many countries there have also been great differences from one region to another in terms of economic growth.

[2] The World Resources Institute, World Resources, 1998–99, Oxford University Press, New York, 1998, p. 245.

THE INSTITUTIONAL/DEMOGRAPHIC CONTENT

A catalog of natural resource issues with which developing countries are grappling would be extensive and would include the following:

- Managing the exploitation of nonrenewable resources, such as oil and minerals
- Managing commercial forest resources and the conversion of forest land to other uses
- Preserving wildlife stocks that have varying local, regional, and international values
- Maintaining the optimal stock of agricultural soil productivity
- Developing and utilizing water resources in efficient and equitable ways
- Maintaining efficient levels of marine resources

But this list looks similar to a list of resource problems facing the developed countries. How different are these problems in the developing world as compared to those encountered in developed countries? Do we need special models and analyses to study them in place of, or in addition to, the ones we have discussed so far? The best answer to this is probably the following: Most of the underlying concepts discussed so far are as applicable to developing countries as they are to the developed world. Notions of efficiency, incentives, the importance of the distribution of net benefits, overexploitation of open-access resources, the important role that property rights play, and the occurrence of market failure and government failure are all ideas that are as important in the developing world as they are in the developed. But in developing economies the institutional landscape can be quite different, leading to an intertwining of political, social, and economic elements in very complex ways. For example, in our discussion of forestry economics in Chapter 12, we used a simple model for showing how efficient decisions were related to, among other things, interest rates. We essentially assumed that there existed a financial market, separate from the timber market, which could accommodate financial transactions in ways that efficiently complemented whatever decisions were made about harvesting trees. This kind of institutional assumption is often not tenable in developing countries.

Another point of difference is that in many developing countries, elements of the natural resource endowment are being relied upon to provide a major impetus for economic growth. Petroleum and mineral deposits, agricultural land, forests, hydropower, and wildlife resources are looked on in different countries as sources of growth. So there are important questions regarding the nature of the connection, if there is one, between resources and growth, and the ways resources should be used if the objective is to stimulate economic growth. In this chapter we take up some of the questions of natural resources and economic growth. Our perspective here is somewhat more macroeconomic than it has been elsewhere in the book. We will take up more micro-related questions of growth and natural resources in the next chapter.

RESOURCES AND GROWTH: TWO PERSPECTIVES

There are two main perspectives from which to view the linkage between economic development and natural resources:

1 A focus on the ways that developing countries may **make use of their natural resource** stocks to achieve economic growth
2 A focus on the **negative impacts** of economic and demographic development on the quantity and quality of a country's natural resource capital

The second of these is perhaps the one most commonly encountered. It is the subject of Exhibit 20-1, which was excerpted from a recent United Nations report. Within the developing world high population growth rates and low incomes are almost the rule, although many countries are beginning to have success in decreasing their demographic rates of growth[3]—hence, the concern with the large-scale degradation of natural and environmental resources that burgeoning populations may produce. Images abound of deforestation, depletion of water resources, loss of productive soil, diminished fish stocks, and so on. These images have frequently produced among observers something along the lines of a Malthusian reaction: fixed quantities of natural resources, populations pushing against some sort of physical **carrying capacity** set by nature, disease, and death because low levels of human skills and technical capabilities make it impossible to increase supply commensurate with demand. The basic cause of the natural resource depletion, according to this view, is population growth and poverty, especially in rural areas.

This viewpoint is oversimplified and misleading. It is certainly true that in some cases there is substantial demographic pressure on natural resource stocks, pressure that would be lessened if populations were lower. But the ultimate productivity with which any natural resource endowment is used, its ability to support and enhance the economic welfare of the people using it, depends on the decisions that individuals make on how specifically the resources are utilized. These decisions are not cast in concrete. The **microeconomic** implications of this will be taken up in the next chapter. From a **macroeconomic** viewpoint, however, the simple conclusion is that in the long run there is no strict, proportional relationship running from population to environmental degradation and natural resource exhaustion. The relationship is, rather, flexible and subject to change. The environmental and resource impacts of economic growth should not be thought of as unfortunate and unplanned implications of economic and demographic growth, but as the result of planning decisions made by the societies in which they occur. These decisions may in many cases be occurring by default. But they need not be.

From a **macroeconomic** standpoint, there is simply no relationship between natural resource endowments and economic growth rates. A way of saying

---

[3] See World Resources Institute, *World Resources 1992–93*, Oxford University Press, Oxford, England, 1992, pp. 76–77.

EXHIBIT 20-1

CHANGING TODAY'S CONSUMPTION PATTERNS—
FOR TOMORROW'S HUMAN DEVELOPMENT

Growth in the use of material resources has slowed considerably in recent years, and much-publicized fears that the world would run out of such non-renewable resources as oil and minerals have proved false. New reserves have been discovered. The growth of demand has slowed. Consumption has shifted in favor of less material-intensive products and services. . . .

So, non-renewables are not the urgent problem. It is two other crises that are nudging humanity towards the "outer limits" of what earth can stand.

First are the pollution and waste that exceed the planet's sink capacities to absorb and convert them. . . .

Second is the growing deterioration of renewables—water, soil, forests, fish, biodiversity.

- Twenty countries already suffer from water stress, having less than 1,000 cubic meters per capita a year, and water's global availability has dropped from 17,000 cubic meters per capita in 1950 to 7,000 today.
- A sixth of the world's land area—nearly 2 billion hectares—is now degraded as a result of overgrazing and poor farming practices.
- The world's forests—which bind soil and prevent erosion, regulate water supplies and help govern the climate—are shrink-

ing. Since 1970 the wooded area per 1,000 inhabitants has fallen from 11.4 square kilometers to 7.3.
- Fish stocks are declining, with about a quarter currently depleted or in danger of depletion and another 44% being fished at their biological limit.
- Wild species are becoming extinct 50–100 times faster than they would naturally, threatening to tear great holes in the web of life. . . .

The severest human deprivations arising from environmental damage are concentrated in the poorest regions and affect the poorest people, unable to protect themselves.

- The fifth of the world's people in the highest-income countries account for 53% of carbon dioxide emissions, the poorest fifth for 3%. Brazil, China, India, Indonesia and Mexico are among the developing countries with the highest emissions. But the huge populations, their per capita emissions are still tiny—3.9 metric tons a year in Mexico and 2.7 in China, compared with 20.5 metric tons in the United States and 10.2 in Germany. The human consequences of the global warming from carbon dioxide will be devastating for many poor countries—with a

---

(continued)

this is that natural resources are neither necessary nor sufficient for achieving high growth rates.[4] We know they are not necessary, because we see many countries (Japan, Singapore, Korea) that have achieved high growth rates despite relatively poor natural resource endowments. And we know they are not sufficient, because many countries (Nigeria, Venezuela, Zambia) with very substantial resource endowments have not only not grown in recent decades, but have actually regressed.

---

[4] Necessary conditions are conditions that **must** hold in order for a certain result to occur. Sufficient conditions are conditions that will produce the result if the conditions hold. A necessary condition need not be sufficient, and a sufficient condition need not be necessary.

EXHIBIT 20-1—*Continued*

CHANGING TODAY'S CONSUMPTION PATTERNS—
FOR TOMORROW'S HUMAN DEVELOPMENT

rise in sea levels, Bangladesh could see its land area shrink by 17%.

- Almost a billion people in 40 developing countries risk losing access to their primary source of protein, as overfishing driven by export demand for animal feed and oils puts pressure on fish stocks.
- The 132 million people in water-stressed areas are predominantly in Africa and parts of the Arab states—and if present trends continue, their numbers could rise to 1–2.5 billion by 2050.
- Deforestation is concentrated in developing countries. Over the last two decades, Latin America and the Caribbean lost 7 million hectares of tropical forest, Asia and Sub-Saharan Africa 4 million hectares each. Most of it has taken place to meet the demand for wood and paper, which has doubled and quintupled respectively since 1950. But over half the wood and nearly three-quarters of the paper is used in industrial countries.

These environmental challenges stem not only from affluence but also from growing poverty. As a result of increasing impoverishment and the absence of other alternatives, a swelling number of poor and landless people are putting unprecedented pressures on the natural resource base as they struggle to survive.

How people interact with their environment is complex. . . . Ownership of natural resources, access to common properties, the strength of communities and local institutions, the issue of entitlements and rights, risk and uncertainty are important determinants of people's environmental behavior. Gender inequalities, government policies and incentive systems are also crucial factors.

The world community has also been active on environmental problems that directly affect poor people. Such areas include decertification, biodiversity loss and exports of hazardous waste. For example, the Convention on Biological Diversity has near-universal signature, with over 170 parties. The Convention to Combat Decertification has been ratified by more than 100 countries. But the deterioration of arid lands, a major threat to the livelihoods of poor people, continues unabated.

And there are other immediate environmental concerns for poor people, such as water contamination and indoor pollution, that have yet to receive serious international attention. Global forums discuss global warming. But the 2.2 million deaths yearly from indoor air pollution are scarcely mentioned.

Source: United Nations Development Program, *Human Development Report*, 1998.

On the other hand, history clearly shows us many cases where natural resource endowments, national or regional, have been instrumental in supporting economic growth. Some countries of the Middle East have achieved high incomes based on petroleum resources; Iceland has grown through using its fishery resources. Many countries have been successful in developing agricultural sectors to help spur national economic growth. This brings us right back to a question similar to those we have investigated throughout the preceding chapters. It is most easily seen in the case of nonrenewable resources. To contribute toward economic growth, they must be used at some nonzero rate. Notions of sustainability, at least in any physical sense, are of little use here. Instead, there are three important questions to answer:

1 What is the appropriate rate of use?
2 How is this rate to be achieved?
3 What is to be done with the resulting rents?

But exactly the same questions arise in the case of renewables. Consider New England in the early seventeenth century. At the time of the arrival of the European colonists it was heavily forested. Over the next two centuries there was a tremendous disinvestment in forests and a large expansion of agricultural land. Present-day observers would probably have pointed with alarm at high rates of deforestation, especially in the hill towns. But this forest conversion permitted a level of economic development that would not have been possible without it. Today the situation has been reversed; much of the land that was converted to agriculture in those times has now grown back to forest. Developing countries face the same choice in their renewable resources such as forests, soil productivity, water, and fisheries. What are the optimal investment, or disinvestment, strategies for these resources? And once these strategies have been identified, what are the best ways of achieving them? This has become substantially complicated because many of the resources in these developing countries have become recognized and valued on a global basis. For example, certain African wildlife, biodiversity in Latin America and elsewhere, and forest resources in Asia and elsewhere are resources for which preservation values are often most strongly expressed in other countries, especially countries of the developed world. This means we have to face the complex task of finding courses of action that are both efficient and equitable from global and national points of view.

HOW ECONOMIES GROW

The study of economic growth has been a major specialty within economics for many years. It is clearly a complex phenomenon, with major interactions among a host of demographic, technological, political, and institutional factors. At bottom, economic growth in any country is related to the growth in its productive capacity relative to the growth of its population. And productive capacity is a function of several factors: the quantity of productive inputs (labor, capital of the traditional sort, natural capital) available to the economy, and the productivity of those inputs in turning out useful goods and services. In this context, therefore, growth requires increases in the quantity of inputs and/or in their productivity. We thus have a way of linking natural resources with economic growth. Natural resources can be thought of as **natural capital,** the quantities and qualities of which are provided by nature. Human beings may make use of this capital, combining it with other inputs to produce goods and services.

  To get an analytical grip on it, we need to use a model that is simple enough to reveal some basic relationships. So we will use what is known as an **aggregate production function** to characterize the production performance and potential of an economy. For a given economy we can express its aggregate output of goods and services for a time period like a year in the following way:

$$Y = f (K, L, Q)$$

where the variables are defined as follows:

Y: Aggregate output of goods and services

K: Stock of physical capital, both private (machinery, buildings, etc.) and public (roads, harbors)

L: The "stock" of human resources, including not just the number of people available to work, but also their skills and capacities

Q: The quantity of natural resources used in the production of the output Q

The letter f denotes the functional relationship between these inputs and output. It tells, for example, by how much output would increase if one or more inputs were increased by some amount. It carries within it a notion of the state of **technological development** of a country at any point in time. This means the technological state of firms in the private sector, such as irrigation technologies used in agriculture and production technologies used in industry. It also includes the particular economic and political institutions used in the country, such as the extent to which natural resources are privatized and the way in which public agencies control resource use.

Suppose that, for the moment, K and L are constant from period to period, and that Q relates to the quantity of a nonrenewable resource that is being drawn upon by the country in question. This might be the case, for example, of a country that is pumping petroleum from a deposit of fixed size.[5] It's clear that output can be maintained as long as the resource is not exhausted; the country simply extracts a given amount each year. If there is no change in any of the other inputs, however, output must decline when the resource is exhausted.

There are basically only two ways of maintaining output in the face of the declining availability of the natural resource. Both involve investment[6]:

1 Investment to augment the quantity/quality of the other inputs
2 Investment in new private and public technology and institutions that have the effect of shifting the aggregate production function itself, in other words, becoming more productive with the inputs available

How much alternative capital must be substituted for the diminished natural resource capital? This depends on the relative productivities of the two types of inputs, which depend on the technological and institutional situation

---

[5] Recall the expression for nonrenewable resources we used in Chapter 2: $S_2 = S_1 - Q_1 + \Delta S$, where S refers to stocks at the beginning of the indicated periods. The variable Q above actually is the same as the Q_1 of the earlier chapter.

[6] Investment involves taking a portion of output and, instead of consuming it directly, devoting it to the production of long-lived capital goods (physical and human) and the institutional changes that will increase productivity in the long run.

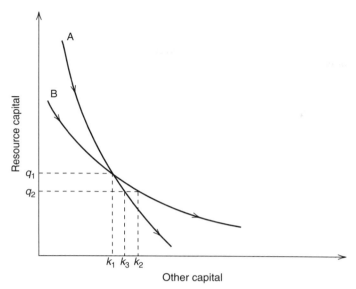

FIGURE 20-1
Substitution of Other Types of Capital for Diminishing Natural Resource
Stocks

in which the developing country finds itself. What is involved conceptually can be pictured, as in Figure 20-1. The two functions labeled A and B show how much alternative capital (machine and/or human) is required to substitute for a given amount of natural resource capital. As we slide down A or B, they show the amount of additional nonresource capital that must be put in place to offset the drop in resource capital and maintain aggregate output at its previous level. The steeper the curve, the easier it is to compensate for the resource reduction. A drop of the latter from q_1 to q_2 requires an increase in other capital from k_1 to k_2 if B is the relevant curve, but only to k_3 if the trade-off curve is A.

The logic of this situation seems clear in the case of nonrenewable resources—like petroleum, minerals, some groundwater aquifers. But it is applicable also to **renewable resources.** A renewable resource harvested from a given area may be managed in such a way as to give a constant resource yield through time. But if population is growing, this implies a diminution in resource yield per capita, and therefore in total output per capita if all other inputs are unchanging in quantity. Thus, to achieve nondiminishing per capita output, this case also requires investment in other forms of capital, either machine capital or human capital. Beyond this, however, is the fact that renewable resource stocks are **variables;** they can be held at high, moderate, or low levels. They can be drawn down to certain levels today, and then allowed to recover at some future time—as long as an **irreversibility threshold** has not been passed.[7] They can be built up and maintained at higher levels than nature itself provides, as in the case, for example, of terracing slopes for sustainable agricultural use or managing a certain habitat to produce a larger stock of a particular type of wildlife. Thus, it is not a case of holding the stocks constant at some arbitrary level, but of figuring out the best time profile of renewable resource stock, from the standpoint of contributing to the overall goal of maintaining or advancing economic growth rates.

NATURAL RESOURCE ACCOUNTING

If economic growth requires that investments in nonresource inputs be coordinated with changes in the stocks of natural resources, then ways must be found to measure the values of these natural resource stocks and the impact that changing stock levels have on the income of a country. This in fact brings us to the subject of **national income accounting.** This refers to the task of measuring the aggregate performance of an economy in terms that reflect the level of economic welfare an economy produces for its participants. The technique of national income accounting was developed in the 1940s and 1950s in order to get a better idea of the macroeconomic performance of a country's economy. Income is usually defined as the maximum amount of money someone can spend in one time period and still expect to be able to spend the same amount in real terms in all subsequent periods.[8] This notion incorporates a concept of sustainability, since at the macro level it refers to the total expenditures a country can make and still be able to spend the same amount in the future. Suppose total expenditures in a given year are the following:

Consumption	$100 million
Investment in new plant and equipment	30 million
Total	$130 million

But in producing its total output, the economy has worn out, say, $20 million of productive capacity; that is, productive capacity has depreciated by $20 million. According to the above notion of income, we cannot count as income the amount that is needed to compensate for the depreciation. Thus, the national income of the country is only $110 ($130 minus the $20 million of depreciation).

The same principle holds for natural resource and environmental capital. If current production causes environmental damage through air, water, or land pollution, this needs to be taken into account in determining national income. If current production also draws down the value of natural resource

---

[7] An "irreversibility threshold" is a stock that is so reduced in quantity or quality that original levels cannot be restored. The classic example is a breeding population of species of wildlife that gets so low that the population cannot recover. Another example is soil that becomes so eroded that it can never be reestablished at its previous fertility level.

[8] To economists this is the classic "Hicksian" definition of income as put forward in John R. Hicks, *Value and Capital*, 2nd ed., Clarendon Press, Oxford, England, 1939, p. 174.

stocks, this should also be adjusted for in determining income. Although there are now widely accepted and employed techniques for estimating the depreciation of such items as buildings and machinery (but not of public infrastructure such as roads), many concepts and procedures for estimating changes in values of natural resource stocks are still being worked on.

The case of **nonrenewable resources** is probably the most straightforward. Suppose a community one morning discovers a mineral deposit within its borders. The deposit consists of 100 tons of the material. The community decides to extract 10 tons of this each year. It costs $3 per ton to do this, for a total annual cost of $30, and this sells in the market for $50. The community thus has a "profit" of $20, which would show up as income produced by this resource. But this cannot be income in the sense described above, because each year the stock of the resource is being depleted. In 10 years, if nothing changes, the resource will be entirely depleted. In this case it is clear that there must be an adjustment to allow for the depleted resource. In a previous chapter we introduced the concept of **user cost** associated with natural resource use. User costs are the future benefits forgone when a resource is used today rather than conserved. In effect, the gross income of resource use needs to be adjusted by user cost in order to determine the level of income net of resource depletion. It is this user cost that must be made good by alternative investment if a community's income is to be sustained.

Strictly **renewable resources** may be somewhat more difficult to assess. When extraction reduces the physical productivity of a renewable resource, this must be taken into account in measuring current income. Going back to our imaginary community, suppose it is an agricultural region, with annual cultivation and cropping, either for subsistence or market purposes. Agricultural production normally extracts a certain amount of productivity from the soil. If steps are taken, by appropriate cultivation and augmentation procedures, to maintain soil productivity, the cost of these procedures is analogous to the cost of maintaining a machine, and ought to be netted out in calculating true income. But if, for one reason or another, soil fertility is not maintained, the value of the reduction must be subtracted from the value of net agricultural output to get a true measure of income. This is analogous to a machine that has diminished in value from use. The job of estimating the value of reduced soil productivity is of course a difficult one. If there were an active market in agricultural land, diminished fertility would imply a lower market price for the land. So the analysis of agricultural land prices might give us the information we need.

Another example is a fishery. If it is harvested at a sustainable rate (i.e., the catch is limited to the natural growth increment so there is no change in the underlying stock), there is no resource depletion adjustment that needs to be made. This is not the case, however, if total catch exceeds natural replenishment, for then there is a diminishing stock that ought to be accounted for. In the case of a forest, the adjustment can be based on the question of whether steps are taken to replant and maintain the overall stock of forests in the long run. The cost of the steps, if taken, are analogous to maintenance expenses, and need to be deducted, along with the temporary reduction in stock of harvestable timber. If the land is abandoned or shifted to another use (e.g., into farms), the adjustment needs to recognize the reduction in the long-run stock of forest resources.

One of the major reasons for valuing reduced natural resource stocks is to measure what could be called the **resource adjusted domestic product** for a country. There are enormous analytical difficulties in getting a single, aggregate number like this—in measuring and valuing resource stocks and then in aggregating them into a believable total. What this has suggested to many people is that this type of analysis be undertaken on a **sectoral** basis. In other words, we must focus on portions of the economy, the use of natural resources within them, and their impacts on the quality and quantity of natural resource stocks. Exhibit 20-2 illustrates the results of a perspective like this, here focused on the forest products sector of Indonesia.

THE CONTROL AND MANAGEMENT OF RESOURCE RENTS

If per capita income is to be maintained or increased, especially in the face of population increases, any disinvestment in natural resources must be offset by investment in other forms of productive assets. This essentially requires a source of monetary resources with which to invest in these alternative assets. One of the most obvious places to look for these investable resources is in **natural resource rents.** There are two essential parts of this process:

1 Using natural resources in ways that maximize their rents
2 Channeling those rents into productive investments

We have talked throughout the book about the conditions that resource use decisions must meet in order that resource rents be maximized. Rent maximization, as a goal, is just as applicable to developing countries as to the developed world. In the next chapter we look more closely at the special problems of maximizing resource rents in developing nations. For the rest of this chapter we focus on condition 2 above: the disposition of the rents.

What happens to resource rents will depend in no small measure on whose bank account they end up in. To whom might they accrue? A list of potential candidates would include the following:

1 **Owners of the resource:** These could be local people, people within the country but residents elsewhere, or foreign citizens.
2 **Local companies engaged in extraction:** Extraction companies may be national, that is, organized and operated by citizens of the country in question. They may or may not be citizens who live in the vicinity of the resource itself.
3 **Foreign companies engaged in extraction:** In this case concession fees (the fees companies have to pay for the right to harvest) may be lower, perhaps

EXHIBIT 20-2

EXAMPLE OF A SECTORAL ANALYSIS OF A NATURAL RESOURCE–USING INDUSTRY IN A DEVELOPING COUNTRY: FORESTRY IN INDONESIA

Some of the questions:

Indonesia has a strong comparative advantage in producing forest products. Consequently, a reasonable development strategy would focus on expansion of the wood processing industries, especially pulp, paper, and wood products. However, Indonesia's forests, which are not always managed sustainably, are barely able to meet current levels of demand. The scale of operation of wood-using industries over the next 25 years is likely to place demands on Indonesia's forestry sector which would decimate its forests. How much wood would be required in the future? Would existing forests be able to meet the demand, especially if a large expansion in the pulp and paper industry is planned? What combination of revised management techniques, including plantation forests, might be needed? Where would land be found for expanded forestry? What would be the cost of this new approach to forestry and what policy changes might be needed to implement it?

Some of the answers[1]:

It was clear from earlier analysis (Duchin and Lange, 1992) that the natural production forests would not be able to satisfy Indonesia's domestic demand for wood products in the near future, even without an expansion of the pulp and paper sector. The sustainable yields of natural forests may already be declining due to poor management practices which cause extensive deforestation and soil erosion. The study now focused on the extent to which plantation forests would need to supplement wood products from natural forests, and on what measures would be required to manage natural forests sustainably, preventing, or at least reducing, further losses.

It has been widely recognized that plantation forests will be needed to satisfy the demand for wood in the future. Plantation forests on a 15-year cycle are projected to account for 40% of log production under S1, and 68% under S2. The study assumes that they will be established on already degraded land not suitable for other crops and, consequently, will not compete with agriculture for land. Some soil erosion will occur when the plantations are first established, but erosion is expected to be negligible thereafter. Changes in the methods of road building, felling, and transportation of timber from natural forests are introduced to reduce soil erosion and deforestation. The net impact of plantation forestry and improved practices in natural forests is to reduce land requirements per unit of forestry output by 35%, soil erosion by 80%, and deforestation by 65% under S1. The figures under S2 are 60%, 92%, and 81%. While in many sectors projected technological changes either reduce costs or increase them only slightly because many inputs to production are reduced, that is not the case in forestry. In contrast to forestry operations in already existing natural production forests where no costs are incurred to establish the forest, plantation forestry requires much more intensive management and is considerably more expensive.

---

[1]The reference to S1 and S2 are to different study scenarios that the analysts considered, each based on somewhat different assumptions about what decisions would be pursued.

Source: Glenn-Marie Lange, "Strategic Planning for Sustainable Development in Indonesia Using Natural Resource Accounts," in Joroen C.J.M. van den Bergh and Jan van der Straaten, *Economy and Ecosystems in Change, Analytical and Historical Approaches,* Edward Elgar, Cheltenham, England, 1997, pp. 320–329. (The referenced work is: F. Duchin et al., "Input-Output Modelling: Development and the Environment in Indonesia," Final Report to EPSS for CIDA, 1992.)

substantially lower, than resource rents. Depending on laws and regulations, a part or all of the remaining rent may be transferred to individuals outside of the country in which the extraction is taking place.

4 **A unit of government, local, state, or national:** In this case taxes or concession fees could transfer all or part of the rent to governmental units or individuals.

How rents are actually divided among individuals and groups such as these depends on a host of factors: how property rights are defined and enforced, taxes, competition in the resource extraction industry and resource industries, the terms written into contracts covering resource harvesting, and so on. The point to be made here, however, is that how these rents are spent, and whether they are devoted to the kinds of investments that are required for economic growth in the region or country in question clearly will depend on how they are distributed among these various potential claimants.

One device sometimes pursued by governments is to appropriate a portion of the rents, via taxes or fees on direct participation in the market, and place them in a **development fund** under the control of political authorities. The stated goal of this type of fund normally is to give governments the means of investing in such things as highways, railroads, and ports that will advance long-run productivity. Of course resources in the hands of political authorities are most likely to be spent for political purposes, which may or may not be the same as investments that advance the true long-run productivity of other parts of the citizenry. Exhibit 20-3 illustrates a particularly egregious example of this in the case of a nonrenewable resource.

EXHIBIT 20-3

ETHNIC GROUPS BATTLE FOR CONTROL OF NIGERIA'S OIL

The ethnic turmoil that has erupted in this riverfront town over control of oil is an ominous sign that Africa's most populous nation is moving into a crisis that could threaten access to the world's sixth-largest supply of crude.

Frustrated by years of corruption and neglect by the government, members of the Ijaw ethnic group have taken hostages and seized dozens of oil platforms owned by companies such as Chevron and Texaco, threatening the country's entire $7 billion-a-year industry. But a rival group, the Itsekiri, is challenging the Ijaw's bid to control the rich oil resources of the Niger Delta, and the government has imposed a dusk-to-dawn curfew to try to stem fighting that has left at least seven people dead.

The unrest in this western region comes in the wake of last week's fire in which at least 700 people were burned to death in the nearby village of Jesse as people tried to tap a few gallons of hard-to-find gasoline from a government fuel line.

"Our oil feeds this country, this corrupt government, the United States and Europe" says Daniel Ekepebide, president of the Federated Niger Delta Ijaw Communities, the group that seized the oil platforms." And yet we don't have electricity. There's no fuel at the stations. We don't move until something changes."

EXHIBIT 20-3—*Continued*

ETHNIC GROUPS BATTLE FOR CONTROL OF NIGERIA'S OIL

Analysts have long concluded that Nigeria—pumping 2 million barrels of oil per day—should be an affluent country. The American Petroleum Institute estimates 8 percent of U.S. oil imports come from Nigeria. But for decades, Nigeria's rulers have enriched themselves from the country's vast oil and natural gas resources, while many poor Nigerians are forced to scavenge or steal oil, as the Jesse explosion demonstrated.

In Warri, Ijaw activists are preventing production at dozens of Western-owned oil platforms that they seized in the past two weeks, shutting down one-third of Nigeria's crude oil output. Brief seizures of oil platforms are common in Nigeria's riverine communities, but the conflict appears to be escalating into Nigeria's worst oil crisis since writer Ken Saro-Wiwa led his Ogoni people, in eastern Nigeria, to protest government oil policy in the early 1990s.

In this latest unrest, youths of the Ijaw and Itsekiri ethnic groups in the Niger Delta are fighting for control of the region's oil and of its local government. The 27,000-square-mile delta is home to more than 7 million people, but the Ijaw, Itsekiri and a subgroup of the Yoruba, the nation's largest ethnic group, vie for dominance.

The region is composed of muddy swamps and tropical forests that are laced by thousands of serpentine creeks and bayous as muddy as the Mississippi. Almost forgotten villages of thatched huts lie in the backwaters, where the only electricity is on the oil platforms, and the only mode of transportation is the dugout canoe.

Both Ijaws and Itsekiris have long claimed ownership of these oil-rich regions. Each demand they hold the local seat of power, so that they can ensure their dirt-poor communities get jobs, clean water and electricity.

The stakes in the battle for control of Nigerian oil are huge, and among the most internationally significant issues in sub-Saharan Africa.

More than 80 percent of total national revenues stem from oil sales. About $25 billion has been made in the past three decades—though most of it has been squandered, stolen or wasted by corrupt and incompetent military regimes. Average income for Nigerians is about $300 per year.

In the late 1970s, when oil was at $40 per barrel, Nigeria ranked as one of the 40 richest countries in the world. Average income was $1,200 per year.

Today, following the disastrous reign of Gen. Sani Abacha, the country ranks as one of the poorest nations in the world. Successive military regimes have siphoned off billions of dollars of oil profits, disregarding the nation's economic health.

Phones don't work. The lights go out. Toilets don't flush. Potholes in roads can swallow small cars.

Worse, Nigeria can't process its own oil into gasoline. The nation's four refineries lie dormant, ruined by neglect.

Source: *The Arizona Republic*, October 25, 1998. Reprinted with permission of Knightridder/Tribune Information Service.

Investments in human capital may be a lot less subject to appropriation by political authorities. In addition, human capital investments can have important impacts on other important dimensions of the overall problem. It is clear, for example, that investments in health, education, and training, especially for women, can have important impacts on fertility rates. Thus, if a portion of natural resource rents is spent on investment in education, it can lead to a substantial fall in the population growth rate, which in turn will lower future demands for natural resources.

THE VOLATILITY OF RESOURCE RENTS
IN DEVELOPING COUNTRIES

A difficult and ongoing problem confronting countries who might think of using resource rents to spur economic growth is the fact that these rents can be very volatile over time. This is because of the volatility of natural resource commodity prices on international markets. The 1970s and 1980s saw massive changes in petroleum prices, with large runups followed by substantial declines. There was a boom in coffee prices in the latter part of the 1970s. Prices of copper and phosphate increased sharply in the late 1970s and early 1980s and then fell back to earlier levels. Since 1995 rubber prices are down by 60 percent, copper prices by 55 percent, and oil prices have dropped to levels below pre-1970s prices.

Figure 20-2 shows the very long run (1850 to today) performance of an index of world primary commodity prices. This index is a composite of major minerals, agricultural, and forestry prices. One can see two major patterns: (1) a long-run trend downward in the twentieth century and (2) the tendency for substantial fluctuations around the trend. In recent decades there were peaks in the early 1970s and in 1980, 1988, and 1995, followed by rapid decreases. A primary reason for the cyclical price swings is the fluctuations in

FIGURE 20-2
Commodity Price Index, in Real Dollars' Terms, 1845–1850 = 100 (Adjusted by U.S. GDP Deflator) (*Source: The Economist,* April 17, 1999.)

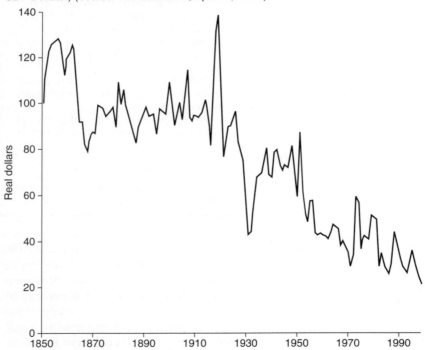

investment in extraction and processing facilities. When prices strengthen, optimism among investors leads to rapid upswings in investment that often will overshoot, leading to overcapacity, market surpluses, and price collapses.

In a world where natural resource commodity prices fluctuate rapidly and strongly, it is hard to develop a sustainable program of public or private growth-producing investment programs based on natural resource rents. When prices increase and rents are high, spending them may not get the close scrutiny it should; projects may be undertaken without adequate benefit-cost analysis. When resource commodity prices fall, projects undertaken earlier may have to be put on hold, or perhaps financed out of risky borrowing.[9]

LAND RENTS AND LAND REFORM

In most developing countries the agricultural sector provides a relatively large proportion of total employment and total output. Thus, agricultural land is a natural resource of immense importance, and the way that land is used has a critical impact on economic growth and peoples' welfare. In our terms, the production and distribution of land rents is of paramount importance. A basic fact of life in many developing countries is that agricultural land is very unequally distributed, with relatively small numbers of people holding large amounts of agricultural land, and large numbers of rural people holding relatively little. The reasons for this are historical, legal, and political; they vary from country to country and region to region. And many local factors are changing, though not as fast as many would like. In some discussions this pattern of land ownership may be expressed as strictly a distributional issue: One group uses the land and accrues the land rents, the other group for one reason or another does not. In this view, redistributing the land would simply shift rents from one group of people to another.

But land distribution is more than an issue simply of who accumulates the rents. It is also a genuine issue of how the land resource is used and how its productivity is enhanced and maintained. Figure 20-3 depicts a very simple and somewhat abstract model that can be used to discuss some of the basic issues of land reform. Suppose there is a small agricultural region populated by just 20 people, all of whom gain their livelihood by farming. There is a fixed amount of land that is to be divided up among the farmers. Since we can't draw a graph with 20 dimensions, let us divide the farmers into two equal-sized groups, whom we will call group A and group B. In reality, of course, the large land-owning groups are usually smaller in numbers than the groups owning little land. But it will be easier if we assume equal size, and we can still get the same intuition from the model. The horizontal axis contains an index of acres; read from the left, it shows the number of acres farmed by group A. The end on the right corresponds to the total amount of land avail-

---

[9] See, for example, I. M. D. Little, *Boom, Crisis and Adjustment, The Macroeconomic Experience of Developing Countries,* published for the World Bank by Oxford University Press, New York, 1993.

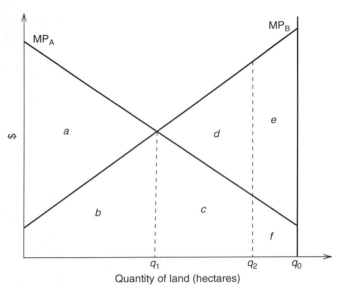

FIGURE 20-3
The Political Economy of Land Reform

able, shown as q_0. Thus, going from right to left shows the number of acres farmed by group B. The vertical scale is an index of value, to be used for showing the value of agricultural output produced by the two groups.

The curves labeled MP_A and MP_B show the **marginal productivity,** in terms of the value of agricultural output, that the two groups can earn on land that they farm. We are not assuming that the groups farm their lands collectively, but rather that they divide it up and farm on individual plots of equal size. We are trying to focus on the relations between the two groups, not on what happens within each one. Both groups have the same human capital in terms of farming. Thus, the MP_A and MP_B curves are perfectly symmetrical. The declining marginal productivity curves illustrate the fact that as the land holdings of either group increase, the marginal productivity, that is, the added agricultural output realized by farming one additional acre, declines. When a group holds relatively little land, it will farm intensively and get high outputs per acre. As land holdings increase, production must become less intensive because the same number of people are farming a larger acreage.

Suppose we wish to have the land distributed between the two groups in such a way as to maximize total agricultural output. It's clear that the land should be divided equally, with q_1 acres farmed by each group. Total output in this case will be equal to $a + b + c + d + e + f$, the total acres under the two marginal productivity curves from where they start to q_1. In fact, most studies of agriculture in developing countries show that, for most crops, greater output can be obtained when the land is divided up into family-sized holdings than when it is worked in much larger units.[10] In fact, however, holdings tend to be skewed, as represented by the point q_2. Here we have a situation in which group A holds considerably more acreage than group B, q_2 acres for A and only $q_0 - q_2$ acres for group B. Total output is now $a + b + c + e + f$. It is smaller than the equal-division output by an amount equal to area d. Note also that **output per person** is much higher in group A than in group B; in the first case the 10 people of the group divide $a + b + c$ of income; in the second case the 10 people divide $e + f$ of income.

Thus, the difference between the equal and the unequal division of land is not just a distributional matter, it is also a matter of productivity; this "society" is sacrificing income equal to area d by virtue of the maldistribution of the land. How the situation represented by q_2 was arrived at is a matter of history in any particular case, normally involving the dispossession of one group by another through political means. If the dispossession is severe enough, per capita incomes of the disadvantaged group will fall to or below subsistence levels, the only practicable response to which may be to migrate into burgeoning urban areas. To the eyes of an outside observer, this may look like a case of a large, poor rural population, with high fertility rates, reaching the "carrying capacity" of the land and having to move into the cities. But this is not what's going on—or at least not primarily what's going on. Instead, what we have is a **political distortion** that makes it impossible to move to a situation where a much larger proportion of the rural population could support itself and provide agricultural output to the rest of the country.

But why doesn't the situation rectify itself? If the land could be redistributed so as to move to q_1, the point of equal distribution, the people of group B would gain an amount equal to $c + d$, while the people of group A would lose c. The gain for the people of group B is high enough that they could compensate those of A fully for their losses and have some left over. Here we run up against a number of factors that make it difficult for this type of adjustment to happen through normal, peaceful, economic transactions:

1 **Monopoly power on the part of large landowners**   A group that is able to gain control of the bulk of the land may also be able to dictate transaction terms for land redistribution. Knowing that group B will experience increased incomes equal to $c + d$ if the land is redistributed, they may be able to set land prices high enough potentially to extract this full amount from any transactions. In this case people in group B would indeed get more land, but their incomes would be no higher than they were.
2 **Lack of credit markets**   The amount c is actual, real income accruing to members of group A. The amount $c + d$ is the **potential** income gain by

[10] For a good review see Hans P. Binswanger, Klaus Deininger, and Gershon Feder, "Power, Distortions, Revolt and Reform in Agricultural Land Relations," in Jere Behrman and T. N. Srinivasan (eds.), *Handbook of Development Economics,* Vol. IIIB, Elsevier, Amsterdam, 1995, pp. 2659–2772.

group B. To purchase the land, group B people have to get a loan based on their potential future incomes. Credit markets in the rural areas of many developing countries are typically very underdeveloped and not up to this kind of need.

3 **Land prices may be higher than their agricultural productivity would imply** In many situations the ownership of agricultural land may confer tax advantages on the owners quite apart from the agricultural productivity of that land. In these cases land prices will be higher than justified strictly on grounds of their agricultural productivity; thus, buyers who expect to use the land for agricultural purposes may be faced with inflated land prices.

The people in group B could "gain access" to a larger share of the land in several other ways. One way is to **lease** portions of it from its owners in group A. In many countries land leasing has been frowned upon, apparently because of the negative political and incentive characteristics this type of institution is said to entail. This may be a mistake because in the long run it may be easier to redistribute land ownership by converting leaseholds to owned land than to start from scratch. The other way to gain access is for people in group B to work for people in group A as hired farm laborers. But if wage levels are determined by the subsistence income levels of people in group B, it will be totally impossible for them to accumulate sufficient financial wealth to be able eventually to convert it into land wealth.

The obstacles to land redistribution through standard market transactions have led to attempts to redistribute land politically either by violence or through a centrally directed redistribution program. The latter involves a central government agency expropriating land, perhaps with some amount of compensation, and redistributing it to new owners. These programs are normally very contentious. Good results are difficult to get because of the extreme political nature of the process.

In recent years a new concept has been developed with the aim of encouraging more, and more peaceful, land reform. It is a new type of negotiated land reform that relies on voluntary land transactions among willing buyers and sellers. In terms of our simple example of this section, it is a technique that tries to create conditions under which members of B will purchase, and members of A will voluntarily sell, portions of land now currently held by the latter. It has been described as **market-assisted land reform**,[11] and contains a number of essential steps:

1 Change the law so as to reduce the incentives that large landowners have to hold onto land for reasons other than agricultural production, for example, as a tax shelter.

---

[11] Johan van Zyl and Hans Binswanger, "Market-Assisted Rural Land Reform: How Will It Work?" in Johan van Zyl, Johann Kirsten, and Hans Binswanger (eds.), *Agricultural Land Reform in South Africa*, Oxford University Press, Cape Town, 1996, pp. 413–422.

2 Develop a means for identifying buyers who are most likely to be able successfully to operate a farm on newly acquired lands; that is, rather than simply giving everybody in group B additional land, identify those who are likely to have a comparative advantage in farming.

3 Establish a system whereby potential buyers can get the credit they need, at reasonable rates, to purchase land.

4 Create effective decentralized systems of courts whereby participants in disputes can settle them according to merits of the cases without resort to central political agencies. The program must lead, not just to a one-time land redistribution, but to a more open and transparent land market at the local level.

5 Develop effective means of providing technical aid to new farmers.

PROJECT EVALUATION

Several decades ago, when the international community began to focus seriously on the economic problems of the developing world, the natural resource decisions that got the most attention were related to large, **resource development projects,** such as dams to provide irrigation water, roads to open up new natural resources to extraction, timber processing facilities, and national parks and forests. Projects of this type are either too large for single individuals to complete or are in the nature of public infrastructure that is the normal province of national or regional governments. Decisions on such projects usually have important economic and political implications; they produce social wealth and they distribute it among various members of society. Economists developed tools for analyzing these project decisions. They were based on some of the **benefit-cost principles** we discussed in earlier chapters[12] and adapted to the special circumstances of developing nations. We review some of these here.

The primary objective of a benefit-cost analysis is simply to estimate and compare all of the economic consequences—benefits and costs—of a project or program, either one that is proposed, or perhaps one that already exists.

Valuing Outputs and Inputs

A project will normally produce one or more goods and/or services as outputs. From an economic standpoint, the most straightforward way of valuing these is by estimating the relevant demand curves, a general version of which is pictured in Figure 20-4. Total benefits are the area under the demand curve, which is $a + b$ for an output level of q^*. If total costs are equal to b, net benefits are equal to a. The types of outputs for which demand functions might need to be estimated would include the following:

- Irrigation water supplied by a new dam
- Electric power produced by a new generating facility

---

[12] See Chapters 8 and 9.

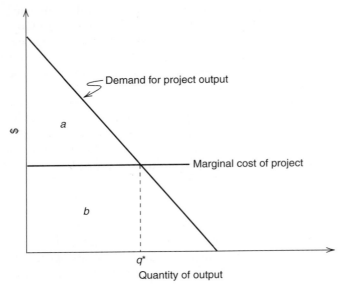

FIGURE 20-4
Demand and Costs for Typical Project

- Hectares of land put into protected status
- Hectares of land cleared for agricultural purposes
- Board-feet of wood produced from a new tree plantation
- Wildlife made available for viewing or hunting
- Information and advice provided to small-scale farmers

Some of these outputs are commercial products and may easily be evaluated with market data. Others are nonmarketed, and will have to be assessed with techniques such as travel cost analysis, hedonic price studies, or the contingent valuation approach.

On the input side the quantities of most inputs can be specified reasonably accurately through engineering means. The amount of pipe needed for an irrigation system, the number of workers needed to construct a dam, the amount of concrete needed to build a road, and the amount of fertilizer needed to establish a forest planting are all examples. The more difficult part is in determining a value for these resources. In theory, the answer is clear: The unit value of an input is the forgone value of economic output that the input would have produced in its next-best use. But determining what this value is can be very challenging. In developed economies with reasonably efficient market systems, the market prices of these inputs are probably the best indicator of these opportunity costs. But in developing economies, markets may be less well developed, and overall resource allocations may be distorted so much that the local prices of the inputs may not accurately reflect these underlying opportunity costs.

As an example, suppose that a public agency is considering the construction of a large dam to supply irrigation water to the farms of a nearby region. Suppose that the construction of the dam will provide jobs for many local people who currently work on the farms and that the wage paid to these workers on the dam project, according to the standard practice of the dam building agency, is (the equivalent of) $10 per day. But suppose this is a labor-surplus region, in the sense that the normal agricultural output of the region could be produced quite easily even with 30 percent fewer people working on the farms. This is frequently a problem in the agriculture of developing countries because of strong demographic growth but few opportunities for alternative employment. In this case the true opportunity cost of the dam building labor, which is the actual amount that the economy will lose in agricultural production when farm workers shift to dam employment, will be substantially lower than the apparent monetary cost of the labor.

The name given to the prices that correctly reflect true opportunity costs is **shadow prices** (or sometimes **accounting prices**), which were encountered in Chapter 9. Another example where it could be important to seek shadow prices is in the valuation of agricultural output (for example, the value of the added farm output in the irrigation project mentioned above). In many developing countries prices paid to farmers are kept low, usually for one of several reasons. If the item is exported, the central government, perhaps by using a central marketing board, can derive revenues by paying low prices to farmers and reselling on the world market at higher prices. In some cases, food prices are kept low so the country's urban dwellers will have access to cheap food. Whatever the reason, the farm price of the output may not reflect the true social value of the outputs, and so we must search for a shadow price for the output.

Accounting for All Impacts

In the case of decisions made in the private sector, we speak of **externalities,** impacts that are real but usually are not taken into account by private decision makers whose actions produce them. In public decision making, such as that involved in publicly funded projects, the imperative is to be sure that all likely impacts have been accounted for. Not only is this necessary if the true social net benefits are to be estimated, but a diligent effort to foresee all of a project's important impacts will reduce the risk of being surprised.

Decision Criteria

A **decision criterion** is both a rule and an index used to decide for or against a project. The criteria most often used are:

1 **Maximization of net benefits** This is consistent with the efficient principle used throughout the book. It is often the case that one will be able to estimate net benefits only for the project as specified; whether higher net bene-

fits would be available from a larger or smaller project may be hard to determine. At the very least, this approach would require that net benefits be positive, even if we don't know whether they are maximum in some sense.

2 **Cost minimization** In some cases project evaluation may be reduced to cost-effectiveness analysis. Where project outputs cannot be easily valued (e.g., projects to preserve biodiversity), the most appropriate objective may be to get the largest physical impact per dollar expended, which technically is the same as cost minimization.

3 **Income distribution impacts** Many developing countries have relatively large populations of poor people who are not well placed either to be the agents of economic growth or to benefit from growth that begins elsewhere. It may be desirable in these cases to undertake projects which, though perhaps having modest net benefits overall, would nevertheless benefit a certain target group of disadvantaged people. The strict efficiency criterion essentially treats a dollar of net benefits to one person as of equal value to that going to anyone else.

If a project is to be evaluated in terms of both its total net benefits and its distribution of these net benefits, this means essentially that we have a case of **multiobjective decision making.** This is a common situation, with respect both to these two goals and also in cases where two or more somewhat incompatible objectives are identified. We would like to stimulate local development but also to conserve a particular local wildlife population. It is important to build a new road to lower the costs of transportation, but we also want to avoid some of the resource impacts the new road could produce. In many cases it will not be possible to reduce all objectives to the same metric (e.g., monetary value) in order to add them up to get an overall net benefits figure. In these cases an explicit multiobjective planning procedure may have to be followed:[13]

In all project analyses, decisions have to be made about how much to focus on the potential **social impacts** of public investments. In developed country settings these are often ignored, on the theory that just adding net benefits in a particular social setting is not going to alter that setting in important ways. In developing countries this is harder to assume. Suppose, for example, a water supply project is to be built in a subsistence-level region, which physically will make it much less time-consuming for households to obtain adequate water supplies. Women who now have to spend a large part of each day traveling to a distant water point will have water available nearby. Possibly, the extra time produced by the project will lead to friction within households because it will upset traditional male/female time allocation budgets. Should this possible im-

---

[13] On multiobjective planning see F. Petry, "Who Is Afraid of Choices? A Proposal for Multi-Criteria Analysis as a Tool for Decision Making in Development Planning," *Journal of International Development,* Vol. 2, 1990, pp. 209–231; C. Romero and T. Rehman, "Natural Resource Management and the Use of Multiple Criteria Decision-Making Techniques," *European Journal of Agricultural Economics,* Vol. 14, 1987, pp. 61–89.

pact be taken into account in planning the project? If so, how should it be handled? Questions like this are much more likely to be present in certain developing country settings than they are in the developed world, where the original benefit-cost principles as established did not deal with questions like these.

SUMMARY

Most of the world's population is located in **developing countries,** those which are trying to achieve faster rates of economic growth that will eventually lead to levels of economic welfare characteristic of the developed world. Many, though not all, of these countries have economies today that are heavily dependent on natural resources, especially agricultural resources. There are two important linkages that need to be looked at closely: the contribution that natural resources can make to **economic growth** and the impact of growth on the quantity and quality of the **stock of natural capital.** Many concepts and models presented in previous chapters are as relevant in developing countries as they are in the developed world, but there are also some important differences. One of these is that in many developing countries a full set of **reasonably efficient economic institutions** may not be present, for example, **capital markets** that resource owners can rely on in making decisions about optimal holdings of natural capital stocks. With nonrenewable resources, economic growth clearly requires that **disinvestment** in resource stocks be compensated for by **investments** in other types of productive capital. With renewable resources and growing populations, it is also true that natural capital, which in this case can be used in a steady-state fashion, should be supplemented with nonnatural capital. The most obvious source of funds to invest in nonnatural capital is **natural resource rents.** Thus, the maximization of rents, and its distribution to those who would invest it productively, is perhaps the most central problem in the relationship of natural resources and economic growth. The chapter ended with a discussion of **project evaluation,** essentially the application of benefit-cost principles to projects undertaken in developing countries.

KEY TERMS

Developing/developed economies
Natural resources and growth
Natural capital
Aggregate production function
Technological development
Irreversibility threshold
National income
Natural resource accounting
Environmentally adjusted domestic
  product

Natural resource rents
Development fund
Land reform
Political distortions
Market-assisted land reform
Resource development project
Decision criteria
Multiobjective decision making

QUESTIONS FOR FURTHER DISCUSSION

1 Discuss the question: Are natural resources necessary for economic growth?
2 Discuss the pros and cons of creating a "development fund" into which revenues are put from the sale of natural resource commodities, with the proceeds to be used for development projects. What are the alternatives to such a fund?
3 How does one reconcile the idea of economic growth, in terms of increasing per capita incomes, and steady-state use rates of renewable natural resources?
4 Many people tend to boil down the development/resources relationship as: large population and high population growth rates, fixed resource base, thus resource degradation and scarcities. Discuss this line of thought.

USEFUL WEB SITES

For a guide to Internet resources on sustainable development see the article by D'Souza and Walton in the Spring/Summer 1997 edition of:

• Review of Agricultural Economics (http://aaea.org/rae.html)

Information on energy and its relationship to sustainable development:

• International Institute for Energy Conservation (http://www.iiec.org)

For information on environmental treaties and resource indicators see:

• Center for International Earth Science Information of Columbia University (http://www.sedac.ciesin.org/entri)
• Pace University Virtual Environmental Law Library (http://willy.law. pace.edu/env/vell6.html)

Online fact book with economic and resource statistics along with lists of environmental concerns:

• U.S. Central Intelligence Agency (http://www.cia.gov/publications/factbook)

For material on the question of population growth and the environment, see the related material on the web site of:

• National Institute for the Environment (http://www.cnie.org)

See also the United Nations Development Program:

• (http://www.undp.org)

SELECTED READINGS

Barbier, Edward B.: *The Economics of Environment and Development, Selected Essays,* Edward Elgar, Cheltenham, England, 1998.
Barham, Bradford L., Jean-Paul Chavas, and Oliver T. Coomes: "Sunk Costs and the Natural Resource Extraction Sector: Analytical Models and Historical Examples of

Hysteresis and Strategic Behavior," *Land Economics*, 74(4), November 1998, pp. 429–448.

Binswanger, Hans P., Klaus Deininger, and Gershon Feder: "Power, Distortions, Revolt and Reform in Agricultural Land Relations," in Jere Behrman and T. N. Srinivasan (eds.), *Handbook of Development Economics*, Vol. IIIB, Elsevier, Amsterdam, 1995, pp. 2659–2772.

Dasgupta, Partha: *An Inquiry into Well Being and Destitution*, Oxford University Press, Oxford, England, 1993.

Dasgupta, Partha, and Karl-Gören Mäler: *The Environment and Emerging Development Issues*, 3 vols., Clarendon Press, Oxford, England, 1997.

Dasgupta, Partha, Amartya Sen, and Stephen Marglin: "Guidelines for Project Evaluation," United Nations, New York, 1972.

Jannson, Ann Mari, Monica Hammer, Carl Folke, and Robert Costanza (eds.): *The Ecological Economics Approach to Sustainability*, Island Press, Coveto, CA, 1994.

Little, I. M. D., and J. Mirlees: *Project Appraisal and Planning for Developing Countries*, Basic Books, New York, 1974.

Pearce, David W., Anil Markandya, and Edward Barbier: *Sustainable Development: Economy and Environment in the Third World*, Earthscan, London, 1990.

Ray, Debraj: *Development Economics*, Princeton University Press, Princeton, NJ, 1998.

Southgate, Douglas, and Morris Whitaker: *Economic Progress and the Environment, One Developing Country's Policy Crisis*, Oxford University Press, New York, 1994.

Squire, Lyn, and Herman G. van der Tak: "Economic Analysis of Projects," World Bank, Washington, DC, 1974.

van den Bergh, Jeroen C. J. M., and Jan van der Straaten (eds.): *Economy and Ecosystems in Change, Analytical and Historical Approaches*, Edward Elgar, Cheltenham, England, 1997.

World Bank: *Expanding the Measure of Wealth*, World Bank, Washington, DC, 1997.

CHAPTER 21

NATURAL RESOURCE DECISIONS IN DEVELOPING COUNTRIES

One of the major themes we have stressed throughout is that to understand how people use natural resources we must first understand the **incentives** they face. Incentives are the individual benefits and costs that accrue to people as a result of their decisions. These incentives explain why people choose certain alternatives over others, and especially why they use natural resources the way they do. They also explain why the decisions made by individuals may not be conducive to maximizing the welfare of society as a whole. This is especially true of decisions that lead to excessive rates of natural resource use. The logic of this extends from diagnosis to prescription; changing the way resources get used can be accomplished most effectively by changing the incentives people face.

The importance of this idea can be appreciated by looking at Exhibit 21-1. It discusses two agricultural situations, one in Kenya and the other in Ethiopia. In the former, colonial policies seriously undermined the ability of local farmers to increase agricultural production. Since independence, however, incentives have been put in place that have led to substantial increases in agricultural output. In the Ethiopian case, on the other hand, heavy taxes and property rights problems have led to impoverishment and soil degradation.

But if this is the same message that earlier chapters sought to give, why devote another chapter to it here? The primary reason is that in many developing countries the political, social, and institutional setting is very different

EXHIBIT 21-1

THE IMPORTANCE OF INDIVIDUAL INCENTIVES: A TALE OF TWO COUNTRIES

Machakos is a semi-arid district in Kenya with poor to middling agroclimatic conditions. In Kenya, the best land was reserved for white settlers. Colonial policy obliged the native population to derive their food supply from a greatly reduced land base. Natives were forbidden to grow the most remunerative cash crops and therefore lacked incentives from the market. In the 1930s, the region was characterized by heavy soil erosion and declining yields. Today, however, Machakos supports a population almost six times as large as in 1932, and agricultural output per unit area (in constant maize units) has increased almost tenfold. Crop yields have risen. Cash crops and horticultural products were successfully introduced. . . . There are more trees, more soil conservation works and greater use of organic manure than in the 1930s.

The necessary investment incentives to bring about these effects are associated with the following conditions which have been assured since independence:

- An agricultural policy which, compared to other African countries, taxed the sector lightly;
- Access to international markets for coffee, and to domestic markets for other cash crops;
- Infrastructure construction associated with rural development projects;
- Access to non-farm and urban employment opportunities in Nairobi;
- Ability to finance investments from sales revenues and labour incomes;
- Security of tenure, provided initially by the traditional communal tenure, and later via land titles;
- New food production technology, especially for maize;

- Locally adapted soil conservation technology and farmer-led initiatives to implement it.

Recent cross-section studies of Ethiopia, on the other hand, find that areas where population density significantly exceeds carrying capacity are characterized by high indices of soil degradation.

Ethiopian farmers were heavily taxed throughout the period via a great diversity of methods. Rural infrastructure construction was limited. Access to international markets and even to domestic markets was often disrupted. Employment opportunities in the rural non-farm and urban economies were extremely limited by the lack of agricultural and economy-wide growth. Periodic famines led to asset depletion and further undermined the peasant's ability to mobilize investment resources.

There was no security of tenure at any time during the period. Under Haile Selassie the farmers were tenants at will, rather than holders of secure ownership or usufruct rights. Under the communist regime the state was the owner of the land; usufruct rights were never securely granted; and peasants were subject to dislocation from villagization programmes and forced migration, and were subject to pressures to collectivize.

There was very little availability of improved technology in food-grains. And there were very few programmes aimed at developing and disseminating improved soil conservation techniques among peasant farmers.

Source: John Heath and Hans Binswanger, "Natural Resource Degradation Effects of Poverty and Population Growth Are Largely Policy-Induced: The Case of Colombia," *Environment and Development Economics,* February 1, 1996, pp. 67–68.

from that of the developed world.[1] In particular, people in developing countries often do not face a set of clearly defined, specialized economic institutions for handling different aspects of economic activity. In developed countries, for example, there are well-developed institutions for handling banking and other financial transactions, insurance, social security, and the transfer of real assets such as land. In developing countries, on the other hand, these institutions often do not exist. Consider the following:

- In Sub-Saharan Africa farmers and nomads do not have access to efficient rural banks and credit markets. This leads them to carry larger numbers of cattle as insurance against droughts. But larger herds lead to extra strain on grazing lands, with resulting soil degradation.
- In developing countries there is typically a lack of institutions for what in developed countries are called welfare systems, systems that help maintain minimal income levels for those who would otherwise fall below subsistence levels. This means that welfare systems must be arranged through customs and practices regarding resource use. One way this has been done historically is to maintain a resource (e.g., firewood or water) on an open-access basis, to which the poor can resort in times of need. Open-access resources, in other words, are primarily devices for welfare assurance. We have seen the conditions of overuse that often result from open-access arrangements.
- In many poor countries it is difficult for families to eke out a living from a natural resource base of low productivity. In this case children are essential to help in this production, and small families are at a disadvantage. Thus, resource scarcities lead to higher fertility rates, which exacerbate the scarcities.[2]

INCENTIVES AND POLITICAL POWER

There is another way in which the situation often differs between developing and developed countries, with important implications for natural resource use. In the developed world, democratic political institutions that are reasonably distinct from economic ones lead to individuals and groups contending for influence over the processes of public policy. In developing countries, on the other hand, political power is often still in the hands of small groups, who can use it directly to gain direct or indirect control of natural resources and of the wealth this makes possible. Thus, although the behavior of individual re-

---

[1] It is worth reiterating here that although we are using just two categories, developed and developing, the countries within each category vary greatly in terms of many important social and economic characteristics. In a review chapter we paint with a very broad brush, using analyses that are generally, but not universally, applicable to all countries.

[2] For an extended discussion of such resource problems in developing countries see Partha Dasgupta, *An Inquiry into Well-Being and Destitution*, Clarendon Press, Oxford, England, 1993.

source users is a function of the incentives they face, it is in the political arena that rules and procedures are established that shape these incentives. Suppose, for example, that political authorities set high income tax rates on farmers, essentially to transfer agricultural rents from the people who created them to those with the power to set the taxes. Under some circumstances this could lead farmers to mine the fertility of the soil, as they try to maintain subsistence incomes in the face of a growing population. This is an incentive problem: High taxes lead to overuse of resources. But it is also a political problem: The authorities have too much arbitrary power and can set high tax rates that the farmers cannot escape. Note also the Kenyan case mentioned in Exhibit 21-1; colonial authorities at one time made it illegal for Kenyan farmers to raise certain cash crops. This is not so much an incentive problem as it is a problem in the exercise of political power.

Thus, the incentives facing individuals are determined by the de facto rules under which people operate, and those who control the political system have the power to establish, change, and enforce the rules. The motives of those in power are not necessarily to ensure that a country's natural resources are used in a way that maximizes social welfare. In many cases their aims are to create conditions that allow them, or their allies, to capture a large portion of whatever resource rents are produced.

Having stressed this political dimension of the problem, however, we nevertheless focus in the rest of the chapter on matters of social efficiency, or the maximization of social net benefits. Clarity in these matters may help in promoting the political and institutional changes that welfare-improving economic growth and development require.

PROPERTY RIGHTS

Nothing can be more fundamental to incentives than **property rights.** A property right is essentially an empowerment that establishes the conditions under which a person, or group of people, can utilize a natural resource. They determine the values that resources will have in different uses to different people, and therefore the incentives they will have to use the resources in different ways. These are abstract notions. The following is a concrete example. In many developing countries low-income farmers are often observed making decisions that lead to soil erosion and reduced productivity of their land. Why would farmers willingly pursue a course of action that undermines the productivity of the resource that is their lifeblood? One major reason could be that their property rights to the land are **insecure** or **attenuated.** Suppose there is a reasonably good possibility, because of political uncertainties in their country, that they could be dispossessed of their land, either because they might be physically removed from it or because they may not be able effectively to stop encroachers. The incentive effect here will be to lead owners to avoid the costs of maintaining long-run fertility—to "mine" the current fertility because the land is likely to be lost anyway in the long run.

People are not motivated to conserve a natural resource they are using if the benefits accruing to them from that act of conservation are lower than the costs. Property rights are the terms of empowerment that determine how these benefits and costs will be distributed. There are two main factors in this determination:

1 The social rules establishing who has the legal right to the benefits, and who has the legal responsibility for the costs
2 The economic costs to resource owners/users of excluding other potential beneficiaries from the benefits and costs arising from the use of a resource

In western developed economies, the normal perspective in property rights economics focuses on the legal specification of the rules of resource use. This is because these countries usually have reasonably effective systems of legislatures, courts, police, or land survey techniques with which property rights can be defined and enforced. Even in these cases, however, there can be differences between the way a property right is legally specified and the way it is actually used. Many landowners, for example, though having complete and secure rights to their land in the legal sense, may find it simply too costly to keep people from entering "their" property and enjoying some of the benefits of its use.

In the developing world, on the other hand, property rights are typically much more complicated. In many countries or regions, formal legal rules and institutions are scarce. In these cases there is greater reliance on **customary rules** and private means of enforcement, such as social norms and pressure. It means also that **extralegal** exploitation of natural resources can be a fairly common occurrence. In some developing countries, for example, illegal timbering by private interests on state land has contributed to large-scale deforestation; in these cases the states have been unable or unwilling to stop the encroachment.

A useful way of classifying property rights is in terms of the two categories:

1 Individual
2 Collective

Individual rights are those exercised by single persons, or perhaps by single families. **Collective** rights, on the other hand, are exercised by some type of group, perhaps a clan, a community, or the central state itself. In pastoral and arid regions, much property, especially of resources, is held communally, with the local village or clan establishing rules for its use. In these settings, however, personal property (like tools or homes) is usually held as individual property. There are many situations around the world in which one part of a resource flow (e.g., hunting or food gathering in a forest) is controlled communally, while other parts (e.g., timber plots) are held as individual property. The appropriate balance between collective rights systems and individual rights systems has been a matter of controversy around the world. On the one hand, many state farms and other collective agricultural enterprises have been dismantled in recent years, in favor of individual farm businesses. The trend in fisheries is also toward individual ownership. On the other hand, most of the forests in developing countries are owned and controlled by state agencies.

Some of the specific property rights problems characterizing natural resource use in developing countries are the following:

1 The prevalence of open-access situations
2 Insecure tenure that has the effect of reducing natural resource user costs
3 Inadequate markets through which resource owners can capture the full value flows associated with resource conservation
4 Inequality in the distribution of resource property rights

Open Access and Rent Dissipation

We have dealt several times with the issue of **open-access resources** and the dissipation of resource rents to which it leads. The open-access problem is thought to be particularly severe in many developing countries, with respect to marine, forest, grazing, wildlife, and water resources. When access to a resource is open to all, **open-access externalities** exist, incentives to conserve are weakened, and resource overuse often results. Traditional societies have often exploited their resource base with communal property institutions, arrangements where resources are open to use by members of the local community but closed to outsiders. Thus, local resources have often been used in common by small, relatively homogeneous, but somewhat marginalized social groups. One of the main functions served by open-access resources is as a community welfare support system. Disadvantaged members of the community may be provided support essentially by giving them access to the natural resource commons. In more recent times, population pressures and resource scarcities have combined to put pressure on these communal open-access institutions. And this in turn has focused attention on finding some means for solving the open-access problem, such as private property, state control, or new communal institutions for managing the resources. Open access has often been evaluated in terms of its implications for resource overuse. If our focus is on economic growth, the stress should also be on the fact of **rent dissipation.** Growth requires that resource rents be invested in productive forms of capital. But if there are no rents, there can be no investment—at least not from this source. Exhibit 21-2 depicts an example of this.

The Absence of Markets

We have mentioned before the problem posed by the fact that natural resource owners may not face a complete set of markets for all the service flows stemming from the resource. This is a problem in the developed world as well. A forest owner may face a well-functioning market for harvested timber, but lit-

EXHIBIT 21-2

RENT DISSIPATION AND ECONOMIC GROWTH

Safi is a small port community in Morocco, about 100 miles southwest of Casablanca. The primary livelihood of its people is fishing, in particular a sardine fishery. Each night a large fleet of sardine boats ply the waters proximate to the town, and each morning the catch is offloaded and trucked to market. The operations are extremely labor-intensive, boat crews are large, offloading is via long (4–6 people) bucket brigades, the docks are alive with men engaged in all sorts of tasks, besides large numbers of onlookers.

Let us look again at the economics of open-access resources like this sardine fishery. The figure shows the typical fisheries effort-yield function, and the open-access equilibrium effort, assuming the cost curve labeled C_0, of e_0. The families of Safi are quite normal: couples form, children are born, the population increases. With few alternative enterprises, the rising population increases the local labor supply. Analytically, this shifts the cost function, actually pushing it downward because of the surplus labor with few alternative job opportunities. Effort levels are increased, stocks are driven lower, and the sardine fishery is in a permanent state of low stocks and productivity.

Clearly, this is not conducive to economic growth, or even to maintaining present income levels of an increasing population. The only way we can turn this situation into one that promotes growth is to invest in other forms of capital, both nonhuman and human, that will lift the productivity of the growing population of the community. But here is the bind. How are we to make these investments? Rents in this fishery have been totally dissipated because of open access. Total costs are equal to total revenues; there is no surplus to devote to other investments.

To promote growth, then, two things must happen. First, some means must be found to limit effort levels. This could be any of the ways we have discussed in earlier chapters: voluntary cooperative action by groups of fishers themselves, public regulation of some sort, ITQs, and so on. Second, some means must be found to transform some or all of the resulting rents into investment that will ultimately provide employment and incomes for the young people of Safi.

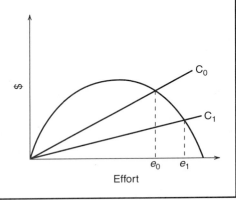

Effort

tle or no market for the amenity values or flood control values produced by the forest. In such cases the decisions of property owners will be biased toward those outputs for which markets exist. This problem is also encountered in developing countries.

Coastal wetlands in many tropical and subtropical countries often contain mangrove forests. These ecosystems support diverse communities of flora and fauna, the harvested products of which have important value. The mangrove forests also produce valuable ecosystem services such as flood control. But they are also under demand in many places for filling and conversion, either to intensive agriculture or to urban development. Private owners of these areas must compare the value of services the mangroves can produce in their natural state, with the price they could get if the land were sold to developers. A careful study in Fiji estimated the following values for natural resource products produced by a mangrove forest area:[3]

1 Forest products gathered on site (e.g., firewood, game animals, fruits) $F9 per hectare per year
2 Fishery products harvested off site (fish that make use of the mangrove for an essential part of their life cycle, but are actually caught elsewhere) $F150 per hectare per year

Thus, a substantial part of the values generated by the mangrove forests, which would be lost if they were converted, is realized by fishers, for whom the mangrove essentially has provided nursery services for the harvested fish in their younger stages. But there is no way for mangrove owners to realize a return on these services; they have substantial social value, but no value to the individual owners. The market in which the demanders and suppliers of these services could conclude transactions on quantities and prices does not exist.[4] Thus, although the mangrove forest owners may have clear and uncontested title to their land (actually wetland), they are likely to be biased toward the development alternative because this will provide higher individual returns than those arising from its use as mangrove forest.

Property Rights, Distribution, and Investment

One common feature of property rights situations in developing countries is a highly skewed distribution of ownership, in which a relatively small number of people own a large fraction of the country's resource capital. We discussed this in the previous chapter, in the context of the distribution of land resources in agriculture. This is very directly an issue of equity; most people would regard it as unfair if 95 percent of the land in a region were owned by 1 percent of its population. What a fair distribution of natural resource assets might be is a matter of ethics and politics. But a skewed distribution of natural capital can have important productivity effects, in both short and long runs. Large amounts of land or other resources that are owned by few people are not likely to be used as intensively as they would if they were more evenly distributed. More than that, the expenditure of resource rents, and hence the long-

---

[3] Cited in John A. Dixon and Padma N. Lal, "The Management of Coastal Wetlands: Economic Analysis of Combined Ecological-Economic Systems," in Partha Dasgupta and Karl-Gören Mäler, *The Environment and Emerging Development Issues*, Vol. 2, Clarendon Press, Oxford, England, 1997, pp. 399–423.

[4] You will recognize the main problem, which is that the nursery services are essentially public goods. Given the way that the fish grow and later disperse, it is not possible to make nursery services available to one fisher without making them available to all the others.

run impacts on growth, will be affected by property ownership distributions. If the rents accrue largely to a small group of owners, they are likely to be spent on things that enhance their own consumption and status and not on investments needed for long-run development. If rents are more broadly dispersed among the population, they are more likely to be spent on such things as education and investments that will increase productive efficiency.

DEFORESTATION

A major issue that has been featured in many developing countries is the over-exploitation of the forest resource, usually spoken of in terms of **deforestation.** In its most general quantitative sense, deforestation might be taken as simply a reduction in the amount of land area devoted to forests of the countries in question. It could also have a qualitative dimension, if one type of forest is replaced by another. The problems to which deforestation contributes are many. Observers in developed countries, fearful of the consequences of rising CO_2 levels in the earth's atmosphere, point to lost **carbon sequestration services** of destroyed forests, as well as to lost **biodiversity resources** that many forests, particularly those in the tropics, harbor. The act of deforestation has also had severe impacts at times, for example, in the air pollution resulting from wide-scale burning. Deforestation has led to severe cases of soil erosion and flooding, as the hydrological buffering services of local forests have been destroyed.

As with many problems, deforestation is a more complex phenomenon than many references to it might suggest. Most forest land in developing countries is **state property,** to which individuals—farmers, foresters, food gatherers, timber concessioners, recreationists, and others—have access on various terms. Individual access may be legal or nonlegal, regulated or unregulated, temporary or permanent. How the forest is used depends on the rules of access and their enforcement, and on the incentives facing the various participants in the process. The entire process can be broken into a two-step combination of alternatives:

1 First step: Clearing the land
   a Harvest
     Commercial
     Subsistence (e.g., firewood)
   b Destruction of trees (e.g., burning)
2 Second step: Using the land
   a Permanent agriculture (commercial or subsistence)
   b Shifting agriculture
   c Forestry (natural or plantation)
   d Nonresource use (e.g., urban expansion)
   e Abandonment

After one of the three land clearing options has been carried out, it is followed by one of the five land use options. In its broadest sense, deforestation refers to any set of decisions that shifts land once forested into another use. Deforestation so defined might not include replacing native forests with forest plantations, though this shift would have substantial impacts on certain forest resources, such as wildlife. A narrower definition of deforestation would be a shift away from forests that is driven by perverse incentives of public policies or institutions. For present purposes we do not necessarily have to agree on a particular notion of deforestation. Instead, we discuss the incentive aspects of several of these conversion options.

Subsistence Agriculture

In some parts of the world forests are cleared for what amounts to subsistence agriculture, which is defined as agricultural production that yields just enough to maintain the people doing it and no more. Consider Figure 21-1. It corresponds to the situation facing a family, or group of families, who clear forest each year (or it could be every 5 or 10 years) for temporary subsistence agriculture. On the horizontal axis there is an index of the number of acres of forest converted each year. The vertical axis contains an index of output, expressed either in monetary terms or, if this is a completely subsistence situation, in physical terms. MP_1 is the initial graph of marginal production; each additional hectare cleared allows the production of MP_1 units of food. MC is the marginal cost function, showing the labor costs of converting land. These labor costs are expressed either in monetary terms or, in the case of strict sub-

FIGURE 21-1
Clearing Forests for Subsistence Agriculture

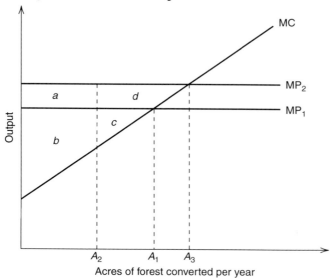

sistence, in terms of food required for its sustenance. As more and more forest is cleared, the marginal costs of clearing additional hectares goes up because of shortages of family labor. If MP_1 and MC are the relevant curves, the total area cleared will be A_1 hectares. By assumption the net return of $b + c$ is just sufficient for maintaining the household.

In a number of cases programs have been sponsored that attempt to raise the productivity of subsistence agriculture so as to lower the number of hectares of forest that must be cleared each year to gain subsistence.

> In parts of the Brazilian Amazon, where smallholders' farming techniques are still very basic, a local environmental group has helped reduce forest loss in one community by getting farmers to adopt a few simple improvements, such as planting their crops in rows rather than scattering seeds, and using hoes for weeding. The biggest potential gains from applying existing farming technology could be achieved in sub-Saharan Africa, where the use of fertilizer, for example, is running at only a quarter the level in India.[5]

Such technical improvements shift the marginal yield function upward, from MP_1 to, for example, MP_2. This increase allows the family to gain its subsistence income with fewer hectares converted. At A_2 and MP_2, for example, net returns would be $(a + b)$, so if area a in the diagram is equal to area c, subsistence income is maintained with a smaller amount of conversion.

There are two closely related problems with an approach like this, however. If the productivity of the farming operations is increased, there will be added incentives for the family to clear more area and try to lift its income above subsistence. Whether the family will succeed depends on how steep the MC curve is. If it is very steep, implying that there is a clear upper limit on the amount of land that can be cleared by one family, then the number of hectares cleared may not have a tendency to increase. If it is less steep, like the one in Figure 21-1, the incentive will be to increase the amount of deforestation. Another factor is that this approach appears to be aimed at perpetuating the subsistence situation of the people who are converting the forests. But subsistence incomes do not leave any resource rents available for investment in other types of productive assets, especially human capital. This is not a viable long-run solution, especially if populations are growing. As populations grow, the diagram of Figure 21-1 would be altered. Adding family members, or new families, would shift the MC curve outward; more people means the ability to convert more acreage. But more people also increases required subsistence income. Both of these will have the effect of increasing the amount of forest conversion.

Commercial Forestry

In many developing countries timber production is an important industry. Its main uses are fuel (roughly 2 out of every 5 people on earth rely on wood as

---

[5] "Development and the Environment," *Economist*, March 21, 1998, p. 10.

TABLE 21-1
COUNTRIES IN WHICH FORESTRY'S SHARE OF GDP IS
10 PERCENT OR HIGHER, AND REGIONAL SHARES

Country	Percentage of GDP
Uganda	23
Bhutan	22
Zaire	21
Swaziland	20
Kenya	19
Zambia	17
Nigeria	16
Solomon Islands	16
Burundi	15
Chad	15
Laos	15
Malawi	15
Sierra Leone	14
Madagascar	13
Rwanda	13
Sudan	13
Central African Republic	12
Gambia	12
Ghana	11
Benin	11
Burkina Faso	11
Papua New Guinea	11
Indonesia	10
Malaysia	10
Africa	6
South America	3
Asia	2
North/Central America	2
Europe	1
Oceania	2
Former USSR	2
Developing countries	4
Developed countries	1
World	2

Source: U.N. Food and Agriculture Organization, *State of the World's Forests*, FAO, Rome, 1997, p. 36.

their primary fuel), wood products, and pulpwood for paper manufacture. Table 21-1 shows a list of countries in which forestry's share of GDP is 10 percent or higher.[6] A substantial amount of deforestation in the developing world is taking place because commercial logging is being pushed well beyond

---

[6] In many countries a substantial proportion of wood harvested may not pass through markets. This is especially true of family fuel-wood gathering.

efficient levels. In Chapter 12 we applied some basic economic concepts to the question of when to cut a tree (or, say, a hectare of trees). We saw essentially that efficiency requires, as it does in most natural resources, a balance between present and future. If trees are harvested today, there are current benefits and costs: benefits in terms of the value of the harvested trees and costs in terms of the costs of the harvesting operation. But there are also future costs, because if the trees are harvested today we forgo future growth and the added value this produces.

There have been many studies of forestry operations in developing countries, focusing especially on factors that make timber harvesting inefficiently high in many cases. Listed below are some of the most important ones:

1 Government actions that have the effect of lowering harvesting costs. In Brazil, for example, the government has built roads to open up forested regions to settlement; this lowers the costs of harvesting the trees and getting them to market. Population growth and other subsidies also led to large-scale conversion of forest land to agriculture, especially cattle ranching.

2 Pursuing forest concession policies that create incentives for timber companies to harvest early and neglect long-run productivity considerations. **Timber concessions** are contracts between governments and private companies, allowing the latter to harvest trees on certain terms, with certain payments to the government. The terms of these concessions shape the incentives facing timber companies and therefore the practices they pursue. In Indonesia, for example, timber concessions are normally 20-year contracts. Thus, the timber companies may have little interest in long-run regeneration of forests for a cycle that may extend over 35 to 40 years.

3 Agricultural subsidies. Some governments provide public subsidies to agriculture, for example, through direct payments to users of pesticides, low prices for irrigation water, favorable import terms on imported machinery, and others. These subsidies increase the private value of land in agriculture, and therefore the pressure to convert forests to agricultural uses.

4 Insecure property rights. In many countries large tracts of forest have been denuded "illegally." This means that timber operators have simply encroached on land the ownership of which rests with somebody else, often the state. If insufficient resources are devoted to stopping this type of encroachment, overharvesting results, because encroachers are not interested in taking actions that maximize the long-run productivity of the forests. This is essentially a property rights problem, in which the titular owners of the forest are unable, or unwilling, to curb encroachment and illegal harvesting.

5 Neglect of the external costs from forestry. As in many resource extraction situations, in both developed and developing countries, the external costs of forestry often go unpriced and, therefore, unaccounted for. These effects include impacts on wildlife habitats and biological diversity and the control of water runoff and protection from floods.

In many countries substantial changes are under way in the management of forest resources. The dominant trends are toward decentralized public management, privatization of land holdings and the forest products industries, and the expansion of protected areas.[7] These goals and trends may often be in conflict.

SOIL EROSION AND SOIL PRODUCTIVITY

The maintenance of soil productivity by farmers in the developing world has long been recognized as an important problem. Instances of substantial soil erosion have been identified, and there are fears that greater efforts to expand agricultural production will increase the phenomenon. But the causal connections among elements of the farming situation that lead to soil erosion are complex. For example, one researcher concluded that "depressing agricultural prices depresses farmer incentives for soil conservation,"[8] whereas another states: "Better farm prices now, if they work as intended, will encourage soil mining for quick, big crops."[9] Can both statements be true?

Recall our earlier discussion about the management of soil erosion.[10] Applying our earlier terminology to soil fertility,

$$S_1 = S_0 - Q + \Delta S$$

where S_0 and S_1 now refer to the "stocks" of soil fertility at the beginning of two successive years, say, this year (S_0) and next year (S_1). Q in this case now corresponds to fertility decreases, while ΔS refers to fertility increases. Fertility is decreased in general by added crop intensification and increased output. Fertility can be increased by investments in such things as terracing, contour cultivation, and the like. In a steady state, $Q = \Delta S$. If this condition does not hold, then fertility is trending either downward (if $Q > \Delta S$) or upward (if $Q < \Delta S$).

Now we can see why the effects of agricultural price increases on soil productivity could be ambiguous, sometimes leading to an increase and sometimes to a decrease. Suppose agricultural prices increase. By itself this would create the incentive for added output, which would have the effect of extracting future productivity from the soil. But higher prices also make more soil conservation and soil building practices more feasible, and these will work in the direction of increasing future productivity. We would normally expect a gradual transition to a steady state, that is, a fertility level that would be maintained over a long period of time, as long as underlying economic factors (e.g., prices of outputs and inputs) do not change. Figure 21-2 shows the path over

[7] Food and Agriculture Organization, "State of the World's Forests," FAO, Rome, 1997, p. 97.

[8] R. Repetto, "Economic Incentives for Sustainable Production," *Annals of Regional Science,* Vol. 21, 1987, p. 45.

[9] M. Lipton, "Limits of Price Policy for Agriculture: Which Way for the World Bank?" *Policy Development Review,* Vol. 5, 1987, p. 209.

[10] See Chapter 6.

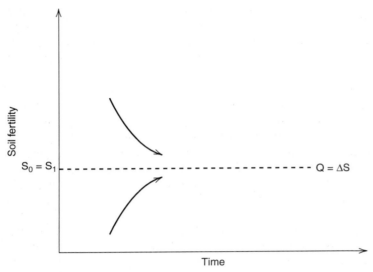

FIGURE 21-2
Evolution of Soil Fertility toward a Steady State

time of soil productivity. Starting from a position either higher or lower than the horizontal dashed line marking the steady state ($Q = \Delta S$), fertility evolves toward that state over time. What we cannot tell with any precision is at what level this steady state will be achieved.

In some cases the steady state will be characterized by complete soil exhaustion. Consider Figure 21-3: It shows marginal costs and returns for a typical farmer in a developing country. These are related to the level of output chosen by the farmer. The curve labeled MR shows the marginal value of output. This could be a marketed output or an output that is used for subsistence, expressed in terms of its subsistence value. The curve labeled MC shows the marginal current costs of production; this increases as output increases. Let us assume, however, that increasing output results in lowering the productivity of the soil. Greater output puts greater demands on soil productivity and results in its diminishment, which has negative impacts for future yields. We can think of this as a user cost associated with increasing today's output rate. The curve labeled MC + MUC shows the total of today's marginal production cost and marginal user cost from lowering the productivity of the soil. The difference between efficient and inefficient courses of action is now clear. Q^* is the fully efficient rate of output, because it balances current returns with the sum of present and future (i.e., user) costs. If decisions were made, instead, simply according to current year costs and returns, output would be pushed out to Q_1.

Can we be sure that the incentive situation facing farmers will lead them to Q^* rather than some higher output? Note that an output higher than Q^*, such as Q_1, involves a trade-off, a higher net return in the current year at the cost of

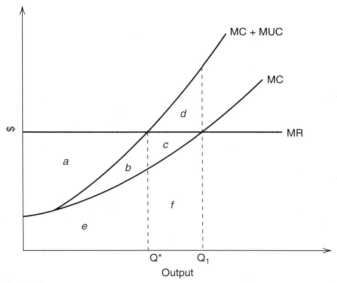

FIGURE 21-3
Output Choices in the Presence of Soil Productivity Losses

lowered returns in future years. Current income will be $a + b + c$ if output is Q_1, and only $a + b$ if output is held at Q^*. If this farmer is a subsistence cultivator or herdsperson, it is entirely possible that the value represented by $a + b$ is below the level needed for subsistence. If this is true, there will be a strong incentive to increase output beyond Q^* because this will increase short-run net returns, even though income in the long run is diminished.[11] This type of situation is particularly common in cases where large numbers of poor people, with limited technology beyond their own labor power, are pushed onto marginal lands through political and economic means. Maintenance of subsistence incomes in the short run may require drawing down the long-run productivity of the soil.

The knowledge required to balance ΔS and Q is not necessarily easy to accumulate. In many countries forests have been cleared in order to devote the land to agricultural production. This represents a massive change in the use of the basic soil resource and usually great uncertainty about how soil fertility will react to intensive agriculture. There is likely to be a strong tendency at first to draw down the basic stock of fertility contained in the soil when first converted, and only later to search for the means of arresting and perhaps reversing the fertility decline.[12]

---

[11] Net income, considering both present costs and user costs, is a when output is at Q^* (revenue of $a + b + e$ and costs of $e + b$), while it will be a − d at Q_1 (revenue of $a + b + c + e + f$ and costs of $b + c + d + e + f$).

[12] See, for example, Kojo Amanor, "Ecological Knowledge and the Regional Economy: Environmental Management in the Asesewa District of Ghana," in Dharam Ghai (ed.), *Development and Environment*, Blackwell, Oxford, England, 1994, pp. 41–67.

LOCAL AND NONLOCAL RESOURCE INTERESTS

A major cleavage in the management and use of natural resources is that between local groups who depend in a direct way on the exploitation of a resource, and nonlocal (regional, national, international) groups who also have
views on how the resource ought to be used. We dealt with an instance of this
in an earlier chapter.[13] There the resource was wildlife, and the conflict was
over the optimal size of a wildlife population from the local and nonlocal perspectives. Another instance is the conflict over a forest between local groups
who gain their livelihood from the forestry industry and nonlocal groups
whose interests are in forest preservation.

This phenomenon is also very common in the developing world. Exhibit 21-3
discusses a case of this sort in Thailand, the resource here being lands that local
people use for swidden agriculture and forest food gathering, but that nonlocal
groups wish to put into a national park reservation. In many cases conflicts of
this type involve the added complication of different ethnicity between local
and nonlocal populations. Situations of this type are very complex economically, socially, and politically. They typically lead to political conflict, often to violence, and usually to major shifts in the way resources are used. But it is possible to explore the issue with some of the simple economic tools we have
employed throughout this book. Consider Figure 21-4: Along the horizontal axis
is an index of the number of acres in the region devoted to a natural resource
reservation. There are two demand curves; D_L is the demand of the local residents for reserved acreage, and D_{NL} is the demand curve of the nonlocal population. In other words, there is some local demand for acreage reservation, but
only at a modest level. The nonlocal demand is much farther to the right; although the per capita willingness to pay of nonlocals may be low, the fact that
these people are much more numerous than the local group implies that D_{NL}
lies well to the right of D_L. The curve marked MC_L represents the marginal costs
of acreage reservation to locals: Reservation makes it impossible for locals to use
the reserved acreage for the purposes it formerly served, such as firewood,
hunting, or temporary cultivation.[14]

Clearly, there is a major discrepancy between the optimal number of reserved acreage from the perspective of locals and nonlocals. For the former
this is a_L, while for the latter it is a_{NL}. In fact, from an overall social viewpoint,
considering both groups combined, the optimal reservation is at a^* acres.[15]
But at a^* there is a major distributional problem: Although net benefits to

[13] See Chapter 18.
[14] There is no function showing marginal costs to nonlocals; these costs could be expected to be
very low in any case, and nothing is gained in terms of the conclusions we can draw from the
model by adding another line.
[15] This conclusion assumes that the reserved acreage is a public good; an acre preserved for
one person (local or nonlocal) is an acre preserved for everyone. Thus, the local and nonlocal demand curves must be added together **vertically** to get the overall, or aggregate, demand curve.
Doing this will show that the point on the nonlocal demand curve above a^* is on the aggregate demand curve for reserved acreage.

EXHIBIT 21-3

LOCAL VS. NONLOCAL INTERESTS

Khao Yai National Park

Established in 1962, Khao Yai is the oldest national park in Thailand. It covers 2,168 sq. km. and is located in the central-eastern region of the country, forming part of the western Phanom Dongrek mountain range. In Thai, "Khao Yai" literally means "high mountains." There are some peaks in the park which rise to over 1,000 m., although much of the area consists of plateaux and valley floors. A number of rivers originate inside the park. These rivers constitute an important water source for irrigation, agricultural industry and urban centres in adjacent lowland areas. Nearly two-thirds of the park's surface is covered with tropical rain forest (i.e., moist evergreen forest). A number of animals found in the park are considered endangered species, including elephants, tigers and gaurs. Since the establishment of the park, a great deal of emphasis has been placed on the protection of these animals, particularly the elephants.

When Khao Yai was proclaimed a national park, there were many settlements within its boundaries. Some of these villages were established long before the government had begun promulgating any forest protection legislation. These settlements were located in fertile areas, usually near rivers or lakes, and generally made use of small patches of forest for housing and crop production. Swidden cultivation was the principal form of agriculture, used with long fallow intervals. Many households supplemented their subsistence requirements with hunting and forest food gathering.

Government officials believed that the slash-and-burn cultivation methods led to frequent forest fires, and that hunting resulted in the indiscriminate killing of wild animals. The existence of the settlements within park boundaries was thus regarded as a serious threat to the protection of wild animals and their habitat. Consequently, settlers from inside the park were evicted, followed by the removal of households settled on the outskirts of the park. Relics of some of the burnt farmhouses can still be seen in the park.

Government officials also sought to include adjacent areas within park boundaries in order to diminish human pressure in the park. This process continues even now, and is justified on the grounds of conservation, especially since the park has acquired a growing national and international reputation in recent years. This has adversely affected the livelihood opportunities of many groups of local people. Another major consequence of this policy has been further deforestation outside the park boundaries, as households losing land in and around the park have moved to new locations and cleared forests for settlement. Those who were unable to migrate tended to over-exploit those forest and land resources which remained relatively accessible. This is especially true in Khao Yai, where the park represents a little 'green island' amidst a much larger grey and denuded settlement area.

Khao Yai has become one of the most popular recreational centres in Thailand. It is regarded as an idyllic retreat from the noise, pollution and humidity which characterize urban life in Bangkok. The park is visited annually by large numbers of city-dwellers, government officials, foreign dignitaries and tourists. Many roads and trails have recently been constructed inside as well as on the periphery of the park to cater for visitors; tourist bungalows, water towers and an 18-hole golf course have been built inside the park, many in areas where local people previously maintained dwellings and farmlands. Motorized generators, which provide electricity and pump water, roar most of the night. Loud music is played by the many groups of urban youth who visit the park. One could question whether the earlier settlers disturbed the wild animals as much as current park visitors. One thing is sure, however: unlike the local residents, the tourists (both Thai and foreigners) bring in money, which is crucial for the maintenance of the park, as well as for the development of the local tourist industry.

Source: Krishna B. Ghimire, "Parks and People: Livelihood Issues in National Parks Management in Thailand and Madagascar," in Dharam Ghai (ed.), *Development and Environment, Sustaining People and Nature,* Blackwell, Cambridge, MA, 1994, pp. 202–204.

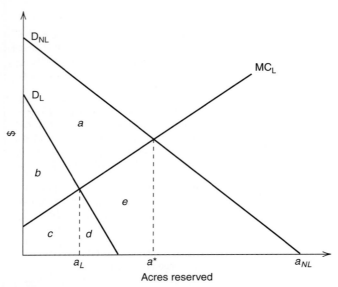

FIGURE 21-4
Conflicts between Local and Nonlocal Groups

nonlocals are clearly positive and large (they are equal to $a + b + c + d + e$), net benefits to locals are small, or even negative; these are benefits of $b + c + d$ minus costs of $c + d + e$, or $b - e$. The net benefits to nonlocals are more than enough to **compensate** the locals for their losses so that the reservation would be welfare-improving for both groups. This now becomes a political/institutional problem as to whether revenues can be shifted to local groups. It requires essentially transferring a portion of the net benefits accruing to nonlocals from them to the locals. How this might be done depends on a number of factors. One important factor is the type of benefits accruing to the nonlocal group, in particular whether they stem from use or nonuse values. If they are based on use values (say, recreation, wildlife watching, or hunting), then income to the locals could be generated in two ways:

1 Through a process of **privatization,** by which the locals are given effective control over the reserved acreage and allowed to levy user charges on nonlocals

2 Through a **political allocation** process, whereby central authorities transfer revenues to locals, raised perhaps through general tax levies or through user charges to direct nonlocal beneficiaries

A position intermediate to these is the development of a local **ecotourism industry,** through which locals may extract a portion of the net benefits of visitors through selling services such as guide fees or accommodations.

The incentive aspects of these alternatives are quite different. When local groups occupy a position in which their revenues and welfare are tied directly to the quality of the resource, they will presumably be led to protect that quality so as to protect their source of welfare. In cases where their support comes from a distant government and is only loosely connected to the physical status of the resource, the local conservation incentive will be relatively weak.

All these possibilities are based on the assumption that the benefits to non-locals are **use values.** If they are **nonuse values,** such as option value or biodiversity existence value, the situation is much more difficult. In this case there are likely to be strong public goods effects so that the revenue gaining potential from local resource conservation becomes quite small. Perhaps one possibility would be to introduce a quasi-market type of situation, in which nonlocal political authorities arrange a compensation plan whereby the amount of payment is linked to the maintenance of certain physical resource qualities by the local population.

SUMMARY

A major theme throughout this book has been how **incentives** shape the natural resource decisions of individuals. This principle holds with great force in **developing countries.** In many of these, market failures and misguided public policy contribute to incentive situations that lead to overuse of natural resources. Although incentives shape decisions of individuals, it is **political power** that determines the rules that shape incentives. This is especially true regarding **property rights.** Deficiencies in property rights institutions can lead individuals to make decisions that do not conserve a country's natural capital. Property rights also determine how the benefits of natural resources are distributed. Our discussion of **deforestation** indicated some of the incentive reasons why excessive amounts of forests might be cleared in many situations, in situations of **subsistence agriculture** as well as in **commercial forestry.** We also discussed the issue of **soil erosion** and the maintenance of soil fertility. Finally, we dealt with a situation that is very common in developing (and developed) countries, in which there are economic conflicts between **local residents** who make use of resources directly and **distant groups** who have their own ideas about how the resources should be used.

KEY TERMS

Incentives	Open-access resources
Incentives and power	Property rights and distribution
Incentives and property rights	Deforestation
Individual rights	Timber concessions
Collective rights	Soil fertility control

QUESTIONS FOR FURTHER DISCUSSION

1 In what way are the incentive aspects of situations facing natural resource users in developing countries the same as those in developed countries, and in what way are they different?

2 In many parts of the developing world (as well as in the developed countries), groundwater aquifers have been depleted because large numbers of withdrawers have failed to put sufficient emphasis on long-run water conservation. What type of property-rights problem is involved here?

3 In some parts of the developing world (and sometimes in developing countries), the productivity of land has been depleted so much that it has been abandoned. Why would individuals willingly choose to degrade land to this extent?

4 Suppose that in a certain developing country subsistence farmers are responsible for substantial amounts of deforestation each year. Suppose also that agricultural extension workers have a way of showing farmers how to get greater agricultural output from the land they clear. Will this increase or decrease the amount of forest cleared each year?

5 What is the likely effect of shifting from communal property rights in natural resources (e.g., a forest that is open to use by all members of a certain community) to private property rights on the rate of economic growth?

6 How is it possible to reconcile the fact that many of the people who are in favor of preserving biodiversity resources in developing countries are located in the higher-income countries of the developed world, whereas many people who wish to continue harvesting these resources in traditional ways are local people who live close to the resources?

USEFUL WEB SITES

Natural resource issues in developing countries, including case studies and management practices:

- World Bank (http://www.worldbank.org)
- Food and Agriculture Organization of the U.N. (http://www.fao.org), under sustainable development
- World Conservation Monitoring Center (http://www.wcmc.org.uk)
- Center for Social and Economic Research on the Global Environment (joint between University College London and the University of East Anglia): (http://www.uea.ac.uk/menu/acad_depts/env/all/resgroups/cserge)

SELECTED READINGS

Barrett, Scott: "The Optimal Control of Soil Erosion," in Partha Dasgupta and Karl-Göran Mäler, *The Environment and Emerging Development Issues*, Vol. 2, Clarendon Press, Oxford, England, 1997, pp. 482–501.

Barbier, E. B., and J. T. Bishop: "Economic Values and Incentives Affecting Soil and Water Conservation in Developing Countries," *Journal of Soil and Water Conservation*, March–April 1995, pp. 133–137.

Barbier, E. B., J. C. Burgess, and A. Markandya: "The Economics of Tropical Deforestation," *Ambio,* 20(2), 1991, pp. 55–58.

Barbier, Edward et al.: *The Economics of the Tropical Timber Trade,* St. Lucie Press, Boca Raton, FL, 1994.

Binswanger, H.: "Brazilian Policies That Encourage Deforestation in the Amazon," *World Development,* 19(7), 1989.

Deacon, Robert T.: "Deforestation and the Rule of Law in a Cross-Section of Countries," *Land Economics,* 70(4), November 1994, pp. 414–430.

Munasinghe, Mohan and Jeffrey A. MacNeely: *Protected Area Economics and Policy: Linking Conservation and Sustainable Development,* World Bank, 1995.

Munasinghe, Mohan (ed.): *Environmental Economics and Natural Resource Management in Developing Countries,* World Bank, 1993.

Repetto, Robert, and Malcolm Gillis (eds.): *Public Policies and the Misuse of Forest Resources,* Cambridge University Press, Cambridge, England, 1988.

Schram, G., and J. J. Warford (eds.): *Environmental Management and Economic Development,* Johns Hopkins Press, Baltimore, 1989.

Southgate, Douglas, and Morris Whitaker: *Economic Progress and the Environment, One Developing Country's Policy Crisis,* Oxford University Press, Oxford, England, 1994.

U.N. Food and Agriculture Organization: *State of the World's Forests,* FAO, Rome, 1997.

Vincent, Jeffrey R.: "The Tropical Timber Trade and Sustainable Development," *Science,* Vol. 256, June 19, 1992, pp. 1651–1655.

Vocke, Gary (ed.): *Global Review of Resource and Environment Policies: Water Resource Development and Management,* U.S. Economic Research Service, USDA, Foreign Agricultural Economic Report No. 251, June 1994.

INDEX OF NAMES

INDEX OF SUBJECTS